T0374903

Correction to *Parliamentary History* Volume 42, Issue S1

Parliamentary History
Volume 42 Issue S1
October 2023

The title of this issue (on the print cover and title page) reads incorrectly as 'Volume Two' instead of 'Volume Three'. This has been corrected online on Wiley Online Library to read as:

Texts & Studies Series 19

Anglo-Irish Politics, 1680–1728
The Correspondence of the Brodrick Family of Surrey and County Cork
Volume Three, 1722–28

Edited by David Hayton and Michael Page

We apologize for this error.

PARLIAMENTARY HISTORY: TEXTS & STUDIES
19

Anglo-Irish Politics, 1680–1728

The Correspondence of the Brodrick Family of
Surrey and County Cork

VOLUME TWO, 1722–28

PARLIAMENTARY HISTORY TEXTS & STUDIES

Alan Brodrick, 2nd Viscount Midleton: painter unknown

Anglo-Irish Politics, 1680–1728

The Correspondence of the Brodrick Family of
Surrey and County Cork

VOLUME TWO, 1722–28

Edited by

David Hayton and Michael Page

WILEY
for
THE PARLIAMENTARY HISTORY YEARBOOK TRUST

Library of Congress Cataloging-in-Publication Data

Library of Congress Cataloging-in-Publication data is available for this book

ISBN 9781394256648

Anglo-Irish Politics, 1680-1728: The Correspondence of the Brodrick Family of Surrey and County Cork / by David Hayton and Michael Page
••

A catalogue record for this title is available from the British Library
Set in 10/12pt Bembo
by Aptara Inc., India
Printed and bound in Singapore
by C.O.S. Printers Pte Ltd
1   2023

Parliamentary History: Texts & Studies

CONTENTS

ACKNOWLEDGMENTS

Once again, our list of creditors is headed by the Viscount Midleton, for allowing us to consult and to publish material in his family papers. We are also indebted to the owners and custodians of the other collections of manuscripts cited and quoted: the Marquess Townshend; the Lord Egremont; the Castletown Foundation; the British Library Board; the duke of Devonshire and the trustees of the Chatsworth settlement; the trustees of the Goodwood collection; the comptroller of Her Majesty's Stationery Office; the director, National Library of Ireland; the Norfolk Record Office; the deputy keeper of the Records of Northern Ireland; the Registry of Deeds, Dublin; Suffolk Archives; the Surrey History Centre; the board of Trinity College Dublin; the West Sussex Record Office; and Manuscripts and Archives, Yale University Library. For help and advice on particular points we are indebted to John Bergin, Andrew Hanham, the late Frances Harris, Richard Holmes and Robert Ingram. David Hayton wishes to acknowledge the assistance provided him by Desmond Crone of the Suffolk Archives, Bury St Edmunds; the staff in Special Collections in the McClay Library, Queen's University Belfast; and archivists in the Public Record Office of Northern Ireland. The general editor of the series, Linda Clark, has once again saved us from errors and inconsistencies, as well as materially assisting research in London repositories.

ABBREVIATIONS

Add. MS(S)	Additional Manuscript(s)
Al. Dub.	*Alumni Dublinenses … 1593–1860*, ed. G.D. Burtchaell and T.U. Sadleir (new edn, Dublin, 1935)
Anglo-Irish Politics	*Anglo-Irish Politics, 1680–1728 …*, ed. David Hayton and Michael Page, vols i–ii (Chichester, 2019–20)
Ball, *Judges*	F.E. Ball, *The Judges in Ireland 1221–1921* (2 vols, 1926)
BL	British Library, London
Boulter Letters	*The Boulter Letters*, ed. Kenneth Milne and Paddy McNally (Dublin, 2016)
Burns, *Politics*	R.E. Burns, *Irish Parliamentary Politics in the Eighteenth Century* (2 vols, Washington, DC, 1989–90)
CTB	*Calendar of Treasury Books*
CTP	*Calendar of Treasury Papers*
CJ	*Journals of the House of Commons*
CJI	*The Journals of the House of Commons of the Kingdom of Ireland* (2nd edn, 19 vols, Dublin, 1753–76)
Cobbett, *Parl. Hist.*	*Cobbett's Parliamentary History of England from the Earliest Period to the Year 1803* (36 vols, 1805–20)
Coghill Letters	*Letters of Marmaduke Coghill, 1722–1738*, ed. D.W. Hayton (Dublin, 2005)
Cork Council Bk	*The Council Book of the Corporation of the City of Cork, from 1609 to 1645, and from 1690 to 1800*, ed. Richard Caulfield (Guildford, 1876)
Cotton, *Fasti*	Henry Cotton, *Fasti Ecclesiae Hibernicae …* (5 vols, Dublin, 1847–60)
Coxe, *Walpole*	William Coxe, *Memoirs of the Life and Administration of Sir Robert Walpole, Earl of Orford* (3 vols, 1798)
Dalton, *Army Lists*	Charles Dalton, *English Army Lists and Commission Registers, 1661–1714* (6 vols, 1892–1904)
Dalton, *Geo. I's Army*	Charles Dalton, *George the First's Army, 1714–1727* (2 vols, 1910–12)
DIB	*Dictionary of Irish Biography*, ed. James McGuire and James Quinn (9 vols, Cambridge, 2009)
Drapier's Letters	Jonathan Swift, *The Drapier's Letters to the People of Ireland*, ed. Herbert Davis (Oxford, 1935)
[E]	England
ECI	*Eighteenth-Century Ireland*
Ehrenpreis, *Swift*	Irvin Ehrenpreis, *Swift: The Man, his Works, and the Age* (3 vols, 1962–83)
[GB]	Great Britain

Hayton, *Ruling Ireland*	D.W. Hayton, *Ruling Ireland, 1685–1742: Politics, Politicians and Parties* (Woodbridge, 2004)
HC 1690–1715	*The House of Commons 1690–1715*, ed. Eveline Cruickshanks, D.W. Hayton and Stuart Handley (5 vols, Cambridge, 2002)
HC 1715–54	*The House of Commons 1715–1754*, ed. Romney Sedgwick (2 vols, 1970)
Hist. Ir. Parl.	Edith Mary Johnston-Liik, *History of the Irish Parliament 1692–1800 …* (6 vols, Belfast, 2002)
HL 1660–1715	*The House of Lords 1660–1715*, ed. Ruth Paley (5 vols, Cambridge, 2016)
HMC	Historical Manuscripts Commission (reports)
IAA	Irish Architectural Archive, Dublin
IHS	*Irish Historical Studies*
ILD	Irish Legislation database (http://www.qub.ac.uk/ild/)
[I]	Ireland
Knatchbull Diary	*The Parliamentary Diary of Sir Edward Knatchbull 1722–1730*, ed. A.N. Newman (Camden Soc. 3rd ser., xciv, 163)
Lib. Mun.	*Liber Munerum Publicorum Hiberniæ*, ed. Rowley Lascelles (2 vols, 1824–30)
LJ	*Journals of the House of Lords*
LJI	*Journals of the House of Lords [of Ireland]* (8 vols, Dublin, 1779–1800)
NLI	National Library of Ireland, Dublin
n.d.	no date
n.s.	new series
N.S.	New Style
OED	*Oxford English Dictionary* (online edition: http://www.oed.com)
Oxf. DNB	*The Oxford Dictionary of National Biography* (online edition: http://www.oxforddnb.com)
PRONI	Public Record Office of Northern Ireland
Reg. Deeds	Registry of Deeds, Dublin
RO	Record Office
[S]	Scotland
SA	Suffolk Archives, Bury St Edmunds
Sainty and Dewar	J.C. Sainty and David Dewar, *Divisions in the House of Lords: An Analytical List 1685 to 1857* (House of Lords RO Occasional Publications, no. 2, 1976; includes a microfiche with list of divisions)
SHC	Surrey History Centre
Swift Corr.	*The Correspondence of Jonathan Swift, D.D.*, ed. David Woolley (5 vols, Frankfurt am Main, 1999–2014)
TCD	Trinity College Dublin
TNA	The National Archives [of the U.K]
Vicars, *Index*	*Index to the Prerogative Wills of Ireland, 1536–1810*, ed. Sir Arthur Vicars (Dublin, 1897)

INTRODUCTION

In February 1722, when this volume opens, the political future of the Brodrick brothers, Alan and Thomas, was uncertain, despite the standing they enjoyed in England as well as in Ireland. Both now occupied seats in the British house of commons. Alan (since 1717 Viscount Midleton) had retained his position as lord chancellor of Ireland, though his influence at Dublin Castle had sunk significantly from its zenith at the time of the Hanoverian succession. In the winter of 1718–19 he had enraged the English ministry, and especially Lord Sunderland, by refusing to support Sunderland's pet project at Westminster, the Peerage Bill. Relations worsened even further during the subsequent Irish parliamentary session, when Alan's son, St John III, led opposition to the government-sponsored repeal of the sacramental test. The lord lieutenant, the duke of Bolton, who had once been very close to the Brodricks, took others into his confidence, notably their great political rival, William Conolly, the Speaker of the Irish house of commons. Following the conclusion of the 1719 session the British cabinet determined on Alan's removal. He was saved by a reconciliation in 1720 between the ministers and the leading figures in the whig opposition, Lord Townshend and Robert Walpole. Walpole argued against Alan's dismissal, as too risky a step given the tension between the Irish and British parliaments as a result of the passage at Westminster in 1720 of the Declaratory Act, asserting appellate and statutory jurisdiction over Ireland.

This was, however, only a temporary respite, and even though Townshend and Walpole strengthened their grip on power in 1721–2, Alan's position had not become secure; far from it. Bolton was replaced as lord lieutenant by the duke of Grafton, who as a lord justice in Dublin in 1715–16 had developed a close friendship, and reliance upon, Conolly, and a corresponding enmity towards the Brodricks. Alan was excluded from Grafton's 'kitchen cabinet', and at the end of the 1721–2 session endured the mortification of being dropped from the commission of lords justices appointed to govern the kingdom in the viceroy's absence, an unprecedented slight on an Irish lord chancellor. Henceforth, he considered himself to be living on borrowed time. His parliamentary seat at Westminster should have afforded some leverage, especially since he and Thomas had been joined there by young St John, in a by-election in 1721. However, of the three, only Thomas attended regularly, and his affected notions of independent-mindedness made him unpredictable, and, as far as government was concerned, unreliable.

The 1721–2 session of the Irish parliament had been something of a 'phony war'. The tension between the Brodrick and Conolly factions was clear enough, as was the fact that Grafton clearly favoured the Speaker, but the principal issue, the proposal to establish a national bank, cut across party lines and there was no formal passage of arms between the followers of 'the two great men' in the Commons. This state of affairs would not last. In July

1722 the crown granted a patent to a Wolverhampton ironmaster, William Wood, to coin halfpence and farthings for Ireland. Wood was a successful businessman who had already branched out in his industrial activities with a contract to supply the Royal Mint, and along with his Irish patent was also entrusted in 1722 with the responsibility of providing copper coin to British transatlantic possessions. But a recent attempt on Wood's part to establish a public company had foundered – as had many similar enterprises in the wake of the South Sea Bubble – damaging his reputation.[1] There was, moreover, considerable resistance among the Irish to receiving quantities of English-made coins of base metal. The lack of small-denomination currency in Ireland was a chronic problem, but so too was the scarcity of gold and silver, and there was a widespread belief that Irish bullion was draining away, into the pockets of absentee landlords, placemen and pensioners.[2] Rumours that Wood had obtained his patent by nefarious means – a bribe to the king's German mistress, Melusine von der Schulenberg, duchess of Kendal – heightened the impression that the patent was a political 'job', concocted in London, which would further depress an already prostrate Irish economy. The sufferings of Irish investors in the South Sea Bubble and the debates over the bank in 1721 had accustomed the political nation in Ireland to scepticism of financial innovations. Moreover, in the popular mind 'Wood's Halfpence' recalled the 'brass money' of James II's Irish regime, a frequently invoked emblem of oppression and poverty. The furore against the patent quickly revived a fierce spirit of 'patriotism' in the Irish parliament.

For the next three years Irish politics would be dominated by vociferous opposition to 'Wood's Halfpence', orchestrated by Jonathan Swift. This 'Irish hurricane' also focused the attention of the British government and parliament, and the English newspaper and pamphlet press, on events in Ireland. At one point it seemed to imperil the very existence of the Townshend/Walpole administration, and although Walpole himself made a point of treating the supposed danger with disdain, the involvement of the duchess of Kendal, and Walpole's identification in Irish prints as the real author of the patent, meant that it was a problem that he had to take very seriously. Indeed, Irish resistance to the halfpence would precipitate a major shift in the ministry's Irish policy.

1

Soon after the Irish parliament was prorogued in January 1722, Alan and his wife set sail for England, intending to join their younger son, Alan II, in London. However, Lady Midleton was taken ill after a difficult crossing, and once Alan, Thomas and St John had all secured re-election to the British parliament in March and April, the Midletons spent the rest of the spring and summer in Bath, before going on to Peper Harow, and then London, so that Alan could attend the parliamentary session at Westminster, which ran from October 1722 until May 1723. It was a long time for Alan to be absent from Ireland, given the importance of the lord chancellor to the transaction of legal business in Dublin, something which would in due course come back to haunt him. It may indicate an intention on his part to tackle the British ministers personally in relation to his estrangement from the viceroy's circle. But it is

---

[1] See the entry on Wood in *Oxf. DNB*.
[2] *Drapier's Letters*, xx.

also possible that he was considering (and not for the first time) a permanent resettlement in Surrey. While Sunderland's death in May 1722 left Townshend and Walpole in command of the ministry, this did not necessarily mean that Alan's own long-term prospects had materially improved. Walpole, in particular, seems to have determined to wait and see what would transpire in Ireland, in the hope that both lord chancellor and Speaker would support government in the event of difficulties over the halfpence.

The approach that Alan took during the British parliamentary session of 1722–3 was to make himself quietly useful rather than noisily disruptive. He and Thomas were both invited to the private pre-sessional meetings of ministerial supporters at Walpole's London residence.[3] Early on, Alan made his mark in the Commons by speaking on the ministerial side over the augmentation of the army.[4] For the remainder of the session, although busy enough, he generally steered clear of controversy. Almost all the committees to which he was nominated were concerned with routine matters, though two dealt with the affairs of Norwich and Great Yarmouth, in which Walpole and his brother Horatio ('old Horace') were particularly concerned.[5] The single exception to this record of humdrum business was the committee appointed in March 1723 to draft a loyal address on the occasion of the discovery of the supposed conspiracy of the jacobite Christopher Layer. The confession extorted from Layer was used to expose what the government alleged was a much more wide-ranging jacobite plot, headed by Bishop Atterbury, whose prosecution (by a bill of pains and penalties) became the political centrepiece of the session. Alan was evidently much exercised by the discovery of the plot and showed his feelings in debate.[6]

The drafting committee on the address concerning Layer was chaired by Thomas Brodrick, who generally outshone his brother as a parliamentary performer and was both more confident and less tactful. Like Alan, Thomas's extensive committee service covered a range of bread-and-butter subjects, including on one occasion a matter that concerned the Walpoles' political interests in Norfolk,[7] but he was also appointed to several of the more politically significant committees. Besides the address relating to Layer, his experience in leading the parliamentary hue and cry after the South Sea Company made him an obvious choice for the committee inquiring into the Harburg Lottery, another dubious financial scheme, and to the committee drafting a bill to prolong the time for hearing claims from the creditors of South Sea directors (a committee which he also chaired).[8] In debate, however, Thomas was impulsive and headstrong: in March 1723, for example, he spoke 'five or six times' on the same day against allowing Bishop Atterbury to confer with his defence counsel in private, even though he could get no one to support him.[9]

Despite Thomas's unpredictability, and presumably as a reward for his own more discreet conduct, Alan was added to the commission of lords justices in Ireland by the end of 1722,

---

[3] *HC 1715–54*, i, 490; *Knatchbull Diary*, 115; *CJ*, xx, 48.

[4] Cobbett, *Parl. Hist.*, viii, col. 46.

[5] *CJ*, xx, 67, 89, 112, 115, 133, 161–2, 172–3, 175, 178, 181, 203, 209.

[6] Cobbett, *Parl. Hist.*, viii, col. 209.

[7] *CJ*, xx, 73, 77, 127, 135, 142, 162, 168, 170, 203, 210.

[8] *CJ*, xx, 75, 33, 168, 170, 202–3. See also Cobbett, *Parl. Hist.*, viii, cols. 53, 195.

[9] *Knatchbull Diary*, 17.

though the appointment process did not go entirely smoothly. The king's letter to Dublin was incomplete and had to be returned. Grafton was rusticating when it arrived in Whitehall and was outraged to discover that Alan had gone directly to the secretary's office to have the letter amended rather than waiting for the viceroy to make the order. If Grafton could not prevent Alan's appointment, he clearly wished it to appear to the world as a favour bestowed by him rather than something achieved against his will or behind his back.[10] There had been unfounded rumours during the winter that Grafton would be replaced as viceroy, but presumably because of the success the lord lieutenant had enjoyed, against expectations, in the previous Irish parliamentary session he could be sure of the backing of Townshend and Walpole.[11]

Since the Brodrick family were gathered together in England during this session of the British parliament, there is naturally a gap in the surviving letters between October 1722 and June 1723, when Alan returned to Ireland and a regular correspondence resumed. Even then some items are missing from the later sequence of letters between Alan and Thomas. Every time a letter went astray Alan blamed the Irish postmaster general Isaac Manley, a crony of Speaker Conolly's, who was widely suspected of tampering with the post, especially when political tensions reached breaking point over the affair of Wood's halfpence. Swift was another who assumed himself to be the victim of Manley's snooping.[12] To get round the problem the Brodrick brothers arranged where possible for their letters to be carried by messengers, and when this was not practicable, to try and disguise the identity of individuals named in the correspondence by means of a cipher, or by some allusive reference comprehensible only to them, which regrettably remains sometimes as obscure to the historian as it was intended to be to the prying postmaster.

Alan's first concern on arriving in Dublin was whether or not he should take up his position as a lord justice, anxious that by doing so he might be committed to resigning his parliamentary seat at Westminster. Under the terms of the English Regency Act of 1706 any member accepting an office of profit under the crown was obliged to seek re-election. On receiving reassurance that he would not have to stand down as an English MP, Alan immediately arranged to be sworn. But he remained dissatisfied, and this dissatisfaction only increased when Grafton returned to Dublin in August. The viceroy was perfectly polite, but his civilities were 'all from the teeth outward', and he reserved his closest confidences for the Speaker, who was 'entirely confided in and caressed'. Grafton even went to stay with Conolly in the country before the session opened in August.[13]

Meanwhile, public opinion in Ireland was becoming increasingly agitated about Wood's halfpence. The first pamphlet denouncing the patent, James Maculla's *Ireland's Consternation* ..., appeared in the middle of August 1723.[14] Alan shared the general concern, and was determined from the outset to defend Irish national interests no matter what the short-term

---

[10] Coxe, *Walpole*, ii, 346–7; TCD, MS 1995–2008/2022: Edward Southwell to Archbishop King, 1 Jan. 1722[/3]; SHC 1248/8/43: papers relating to 'the obstructions given and difficulties made in spring 1722/3 to my being made one of the lords justices of Ireland'.

[11] TCD, MS 1995–2008/2022: Edward Southwell to Archbishop King 1722[/3]; 1995–2008/2026: William Trench to King, 26 Jan. 1722/3.

[12] *Swift Corr.*, ii, 433, 540.

[13] See below, Letters 551–2.

[14] Sabine Baltes, *The Pamphlet Controversy about Wood's Halfpence (1722–25) and the Tradition of Irish Constitutional Nationalism* (Frankfurt am Main, 2002), 114–17.

cost to himself. He had little confidence in Walpole and Townshend, but there were others in England to whom he might turn. The most important was the secretary of state, Lord Carteret, who had ambitions to take over the leadership of the ministry himself. Thomas also had a range of influential contacts, including the duchess of Marlborough.[15] A letter written in August 1723 – perhaps under the assumption that it would be intercepted – provides ample testimony of Alan's state of mind as the crisis approached:[16]

> I shall consider myself as only one who will suffer no more in proportion than his neighbours, if he lies still; and doth not irritate those who have power and inclination to bear down all opposers. But shall be sure to feel the continuance of the resentment of the great ones if I make myself the butt of their fury by taking the lead in opposing the loading this kingdom with that provision for favourites which will not be born elsewhere. I scorn to make my interest (as a certain person [*Conolly*] doth) by sacrificing the trust reposed in him by the country and lying forward and backward and swearing he never was nor will be in any of the projects … and having done this I think I shall acquit myself from any imputation of being instrumental in the ruin of the country: but if those who are chosen its representatives in parliament, think fit to be silent, I do not think I am under any obligation to do more than vote according to honour and conscience if anything comes before the house of lords, in which the welfare of Ireland appears to me to be much concerned.

2

Once in Dublin Grafton consulted those whom he called the 'principal persons' in parliament, and quickly formed the view that opposition to Wood's patent would be insurmountable. Not even Conolly could be persuaded to support it. The viceroy correctly predicted 'disagreeable proceedings'.[17] But he was unable to persuade the cabinet of the danger: Walpole saw no rational ground for Irish objections.[18] Grafton was sent back to do more canvassing, which only increased hostility to the project. Panicking, he pointed the finger of blame at the Irish lord chancellor.[19]

The storm broke on Friday, 13 September 1723, in an ill-tempered debate in the Irish house of commons resulting in a request to the lord lieutenant to supply a copy of the patent and other relevant papers. To MPs' surprise, the chief secretary, Edward Hopkins, informed the House that Grafton did not possess a copy of the patent. Fortunately, by the following Monday one had been discovered, misplaced among the baggage brought from England. This saved the viceroy from a complete political catastrophe: at least the proceedings on supply could continue while the Commons discussed the halfpence. Grafton's initial refusal had threatened to bring all parliamentary proceedings to a standstill.[20] But the sight of

---

[15] See below, p. 8 and BL, Add. MS 61476: Thomas Staunton to St John III, 8 Feb. 1723[/4].
[16] Below, Letter 553.
[17] Coxe, *Walpole*, ii, 347–8.
[18] Coxe, *Walpole*, ii, 348–9.
[19] SA, 423/880: Grafton to Walpole, 14 Sept. 1723; Coxe, *Walpole*, ii, 349.
[20] Burns, *Politics*, 140–1.

the viceroy so clearly floundering encouraged opposition. The Commons secured a report from two local assayers that the coins were of low quality, and passed a set of resolutions condemning Wood's halfpence, embodying these into an address. According to the lord lieutenant, St John was 'at the head' of the party in the Commons which was pressing for the most vigorous response.[21]

Grafton tried to make the best of things in his despatches to Whitehall, arguing that nothing could have been done to stem the tide, and that the outcome might have been worse. St John's followers in the Irish house of commons had been foiled in an attempt to censure those who had advised the passing of the patent. Grafton told Walpole that St John, 'as much as parliamentary terms would allow, pointed his malice at yourself and me', and had moreover vowed that 'by the blessing of Almighty God, he would in a parliament in another kingdom move to have this iniquity looked into'. Grafton added that Midleton's professed ignorance of these proceedings could not be taken at face value, since those supporting St John had included the chancellor's secretary, purse-bearer 'and three or four other dependants'.[22] Then the upper house took up the cudgels, with an address of their own to the king, which Alan himself played an important part in framing. The line that he followed, arguing that the king had been misinformed (without saying by whom), could be presented as reasonable and moderate, but its implications were confrontational: while the Commons contented themselves with denouncing Wood and calling for the revocation of the patent, the upper house was in effect seeking assurances that all those responsible would be subject to the king's displeasure.[23]

Not surprisingly, Walpole and his colleagues were outraged. Walpole immediately sent a blistering letter to Grafton, refusing to give way over the patent, and insisting that detailed objections be sent over. He had no intention of humiliating himself, and antagonising the duchess of Kendal, simply in order that Grafton should have an easy time.[24] Walpole did not need convincing that Midleton was the instigator of fireworks in the Irish house of commons, and shared Grafton's belief that the Brodricks were intriguing with Carteret; indeed, he was reliably informed by Townshend (who was then in Hanover with Carteret and the king), that Alan Brodrick II had shown Carteret a letter from his father about the halfpence. But Walpole was equally exasperated at the lord lieutenant's apparent incompetence and the inability of Conolly and other so-called 'faithful servants of the king' to defend the patent. He rejected out of hand Grafton's explanation, that the complaints of 'the country party' in the Irish parliament had already acquired impetus through the existence of other grievances, especially the increase in pensions on the Irish establishment.[25]

For the time being, Grafton was left to soldier on, consumed by self-pity. He had been mauled by letters from Walpole, and was unable to make any satisfactory concession to the

---

[21]SA, 423/881: Grafton to Walpole, 23 Sept. 1723. For St John's importance in the House, see *CJI*, v, 14, 22, 31–2, 114, 118.

[22]BL, Add. MS 47030, ff. 17–18: Philip Perceval to Viscount Perceval, 22 Sept. 1723; SA, 423/881: Grafton to Walpole, 23 Sept. 1723.

[23]Burns, *Politics*, 143; SA, 423/884: Grafton to Walpole, 20 Oct. 1723.

[24]SA, 423/882: Walpole to Grafton, 24 Sept. 1723.

[25]Raynham Hall, Townshend MSS: Grafton to Townshend, 24 Sept. 1723; SA, 423/883: Walpole to Grafton, 3 Oct. 1723; SA, 423/884: Grafton to Walpole, 20 Oct. 1723; BL, Add. MS 32686, f. 237: Townshend to Walpole, 2 Oct. N.S. 1723; ff. 387–8: Newcastle to Walpole, 2 Nov. 1723.

Irish parliament about the halfpence.[26] For his part, Walpole was 'at a loss to know what answer to give' to the addresses, which he considered to be 'no less than a civil remonstrance'. In his view, the king could not concede that passing the patent had been wrong, or promise to make no similar grant in future; an answer to the addresses of the two houses could only be couched in the most general terms.[27] As for the Brodricks, neither Walpole nor his closest colleagues, Townshend and the duke of Newcastle, were under any illusions about them. Alan I had written to Walpole to explain himself, but his critical remarks on the patent, his attempt to lay all the blame for what had happened on political rivals in Ireland, and veiled threats that the affair might lead to 'storms in England', were dismissed by Newcastle as 'insolent'.[28] In discussions with Townshend in Hanover, George I had already agreed to appoint a new lord chancellor whenever Townshend and Walpole thought fit. But Walpole lacked confidence in Conolly and his followers: were they willing, or able, to support government over the halfpence?[29] So, for the time being, the decision was not implemented.

The king's answer to the addresses arrived the day after Grafton had adjourned the Irish parliament for its customary mid-term recess, taken once bills had been sent to England to be scrutinised by the British privy council. The terms were exactly as Walpole wished: brief and anodyne, expressing concern that the grant of the patent had caused so much uneasiness, and promising to do everything possible to satisfy the Irish, including ordering an inquiry as to whether abuses had been committed by the patentee. Grafton withheld the text from the privy council until the day before parliament resumed sitting in December. When councillors were informed, Archbishop King of Dublin was incandescent, and Midleton also expressed himself dissatisfied, but promised not to speak out in parliament. He honoured the letter of this promise, but in debate evidently managed to make his true feelings clear. Even so, the Lords accepted the answer by a clear majority. In the Commons stronger sentiments were vented, and although there was a vote of thanks, St John Brodrick secured an amendment requesting the king to order revenue officials in Ireland not to accept the coin.[30]

Grafton's animosity towards Midleton knew no bounds. In lengthy, impassioned letters, he again urged ministers in London to dismiss the chancellor, making a raft of accusations; not only that Midleton had obstructed the king's business, but that he was 'shaking hands with the Tories here' and advancing politically dubious individuals to the county magistracy, including 'new converts from popery'. It was crucial that the king make a clear statement, so that all might see who had the greater credit in England, lord lieutenant or lord chancellor.[31] In response, Grafton was privately reassured, by both secretaries, Townshend and Carteret, that the king was 'very much dissatisfied' with Midleton's conduct, blamed the chancellor

---

[26] BL, Add. MS 32686, f. 362: Walpole to Newcastle, 24 Oct. 1723.

[27] BL, Add. MS 32686, f. 374: Walpole to Newcastle, 30 Oct. 1723.

[28] BL, Add. MS 32686, ff. 372–3: Newcastle to Walpole, 28 Oct. 1723; Coxe, *Walpole*, ii, 349–51.

[29] BL, Add. MS 32686, f. 367: Townshend to Walpole, 25 Oct. 1723; f. 357: Newcastle to Walpole, 22 Oct. 1723; SA, 423/885: Walpole to Grafton, 26 Oct. 1723.

[30] Burns, *Politics*, 148.

[31] Coxe, *Walpole*, ii, 352–63; TNA, SP 63/383/103–4: Townshend to Grafton, 23 Jan. 1723/4.

entirely for the 'unquietness' of the parliamentary session, and was determined to remove him from office, even if not quite yet.[32]

The situation was complicated by the connections the Brodricks were continuing to forge with British politicians and by their presence in the Westminster parliament. Grafton's Irish troubles threatened to become a central element in ministerial intrigues. Thomas was joined at Westminster in January 1724 by St John III, whose letters show contacts with various persons of influence.[33] From the evidence of the many committee appointments of 'Mr Brodrick' recorded in the Commons' *Journals* it is clear that one (and probably both) attended regularly until the prorogation in late April 1724.[34] Little is known of their conduct in the Commons beyond this bare record. Thomas certainly wrote letters to the duchess of Marlborough over the winter of 1723–4 which professed his disgust with the current set of ministers, who, he said, were acting on 'no other principle than securing themselves'.[35] While he may of course have been telling the duchess what she wanted to hear, the one speech of his that is recorded during this session, on the malt tax in Scotland, was certainly at variance with the ministerial line. Thomas argued in favour of obliging the Scots to pay the duty, contrary to the intention of Walpole, who was determined to avoid any inflammation of Scottish opinion.[36]

Although there can be no doubting the unpopularity of Wood's halfpence, manifest in a shower of pamphlets published in Dublin during the autumn and winter of 1723–4,[37] the viceroy's difficulties were also grounded in the chronic rivalry between Alan Brodrick and William Conolly. While Conolly was publicly seen to have the ear of the viceroy, who continued to pay visits to the Speaker's country seat at Castletown in County Kildare,[38] Alan's retention of the seals, his restoration to the commission of lords justices, and the influence he was rumoured to enjoy in England, made for mixed messages. This situation undermined the Speaker's authority in the Commons, and enabled the Brodricks to mobilise an alliance of their traditional supporters (concentrated in the province of Munster) with malcontent whigs, tories and 'independent country gentlemen', in order to carry some (though not all) crucial divisions.

After the recess the Speaker's friends hit back. Lord Fitzwilliam, a personal enemy of the chancellor, as well as an intimate of the viceroy, moved for a committee of the house of lords to inquire into Alan's prolonged absences in England. Although these absences had been properly authorised, the Lords drew attention to the serious detrimental effects on the administration of justice in Ireland, and criticised Alan for not properly informing the king of the likely consequences. Judging by his letters, Fitzwilliam's attack alarmed Alan considerably, even though the end result was less painful than it might have been, and Francis Bernard, the ex-tory who was leading the Brodrick faction in the Commons in St John's

---

[32] SA, 423/881: Townshend to Grafton, 7 Jan. 1723–4; Coxe, *Walpole*, ii, 363.

[33] No further mention of St John occurs in *CJI* after 20 Dec. 1723 (v, 180).

[34] *CJ*, xx, 244, 246–7, 251, 258–9, 262–3, 266, 268, 272, 274–5, 278, 288, 295, 306, 309, 329.

[35] BL, Add. MS 61476, f. 74: Thomas to the duchess of Marlborough, 21 Feb. 1723[/4].

[36] *Knatchbull Diary*, 12.

[37] Baltes, *The Pamphlet Controversy about Wood's Halfpence*, 122–32.

[38] *Swift Corr.*, ii, 485.

absence, managed to engineer a resolution in the lower house vindicating the chancellor.[39] The extent to which parliamentary politics had become personalised was shown in January when followers of Conolly and the Brodricks were on opposite sides in a commons debate on a controversial by-election for County Westmeath. This episode gave rise to a popular ballad, in which Conolly was satirised as 'Sir Owen McHugh' (in reference to his Ulster catholic origins), which was frequently sung by members of the Brodrick faction attending performances in the Smock Alley theatre and came close to provoking violence among the audience.[40]

By the end of the Irish parliamentary session, in February 1724, Grafton had secured a supply, even surviving a scare over the British privy council's suppression of a popular popery bill. He could therefore breathe a little easier.[41] Nevertheless, it was clear that Irish politics, if not the Irish administration, had become dysfunctional, a turn of events which left Walpole and his colleagues in a cleft stick. It was popularly assumed, in both Ireland and England, that Wood's patent would have to be withdrawn, but – besides repercussions at court – such a decision would mean not only bowing to public opinion in Ireland but allowing the Brodricks to claim a moral victory. In casting around for a solution to their problems, ministers seem briefly to have returned to a desperate expedient which they had already considered and rejected during a crisis in Irish parliamentary management in 1720, namely trying to make the Irish government self-sufficient, by reducing expenditure and improving the yield of the hereditary revenue, so as to render further meetings of parliament unnecessary. When Grafton was asked to stay on in Dublin for a time, something he regarded as a 'penance', it was to undertake just such a review of the Irish establishment and the management of public finance. But the recent increase in civil list pensions – principally to English recipients – made retrenchment problematic, and it was also highly unlikely that Conolly and the 'Castle party' would co-operate with the project.[42] Unsurprisingly, by the time Grafton embarked for England he had made no progress.

3

Already, before Grafton's departure from Dublin, Walpole and Townshend had determined on drastic action, in the form of a ministerial reshuffle in England. The prime necessity was a new viceroy, and evidently they first fixed on the duke of Bolton, indicating their determination to take a tough line. Only subsequently did they alight upon a more in-genious 'scheme', which promised to solve both their problems, the crisis in Ireland and the intrigues of Carteret at court. The relatively short and trouble-free British parliamentary session of January–April had confirmed the king's confidence in Walpole's managerial abilities, and enabled the minister to take action against his most dangerous rival. Carteret was announced as lord lieutenant of Ireland, with Grafton moving across to become lord chamberlain. The vacant secretary's place went to Newcastle. In this way the problem of

---

[39] Coxe, *Walpole*, ii, 358–63; *LJI*, ii, 773–6; *CJI*, v, 182; BL, Add. MS 9713, f. 15: Sir Richard Levinge to Edward Southwell, 10 Feb. 1723/4; Burns, *Politics*, 150–2.

[40] D.W. Hayton, 'Two Ballads on the County Westmeath By-election of 1723', *ECI*, iv (1989), 7–30.

[41] BL, Add. MS 32687, ff. 1–2: Grafton to Newcastle, 19 Jan. 1723/4; Burns, *Politics*, 155–6.

[42] BL, Add. MS 32687, ff. 4–6: Newcastle to Grafton, 28 Jan. 1723/4; SA, 423/888: Grafton to Townshend, 8 Feb. 1723/4; BL, Add. MS 32687, ff. 9–11: Townshend to Grafton, 22 Feb. 1723/4.

dealing with the opposition to Wood's halfpence was dumped on Carteret, who had, it was thought, encouraged Irish recalcitrance for his own ends. Since Walpole never took very seriously manifestations of Irish indignation at the patent, he appreciated Carteret's predicament solely in terms of practical politics and the management of factions: the new viceroy would have to choose for himself between Lord Midleton and Speaker Conolly; in other words, to 'take his party betwixt the two great men there'.[43]

In their reports to Midleton, Thomas and St John Brodrick were cautiously optimistic. Carteret was making appropriately reassuring noises, even visiting Thomas at his home rather than waiting for a courtesy call. The viceroy made a point of including St John among several recommendations for admission to the Irish privy council, a remarkable gesture given the young man's behaviour in the previous parliamentary session in Dublin.[44] Francis Bernard was also readmitted to office, as prime serjeant.[45] Carteret gave an even more substantial proof of his friendship by nominating Alan alongside Conolly and the commander-in-chief, Lord Shannon, to the commission of lords justices which would govern Ireland until the viceroy was able to make his way to Dublin himself. In taking the initiative to make the appointments while Grafton was technically still in post, Carteret was consciously breaking with protocol in order to send a political message. He would take sole responsibility for Irish business (as Walpole and Townshend indeed wanted him to), and there would be no more underhand correspondence between Dublin and English ministers. Of course, during Grafton's viceroyalty the most serious subversion of normal channels of communication had been the contacts between the Brodricks and Carteret himself, but what the new lord lieutenant was trying to show was that the Speaker ('Sir Owen', as Alan and Thomas now derisively referred to him in their letters) would not be able to write privately to his friends in Whitehall. Alan gleefully reported his rival's discomfiture, and the cringing tone Conolly was adopting to Grafton's successor.

At the same time, the affair of the halfpence did not look at all promising, and St John in particular, even in his most sanguine letters, could not avoid expressions of gloom, reflecting what would seem to have been the popular mood.[46] Anxieties were heightened by events in England, where the promised inquiry into the halfpence was being carried out by a committee of the British privy council. Wood had requested an official assay of his coinage at the Royal Mint, which declared it sound, except for the fact that some individual pieces were 'not so equally coined in the weight as they should have been'. Wood then offered to limit himself to £40,000 worth of copper currency for Ireland if the Irish government would offer no hindrance to its circulation. The committee accepted his proposal, and ordered the Irish revenue commissioners to revoke any directions given to their officials not to accept the coinage. (In a private letter to Newcastle, Conolly, as *de facto* chief commissioner, vehemently denied they had ever done so.) While all this was going on the Irish privy council, provoked by reports in the London press of the progress of the inquiry,

[43] BL, Add. MS 32687, ff. 54–5: Walpole to Newcastle, 1 Sept. 1724. See Hayton, *Ruling Ireland*, 127, 233–4; Burns, *Politics*, 160–2; Patrick McNally, 'Wood's Halfpence, Carteret, and the Government of Ireland, 1723–6', *IHS*, xxx (1996–7), 360–1.

[44] TNA, SP 63/383/244: Carteret to Newcastle, 14 May 1724.

[45] McNally, 'Wood's Halfpence', 365.

[46] See, for example, *Swift Corr.*, ii, 489, 493, 496; NLI, MS 29766/5: Patrick Sherlock to Caesar Colclough, 28 Apr. 1724.

agreed an address to the king in the same terms as the parliamentary addresses and repeated the request that revenue officers be told to refuse Wood's money. This was supported by addresses from the grand juries of the city and county of Dublin. Alongside Lord Abercorn and Archbishop King, Alan Brodrick was a prime mover in the privy council's address. Predictably, it only intensified Walpole's fury: he was more than ever convinced, following the Mint's assay, that Irish objections were the product of ignorance, bigotry, and factional malice, and demanded that the Irish council send over papers and witnesses to prove their case, which they were unable to do. Publicly, the ministry let it be known that, although the patent would not be recalled, some effort would be made to mitigate detrimental effects to the Irish economy.[47] Opinion in Dublin remained obdurate: the patent had to be recalled in its entirety.[48]

Now Swift entered the fray. His *Letter to the Shopkeepers, Tradesmen, Farmers, and Common People of Ireland, Concerning the Brass Halfpence Coined by Mr Woods* [sic]…, the first of the so-called 'Drapier's Letters' (after the pseudonym Swift adopted, 'M.B. Drapier') appeared in March 1724. Swift scholars have suggested that Alan Brodrick may have been one of those who encouraged the dean to take up his pen, and that the chancellor may even have given advice on some legal and constitutional aspects, though Alan was careful not to make any such admission in his letters.[49] A sly reference in Swift's text to 'Squire C———y' and his great wealth might be taken as further evidence of Alan's involvement.[50] A second pamphlet, in the form of a letter to the printer Harding, appeared in August, protesting that the 'universal sense and opinion of the nation' had already been made clear, through the addresses of parliament and privy council.[51] Soon afterwards the report of the British privy council's inquiry was published, and Swift launched his third and longest letter so far, a comprehensive demolition of the government case.[52]

All that the ministry had achieved by carrying out its inquiry was to raise public opinion in Ireland to fever-pitch. In August and September 1724 petitions and addresses against the halfpence flooded in; associations of tradesmen in towns across the country pledged that they would never receive the hated coin, and published their declarations as broadsheets; there were public demonstrations and threats of physical violence against ships bringing the coin to Irish ports, which in one case seem to have deterred a captain from landing.[53] Francis Bernard wrote from County Cork that 'The spirits of the people in general are raised to that degree by the late proceedings in favour of Wood's copper money that if any attempt should be made to utter it or even land it I know not what mischiefs may follow.'[54] The king's

---

[47] *Drapier's Letters*, xxiv–xxxii; Albert Goodwin, 'Wood's Halfpence', in *Essays in Eighteenth-century History …*, arr. Rosalind Mitchison (1966), 129–30.

[48] BL, Add. MS 47030, ff. 65–6: Viscount Perceval to Philip Perceval, 6 May 1724; ff. 66–7, Philip Perceval to Viscount Perceval, 26 May 1724.

[49] *Drapier's Letters*, xxiii; Irvin Ehrenpreis, *Swift: The Man, His Works and the Age* (3 vols, 1962–83), iii, 206.

[50] *Drapier's Letters*, 8.

[51] *Drapier's Letters*, 26.

[52] *Some Observations upon a Paper, Call'd, The Report of the Committee of the Most Honourable the Privy Council in England, Relating to Wood's Halfpence* (Dublin, 1724).

[53] *Drapier's Letters*, xxxiii–xl; *Coghill Letters*, 10–11; NLI, MS 4177/30: earl of Orrery to Brettridge Badham, 8 Sept. 1724; Chatsworth House, Derbyshire, Devonshire MSS: Bernard Hale to duke of Devonshire, 10 Sept. 1724 (I owe this reference to Dr A.P.W. Malcomson); BL, Add. MS 32687, ff. 56–62, Walpole to lords justices [I], 3 Oct. 1724 (draft).

[54] BL, Add. MS 60583, ff. 41–2: Francis Bernard to Edward Southwell, 25 Aug. 1724.

instructions to the Irish administration not to hinder the currency of the halfpence were naturally interpreted by the recipients as a command 'in court language … to the officers of the revenue to receive them', and by this means to ensure their circulation. But as one of Conolly's colleagues on the revenue commission pointed out, 'the general aversion of all people here to those halfpence is such, that … nothing but force can make them pass'.[55] And force was not something the authorities in Dublin Castle were prepared to use, even if given a direct order.

By September 1724 popular opposition in Ireland to the halfpence had become an even greater political danger to Walpole. Ministers were already prone to suspect that Irish protestants were infected with a passion for 'independency'. This assumption had been a feature of some of the polemical literature arising from the Woollen Act of 1699 and the resumption of the forfeitures in 1699–1703. It had resurfaced in the correspondence of English politicians during the jurisdictional dispute between the Irish and English Houses of Lords in 1717–20, and in British parliamentary debates on the Declaratory Act. Indeed, the notion that, left to their own devices, Irish politicians would seek to establish some form of constitutional autonomy seems to have been an obsession with English politicians, despite protests to the contrary from Dublin. The campaign against the halfpence was also coming closer to Walpole himself. The Drapier had taken care to direct his fire against Wood and his accomplices, but others were less circumspect, including Swift himself in different guises.[56] There were attacks on the duchess of Kendal, and in one notorious instance, a Dublin newspaper, *Dickson's Dublin Intelligence*, printed a report that:

> A certain nobleman of England, my L— W—e, who was the chief in gaining Wood his patent, hearing of the joint declaration of the people of Ireland against the brass coin, has sworn that since he gained the patent, if the people of Ireland still persist in their refusal of the brass coin, he would make them swallow it in fireballs.[57]

Clearly there was no point in waiting to send Carteret to Dublin until the 'additional duties' ran out and the Irish parliament would have to be recalled, since the lords justices could not be trusted to deal with this escalating situation. Already, Walpole and Townshend had given a hint of the way their thinking was developing – towards some form of 'direct rule', or at least attempting to curb the power of those Irish politicians on whom viceroys depended – and then in July the death of Archbishop Lindsay of Armagh created a vacancy at the head of the Church of Ireland. As a high churchman and a tory, Lindsay had been cold-shouldered by government ever since the Hanoverian succession. Whereas it had become customary before 1714 for the primate to be included, *ex officio*, on the commission of lords justices, successive whig administrations had turned instead to the politically more reliable archbishop of Dublin, William King. But King, although a whig in his politics, was also a staunch Irish patriot, and in playing a vigorous part in the assertion of Irish constitutional rights had forfeited ministerial goodwill. More recently he had been at the forefront of the agitation against the halfpence, and was strongly suspected of having given

---

[55] *Coghill Letters*, 9; NLI, MS 16007, pp. 135–6: revenue commissioners [I] to treasury commissioners [GB], 29 Aug. 1724.

[56] Baltes, *The Pamphlet Controversy about Wood's Halfpence*, 155–214.

[57] Reprinted in *Flying Post*, 12 Oct. 1724.

encouragement to his old friend Jonathan Swift to write against Wood. In fact, Walpole and Townshend did not trust any Irish-born bishop, and instead secured the nomination of Hugh Boulter, bishop of Bristol.[58] This was the first step in a considered strategy of advancing Englishmen to leading positions in the Irish establishment, in the church and in the law, in order to establish a permanent 'English interest' in Dublin Castle. The so-called 'undertaker system', by which Irish politicians managed the Irish parliament in return for influence over patronage, and the direction of policy, had clearly failed the test of pushing through an unpopular policy, and a new scheme of management was called for.[59]

Walpole does not seem to have had any faith in Carteret's ability to solve a problem the viceroy had himself helped to create. Indeed, in a private letter to Newcastle Walpole gloated over what he expected would be the lord lieutenant's inevitable failure. He would not have agreed to send Carteret to Dublin, he said, if he did not think matters would end in a rapid recall. Carteret was on the horns of a dilemma: he would have to press the retention of Wood's patent and lose his credit with his Irish friends, or espouse the cause of Irish 'independency' and lose his credit with the king, leaving the way open for Walpole and Townshend to impose a harsh settlement on the Irish.[60] This proved to be a major underestimate of Carteret's abilities as a politician. In their expectations from the new lord lieutenant, both Walpole and the Brodricks were to find themselves mistaken.

4

Carteret's initial approach to his task could be characterised as a form of 'masterly inactivity'. After his arrival, Dublin was awash with contradictory rumours: some reports from England suggested that Wood would be abandoned, while at the same time many in Ireland assumed that Carteret had been ordered 'to oblige us to receive' the coinage, and, to this end, would dissolve the parliament and call fresh elections.[61] The viceroy himself gave nothing away. As Alan's letters make clear, Carteret cultivated the impression that he would do nothing to force, or even persuade, the Irish to accept the halfpence, but equally would not promise that the patent be withdrawn. No one was able to guess at the likely outcome. The lord lieutenant was similarly non-committal in his personal dealings with local politicians. He treated the chancellor kindly, but was equally civil to the Speaker and his cronies. One observer thought him 'very reserved', which was true in so far as he seems to have guarded his true feelings, preferring to keep up a façade of general affability, and welcomed all to the viceregal court, whether old friends or potential enemies. His main diversion was hunting in the Phoenix Park, with hawk or gun, and his closest companions were his chief secretary, Thomas Clutterbuck, and members of the viceregal household.[62]

<hr/>

[58] Patrick McNally, '"Irish and English Interests": National Conflict within the Church of Ireland Episcopate in the Reign of George I', *IHS*, xxix (1994–5), 295–314; Philip O'Regan, *Archbishop William King of Dublin (1650–1729) and the Constitution in Church and State* (Dublin, 2000), chs. 8–9; *Boulter Letters*, 44–7.

[59] Hayton, *Ruling Ireland*, 126–7, 240–1.

[60] BL, Add. MS 32687, ff. 54–5: Walpole to Newcastle, 1 Sept. 1724.

[61] TNA, C 110/46/348: Owen Gallagher to Oliver St George, 17 Oct. 1724; TCD, MS 1995–2008/2117: Francis Annesley to Archbishop King, 27 Oct. 1724; NLI, MS 4177/38–9: earl of Orrery to Brettridge Badham, 14, 21 Nov. 1724; HMC, *Various Collections*, viii, 377.

[62] W. Sussex RO, Egremont MSS: James Hamilton to earl of Thomond, 21 Nov. 1724 (a reference I owe to Dr A.P.W. Malcomson); W. Sussex RO, Goodwood MS 103: Michael Broughton to duke of Richmond, 21 Nov.

One incident did force Carteret to act, and he did so decisively. His arrival in Dublin coincided with the publication of the next in the series of 'Drapier's letters', the *Letter to the Whole People of Ireland*, which not only attacked Walpole directly, but openly denied the presumption that Ireland was constitutionally dependent on England, and invoked William Molyneux's notorious *Case of Ireland …* (1698) in support of its arguments. Carteret could not afford to ignore this challenge: to have done so would have rendered his own position untenable. So he summoned the Irish privy council, and, having given his personal opinion that hatred of the halfpence was being exploited by malicious individuals pressing the case for 'independency', proposed that a proclamation be issued for the arrest of the printer, Harding, and the offering of a reward for evidence leading to the discovery of the author. After some debate, it was agreed that the proclamation be directed not against the *Letter* as a whole but against particular passages within it. Even so, some councillors refused to sign.[63]

Midleton was not one of them. He too had no choice but to take a firm line unless he wished to resign his post, which at this stage he did not. Although he had gone too far in opposition to the halfpence to be able to backtrack, he had to be careful. Not long before writing the *Letter to the Whole People of Ireland*, Swift had composed a more moderate statement of the case against the halfpence, in the form of *A Letter to the Lord Chancellor Middleton* [sic], which was not published at the time.[64] it assumed that the author and the lord chancellor were fundamentally on the same side. But Midleton could not appear to endorse the extravagant claims that Swift was now making. And he seems to have been genuinely concerned that extreme rhetoric of this kind risked endangering the Anglo–Irish constitutional settlement which had been established since the Glorious Revolution and which gave Irish protestants a level of practical independence within the overarching security of the English connection. According to his own testimony, he told Carteret that in his opinion the pamphlet was seditious and should be the subject of a judicial inquiry.

Carteret may even have been grateful for an opportunity to demonstrate to the king his own loyalty: the issues raised by the *Letter to the Whole People of Ireland* were much broader than Wood's patent and enabled the viceroy to take a stand in defence of constitutional principles without compromising his non-committal approach over the halfpence itself. Moreover, as the affair developed, tensions in Dublin escalated, enabling Carteret to make the case more persuasively to Walpole and Townshend that a graceful withdrawal over the patent was the wisest course of action. In November 1724, soon after the proclamation, Harding was arrested, but refused to name the author of the pamphlet. Before Harding could appear before a grand jury, Swift had written, and published clandestinely, a short paper of *Seasonable Advice* to the jurors. It included a passage which contrasted the members of the grand jury – 'merchants and principal shopkeepers' who 'can have no suitable temptation offered them' – with those, including signatories to the proclamation, who enjoyed 'great employments, which they have a mind to keep, or to get greater', and thus might 'make up in their own private advantage, the destruction of their country'.[65] Although Midleton

---

[62] *(continued)* 1724; HMC, *Various Collections*, viii, 377; Ehrenpreis, *Swift*, iii, 223–5; Rachel Wilson, 'The Vicereines of Ireland and the Transformation of the Dublin Court, *c.* 1703–1737', *The Court Historian*, xix (2014), 19–22.

[63] *Drapier's Letters*, xli–xlii, 65–87; BL, Add. MS 34265, f. 226: Bishop Downes to Bishop Nicolson, 22 Oct. 1724; Ehrenpreis, *Swift*, iii, 253–70; *The Proclamations of Ireland, 1660–1820*, ed. James Kelly and Mary Ann Lyons (5 vols, Dublin, 2014), iii, 143–4.

[64] *Drapier's Letters*, 123–42.

[65] *Drapier's Letters*, 91.

was stung by this remark, regarding it as a personal attack on himself, he was unhappy with the Dublin government's aggressive response, rightly predicting that over-reaction would rebound against the Castle. Carteret insisted that the *Seasonable Advice* be brought before the grand jury as 'scandalous and seditious'. Despite the efforts of the principal law officers the jurors refused to present, whereupon Lord Chief Justice Whitshed dissolved the jury and summoned another. However, the new jurors proved equally intractable, and eventually brought in an alternative presentment, 'of all such persons as have attempted, or shall endeavour by fraud or otherwise, to impose the said halfpence upon us'.[66]

The decision to send Carteret to Dublin, which Walpole had considered a master-stroke, had blown up in the ministry's face. The behaviour of the grand jury had made a striking impression on English public opinion, and there was renewed talk in London that the affair of the halfpence would be raised in the British house of commons.[67] Carteret seized his opportunity to press for a settlement. He told Newcastle that Dublin was 'in the greatest apprehension and ferment, looking upon it as an act of violence to introduce Wood's halfpence'. Furthermore, many believed that what Whitshed had done, in discharging the jury, was 'contrary to law'.[68] Matters were going from bad to worse. Carteret suggested an obvious way out, which he said he had discussed with the king's principal servants in the Irish house of commons: to withdraw the patent and pay Wood compensation. This did not go down well with the English ministers or at court, and the viceroy was told to repeat the previous mantra, that the king had no intention of forcing his Irish subjects to accept the coinage.[69] But English resolve was beginning to weaken, especially when Archbishop Boulter echoed Carteret's assessment: Ireland was 'in a very bad state'; minds were 'poisoned' against the halfpence; and notions of 'independency' were growing in popularity. 'Those of sense and interest' in Dublin agreed that the withdrawal of the patent was the only solution.[70]

It took time for Walpole and Townshend to be persuaded, and to persuade the king. In the meantime Carteret did what he could to reassure Irish politicians, and the Irish public at large, that there was no need for further anxiety on the score of the halfpence, without committing himself.[71] This outpouring of oil seems at last to have had an effect on the troubled waters of Irish public opinion, or perhaps, as in the aftermath of the Declaratory Act, Irish protestants were drawing back from the extreme position Swift had set out in the *Letter to the Whole People of Ireland*. The Drapier did contribute a further, more moderate, letter, but otherwise the storm began to die down.[72] As the revenue commissioners' secretary reported, 'Our apprehensions of the copper halfpence are not quite removed, nor do they seem to increase'.[73]

---

[66] *Drapier's Letters*, xlix–lv; Burns, *Politics*, 181–5.

[67] HMC, *Portland MSS*, vii, 392–3.

[68] SA, 423/892: Carteret to Newcastle, 24 Nov. 1724.

[69] Burns, *Politics*, 185–6.

[70] *Boulter Letters*, 102, 106–7. The despondent frame of mind to be found among Conolly's supporters is clear from TNA, SP 63/385/7: Isaac Manley to [Charles Delafaye], 9 Jan. 1724[/5].

[71] Burns, *Politics*, 187, 191.

[72] Baltes, *The Pamphlet Controversy about Wood's Halfpence*, 255–65.

[73] PRONI, D1556/16/4/3: James Forth to Henry Maxwell, 5 Dec. 1724.

In the meantime, Carteret occupied himself conducting a detailed review of every aspect of Irish government, which exposed a number of instances of maladministration.[74] This helped to nourish his popularity, but it may well have had another motive, following on from the proposed review of finance and expenditure that Grafton had been asked to undertake, with a view to decreasing dependence on Irish parliamentary taxation. Viceregal inquiries laid bare a chaotic situation in almost every branch of government. Carteret identified Captain John Pratt, the deputy vice-treasurer, as the principal culprit. Pratt had not simply neglected to pass his accounts promptly, he had made use of public money for his own private purposes, with the result that there was a deficiency in the treasury of over £80,000. Pratt was promptly dismissed in June 1725 and committed to the Marshalsea prison in Dublin, and an action was taken against him for the money owed.[75]

It was difficult for the leading Irish politicians to know what to make of Carteret. He had not admitted any individual or faction into his confidence; and although he may have talked to Midleton more often than to Conolly, their conversations were not reassuring as far as the chancellor was concerned.[76] There was no confirmation that Wood's patent would be revoked, and indeed Alan seems to have come to believe that, when the parliament met he would be expected to actively support the introduction of the halfpence. Rumours from England, relayed in Thomas's letters, made Alan more and more uneasy: that the patent would not, after all, be given up; that Carteret would be recalled; and that Alan himself would soon be dismissed. The English ministers, it was said, believed the Brodricks and their followers in Ireland to be as violent as ever against the halfpence, and were considering various alternative candidates for the Irish lord chancellorship. As usual, Thomas, the only member of the family to attend the British parliamentary session of November 1724 to May 1725, did not help by his conduct in the Westminster house of commons. He attended regularly but does not seem to have done very much to assist the court on essential business, while his occasional forays in debate, over the impeachment of the English lord chancellor, Lord Macclesfield, and the ministerially-sponsored attempt to rehabilitate the tory Lord Bolingbroke, stirred up backbench emotions in ways of which Walpole did not approve.[77]

The evident hostility of Walpole and Townshend, and the lukewarm reception he himself was meeting at the Castle, seem to have determined Alan to take the dramatic step of resigning the seals before he was dismissed. His letters show that he began to think of doing this in March 1725, and after some further rumination, and advice from Thomas, eventually tendered his resignation at the end of April, although this was not accepted until 10 May, and for administrative reasons he was kept in office until a successor was appointed in July.[78] After the event chancellor and viceroy gave conflicting, and essentially self-serving, explanations: Alan alleged that Carteret had required his support for the maintenance of Wood's patent; Carteret told one of Conolly's political allies that the Brodricks had insisted he 'trust all to

---

[74] *Coghill Letters*, 20.

[75] *Coghill Letters*, 21; Burns, *Politics*, 189–90; *Hist. Ir. Parl.*, vi, 113.

[76] Christ Church, Oxford, Wake MSS, Epist. xiv, f. 263: Bishop Godwin to Archbishop Wake, 18 May 1725; TNA, C 110/46/313, 366–7: Owen Gallagher to Oliver St George, 9 Jan. 1724[/5], 22 May 1725.

[77] *CJ*, xx, 348, 350–2, 363, 369–70, 372, 374, 384, 386–9, 408, 418, 428, 439; *Knatchbull Diary*, 36, 48.

[78] TNA, SP 63/385/90, 138: Carteret to Newcastle, 29 Apr., 8 June 1725; SP 63/385/109: Newcastle to Carteret, 10 May 1725.

their conduct and management'.[79] Perhaps this was how each of the protagonists perceived the other's position. But the simple truth is probably that Alan was becoming tired: he was concerned about his health, and the fatigue of chancery business was taking its toll. His previous, very visible, opposition to the halfpence afforded him no flexibility should the affair once again come to a crisis, and he was more than ever certain that dismissal was inevitable. Resignation gave him freedom.

Ironically, it was not long after Alan had unilaterally cut the Gordian knot into which high politics in Ireland had become entangled that a final decision was taken in England about Wood's patent. In July an English whig lawyer, Richard West, was nominated as lord chancellor of Ireland, against the viceroy's recommendation to promote the chief baron of the Irish exchequer. This was another step towards creating a permanent 'English interest' at Dublin Castle, and to underline this fact, West was instructed, once he had arrived in Dublin, to talk to the primate first.[80] The two men were soon in 'perfect agreement'.[81] Alan made sure that he was not present when his successor was sworn, taking a coach and going a dozen miles out of town in a deliberate, if futile, snub.[82] Carteret was then asked by Newcastle to state what was necessary to make the forthcoming parliamentary session go well. He replied that without the removal of the threat of Wood's halfpence no lord lieutenant could carry out the king's business. Crucially, his argument was strongly supported by Boulter.[83] At this point, Walpole and Townshend had other things to worry about. The recent parliamentary session at Westminster had been considerably more fraught than the previous year, with Lord Chancellor Macclesfield's impeachment, a controversy over remodelling the government of the City of London, and the defection to opposition of a leading whig, William Pulteney; the Shawfield riots in Glasgow against the malt tax in the summer of 1725 had created a political crisis in Scotland; and the international situation had become both more complicated and more dangerous with the signing of the Treaty of Vienna between Spain and Austria. In these circumstances, Walpole seems to have lost his appetite for a hard line approach to the halfpence, especially since Midleton was now out of office and free to declare his opinion unambiguously. The decision was taken on 12 August, while the king was abroad, and communicated to Carteret in an official letter a week later. But the precise terms – Wood agreed to surrender his patent in return for a pension on the Irish establishment held in trust for him by a nominee – were kept quiet for as long as possible.[84] The immediate reaction in Ireland was reportedly one of 'great joy', with bonfires in the streets of Dublin; one, pointedly, right outside the door of Speaker Conolly's mansion in Capel Street.[85]

---

[79] McNally, 'Wood's Halfpence', 364.

[80] Yale University, Sterling Library, MS 114: Newcastle to West, 7 Aug. 1725; *Boulter Letters*, 123–5.

[81] *Boulter Letters*, 125.

[82] NLI, MS 41675/6: Alan I to Rachel Courthope, 27 July 1725.

[83] Burns, *Politics*, 193.

[84] TNA, SP 35/57/230: Walpole to Newcastle 12 Aug. 1725; SP 35/57/248: Charles Delafaye to Newcastle, 19 Aug. 1725; Burns, *Politics*, 194.

[85] BL, Add. MS 9711, f. 65: Darby Clarke to Edward Southwell, 27 Aug. 1725; TNA, C 110/46/389: Owen Gallagher to Oliver St George, 31 Aug. 1725.

5

Carteret was now free to make his choice between 'the two great men'. It was obvious that Conolly would return to his previous role as the government's principal parliamentary manager, and indeed in August Carteret's butler was sent to Castletown, possibly to make arrangements for a viceregal visit.[86] At the same time, Carteret did not intend to hand himself over to a single 'undertaker', and continued to court potential allies on his own account, some of whom acknowledged very different allegiances than Conolly's friends. The lord lieutenant seems to have ignored the Brodricks entirely; at least Alan claimed that after his resignation as chancellor Carteret never 'looked straight upon' him.[87] But other erstwhile oppositionists found themselves the subject of viceregal attentions. Francis Bernard, for example, was 'spoken to with some freedom' by the viceroy, and consulted about sensitive political matters: he would eventually get his reward in June 1726, when he was restored to the bench as a judge of common pleas.[88] Carteret enjoyed less success with his attempts to win over two more of St John Brodrick's principal lieutenants, Thomas Carter, who was allowed to purchase the office of master of the rolls but remained obdurate in opposition, and Henry Boyle, knight of the shire for County Cork, who when the session opened in September 1725, was asked by the chief secretary to second the motion for the loyal address.[89]

By this time it was too late for irenicism or inclusivity in parliamentary management. Carteret may have assumed, along with some other observers, that his administration would surf a wave of public relief and rejoicing at the surrender of Wood's patent and enjoy a trouble-free session, but this was not to be the case.[90] In the Lords things went badly at first, before improving. There was significant opposition, led by Alan and Archbishop King, to an address thanking the king for putting an end to the halfpence.[91] Although Alan had wisely refused the intended dedication of a collected edition of the Drapier's letters,[92] he was determined to make some political capital out of the surrender of the patent. The loyal address could not be stopped, but could be doctored, and he and King secured the insertion of a phrase praising the monarch's 'great wisdom' in ending the patent, a phrase whose implications were too obvious for the court party to let it pass unopposed, but which was still added on a division.[93] Although this was embarrassing, it was the last real success the opposition was to enjoy in this session in the upper house, where the court party, under Boulter's leadership, established its dominance, symbolised in the severe response to the anonymous publication of Swift's poem *On Wisdom's Defeat in a Learned Debate*, a satire

---

[86] TNA, C 110/46/387: Owen Gallagher to Oliver St George, 21 Aug. 1725. Unfortunately, 'by some accident', the butler 'fell off Mr Conolly's house and was killed'.

[87] See below, Letter 702.

[88] *Coghill Letters*, 22.

[89] McNally, 'Wood's Halfpence', 365; PRONI, D2707/A1/2/8D: Thomas Clutterbuck to Henry Boyle, 11 Sept. 1725.

[90] PRONI, D2707/A1/2/8F: earl of Inchiquin to Henry Boyle, 12 Oct. 1725.

[91] *Boulter Letters*, 126–7.

[92] Coxe, *Walpole*, ii, 437–8; *Swift Corr.*, ii, 603.

[93] See below, Appendix 1.

on the Lords' debate on the address. The poem was ordered to be burned by the public hangman and the printer, John Harding's widow Sarah, was committed to custody.[94]

In the Commons, events followed a very different trajectory. At the outset MPs 'came to a proper resolution for an address without anything worth calling opposition',[95] but the Castle party came under fire on a range of different issues, most importantly over the supply. The opposition was again led by St John Brodrick and Thomas Carter. With the addition of a body of tory MPs headed by the Hon. Richard Stewart,[96] they seized upon a confusion in the public accounts over the extent of the government's debt. Information given to the House by the deputy vice-treasurer reported the total at £187,000, as against the auditor-general's estimate of £140,000. St John and his friends were able to exploit suspicions already aroused by the exposure of Captain Pratt's misdeeds to persuade the House to vote that the debt did not exceed £120,000. The end result was a grant of additional taxes for two years with nothing extra to service the national debt.[97] It was a blow to Carteret, but he was not entirely downcast, since the majority in the crucial division had been relatively narrow, 114–105. In his view the 'king's servants', that is to say Conolly's party, had worked hard to persuade the country gentlemen, and it was only the incompetence of those responsible for presenting the accounts which had brought about this defeat.[98] Boulter's letters to England were even more optimistic: in the long run, the influence of the Brodricks was certain to decline, since Midleton was on the point of retiring to live in England, while, despite recent parliamentary successes, his son was not at all popular.[99] Nonetheless, as the recess approached there was a great deal of talk in Dublin of the likelihood of new elections, so much so that some prospective candidates began to spend money in advance of a dissolution.[100]

One Irish critic blamed Carteret personally, and his reluctance to wine and dine 'the country gentlemen', as his predecessors had done.[101] His pose of standing above politics had been his undoing. The duke of Newcastle, as surprised as any other English minister by the turn of events, speculated that 'the conduct of affairs in the House, was not time enough put into the hands of the Speaker and his friends'.[102] This was not entirely fair, as in advance of the crucial debate Boulter had reported that, in relation to 'paying the debts of the nation', 'the management of that affair is put into the hands of the Speaker'.[103] However, Carteret had learned his lesson and henceforth made the direction of viceregal favour entirely clear.

---

[94] *Swift Corr.*, ii, 621; Ehrenpreis, *Swift*, iii, 314–16. Alan Brodrick deplored the poem and considered that the Lords had acted justly in condemning it.

[95] *Boulter Letters*, 126; TNA, SP 63/386/138: Thomas Tickell to Charles Delafaye, 24 Sept. 1725.

[96] *Boulter Letters*, 136; *Coghill Letters*, 25–6.

[97] Norfolk RO, WKC7/34: Thomas Wyndham to Ashe Windham, 15 Sept. 1725; BL, Add. MS 9711, f. 70: Darby Clarke to Edward Southwell, 29 Oct. 1725; *Boulter Letters*, 130, 136; Burns, *Politics*, 208–10.

[98] BL, Add. MS 38016, ff. 1–2, 3–4: Carteret to Edward Southwell, 14 Oct. 1725, 9 Jan. 1725[/6]; TNA, SP 63/386/292: Carteret to Newcastle, 16 Nov. 1725; *Coghill Letters*, 28–9; HMC, *Portland MSS*, vii, 404.

[99] *Boulter Letters*, 136; Victoria County History, *Surrey*, iii, 49–52.

[100] NLI, MS 38599/8: Robert Jones to Thomasine Howard, 11 Nov. 1725; MS 29766/5: George Le Hunt to Caesar Colclough, 11 Dec. 1725; John Cliffe to Colclough, 4 Dec. 1725; MS 11481/1: — Hely to William Flower, 30 Nov. 1725; James Tynte to [Flower], 10 Dec. 1725; MS 11481/3: Major Flood to Flower, 9 Dec. 1725, Ephraim Dawson to Flower, 7 Dec. 1725, Flower to Sir Thomas Vesey, 30 Nov. 1725.

[101] BL, Add. MS 47031, ff. 93–4: Philip Perceval to Viscount Perceval, 1 Feb. 1725/6.

[102] BL, Add. MS 32687, ff. 181–2: Newcastle to Townshend, 5 Nov. 1725.

[103] *Boulter Letters*, 130.

In January 1726 he finally paid a visit to Castletown, staying with Conolly for several days.[104] He also played his part, in support of his 'undertaker', in canvassing MPs.[105]

The results were seen when the Irish parliament reassembled in late January. At the opening of the Westminster session a week earlier, the king's speech had drawn attention to the potential danger of a jacobite invasion and the Commons had responded with resolutions for the augmentation of the armed forces. When Carteret communicated this news to the Irish parliament and asked MPs to 'express their duty to his majesty in such a manner as the present state of affairs in Europe seemed to require', the response was enthusiastic, the Commons promising in an address to take the most effectual means to put forces on the Irish establishment in a condition of readiness. This drew St John Brodrick into a false move. He proposed an amendment critical of the present administrations in England and Ireland, but suffered a crushing defeat.[106] On the same day he requested permission to go to England, to attend the Westminster parliament. Although he in fact stayed in Dublin for the remainder of the session this was another *faux pas*, buoying up still further the new-found confidence of the Castle party.[107]

After another recess, the final trial of strength occurred in the Commons on 27 February, when Conolly's henchman Henry Singleton moved to advance £10,000 immediately for the Irish army, with an assurance that should the funds granted in this session prove inadequate the Commons would make appropriate provision when they met again. St John protested that this was undoing all that had been achieved in keeping the government to reasonable financial demands, but found himself defeated once more. The outcome was seen as 'a victory over [*the*] Brodricks', and Carteret could crow that:

> Our affairs have taken a happy turn ... and this session of parliament will now be universally allowed to have been one of the best that has been held for the service of the king and the kingdom ... The few discontented people have lost their credit now with the country gentlemen, who for some time they misled by lies and nonsense, and the bulk of the gentlemen of all parties go down to their countries persuaded that they have been honestly dealt with.[108]

Carteret duly prorogued the parliament in March 1726 and returned to England, leaving Archbishop Boulter, Lord Chancellor West, and Speaker Conolly to act as lords justices in his absence.

6

Political defeat caused the Brodrick family to take stock. Alan had been a sedulous attender at the Irish house of lords in the 1725–6 session, missing only eight out of 38 sittings

[104] *Swift Corr.*, ii, 621.

[105] TNA, SP 63/387/50–1: Boulter to Charles Delafaye, 22 Feb. 1725/6.

[106] Burns, *Politics*, 212–13.

[107] *Coghill Letters*, 34; *Boulter Letters*, 142; BL, Add. MS 47031, ff. 93–4: Philip Perceval to Viscount Perceval, 1 Feb. 1725/6; BL, Add. MS 38016, f. 5: Carteret to Edward Southwell, 7 Feb. 1725/6.

[108] Yale Univ., Sterling Lib., MS 114: Richard Edgcumbe to Richard West, 8 Mar. 1726; BL, Add. MS 38016, f. 7: Carteret to Edward Southwell, 1 Mar. 1725/6.

according to the presence lists published in the *Journals*, but he confessed himself 'weary of going to Chichester House [where the Irish parliament met] … and … shall not be easy till I get to Surrey'.[109] He set sail for England as soon as the Irish parliament was prorogued, and after a month at Bath, settled himself at his Surrey estate, Peper Harow. Since its purchase, the property had been looked after by his 'sisters', Martha and Rachel Courthope (in reality his second wife's aunt and sister-in-law respectively), supplemented by an occasional inspection by Thomas. Now Alan took the reins himself. He was in residence until January 1727, when he went up to London for the British parliamentary session, and after another spell at Bath, finally returned to Dublin at the end of June. Despite his age (he was now over 70), his declining health, evidenced by his trips to take the waters, and protestations that he had supped his fill of public affairs, he did not abandon either the Irish or British parliaments. His principal interest, however, was in managing his estate and providing for his children. Once he resigned the lord chancellorship he seems to have given over his time to his financial affairs, and the maximisation of income from his property.[110] With his customary attention to detail, he prepared inventories of his property and rentals, both in Ireland and England, principally to assist his younger son, Alan.[111] The elder, St John, had already been provided for and set on a career, but Alan junior still had his way to make in the world.

After an undistinguished career at Cambridge, 'Nally' (as the young Alan was called within the family) was admitted to the Middle Temple in 1721, but seems to have had no intention of pursuing a career in the law. In the summer of 1723 he was sent to Hanover, to wait upon the king and to make himself known to the court and to those ministers in attendance on the monarch. While there he also seems to have acted as a conduit for correspondence between his father and Lord Carteret, who was in Hanover in his capacity as secretary of state. This experience gave the young man a yearning for continental travel. His father approved, up to a point: in respect of himself and his children Alan senior seems always to have been torn between the prospect of making a grand figure in England and nurturing the family's Irish power base. He told 'Nally' in September 1723 that:

> The chief end I had in sending you abroad was that you might pay your duty to the king; and I made no doubt of your endeavouring to improve your understanding by such observations as you should be able to make of the wisdom and defects in the constitution of such foreign countries as you shall travel through before your return; but since … a good part of your fortune lies in this kingdom, I cannot but be of opinion, that the most useful knowledge you can acquire will be that of the kingdoms to which you belong; and in particular of Ireland.[112]

There may also have been an element of parsimony in his attitude; unlike his brother Thomas, Alan spent money carefully, and was always wary of any spendthrift tendencies among his offspring.

[109] Below, p. 262.
[110] NLI, MS 41675/6: Alan I to Rachel Courthope, 27 July, 21, 31 Aug., 20 Oct. 1725; SHC, G145/box98/1: Nathaniel Evans to Alan I, 25 Aug. 1727.
[111] SHC, G145/box102/5: inventory of Alan Brodrick I's Irish estate; SHC, G145/box 1: volume relating to Peper Harow estate; SHC, G145/box102/4: rent rolls of Irish and English estates.
[112] Below, p. 50.

Alan junior was to spend two years wandering around Europe, at his father's expense. In the winter of 1723–4 he was at Cambrai, observing at first hand the snail-like progress of the diplomatic congress, which bored him to distraction. During the summer he made a long journey across the German states, from Düsseldorf to Regensburg (Ratisbon), where he witnessed a meeting of the Imperial Diet, though he was more interested in sightseeing, aided by various travel books that he had brought with him.[113] Then it was on to Venice, and slowly through Italy, spending most of his time looking at art, and consulting 'virtuosos' to improve his connoisseurship.[114] He spent six or seven weeks in Rome: 'the first half of the time I spent in seeing the curiosities and antiquities of the place, and the last in reviewing and attempting to fix in my memory the most material things'.[115] Then it was north again to Genoa and Turin, on to Vienna and Berlin, and home via Hanover again, and Holland, with a short diversion to see Paris. He wrote to his father:

> I hope you will have no reason to be discontented with … my travels, since I have used my utmost endeavours to improve myself in whatever the place I was in, could inform me of. I have done what has been in my power towards perfecting myself in French; and have learnt as much Italian as the small share of conversation, which strangers can have with the people of the country, would admit of.[116]

The paternal welcome, when he eventually returned to London in the autumn of 1725, was warm, but there was a schoolmasterly tinge to the long letter Alan senior sent to his son, which implies that the young man's enthusiasm for arts and antiquities, the beauty of ancient churches and the glittering spectacle of court life did not entirely meet with approval:

> I hope what you have seen abroad will make you more sensible of the happiness we enjoy under the mild and free government both in church and state at home, and particularly of our living where the religion established is that which our Saviour planted in the world … I cannot have the least doubt but that you have brought back the same principles of religion which you have been early and carefully instructed in; and that you have seen too much of the misery which the people of the countries through which you have travailed labour under, not to be confirmed in your love to the laws and constitution of your own country …[117]

There remained the problem of what 'Nally' was to do with himself. For the time being he stayed in England, not venturing to Ireland at all, and moving between London, some Courthope relations in Middlesex, and Peper Harow. He declined the opportunity of a seat in the Westminster parliament, and instead took up a position in Edinburgh in September 1727 as a customs commissioner.

Nally's sister Alice, the other surviving child of Alan's second marriage, was equally problematic. She too spent her time in England, principally with her Courthope relations in

[113]SHC, 1248/6/62–3: Alan II to Alan I, 4 Sept. 1724.
[114]SHC, 1248/6/86–91: Alan II to Alan I, 7 Oct. N.S., 8 Nov. N.S. 1724, Alan II to Thomas, 8 Nov. N.S. 1724.
[115]SHC, 1248/6/209–10: Alan II to Alan I, 25 Apr. 1725.
[116]SHC, 1248/6/302–3: Alan II to Alan I, 11 Sept. N.S. 1725.
[117]Below, Letter 711.

Surrey and London (where Martha had a house). Attempts to marry her off in 1724 to a baronet with a large fortune foundered on her dislike of the would-be husband. Her determination on this point greatly resembled that of her maternal aunt, Alan's sister Katherine, whose refusal to accede to paternal preferences over two decades earlier had caused a rupture in relations between father and daughter. Perhaps remembering this unhappy history, Midleton allowed his beloved 'Ally' the freedom to choose. Some years after his death, in 1736, just as her aunt had done, she married an English clergyman, in her case John Castleman or Castelman, a young gentleman of a Gloucestershire family who was then a fellow of All Souls, Oxford, and soon afterwards became a prebendary of Bristol cathedral, where he remained until his death in 1761.[118]

St John was an altogether different proposition. Significantly older than his half-brother and -sister, he was already making his way in the world, balancing a career at the bar with the demands of membership of the Irish and British parliaments. He was also primarily responsible for managing the family interest in Cork, in his parliamentary role as knight of the shire for the county, and more practically, as his uncle Thomas's tenant in Ballyannan, where he spent as much time as he could, nursing the family's influence and connections in Cork city, the borough of Midleton and the surrounding countryside, and ensuring that his father's rents were paid and the property maintained. Claims were made that St John also attempted to 'improve' the house and estate at Ballyannan, although his letters reveal a hard-headed approach to estate management typical of the family, focusing on the ways in which returns could be maximised and potential assets like timber turned to material advantage.[119] But the senior members of his family were hard taskmasters. His father was not always sympathetic to his financial difficulties, and was disinclined to spend money in helping out, while at the same time insistent that St John do his duty in both parliaments, even at the expense of his legal practice; so there were some sharp exchanges, which occasionally drove St John to exasperation. His uncle Thomas was even more demanding, particularly when looking for rents and remittances, although he generally preferred to get St John's father to write dunning letters on his behalf. Thus the tensions and occasional outbursts of bad temper that had characterised the relations of Alan and Thomas with their own father were repeated in the next generation.

By the mid 1720s Thomas was firmly settled in England, the limits of his travel encompassing the Brodricks' ancestral seat at Wandsworth in Surrey, his lodgings in Whitehall, and parliament at Westminster, with occasional visits to political friends in the country, race meetings at Newmarket, and cures at Bath. Ireland no longer figured on his itinerary. His health was also giving cause for concern: he spent time taking the waters in the summer of 1725, returned to Bath in the spring of 1726 following a painful inflammation of his leg, and was back there again in September 1727. He still contributed to debates in the British house of commons but his heyday had passed. In the session of January to May 1726 he was handicapped by ill-health, but even when present he was not especially busy: his number of committee appointments was the lowest for many sessions, and none were of particular

[118] *Historical Register*, 1737, Chron., 189; *A Bristol Miscellany*, ed. Patrick McGrath (Bristol Record Society, xxxvii, 1985), 44; TNA, PROB 11/862/413: will of John Castleman, 1761.
[119] D.W. Hayton, *The Anglo-Irish Experience, 1680–1730: Religion, Identity and Patriotism* (Woodbridge, 2012), 93–4.

importance politically.[120] His lifestyle, however, was as extravagant as ever. Unfortunately, the family's surviving estate papers do not provide details of his rental income. The only estimate comes in the Irish economist Thomas Prior's published list of 'absentees' in 1729, which included Thomas Brodrick with an estate of £2,500 a year, substantial enough for an Irish landowner but insufficient to enable him to live in the manner he wished; hence the irritation at what he perceived to be inadequate returns from St John.[121] While travelling around Europe Alan Brodrick junior was constantly on the lookout for pictures which his uncle had commissioned him to purchase: works by Tintoretto and Veronese in Venice, Carracci and Correggio in Bologna, Lutti and Poussin in Leghorn. He bought five pictures for Thomas in Italy at a total cost of £260, and then a Rubens and a Caravaggio in Flanders, to add to what was by all accounts an already substantial collection.[122] But the principal drain on Thomas's pocket was his passion for the turf. Right up until his death he financed a stable of racehorses, whose exploits kept him within the circles of gamblers and gamesters which his brother Alan had always deplored.[123]

7

Thomas, Alan and St John all attended the Westminster parliament in the last session of George I's parliament, from January to May 1727, and while Alan did not make much impact on proceedings,[124] his brother and son were much busier.[125] A 'Mr Brodrick' was appointed to the committee of 13 March to draft an address on the Imperial Resident's memorial,[126] and both Thomas and St John were recorded several times as speaking in debate. On the whole they seem to have supported the court, especially on issues relating to foreign policy. This would have been consonant with the strategy Alan had adopted before the eruption of the crisis over Wood's halfpence, which involved speaking and voting as a loyal whig at Westminster however much he might dislike and even oppose aspects of government policy in Ireland. There were still bumps in the road: on 12 April, for example, both Thomas and St John sided with the opposition on the motion for a vote of credit, and on another occasion Thomas was reported to be 'angry' with the ministers.[127] But overall it began to seem as if a rapprochement between the Brodricks and the ministry was possible, and Carteret and the Castle party in Dublin began to feel concern, especially since Carteret was increasingly uncertain of his own standing with Walpole and the king. A recent batch of senior appointments had been made in Ireland directly contrary to the recommendations

[120] *CJ*, xx, 546, 566, 570, 585, 587, 593, 596–8, 619, 687, 693.

[121] Thomas Prior, *A List of the Absentees of Ireland, and the Yearly Value of their Estates and Incomes Spent Abroad* … (Dublin, 1729), 3.

[122] SHC, 1248/6/82–3, 97, 100–1: Thomas to Alan II, 6, 19 Nov., 4 Dec. 1725; 1248/6/127–8, 219–20: Alan II to Thomas, 19 Jan. N.S., 4 May N.S. 1725.

[123] SHC, 1248/6/55–6: St John III to Thomas, 16 Aug. 1724; John Cheny, *An Historical List of All Horse-matches Run … in 1729 …* [1729], 161.

[124] *CJ*, xx, 739, 769, 799, 819–20, 827, 835, 838.

[125] *CJ*, xx, 731, 741, 775, 797, 799–800, 802, 810, 813, 817–20, 827–9, 851, 854, 863. It is impossible to distinguish between uncle and nephew in respect of the references to 'Mr Brodrick'.

[126] *CJ*, xx, 799.

[127] Cobbett, *Parl. Hist.*, viii, cols. 548–9, 551, 563; *Knatchbull Diary*, 61, 70.

of the viceroy and his 'undertaker'.[128] The younger Alan's appointment to the Scottish customs commission was also interpreted by some as a sign that the Brodricks might be coming back into favour in England.[129] However, the tragic events that were to follow would bring everything to ashes.

At first things had looked promising. St John let it be known that he intended to challenge Conolly for the Speakership of the Irish house of commons when a new parliament would open (the death of King George I in June 1727 meant an automatic dissolution), and his friends' vigorous canvassing was enough to give the authorities at the Castle cause for anxiety.[130] Carteret had sent reassurances that Conolly would carry the viceregal nomination, and had further encouraged the Speaker by promising William Brodrick's place as second serjeant to Conolly's nominee, on the grounds that William had been out of the kingdom – in Jamaica – for such a long time.[131]

Although Thomas did not seek re-election at the British general election in August 1727, Alan was brought in again by the duke of Somerset at Midhurst. For a time St John thought himself likely to be excluded at Bere Alston, when Sir Francis Drake, on whose interest St John had been returned, felt that he needed to stand himself in case of defeat elsewhere, but in due course Drake opted to sit for another constituency, leaving the way open for St John to take up the vacancy at a by-election. As things turned out, there was not enough time for this to happen.[132] In the Irish general election, which took place at the end of September, and was fiercely contested across the country (there having been no general election in Ireland since 1715),[133] St John was 'unanimously' re-elected for County Cork, alongside Henry Boyle, despite the threat of opposition, and despite falling ill before the poll with a 'rheumatical fever'.[134]

This sickness stayed with St John all winter, the ministrations of Cork doctors only making things worse. He did not come to parliament at all, and a relieved Conolly resumed the chair 'without the least opposition'.[135] Not only was St John confined to bed, Henry Boyle, the second-in-command of the 'Munster squadron', was in England, leaving the opposition coalition without leadership. Despite ongoing concern about the recent growth in the Irish pension list, and the underlying economic uncertainty caused by a succession of poor harvests, the session went smoothly for government.[136] The only issue to trouble Carteret was a bill to restrict the use of parliamentary privilege, which led to a minor revolt in the upper house, where otherwise there was said to be 'not enough business to keep them in countenance'.[137]

---

[128] Hayton, *Ruling Ireland*, 249.

[129] *Boulter Letters*, 223.

[130] PRONI, T2774/1: Thomas Tickell to Carteret, 23 June 1727; *Boulter Letters*, 206.

[131] NLI, MS 41583/7: Michael Smyth to William Smyth, 4 July 1727; IAA, Conolly MSS, box 53: Theophilus Clements to Conolly, 27 July 1727.

[132] *HC 1715–54*, i, 225–6, 329, 336.

[133] BL, Add. MS 47032, ff. 21, 25: Philip Perceval to Viscount Perceval, 20, 27 June 1727; TCD, MS 750/9, p. 28: Archbishop King to Edward Southwell, 3 Oct. 1727.

[134] BL, Add. MS 46978, p. 157: William Taylor to Viscount Perceval, 2 Nov. 1727.

[135] *Needham's Dublin Post-man*, 4 Nov. 1727.

[136] *Coghill Letters*, 41; Burns, *Politics*, 230–2.

[137] Burns, *Politics*, 233; NLI, MS 8802/1: Edward Cooke to [Sir Richard Cox], 2 Feb. 1727[/8].

Alan had been present in the Irish house of lords at its first sitting in November 1727, but thereafter attended infrequently. According to the presence lists, he was in the House once between 19 January and 15 April 1728, and in total attended only 16 sittings out of a possible 65. The principal reason for his absence was the need to be close to St John, whose prolonged suffering, punctuated by brief rallies and punishing relapses, finally came to an end with his death on 28 February 1728. Alan was heartbroken at the loss of another child (Courthope, his second son by his second wife, had died in infancy in 1701), and his ability to endure this blow was not helped by a brutally tactless letter from Thomas, written and received while St John was on his deathbed, which accused Alan of favouring the children of his second marriage and made disparaging remarks at the expense of the still unmarried Alice. 'I am sure', wrote Alan in reply, that 'all my children … hath been most dear blessings and … I shall be very little obliged to them who take the worst and wickedest way of expressing regard to and affection for them, by unjust suggestions of want of love toward them and too great partiality in favour of others.' It was an exchange that was not untypical of the family but even at this distance seems shocking.[138]

St John's death seems to have broken his father, who followed his eldest son to the grave in August 1728. Thomas died two years later, in October 1730, leaving his nephew, 'Nally', as his sole heir.[139] William Brodrick, whose health had been a cause of concern in May 1728, was still living in Jamaica in 1733: the date of his death is unknown. Laurence, the youngest of the five brothers, held various parish dignities in the diocese of Oxford until his death in 1748. Since St John had left no heir, nor much by way of an estate (he had, it was said, 'made a purchase', but was seriously in debt), the extensive Brodrick patrimony, in Cork as well as Surrey, passed to the younger Alan, now second Viscount Midleton.[140] Neither he nor his sister seem ever to have cared much for their stepmother, something their father was sufficiently aware of to be hypersensitive to their failure to pay his wife courtesy visits when she was in England, despite excuses offered and promises made. After Alan's death this hostility came out into the open. Lady Midleton had been left as executrix under her husband's will, which took several years to prove, presumably because the second viscount challenged the dispositions to the widow and her daughters by her previous marriage, who had to be provided for.[141] 'They are resolved to do everything they can to distress me', Lady Midleton complained to a correspondent, 'for my dear friend is gone and they may do what they want with me now'.[142] 'Ours is a melancholy family', Alan Brodrick had written as far back as 1683, and so it remained.

The second viscount did not attempt to make a name for himself in parliament but quietly enjoyed the emoluments of an official career. After the death of his uncle and the settlement of his father's estate, he moved from the Scottish customs to become joint comptroller of army accounts in Whitehall. The family focused on their English estates, and when Alan junior died in 1747 he was buried at Wandsworth. He had married Lady Mary Capell, daughter of the earl of Essex. Their only surviving son, who succeeded as third viscount, sat in the Westminster parliament from 1754 to his death in 1765, as a follower of the duke

[138]Below, pp 347–52. See also Hayton, *Anglo-Irish Experience*, 89.

[139]TNA, PROB 11/640/97: will of Thomas Brodrick, 1730.

[140]NLI, MS 41580/4: Jane Bulkeley to Jane Bonnell, 9 Apr. 1728.

[141]*Genealogical Memoranda Relating to the Family of Brodrick* (privately printed, 1872), 8.

[142]NLI, MS 41580/3: Lady Midleton to Jane Bonnell, 3 May 1730.

of Newcastle, without making much of an impression.[143] His son, the fourth viscount, employed the architect Sir William Chambers to rebuild Peper Harow in a classical style, and 'Capability' Brown to redesign the park.

The deaths of St John Brodrick and his father in 1728 were part of a broader generational change in Irish politics. A year after Alan's death his great rival William Conolly suffered a fit in the Commons chamber and was obliged to resign as Speaker on 12 October 1729. Less than three weeks later Conolly was dead. The leadership of the Castle party passed to the chancellor of the exchequer, Sir Ralph Gore, who took the Chair. On the other side of the House the 'Munster squadron' was now headed by Henry Boyle, whose own power base, concentrated in County Cork, brought together the various strands of the old Brodrick interest, families like the Bettesworths and Hydes, with the extensive electoral interests of his Boyle kinsmen, the earls of Burlington and Orrery, which he was able to manage for the absentee proprietors.[144] Thus Irish politics followed a familiar path, until Carteret's replacement in 1730 by the duke of Dorset, and Gore's death in 1733, ushered in a new era. Henry Boyle's election as Speaker in 1733 might perhaps be seen as a posthumous victory for the Brodricks, although by this time the family had long since ceased to think of themselves as a force in the Dublin parliament, or indeed in Ireland more generally. They were once more an English, rather than an Anglo–Irish family.

---

[143] *The House of Commons 1754–1790*, ed. Sir Lewis Namier and John Brooke (3 vols, 1964), ii, 120.

[144] NLI, MS 13296: —— to Edward Corker, 17 July 1728; NLI, MS 4177/62: Orrery to Brettridge Badham, 19 Oct. 1725; PRONI, D2707/A1/2/18: Burlington to Boyle, 13 July [1727]; NLI, MS 13296: Burlington's instructions to his commissioners, agents and receivers, 14 Aug. 1729; PRONI, D2707/A1/1/21A: Andrew Crotty to Henry Boyle, 15 Aug. 1729.

NOTE ON EDITORIAL PRINCIPLES

The bound volumes of Brodrick papers contain a variety of materials: letters to and from various correspondents belonging to or connected with the Brodrick family, together with assorted papers. In order to give some system to the selection of letters and to reduce as far as possible the element of subjectivity, we have chosen to print only the correspondence between Alan Brodrick I and his siblings and offspring: his brothers St John II and Thomas, his sons St John III and Alan II and his daughter Alice. There is one exception to this rule: sometimes, in order to evade the prying eyes of political and personal enemies, Alan I addressed letters to his second wife's aunt Martha Courthope in England, who was clearly expected to pass them on to his brothers or his son. These letters have therefore been included in the edition. We have also exercised a limited discretion in omitting material of an entirely domestic nature, including references to the management of property and the pursuance of cases at law, where these have no discernible relevance to the political and public lives of the principals. We have indicated such abridgments by ellipses.

In presenting the text, we have generally sought to preserve the original spelling and punctuation, including underlinings. We have silently modernised thorns, extended standard contractions (including ampersands), and lowered superior letters. (Contemporary material quoted in footnotes and in the introduction, has, however, been modernised throughout.) Words or short phrases repeated by the writer in error have also been deleted. A full point has been added at the end of each sentence where the writer has omitted to do this (usually when the sentence ends with a closing bracket). We have not reproduced subscriptions, superscriptions and signatures to the letters. Square brackets have been used to indicate editorial interpolations: doubtful readings are printed in roman type, editorial extensions in italics. Dates are given, in letter-headings and in footnotes, in the customary fashion, that is to say in Old Style (the Julian calendar) but with the year beginning not on 25 March but on 1 January (which was the case with New Style, under the Gregorian calendar). Where a letter is dated using both year-dates, as for example 1 Mar. 1712/13, this has been preserved; where the year-date given is only in Old Style, the New Style year-date has been added in square brackets.

Every effort has been made to identify persons who figure in the letters, but not always successfully, since the Brodricks often wrote allusively or elliptically, in the hope of mystifying those in the Irish post office (in particular the postmaster-general Isaac Manley) whom they suspected of attempting to intercept their correspondence. To prevent repetition in the footnotes, biographical information relating to family members and connections, and to members of the Irish parliament (the house of lords – including bishops – as well as the house of commons), has been gathered into appendices. On occasions where the letter-writer provides a full name, and the context makes it clear that the person concerned was an Irish MP or a member of the Irish house of lords, no footnote reference is given. Similarly, in order to conserve space, an individual mentioned by his or her full name in the text is identified in a footnote only on their first appearance. Unless otherwise stated, basic biographical details (dates of birth and death, place of residence, offices held, constituencies represented) have been drawn from standard sources, such as the *Complete Peerage* and *Complete Baronetage*; the relevant volumes produced by the History of Parliament Trust; Edith Mary Johnston-Liik's *History of the Irish Parliament*; the *Dictionary of Irish Biography*; and the *Oxford Dictionary of National Biography*.

CORRESPONDENCE 1722–1728

532. *Alan I, Holyhead, to Thomas, Westminster, 26 Feb. 1721[/2]*

(1248/5/190–1)

It is a melancholy thing that I am forced to write first from this place to you after our landing. We sailed from Dublin on Fryday about noon with a flattering wind, which ended in a calm and as soon as we came up with the Welsh land chopped about to South South East and more Easterly afterward; soe that we were forced to make this place and it is very well we did soe; else we must have lain beating it out at Sea without any reasonable hope of getting over the bar. I suppose our good Lieutenant will have been long in London before this can reach that place;[1] I doe assure you he hath left an extraordinary character behind him in the place whence he comes, the particulars will be as fit for the subject of private conversation as for a letter. I observe by the Thursday news letter from London which came in here this morning, that the numbers on one question in the house of Lords were 32 against 50: the minoritye is far short of the others but exceeds the number of the minoritye on any former question that I have observed.[2] The ilnesse of my wife makes me much doubt stil in what maner we shal attempt reaching Chester; her dread of going again on ship board is inexpressible and indeed she was ready to dye and actually fainted on her going into her chamber in this place. But stil I doubt she will not be able to perform the journey on horseback. This will make my getting to London later then I could wish and once hoped.

533. *Alan I, Parkgate,[3] to Thomas, Westminster, 4 Mar. 1721[/2]*

(1248/5/192–3)

We left Holyhead on Fryday in the evening and gott hither yesterday about ten in the morning. But my wife was so weak with her voyage that she dared not undertake her journey last night to Chester, tho my Coach was here to carry her. Her late sicknesse and

---

[1] Grafton had departed from Ringsend on 22 Feb. Alan intended to sail at the same time but in a different vessel (BL, Add. MS 34778, ff. 116, 118: Thomas Medlycott to [Edward Southwell], 20, 22 Feb. 1721/2).

[2] Among recorded votes the closest to these numbers would be the division on 3 Feb. 1722 on a motion to adjourn the House relating to the absence of the lord chancellor (31–49) and that of 13 Feb. on the committal of the elections bill (30–48): Sainty and Dewar, microfiche.

[3] Parkgate in Cheshire, a port on the western side of the Wirral peninsula, was a principal point of embarkation for travel to Ireland.

the fatigue of her voyage have made her soe excessively weak that I think it might have cost her her life to have attempted stirring her yesterday, or indeed on this, soe that we resolve not to begin our journey hence till to morrow morning, and shal be obliged to make very small and easy journeys on the road. I am sensible how inconvenient it will be to me to have his Grace[4] soe long before me in town, but that is now out of my power, nor can any hast to be now made be of any service to me. I will write from Chester either to Ally or to one of my sisters[5] and if I can be more particular as to the time of my getting to London then I now can, will then tell you: but I apprehend it will not be before Monday or Tuesday sevennight. You will be surprised to hear that the Custom house Officers both at the Head[6] and here seemed to me to be a good deal in doubt (notwithstanding the great interest making in Cheshire Chester and Anglesey) whether the P[arliament] will be dissolved. As they are not the wisest men, they are the most likely to know the sentiments of their superiors; but I think there remains no room for doubting that matter: It is gone too far to be recalled …

[PS] My wife is better after a good nights rest which she had since her landing here.

534. *Alan I, London, to Thomas, Guildford, 16 Mar. 1721[/2]*

(1248/5/196–7)

Mr Barnes the postmaster of Petworth[7] brought me (I should say to my sister) your letter to her of the 15th[8] and the two inclosed from my son to you. By him I write to my Lord Duke of Somersett[9] and assure him that I will wait on him very soon and be at Midhurst some time in the beginning of the next week, where I am sensible how difficult a task your Nephew hath had as well from the reasons he assigns, which would confound one of more years and experience then he is yet arrived at how to behave oneself as from his being perfectly unacquainted with the maner of these things; but I presume he will be careful not to doe anything but entirely conformable to the directions given him by my Lord Duke who is not to be disobliged on any score whatever. Pray if you have leisure, give him instructions how to conduct himself in such maner as you think he ought. I write to him this night: I hope my state of health will allow of my being at Petworth on Monday, which I doe not see how I shal be able to compasse unlesse I can gett to Peperhara on Sunday night. I hardly know how to reconcile one part of your letter to my sister about Mr Randyl with what your Nephew writes of his shrinking,[10]

---

[4] The duke of Grafton.

[5] Martha and Rachel Courthope (see below, Appendix 2).

[6] Holyhead.

[7] Petworth House in Sussex was the principal seat of the duke of Somerset.

[8] SHC, 1248/5/194–5: Thomas to Martha Courthope, 15 Mar. 1721[/2], with a message for Alan that his presence was needed at the Midhurst election.

[9] Charles Seymour (1662–1748), 6th duke of Somerset, patron of Midhurst borough (*HC 1715–54*, i, 336).

[10] Morgan Randyll (1649–aft. 1735), MP [E & GB] Guildford 1679–81, 1690–1705, 1708–10, 1711–22. He had incurred heavy losses in the South Sea Bubble, and in 1720 sold his estate of Chilworth in Surrey. However, he maintained his candidature at Guildford in 1722 as far as a poll, where he trailed in a distant third behind Arthur Onslow and Thomas Brodrick (*HC 1715–54*, i, 329).

unlesse you should in some letter before the date of yours to my sister have given your Nephew your thoughts that he would not stand it. I cannot but think you were in the wrong not to have stood for Westminster, where I think you would have succeeded, but I doubt Lord Onslow[11] took you in to support the interest of that family in Guilford, which I hear declines apace there as well as in the County at large by the folly of one man.[12]

535. *Alan I, London, to Thomas, Guildford, 17 Mar. 1721[/2]*

(1248/5/198–9)

Last night I gave into the hands of Mr Barnes a letter for my Lord Duke of Somersett, another for you and a third for your Nephew which he assured me should be delivered without losse of time; in mine to my Lord Duke I told his Grace I resolved to wait on him at Petworth before going to Midhurst, which I doubt his having ordered matters soe as to have the election on Tuesday will make impracticable without great prejudice to the successe of the affair, if what Sir Ri. Mills[13] told your Nephew hath any foundation: for I know how Petworth lies with respect to Peperhara and consequently am in the dark whether I may take it in the way to Midhurst on Tuesday morning. You know his Grace must be followed in his own way and I refer my self entirely to you in the matter and beg you will write such a letter to him about my not waiting on him at Petworth before I goe to Midhurst as will be proper, if that shal be found impracticable; but a complement must be paid him on this occasion, or he may be piqued if I should goe to the corporation directly without being introduced by his Grace. Now I apprehend the losse of a very little time in the morning of the day of election may be of very ill consequence and give our adversaryes an advantage over us, as if I were not in England. This night my wife and I resolve to lye at Cobham in our way to Peperhara where we shal be to morrow night, and see you at Guilford. We will enquire for you at Mr Storers house[14] and desire you will bespeak us a good dinner at such house in the town as you see most fit.

[11] Thomas Onslow (1679–1740), 2nd Baron Onslow.

[12] Lord Onslow. A short account of his various follies, political and financial, is given in *HC 1715–54*, ii, 311–12. In August 1723, while Onslow was travelling on the road near Guildford, a local man named Edward Arnold shot him in the shoulder and neck. When questioned, the assailant said 'that many persons having complained of my lord's zeal and activeness in public matters in the country and that he was the occasion of all disturbances there, he thought if my lord was out of the way all things would be quiet' (*A Portrait of Influence: Life and Letters of Arthur Onslow, the Great Speaker*, ed. Mary Clayton (*Parliamentary History Texts and Studies*, xiv, Oxford, 2017), 34–5; HMC, *Various Collections*, viii, 365).

[13] Sir Richard Mill (c. 1689–1760), 5th Bt, of Woolbeding, Sussex, elected MP for Midhurst at a by-election in November of the previous year.

[14] Jude Storer, admitted a freeman of Guildford in 1721 (*Guildford Freemen's Books 1655–1933*, ed. Hector Carter (Guildford, 1933), 48); postmaster there in 1745 (*Surrey Archaeological Collections*, xxxiii (1920), 128); and mayor in 1743, 1751 and 1759 (Owen Manning and William Bray, *The History and Antiquities of the County of Surrey ...* (3 vols, 1804–14), i, 40).

536. *Thomas to Alan I, Bath, 3 May 1722*

(1248/5/215–16)

The King has putt of his going to the fifth of next month, whither upon account of domestick, or forreigne affairs, I know nott, probably both the one and the other have a share; accounts from abroad are sayd to bee what are nott to bee wisht.

Charles Churchhill went hence a weeke since, tis generally given out for Vienna, butt I know hee was mett upon the Canterbury road, I beleive him gone to Paris, and thence perhaps to Madrid, his going was a secrett.[15]

Our great men (including land and sea officers) frequently have been consulted, which gives rise to many speculations. The meeting of the parliament uppon the tenth has been a good deale talkt of, butt I am confident without grounds.[16] A hundred storyes are raisd in relation to the effects Lord Sunderland left, and groundlesse reports of the ministers having taken a great share of them out of his closett, in order to conceale the quantum, which occasions more free talking then is reasonable.[17]

Whither the whisper of the Princes Regency bee att this time (as is sayd) under consideration,[18] or given out, to feele the pulse of people, I doe nott pretend to guesse.

537. *Thomas to [Alan I], 8 May 1722*

(1248/5/213–14)

I cannott give you any well grounded perticular accountt of the scence of villany now carrying on, though I am told the bottom of the designe is fully fathomd as far as itt relates to what was to bee reduct into act here.

I take for graunted that the minute the King should bee under saile an insurrection was to have been both in London and Westminster, and make noe doubt of great numbers of miscreants being come hither to joine those of their party, whoe are butt too many in both places. I am told that this intention has been communicated to their freinds abroad, in order to induce them the more readily to prepare for seconding; a second attempt like that in Scotland of invading before the party here (whose numbers have been prodigiously magnifyd) should convince them that they were ready and willing to putt themselves in

---

[15] Charles Churchill (c. 1679–1745), MP [GB] Castle Rising, col. of dragoons and groom of the bedchamber to the prince of Wales. The *Daily Post*, 4 May 1722, reported that he had set out for Spain on 'special affairs'.

[16] The British parliament was summoned for 10 May, but did not meet until 9 Oct.

[17] Sunderland had died at his London residence (Sunderland House in Piccadilly) on 19 Apr. His papers had been immediately locked up and sealed by his executors, Lord Carteret and Daniel Pulteney, MP [GB]. Subsequently, however, Carteret and the other secretary of state, Lord Townshend, together with other leading ministers, broke the seals and removed various letters and papers, possibly with the aim of implicating Sunderland in the flight of the South Sea Company cashier, Robert Knight, the previous year. There was also speculation that the papers contained proof of Sunderland's extensive gains from the South Sea Bubble or of dealings with the Pretender (HMC, *10th Rep.*, iv, 345). See Clyve Jones, 'Whigs, Jacobites and Charles Spencer, Third Earl of Sunderland', *EHR*, cix (1994), 60–9.

[18] The possibility that the prince of Wales could act as regent in his father's absence in Hanover.

the front of the battle;[19] Time must shew whither our good allyes to the southward[20] will pursue what was certainly intended, or leave the party here to undergoe the fate they deserve, if the former the affair will nott bee soone over, butt the latter I thinke will, for sufficient care is taken to prevent the first designe being putt in execution, and att the same time provision is making against the worst, every thing (as itt ought) is kept very secrett, butt I fancy my information good.

This discovery may probably (because I am sure most reasonable) prevent the Kings leaving us this year. Orders are sent for having six Regiments ready to imbarque att Corke and Kingsaile uppon occasion, and such as are quarterd nearest those places are pitcht uppon.

I hear Sir J. Montague[21] is to bee Cheife Baron,[22] and to bee succeeded by Gilbert,[23] butt the latter nott soe certain … My going towards you the latter end of next weeke (as I intended) will depend uppon what may farther happen, which hitherto you may bee sure I cannott foresee, if I doe nott goe directly from Pepper Hara, I will immediately returne to towne, and from time to time give you the best accounts I can.

538. *Alan II, London, to Alan I, 8 May 1722*

(1248/5/217–18)

This Morning a Camp was pitched in Hyde Park, and the Guards lye Encamped there to night.[24] There is a talk that all the Officers of Marching Regiments are to be ordered down to Quarters, and to be in a Readiness at an Hours warning; and some are at this time on their March towards London. There is a Report that the Government have received Information of a Place, where there were Arms for six Thousand men, and that they have been seized; and one of last Saturdays Prints mentions One Bolton a Sword Cutler, who has been taken into Custody of a Messenger.[25] How true these Reports are, I know not, for I have only heard them in Coffee House Talk; but if there is any such Design on foot, may it fare as their last did; but I think they can not expect to meet with that Clemency, with which the King so tenderly used the Rebels at Preston.[26] If I hear any thing to be depended upon, I'le not fail of Giving your Lordship an Account of it …

---

[19] The unsuccessful jacobite rising in Scotland in April 1719, which was to have been accompanied by a simultaneous landing of Spanish troops in the south-west of England, before the Spanish fleet suffered storm damage off Cape Finisterre in March and their part in the joint invasion scheme was cancelled.

[20] The French.

[21] Sir James Montagu (1666–1723), MP [E & GB] 1695–1700, 1705–13, baron of exchequer [E].

[22] Of the English exchequer.

[23] Jeffray Gilbert (1674–1726), chief baron of the Irish exchequer.

[24] Confirmed in *Post Boy*, 5–8 May 1722.

[25] *Evening Post*, 3–5 May 1722; *Daily Journal*, 5 May 1722. Other cutlers were also taken into custody at the same time. In Bolton's premises, on Ludgate Hill, were found 'a great number of basket-hilted and other swords with these words engraven on them "For James and my country's good"'. (BL, Add. MS 47077, ff. 45–6: newsletter, 5 May 1722.)

[26] After the defeat of the English jacobite forces at Preston in November 1715.

[*PS*] The Prorogation of the Parliament to the 5th of June can be no News to your Lordship.[27]

539. *Alan II, Peper Harow, to Alan I, 23 May 1722*

(1248/5/219–20)

I have been in Surry these ten Days, and have mett with nothing worth giving your Lordship an Account of. I knew an History of the Races[28] wou'd be no Diversion to you, and we had no Company to furnish out a subject for a Letter; so that these have been the Reasons why your Lordship has not heard from me. My Uncle will give you an Account of this Place, and a sad one it will be as to the Fruit, for the Frosts have spoiled almost all. I shall go to London soon, so as to be at the Birthday, which I will not fail giving your Lordship an Account of ... there I shall learn whether the King goes abroad this summer, for we have Different Reports about it, some being as Positive that He will, as others that He will not; however by that Time I beleive one may come to a Certainty ...

540. *Alan II, London, to Alan I, Bath, 29 May 1722*

(1248/5/221–2)

I think my self obliged to give your Lordship an Account of yesterdays Diversions,[29] and tho' I have no great Talent that way, shall begin with telling your Lordship that we had as much Company, and as little Finery, as ever appeared on such an Occasion. The Prince, Princess, and the young Ones,[30] who were all three there, were extreamly fine; some few Ladies wore very rich Cloths, but the Men in Generall very Plain. Princess Ann[31] and Lord Essex[32] (who was the Finest of any Gentleman there) began the Ball; and his Lordship and the Dutchess of Newcastle the Country Dancing.[33] In the Evening the Princess went to my Lord Cadogans Tent, and was Entertained there by him;[34] The Artillery fired, and after them the Guards a Running Fire; of this We had three Vollies; and I own that no Part of the Days Diversion was so great an Entertainment to me; the Park was thronged with Coaches, and I do not wonder at it, for it was richly worth seeing. There were Fire=works at Night, but those I did not see, so can give no Account of them ... We have no certain accounts how his Majesty intends to spend this summer; some say att Kensington, others at Hampton

[27] The British parliament met on 10 May, according to order, only to be prorogued again to 5 June (*LJ*, xxii, 3–4).

[28] Results from horse races at Epsom and Guildford were reported in the *Weekly Journal*, 26 May 1722.

[29] The celebrations of the king's birthday.

[30] George, prince of Wales (1683–1760) and his wife, Princess Caroline (1683–1737), with their three youngest children, Amelia (1711–86), Elizabeth Caroline (1713–57) and William Augustus (1721–65).

[31] The 13-year-old Princess Anne (1709–59), later wife to William IV, prince of Orange.

[32] William Capell (1697–1743), 3rd earl of Essex, gentleman of the bedchamber to the prince of Wales.

[33] Henrietta (*d.* 1776) wife of Thomas Pelham-Holles (1693–1768), 1st duke of Newcastle-upon-Tyne.

[34] William (1672–1726), 1st Earl Cadogan.

Court, some that He intends to take a Tour round England, others that He has not given over the Thoughts of a Longer Journey.

541. *Thomas to Alan I, Bath, 4 July 1722*

(1248/5/223–4)

Mrs Courthop writing last post, excusd my nott doing soe; I might have continued drinking the waters a weeke longer, the quarter session nott beginning till Tuesday next, however coming away when I did may probably prove lucky, for the weather is exceedingly bad, great rains with violent stormes of wind, and likely to continue … I find you have wrote for Dr Hale's opinion,[35] which I take for graunted will governe the time of your coming, the waters may bee now dranke as well as att any time, and I hope Miss takes the benefitt of them … I have had noe letters from London, nor seen anybody, soe that I know nott how the world goes, save that the insolence of the Jacobites is nott att all abated, by the discovery of their traiterous designes, I thinke this spiritt will nott bee layd, till itt comes to a better and worse between us, this I observd the whole road I came …

542. *Thomas, Whitehall, to [Alan I], 14 July 1722*

(1248/5/225–6)

Noe letter having come from any of you since my leaving the Bath, except that from Mrs C[*ourthope*] to her sister, wrote the Saturday after, gives reason to thinke there might bee one in the male of Wensday, when all the bags were carryed of by a single high way man.

   I stayd att Guilford till the session ended att two a clock on Thursday, came to Cobham that night, and yesterday hither; Dr Butler stands all defiance,[36] Lord Onslow was told that hee sayd hee would nott yett take the oaths, for that att present noe body could tell what would bee uppermost.

   I heare that Mr W[37] sayes publiquely att his levey, that if the S[*outh*] Sea Com[*pany*] would bee good boyes for the future, the remission of the two millions would bee recommended,[38] to what end this soe long before hand can bee, I know nott, unlesse to sound peoples opinions, itt may be carryd as the S[*outh*] S[*ea*] scheme was, but I thinke cannott any other way; att the same time this is thus talkt, I am throughly perswaded they are in more doubt of this H[*ouse*] of Commons then can bee easily imagined; this I heare from good hands.

---

[35] Richard Hale (1670–1728), the distinguished London physician (*Oxf. DNB*).

[36] Possibly Edward Butler (c. 1686–1745), a high-flying tory and the newly installed president of Magdalen College, Oxford, who had been awarded a DCL in 1722. He would go on to represent the university in parliament from 1737 until his death (*HC 1715–54*, i, 510).

[37] Robert Walpole (1676–1745), of Houghton Hall, Norfolk, MP [GB] King's Lynn; 1st lord of the treasury and chancellor of the exchequer [GB]; later 1st earl of Orford.

[38] By the National Debt Act of 1721 (7 Geo. I, st. 2), the South Sea Company had been excused part of its liability. Two million pounds of its capital was to be cancelled at midsummer 1722, and in return the company would have to repay £1,000,000 in exchequer bills. However, the directors were currently pursuing further negotiations with the Bank of England. (P.G.M. Dickson, *The Financial Revolution in England: A Study in the Development of Public Credit, 1688–1756* (1967), 176–9.)

The prints tell you Mr Smelt (of our house) is of the board of Ordnance,[39] butt doe nott mention its being done by W[alpole] against Lord C.[40] will, and indeed carryed over his belly, for I am very well informed his Lordship opposd itt with might and maine.

I am told what wee know of the plott,[41] or att least somuch as may bee fitly divulged, is digesting, in order to acquaint the Parliament therewith att the opening of the session.

Tis whisperd that Mr Clayton (of the Secrett Committee) will succeed the late Speaker, in the Princes service[42] … If you thinke of continuing att the Bath (which the coolnesse of the air may possibly incline you to) shee will bee able to gett the cellar I formerly mentioned, finisht, and in addition to itt, a little more of the outward repair of the house, which indeed itt wants.

If that bee the case may itt nott bee reasonable that your sonne make you a short visitt, hee may have my horses, for I have nothing for them to doe my selfe.

All the hay which is cutt, is gott in, I can not say in very good condition, for few dayes have passed without more or lesse raine …

[*PS*] I should have told you that Mr W[alpole] says Lord Sunderland made his request for Mr Smelt. How far tis beleivd I know nott.

543. *Alan I, Bath, to Thomas, Privy Garden, Whitehall, 8 Sept. 1722*

(1248/5/231–2)

I am to acknowledge your last letter of the sixth instant and those of the 25th and 28th of last month. By the later I find that the farther promised conference hath not been had with you since my leaving town, which I understood was intended and that you would not have only such hints as were to be collected by what was communicated in my presence: for I confesse I should be much surprized if something more close is not capable of being shewn and (considering the steps which have been since taken) I can not but think it will be of very ill consequence if some thing particular cannot be shewn; for that there are people disaffected to his Majestye and consequently well wishers to the P[retende]r nobody ever doubted, or that some of these people have all along had designs to bring their wishes to effect: but when a particular man of the B[ishop] of R[ochester']s figure is committed for high treason people will be desirous to know what the particular charge against him is, and unlesse something can be made out by proof against him, as little as I love him, I cannot but wish he may not be able to doe those whom he thinks his enemyes more harm then they

---

[39] Leonard Smelt (c. 1683–1740), of Kirkby Fleetham, Yorks., MP [GB] Northallerton, appointed clerk of the ordnance [GB] in 1722.

[40] Earl Cadogan, master-gen. of the ordnance [GB].

[41] The so-called 'Atterbury Plot', associated with Francis Atterbury (1663–1732), bishop of Rochester, which the government had begun to investigate in earnest in April. The first conspirator to be arrested had been taken on 19 May, and had been examined by a committee of the privy council, after which the whole affair became common knowledge even though not publicly announced: see G.V. Bennett, *The Tory Crisis in Church and State 1688–1730: The Career of Francis Atterbury, Bishop of Rochester* (Oxford, 1975), 246–53.

[42] William Clayton (1671–1752), of Sundon, Beds., MP [GB] St Albans, eventually became auditor-gen. to the prince of Wales in 1725. Hon. Spencer Compton (c. 1674–1743), MP [GB] Sussex, and later 1st earl of Wilmington, retained the Speaker's chair in the 1722 parliament, and also his place as treasurer to the prince of Wales.

have done him by his Committal.[43] Pray doe you hear from any good hand that there is any evidence of his having remitted money to any of the traitors beyond sea, for (as far as I can guesse by the news papers) that is the matter cheifly alledged against him. You will also tell me whether you have any account of the contents of any papers of his own handwriting; for that will be home evidence on him. As to the letter of Mr Ward I know not what to say to it, nor how to advise in affairs of that nature.[44] I doubt the truth of the case is this that some silly weak man had a mind to marry his daughter, whom he thinks to be a better match then she is ever like to meet, if she misses him. But if that be the case I am sure I would not be assisting to him in such an affair, tho the woman were much nearer of kin to me then his daughter is; nay I would not surprize any man into a match with my own daughter who were not of prudence and sufficient understanding to know what would be a fit match for him, without the privity of his parents etc. And this I doubt is the Case: And if soe I am sure you will have no hand in it; nor doe I know what power a Chaplain of a Regiment hath to grant licences, or what obligation he lies under to doe it, or what compulsory methods are proper to oblige him to doe it, if it be his duty. The Dutchesse of Marleborough[45] is well and soe is your sister and all here. I think it will be advisable to leave this place the end of this month, and to spend a few dayes at Peperhara before the Parliament meets …

544. *Alan, Bath, to Thomas, 26 Sept. 1722*

(1248/5/237–8)

I have your letter of the 22th, and had a visit made me by a Gentleman (whose name I forbear to mention) on the 24th in the evening; but you will know whom I mean when I tell you he goes by the same Nickname which the old Earle of Orrery[46] gave a very near relation of yours and mine, from his having a contest with him before the Court of claims about the will of Sir John FitzGerald and indeed for the estate of Midleton.[47] You cannot but recollect that he used to call our relation B—. — and for another reason this Gentleman passes by the same name.[48] This Gentleman told me he had received letters from London giving an account of what is contained in such papers as have been either intercepted or sent from beyond Sea in reference to the plot here; he owned his letter came from his colleague, and it contained a short abstract of all which two Gentlemen saw on

[43] Atterbury had been arrested on 24 August, examined by a cabinet committee, and remanded to the Tower of London on a charge of high treason (Bennett, *Tory Crisis*, 256–7).

[44] Conceivably one of the two daughters of Michael Ward, MP [I], but they would have been very young (the elder, Sophia, did not marry until 1739). More likely the sought-after bride was 'Deby', daughter of Michael Ward's uncle, Rev. Charles Ward of Mount Panther, Co. Down: her marriage was agreed the following year (PRONI, D2092/1/2, p. 40: Charles Ward to Michael Ward, 21 Oct. 1723).

[45] Sarah Churchill, née Jennings (1650–1744), widow of the 1st duke of Marlborough, who had died on 16 June 1722.

[46] Roger Boyle (1621–79), 1st earl of Orrery.

[47] Presumably their father, St John I.

[48] Possibly a reference to Grey Neville (1681–1743), of Billingbear, Berks. MP [E & GB] 1705–10, 1715–23, who was known as 'Bishop Neville' on account of his unusual religiosity (and possibly with a dash of irony, given his membership of an Independent congregation) (*HC 1690–1715*, iv, 1014).

the Saturday before I left London, indeed very well abstracted; which the writer might doe the better having had the perusal of the original papers (as he said) which were sent to him on his coming to town, and not only an abstract of them.

His letter also contained a summary of other papers which related more nearly to the Bishop of R[ochester] much to the purpose those two Gentlemen were told that there were papers in safe hands. But the letter also imported one thing which I have a great while suspected that a certain person (who is dead) was (in the opinion of the writer) playing a double Game for some time past, and that among some letters seised since the discovery of this conspiracy the conspirators mention his death with great concern, and say matters must be carryed more cautiously now for that there will be more care and watchfulnesse now used then would have been if he had lived.[49] The writer goes on to say that among his papers was found a very kind letter to the deceased from the P[retende]r, which had been shewn to the K[ing] and that he expressed himself in such a maner that it had never been intimated or communicated to him by the person, to whom it was wrote. You have the best oportunitye of any body to find out whether this fact be true: for if it be it is plain something hath been intrusted to the writer which two other Gentlemen were not to be intrusted with. Use all methods to come at the knowledge whether such a letter was found and what the contents were; for a great deal depends on the knowledge of it.

The Gentleman also told me that the Bishop of R[ochester] would be brought to his tryal in the Kings Bench and be acquitted before any thing could be done in Parliament; for by his discourse he was entirely for proceeding by way of bill of attainder, in which he seemed desirous to know my sentiments, but I no other way let him into them then as he might guesse what they were by perfectly concealing them. He added that he resolved not to go to London, for that nothing would be done but the remitting the two Millions to which he seemed to be averse (tho he had formerly argued for it with me) and an encrease of troops, which he seemed to think absolutely necessary.[50] He seems to be very angry with our great men, as not having necessary courage. We begin our journey toward Peperhara on Fryday, to which place I desire you to direct the answer to this, and to let me know when we may hope to see you. I have bestirred my self in behalf of our freind and beleive a good many (who differ in their sentiments from us in other matters) will be his hearty freinds against his competitor. You have one short way to know whether a certain person keeps that exact neutralitye in the matter which he professeth. If C[harles] C[hurchill] be for Mr E[velyn] soe is Mr W[alpole].[51] Our freind will have an oportunitye to speak to the former soon, for he went for London yesterday; and our freind hath an intimate acquaintance with him which will certainly intitle him to his freindship; if the others being in the opposite interest doth not prevent it; as it certainly will if he be. Pretty Master Evelyn is gone hence

[49] Lord Sunderland.

[50] The £2,000,000 owed by the South Sea Company to government. On 12 Dec. 1723 the company petitioned parliament for permission to convert part of their capital into annuities. The petition was referred to the committee considering the public credit and national debt, where a motion was made to remit the £2,000,000 debt and convert a moiety of capital into annuities. This was supported by the court but 'strenuously opposed' by several whig MPs, including Thomas Brodrick. (Cobbett, *Parl. Hist.*, viii, col. 53.)

[51] Charles Churchill, MP [GB] was a close political associate of Robert Walpole. Mr Evelyn is presumably George Evelyn (1678–1724), of Rooksnest, near Bletchingley, Surrey, MP [GB] Bletchingley, and clerk of the prince of Wales's household, who was being considered for an appointment which does not seem to have materialised. Churchill was groom of the bedchamber to the prince.

to school; if I can make any judgement of things future that sweet youth will make a very considerable man.[52] My humblest services to my Lord Godolphin[53] and such freinds as I have at Newmarkett, and to honest Mr Frampton in particular.[54]

545. *Thomas, Newmarket, to Alan I, Peper Harow, 2 Oct. 1722*[55]

(1248/5/239–40)

I have enquired from the person whom you hint att, touching the letter wrote by the — and doe nott find any grounds for what you were told, as to that perticular, att least I am confident hee is a stranger to itt, butt att the same time hee seemd to give into the notion of the persons playing a double game, to whom twas suppos'd to bee writt, uppon which topick I have talkt to him formerly, and always found him full of suspition of the truth of that matter, indeed hee has almost own'd conviction.

What the Bishop[56] could meane by trying [*Atterbury*] att the Kings bench bar, I cannott devise, unlesse in order the better to feele your pulse as to the other way of proceeding,[57] for I am confident there never was a thought of the former, the consequence of which would undoubtedly bee what hee sayd, and for that reason would nott bee attempted. I doubt his anger to some people is nott somuch uppon account of defect of necessary courage, as that they are a little too close handed to him, in perticular, for surely somuch meritt as his, claims great returnes.

Here is more company then any one can imagine, since their coming can bee butt for three or four days, the presize time when wee shall decamp is nott fixt, butt tis agreed on all hands, that none of us is to be absent from Westminster this day sennight. I have mett with like successe as you did in relation to Lord H. affair,[58] I thinke his Antagonist will hardly stand itt.

546. *Alan I, Dublin, to Thomas, 13 June 1723*

(1248/5/280–1)

I ought to give you the earliest account of our landing yesterday; we sett sail from Park Gate about one at noon last Monday, with a flattering South East wind in Chester river,[59] but

---

[52]John Evelyn (1706–67), of Wotton, Surrey, eldest son of Sir John Evelyn, 1st Bt, who was then at Eton and went up to Oxford in 1725. He was elected MP [GB] for Helston in 1727 and succeeded his father as 2nd Bt in 1763.
[53]Francis Godolphin (1678–1766), 2nd earl of Godolphin.
[54]Tregonwell Frampton (1641–1728), of Newmarket, Suff., sportsman and gambler (*Oxf. DNB*).
[55]Letter endorsed by Alan I, '… nothing found in Lord Sunderlands papers as to the plot: but Lord Godolphin beleived Lord S[*underland*] was playing a double game'.
[56]Grey Neville, MP [GB] (see above, p. 38).
[57]The method chosen by the ministry to proceed against Atterbury was by a parliamentary bill of pains and penalties.
[58]Probably Trevor Hill, Lord Hillsborough, Alan's stepson.
[59]The River Dee.

no sooner were we gott below Ormes head[60] and soe free from the draught of the wind between the English and Welsh coast but we mett with Westerly winds and ugly squawls; to be short the wind was soe bad that we were not able to gett into the Bay[61] till yesterday morning about three of clock; and if we had not been in a very good ship commanded by a very expert and diligent officer we never could have made our passage with the winds we had ... I was received here with great respect civilitye and kindnesse, had a visit made me by two of the Lords Justices as soon as I had refreshed my self after landing, but the Archbishop was out of town.[62] And upon the advice of my freinds here am determined to be sworn this day one of the Lords Justices; tho I confesse when I left London, my own sentiments were that it would be more advisable not to be sworn nor to take on me the Justiceship, to prevent any dispute about my accepting it making my election void; but when I consider that Mr Craggs being made one of the Lords Regents of Great Britain was not looked on to vacate his election, and that Mr Walpole is now made one of the Lords Justices of Great Britain I cannot see the difference between the Cases as to this point.[63] This I am sure of that unlesse some people incline to goe into that side of the question which is least favourable to me, it will not be in the power of others to hurt me: and I can not think that it will be thought expedient to doe me an ill office unprovoked; since if I have not done them some service, I am certain I have not disserved them, and may hereafter have it in my power to remember ill usage. If I should meet with ill treatment (which I will beleive I shal not meet) the worst will be my being put to the trouble and expence of a new election, or perhaps a disappointment in that attempt: which I hope and beleive will hardly be the case if early care be taken in the matter, and my Lord Duke of Somersett continue his goodnesse to me: It was most unfortunate that by the sicknesse of the Dutchesse it was impossible for me to wait on his Grace for many weeks, I may say some months before his going to Petworth upon the Dutchesses death[64] and you know our constant attendance in the house and the sicknesse of your sister hindred me from going over to Petworth to wait on his Grace there before my leaving London. I desire you will take the first favourable oportunity of discoursing his Grace on this subject; and that you will let me have your thoughts and those of other freinds as to the vacating my election by my taking on the office of one of the Justices. But if it should doe it, I know the worst that can happen and even that seems to me not to be an undesirable thing; at least the time will soon come when in prudence and for my own sake I ought to make it my own act to desire to retire: which I think I shal be admitted to doe honourably and with some mark of his Majestyes favour to a faithful servant who hath done something and hath suffered a great deal in his Majestyes service. Pray let me know your thoughts of this matter at large. I have wrote to my sister Courthope to offer the use of Peperhara to her this Summer and desire you to urge her to it; the cheif reason I have given her for doing it is that it will be for her and

[60] The Great Orme, north-west of Llandudno, Caernarvonshire.

[61] Dublin Bay.

[62] Lord Shannon and Speaker Conolly, Archbishop King being absent.

[63] Relating to the provision in the English Regency Act of 1706 (4 Anne, c. 8), that 'no man to take any place after his being elected a member of parliament, but accepting such a place shall make his election void': see John Cannon and W.A. Speck, 'Re-election on Taking Office, 1706–90', *BIHR*, li (1978), 206–9.

[64] Elizabeth, née Percy (1667–1722), 1st wife of Charles Seymour, duke of Somerset and *suo jure* Baroness Percy, died on 24 Nov. 1722.

other peoples healths for her to go thither, but there is a farther reason, which hath weight with me, which you will soon hit upon, when you consider what may be the consequences of our freinds in Bond Street staying in town during the whole summer; beside I think it will be a pleasure for all of you to spend the hot months in so cool a retirement, after so much hurry as you have lately undergone. Your nephew[65] is not returned from Munster but is expected this night. If you should see Mr Walpole I wish you would talk with him about the matter of my taking on me the Justiceship and feel his pulse in it. What was the Commission which is said to have been to my Lord C[*arteret*] and which was afterward ordered to be cancelled or vacated, for I heard it very imperfectly at Chester and not from a good hand. Give my humblest services to your most valuable and worthy freind when he gives himself the trouble next to sit with you in an evening. God be thanked your sister and I are both better since we began our journey then when we left London. Pray tell me whether you pay postage for your letters since the time of the Parliaments rising, or whether that among your other privileges continue for any and how many dayes after.[66]

547. *Alan II, to Alan I, 11 July [1723]*

(1248/5/284)

I have received your Lordships of the 4th, and set out for Petworth to morrow morning to deliver that to his Grace. I can never sufficiently acknowledge my thanks to your Lordship for your offer of procuring me a seat in Parliament, even at the Expence of your own; but sure you can never think that I cou'd have such a desire, or woul'd accept of it on those terms, even tho' there were no other Difficulty. But, my Lord, I fear I can not propose that to my self, for there are such struggles every where, that there will be the strictest scrutinies into whatsoever may be disadvantagious to any Candidate.

I have only time to tell you that I will do every thing in the best manner I can at Midhurst, and I hope never to do any thing that shall give you Reason to doubt of my being … [*etc.*]

548. *Alan II, London, to Alan I, 23 July 1723*[67]

(1248/5/285–6)

I sett out on my Journey to Hannover tomorrow, and will take great Care of your Lordships Letter and the Paper which you have Entrusted me with. I shall always do every thing in my Power to obey your Lordships Commands in the best manner I am able, and hope you will never have any Reason to think me wanting in my Duty to you … My Uncle is still at Guildford, for the Mint Bill has made a long and troublesome sessions for the Surry

---

[65] St John III.

[66] For the privilege by which the correspondence of members of the Westminster parliament was carried free of charge within Britain and Ireland ('Members Franks') see Kenneth Ellis, *The Post Office in the Eighteenth Century: A Study in Adminstrative History* (1958), 39.

[67] Letter endorsed by Alan I, 'Nally … Will deliver my Letter and paper to Lord Carterett'.

Justices.[68] I hope however that He will soon go to the Bath, for He seems to think it will be of great service to him.

549. *Alan II, Hanover, to Alan I, Dublin, 17 Aug. N.S. 1723*

(1248/5/294–5)

I came hither last Friday, and went next morning to my Lord Carterets[69] and delivered your Lordships Papers to him, and received great Civilitys from him. My Lord Townshend[70] too has been extreamly obliging to me, and so have all the great men both English and German. The Queen of Prussia went away from hence two or three Days before we came hither,[71] but the Duke of York is still here,[72] and I beleive will stay till the King goes into the Country to hunt. He has the most obliging Manner in the World to strangers that go to Osnaburgh, but as He was here when we passed through it we made no stay there. We left Gravesend on Friday morning, and reached this Place that day sevennight, after a Journey tiresome enough from Utrecht hither. The sea was not so bad as I expected, for we had a fair Wind and good Weather, and landed on Saturday Evening at Rotterdam. If your Lordship has any Commands for me, a Letter directed either in French or English to me at Hannover will come safe.

550. *Thomas, Bath, to Alan I, 17 Aug. 1723*[73]

(1248/5/292–3)

I send nott the inclosed as a motive to your dealing, in what I dare say you never will.

If something very strong bee nott done in your next sessions, perhaps before the succeeding one, parliamentary aids may bee necessarily doubled for supporting the establishment, since every day soe far lessens the revenue, as that before Whitehall can bee built by grauntees, the Hereditary Revenue of Ireland may bee disposed of.[74]

---

[68] In April 1723 parliament passed an act (9 Geo. 1, c. 28) to remove the privileged status of 'the Mint', a liberty of the archbishop of Canterbury in Suffolk Place, Southwark, where insolvent debtors claimed sanctuary. Both Alan and Thomas were members of the second-reading committee on the Bill (*CJ*, xx, 203). The Mint was suppressed in July 1723, resulting in a mass exodus of families with their belongings, who were then cleared of their obligations at Guildford quarter sessions (*CJ*, xx, 132, 154–7, 220–1; Nigel Stirk, 'Arresting Ambiguity: The Shifting Geographies of a London Debtors' Sanctuary in the Eighteenth Century', *Social History*, xxv (2000), 316–29, esp. 325).

[69] John Carteret (1690–1763), 2nd Baron Carteret.

[70] Charles Townshend (1675–1738), 2nd Viscount Townshend.

[71] Sophia Dorothea (1687–1757), daughter of George I and wife of Frederick William I of Prussia.

[72] Ernest Augustus (1674–1728), duke of York and prince-bishop of Osnabrück, younger brother of George I.

[73] Letter endorsed by Alan I, '... that we are like to be overladen with pensions'.

[74] Parts of the former Whitehall Palace were leased. A great deal of building work was being undertaken in 1723, including the demolition of the King Street gate and the gun platform, the expansion of the privy garden, and the construction of new admiralty building (Edgar Sheppard, *The Old Royal Palace of Whitehall...* (1902), 80, 172–3, 178–9).

I have spent between a fortnight and three weekes here, the waters passe very well, and sitt easy on my stomach, as usually, notwithstanding which the paine remains, especially in my right kidny, from whence I doubt I may too assuredly conclude the encrease of the stone in that part, the rather because noe gravell comes away; if soe I must with what patience I can, submitt to what I take to bee unavoidable, as well as past remedy.

I hear his Majestys returne may possibly bee sooner then expected, you will therfore consider what directions to give relating to my nephew, whither to returne, or take this opertunity of seeing Italy.

551. *Alan I, Dublin, to Thomas, Bath, 24 Aug. 1723*

(1248/5/296–7)

… We are at the Castle just as formerly, Mr C[*onolly*] entirely confided in and caressed, not but that care is taken to appear upon every publick occasion as civil as possible elsewhere; but it is all from the teeth outward. Our patent for coyning halfpence granted to William Wood[75] gives us more uneasinesse then was expected; I was spoken to about it in this maner, that it was the Kings patent and that all his Majestyes servants should doe all in their power to support the grant, which indeed a Clause in it doth require of them.[76] But by this speaking to me I could not but beleive that it is for the benefit of some freind: and considering the Lord Cornwallis deceased[77] did in the later end of King Williams reign apply for a new patent for coyning halfpence here,[78] after the expiration of Knoxes patent, as intitled to an interest in it by the marriage of Lord Arrans daughter and heiresse[79] and that the same Lord renewed his application about the year 1717. I am apt to think considering how well he stands with the now ministry that his son may think this as proper a time to hope for a favourable event as he is likely to meet with.[80] But people here are greatly distasted at this grant and think it will turn much to the detriment of the Kingdome. They think that since we could not last Session be perswaded to part with all our gold and silver for paper,[81] that [?it is] hoped we will doe it now for a little Copper: but there seems soe general an aversion in most people to the thing that now I hear it whispered that this grant

---

[75] William Wood (1671–1730), ironmaster, of Wolverhampton, Staffs., for whom see *Drapier's Letters*, 189–90; *Oxf. DNB*.

[76] Grafton had in fact spoken to all 'the principal persons' in Dublin about the patent, making what arguments he could in its favour and emphasising that it was 'a point I had much at heart' (Coxe, *Walpole*, ii, 347–8).

[77] Charles Cornwallis, 4th Baron Cornwallis (c. 1675–1722).

[78] In 1700 (*CTB*, xv, 61, 316).

[79] Sir John Knox (*d*. 1687), who in 1685 obtained the remainder of the term of the patent granted in 1680 to Sir Thomas Armstrong (c. 1633–1684) and George Legge (1648–91), 1st Baron Dartmouth, to manufacture copper halfpennies for Ireland for a period of 21 years. Knox's patent then came into the hands of his brother-in-law Roger Moore (*d*. 1705), MP [I] 1692–9, whose coinage was the subject of an inquiry by the Irish house of commons in 1697. Cornwallis had married Lady Charlotte Butler, daughter and heiress of Richard Butler, 1st earl of Arran.

[80] Charles Cornwallis (1700–62), 5th baron, was Lord Townshend's son-in-law, having married Hon. Elizabeth Townshend in November 1722. He had also been a groom of the bedchamber until his appointment in May 1722 as chief justice in eyre south of the Trent (J.M. Beattie, *The English Court in the Reign of George I* (Cambridge, 1967), 62).

[81] An allusion to the failure of the project for a national bank in the 1721–2 session.

is for the benefit of a certain foreigner; by which means the odium will fall on the [*king*] and not on the person who gott it for any other person. But I think the greatest care will be used to prevent the Parliaments falling on this patent; but the successe of such an attempt time must shew.

552. *Alan I, Dublin, to Alan II, 24 Aug. 1723*

(1248/5/298–300)

… Be sure on receit of this to wait on the person to whom I wrote by you,[82] and make my complements to him, and let him know that matters here goe on as they formerly did: with this only difference that a freind of yours[83] is treated very civilly, but with just the same degree of confidence as formerly. It was impossible for me to foresee the difficultyes which might arise in our Parliament from the patent granted to William Wood for coyning three hundred and sixty tuns of Copper into half pence and farthings for this Kingdome; which at the rate of one pound of Coppers being coyned into 60 halfpence or 120 farthings will amount to no lesse a summe then £90000 which at some time or other will become of just soe much value to the possessors of that kind of money as the mettal of which it is made will be then worth here. For whose advantage this patent was intended or is to be we are a good deal in the dark; but I confesse I am apt to think from some papers being lately produced by a certain under Secretary who seemed to me to be pretty much concerned for Mr Wood,[84] I cannot but conjecture that this grant is grafted on a pretension which the late Lord Cornwallis had to renew a former patent granted to one Knox, in trust as to one third part for the late Earle of Arran, to whose daughter and heiresse the Lord Cornwallis was marryed. On this ground the Lord Cornwallis did about the year 1700 apply for a new patent, and I think renewed his application in 1717 but nothing was then done, the Lords Justices in the year 1700 having referred the matter to the then Attorney and Sollicitor General, and they having made a report that it was expedient that great care should be taken that the mettle to be coyned should be intrinsically worth very near as much as the peices were to be current for, deducting the expence of coynage, and that securitye should be given to exchange this kind of money when it should cease to be current.[85] I was at that time Sollicitor General, and did then think those matters were very necessary to be provided for, and our report not being soe favourable to the person who desired the patent I doe not find any thing was then done farther in it: And as far as I can judge of the minds of other people there seems to be no great prospect of the project succeeding at this time; for tho the patent contains a mandatory clause to all Officers etc to be aiding and assisting to the patentee that he may reap the advantages intended to him by the patent yet I confesse I have given my opinion that people are generally perswaded that this patent will not be for the publick advantage of the Kingdome: and this I did after the person to whom I had given that opinion told me that it must be considered as a patent actually passed, and that

---

[82]Lord Carteret.

[83]Alan himself.

[84]Charles Delafaye, MP [I].

[85]*CTB*, xv, 61, 316; W.E.H. Lecky, *A History of England in the Eighteenth Century* (8 vols, 1878–90), ii, 458–9.

all the Kings servants should support it as far as it might be supported. Some other people with whom I doe not alway agree in other matters were of the same mind, and I rather attribute it to their being soe then to the arguments which I used that I observed the person to whom we were speaking seemed a good deal staggered in his opinion of the successe of the matter, and to give it up in some measure, provided it could be so ordered that noe notice might be taken in either house of Parliament of this patent. But how that matter will be time must determine; for some people say there will be a necessitye to take it into consideration to prevent the mischeif taking place, since the patent is actually passed, and the patentee may and probably will proceed to coyne and utter his coyne to the great prejudice of the Kingdome; unlesse prevented. But it is hoped that as in a case not altogether unlike this, both houses were prevayled upon not to take a resolution to addresse the King that we shal be in as good temper now: and this seems to be very likely to be attained. But if the patent come under the consideration of either house I cannot but think it will be next to impossible to prevent their giving it their ill word. I heard very lately as if the benefit of this grant was to redound to a certain foreigner Monsieur F—[86] but this is new with us, and for ought I know thrown out to cast the odium where it ought not to be laid: for it is most certain the thing is very much disliked here and creates more dissatisfaction then one would easily imagine. Your own prudence will tell you that this is a matter which you are not to speak of in conversation; nor must you shew this letter to more then one person. Let me remind you of being very careful in your conduct and behavior, considering you are now stepped into the world and the least false step will be taken notice of, and men will be apt to form their judgements of what you will be, by the manner of your setting out into the world. I know you have a natural modestye; let nothing prevail with you to foregoe it; I say the same to you as to good nature and civilitye: doe all the good offices you can where they are wanted. Avoid giving offence to any body and consequently you must avoid every degree of intemperance: but this is what I know you are not addicted to: But the world hath given Germany the character of being more addicted to wine then were to be desired: yet I doe not find that part of it where you now are labours under the imputation soe much as other parts of the countrey, which I impute to the example which their and our great and good Prince sets them. Give my humblest services to my Lord Carterett, my Lord Townesend, and to the Grand Marshal.[87]

[PS] My Lord Lieutenant goes this day to Mr Conelyes, they say to dine; but possibly he may lye there two or three nights before the Parliament meets.

553. Alan I, Dublin, to Thomas, 26 Aug. 1723

(1248/5/302–3)

I have your letter of the 17th from Bath, with the enclosed from your freind which makes you an offer of such a nature as I should (without your telling me soe) presently conclude you never would embrace; The penny worth he mentions can never be esteemed a good

---

[86] Probably Friedrich Ernst von Fabrice (1683–1750), a Hanoverian courtier; *Kammerherr* (gentleman of the bedchamber) to George I as elector of Hanover from 1719.

[87] Possibly Earl Cadogan is meant.

one by him who thinks the thing to be purchased ought never to have been granted to the seller: and that there may come a time when neither the grantees right nor the more compassionate consideration of the purchasers having paid a full value for it may be esteemed a sufficient reason to continue the paiment of the thing granted. For my part I think as things are managed in this respect something of this kind must necessarily follow: When an horse hath more weight put on his back then he possibly can bear, it is very natural for him to kick and endeavour to throw it off which if he cannot effect, there remains nothing for him to doe but to lye down and sink under it. As to what you foresee will be done for the future here as to loading us with more pensions (then we can bear, without resorting to new taxes) I have long found what is intended: but very much doubt whether the method you propose to be taken to prevent it, would be effectual altho it should be heartily gone into, which I am of opinion it will not (for we hunt under a pole[88] in imitation of our betters and make our Court the same way that they doe). I have had soe very little thanks, for the endeavours I used to reduce our establishment (in the beginning of his Majestyes reign) from those people who would have been savers if my endeavours had taken effect, and have been so treated by the very ministry by whose direction the Justices (of which number I was then one) acted in that matter that I shal consider my self as only one who will suffer no more in proporcion then his neighbours, if he lyes stil; and doth not irritate those who have power and inclination to bear down all opposers. But shal be sure to feel the continuance of the resentment of the great ones if I make myself the but of their fury by taking the lead in opposing the loading this Kingdome with that provision for favourites which will not be born elsewhere. I scorn to make my interest (as a certain person doth[89]) by sacrificing the trust reposed in him by the countrey and lying forward and backward and swearing he never was nor will be in any of the projects, as the Bank, patent for Copper money or the like; and having done this I think I shal acquit my self from any imputation of being instrumental in the ruine of the countrey: but if those who are chosen its representatives in Parliament, think fit to be silent, I doe not think I am under any obligation to doe more then vote according to honour and conscience if any thing comes before the house of Lords, in which the welfare of Ireland appears to me to be much concerned. Perhaps you will think I ought to go farther, but I think not. The pention Mr V—[90] means is that granted to Lord H— and Lady H— for their lifes;[91] the purchase demanded amounts to £10500 which is too great a portion for this poor Kingdome to give with a Lady perfectly a stranger to it. Pray where is the odds between taxing us with such a summe directly or giving such an annual summe as will sell at a market rate for soe much money; nay and be a good penny worth in the opinion of the proposer.

---

[88] Another term for 'stop-hunting', where dogs are so well trained that they will stop their pursuit at the word of command, or a flourish of the hunting-pole, and follow the huntsmen until told to move forward (Thomas Fairfax, *The Complete Sportsman; or, Country Gentleman's Recreation* … (1765), 107–8).

[89] Speaker Conolly.

[90] Agmondisham Vesey, MP [I].

[91] Emanuel Scrope Howe (c. 1699–1735) and his wife Maria Sophia Charlotte (1703–82), the illegitimate daughter of George I by Charlotte Sophia, countess of Darlington, who were provided for on their marriage with a pension of £750 p.a. for life on the Irish establishment (A.P.W. Malcomson, *Nathaniel Clements: Government and the Governing Elite in Ireland, 1725–75* (Dublin, 2005), 78).

I begin to think that the affair which I thought when I wrote to you last would be dropped, will be endeavoured to be carryed on. If it be, the successe will be the same with what the grand project of the last Session mett.

554. *Thomas, Bath, to Alan I, Dublin, 5 Sept. 1723*

(1248/5/308–9)

… I have this morning one of the 7th new stile, from my nephew,[92] with very good observations of different natures, you will (which I mentioned in my former[)] determine what relates to his stay where hee is, till the Kings returne, (which I thinke will nott bee soone) or going towards Italy, before the season shall make the passage over the Alps both difficult and dangerous.

555. *Alan II to Alan I, 21 Sept. N.S. 1723*[93]

(1248/5/316–17)

Your Lordships of the 24th of last Month came safe to me yesterday, enclosed in one from my Aunt; and since by that method it has succeeded better, than I have Reason to beleive any of mine to your Lordship have done (which have gone by the Post) I shall convey this by the same Hand.

The Gentleman whom I was ordered to wait upon, went yesterday out of Town, and is not expected again till late this Evening; and it's being Post night will (I fear) make it difficult to gain Admission; However I will attempt it, and if I succeed early enough to write, your Lordship shall not fail of another Letter by this Post. If I do not, I will wait on Him early tomorrow, and give an Account by the next Opportunity. It was no longer ago than the Day before Yesterday, that the same Gentleman ordered me to make his Compliments and Excuse to your Lordship, for his not having wrote to you, and bid me promise for Him, that He wou'd do it very soon.

I do assure your Lordship, that as to the Letter which I mentioned in one to my Aunt, it must have miscarried by the ill Regulation of the Post, on this side the Water, as severall between my Aunt and me have done; but I hope she has now found out a Method of sending them safe as long as I stay here; how long that will be, I do not know, for I have received no Directions from your Lordship on that head; but I shoud be very glad to know what Course you wou'd please to have me steer. It is generally believed here, that the King intends to go to Berlin, and we have a Report that He sets out on this day sevennight; if so, and I receive no other commands I propose going thither, but beg that I may have orders what I am to do, as soon as possible; for the season is so far advanced that the

---

[92] Alan II.

[93] Letter endorsed by Alan I, 'Nally … will shew mine of 24 Aug. O.S. to Lord Carteret who excuses himself for not writing to me, but promises soon to doe it (which he <u>took care not to doe</u>)'.

King cannot possibly make any long stay there, before He goes to the Guere.[94] The Duke of Yorks Intention of leaving this Place on Fryday next, gives great Credit to the Berlin Expedition …'

556. *Alan I, Dublin, to Alan II, 12 Sept. 1723*[95]

(1248/5/310–11)

Your curiositye as well as good wishes to the countrey probably incline you to wish you knew what is doing here this busy season. I once thought we should not have mett with any thing during the Session which would create us any sort of uneasinesse. But am sorry to find that a patent some time since past in England for coyning Copper halfpence for Ireland hath greatly alarmed people; and the Commons have on Monday last ordered a call of the house on Monday next, and likewise directed the Speaker to write circular letters to the Sherifs of the several Countyes requiring the members to have notice from them that the house expects their attendance. I am told this order was made after the house had voted to resolve itself into a Committee of the whole house on Fryday sevennight next to take the State of the nation into their consideration, and particularly in relation to the Copper halfpence and farthings.[96] If you are desirous to know who were for and who against the Copper halfpence I can make no other answer then that (as I hear) every body who spoke expressed great dislike of them and of the patent obtained by William Wood for coyning them. But there was some difference in opinion among Gentlemen about the time of ordering the matter to be considered and the house to be called over. Some wished it might not be soe soon as others moved it to be; but such was the zeal of the house against the thing that there was no possibilitye of stemming the current; and tho the votes are not printed in that order yet I am told the order for writing circular letters was moved just after the house had resolved to goe into a Committee to consider the State of the Nation and had that cheifly in view to have the house full when the matter of the halfpence came to be considered. As far as I can judge there can not be any method found to hinder them from doing all they justly can to prevent this patent taking place or Mr Woods coyne passing among or upon ignorant people, which they say is far short in value from what it is to be passed for, and of the finenesse he is by his contract obliged to make them of. But (as far as I can find) Gentlemen are as unanimous in determining to doe every thing which they apprehend necessary for the preservation of the countrey from the calamity which they apprehend will fall upon it if these halfpence come once to be current, in the most respectful and easy maner they can light upon which will effectually attain this end, as they are zealous to get rid of the coyne and of the patent. But I doubt whether such an expedient will be found out as will satisfye the house that the Kingdome will not be sufferers by this

---

[94] George's hunting-lodge at Göhrde, in Celle. Carteret's private secretary reported from Hanover on 20 Sept. N.S., 'There is no day fixed as yet for the king's going to the Gohr, though the *equipage de chasse* was sent there on the 16th' (HMC, *Polwarth MSS*, iii, 306).

[95] This may well be the letter referred to by Lord Townshend when he wrote to Walpole from Hanover on 2 Oct. N.S.1723, that Carteret had seen a letter from Alan I to his son about Wood's coinage (BL, Add. MS 32686, f. 237).

[96] These orders, which were given on 9 Sept., are confirmed in *CJI*, v, 17–18.

Coyne, and then the great care must be to prevent warm people from doing things in an improper maner. It is an hard case that soe soon after the Bank we should have this bone of contention thrown among us; the former had some advocates for it, who thought it an useful thing and of publick benefit: but this hath not one creature that will appear for it, or pretends to vindicate it any farther then by saying Wood hath the Kings patent for it. Be not too free in shewing my letters; particularly this I desire this may not be seen by more then one person except yourself.

557. *Alan I, Dublin, to Alan II, 18 Sept. 1723*

(1248/5/312–15)

The Chief end I had in sending you abroad was that you might pay your duty to the King; and I made no doubt of your endeavouring to improve your understanding by such observations as you should be able to make of the wisdom and defects in the constitution of such foreign Countrys as you shall travel through before your return; but since his Majestys British Dominions are like to be your place of abode, and since a good part of your fortune lies in this Kingdom, I cannot but be of opinion, that the most useful knowledge you can acquire will be that of the Kingdoms to which you belong; and in particular of Ireland. For that end I have in some late letters given you such insight into the affairs of this Parliament as at that time I was able; since my last the House of Commons, on the 7th of September resolv'd, that their House should be calld over on the 16th and this was movd by a Gentleman who had on Saturday before given reason to believe that he would on Monday move the House to take the matter of the new Copper Halfpence into consideration; I presume my Lord Lieutenant had notice of it, for that Gentleman din'd at the Castle on Sunday, and was inducd to promise that he would not make the motion the next day; but he says he then told my Lord Lieutenant that he was resolvd to move for a Call of the House the next day; and accordingly did so; the same day another Gentleman said that after the House was full he thought it proper to take the affair of the Copper halfpence into consideration, and upon that motion it was orderd that the House should resolve itself into a Committee of the whole House on Fryday the 20th instant to consider of the State of the nation and particularly in relation to the Copper halfpence: my Lord Lieutenant seemd a good deal uneasy not only at the thing, but at their beginning it so early in the Session, and I apprehended that his Grace from the part my Son took in the debate which I dare say was misrepresented to him, had some suspitions infus'd into him that I was privy to these transactions; but I can with great truth affirm I never heard either that those motions were intended to be made before the House had come to resolutions upon them, nor did I ever discourse one word with any of the Gentlemen concern'd in making them; but the truth is the whole Parliament was so full of the matter of the halfpence, and of the mischief which would fall on the nation if a stop was not put to their obtaining a currency that it was impossible to hinder Gentlemen from speaking the sense of the Countrys from which they came upon the Subject; this my Lord Duke plainly saw, and expressd himself once to this effect in my hearing; that the late prospect of a Bank here had some friends but that he did not see one man but what was against the halfpence; to enable themselves to proceed regularly, they voted an Address to my Lord Lieutenant that he would give directions that the exemplification or Copy of the Patent, and all papers which his Grace had in relation to the Coyning of halfpence be laid before the House; this motion was oppos'd by some few with great violence; particularly one Gentleman, Mr Ward,[97] took upon him to say he believd my Lord Lieutenant had no papers but if he had, he thought he would not send 'em to the house, which enflam'd the House exceedingly; and on the question being put in was carri'd nem: con: On Saturday Mr Hopkins[98] carryd my Lord Lieutenants answer to the address of the day before in these words; that his Grace has no exemplification or copy of the Patent for coyning halfpence or any other paper that would give the House satisfaction upon that subject: I had the misfortune to be abroad that morning, when his Grace sent for me to the Castle, and indeed I could wish, if he intended to ask my opinion in relation to his answer, that he had commanded me to attend him that morning the night before when I was with him at the castle; if he had done me the honour to have consulted with me, I should certainly have repeated my advice to him to let the Commons have a view of the Patent, for I could see no ill consequences arising from his so doing; but his keeping it a secret only encreasd peoples jealousies that something very bad was contain'd in it, which perhaps the sight of it might remove, or at least keep 'em in temper; but if such advice had not been taken I should certainly have been for softening the answer as to the manner of it; which I told my Lord Lieutenant assoon as he was pleasd to communicate it to me, for that I feard it would not be very satisfactory to the House; he answer'd me that I was come too late, for that Mr Hopkins, with whom I presume he had consider'd it, was gone down to deliver it to the House; some Gentlemen, when it was deliverd had a mind to vote it unsatisfactory, but were perswaded to put it off for that time, and so it was enterd in the Journal;[99] but at a meeting that day, as I am informd, several members resolvd to move the House to go into proper methods to obtain a more satisfactory one; and I have reason to believe my Lord Lieutenant had notice of their intention; on Monday Morning I waited on him and told him that I had receivd an account that some of the Members pretended to be able to prove, that an exemplifyd Copy of the Patent, which was in some persons hand in Town, was actually deliverd into the Castle; that I did not know what truth there was in this, but if it could be made appear, it would in no sort tend to his honour, and lest, if it was so, they should come to the bottom of it I advisd him to have the Copy return'd into the persons hand from whom it came; and then he might of his own accord lay it before the House; whether it was from what he had heard of the intention of the Commons, I dont know, but that very day Mr Hopkins carryd a message to the house to this purpose; that since my Lord Lieutenants answer of the Saturday before, an exemplifyd Copy of the Patent had come to his hands, which he had orderd to be laid before the house;[100] you may easily imagine what different speculations there are, about these two very different messages; for my part I am not master of the thing enough to inform you of the reasons of 'em; but I

[97] Michael Ward, MP [I].

[98] Edward Hopkins, MP [I], chief secretary.

[99] On Friday, 13 Sept. the Commons addressed the lord lieutenant to lay before them the exemplification of Wood's patent and other relevant papers in his possession. Grafton's response the following day, as relayed by Hopkins, was that he did not have in his possession either the exemplification or any documents which might answer the purpose of the request. (*CJI*, v, 21–2.)

[100] On Monday, 16 Sept., Hopkins informed the Commons that since his original message the lord lieutenant had received the exemplification and other papers and was therefore now in a position to comply with their request, for which thanks were voted (*CJI*, v, 21, 23–4).

am not without fear that this little incident of the first answer, and the other conduct in this affair may incline people to a more nice examination of the Establishment, than I think the Generality of 'em was once dispos'd to; and if this should prove the case, it must be imputed to none but Mr Woods friends, or those he represents; who, are now loudly spoke of, as if they were some great ones among ourselves; I thank God I am tolerably well but under great anxieties upon account of this matter; the part that I shall take in it shall be to incline as many as I can to be easy and complying in the matter of the establishment, and as to the halfpence that they do nothing misbecoming the most dutiful subjects to the best of Princes; but I confess I am mightily afraid that peoples tempers are so ruffled by these proceedings that it will be hard to keep em within any bounds; in short if there dos happen any thing untoward it is easy to see whence it takes its rise present my most humble respects to Lords Carteret and Townshend and the Grand Marshall.

558. *Alan I, Dublin, to Alan II, Hanover, 27 Sept. 1723*[101]

(1248/6/70–1)

You will see by what is contain'd on the other side of this sheet[102] whether the resolutions the Lords came to yesterday relating to the coyning and uttering Copper half pence for this Kingdom, be more soft or more severe and warm than those of the house of Commons, which I beleive you must have seen before the receite of this Letter. If they be not more moderate and Less warm than those of the Commons, I perswade myself that the noble viscount who was the ocasion of this affair being atal taken into the consideration of the house of Lords, missed his Aim: for I did aprehend my Lord FitzWilliams when he proposd the moveing of the matter to the Archbishop of Dublin did it with a view to soften things, and it was after that he had proposd it to the archbishop of Dublin to move (that the house would take that matter into consideration) that the Archbishop of Tuam made the motion for it, the Archbishop of Dublin haveing refused to Doe it for this reason that there had hardly one mocion been made in our house this session but by him. My Lord FitzWilliams is putt into the chair to draw the addresse to his Majesty on these resolutions and will have a Difficult task out of such materials to form an agreable addresse, when it is prepared and reported by him to the house I will endevour to soften any expression which I aprehend may be chocking or give offence; but such is the resentment of several Lords against these

---

[101] Copy in an unknown hand.

[102] ‘(1)   Resolved that it is the opinion of this Comittee that the Letters patents granted to William Wood Esq for coining copper farthings and half pence for this Kingdom have been obtained in a cladestine and unpresedented manner and by a gross misrepresentation of the state of this Kingdom.

(2)   Resolved that it is the opinion of this Committee that whatever persons have confederated with the said William Wood in procureing the said Letters patents are justly chargeable with a Design to enrich themselves by the Impovrishment of this Kingdom.

(3)   Resolved that it is the opinion of this Committee that the uttering in this Kingdom the copper halfpence and farthings coined by William Wood would tend to the Diminution of his Majestys Revenue the Impoverishing of the people and the Ruin of trade.

(4)   Resolved that it is the opinion of this Committee that it would be for his Majestys service and the great good of this Kingdom, for the King to Reserve the coining of half pence and farthings to the Crown and not to intrust the same with any private person, body politick or corporate.’

half pence that I know not what sucksess such an attempt will meet but I resolve to try and will not despond.

I am sorry to find that my fears, which I formerly expressed Least this unhapy affair might create Difficultys in other matters, which otherwise probably would have passed over more easily, were to well grounded: for I find the Committee of accounts are more than ordinarily nice in their enquiry's. Several Letters from Mr Wood (the patentee for coyning half pence) to his corispondents here have been read in Both houses[103] in which the names of Mr Hopkins and Mr Whichcotte[104] are mention'd in such a maner as perhaps gives room for weak and malicious people to suspect they might have more knowledge of this transaction than one would wish. But after the professions and protestations of both that they are perfectly unconcern'd and no way privy to any thing relateing to the obtaining the patent I canot entertain the Least aprehension of either of them to have prevaricated. I will soon Lett you see copyes of the Letters which have been proved and read in the house of Lords, present my humblest services to Lord Townsend and Lord Carterett and those few others with whome I have the honour of any acquaintance.

559. *Alan I, Dublin, to Alan II, 30 Sept. 1723*[105]

(1248/5/318–19)

On Saturday I sent your Uncle the addresse which the house of Lords agreed to make to his Majestye about the Copper halfpence coyned by William Wood for this countrey: Both houses of Parliament were of one mind that his Majestye had the good of the Kingdome in his view, and that he was informed that the coyning such a number of half pence as Wood was empowred to coyne would be for the benefit of it; but they were also of opinion that his Majestye had been misinformed very much to the detriment of Ireland, and to the advantage of Wood and of those concerned with him in the profit that would accrue by the coynage of soe great a summe of base money.[106] Soe both houses have applyed to his Majestye for his protection and that he would prevent soe great an evil from falling upon us: but I cannot but say I think the Lords have done it in a more handsome and agreeable maner then the other house. They say for themselves that at the time the Lords addressed, the Commons had actually delivered their addresse, and that the upper house was not at that time in soe much fear as the Commons were (while their addresse was stil under consideration) least the project might take place: but that the Lords beleived all would doe well when the Commons had with soe much zeal expressed their detestation of Woods scheme, which gave the Lords a fair handle for being very temperate in their application.

It is certain that the necessity of the thing (which both houses were equally sensible of) extorted from them the applications to his Majestye; being very unwilling to approach his Majestye with any thing in nature of a complaint.

[103] They are listed in *LJI*, ii, 748.

[104] Paul Whichcote (c. 1690–1760), 2nd sec. 1720–4 (for whom see J.C. Sainty, 'The Secretariat of the Chief Governors of Ireland, 1690–1800', *Proceedings of the Royal Irish Academy*, lxxii (1977), sect. C, 33).

[105] Partly printed in Coxe, *Walpole*, ii, 368–72. In the extracts he published from the Brodrick papers Coxe made emendations to punctuation, paragraphing, spelling and capitalisation.

[106] The Lords' address was agreed on Saturday, 28 Sept. (*LJI*, ii, 750–1).

We read over all the letters and papers relating to this affair on Wednesday 25 Sept. and adjourned the consideration of them and the debate till the following day.[107]

You shal soon have copyes of some pretty extraordinary letters which were proved before us and read, in which some persons are named, who doe assure us here, they knew nothing of the matter; but Wood must be a very silly fellow to order his correspondents to apply to men for advice and assistance in forwarding the project, who are perfectly strangers to the thing.[108] I told you in my postscript under the Copy of our addresse that two Lords named in it were instrumental in softning matters, by which I meant in the wording the addresse: but I think I may without vanitye say I pressed the prudence and necessitye of our approaching the King in the most humble and dutiful maner as far as any Lord in the house did, and I beleive with as much successe. I hope his Majestyes goodnesse will incline him to give us such an answer as (we hope) we may reasonably expect, considering that we think without such application to him we must have been ruined: and that we may have the satisfaction to hear what we have been obliged to doe in this unhappy affair is not taken to be the result of any inclination to complain unnecessarily. The sooner such an answer comes over the more chearfully will all matters of the Session proceed. It is very mortifying to us that the next Session after the bank was attempted to be settled among us, we should be forced to struggle with the Copper coyne which in another shape would have carryed away all our gold and silver in exchange for that base mettal, as the Bank would have done in exchange for the Bankers paper. No project was ever carryed on soe sillily as this hath been; the patent was concealed, and made a great secret here, after it was very well known that it had passed the great Seal in England, nay after several Copyes were in the hands of people; which induced those who had never seen them to suspect there was something contained in it more mischeivous then perhaps they would have thought if the patent had been made publick. Nay Wood the patentee had the folly to write in the postscript of a letter that he had power to make 200 Tuns of Copper money at any time as soon as he could, which at the rate of one pound of Copper being coyned into sixty halfpence or one hundred and twenty farthings amounts to £50000, and soe much of our Gold or silver might have been carryed away from us in one year if the halfpence had been received; This letter was written by Wood to his brother in Law and correspondent John Molineux, and bears date the 9th of February 1722 and the contents of it became publick by Molineux shewing it to some persons here to incline them to come into the scheme.[109] Now if the patent had been shewn as soon as it was passed it would have appeared by it that Wood had not a power to coyne more then one hundred Tons of Copper the first year; and this would have shewn people that there was not danger of having soe great a summe as £50000 being powred in upon them at once.

There was another letter written by one James Hudson dated the 23 Dec. 1721 to his cousen Tristram Fortick in which he insists on Forticks laying down at the delivery of the patent £5000 for managing £100000; and Hudson tells him that they can gett a Gentleman in London that will lay down that summe for one fourth part of the profits, giving him

---

[107] In a committee of the whole House on the state of the nation (*LJI*, ii, 748).

[108] The letters are among a schedule of listed documents in *LJI*, ii, 748.

[109] Letters from Wood to his brother-in-law John Molyneux (*d. c.* 1735), an ironmonger of Meath Street, Dublin, dated 18 Oct. 1718, 9 Feb. 1722, and 10 and 15 Aug. 1723, were among the listed documents examined by the Lords (*LJI*, ii, 748). For Molyneux, see *Drapier's Letters*, xiv–xv, xxxvii, 321; Vicars, *Index*, 350.

liberty first to pay himself the summe laid out before any of the other three receive any thing, soe that the sharers reckoned on £20000 profit.[110]

This letter and others from merchants in Bristol and London which offered to send over to their correspondents quantityes of these half pence at a great discount together with the nature of the coyne, both for finenesse and weight convinced people that the Kingdome must suffer extremely if such a quantitye should be imported and uttered as might be made of 360 Tons of Copper, and all the members of Parliament came up full of the complaints and resentments of the countrey against them. Beside the Privy Councel thought themselves very injuriously treated and aspersed by Wood in his letter 9 Febr. 1722 in which he tells his correspondent if a proclamation is necessary in Ireland for to make it current, he can have it; or any thing that is wanting. Wood in another letter dated 10 Aug. 1723 writes to Molineux that he had sent by Mr Whichcotte the Duke of Graftons secretary an exemplification of his grant with the great Seal affixed to be registred in Ireland, and in the same letter tells him that he hears of a complaint or remonstrance to be made in Ireland, which he is pleased to say will in effect be noe other then against his Majestye and ministry for making the grant. My Lord Lieutenant landed here on the 13th of August, and this grant was soe mislayd or soe little minded by Mr Whichcotte that it was never brought to light till the 16th of September (after my Lord Lieutenant had returned his answer on the 14th to the addresse made by the Commons on the thirteenth) that his Grace had not the patent, nor any Copy of it, nor any other papers which would give them any satisfaction. The maner of this grants coming to light I never could hear an account of, such I mean as I am fond of setting down in writing. But certainly either Mr Whichcotte or another of his Graces servants was much to blame for his negligence.

There was a letter written by Eleazar Edwards to his correspondent Thomas Bailie in Dublin dated 14 Sept. 1723 in which Edwards informs Bailie that Wood said if the halfpence would not go in Ireland he shal have a licence to passe them in England, and thereupon Edwards directs Bailie before he sends the halfpence back to him to let him know what Secretary Hopkins saith to it, and what Bailie finds is like to be done with them here.[111] Nothing soe much employes mens conjectures as what person or persons is or are to reap the benefit that will accrue to somebody by this coynage, if it should take place; I should have expressed myself otherwise viz. who were to have had it if the thing had succeeded. For I will not entertain a thought that a thing soe very disagreeable and pernicious to a countrey which hath at all times signalized itself for its affection and duty to his Majestye will be farther carryed on for the advantage of particular persons, since it appears by Mr Woods letter dated 10 Aug. 1729 that tho the obstructions he hath mett with in uttering his halfpence in Ireland have been of great disservice to him, yet he hath such interest that he fears no ill consequences, and if Ireland refuseth the Coyne it will easily be disposed elsewhere.[112] I wish if Mr Wood be a man who hath deserved well of the Crown, some

---

[110] Letter listed in *LJI*, ii, 748. Tristram Fortick (*d.* 1755), was a wealthy saddler of Capel St., Dublin, and Grange, Co. Dublin (Reg. Deeds, 31/164/18368; *Gentleman's Magazine*, Sept. 1755, p. 428; NLI, MS 45909/3: will of Tristram Fortick, 1755; *Hist. Ir. Parl.*, iv, 219); Hudson was his cousin.

[111] Eleazar Edwards was a member of the court of assistants in the Royal Mines Company (*Daily Courant*, 13 Aug. 1720); Thomas Baillie, of Pill Lane, Dublin (*CJI*, v, 21), may have been one of the sons of Robert Baillie, a wealthy upholsterer of Capel St., Dublin and Kildrought House, Co. Kildare (*The Letters of Katherine Conolly 1707–1747*, ed. Mary-Louise Jennings and G.M. Ashford (Dublin, 2018), 266; Reg. Deeds, 57/308/38610).

[112] To John Molyneux (*LJI*, ii, 748).

other method could have been found to reward his merit. Present my humblest services to my Lord Townesend and my Lord Carterett. I hope now this affair is over we shal not meet with anything that may create farther warmth in our Session. Possibly you may think my letters worth laying by; if you doe keep them let me in answer to this know the date of every letter you have had from me since you left London and tell me what the conjectures are at the Court where you are, what person or persons is or are at the bottom of this affair.

560. *Alan I, Dublin, to Thomas, 21 Oct. 1723*

(1248/5/323–4)

I take it for granted that you will be back in London from Newmarkett before this letter can reach that place. It will be surprising to you to find that the same house of Commons, which at the beginning of the Session was unanimous in one point (I mean the matter of our Copper half pence) and soe firmly determined that it was not in the power of man to gett one single person who would speak in behalf of Mr Woods patent, soe very soon after as on Saturday last to be as equally divided as an odd number can be divided; especially if it be true that it was with the strongest sollicitation and application that Mr Levinge[113] the sitting member had the good fortune to have 89 yeas for agreeing with the Committee of elections (which voted him duly elected) against 88 who were for disagreeing with the Committee.[114] It was in everybodyes mouth that Levinge had carryed it by a very small majorytye; but one Gentleman hearing that said declared he was convinced that nothing could have carryed it for him but a very great majorytye; It was very observable that the resolution of the committee had not such a foundation, as would induce the two Dr Coghils, who are very near relations by marriage to Captain Levinge[115] or the Chancellor of the Exchequer,[116] or Attorney General,[117] or Brigadier Creichton to stand the division but they absented themselves; and yet I have very good reason to beleive it was not for want of sollicitation from those who espoused Mr Levinges cause. The Case as I hear it was that the Sherif without any ground closed the Poll when about 100 freeholders (who had not polled) desired to have their votes received; but the Sherifs refused to doe it, and yet the election is it seems a good one.[118] Young Rotchfort[119] was Levinges competitor, who had a good many Whigs for him, who thought it better to have a Tory sit in the house if he were fairly elected; then to establish a precedent that a Sherif might return whom he pleased for Knights of the shire. Your Nephew was chairman of the Committee and moved that the report of this Case might be printed to silence or refute the clamours of those who represented the vote of the Committee without doors to be a very ill grounded one; but he could not prevail, which those who are favourable to Mr Rotchfort would use as an

---

[113]Richard Levinge, MP [I].

[114]Confirmed in *CJI*, v, 129. See also Hayton, 'Co. Westmeath By-election', 7–40.

[115]Richard.

[116]Sir Ralph Gore, MP [I].

[117]John Rogerson, MP [I].

[118]See Hayton, 'Co. Westmeath By-election', 9–10.

[119]George Rochfort (1683–1730), of Gaulstown, Co. Westmeath, MP Co. Westmeath 1707–14, 1727–*d*.

argument to induce people to beleive that the majoritye might apprehend that the facts reported might possibly in the judgement of others be a foundation for the house to have disagreed with the Committee. Whereas say those of the majoritye, it is not usual to appeal to those without doors by printing the special reports from the Committee of elections. I confesse when I saw the list of the members who voted for agreeing with the Committee, I could not but think that Rotchfort must have something in his cause to induce so many Gentlemen to vote for him, as to bring it to an equalitye within one single vote: especially considering what the quota from the revenue amounted to. I mean those who voted for Levinge of which number take the following persons.

Collectors and concerned in the revenue

Clements	May. Maynorrd.	Ben. Parry. A Ranger of the Park
Bindon[120]	George Ram. hath an emploiment in the Exchequer	
Pearson		
Col. Henry Sandford		
Mr Medlicotte		
Mr Manley Postmaster.		
Trotter Sollicitor of the Crown in civil and revenue Causes.		
Marlay Sollicitor General.		
Mr The: Upton Councel of the Barack board.		
Mr Rose Councel to the Commissioners of the revenue.[121]		

Army

General Winne.	Lt Col. Rich. St George, half pay.	
Owen Winne jun.	Lt Col Brasier.	Mat Penefeather.
[?Ste]ph[?enson][122] Commissary	Lt Col Bligh.	Pat Fox.
	Purefoy	Lt Col. Berry.
	Freeman.	Lt Col. Whitshed.

But that which will seem to you as indeed it did to me very odd, I am told the Speaker should have the weaknesse to declare that the contest was not between Rotchfort and Levinge but was between him and Mr Brodrick; which of them should guide the house of commons. I think it is insolence in either of them to pretend to doe it, or to aim at, and I am sure one of them understands himself too well to entertain such a thought: but nothing could be lesse for the service of Mr Speaker then to make such a declaration just before the day on which the sense of the majoritye was to be declared, and then with the concurrence of many who depended intirely on another place not to be able to carry the question of agreeing with a Committee in favour of a sitting member by no greater a majoritye then one voice. This division I apprehend hath cemented a body of men in a common interest to preserve the Libertyes of their countrey against the attempts of them who would sacrifice everything to their ambition. And faith I think people doe apprehend there are such among us, and I wish there may not be too much ground for it. But it is plain whom the Castle supports, and alway will; viz. those who will goe into all their measures without reserve.

---

[120]David Bindon, MP [I] or Samuel Bindon, MP [I].

[121]Recommended to that position the previous year by Grafton, presumably on the advice of Speaker Conolly (NLI, MS 16007, p. 98: Grafton to revenue commrs. [I], 22 May 1722).

[122]MS blotted.

561. *Alan II, Brussels, to Alan I, Dublin, 3 Nov. N.S. 1723*

(1248/5/331–2)

I hope my last from Hannover, which I for the greater security got Leave to send by my Lord Carterets Packet, came safe to your Lordships hand; tho' I cou'd wish I had received my Answer sooner. But this I do assure your Lordship, that I wrote the very moment I was told what I was to say … I must say something about an Inhabitant of this Town, whose settlement here your Lordship promoted as far as you cou'd; I mean Dr Atterbury, for He goes by no other Name, even amongst the Poorest People, and I beleive leads a Life here as uncomfortable as can well be conceived. He is contemned and despised by every Creature, and sees scarce any Body but his own servants, with whom He quarrels daily; insomuch that He turned away, and set a starving that very servant to whom, your Lordship remembers, He intended a great kindness in a Letter which was intercepted. But He was at Daggers drawn even with Mr Morris when He was here,[123] and their Quarrels were the cheif Discourse and Entertainment of the Town. But He still maintains his Pride, and refuses to take a Receipt from a Tradesman unless He is styled Monseigneur; the Title which they always give their Bishops here.

562. *Alan I, Dublin, to Thomas, 1 Nov. 1723*[124]

(1248/5/325–8)

The pacquets went from this place soe very irregularly and uncertainly about the later end of the last month and the beginning of this while the proceedings of the Parliament in relation to Mr Woods patent were probably in great measure the subject of most letters that I chose to write to you and to my sister by private hands; and yet for any thing I can find I might as safely have trusted what I had to say to the common post, as by the way I took: yet I can hardly think the Gentleman by whose hand I wrote to you could neglect to give or send you the letter … Your being at Newmarkett possibly prevented your owning the receit of it, but I am strangely at a losse how it comes to passe that my sister should not have received a letter which I putt into Charles Stewarts hand[125] who was to have done me the favour to deliver it to her with his own hand; but my Lord Lieutenant prevailed on him to stay longer here to attend the Parliament soe he tells me he gave it to Lord Montrath who sailed hence on Thursday the third of October, and as I hear reached London on the tenth. But she in her last letter dated 23 Oct makes no mention of her ever having received it. I doe beleive people will be lesse curious then they have been for some time past to know Gentlemens thoughts about the Proceedings of our Parliament with respect to the Copper money intended for us and for our good. For our sense of that matter is so fully understood and there needs no industry to be used to know the thoughts of every man in the Kingdome who hath a dram of sense or a penny of money, or the least love for the

---

[123] Atterbury's son-in-law, William Mor(r)ice (1691–1755), husband of the bishop's only child, his daughter Mary.

[124] Partly printed in Coxe, *Walpole*, ii, 372–5.

[125] Hon. Charles Stewart, MP [I].

countrey. I have seen a paper well written (as far as I can judge) upon that subject which from the maner I conclude is intended for the presse; but I have not been able to get a copy of it: for which my freind in whose hand I saw it gave me this reason: He said that as he never had contributed to the raising or increasing the heats which had hapned by occasion of this Copper money, soe he resolved not to doe any thing which might continue or revive them: As he apprehended giving a Copy might do; for that it would not be in his power after doing soe to prevent its being made publick, which he never designed, unless there should be a necessitye for it from Mr Woods and his freinds behavior in justification of his scheme. But in that case he would speak his mind in the plainest and most publick maner, which he declined to doe till he saw there was a necessitye for it, because he should be forced to speak some truths which might disoblige. I gave Mr W[alpole] an hint of my having seen such a paper and that I hoped to be able to send you a copy of it soon; and so have enabled you to shew it to him which I intend to doe soon as possible: and I wish there may not be an oportunitye sooner then I desire. For yesterday my Lord Lieutenant delivered to me his Majestyes answer to the Addresse of the house of Lords at the beginning of the Sessions, and expressed him self in this maner that he had received his Majestyes answer to the Addresses of both houses of Parliament, which I hoped and was willing to understand meant the several Addresses of both houses, the first being only an addresse of congratulation on the discoverye and disappointment of the designs of his Majestyes enemyes; the other against our being impoverished by Mr Woods lean Kine eating up our fatt.[126] But I soon found that the answers were only to the addresses of congratulation,[127] and cannot but say that his Graces maner of speaking gave me lesse hopes then I desired of our soon receiving a gracious answer to the other Addresses: I shewed how much it imported his Majestyes service, the good of the Kingdome, his Graces honour, and how much it would be to the satisfaction of all the Kings servants and well wishers that the Session might have an easy and speedy issue: and that to attain all those desirable things it were to be wished that such answer might come soon and remove the dismal apprehensions the countrey lyes under of being ruined and impoverished by a thing which we are told is intended for our good. His Graces answer was that I might be sure he wished we might receive such an answer: but he gave me no other reason to think he beleived that we were like to receive an answer such as is here not only desired, but (if I thought the expression proper to be used) I might add (I think) expected. I doe not know but your plain way may doe his Majestye and this Countrey service, if you would wait on Mr W[alpole] and tell him that they doe not act with candor or judgement who think or may pretend to give hopes that the Kingdome is capable of being perswaded to receive this money voluntarily; if such people have been found who formerly gave hopes that methods might be taken here to reconcile people to this Copper money, they must now see they misjudged the thing and must confesse that they have not the power to doe every thing which they undertake.

For we are not without our suspicions that hopes have been given from this side that there should such methods be taken here, as should make Mr Woods money current, and among Mr Woods letters to his Brother John Molineux there is one expression which points strongly this way.[128] But you may assure Mr W[alpole] that all hopes which may

---

[126] A reference to Pharaoh's dream in Genesis, 41: 4.

[127] These had been presented by Hopkins on 31 Oct. (*CJI*, v, 550).

[128] The relevant letters were of 10 and 15 Oct. 1722 (*LJI*, ii, 748).

have been given or which shal be given that the people here will receive them of their own accord are without any sort of foundation; nothing will ever create a currencye of them but what this countrey promises themselves they shal never see in his Majestyes reign. I will now let you into a secret that nothing was ever managed with lesse skill then this whole affair hath been since it was first mentioned after the Dukes landing. He declared himself perfectly unconcerned how the thing went, and that he had no instructions about it from the King or the M[inistr]y; but added that honour was to be done to the Kings patent, which had passed before ever he was made acquainted with the matters being in agitation. The Exemplification of the patent which Mr Wood in one of his letters to his brother Molineux saith he had sent by Mr Whichcotte my Lords private Secretary was not forthcoming altho there were forty Copyes in several hands in the town. But at length the Exemplificacion was (we find) not given by Mr Woods as he said to Mr Whichcotte, but to one Mr Brumstead a Gentleman of the Dukes,[129] who had mislayd it, and at length found it on the 14th of September among some lumber and goods which were brought over. But this finding hapned to be unfortunately after my Lord Lieutenant had given an answer to the address of the house of Commons in which he told them he had no papers etc relating to it which would give them any satisfaction: The town knew how agreeable the answer was to the majoritye of the house of Commons and I have reason to think my Lord Lieutenant was told by several that wished him well that there would be an humble application for a more satisfactory and explicite answer: but this was fortunately prevented by Mr Brumsteads finding the exemplification between the deliverye of the Lord Lieutenants answer on Saturday and the houses meeting on Monday, when Mr Hopkins (as soon as the Speaker was seated in the Chair) told the house that a Gentleman attended at the door with the exemplification.[130] Now if instead of three persons going together into an upper room in Mr Conelyes house on Fryday the sixteenth day of August (when the Lord Lieutenant dined with the Speaker and I had the honour to be of the company) the number had been made fowre It is very possible that a fourth man might have been of opinion (supposing he could have been induced to have gone into the Copper scheme) that the way to have succeeded would have been to act avowedly and above board, and either wholly to have dropt the thing as wholly impracticable and inconvenient or else to have appeared for it heartily and fairly. The other method was the result of the poor temper and spirit of one man, who hopes he shal be able to blind people as to his being a well wisher to the thing, and hath obtained his end of convincing one man that he would doe all in his power which indeed he hath done, and that is nothing.

You will wonder at my mentioning three persons going into an upper room, one of them I need not name to you, but Mr Hill[131] was told this (in a vaunt) by a creature of Mr C[onolly] that after the Chancellor was gone away, the D[uke] the Sp[eaker] and Mr H[opkins] went into an upper room and were together for two hours and then settled the measures to be taken in the publick affairs. Indeed one would admire how it should be possible for men who have soe many troops at command should be soe ill Generals as to receive so many disgraces as our great men have done this campaign. The truth is instead of carrying

---

[129] Probably Charles Brumpstead (*d.* 1744), later an officer in the royal household (keeper of the standing wardrobe and clerk of the wardrobe at Whitehall) (*London Magazine*, Feb. 1744, 102).

[130] On 16 Sept. 1723 (*CJI*, v, 23).

[131] Arthur Hill, MP [I].

matters on with temper and prudence and good manners, some Gentlemen depending on numbers in all events chose to act with hauteur and to place indignityes on Gentlemen, who would not bear them and were very able to shew how inconsistent such proceedings were with the very being of Parliaments. Civil treatment and common countenance shewn to your Nephew might have made him lesse ready to give them the chagrin which they were often put into by his means. In short if they had considered better they would not have provoked a man whom few of them could hold a debate with, nor laid him under such impressions at a certain place that it was impracticable for him to explain himself and undeceive the other, where he had been misinformed. It is time to conclude and I know not how to do it better then by saying that in my opinion there are several who will think it will be time enough to passe the bill of Supply when they find reason to think the danger of the Kingdome from the Copper money is over, but I will not pretend to guesse at the numbers they may amount to. But of this I am fully convinced that a very great majoritye of both houses (if we should not have the happinesse of his Majestyes gracious answer to our Addresses) will come to resolutions which one would wish there might be no motive to come to, but what they may be I will not presume to guesse; least I should be thought a promoter of them. Possibly some may think that the least they can doe will be to lay those who shal countenance the currencye of Copper money by voluntarily receiving them in payment under such characters which few men would willingly have fixed on them by the body of the Nation: and I heard one man talk lately of sending over some members of both houses on an errand for which I hope there will be no occasion.

563. *Thomas to Alan I, Dublin, 5 Nov. 1723*

(1248/5/321–2)

I received (att Newmarkett) last Sunday the coppy of the deed, which brought mee to towne, sooner then I intended, having thoughts of spending the remainder of our fine weather with Lord Godolphin, whoe I left there … I doe nott att all wonder att that wrote to you, relating to the halfe pence, for twere a jest to fancy the benefitt arising thereby, should belong to the Pattentee, noe, that is a morsell fitter for his betters, I have never heard any one indifferent person of another opinion, or whoe thinks other then your Parliament doe; therefore I beleive those whoe say itt must yett bee rammd downe your throats spoake their wishes, nott opinions.

There is yett noe account come (that I hear of) what reception it meets with, in Jamaica,[132] in the citty I shall bee informd better. I am told Justice Eyre is to bee Chief Baron,[133] Mr Reeve a judge,[134] and Mr Werge[135] to succeed him as Kings Councill. I

---

[132] Wood had been granted a patent to coin small copper denominations for the use of the king's 'dominions in America' (*CSP Colonial*, 1724–5, 462).

[133] Sir Robert Eyre (c. 1667–1733), of New House, Whiteparish, Wilts., MP [E & GB] 1698–1710; solicitor-gen. [E] 1708–10, justice, queen's/king's bench [E] 1710–23, appointed lord chief baron of exchequer [E] Nov. 1723.

[134] Thomas Reeve (c. 1673–1737), of Maidenhead, Berks., attorney-gen. of the duchy of Lancaster, was appointed to succeed Eyre.

[135] Clement Wearg (c. 1687–1726) of the Inner Temple, appointed solicitor-gen. [E], and knighted, in February 1724.

cannott learne the Kings being expected till towards Chrismas. I left the D[*uke*] of De-von[*shire*][136] ill, having a tendency to the Gout in his stomach, butt when I came away hee was better, and his Doctor had good hope of diverting itt.

564. *Thomas to Alan I, 12 Nov. 1723*

(1248/5/333–4)

Lord G[*odolphin*] att his returne on Sunday night from Newmarkett, brought mee yours of the first; and yesterday morning your other of a very old date ... came ... Your letter by Mr Alcock desires that Mrs C[*ourthope*] and my selfe would settle the matter as to your sonne, of which you are certainly the best, and indeed onely judge, I will therefore tell you my sentiments. The sooner your directions come the better, for the year is very far advanced, which must render his going farther more difficult and hazardous then twould have been sooner. I know you had a promise of his being provided for, butt I owne (for several reasons) I lay little stresse on that, the treatment your selfe has mett with, I fancy must convince you that this is well grounded; seeing the world, and becoming acquainted with the different interests in Europe, quallifies a man for every sort of businesse, which alone enables him to stand upon his own leggs, and will allwayes have more weight then the favour of Courtiers, even supposing their professions reall, which they very seldome are, beside that a man recommended by his owne meritt is lesse liable to the caprice of those whoe pretend to bee his patrons, then any other, and likelyer to stand his ground when his freinds may nott bee able to maintaine theirs.

From what I have heard both of and from him, I thinke there is noe manner of danger of ill conduct, and I am very sure the remarkes hee has hitherto made, have been just, and his reasoning very strong. Consider this matter, and give directions assoone as possible.

If what Mr Clarke this morning told mee, bee fact, that an answer was come, and sent towards you relating to the halfe pence, which would bee satisfactory, noe more need bee sayd in relation to my speaking uppon that subject to Mr ———. Butt supposing itt otherwise what you mention would bee of noe significancy, for from what hee wrote to your selfe, and has lett fall to some here, you cannott doubt his being in the secrett, nay particeps criminis;[137] when I have a safe conveyance ile speake plainer, then I care to doe by post, for you may bee very sure both yours and my letters are opened, att least have been soe for some time past, and what reason can there bee to expect a discontinuance of that vile practice.

The generall opinion is that the Parliament will nott meet till after Chrismas, and some pretend to fix the 15th of Jan. for the time.[138]

I need nott tell you your mony Bill will bee readily agreed to, That for Chappells of ease will bee soe too, That against maiming, with an amendment to make itt conforme to ours,

---

[136] William Cavendish (1672–1729), 2nd duke of Devonshire.

[137] An accomplice in a crime.

[138] Currently the Westminster parliament stood prorogued until 19 November, but subsequent prorogations delayed its meeting until 9 Jan. 1724 (*CJ*, xx, 224).

of shooting in other place then houses, and I guesse made temporary, that for pious uses, will I beleive sleep, as a former did, or bee very much altered ...[139]

565. *Thomas to Alan I, 16 Nov. 1723*

(1248/5/335–6)

... You would hardly beleive what is sayd in excuse for the Halfe penny pattent, I did indeed heare itt some time since, from a man of honour and probity, which I then lookt uppon, onely, as what occurred to him, possible, butt I am satisfyed of his having heard itt from other hands since tis now publiquely given out, and with a good deal of industry, being the most plausible excuse that can bee made.

The house of Commons say they tooke three (butt I thinke four) different kinds of halfe pence, made an essay from all, and by a medium of the whole formd a computation of value, which falling a great deale short both of the conditions of the pattent, and intrinsick value, they charged as a grosse abuse and deceipt on the Pattentee, whereas the three baser sorts were counterfeits, never coind by him;[140] Risum teneatis[141]

Butt these are the shifts to which they are driven, to serve a present turne, without considering the consequence, how very strong an argument this (if true) is against coining any considerable quantity of base mony; butt bee that as twill, if my information bee true, the patent is to bee supported, and Ireland to have the benefitt of the currency of this mony, for people of noe better understandings then those whoe can find out that a hundred and fifty may bee lost by laying out a hundred, ought to bee under the care and direction of guardians of more sence, then those of that country are; I should nott take much notice of such stuff, if itt went noe farther then those (employd or concernd in this pattent) whoe in coffee houses endeavour to amuse and banter their auditors, butt if (as I heare) itt bee publiquely maintaind by men of figure, that such is the intrinsick value, as the Pattentee must and would necessarily bee a looser, were hee nott savd from such losse, by having copper mines of his owne.[142] The resolutions were somany absurd Bulls,[143] the produce of Irish understandings.[144]

---

[139] The British privy council rejected the Bill 'explaining and amending an act for the maintenance and execution of pious uses', and amended the Bill 'to prevent malicious maiming and wounding' in such a way that it was lost in the Commons on its return to Ireland. The Bill 'for explaining and amending an act, entitled, an act for real union and division of parishes', though amended, passed into law as 10 Geo. I, c. 6. (ILD.)

[140] James Maculla, a Dublin 'brazier', and William Maple, an operating chemist at Trinity College Dublin, had, on the instructions of the Irish revenue commissioners, made an assay in 1723 of some of Wood's coins that were already in circulation in Ireland and reported to the Irish house of commons in September of that year (Jonathan Swift, *Irish Political Writings after 1725* ... , ed. David Hayton and Adam Rounce (Cambridge, 2018), 130; *DIB*, vi, 354–5; Baltes, *The Pamphlet Controversy about Wood's Halfpence*, 119).

[141] A well-known Latin phrase, meaning 'Can you help laughing?'.

[142] As well as being an ironmaster, Wood is said to have owned and operated various iron- and copper-mines (*Drapier's Letters*, 189–90).

[143] 'An expression containing a manifest contradiction in terms or involving a ludicrous inconsistency unperceived by the speaker', usually associated with the Irish (*OED*).

[144] The derogatory phrase 'Irish understanding' was in common use. For an example dating from 1666, see Hayton, *Anglo-Irish Experience, 1680–1730*, 10.

I make little doubt of this letter being lookt into, and perhaps stopt as others have been between us reciprocally, therefore I declare for my selfe that if the asses ears are called hornes, I shall submitt to wiser men,[145] though for my soule I shall never bee able to bring my selfe to disclaime the use of my senses in this or any other perticular uppon being answerd by way of argument Ipse discit,[146] I have nott, or ever shall have implicit faith, against the evidence of reason, or my owne senses, this determines mee against Transubstuntion[147] and will hold in other things especially having heard in publique, that jealousyes were unreasonable and that relyance, I thinke the word entire was nott made use of, though strongly implyd or the position falls to the ground; wee shall see how far this matter will bee carryed, butt surely itt had been more prudent to have left out the caution given to the people of England against taking these halfe pence, which says that paper (lookt uppon to bee of some autority) I meane the daily courant,[148] for that they were nott of vallue they ought, and subjoins their been coind onely for Ireland.

Perhaps the losse to England may bee thought on, though that of Ireland may nott, for when rents come to bee payd in this coine, I beleive fifty per Cent will bee under the currentt Exchange, from whence twill follow that an entire stop must bee putt, as well to what is spent in living here, as to what is layd out in the manufactories and other commodityes exported hence.

The brasse mony in King James' time I take to have been of the same nature,[149] though I never heard the advantage accruing to Ireland from itt, pretended to bee maintaind.

This being a leisure day, has lead mee into this long letter, butt I question whither when itt comes to your hand (if itt ever doe) the reading will bee as easy as the writing is to mee.

Reading itt over gives mee reason to thinke youl mistake what I meane by the expression, I will submitt. Therefore you are to understand itt as in my private capacity, for in this and every other case, where I am to give my opinion I shall doe itt without reserve, or fear of the consequences which may attend itt as to my selfe, for as I never did, I never will betray any trust reposd in mee

566. *Thomas, to Alan I, Dublin, 7 Dec. 1723*

(1248/5/337–8)

I have little more to say then that my nephew[150] gott nott to towne till yesterday, I determined nott to give trouble to our ministry till after his coming, to the end I might bee fully apprised of every fact, and as far as possible into the rise as well as progresse of your affair,

---

[145] From the proverb, 'You will make me believe that an ass's ears are made of horns' (James Howell, *Paroimiographia Proverbs* … (1659), 6).

[146] *Ipse dixit*: a statement of opinion, without proof.

[147] Transubstantiation: in catholic belief, the literal conversion of the eucharistic elements during the mass into the body and blood of Christ.

[148] The relevant issue of the *Daily Courant* has not been traced.

[149] The so-called 'gun money' issued on King James's behalf in Ireland during the Williamite war, minted from various base metals, and popularly supposed to have been made from ordnance which James's forces had been obliged to melt down: it rapidly became a symbol of the economic hardship to be expected from a jacobite regime.

[150] Alan II.

which I thinke I am now pretty well master of, wherefore I resolve tomorrow morning waiting uppon them ...

567. *Alan I, Dublin, to Thomas, 8 Dec. 1723*

(1248/5/339–40)

I received your letter of the 26th of last month ... I will doe all I can to bring Randal Clayton to doe reasonable things with respect to his unfortunate younger brother,[151] whose strait condition I have laid home to him, and told him that in my opinion he was in a great measure the means of his ruine in the South Sea. On the other hand he rather attributes his own misfortunes in London to the encouragement which Courthope gave him to come over and make his fortune in the South Sea. I wish there was not some ground for this: since that poor young man like the rest of the young fellows about the Court and town was possessed with the epidemick phrenzy which at that time had infected people of more years and discretion: and that which gives me the greater conviction that the younger brother was the 1725 first mover to dabble in the South Sea is that he hath lost his whole fortune in it, and very probably out of good nature to his brother put him on going into a thing from whence he apprehended so advantagious returns. That poor young man puts his brother on asking from me some civil emploiment, and thinks that out of gratitude to his fathers familye [memorye *written above*] I can doe no lesse then grant him one: Now he lies under a double mistake; for really instead of my being a debtor in point of gratitude to my brother Clayton,[152] the ballance lyes very much on the other side: However for relation sake and because of the unfortunate condition to which my Cousen hath reduced him self, I should be very willing to make a grant to him of a civil emploiment, or (as Courthope terms it) sinecure if I had any such in my power. But alas! that is not my case; nor would my recommendacion be of any avail here, unlesse I laid down the current value of the thing desired; nay I doe not think I have interest enough to have the preference of the markett. On the contrary I cannot but think my recommending him and his being my relation would in all probabilitye put him on a worse foot then a meer stranger. For Brother I find it is like to continue my fortune, never to be well with the great people, for I can not court their smiles at the expence of my countreys ruine; and indeed my judgement is that the Bank or Woods Copper money would have effectually taken the whole gold and silver out of the Kingdome and I chose to declare my sense to be soe, when those matters came under consideration in parliament: By these steps I fell into the high displeasure of a great man, who would not have been a loser if either of those destructive schemes had succeeded, and have been treated ill enough on the score of the Bank, as you already know; and truly very little better since the halfpenny patent hath been rufled in both houses of Parliament as it hath been. In soe much that after the Kings answer to the Addresses of both houses about Woods patent were come to my Lord Lieutenant, he told me that they were come to his hand, and were very gracious and good and would be satisfactory to all reasonable men: but what the answers were in particular he declined communicating to me, tho I

---

[151] Courthope Clayton (see Appendix 2).
[152] Laurence Clayton (see Appendix 2).

urged him to it, and only had his leave to let people know so much in general. About two dayes after I told his Grace I had obeyed his commands and told Gentlemen what his Grace had said, who expressed great earnestnesse to know what the answers imported in particular, and I expressed a desire to be able to gratifye them, but was in plain terms given to understand that till the meeting of the Parliament he would not let them be known: How far he hath pursued that resolution he knows; but I beleive I shal be able to give him a copy of them before the twelfth of December. But this I am sure that some minions have not been sparing in letting the world know what they understand it to be. By this conduct in this particular and by his never consulting with me (as usual) in pricking Sherifs I see plainly his intent is to doe every thing disagreeable to me, and I beleive to endeavour to have the same slight upon me as he did when he last left Ireland: I am heartily sorry your health or other businesse calls you at this time out of town, since probably his Majestye will be come to London before you receive this. And noe doubt the matter of his Graces going into England and appointing Justices will be determined very soon after. If you find that I am designed to bear that diminution, which I would not endure the last time, and for which I had a sort of reparation (with promises of better treatment for the future) I doe entreat and empower you without farther authoritye or direction, as soon as ever you have good ground to be convinced that it is intended I shal remain here as Chancellor (without being one of the Justices) to have either a peticion or memorial to his Majestye, expressing my having faithfully served his Majestye to the best of my power for several years past, to the impairing my health; which with some discouragments I have mett oblige me to beseech his Majestye to allow of my retiring and surrendring the Great Seal. This is my fixed and determined purpose, and I desire you to act accordingly, and let those know to whom it is proper to speak on this occasion what I have resolved on: but if I meet with this treatment I shal think promises have not been performed, and instead of having had right done me, I must look on the last part of my treatment more unsupportable then the first, and take measures accordingly: but I shal alway know that all the services in my power are due to his Majestye and shal never fail to doe every thing for his Majestyes service and the good of such of his Kingdomes as I shal have the fortune to be in. I have not heard of your having received a letter which went by Mr Mathews servant[153] with a Ballad inclosed …

568. *Alan I, Dublin, to Thomas, at his lodgings in the Privy Garden, Whitehall, 28 Dec. 1723*

(1248/5/344–5)

Sure I am very unfortunate not to have received one line in answer to the many letters I have wrote lately, when they soe much concern me; If I had not reason to think noe methods are soe wicked as would not be gone into by some people I should not suspect any unfairnesse in the post office; but my late treatment hath worn out my charitye, and made me apt to beleive men that are proud and disobliged are capable of doing the worst things to destroy those against whom they have been pleased to take up a displeasure. Senny

---

[153]John Matthews (1683–1733), rector of Kilkeel, Co. Down; a connection of Alan through his wife (see *Anglo-Irish Politics*, ii, 192).

intends to set sail as soon as possible and will be able to set all matters in a most clear light: and I hope you will be in London at the time he gets thither. The ill offices done me by some late votes and the fair character under which I am laid by another vote must be left to be weighed by his Majestye and his ministry:[154] but of this I am certain that I am here in the hands and power of people who are able to have a majoritye say and declare any thing to my prejudice which is never soe undeserved and ill grounded. I should be unwilling to say or think this if I had not too late proof how much people are under the command and direction of ——[155] from whom I expect just the same treatment that a Lambe meets from an hungry wolf. I cannot doubt your care and endeavours not to have me overborn in a just and honourable case. Let not your stifnesse hinder your doing what you are able even tho you are forced to take the pains to go from White Hall to Arlington Street.[156] Whatever the event of this matter shal be to me I have the comfort to know I fall a sacrifice to the opposicion I gave to Woods halfpence: and I had rather fall for then with my countrey. But it is also a pleasure to me to be sensible that Strafford will not be thought fit to doe as he hath done much longer.[157] Pray answer this letter as soon as it comes to hand, and let me know what is like to be our fate as to the halfpence. Sure the Lord Treasurer,[158] Vice Treasurer,[159] and Master of the Rolls[160] will think themselves concerned in the hint given in our resolutions how unfit it is for them to be out of the Kingdome: Ten to one but the Commons may at next meeting impute as much delay of justice to their absence as the Lords have done to mine: and in time it may come to the Commissioners of the revenue Officers of the Army etc. In truth I doubt the whole strikes farther then is yet seen at the Kings power, but how the ministers will understand it considering who is at the head of the prosecution against me time must shew …

[PS] If a former letter is come to your hand in which I desire you to lodge a memorial or petition to the King [in] my name that I will lay down, in case I be left out of the Governement: I have thus far altered my mind, that in case there be not people put in whom I scorn to serve under I would not have you put that desire of mine into immediate execution, but if that St Omers bird FitzWilliams (for there he had his education)[161] be put in, it is plain that is done on purpose to pique me and if that be shal happen to be the case pray make no delay to let them know no consideration shal make me serve one hour after that indignitye put on me. If men of figure (who have not basely insulted me) be made Justices I can bring my mind to bear that for a time till I can lay down with more consideration: for after these rufles you may be sure I desire rest and retirement. If there must be either a Bank or a patent for halfpence or some such contrivance carryed

[154] For the campaign against Alan in the Irish house of lords, see below, pp. 81–2.

[155] Presumably Speaker Conolly.

[156] Robert Walpole's Westminster residence.

[157] A disparaging reference to Grafton, likened here to Thomas Wentworth (1593–1641), 1st earl of Strafford, Charles I's lord deputy in Ireland 1632–9.

[158] Richard Boyle (1694–1753), 3rd earl of Burlington and 4th earl of Cork, held the patent of lord high treasurer of Ireland.

[159] The vice-treasurership was held jointly by Hugh Boscawen (c. 1680–1734), 1st Viscount Falmouth, and Sir William St Quintin (c. 1662–1723), 3rd Bt, of Harpham, Yorks., MP [GB] 1695–d.

[160] William Berkeley (c. 1664–1741), 4th Baron Berkeley of Stratton.

[161] Richard, 5th Viscount Fitzwilliam had been brought up a roman catholic but had conformed to the Church of Ireland in June 1710 (*The Convert Rolls …*, ed. Eileen O'Byrne and Anne Chamney (Dublin, 2005), 95, 351).

on every Session I am fated to be alway opposite to the Governement here and shal be content to be out of the strife. But I hope the Kingdome hath shewn it will not easily allow such things [to] be imposed: and that we are not soe far under the direction of any Lord Lieutenant, assisted with his Conollyes and other Sycophants to perswade us to swallow our own destruction. I think his Graces sage conduct hath secured us against seeing his face standing that way which his back will when he leaves Ringsend:[162] I am also of opinion that the ministry will but little beholding to his prudence, which hath not thought it his affair to interpose in stopping the Lords from coming to resolutions which will in time reach more of the Kings servants then his Chancellor. I think too that they will see there is or will be a necessitye of not letting C[onolly] wholly govern the Kingdome. Pray write to me.

569. *Thomas to Alan I, 4 Jan. 1723[/4]*[163]

(1248/5/348–9)

Uppon New years day came yours of the 8th of last month, postmarked as coming in that day, soe that you may bee very certaine twas stopt on your side, and probably a coppy sent over, before twas lett goe forward, for of the many you say you wrote, nott one came to hand, the same I perceive has happened to those from hence.

Last night I receivd that of the 28th. You may bee very sure I will strictly follow your directions in what relates to your selfe, butt this must appeare (in the opinion of all impartiall men) calculated for a family indignity, uppon which foote I take my selfe to bee very nearly concern'd, and shall uppon my owne account, (and soe I will explaine my selfe) speake my mind freely, without mincing,[164] I know what ground I stand uppon, and make noe dispute of maintaining itt; the attempt is noe surprize to mee, otherwise then uppon account of the folly of itt, for I expected nothing lesse from that treatment which you receivd as well before, as after your coming over; for which reason you know I told you my mind, uppon doing which you tooke mee up very short, saying that my Lady Midleton (to whom I perticularly directed my discourse) would alwayes have a just sence of the honour of family, had my advice been followd, this slur had never been cast uppon itt, nay I am very confident you had mett with better treatment, for people that will bear, shall bee sure to bee well loaded, butt somuch as expressing dissatisfaction att your usage in the manner you had sufficient ground to have done, was nott to be thought on, the reason to mee both then and still appears very plaine. Noe recommendation of Justices is yett come that I can learne, I am sure nott to the proper person, though very possibly itt may privately to others, I will watch itt narrowly, and unlesse things are turned upside downe am confident wee shall nott (all of us) meet with like insults as you have; tis very probable this as well as all my other letters may bee opened, or stopt, the latter is the onely thing I feare, for I would nott vallue my thoughts and resolutions being printed and posted up att the markett crosse. As to your

---

[162] Ringsend, near Dublin; the usual point of embarkation for England.

[163] Letter endorsed by Alan I: 'Tho: Brodrick … resents and despises the insult made on me in the house of Lords'.

[164] Prevarication or reticence (*OED*).

copper coine I can say noe more then that every body thinks that att an end; the Pattentee offers itt to sale, and by way of ridicule on the calculation made by your house of Commons, I was askt whither I would give six thousand pounds for itt, my answer was Noe, nott six pence, I will write constantly lett therefore a servant attend att coming in of each packett.

570. *Alan I, Dublin, to Thomas, at his lodgings in the Privy Garden, Whitehall, 8 Jan. 1723[/4]*

(1248/5/350–1)

This letter will be delivered into your hand by a near relation of your old freind Sir Thomas Smith[165] who is his Nephew, Dr King:[166] Half an hours conversation will convince you he is a man of very good sense, but the other part of his character (his probitye and honour) are what he is most truly valued and beloved for by those who have had the happinesse of a longer acquaintance with him. He is a petitioner for a seat in the house of Commons against a potent Antagonist and interest which you will beleive when you find Mr Bromley to be the sitting member against whom he peticions[167] and consequently that he will meet all the opposicion that the Universitye and its bigotted disciples can give him. I hope you will find his case to be of that nature that you will think it ought to be espoused and supported and then I am certain you will doe it zealously and with pleasure. I have had the favor of some acquaintance with him by means of his Uncle, and have had the additional happinesse of his being an eye and ear witnesse of the late proceedings in the house of Lords against me: he is able and I think will not decline telling the story as it appeared to all indifferent people and I think it only needs to be barely related without the least favor or affection. Our Lords seem not to be extremely pleased at their own report, and some of them say they will question the Clerk for printing the Protest as part of the proceedings,[168] and one Lord expressed himself thus that as the report was printed it was an heap of nonsence: Whose fault is that? I doe assure Brother the man whose character was intended to be sullyed hath suffered much lesse then his enemyes have in the opinion of people here: The indignation and resentment which the Commons conceived at the nature and maner of the proceedings appear sufficiently in the vote they came to in my favor, which neither the sollicitations nor power of [*the Speaker*] and of all his Sycophants could withstand or prevent. Lord Molesworth would not have Senny prefer his peticion unlesse he finds the tyde turned, that is his own expression and he explains himself thus that he would not throw good money after bad. He hath been most freindly to me in my affair and soe hath my Lord Montjoy. You will probably have one of the reports come to you under cover before this will be delivered: Pray carry or send it by your nephew to my Lord Carterett.

[165] Sir Thomas Smyth (*d.* 1732), 2nd Bt, of Radclive, Bucks., ranger of the Phoenix Park 1705–11 and master of the game [I] 1722–30; MP [I] 1703–13 (*Hist. Ir. Parl.*, vi, 298).

[166] William King (1685–1763), principal of St Mary Hall, Oxford: in fact a high tory, with pronounced jacobite sympathies, who had been the defeated candidate at the parliamentary election for Oxford University in 1722 (*Oxf. DNB*).

[167] William Bromley (1663–1732), of Baginton, Warwicks., MP [GB] Oxford University; a former Speaker of the house of commons, and himself a tory, albeit a less violent one than King. For a moderate tory's exasperation at this division of the 'church interest' which might have let in a whig candidate, see *Remarks and Collections of Thomas Hearne*, ed. C.E. Doble et al. (11 vols, Oxford, 1885–1921), vii, 328–9.

[168] In the *Votes* of the House.

Our storms have hindred all intercourse of late between you and us: we have had abundance of shipwrecks and the losse is greivous to our merchants: but nothing so affects us as the apprehension of our losing all by the halfpenny patent …

[PS] Pray let me hear from you.

571. *Thomas to Alan I, 9 Jan. 1723[/4]*[169]

(1248/5/352–3)

Yesterday I waited on Lord T[*ownshend*] and this morning uppon Lord C[*arteret*] and gave them (I am sure) a true and faithfull accountt of what had passt on the subject of your affairs.

I was told by the former that Lord Lieutenant absolutely denyd having any hand in, or even knowledge of itt, to which my reply was, that last winter (and I thought with great truth) concurring circumstances were proofs of a stronger nature, then generally positive oaths That I must appeale to his Lordship whither in the house of Lords hee did nott bid mee tell you hee had layd before his Majesty the desire you expressed of having leave to returne, that hee was to tell you that must nott bee as yett, hee sayd hee perfectly well remembred itt; I told him that some time after you applyd againe, and that by the D[*uke*] of G[*rafton*] hee sent you word, that after such a day, and nott sooner you should bee att liberty to goe, and that you might prepare accordingly, this hee sayd hee remembred alsoe, I then told him you had reminded his Grace hereof, whoe could nott call perticulars to memory; which I thought wanted some explanation, for reconciling his ignorance of the whole affair, besides which I went into other perticulars, from whence I ownd my opinion different from what was pretended, and must leave the consideration to his Majesty when hee should bee informd of facts, to which I beleivd him att present a stranger, hee told mee att parting that hee thought hee could recollect what I had sayd, and bid mee assure my selfe hee would fairly repeate what I had sayd, my answer was that I had nott the least doubt of his doing soe, nor was I under any apprehension that a family whoe have always acted zealously for his service, could possibly (from his Majestys great goodnesse) faile of being rightly understood, and accepted by him; hee then told mee hee would assoone as hee could, informe mee of his Majestys thoughts uppon the whole.

I had this morning the opertunity of a little longer time with Lord C[*arteret*] and had like assurances from him, and have as little doubt of his performance, as of the others; uppon the whole I am satisfyd, his Majesty will bee fully apprizd, and am under noe manner of uneasinesse, since I am throughly convinct, you have acted both discreetly and honestly, in every perticular, and for his Majestys service in every instance.

I write by night, after a pretty long day in the house, wherefore you are nott to wonder that I am nott soe perticular or explicite as I should att another time, butt beleive, you will bee satisfyd what is necessary has been done, and I am sanguine enough to thinke twill have a good effect …

[169]Letter endorsed by Alan I: 'Tho: Brodrick … that he had discoursed both the Secretaryes about the treatment I had mett with in the house of Lords, gives me reason to hope the designs of my enemyes will be disappointed'.

572. *Alan I, Dublin, to Thomas, 11 Jan. 1723/4*

(1248/5/354–5)

I am to thank you for yours of the second which promises that you will write to me every post; but I can assure you that the pacquet which brought in the London letters of the 4th brought me none from you of that date.

Matters are in much the same scituation here as when I wrote last, only the Castle people who pretended to be very angry at the printed report, and that they would complain to the house on that subject (1. Because the Protest was printed (as they pretended) without authoritye. 2. Because say they the report as it is printed is an heap of nonsensical stuffe, to that purpose I hear a certain dependant Lord expressed himself to an officer in the house concerned in the printing it.) are now upon second thoughts become cooler and instead of pursuing those warm resolutions have let Tuesday and Fryday last passe without any such attempt: But the great view was to get a vote in the house of Commons in favour of a certain person, which those who are against the thing say is to desire them to wipe one (that is be —) clean but alas this is received with indignation; and if the question were put whether he should be — I think it would be more easily carryed in the affirmative. In short it is incredible what the resentment of Gentlemen is of the late impotent malicious ill judged attack on me. Every body sees whence it comes and what the reason is why I have been soe treated: I doe not mean by the Lords but Castle. The town swarms with Lampoons and Ballads on the managers and on Wednesday night between every act the [ballad?]of Sir Owen (which your Nephew will explain) was plaid between every Act with most profuse laughter of the Auditorye which clapped all the time (except a very few hissers who at the third time perceived the joke;[170] and I am told the Nephew and heir apparent of Sir Owen could not stand it but went out of the house).[171] This I am sure of that Punches Addresse to the Ladyes to intercede with Monsieur Vanderhop on his behalf[172] was read publickly by young Conyngham[173] at Lady Montjoyes[174] house in the full companye on her visiting night. The truth is never people were in lower esteem or lesse beloved then some who with you pretend to be Masters of the hearts of all men here. The most that is now hoped for by them is to retreat with their broken troops without any farther action: For I hear all thoughts of complaining of Mr C[*onolly*] for a supposed insult on a certain Viscount is dropped: but I am a good deal of opinion that when they decamp the weaker

[170]A ballad satirising William Conolly as 'Sir Owen MacHugh', in reference to his supposed catholic origins in north-west Ulster, was played several times at theatrical performances in Dublin 'on purpose to affront the Speaker or such of his friends as were there' (BL, Add. MS 47030, ff. 57–8: Philip Perceval to Lord Perceval, 30 Jan. 1723/4; Hayton, 'Co. Westmeath By-election', 26–9 (which prints a surviving version of the words, from a MS in the BL)).

[171]Confirmed in BL, Add. MS 47030, ff. 57–8: Philip Perceval to Lord Perceval, 30 Jan. 1723/4. The nephew was William James Conolly (*d.* 1754), later MP [I] 1727–54, and [GB] 1734–*d.*

[172]'Punch's Petition to the Ladies', a poem once attributed to Swift, includes the lines 'Nor did we show the least affection/To Rochfort on Westmeath election/Nor did we sing MacHugh …'. Vander Hop, mentioned in the poem, was the chief secretary Edward Hopkins. See *Swift's Poems*, ed. Harold Williams (2nd edn, 3 vols, Oxford, 1958), iii, 1108–9.

[173]William Conyngham (c. 1698–1738), of Slane Castle, Co. Meath, MP [I] 1727–*d.* Conolly was his uncle by marriage and had been his guardian.

[174]Anne, née Boyle, wife of the 2nd Viscount Mountjoy.

army may chance to receive a parting blow. A certain person hath been heard to say he is dying, and that he wonders people will not let him dye in peace. Sure those on your side will not wonder if one soe unfairly attacked as your freind should endeavour to return the complement. He cautioned the person concerned not to give into the thing and told him how much it would be for the Kings service and his own honour and the quiet of the Kingdome not to have that affair proceeded upon, and of this I gave an account to a certain person (whom you will guesse) by letter dated 7 Jan. which I would know whether it ever came to hand having had no answer to it: But this was not hearkned to, the pretence now is that the Archbishop of D[*ublin*] and F[*itzwilliam*] would not be advised: But methinks it is not much for one mans honour that he had not interest enough in his two favourites to prevent their proceeding in a matter, which had so little in it that with all the support and countenance given could not be brought to the desired effect. For I think the person who was to be humbled hath hitherto had much the better of the battle. Senny promised to write to me, and indeed he did soe from Chester, but not since that I can hear; and I take it for granted he came late to London. Pray let me know in plain terms from —— and Mr [?W] what I am to trust to as to my future treatment: for I neither [?can] expect to know any thing from this side, nor can depend on any one thing which is said to me. It will import me to be at a certainty soon that I may dispose my affairs accordingly. The wise men with you cannot but see that we have been woful politicians during this whole Session; which might have been most easy and quiet with the least prudent conduct: But our pride would not allow us to give ear to any thing which came from a certain quarter, and as soon as we landed a certain <u>spirit</u> possessed a great man, and carryed him farther then was to be wished.

573. *St John III, London, to Alan I, 11 Jan. 1723[/4]*[175]

(1248/5/358–9)

I wrote to you the night after I came to this place, but not having seen or spoke to any body at that time, I could then say very little to you; and indeed I am now at a loss in what manner to write, knowing that tis more then probable that my letter will be open'd before it reaches you. My Uncle gave you an Account of a conference he had with the 2 S[*ecretaries*],[176] upon the subject of our late proceedings in Ireland, so that I need not trouble you on that head further then to tell you that every word he said was that day laid before — by one, in presence of the other, in the plainest manner, not without reminding him of the constant zealous affection of our family etc, particularly in the last session here, the quiet and success of which, he was told was in a good measure owing to it. I had yesterday a conference of near 2 hours with the person to whom you have some times wrote upon this subject, and did, in the best manner I could open and explain to him the whole History of our session, particularly with relation to the Patent; at which he seem'd a good deal surpriz'd, and told me I had put that matter in a very different light from what it had been represented in by those who had transmitted constant Accounts of it over hither. I found that every one of the resolutions

---

[175] Partly printed in Coxe, *Walpole*, ii, 376–8.
[176] Lords Townshend (northern department) and Carteret (southern).

had been said to have been of mine, and consequently your, framing, particularly the two which seem to have given the greatest offence, those about the notorious misrepresentation of the state of the Kingdom, and Addressing the King against granting the power of coinage to any private person whatsoever.[177] When I mention'd the person that mov'd them, Singleton,[178] the meeting at the Rose[179] the night before we went into the Committee, the manner of opening it by the Chancellor of the Exchequer, the proposing one or both those resolution by Mr Ward, and in short every thing that was said or past there, which I did very fully and truly, he said he confest some peoples proceedings and Politicks were a good deal out of his depth, and could hardly beleive me when I acquainted him with Mr Uptons[180] motion at the close of the Debate, to declare Wood incapable of any Employment, Pention etc from his Majesty, fearing, as he said, that he might be made a Commissioner of the Revenue, or be put upon us for a Pention of £1000 per Annum, as a satisfaction for the loss of his Patent. You may be sure I did not forget telling him whose Creature and confident he was; nor that the Question of the 150 per Cent loss was mov'd by the Kings Sollicitor, member for Newtown.[181] He was very exact about the names of the particular persons who mov'd the several Questions, which he made me repeat 2 or 3 times; and assur'd me that as my Uncle had the day before told him a good deal, so I had explain'd and enabled him to say many things which he had omitted, which he would not fail to represent to — immediately.

I had the satisfaction to be told, when I gave him an Account of the first matter of heat which past in the House, (a certain grave persons most irregularly calling me to orders) that whatever the consequences of that behaviour were, he thought, the person who was the occasion of them, and not I were answerable for them.

When I began to enter upon the Proceedings of the 2 houses about you, he told me, I need not labour that Point, for that it was very well understood, and that no great stress was laid upon it.

This is the substance of what past between us, at least as much as is proper to be trusted to a letter that is to pass thro' Manleys hand;[182] when I can meet with a proper opportunity, I will write more explicitly, and let you know several particulars which I beleive wont displease you. In general I think our late Proceedings will in no sort answer the end propos'd; but on the contrary, will take a very different turn from what those who set them afoot expected.

I go very little abroad, so cant send you much news. Our session open'd very quietly, not a Debate upon or negative to the Address, and people seem to think, twill be a very short and easy one; but of this I dont pretend to give any opinion.

---

[177] The Lords' address claimed that Wood had obtained his patent by 'a gross misrepresentation of the state of the kingdom', while the Commons declared that the patent 'could not have been granted had not Wood and his accomplices greatly misrepresented the state of the nation to his Majesty'. The Commons were open in stating that granting to any private individual the right to mint coins 'has been highly detrimental' to the king's loyal subjects in Ireland, the Lords more circumspectly stated that preserving the crown's exclusive right would always be for the king's service and the good of the kingdom. (*LJI*, ii, 750; *CJI*, v, 36.)

[178] Probably Henry Singleton, MP [I].

[179] The Rose Tavern in Dame St., Dublin.

[180] Probably Clotworthy Upton, MP [I].

[181] Thomas Marlay, solicitor-gen. [I].

[182] Isaac Manley, MP [I], postmaster-gen. [I].

The town says Lord Cadogan has stood his ground, notwithstanding a very strong Attack made upon him. The scheme was, Cobham[183] to command the Army, Argyle,[184] for the present, to take up with the ordinance, and Dorset[185] to be Steward; If this had succeeded, twould hardly have stopt there; but as it has been disappointed, people who know nothing, make various conjectures upon the consequences of it. In short we are in a strong rumble here; who will turn up, God knows; Particulars you must not expect by the Post, any more then Answers to your letters to the person who is the cheif subject of this; who bid me tell you that writing would only prejudice you and himself, but that he is, and I verily beleive him, much you servant.

For the future I should advise your writing either to my Uncle or me, rather then directly to him …

574. St John III, London, to Alan I, 12–13 Jan. 1723[/4][186]

(1248/5/356–7)

I wrote to you by last nights Post, but having an opportunity of sending this by a private hand, Mr Hamilton, I shall mention some things now, which in prudence I could not do yesterday, without repeating any thing I then wrote.

You cannot imagine what a noise your Affair has made on this side the water, nor how tis resented by almost all sorts of people. I speak not my own words when I tell you tis the luckyest incident that could have befallen Lord Carteret, Roxborough[187] etc, who you may be assur'd have and will pursue it to the utmost with the King, whom it has very much sower'd already; these are the words of one of those Lords to me. I need not tell you that the breach between those 2 Lords and Mr Walpole is so great as to be past a possibility of reconciliation or even acting together. The former have withstood many home pushes at them and their freinds at Hanover, and as I told you yesterday have been able to support Lord Cadogan, even after positive promises made to the 3 Lords I then mentiond of his Employments, which has not only a good deal Chagrin'd them, but is lookt upon as a great blow to W[alpole], especially considering the time of pressing and denying him this, the beginning of a session, when he and his freinds fancy they have a right to ask and insist upon any thing. He is certainly a very considerable man, and has great influence in the House of Commons; but then, many things which pass there purely by the zeal and affection of Gentlemen to the Kings person and Government, are, by his Creatures, ascrib'd wholly to his conduct and Interest. In short while he pursues the Kings Measures he has, no doubt, great opportunitys of serving him, but if thro Pique, or any other pretence, he should again think fit to oppose them, be assur'd there are Gentlemen enough, even in this Parliament, to do the Kings business, without him or his freinds, and tis not impossible but that you may in a little time see what I say come to pass. I mention this purely that you may not be under

[183] Richard Temple (1675–1749), 1st Viscount Cobham, a lieut.-gen. and col. of the 1st Dragoon Guards.

[184] John Campbell (1680–1743), 2nd duke of Argyll and 1st duke of Greenwich.

[185] Lionel Cranfield (1688–1765), 1st duke of Dorset, eventually appointed lord steward in 1725.

[186] Printed in Coxe, *Walpole*, ii, 378–9.

[187] John Ker(r), 1st duke of Roxburghe.

any apprehensions from the omnipotence of his power; He certainly has a great deal, but your freinds have at least as much Credit with the King, and are infinitely better esteem'd by the disinterested part of mankind. What the Event of this contest between them will be, I cant pretend to say; and am afraid I shall be thought to speak my inclinations rather then my judgment, when I tell you I have very little apprehensions about it. Tis certainly prest on both sides with the greatest application and vigour, and is a fair Trial of their Credit and Interest with the King; so that the Event of it will, in all probability, determine the fate of one of the Partys. By all the observation I could make, our freinds seem to think they have gain'd a great advantage over the others, and to determine to pursue it to the utmost, and Lord C[arteret] went so far tother day as to tell me he did not think doing you justice by continuing you in your Employments, was a sufficient reparation for an injury which he thought was done and meant to the whole family, and therefore advis'd both my Uncle and me to insist upon some particular mark of the Kings favour being shewn one of us and to mention this to Mr W[alpole] in the strongest Terms. I have great reason to know he Mr W[alpole] is both asham'd and uneasy about his freinds behaviour in Ireland, which has brought him into the greatest difficultys he ever was involv'd him [*sic*] since his last getting into the Ministry. For this reason, great pains are taken to shift the load from our great man in Ireland, who pretends to disavow even the knowledge of it, and the whole blame is laid upon that most inconsiderable tool of his Jack Rugby.[188] When I was told this by a very great Lord and freind of theirs, I took the liberty to say I could hardly beleive he was in earnest; but that if he were, he was not very well acquainted with the complexion of our House of Lords, to imagine they dar'd have taken such a step without orders from their superiors, or that 11 Bishops and 9 Temporal Pentioners could have been influenc'd by a little inconsiderable Papist in Masquerade, whose person every one of them hated and despis'd.[189]

Tomorrow I shall hear the result of my Conference with Lord C[arteret], having been order'd to attend him to that purpose; you shall be sure to hear from time to time whatever is fit to be trusted by Post, and as often as possible by a private hand. I beleive my Uncle will make use of the opportunity of this, and hope the Account he gives you will be satisfactory.

I will keep my letter open as long as possible, not knowing but I may hear something further before I send it away.

I have nothing more to add, not having seen Lord C[arteret] since I began my letter; only that this day in the House Mr W[alpole] appointed me to be with him on Wednesday morning; I shall say nothing without advice, and will give you the earliest Account of what passes.

God Almighty preserve your Lordship, and disappoint the devices of all your Enemys. Monday noon the 13th.

---

[188] Dr Caius' servant in Shakespeare's *The Merry Wives of Windsor*, used as a nickname for Lord Fitzwilliam, possibly in reference to the passage in Act 1, sc. iv (ll. 9–14) in which Mistress Quickly describes Rugby as 'An honest, willing, kind fellow, as ever servant shall come in house withal; and I warrant you, no tell-tale nor no breed-bate; his worst fault is that he is given to prayer; he is something peevish that way …'. The Brodricks continually emphasised Fitzwilliam's catholic upbringing.

[189] The figures for divisions in the Irish house of lords are not given in *LJI*, but Grafton informed Walpole that the majority against Midleton had been of the order of 21–10 in both the divisions which he had lost (Coxe, *Walpole*, ii, 360).

575. *Alan II, Cambrai, to Alan I, Dublin, 27 Jan. N.S. 1724*

(1248/5/133–4)

I think it my Duty to inform your Lordship that the Congress opened yesterday at One a Clock, which is three weeks sooner than what was generally expected here.[190] The Ambassadors met at the Townhouse, without any Intention to do Business, any farther than the settling the Rooms and private Apartments which They are to have to retire into. The Embassadors from France did the Honours, in giving all the others the Choise of their Apartments; and after many Compliments, and settling those kinds of Things which I have mentioned, They parted; and it is thought that They will meet very soon to proceed upon Business. However the Congress is already opened, before People (even on the spot) were aware of it; and as the most materiall Points are beleived to be already adjusted, and the measures well concerted, no body doubts but it will be brought to a speedy Conclusion. Your Lordship will pardon my Boldness in congratulating you on a late Resolution of the House of Commons of Ireland, wherein they give the most publick Testimony of your Lordships Merit, and their own sense of it.[191] I cannot but observe how bitter it must be to your Ememies (if you have any, and who is there but has?) to see your Lordship triumph over all Opposition, and to find that Those who have known you most, have the greatest Honour and Respect for you. I fear I shou'd offend your Lordship in saying any more on that head, and will therefore conclude …

576. *St John III to Alan I, 17 Jan. 1723[/4]*[192]

(1248/5/360–1)

I deferr'd answering 2 of yours of the 2d and 3d Inst by last Post, being appointed by Mr Walpole to attend him this morning, and consequently desirous of letting you know what past in that conversation. I was with him above 2 hours this morning, and in the best manner I could gave him a particular Account of what past in our Parliament, especially with relation to Woods Patent, which I do not repeat to you who are so well appriz'd of it. He heard me with great Attention, and in the conclusion told me he had been inform'd of most of the particulars I mention'd, but that some of them were new to him; by which I understood he meant the history of all the Resolutions we past, except the first, the persons that mov'd them, and the motives of their doing it. He then began with a Protestation of

---

[190] The Congress of Cambrai, described by one historian as 'that most solemn farce', had been called in order to settle the differences between Spain and Austria through the joint mediation of England and France. Having officially opened in 1722, it did not get down to business until 1724 (J.C. Walker, 'The Duke of Newcastle and the British Envoys at the Congress of Cambrai', *EHR*, i (1935), 113–19).

[191] On 23 Dec. the Irish house of commons resolved, in response to the attacks on Alan in the Lords, that the lord chancellor 'has behaved himself with the utmost zeal and affection to his majesty's person and government and to the Protestant succession …with the greatest regard to the properties and welfare of his fellow subjects, and for his faithful and eminent services to his majesty and to his country, is a person highly meriting his majesty's favour (*CJI*, v, 182).

[192] Printed in Coxe, *Walpole*, ii, 409–13. Letter endorsed by Alan I: 'Senny … that he had a long conference with Mr Walpole about the halfpence and the persecucion that I have undergone in the house of Lords, in which the Duke of Grafton denyes to have had any hand'.

his not having the least hand in advising or promoting that Patent, further then as first Lord of the Treasury it must of necessity go thro his hands; and took particular pains to disclaim having had the least share of the Advantage, or prospect of any, by it. He said that these things were intended as boons from the Crown, and consequently that it must be suppos'd and was intended that the Patentee should have some profit by his Grant, and added that he thought those who had with so much zeal appear'd against this Patent, should be sure that no Petition or Paper could be produc'd under their hands, desiring a Grant of the like nature; but a good deal more to the prejudice of Ireland, it being propos'd that a Pound of Copper should be coin'd into 3 shillings, whereas Woods was only into $\frac{1}{2}$ a Crown. This he mention'd and repeated in such a manner that I imagin'd you were the person intended, and when I prest him to explain himself, he desir'd to be excus'd from naming any body, so left me to my own conjectures. Tho I know you never had any share in a project of this kind, yet I should be glad to have your opinion of the person he intended, and exprest himself against with great bitterness.

He then proceeded to talk of the extraordinary method of our Proceedings, which he said he was afraid would hardly answer the end not being founded even upon truth; that the Calculations were false, and that there never was but one sort coin'd by Wood, and those strictly according to the Patent, and that all the other sorts were Counterfeit, having been assur'd so by Wood. He said he was the more positive in this matter, because particular care was taken by the Lords of the Treasury to appoint a Comptroller who was very far from being a freind to Wood; that Sir Isaac Newton was the first that was appointed, but that he, being old, desir'd, and accordingly obtain leave to resign to Barton his Nephew, who had made several Assays, by which it appear'd that the $\frac{1}{2}$ pence were not only better then any that were ever coin'd before, but even exceeded the Terms requir'd by the Patent.[193] He could not conceal his resentment at what past in our Parliament, which he said he was afraid would hardly attain the end propos'd; every thing there being hurryed in such a manner as not to give people time to consider of what was proper to be done, and therefore they were oblig'd to advise general Answers, that when Gentlemen were a little cool the ministry might consider of some reasonable scheme, which he hop'd might be agreable. To this I answer'd that the hurry and heat with which this affair was carryed, if any such there were, was to be imputed wholly to them who had declind and indeed rejected all freindly proposals; that if Gentlemen had understood and could have trusted one another, I was assur'd things would have taken another turn, and any reasonable thing that could have been propos'd either by the Castle or Ministry here would have been gone into; but that since all measures of this kind were declin'd, I thought they who gave such advise, and not our freinds, were accountable for the consequences, to which he seem'd to agree. He insisted a good deal on the legality of the Patent, and was afraid that bringing a scire

---

[193] Sir Isaac Newton (1642–1727), the master of the mint, had been appointed in 1722 as comptroller of Wood's mint at Bristol but employed Matthew Barton (*d.* by 1726) to undertake the work as king's clerk and comptroller of coinage for the service of the king's dominions in America. No family relationship has been found between the two men, though one of Newton's nieces by marriage was Catherine Barton, whose husband, John Conduitt, MP [GB] took over much of the work at the mint and eventually succeeded Newton as master. (*CTP, 1720–8*, pp. 221, 318, 404; *The Correspondence of Isaac Newton*, ed. H.W. Turnbull et al. (7 vols, Cambridge, 1951–72), vii, 217–18, 272–8; R.S. Westfall, *Never at Rest: A Biography of Isaac Newton* (Cambridge, 1980), 865.)

facias[194] against it in Ireland or questioning it in the Parliament here, would rather establish then avoid it. I told him, as to the first, that I was in hopes his Majestys Answer and the proceedings of our Parliament, would in a good measure secure us, for the present at least, from the pernitious consequences of that Patent; and that I saw no sort of occasion for a scire facias, unless it was intended, in all Events, to establish it; As to the second, I thought he would consider how far that might be adviseable, and whither it might not create some uneasiness in a session which hitherto had, and I hop'd would continue to proceed with the greatest Unanimity and quietness. He seem'd, in this particular, to have overshot himself, at least to have intended to feel my Pulse; but I had before given assurances that I would not attempt bringing it into Parliament here, and had very good reason to beleive other people would at least not be at all displeas'd that it were done, upon an Assurance that the House here might have had another opinion of that project then ours in Ireland exprest. This is, as near as I can recollect, the substance of what past between us, which I have set down in the very order it was deliver'd, having taken notes of all that was said as soon as I came home. Upon the whole, I am [of] opinion this Affair is far from being over, and that as soon as the Parliament rises, something or other will be attempted, but what in particular I do not even pretend to guess.

From the subject of Mr Woods Coinage we past to that, which was the principal part of my Errand, your Affair, which I was advis'd only to talk of in general, without entering into particulars, or expecting a positive Answer to any thing. In this I found we entirely agreed, so that after having open'd the several steps taken by FzWilliams[195] etc preparatory to the Resolutions, and the certainty we had of his G[race] being at the bottom of the whole, (which however was denied;) I told him I was sure I need not remind him of the consequences which might attend the giving any Countenance to such a proceeding, which every body here lookt upon as a Contest between his Majesty and the Lords, and not between the Lords and you. These were the very words L[ord] C[hief] j[ustice] King[196] us'd to me. I then mention'd the constant good affection of our family in general, and yours in particular, to his Majestys person and Government; especially the services which he knew they did him last session here; and therefore concluded that when they were fairly represented, as I did not doubt they would be, to his Majesty, he would be graciously pleas'd to take them into his consideration, and that we entirely depended on his goodness and justice. I said something of my self, and that my principal Errand was, by my behaviour in Parliament to convince his Majesty and the world, that I had been most vilely misrepresented. In Answer to this I was told, that however he might have been lookt upon as an Enemy to our family, he never had done any Act to disoblige any one of them; but on the contrary had done us all the good offices he could whenever it lay in his power. That he was sure he had never given my Uncle reason to resent any thing, except it were his not being restor'd, as others were, to his Employment, the beginning of the Kings reign.[197] That he was not

---

[194] A writ directing a sheriff to require a person to show cause why a record should not be annulled or why another person should not have advantage of it (*OED*).

[195] Lord Fitzwilliam.

[196] Sir Peter King (c. 1669–1734), of Ockham, Surrey, MP [E & GB] 1701–15; judge (not lord chief justice) of common pleas [E] 1715–25, lord chancellor [GB] 1725–34; cr. Baron King of Ockham 1725.

[197] Thomas had held the office of joint comptroller of army accounts from 1708 until his dismissal in 1711.

then in the Administration, and therefore that could not be justly imputed to him, and that since he was so, he had it not in his power to shew his regard for him.

As to your particular, tho he was sensible the putting you in the Government[198] was ascrib'd to the Interest of other people, yet he assur'd me twas principally owing to him, for that unless his G[race] had consented to it, the King would never have order'd it to be done, without removing him, which he was sure could not have been done. That he was the person who obtain'd his G[race's] consent, and that, not without great difficulty, being oblig'd to make it a point between them, and to put an old freindship that had been between them, upon it.

That after this Affair was settled, he thought some trifling punctilio's,[199] as not sending the order over under Lord Lieutenants Cover, were unnecessarily insisted upon, and exprest himself with some warmth against a freind of yours, whom tis not proper nor necessary to name.

He then made professions of the regard and good opinion he had of me, and of his having taken all opportunitys of shewing it when I was last here, which indeed was in a good measure true, that he had endeavour'd to serve me in the Affair of the Sollicitorship,[200] but was prevented by Lord Sunderlands power; and concluded with general professions of regard to our family, that he would consider of what I had said, and lay it before the King.

I told you before I was instructed not to make any particular request, nor desire particular Answers; the reason of which I must not now tell you, and so our conversation ended.

I wont take up your time with making any reflections upon it, which you are much better able to do; but will in a few words tell you my impartial opinion of your Affair. You have certainly 2 or 3 very sincere freinds, who have and will employ all their Credit and Interest to serve you and have laid every thing in a full and true light before [*the king*]. No body has yet declar'd themselves openly against you; and tho I am not sanguine enough to beleive, as some of your freinds do, that no attempt will be made to lay you aside, yet I am of opinion that you are upon a much better foot then you were last year, and that FzWilliams's and his wise freinds scheme, have been the luckyest incident that could possibly have befallen you. Tis certain W[alpole's] Interest, if employed against you, is very great; but I assure you very far from being omnipotent, of which we have had very late proofs; and I cant beleive he will be brought to lay all his strength to do a partiuclar Injury to a family who have never disserv'd him, but have and probably may have it in their power to be of use to him; and all this to gratifye the private malice and pique of 2 or 3 the most inconsiderable wreches in the world.

But what I cheifly depend on is his Majestys goodness and justice, who I have reason to know has a good opinion of yours and my Uncles Integrity and services, and will therefore not be prevaild on to shew a particular mark of disfavour to a family who, he is sensible, have upon all occasions, appear'd most signally in his Interest, and without vanity, done him considerable service.

I at first intended this letter only as a rough Draught, but tis spun out to that unreasonable length that I have not time, nor indeed am I able to write it over. You must therefore excuse the faults of it …

---

[198] As a lord justice [I] in 1722.

[199] *Punctilio*: a strict adherence to correct form.

[200] See *Anglo-Irish Politics*, ii, 290.

577. *Alan I, Dublin, to Thomas, 19 Jan. 1723[/4]*

(1248/5/362–5)

I will venture to speak my mind fully and plainly in this letter which will be delivered by a freind and not passe the Castle inquisition, which I make no doubt the letters which I write or which are addressed to me constantly doe.[201] our wanting soe many letters which ought to have passed of late between us leaves no room for our doubting this. To which I may add that on my word I received no letter from Senny dated the seventh of this month, altho he mentions in his letter dated the 11th (which is come to hand) one dated the day after he reach'd London: if he is sure he wrote a letter to me on that day I am most certain that I never received it; pray enquire of him and let me know what he saith. It is not at all surprising that a man should be unwilling to own his having sett on foot the late enquiry made in the house of Lords in reference to me, because nothing was ever worse judged or more improper for a certain person to countenance. But I cannot but be concerned to find that he denyes he had any hand in it or even knowledge of it, whereas what I am going to subjoin is capable of being proved by witnesses of undoubted credit: viz. that a certain person spent near two hours on the Fryday night (immediately preceding the Saturday on which the Committee came to their famous resolutions) at the house of the Bishop of Kildare who had the Proxyes of the Lord Primate and Bishop of Cloyne, and employed a certain Lord to secure Lord [*written above, in a different hand*: Strangford] who had given the Earle of —— [*written above, in a different hand*: Meath] great reason to beleive he would have been a freind, but alas he was too much in the power of —— [*written above, in a different hand*: the Duke of Grafton]. But to come to farther facts messenger after messenger was sent to find out and secure poor Lord —— [*written above, in a different hand*: Blessinton] whose condition had inclined him to apply for a Commission and for the arrear of his half pay since he had been struck off that list. But he was too honourable to be prevailed on to goe to the Castle, or to break his word which he had given to Lord Meath Lord Rosse and me that no consideration should induce him to join in that persecution of me, and indeed he acted as his father would have done if he had been living. To this I must add what I had out of the mouth of the Bishop of Ossorye that he was sent to on the Saturday morning to goe to the Castle, when he was actually putting on his robes to goe to the Parliament house, before he went thither, and having said he could not goe thither before he went to the house, he was desired not to go thither at all, which he received with resentment and said he thought he should not go again to the Castle at all, and hitherto he hath kept his resolution and I think will continue to doe soe. But what puts the matter out of all doubt is this, that Lord [?Blaney] having staid in town and voted as — [?*the lord lieutenant*] wished on Saturday, his occasions called him the next day to go out of town toward the North, and indeed I think I have reason to beleive that he was unwilling to be farther concerned in that affair, having on Saturday declared he had been doing dirty worke: but after he had sett up in his Inn at Bellagh[202] on Sunday night there came a letter to him from a certain person, telling him that he must attend on Monday when the report was to be made to the house, and so strong were the orders that the poor Gentleman was under the necessitye of

---

[201] That is to say, being opened and inspected by the postmaster-gen., Isaac Manley, MP [I].

[202] Possibly Belragh in Co. Tyrone.

complying and returning to town by night (as I hear) and entring on the same dirty work on Monday which his stomach had taken offence at on Saturday. We have not many military Lords in our house, nor many pentioners; but some we have of both kinds; and it was my misfortune to have three Lords, Shanon, Santry and Kilmain, two of which have regiments and the third is Governor of Londonderry among the majorityе.[203] I am sorry to be forced to say that the circumstances of some of our nobilitye obliges them to receive pentions from the Crown. Of this number are the Earle of Roscommon the Lord Strangford, and the mother of another Earle (Cavan) is also on the list of pentioners,[204] and I hear Lord Mount Alexander and Altham are solliciting and in hopes of being recommended to the same favor: The Lord Cavan is on our half pay list as Lieutenant Colonel, and about this time the death of Col. Ramsey[205] made it possible that he might be recommended to succeed him: but I would not have you apprehend that any one of those Lords voted on any other motives but the pure service of their countrey, tho in a point which concerned the Crown and Prerogative so much as the commanding the attendance of the Chancellor of Ireland in the British Parliament for his Majestyes service, one might have not at all been surprised if someone of these Lords had hapned to have voted on that side of the question in which the Prerogative may seem to be something concerned; but it soe fell out that all these noble Lords had such arguments used to them that they thought it proper to take the other side of the question. You know the Bench of Bishops never have any regard to the inclination or disposition of the Castle in any question, especially when —— [*written above, in a different hand*: the primate] is in a very ill state of health which may cause a good many useful removes. And indeed I was soe unhappy to have no more then two of that Bench who voted for me viz. Tuam and Ossorye. But this ought to be imputed wholly to their love of their countrey: Yet I cannot well account for the Proxyes of those Peers of this Kingdome who were in London when a certain person left it, all falling into the hands of Lords who were for sousing me: If I should say the D[*uke*] of G[*rafton*] brought over the Marquesse of Carlows and Lord Grimstons Proxyes and some others I am satisfyed I should speak truth; but perhaps it might be accident that lead him to put them into such hands as were of opinion against unfortunate me. But that which leaves this thing beyond contradiction is his not interposing by doing me the justice to declare that he knew my absence was in obedience to his Majestyes commands: this I told him on Wednesday the 18th of December (the day after FitzWilliams made the mocion[206]) would have put an entire stop to the matter, but he refused to declare he knew or remembred any thing of it: I must therefore say Qui malum cum potest non prohibet jubet.[207] After all I am apt to beleive

---

[203] Shannon was col. of the 7th Horse, Kilmaine col. of the 7th Foot, and Santry the governor of Londonderry and Culmore Fort.

[204] Roscommon (£300 p.a.), Cavan (£200 p.a.), and the countess of Cavan (£100 p.a.) were all in receipt of pensions 'during pleasure', while Strangford was being paid £250 p.a. 'till otherwise provided for' (*Hibernia Notitia* … (Dublin, 1723), 9–10).

[205] Possibly John Ramsey, lieut.-col. of Harrison's regiment in 1715 (Dalton, *Geo. I's Army*, i, 334).

[206] On Tuesday, 17 Dec. the Lords resolved to go into a committee the following Saturday to consider the grievances caused by the absence of office-holders from Ireland, and in particular the delay to matters of business and the administration of justice (*LJI*, ii, 767). Fitzwilliam's role is confirmed in BL, Add. MS 47030, pp. 44–5: Lord Perceval to Philip Perceval, 8 Dec. 1723.

[207] 'He who does not prevent an evil, when it is in his power to do so, abets it'; a maxim frequently quoted, among others by William Prynne in his *Letter* to Cromwell of 1649 (in *A Collection of Scarce and Valuable Tracts …*, ed. Sir Walter Scott (2nd edn, 13 vols, 1809–15), v, 185).

that he did endeavour to have put some stop to the proceeding on Thursday, but he had let the thing go soe far that instead of being able to govern his two freinds the ArchBishop and Viscount,[208] they had framed to themselves such promising hopes of successe, through the assurances given them by other Lords before his G[*race*] began to bethink himself and to draw back, that they were not to be governed. The Prelate might beleive that they were in an hopeful way to lessen the number of the —— [*written above, in a different hand*: Kings] freinds in the house of Commons, and the temporal Lord I think proposed to him self to gratifye his spleen and malice on a man whom without cause given he is pleased to hate more then I think he doth any man alive, but himself since his disappointment. But it is observable that since the proceedings in the two houses were over, FitzWilliams is his constant attendant, alway in his Coach, and at the playhouse and musick meeting with him. Perhaps that may proceed from the Castle being almost wholly deserted, and indeed the Levees are not so full as one would wish. This is a long story, yet contains not half the proofs that a certain person was not ignorant of this intended attack before it was made: of which this may be a farther evidence.

Ned Crofton (son of Sir Edward) a member of the house of Commons was in the house of Lords on Monday 23 December and went out to dinner; after his return he stood at the bar next to one of my Lord Lieutenants Gentlemen (by name Eldred)[209] and asked him what the Lords were then upon: Eldred answered they were going on with the same businesse in the same maner as he left them. Crofton said that they who had advised my Lord Lieutenant to goe into this affair (so universally offensive to the Kingdome) were the worst freinds he had in it. Eldred asked him if that was really his opinion, Crofton said it was, to which the other made this reply; Nay the Dutchesse advised that the thing should never be begun unlesse they were sure to be able to go through with it: And during the whole time of the hearing all the Gentlemen of and dependants on the Castle were constant attendants on the house, and the Pages rouled about the Streets in one of the Coaches or Charitots from one Lords door to another while the thing was carryed on. But since the matter hath been unsuccesseful and given a deal of offence it is very industriously given out that —— [*written above, in a different hand*: his Grace] had no hand in it. But a certain favourite —— [*written above, in a different hand*: Bishop of Fernes] was heard to say after the Commons had come to their resolution, that if his advice had been taken and the matter had not been brought on untill after Christmas all had done well in both houses; for you must know some peoples power lies in a thin house of Commons … Farewell after thanking you for the infinite pains you have taken to prevent an honest man from being torn down by rage and power.[210]

I had forgot to tell you that tho you say your Nephew did not gett to London till Monday the sixth of this month that his good freinds in this town gave out that they

---

[208] Archbishop King and Lord Fitzwilliam.

[209] John Eldred (TNA, SP 63/383/910: Grafton to Newcastle, 9 Apr. 1724), probably identical with John Eldred (c. 1691–1744) of Great Saxham, Suffolk (Joseph Foster, *Alumni Oxonienses: The Members of the University of Oxford* (2 vols, Oxford, 1891–2), i, 455: TNA, PROB 11/753/474).

[210] After the House had discussed on 21 Dec. the evidence given them concerning the absence of office-holders from Ireland (including Alan) a committee of the whole House was appointed to consider the matter. The committee reported on the 23rd and resolutions were passed declaring that the lord chancellor's absence from Ireland had led to a 'failure of justice'. Alan was among the lords who protested. (*LJI*, ii, 769–6.) St John III and Arthur Hill had been among those called by the Lords to give evidence in person.

had letters from London by the former pacquets dated 4 January which assured them of his not being then in town but of his having waited on the ministry and particularly on the Duke of Dorset and that he had laid a scheme before him in relation to Ireland, but was repulsed with great contempt. By this story I see they apprehend that Duke to be a likely man to succeed this: therefore I think your Nephew should not fail waiting on him and being as well with him as he can. Tell him too that it is of absolute necessity to write to some of his freinds in the house of Commons a letter about our publick affairs here; for they ought not to have room left to beleive he neglects or forgets them as soon as he gets to London. Something will be done here in reference to the halfpence if we have no answers to our addresses, and I think if any body proposed the sending over some members to follow it, it would hardly be stemmed. Of this you may make your use with the great men, but pray loose not a minute in giving me your thoughts in the matter whether it would be a service or disservice to the Kingdome, which I confesse I am a little in doubt of.

This letter will be delivered by a freind of Colonel Jos. Paule[211] who hath a company in the Guards and having a very good estate here and being in very good esteem with all honest men here thinks he may be more useful to his Majestyes service and interest to reside here then to return into England. He is therefore desirous to dispose his command in the Guards there in order to exchange it for a Lieutenant Colonelship here, and being a very particular freind of mine hath prayed me to write these few lines in his favor and that you will give yourself the trouble to mention him to my Lord Cadogan as one who lives here in a very handsome maner and in as good credit as any one Gentleman in the County of Carlow where his estate lies. He deserves all the offices in my power for his service and if you knew him you would think him worthy your freindship.[212]

578. St John III, London, to Alan I, 21 Jan. 1723[/4]

(1248/5/368–9)

… I have received but 2 letters from you since I came hither, nor have I heard one word of any thing that past in your Parliament since it sat last; except what you mention in your letter of the 14th to my Uncle, which he bids me own the receit of to you, and to tell you he never received that which you say you wrote under the Cover of his freind in Chancery Lane. Twould be but kind in Arthur Hill[213] to let me know, from time to time, what is done in Particulars of it; and if you please to order him to do so, twould be of service, for I assure you our Proceedings in Ireland are more enquird after, and are of more consequence at present, then you can imagine. Nothing material has hapned since I wrote last, at least nothing that I will trust honest Mr Manley[214] with the knowledge of. In general he and

---

[211]Joshua Paul (*d. c.* 1729), eldest son of Jeffrey Paul, MP [I] Co. Carlow, capt. and lieut.-col., 1st Foot Guards since 1713 (*Hist. Ir. Parl.*, vi, 32; Dalton, *Army Lists*, vi, 51, 53; Reg. Deeds, 57/350/38822).

[212]A year later Paul was being recommended by Speaker Conolly as 'a very honest gent' (TNA, SP 63/385/19: Conolly to [Charles Delafaye], 20 Jan. 1724[/5]).

[213]See Appendix 2.

[214]Isaac Manley, MP [I].

his freinds may have the satisfaction to know that every thing goes as we could wish, and that their wise schemes are thought here unlikely to attain the end propos'd, as they were improper to carry on his Majestys Affairs with ease or honour.

Dont be concernd at any little paltry slights that are endeavour'd to be plac'd on you; and be assur'd the Authors of them will not be thankt for their behaviour, which has been very fully explaind. Put your self as little in their way as your Duty will allow; and remember your own Answer to justice Upton upon a like occasion, Afflictions are Circular etc.

If any thing worth your notice happen to morrow in the Debate about the 4000 Additional men, I will give you an Account of it … God Almighty preserve your Lordship, and confound the devices of all your Enemys.

579. *Thomas, London, to Alan I, 25 Jan. 1723[/4]*

(1248/5/366–7)

What will be the consequence of the wise Philip of Spaines abdicating, time must shew;[215] Grimaldos going of with him is a sufficient proofe, that tis nott out of a principle of Religion, the turne industriously given out, for this man has more sence and weight then the whole ministry beside.[216]

I thinke itt tends directly towards an union of the two crowns, perhaps nott immediately in the same person, butt beyond question in interest, which is the same thing to us, Alberoni noe doubt will bee the Primier in Spaine,[217] whose attachment to the Pretender you very well know.

Yesterday I movd for an accountt of the neate produce of the mault tax for the last seven years in Scotland, I thinke this will putt our leaders under a necessity of putting that matter on a better foote then hitherto, unlesse they will tell the people of England in plaine termes that they shall bear the whole burden, whilst the others have the profitt of trade with us, without paying towards the charge of the Government. How theyle mumble the thistle[218] I know nott.

I beleive you will remember Mr Smith from whom the inclosed is, hee's a very worthy honest man.

Mr Molyneux[219] (whoe might have carryd his election without opposition) complimented our great men in favour of Deane,[220] the candidate att the late election, butt hee is

---

[215] Philip V (1683–1746), king of Spain, abdicated in favour of his son Louis in January 1724 but reascended the throne on Louis' death the following September.

[216] José de Grimaldo y Gutiérrez de Solórzano (1660–1733), marquis of Grimaldo, Philip's chief minister, left office with him.

[217] Cardinal Giulio Alberoni (1664–1752) chief minister of Spain 1716–19 but not reappointed.

[218] Mumble in the sense of chewing, and thus to chew something difficult; the phrase was commonly used to mean prevarication (*Another Letter from a Country-Whig to Richard Steele, Esq; on His Defence of his Guardian August the 7th* [1713], 7; John Toland, *The Second Part of the State Anatomy* (1717), 14).

[219] William More Molyneux (1690–1760), of Loseley Park, Surrey.

[220] George Deane (c. 1685–aft. 1739), of Bishop's Hull, Somerset, MP [GB] 1726–7.

baulked by young Elton whoe sett up butt two dayes before the choice,[221] our eyes begin to open.

580. *St John III, London, to Alan I, 1 Feb. 1723/4*[222]

(1248/5/372–3)

I did not receive yours of the 16th till yesterday, and not finding any Post Mark upon it, I dont know to whom to impute the blame of its not coming sooner. I am surpriz'd that you did not acknowledge the receit of any one letter from me in it, having wrote no less then 6 since I came to this town, and every one of them upon business. I should be glad we could fix any tampering or roguery at the Post office, because Mr Carterett[223] has promis'd, if any thing of the kind can be prov'd, to do us ample justice; and has already wrote to Mr Manley on that subject. In order to it, I beg you will let me know the Dates and number of letters you have received, for if there has been any foul play, depend upon it we shall have reparation.

I wrote on the back of one of Nancys[224] to her Mother all that I knew of your Affair, and since that time have found no reason to alter my opinion of it, but very much the contrary. I had yesterday a long conference with one to whom you are under very great obligations both upon this and a former occasion. He assures me that matters are upon so good a foot, that he does not beleive that leaving you out of the Government will be even Attempted. On the contrary that orders are gone from hence to name you, among others, in the letter which is soon to be wrote. I told you in a former that your being put in when you went over last was owing to the personal Interest of a great man with his freind, and by no means to those to whom you may fancy your self under some obligations upon that Account. If this be the scheme now, you may be sure we shall be told the same story and with equal truth. Till this great point is settled, I dont think it adviseable to insist or even mention any thing else; but when that is over, I think we ought to speak plain English, and insist, that as you are equal in Commission, so you ought to be in power of Credit with that little fellow, who I may venture to tell you is now pretty well understood here. If this had been done formerly, I fancy we should not have been under some difficultys that we have been of late. What gives rise to this Advice at this time, is an expression of the persons I mentiond to me yesterday, That the King and every body here were sensible where the influence and Interest of Ireland lay, and therefore he was of opinion that those ought and would be employed who were most capable of serving him. That if people could have been contented with doing the Kings business only, he was sensible it might have been done in the most unanimous and quiet manner; but if his Majestys name and Authority were to be made use of to gratifye the private pique and resentment of — [*the*

---

[221] Abraham Elton (1679–1742), of Clevedon Court, Somerset, son and heir of Sir Abraham Elton (1654–1728), 1st Bt, one of the MPs [GB] for Bristol, was returned to the Westminster house of commons at a by-election for Taunton on 18 Jan., with Deane and Molyneux among the defeated candidates (*HC 1715–54*, i, 317).

[222] Partly printed in Coxe, *Walpole*, ii, 379–80.

[223] Edward Carteret (1671–1739), of St Clement Danes, Middx, MP [E & GB] 1698–1700, 1702–5, 1717–21; jt postmaster-gen. [GB].

[224] His wife Anne, née Hill (see Appendix 2).

duke of Grafton], he thought they were accountable for the consequences who had been prevaild on to enter into such weak measures. These are, as near as I can recollect, his own words.

There is very little publick news stirring. Every thing goes on very quietly in Parliament, and there is great probabilitye of a short and easy session. The great ones are, to outward appearance, upon a very freindly foot. Towards the close of the session we shall know how far they are sincere. The Dukes of Dorset and Bolton[225] are now said to be the Competitors for our Government; both W[*alpole's*] freinds, and they say, both promis'd; I am glad however his Grace is like to have a successor; I doubt we shall never have his fellow.

There are letters in town which say the Pretender was gone, very privately, from Rome towards France. Perhaps there may be nothing in this, but every body here is at a loss to think what turn the extraordinary Event of the King of Spains Cession will take, for that twill be attended with some remarkable consequence, is most certain.

I must repeat my request that you would direct Arthur Hill to give me an Account of what passes in Parliament, because I assure you other people write constantly.

581. *St John III, London, to Alan I, 8 Feb. 1723/4*[226]

(1248/5/374–5)

I am to acknowledge the favour of 3 of your letters, of the 25th, 27th and 30th of January. The 2 first came by Wednesdays Post, but dining the next day with the Duke of Roxburgh and staying pretty late there, I could not answer them at that time.

Before I enter into particulars, I think it necessary in general to tell you that as the letter for constituting or naming Lords justices is not yet come, so you must not expect any other Account of your Affair but that it still continues upon as good a foot as possible, nor can I yet see the least danger of its miscarrying. Tis very easy however to discern the different inclinations of some of our great men by their very different behaviour to me. From one side I meet with more civility and goodness then I can well express, and I am persuaded they are very sincere in their professions. Other people talk always in general terms, but so as they would have me beleive they are and always were very good freinds to our family, and that even at this time they have not a thought of doing the least injury to any one of them. These are their own words, and as they will in a very short time have an opportunity of explaining themselves, so I shall defer giving my opinion of them till then. I could wish however that the business of the Scoch Malt Tax had not hapned, at least that my Uncle had not appear'd so warmly in it, till yours were over. The Case is this. Ever since the end of the war they have been charg'd with the same Duty upon Malt, 6d per Bushel, with England; but this being more then that commodity will bear, as they say, they have never paid one farthing to that Tax, which you know is a very greivous one here, and consequently must imagine the English Members were not well satisfyed to see them escape without paying one farthing, where they pay £750000 per Annum. My Uncle,

---

[225] Lionel Cranfield Sackville (1688–1765), 1st duke of Dorset; Charles Powlett (1685–1754), 3rd duke of Bolton. Dorset had been spoken of as a possible replacement for Grafton in January 1723 (TCD, MS 1995–2008/2026: William Trench to Archbishop King, 26 Jan. 1722/3).

[226] Partly printed in Coxe, *Walpole*, ii, 438–9.

among others, has always roar'd at this, and mov'd yesterday to adjourn the Committee of Ways and Means, where the Malt Tax was proposd, till Monday, in order to think of some Method to oblige Scotland to pay something to it. This was oppos'd by Mr W[*alpole*], but after some Debate he was oblig'd to give it up, and I beleive twill admit of a pretty long [*debate*] a Monday, and if not carryed there will be at least a pretty close division upon it. I own I dont see how insisting upon so just a thing can reasonably give any offence; but as tis a method with some people to tax those who either refuse to go into or oppose their jobs with obstructing the Kings measures, so tis not impossible but that this turn may be given my Uncles behaviour; and for that reason I prest him and made use of all the little Interest I have to prevail with him not to take the lead in this Affair, but to no purpose. I own I cannot enter into their reasons, tho I submit entirely to their advice, who think the way to attain what every honest man wishes for, the humbling ——,[227] is to go thro this session as quietly and with as little opposition as possible, and therefore I resolve not only not to enter into the Debate on Monday, but to divide with those who are for keeping things upon the foot they now are, being convinc'd of this certain truth, that tis necessary sometimes to give up ones opinion in lesser matters, in order to attain those of greater consequence.

I hear the Post Bell so that I must conclude this letter much sooner then I intended, but will write to you more at large soon. Dont be angry at my sitting down so late as not to allow my self reasonable time to write. I did not receive your last letter till 3 this Afternoon, and was engag'd to dine to day with some great people, from whom I have stole out to write this. Before I conclude I must tell you that I spoke to Serjeant Pengelly,[228] not having yet been able to see L[*ord*] C[*hief*] j[*ustice*] King, about the business of appointing the Circuits. He seems to think, but is not clear in opinion that the Chancellor has the sole power of doing it. The method is this. The judges meet and agree among themselves who shall go the several Circuits, and when that is done they send a Paper to Lord Chancellor, with the names of the judges as agreed on by them, which he signs, and this when returnd is lookt on as their warrant for going. He says their appointments have been alter'd by the Chancellor,[229] and even this Term justice Raymond[230] was desird to go the western Circuit, contrary to what was before agreed on; but this is lookt upon to be rather an intimation of the King['s] pleasure, then the power of the Chancellor, and therefore submitted to. Upon the whole, since the point is not very clear, and as the world now goes your inclinations or orders may probably be contradicted. I should think tis not worth your while now to enter into a dispute of this kind, but rather let it rest upon the foot it now is.

The Bell waits therefore I must conclude.

---

[227] Walpole.

[228] Sir Thomas Pengelly (1675–1730), of Cheshunt, Herts., MP [GB] 1717–26; prime serjeant [E] 1719–26; chief baron of the exchequer [E] 1726–*d*.

[229] Thomas Parker (1667–1732), MP [E & GB] 1705–10, 1st earl of Macclesfield, lord chancellor [GB] 1718–25.

[230] Sir Robert Raymond (1673–1733), of Langleybury, Herts., MP [GB] 1710–17, 1719–24), solicitor-gen. [E] 1710–14, attorney-gen. [E] 1720–4, appointed a justice of king's bench [E] in Jan. 1724.

582. *St John III, London, to Alan I, 25 Feb. 1723/4*

(1248/5/378–9)

I have sat up no less then 3 nights attending Dr Freinds Election,[231] which has given me so great a Cold, and put me so much out of order that I really am hardly able to write; however I resolv'd to make any shift rather then not thank you for your 2 last letters which I desir'd Lady Midleton to do in the letter I wrote to her.

You may easily imagine the matter of Freinds Election was made a point by all partys, and indeed he was well defended, and as weakly attackt. I had reason to know he was personally obnoxious, and with great reason, to [*the king*], so that when I found Mr W[*alpole*] and his Creatures made great merit, and intended to arrogate the whole credit of turning him out to themselves, I thought it adviseable, for many reasons, to take my part in that Affair, and if I am not flatterd, did a good deal of service in it. Whatever the reason is, I have received abundance of Civil treatment of late from those who, when I first came over, affected a great Air of coolness and neglect, and no longer ago then yesterday, a person, from whom even a nod is lookt upon as a great favour, left his place in the House, sat by and talkt with me a good while about a scheme for reducing the publick Detts, which is to be open'd to the House in a day or 2.[232] I am too well acquainted with the sincerity of some people, to depend upon any professions they make; however I still continue of opinion that since the removing you is found to be pretty difficult, it will not even be attempted, but that whenever the letter comes over, which it is not yet, you will be recommended.

I cant write much more, but in general desire you will be assurd that your freinds here are not idle, and think their Game grows better and better every day.

The Secretary is to be restord to his Commissioners place,[233] Young to succeed Edgcumbe in the Treasury here,[234] and Edgecumbe St Quintin in Ireland.[235]

583. *Alan I, Dublin, to Thomas, 28 Feb. 1723[/4]*

(1248/5/376–7)

I presume there will be noe cause of farther complaint of the stagnation of justice by the great delayes given by the Lord Chancellor in causes in Chancerye, whether by his absence

---

[231] The hearing on the petition against the election for Launceston (in 1722) of the jacobite John Freind (c. 1677–1728), of Hitcham, Bucks., MP [GB] 1722–4, 1725–7. Freind was eventually unseated on 17 Mar.

[232] On 26 Feb. the Commons appointed a committee to sit in a week's time to consider that part of the king's speech relating to the national debt. The scheduled sitting was repeatedly postponed and eventually took place on 24 Mar. (*CJ*, xx, 274, 280, 291, 296, 300, 303–10).

[233] Edward Hopkins, Grafton's chief secretary, had previously served as a revenue commr. [I] 1716–22. He was not restored on ceasing to be chief secretary.

[234] William Yonge (c. 1693–1755), of Colyton, Devon, MP [GB] Honiton, replaced Richard Edgcumbe (1680–1758), of Mount Edgcumbe, Cornwall, MP [GB] Plympton Erle, in one of two changes made to the British treasury commission on 2 Apr. (J.C. Sainty, *Treasury Officials 1660–1870* (1972), 19).

[235] Edgcumbe did not take the place on the Irish revenue commission, vacant since the death on 30 June 1723 of Sir William St Quintin, 3rd Bt (*HC 1715–54*, ii, 405), but instead became vice-treasurer [I] on 7 Apr. 1724 (*Lib. Mun.*, pt 2, p. 47).

or on any other pretence: for yesterday I heard and determined every cause that was ready for hearing and to morrow is the last Seal after this term[236] when I shal be able to give the same dispatch to all the motions. I doe assure you if you did not much alter the resolution you said you had taken in your letter soon after you had notice of the proceedings against me in the house of Lords, that you would write to me every post; I have been very unfortunate in having a correspondence I soe much value intercepted, for I think I never received more letters from you then two since that in which you promised a more punctual intercourse. But this I am morally certain will come to your hand being to be sent by a particular messenger who goes over to sollicite a private bill relating to the settling the differences in the Bellew familye here and paying their debts in which your old freind Sir Thomas Smith hath involved himself farther then one would wish.[237] It is at his desire that I intreat you to give the bill all the freindly assistance in the dispatching and carrying it through that is in your power: and I hope you will tell Senny that I hope he will doe the same. This is an affair which concerns a freind; but that which I am next to mention relates nearly to my wife and to my self. You are sensible that my Lady Hillsborough hath been on this side of the water for some time past and that her errand was to perswade Arthur Hill and others to come into a scheme for raising a summe of £25000, for payment of my Lords debts (as is pretended). She hath posted notice of a bill intended to be passed this Session at Westminster to enable him to charge his estate with soe much money, and to induce people to think the scheme reasonable she saith that an estate of about £1400 per annum which he hath in his power to sell or dispose of shal be settled as an equivalent to the same uses as the Lands to be charged by the bill stood settled. Now tho this may seem at first to be an equivalent, yet these things are to be considered; first that it will ill become your sister to consent to the selling or charging an estate in the hands of her grandchildren of which she was a purchaser by marrying my Lord Hillsboroughs father and by her marriage porcion, and more soe by preserving and clearing that estate from being eaten out by the debts which affected it when it came into the possession of her husband. If a person whom I will not name had been half as careful to prevent its being plunged into the heavy load of debt which it is now said to lye under as my wife was to pay off the debts which affected it when it came first into Mr Hills possession, there would be no need of an Act of Parliament. But it is to be farther considered that (as the printed advertisement imports) the equivalent to be settled in lieu of the power to charge the settled estate with £25000 the estate soe to be settled is intended to be settled subject to the debts affecting the same; now who knows what those debts are or consequently what the real value of the supposed equivalent is above the debts which affect it? I have reason to beleive those debts amount to above £10000. In the next place the equivalent Lands are I think all or most of them leasehold Lands and not Lands of Inheritance: now I need not remind you what a difference there is between those two. But if the Lands proposed to be settled be a just equivalent to what is proposed to be charged on the settled estate why doth Lord Hillsborough make use of those powers

---

[236] The last 'seal day' of the legal term: a day in which writs were sealed in chancery.

[237] Sir Thomas Smyth (aft. 1657–1732), of Radcliffe, Bucks., MP [I] 1703–14. On 3 May 1723 a petition had been presented to the Lords at Westminster by John, 4th Baron Bellew and others, including Smyth, for leave for a bill to dispose of parts of Bellew's estate for the payment of his late father's debts. It was referred to two judges to inquire into and report, but nothing more was heard of it. (*LJ*, xx, 180; *Failed Legislation, 1660–1800, Extracted from the Commons and Lords Journals*, ed. Julian Hoppit (1997), 298.)

which he saith he hath over the Land which he hath power over to raise the £25000, if there be occasion for raising so much money? And why must he put the difficultye on his Mother and brother of consenting to an Act of Parliament which they are no way inclined to consent to meerly to raise that money which he saith he will give as good a thing for? I must therefore desire in the first place that your acquaintance with Lady Hillsborough nor her insinuations may not prevail on you either to be concerned in promoting that bill, or to shew this letter: My wife and I both of us depend on your opposing any bill that may affect her younger son or grandchildren (who are infants) or which for ought I know may be soe drawn as to weaken her jointure settled on her or the additional jointure given her by the will or her husband. This is a justice due to every stranger to have nothing done in any act which may affect any person not consenting to it.

584. St John III, London, to Alan I, 2 Mar. 1723/4[238]

(1248/5/380–1)

Last Friday I received your Lordships of the 19th, with an Account of Stanfords Affair, and a Conversation that lately past between you and a certain person in relation to the putting disaffected persons into the Commission of Peace. I should be sorry that any little indirect insinuation upon that head, should have given you the least thought or uneasiness, because they are first beneath your Notice, and in the next place have no other Effect here then to shew the poor Impotent Malice of your Enemys, in spight of all their Asseverations and professions of not being concern'd in a late notable scheme. While you stand acquitted to the only valuable part of mankind and your own conscience these poor Attempts can never hurt any body but the Authors of them, and I hope you will in a little time be convinc'd of this. I need not I am sure caution you in the mean time against giving way to any importunity, or saucy Application on this head, which only emboldens those who make them to rise in their demands; whereas a steady spirited behaviour and resolutely acting up to the Dignity of your Post, will certainly prevent a great many of them, and whenever you think fit not to comply with those that are made, will always put you in the right of the contest, let who will support it.

I find I made a right judgment of the reasons of [*the duke of Grafton's*] staying so long in Ireland, when in my letter to Lady Midleton I told her it must be by directions from hence, to see whither the Affair of the Government could be carryed to some peoples satisfaction; or else, by keeping possession, to prevent the immediate declaring a successor, and of course receiving another years salary. That matter is now fully explain'd and gives some people more uneasiness then you can imagine. The contest formerly lay between his Grace of B[*olto*]n and Do[*rse*]t, but of late another Competitor has appear'd who declares he <u>must</u> not be denyed his request; you may perhaps have heard that when a certain

---

[238]Partly printed in Coxe, *Walpole,* ii, 380–1. Letter endorsed by Alan I: ' Senny … about Mr Nisbetts application against Mr Stanfords being in Commission of peace. That Lord Lieutenant stay in Ireland is in hopes he may stil attain his end and prevent my being left one of the Lords Justices: thinks he will fail doing it. That Duke of Argyle puts in hand for it, which gives great uneasinesse to Mr W[*alpole*]'. 'Mr Nesbitt' was Thomas Nesbitt, MP [I]. Captain John Stanford (c. 1686–1745), of Carn, Co. Cavan, the son of Luke Stanford (*d.* 1733) a merchant of Belturbet, Co. Cavan, was appointed a j.p. for Co. Cavan on 16 Jan. 1724 (H.B. Swanzy, *The Families of French of Belturbet and Nixon of Fermanagh and their Descendants* (privately printed, 1908), 28–9).

person parted with a Generals staff for one of a less size, he obtain'd it upon positive assurances never to expect the former, or any way to intermeddle with the Army; but this is now explaind, <u>and very reasonably</u>, to extend only to England; and that the Government of Ireland could never be construed to be comprehended within the promise, being entirely a Civil Employment, tho by Accident the Command of the Army is Appendant to it.[239] Without entring into the Nicety of this way of reasoning, tis certain he has askt it, and in a pretty positive manner, and those who best know him think he will not be very easy if denyed. On tother hand, to have an Employment of so much consequence and value taken out of the hands of a Favourite, by such means, seems a little to strike at that omnipotence, upon the notion of which a good deal of our present Interest is founded.

By this time I beleive some people begin to repent the taking Sir Simon[240] into such a degree of confidence, indeed into the Administration; because if I am not misinform'd he has struck into this new scheme; and if people could have been prevaild on to have shewn a little good nature to honest Harry Madrigal,[241] we should have had a very pretty Triumvirate, but this unexpected incident, together with what lately past in the House of Commons, an Account of which you will see in Lord M[olesworth']s letter, has put a stop to that Affair, for the present at least.

Lord C[artere]t and his freinds seem to be perfectly unconcern'd in this scrape, knowing it can not hurt them, let it take what turn it will; tho if it succeed, <u>we</u> must alter our disposition, and take entirely new measures, of which I should be glad to have your thoughts. I told you when I first came over, and observ'd the scituation of our great men and their Interests, I was of opinion, the sullen Calm and seeming unanimity that appear'd at the opening the session, would probably end in a storm, having learnt so much skill in Navigation, as to know, one is generally the consequence of the other. The session is now so near a Conclusion that I beleive nothing will appear till tis over; but I am strangely out in my Politicks if the next dont prove a warm one.

You must imagine this new Contest has put a full stop to your Affair, of which I can say nothing new. In general I think you and all your freinds are upon as good a foot as possible; and you may depend upon my utmost care and vigilance, and that the only thing I have in veiew here, is how to conduct my self so as to be able to be of service to you.

I have wrote to Lord M[oleswor]th a long letter by this Post, which contains the little I know or can learn of publick Affairs, to which I must beg leave to refer you, not being able to enlarge upon them in this, which has already run out into an unreasonable length.

[239] The duke of Argyll.

[240] The former tory lord chancellor Simon Harcourt (1661–1727), readmitted to the British privy council in 1722 and appointed to the commission of regency in the king's absence in 1723. He had promised at that time 'entirely to support the king and Whig interest' (BL, Add. MS 32686, f. 236: Newcastle to Dr ——, 25 Aug. 1722).

[241] The former tory secretary of state and jacobite exile Henry St John (1678–1752), 1st Viscount Bolingbroke. In the satirical squib *The Last Words of William Parry a Lawyer Who Suffered for Endeavouring to Depose the Queen's Highness, and Bring in Q[ueen] Mary and her young son James,* an ostensibly historical document with strong contemporary resonances, and almost certainly published during the last years of Queen Anne's reign, the hapless Parry, convicted of treason against Queen Elizabeth I, blamed the bad company he had kept, especially two 'secret Enemies to the queen's highness'. These were 'Robin Trickster a turn-coat scrivener' (an obvious reference to Robert Harley, 1st earl of Oxford), and 'Master Harry Madrigall of St John's parish, clerk of her grace's guards'.

I still think we shall rise before Easter, and hope every thing will be settled to our satisfaction before that time, for I long extremely to get out of this, (to me) disagreeable, expensive place.

Nancy begs Lady Midleton and you to accept her humble Duty. We are both extremely pleas'd to hear she and your Lordship are so well, and have no doubt but you will both live to triumph over your Enemys, and to see them expos'd in their proper Colour.

585. *Alan I, Dublin, to Thomas, 9 Mar. 1723[/4]*

(1248/5/384–5)

This letter will be carryed as far as Chester by Arthur Hill toward which place he intends to sett sail to morrow if the wind come about which is now at South East: by this means I take it for granted that it may in likelyhood escape the perusal of those who are most inquisitive into what passes between you and me and everybody that corresponds with me. And I chuse in this to mention what I formerly hinted that for certain the most pressing instances have been made from this side of the water to have one very deserving man removed,[242] which point (if they can carry) they propose this advantage to themselves in doing it. His open and avowed honesty in giving such opposition to the matter of Woods Copper money as was fit for one in his Station to give, by declaring his thoughts that the project if once brought to bear would end in the impoverishment and ruine of Ireland, and would in consequence be very detrimental [t]o the Kings revenue here, added to the resentment which his sons and brothers behaviour in that matter as members of the house of Commons gave great offence: insomuch that a Privy Councellor came to him (as in freindship but no doubt by direction) to let him or his wife know that he might suffer on the score of his son, to which it was answered that he was independent on the father and in a much greater matter (in marrying himself contrary to expresse commands of his father) had shewn he looked upon himself as noe sort obliged to follow his fathers directions when ever his judgement differed from that of his father. This matter I beleive is aggravated against the father, as if all was done by the son at the instigation as well as with the privity of the father; and this is the handle taken against him: And there is a farther view in this matter, for if a Cushion[243] can be made vacant there will be room for one to succeed who by his behavior during the Last Session here hath lost all maner of credit and character and is so fallen from the practice he once was in at the bar that I think he is almost weary if not ashamed to appear in Court. The triumph would be great if the party could mortifye an honest man and a good Lawyer and at the same time gratifye a favourite who hath purchased some peoples good will at the expence of what a good man would not part with for any consideration; but the design lyes deeper, for it is not improbable that Sir O[*wen*][244] and the Cabinett may propose to see the vacancye that will be made by this new promotion filled by one for whom you and I wish too well to, ever to desire he may succeed in that Station upon the ruine of another mans interest and when he must be first disgraced before

[242]Alan himself.
[243]The seat of a judge or senior legal officer.
[244]William Conolly (see above, pp. 9–10.).

the favourite can be preferred. My former letter will be a sufficient explanation of this; or Senny on first seeing it will explain it to you. I must not forget the freindly assistance the old man gave me in my persecution, which I think is as much the reason of one mans fury against him, as any other thing which is or can be pretended: and I am sure it would greive myself to see him suffer on my account, and I ought to be despised if I could stand stil unconcerned when any thing is designed to his prejudice. The whole Cabinett is with his Grace at Castletowne, viz. FitzWilliams, Hort Bishop of Fernes Hopkins, and Mr Manley[245] was there but is returned yesterday. Mr Ponsonbye lives soe near the place[246] that he can be there on an hours warning. Every thing is managed with great secrecye not the least intimation of the time when his Grace thinks of leaving Dublin, or of the persons whom he hath or shal recommend to be Justices in his absence, and if you will credit what the little people about the Castle say, it is not at all fixed when he intends to sail; nay Lord Tullamore told me that he went lately to take his leave of the Duke and to let him know that he did not think of being in town till May; soe as he supposed he should not have oportunitye to take leave of his Grace before he went for England unlesse he did it then: The answer was that the Duke knew no more of the time when he should leave Ireland then his Lordship did. I desire that my daughter Brodrick may be invited to spend her Easter with you and my sisters and Allys at Peperhara, and that you will speak to them all upon the subject. It is incredible how little a figure some people make at present, and how low reputation runs …

[*PS*] I fear that your silence proceeds from ilnesse or that Senny hath acted in some matters not (as you think) he should have done. [*in a different hand*] Dont tell Lord H[*illsborough*] that his brother is in England.

586. St John III, London, to Alan I, 11 Mar. 1723/4[247]

(1248/6/161–2)

I wrote Arthur a long letter by last Post, but some thing having hapned since that time which I think worth your notice, must beg leave to give you a second trouble. Lady Hillsborogh came to town on Monday last, and among other things told us that the common talk of Dublin was, that his Grace was determin'd not to leave it till the Affair of the Government was settled to his satisfaction; and that he was assur'd it should be so as soon as the Parliament here was up, and nam'd old Monmouth[248] as the person from whom she receiv'd this notable intelligence. Tho I was not under the least apprehension from this ridiculous peice of boasting, yet I thought a proper use might be made of it, by taking occasion to feel the

---

[245] Isaac Manley, MP [I].

[246] Brabazon Ponsonby, MP [I], had acquired through marriage property at Bishop's Court, near Straffan in Co. Kildare (*Hist. Ir. Parl.*, vi, 81).

[247] Printed in Coxe, *Walpole*, ii, 382–6. Letter endorsed, by Alan I, 'Senny … that my brother and he had waited on and expostulated with the ministry about the design of the D[*uke*] of G[*rafton*] to have me out of the government which they disclaimed intending. Gives reason to beleive he will not be able to accomplish his design'.

[248] Isaac Manley, MP [I], had taken part in Monmouth's rising in 1685, escaping afterwards to Holland, and had been among those excepted from the pardon issued by James II in 1686 (George Roberts, *The Life, Progresses and Rebellion of James, Duke of Monmouth* (2 vols, 1844), i, 262; ii, 51, 260). The popular ballad of 'Sir Owen Makue' identified him as 'the old Whig' who 'scour'd of vid Monmouth' (Hayton, 'Co. Westmeath By-election', 28).

Pulse of the Ministers a second time, and making this report the handle for renewing our Application to them. Accordingly My uncle and I waited upon the 2 Secretarys, and after speaking his mind very fully and plainly to each of them, he concluded with desiring they would acquaint the King with his humble request that he might have the honour of an Audience, whenever his Majesty was pleas'd to think it proper. This had been concerted before, and when it was mention'd, one of the great men seem'd a good deal surpriz'd; said he was satisfyed we were alarm'd without reason, and why should people complain before they were hurt? However when we persisted in the thing, they both promis'd to do what was desir'd and to let us know his Majestys pleasure. I dont repeat the particulars of the conversation, because I take it for granted my Uncle has or will soon give you an Account both of that, and what he says to the King; to whom I assure you he is resolv'd to say a great many bold honest truths, which I am confident his Majesty will receive with his wonted goodness, having as good an opinion of the Author as of most men in his dominions. We shall, to morrow, know the day he appoints for his waiting on him.

It came to my turn to speak to Mr W[alpole], my Uncle not visiting him, and if in telling you what past between us I mention any thing which perhaps Modesty forbids me to do, you must not impute it to my vanity, but the desire I have to lay every thing in a just and true light before you, that you may by that means be the better able to judge of the scituation of your own Affairs. I began with telling him that the last time I waited upon him, my principal Errand was to justifye my own Conduct in the Irish Parliament which I had reason to know had been vilely misrepresented to him, and that besides what I then said, I hop'd my behaviour in this had effectually given the lye to all those silly malitious reports; That I now came to him to demand a peice of justice on behalf of a person who had been most basely traduc'd and ill treated. I told him I was too well appriz'd of the freindship and intimacy there was between him and his Grace to imagine any thing I could say would induce him to espouse your Interest, or decline his; but that I apprehended this was not the case at present, and that his Grace was no otherwise concern'd in the Question, then as his name was made use of to gratifye the private resentment and malice of 2 inconsiderable fellows; and therefore hop'd he would not contribute to the doing so great an Injury to our family, who he knew had, on many occasions, done the King Eminent services, and had in no one Instance, disserv'd him, Mr W[alpole], or his Interest. I then went thro the whole detaile of our Session, and concluded with the Account I mention'd of his Graces stay in Ireland, and the reasons assign'd for it. In answer to this he began with telling me he was surpriz'd at my taking any umbrage at his Graces stay, and that the expostulation on that head should came from our Quarter which he was sure it would not, had I known the true reasons of it; that tho there had not been any <u>orders</u> sent, yet he beleiv'd he had received some <u>Intimations</u> from his freinds here, that twould be convenient he should continue where he was for some time; that they were winding up their bottoms as fast as they could, and should be glad to have a little time <u>to look about</u> them after the Parliament was up; that as he could not deny but that my reasoning about his Graces stay was just, so he beleivd I must own that another, and that a very good one, might be assign'd for it, but that twas not proper for him to explain himself further on this subject, however he was sure I understood what he meant.

I told you in a former, or one I wrote to Lord Molesworth, that the Duke of A[rgyl]es insisting on our Government at the time and in the manner he did, had given the Ministry some uneasiness; and that I beleiv'd his Grace of G[rafton] was directed to stay some time longer purely to give them time to look about them till the Parliament was up, ther reason for which you will easily apprehend. I am now fully convinc'd that I judg'd right, and that it is the only reason for his doing so; that which his freinds in Ireland assign for it, not having been so much as mention'd here, not even in his private letters, if I can beleive the solemn asseverations of those who ought to know that matter best; and I must again repeat my opinion, that however valiant and sanguine Sir Owen and his freinds may appear, they will not even venture to propose the leaving you out of the Government, at least not in their publick letters. But to return. Mr W[alpole] proceeded by telling me he beleiv'd I did not apprehend any ill offices from one part of the Ministry; but that, whatever my opinion might be of them, perhaps the others were as sincerely our freinds as they who made larger professions. I took the liberty here to interrupt him, by saying I was sorry to hear such an Expression which he understood I meant of the dissentions among the great men, and said the matter was publick, and that he did not disown being upon ill Terms with Lord C[artere]t; but I went on and explaind my self, that my concern arose from his beleiving I had entred into measures, or chose to make my Court to one part of the Administration rather then another; that if justice were done you, I was assur'd you would as willingly own the obligation to him as to any body; and that for my own part, I would always endeavour to behave my self in such a manner as to merit the freindship of all the Kings Ministers, and should be particularly happy if I could obtain his. This gave him an opportunity of saying a great many things of me that neither he nor I thought I deserv'd. He told me that he had never received more satisfaction, then in my last Conversation with him; that I had Explain'd the History of our Session so clearly and with such an Air of sincerity, that what I said had made a great impression on him. That he had laid every thing that past then, before the King in the best manner he could; and that he had the satisfaction to tell me that my behaviour in Parliament here was entirely agreable to the King, that he had constantly acquainted him with it; and that it was the greatest confirmation of the truth of every thing I had said relating to the Affairs of Ireland. He continued, that twas natural to imagine people in his scituation were glad of the freindship of men of Character and understanding, and that without Compliment, he thought our family were possest of both, and therefore should always desire our freindship, and would give me any instance I could desire of his sincerity and regard for me. I told him I had nothing to ask for my self, that I never yet had, nor did I beleive I ever should ask for an Employment; that doing you justice was the only favour I desir'd, and that I should make my judgment of the sincerity of the many professions that had been made me, by the steps that were taken in that Affair.

He told me he hop'd he had said enough to convince me he was not so naughty as he had been represented, and that I would not think him so, for not having explain'd himself further upon the subject of our conversation, which he was sure I would not take amiss, when I consider'd either his publick or private scituation. We parted upon the civillest terms, and I must tell you, he talkt to me with infinitely more freedom and freindship then when I came first to town.

I have been the more particular in this Account, not knowing but the prating and lying of some people may give you some uneasiness. You will form your own judgment upon what I write, and tho I am too well accquainted with the professions of great men to build much upon them, yet I am so entirely satisfyed that they know tis their Interest to do you justice, that I have not the least doubt of their doing so, and often think, that we give too much Credit and weight to the Interest of our Enemys, by laying so much stress upon a point which I know they cant carry, and notwithstanding all their boasting, I verily beleive dare not even propose.

I this moment received a message from Lord Townsend to be with him tomorrow morning, and will let you know what passes in my next. In the mean time let me entreat you, by your behaviour, to let [*Conolly*] and his freinds see, you know you are out of their power. Indeed My Lord their Interest and Credit here is at a low Ebb; and I should be very sorry to think you had no better Tenure in the Great Seal, then Sir Owen has in his power.

I forgot to tell you that as an Instance of Mr W[*alpole's*] sincerity, I was employed by him yesterday to move for the discharging the Committee of Elections from hearing any more Petitions this Session.[249] The 2 next were the D[*uke*] of Ar[*gyl*]es Uncles and Couzin Germans;[250] from which you may form your own Conjectures, for I assure you the thing will bear it.

587. *Thomas to Alan I, Dublin, 19 Mar. 1723/4*

(1248/5/386–7)

Last night I received yours of the 9th about four days since a letter was deliverd mee in the house (from the person whoe is the subject of yours) by one under whose cover I presume itt came, for greater security, which I assure you was a necessary precaution; I know nott how far some peoples malice and resentment may carry them, butt this you may bee very sure of, that I will omitt neither application nor paines for frustrating their designes, I make noe doubt butt what you mention will bee the sheet anchor, as being the most likely to take place, butt even that I hope will nott hold.

The reason of my silence was, that my nephew[251] was better able to write from time to time then my selfe, for though I have hitherto been able to attend the house, except during a few dayes intervall, when I was ill, I have been and still continue weake, and extremely despirited, the effect of bodily illnesse, nott any uneasinesse of mind.

I assure you hee has acted after such manner as has created a character which every honest man would desire, the establishing which must bee the worke of time, this is in his own power, and I beleive heel doe itt ...

[*PS*] I have promisd excusing my nephews nott writing by this post, hee dines with Lord Burlington, nor may you possibly hear from him by the next, for wee both goe tomorrow to the Assizes att Kingston.

When you see O[*liver*] St George[252] tell him I beleive wee may putt his mind att ease by the standing order of thirty dayes space between the first and second reading of any Bill

---

[249] On 11 Mar. 1724 the committee was instructed not to proceed on any petitions once they had heard the petition for Northumberland (*CJ*, xx, 290).

[250] The petition for Dunbartonshire, brought by the defeated candidate Hon. John Campbell (c. 1660–1729), of Mamore, Dunbartons., who was eventually seated on 22 Jan. 1725, and that for Elgin Burghs, brought by Campbell's son and namesake (c. 1693–1770), who was eventually seated on 25 Jan. 1725 (*HC 1715–54*, i, 384, 399, 522, 523).

[251] St John III.

[252] MP [I].

relating to Ireland,[253] Lord Lowths nott being yett come to us.[254] I hope this will appeare tomorrow, when a Bill this day sent by the Lords will bee read the first time, for though I shall nott bee in the house, I thinke that matter secure.

588. *St John III, London, to Alan I, at his house in Dublin, 24 Mar. 1723/4*

(1248/5/390–1)

I have not heard a word from you a long time, tho I have wrote 2 or 3 letters since I received any from you. The first was sent under Arthur Hills Cover, and perhaps his being in England may have prevented your receiving it in time; besides, unless you read his letter you will be surpriz'd at its being directed to you, tho Addrest to Tom Carter,[255] but the truth was I wrote so plainly upon 2 or 3 subjects that on second thoughts I chose rather to send them to you then him, and desir'd Arthur Hill to tell you so.

I am a little uneasy till I hear you received another long letter which I wrote a Post or 2 before that, to give you an Account of a long Conference I had with Mr W[alpole], and for fear of its falling into old Monmouths hands, sent it under Lady Blessintons[256] Cover. By it you will fully understand my sentiments of a Certain Affair, which I do not yet see the least reason to alter, every thing continuing upon the same foot as when I wrote. There is no letter in form yet come from his Grace, tho I hear to day he intends to come away the beginning of May; if so, he must certainly write soon, that there may be time for the Kings Letter to go thro' the common forms of the offices. I own I could wish, for many reasons, this Affair were settled before the rising of the Parliament; not that I suspect any Attempt will be made against you on this side the water; but your freinds will be better able to speak plainly while the house is sitting then after it is up.

The Kings going abroad is now generally beleiv'd; if so, twill probably hasten his Graces coming over, who I take for granted will think it proper to kiss his hand and give an Account of his Administration, before he goes away. The town talks of misunderstandings between the great men, that they will probably come to an open rupture as soon as the Parliament is up. I hope there is no foundation for this report, but if there be, I cant but think W[alpole] must prevail, and for that reason endeavour to be as well with him as I can. Tis certain his Interest in our house is prodigious, and while that continues twill be pretty hard to withstand him … I hope we shall be in Ireland before the first of next Term; The House will certainly rise in a few days after Easter, and I hope before that time the main Affair will be settled to our satisfaction; if not, I am resolv'd not to stir till tis determin'd. In the mean time I beg you will be under no uneasiness about it, for I think tis impossible it should miscarry.

[253] Any private bill: this standing order was made on 6 Feb. 1707[/8] (*A Collection of Rules and Standing Orders of the House of Commons; Relative to the Applying for and Passing Bills …* (1774), 22).

[254] Matthew Plunkett (1698–1754), *de jure* 9th Baron Louth, hailed from a catholic family which had fought for James II, but had himself been brought up as a protestant. In October 1723 heads of a bill to enable him to make provision for his wife had been introduced into the Irish house of commons, but had not progressed (ILD). There is no record in *CJ* of a similar bill being brought into the Westminster parliament in the 1723–4 session.

[255] Thomas Carter, MP [I].

[256] Either Anne Boyle (née Coote) (*d.* 1725), dowager Countess Blessington, or her daughter-in-law, Martha (née Matthews) (*c.* 1683–1767), wife of the 2nd viscount.

589. *Alan I, Dublin, to Thomas, 27 Mar. 1724*

(1248/6/183–6)

… After Sennyes writing to me on the eleventh instant that he was ordered to attend a certain person the next day, and that you resolved to make a vist to [*the king*] [I] cannot but be surprised that neither he nor you wrote one line to me on the 12th 14 or 17th of this month; but indeed I have one of the 19th from you which leaves me at least in the dark as much as I was before. Unlesse I am to construe your saying nothing to me in this sense that either you have nothing to say which I desire to hear or you think worth writing. Indeed Senny might before his going to dine with Lord Burlington have sate down and wrote two lines for my information if not satisfaction. The Bishop of Dromore I hear talks it aloud about the town that upon the death of the late Bishop of Meath,[257] he wrote to some great man in London (his patron I suppose the Duke of Montague[258]) to apply on his behalf to succeed in that See; but that he had for answer that the great man had spoken to the King too late, else he should have been the man: But the coming too late is said to have proceeded from some directions from this side of the water to the post office in London that no letters which came by that maile should be delivered out till fowre and twenty hours after the letters of [*the duke of Grafton*] and of Mr C[*onoll*]y were delivered. To whom these orders from hence should be sent or by whom I cannot account for, nor am I willing to beleive that any regard would be paid to them, if such went: but you have the story as it was very lately told by one who heard it (as she said) out of the reverend Prelates mouth. To tell you the truth next to the two persons who have been successeful in their applications to be translated, there was not one of the whole Bench who seemed to me to have taken more pains to merit the good graces of the Castle and who really had more personal merit by shewing his zeal in an affair which was in agitation very near Christmas day last then this disappointed deserving man: but it is impossible to reward everybody according to their deserts; when there are so many. The meeting at the Castle on Monday last to advise his Grace in what maner to answer Lord Carterets letter about sending over the witnesses against Mr Wood and the objections to his patent[259] ended thus. Everybody agreed in opinion with my Lord FitzWilliams Mr Hopkins and Mr Parry[260] that all who were summoned had reason to think it to be an honour and favor to be advised with upon such an occasion, and that everybody ought to assist my Lord Lieutenant with the best advice they could give in soe nice and difficult an affair. Beyond this no one of those three went nor proposed what seemed to them to be fit to be done upon the occasion. But the

---

[257] John Evans (c. 1652–1724), bishop of Bangor 1701–16, Meath 1716–*d.*, died in Dublin on 2 Mar. 1724 (*Oxf. DNB*).

[258] John Montagu (1690–1749), 2nd duke of Montagu.

[259] Carteret, as secretary of state, had written to Grafton on 10 Mar. 1724 to ask that papers and witnesses be sent over to London to support the objections which had been made to the patent and the patentee (TNA, SP 63/383/84). Grafton replied on 20 Mar. that he had consulted some members of the Irish privy council and would take further soundings (TNA, SP 63/383/99). On 24 Mar. he wrote again to Carteret that after further consultation he had been advised that witnesses could not be sent into England without their consent, and therefore awaited further instructions (TNA, SP 63/383/119–20). Newcastle replied on 14 April that although it was never the king's intention that witnesses be sent over against their will, he nevertheless hoped that Grafton could persuade some to travel (TNA, SP 63/383/158–9: Newcastle to Grafton, 14 Apr. 1724).

[260] Benjamin Parry, MP [I].

rest of the company, who spoke at all saw such difficultyes as to be forced to own they knew not what advice to give. That if this had been proposed while the Parliament was sitting, the houses which had come to resolutions and addresses about the patent granted to Wood, and they only could send over the original papers and evidences which they found to be material against Wood and his patent, as they only knew what the objections were which they thought made the patent an illegal grant. They thought it was neither prudent nor safe, for any persons to advise the sending over such and such evidences against Wood, or objections to the patent, which would be understood to be all that were to be found or made whereas possibly the Parliament might be of another opinion, and others as strong might be omitted. So the meeting came to no resolucion nor can I tell what answer is gone to Lord Carterett. But this I know that if I understood Jack R[*ugh*]y right, in saying he hoped that the meeting would have a good effect toward the preventing the halfpence coming among us, an healing mocion (if anybody had been soe kind to make one) would have been hearkned to: but this is only a bare conjecture; however I was not a little confirmed in it by one Gentlemans saying toward the end of the consult, he hoped and did beleive the King out of his goodnesse would (if there should not be found any way to avoid this grant by a Legal cause) doe it by giving Mr Wood some other satisfaction in lieu of it. But no body was publick spirited enough to speak plainer. The matter hath much alarmed the nation, which was perswaded into a beleif that the thing was dead (for so was the language of a certain place) and never would be thought of again, and the common people talk of applicacion by way of addresses or presentments in the several Countyes of the Kingdome; Of what avail that can be I doe not see, for sure no body doubts but that the sense of the Kingdome is sufficiently known to be very opposite to Mr Woods coyne and patent.

590. *Thomas to Alan I, Dublin, 31 Mar. 1724*

(1248/5/392–3)

I have just received yours of the 24th to your sonne, which I opened, hee, his wife and Mrs C[*ourthope*][261] being gone out of towne this morning, you may bee sure you had nott remaind in the darke, if I could have given an accountt of the event of the subject you mention, butt hitherto nothing has been done towards itt, for what reason I know nott, butt am of opinion tis delayd till matters of greater importance (which I take to bee on the [?Tappe][262]) are resolved uppon, wherein I am the more confirmd, from this dayes newes, which I take to bee a beginning; Mr Treby Secretary att war to bee a teller,[263] Mr Pelham Secretary att war,[264] Mr Edgcomb to succeed Sir W[*illiam*] St Quintin, and Mr Young in the Treasury, itt seems to mee an odde jumble, and such as I cannott conclude any thing from, butt a little time will explaine things. I deferd owning yours of the 28th of last month, (which was left for mee about ten dayes since), surely sending over one to sollicite Sir Tho

---

[261] Martha Courthope.

[262] On the tapis (carpet): under consideration.

[263] George Treby (c. 1684–1742), of Plympton, Devon, MP [GB] Plympton Erle, sec.-at-war [GB] since 1718, became a teller of the exchequer [GB] in April 1724 (*HC 1715–54*, ii, 476).

[264] Hon. Henry Pelham (1695–1754), of Esher Place, Surrey, MP [GB] Sussex, currently a lord of the treasury, did succeed Treby in April.

Smiths affair was very ill judged, since by a standing order, bills relating to Ireland cannott bee read a second time, till thirty dayes after the first, for which reason (I suppose) wee have heard nothing of itt.[265] Noe insinuations of Lord H[*illsborough?*] or any other person shall prevaile on mee to doe a thing which I thinke nott right, noe more then I will omitt doing what is soe, according to the best of my understanding, if I mistake itt may perhaps justifie Mr H[*ill's?*] opinion of mee, that when I gett a thing into my head, there is noe convincing mee, I have nott this charecter with others, and I doe nott foresee his thoughts likely to prejudice itt.

Tis nott my businesse to enquire into the equivalent, att least att present, tis of noe use, butt this I am sure of, if Lord H[*illsborough?*] lives till hee has a sone of age, twill bee in their powers to putt Mr H[*ill's?*] expectancy out of the case. Wee shall adjourne next Thursday to the Monday sennight,[266] during which time (att least) I intend to take the benefitt of air, which I extremely want, in case my presence bee necessary I can very soone returne.

591. *Thomas to Alan I, 4 Apr. 1724*

(1248/6/1–2)

... I endeavourd yesterday waiting on Lord Lieutenant[267] butt was told hee was gone out, and did nott dine att home, which I understood as forbidding my coming in the evening, though I know Lord C[*hancellor*] and some others were with him, to bee sure his time will bee fully taken up for a while in making his own preparations, my compliment is made by leaving word with his gentleman that I was oblidged to goe out of town very early this morning, how your good freinds will receive the news may bee easily guesst. I thinke the management att the consultation very right, att least in all but the three whoe mentioned the honour of being advisd with, and presst others to give their best assistance, I should think itt incumbent on them more perticularly to have spoake their thoughts, for surely they could nott have soe mean an opinion of the rest as to beleive them capable of being made the catts foote,[268] butt that was certainly intended. The story of stopping the letters is such a jest as none butt hee whoe tells itt could have imagined, had such an order come they might bee very sure proper use would have been made of itt, and that without attaining the end proposed.

You will of course congratulate Lord Lieutenant which may bee very heartily done in general termes, without descending to perticulars. By what followes you will see I wrote what goes before in the evening, since writing itt I have a message from Lord Lieutenant that hee would gladly see mee, and would therefore send word when hee came home, if hee doe soe, what happens shall follow.

Instead of sending his Lordship surprizd mee by coming to my house, hee has named you Lord Shannon and Mr Conelly to bee justices, and has his Majestys approbation; by next post directions will goe to his Grace for constituting you soe.

---

[265] This was a standing order of the house of commons.

[266] On Thursday, 2 Apr., the Commons adjourned for a week (*CJ*, xx, 318).

[267] The new lord lieutenant, Lord Carteret. Grafton had been informed of Carteret's appointment by a letter sent from London two days earlier (SA, 423/890: Newcastle to Grafton, 2 Apr. 1724).

[268] A person used as a tool by another (OED).

Hee is nott to goe over this year, his Majesty having told him hee would keep him near himself long as hee could, this will putt matters in Ireland upon a better foot then for many yeares past, keep this to your selfe, what will your back freinds thinke hereof, since contrary to custom the new Lord Lieutenant has recommended, without waiting his Predecessor doing itt. The matter of the half pence I take to be att end, those that will take them may, butt noe compulsion which shews how rightly you judgd of what was dropt att your meeting, to which the behaviour there has in great measure contributed. Mr Clutterbuck of our house is to bee Secretary.[269] Hees a sensible young gentleman, and I beleive will please. You are infinitely oblidged to his Excellency for the many good offices hee has done you, in returne of which you will I am sure make his Government as easy as you can.

One thing I beleive you shall soone perceive, that hee is cheif Governor in the strictest sence, since I am convinct every thing relating to that Kingdom will bee to passe through his hands, without the interposition of others, soe that the private correspondence hitherto held, will cease, or what is the same thing, signify nothing, for cleare open dealing will obtaine, and this is all that can bee wisht for, or desired, doing the King and countryes businesse will bee his veiwe, without any private ends, in this hee was very explicit, and hopes for successe in carrying matters on, uppon noe other termes.

I wrote what goes before Lord C[arteret] left mee, when twas very late, soe that I doubt youl scarcely read itt.

592. St John III, London, to Alan I, 14 Apr. 1724[270]

(1248/6/7–8)

I design'd to have wrote by last Post, but Lord Carterets being out of town prevented me. He returned on Sunday morning, and I had a good deal of discourse with him about the Affairs of Ireland, the particulars of which it is not proper to send in a letter that is to go thro Manleys hands, and indeed I am enjoin'd not to mention many of them till I can find a more secure conveyance. In general you may be assur'd he is enclin'd to do every thing in his power that can be thought for the service of the Countrey, or is agreable to the inclinations of some of your freinds, towards whom he expresses himself with uncommon regard and Esteem. The thing which is likely to create him the greatest uneasiness is that pernicious scheme of the halfpence, which I now apprehend more then ever. You must no doubt have seen the Account that was lately given by Mr Wood in the publick News Papers, of a hearing before a Committee of Council, at his instance, and the order that issued thereupon for an immediate Assay of some of his Coinage.[271] I endeavour'd to inform my self as well as I could of what past there, but could learn little more then what is mention'd in the Papers,

[269] Thomas Clutterbuck, MP [I].

[270] Partly printed in Coxe, *Walpole*, ii, 388–9.

[271] The *Daily Courant*, 10 Apr. 1724 reported a meeting of a committee of the British privy council at the Cockpit on the previous day, to consider the representations of the Irish parliament against Wood's patent. No evidence was presented in support of the assertions of the representations, and Wood was heard 'in justification of himself', after which, 'at his desire, orders are given for an essay to be made immediately of the fineness, value

nor do I beleive there was any Debate on that subject in Council. When the Report of the Assay is made, we shall know what is determin'd about us; in the mean time it seems pretty plain to me that this Affair is to be pusht to the utmost, not only as tis a darling Project of one who cannot bear contradiction, but as twill lay some other people, for whom he has not much regard, under the greatest difficultys imaginable. I am not acquainted with the forms of Issuing Proclamations in Ireland, but if any thing of that nature is to pass thro the hands of a freind of mine, which he imagines destructive to the kingdom, I hope he will have little doubt with himself in what manner to act; I could say a great deal on this subject, but dare not, for the reasons I have given, enlarge upon it. I am to be with Lord C[arteret] again to morrow by appointment, and as soon as I can meet with a safe hand, you shall know every thing that pases.

Tis whisper'd among some people that he will not go into Ireland, but have the same successor there that he had in his former Employment.[272] This possibly may be in some peoples thoughts, but if [*the king*] has assur'd him, as tis said, he shall go over, I beleive twill be pretty difficult to perswade him to alter his resolution. Tis certain he is as well there as ever he was in his life, and the night after the alterations were declard [*the king*] talkt to him near half an hour in the Drawing room, and hardly spoke to any other person; so that his freinds are sanguine enough to think he will, even yet, be able to make his party good.

We are told the Parliament will be up in a few days, but as far as I can judge by their manner of proceeding, they will not rise so soon as is expected. Be that as it will, unless something extraordinary happen, I will endeavour to get away so as to overtake the very beginning of next Term, for I am heartily tir'd of this town, and long, more then I can express, to see you and my freinds in Ireland. I hope in a day or 2 to hear how Sir Owen and his Creatures received the news of your being put into the Government; they certainly must have been a good deal mortifyed, especially considering how high their expectations were rais'd; but they have been so much mistaken in their Politicks of late, that disappointments of this nature sit easier upon them then they did formerly …

[*PS*] I have received no letter from you since that of the 2d.

593. St John III, London, to Alan I, 18 Apr. 1724[273]

(1248/6/3–4)

Yesterday I received your Lordships favour of the 9th, by which I find you had heard the agreable news of Lord Carterets being appointed our Governour, and of your being nam'd one of the Lords justices in despight of all the attempts and malice of your Enemys. You may be sure I did not omit paying all the respect and Compliments imaginable on this occasion, to a person who has been so remarkably freindly to you, and by that means laid our family under such obligations as ought never to be forgot. I shall see Mr Clutterbucke

---

[271] (*continued*) and weight of this coinage, and its goodness compar'd with the former coinage of copper money in the kingdom of Ireland'.

[272] Carteret's successor as secretary of state for the southern department was the duke of Newcastle.

[273] Partly printed in Coxe, *Walpole*, ii, 386–8. Letter endorsed by Alan I, 'Senny … had seen Lord Carteret and Mr Clutterbuck and made my complements. Gives an account of what the Court designs to doe on Woods complaint'.

to day and will then obey your Commands to him. I had, upon the general good Character of the man made my self well acquainted with him before I imagin'd I should see him in the Employment he now is, and you must beleive I shall now do every thing in my power to cultivate his freindship, and hope before I leave this place to put it upon such a foot as that no little malitious lyes or insinuations will be able to shake it. I have had a good deal of discourse both with my Lord and him about the Affairs of Ireland, and have honestly told them my opinion of them, and I look upon the difficultys and indeed disgrace which his Predecessor met with by espousing that pernicious Patent, and giving himself entirely up to the freinds of it, as a peice of very good fortune to Ireland, because they will effectually prevent his treading in the same steps.

From the time of his being declar'd Lord Leiutenant I confess I was more then ever apprehensive of the halfpence, both because I knew the power of their great Patron was vastly encreast, and as I was of opinion that the prospect of laying my Lord under difficultys, might be an Additional Motive to the others insisting on the Establishment of the Patent, and I now find I was right in my Conjectures. I gave you a hint in my last of what past in the Committee of Councel about them, and am promis'd a Copy of the order then made, which if it come time enough, I will send you by this Post. All that is said to be design'd at present is only to send over an order to the Commissioners of the Revenue, to revoke one lately made by them forbidding their officers to receive or pay any of that cursed Coin, so as the Patentee may be upon the same foot he was at the opening of the Parliament. I never till lately heard our Commissioners had vertue enough to issue so honest an order, nor can I yet bring myself to beleive it, tho I have been assur'd of the truth of it from very great hands; but if they did, I am afraid some of those honest Gentlemen will find themselves in a good deal of difficulty how to act upon this occasion. If they revoke the order, I doubt whenever the House of Commons meets they will expect a very good reason from their Members for acting in direct opposition to their unanimous and repeated sense, and will hardly think any orders from their Masters here, can dispense with their obligations to them. On the other hand, should they persist in what they have done, you know you have to do with people who are pretty impatient of contradiction, and will hardly bear to have their orders disputed by those whom they look upon as their servants.

Tis now pretty plain with what veiew so many resolutions were fram'd at a certain place against the abuses of the Powers of the Patent, and I hope, if ever it should prevail, the Countrey will be made sensible to whom they owe that blessing. I have reason to know that the Plan of all those wise Questions was sent from hence, with design to make the use that is now intended of them viz. The Parliament complains only of the misexecution of the Patent, but there has been none such; therefore no cause of Complaint.

You and I are too well acquainted with Mr S[ingleto]ns sincerity to imagine he could have any indirect veiew in proposing the Question for Addressing against granting any Patent for Coining etc to private persons; but as the best Actions are liable to misconstructions, so a handle is taken from hence to say that his Majestys Prerogative is struck at by this, and in such an Article as that not even an English Parliament ever ventur'd to question; and therefore, if for no other reason, his Ministers are oblig'd to justifye the Legality of this Patent.

This is the foot upon which the abuses complain'd of are put; As to the objections made to the Quantity, they are allow'd to have some little weight; but may be answer'd by the Patentees condescending to lessen it, perhaps half, and then surely all uneasiness will be remov'd. I dont trouble you with the Answers made to these weighty objections; but upon the whole I beleive revoking the order I mention'd above, and agreeing to lessen the Quantity is what is at present design'd, and in all other respects the Patent is to stand upon its own bottom; without the assistance of a Proclamacion or order for receiving them, both which are positively disavow'd, and I hope will never be given into.

I dont trouble you with Politicks, not caring to trust my thoughts to a letter, which other people may perhaps look into; besides I hope to see you very soon, tho I am afraid twill be impossible for me to overtake Term. We shall have finisht in the House of Commons by Thursday next, and shall then Adjourn till Monday for the Lords to wind up their bottoms,[274] however I have thoughts of staying a few days longer to see what turn things will take, which are now in their Crisis, and since tis not possible to overtake Term, will make Bristol my way home.

594. St John III, London, to Alan I, 21 Apr. 1724[275]

(1248/6/9–10)

I wrote you a long letter by last Post, and was then in hopes I should not have had occasion to trouble you with another, unless it were to give you an Account of my having left this place, which I intended to have done to morrow, and had settled all my Affairs accordingly, but was oblig'd to alter my resolution by an Account I received, and which went Current for 2 or 3 days, of some further changes intended, and particularly one lately made, I dare say a good deal to your satisfaction. I endeavour'd to inform my self of the truth of this matter, but dont find there was any other foundation for the report then a letter lately sent over by your very good freind, complaining of ill usage in being superseded while in Ireland, contrary to all President as he alledges, and desiring that the Commission appointing Lords justices may not pass till he is ready to come away, for if it does, <u>he must steal away by night</u>, rather then stay or go off as a private man. This letter I hear was communicated to his successor, who was desird to make this matter easy by consenting his Grace should have the pleasure of passing the Commission for Lords justices in his absence (which by the by he has a thousand times said he would never do if you were to be in it) and that as soon as he was landed, Lord Carteretts should be put under the Seal, and then a new one for appointing the same Lords justices during his absence, should pass the Great Seal of Ireland. This is the foot upon which this matter is put, and you may depend upon it there is no other veiew in it then what I mention, and that repeated orders are sent to hasten his Grace over, who I beleive will have left Ireland before this reaches you.

Besides the letter Sir Owen has wrote in answer to the publick one wrote him by Lord C[artere]t, I hear there is another sent to a certain Minister, whom I must not name nor even describe, desiring him to assure our freind of his best services, and of his desire to make him easy in every respect; that he is perfectly easy in the Company he is put, and is very desirous

---

[274] Both houses continued working until they were prorogued on 24 Apr. (*CJ*, xx, 329–30; *LJ*, xxii, 334).

[275] Partly printed in Coxe, *Walpole*, ii, 389–91. Endorsed by Alan I, 'Senny … about the alteration of the Kings letter to the Duke of Grafton to appoint Justices etc.'.

of living well <u>with every one of them</u>. How strangely is that servile Abject Creatures tone alter'd! He would have talkt in another style if his freinds scheme could have been brought to bear; but I find he is resolv'd to continue his power by the same base unworthy Methods he attain it, viz the most servile mean Compliance with every thing that he thinks has power either to hurt or serve him.

I dare say you must be impatient to know how matters go here, and what further alterations are likely to be made since the late great ones. Every body expected the Command of the Army would have been put into other hands immediately; but hitherto the person who has it has stood his Ground beyond expectation; and the town says, has a freind who has positively declar'd he will not part with him;[276] If this be fact, such a Repulse is more then an overballance for the late victory; tho for my own part, I know the Power and Temper of a certain person[277] so well, as to be firmly of opinion that he <u>will</u> carry this and every other point he insists upon; and will leave no body in Employment but his own relations and Dependants.

The Commission for the Admiralty, they say, will be soon alterd; and that there are thoughts of putting it upon the same foot as it was in the Prince of Denmarks time; but I beleive it much more likely that Lord Tor—n[278] will succeed B—ey,[279] and that 2 or 3 of his freinds will be joind with him in the room of so many of the others.

Your freind at Ockam is like to have the Purse; The Cheif Baron to preside in the next Court, and he that was lately ours, in the Court he now is.[280]

These changes make a good deal of uneasiness among every body but those immediately concern'd in them, and the Toreys, who seem extremely pleas'd, and have hopes of being taken in. Tis certain the present bottom is very narrow considering the Prodigious superstructure; but I am of opinion twill be as dangerous to endeavour to enlarge it by those means, as tis impossible it should stand long upon the present foot.

The Publick Papers tell you that Kensington is fitted up, for the next Summer; but as the Air there cannot be suppos'd to be so good by reason of its neighbourhood to this unhealthy town, tis possible a more remote and agreable place may be thought of.

I told you in my last, what I now find is resolv'd, that there would be an order sent to the Custom house to revoke one lately issued from thence, forbidding the several Collectors to receive or utter any of Woods halfpence, which, however agreable to the sense of both houses of Parliament, is said to have been very irregular, as not being warranted by any directions from hence, and pretending to Controul or Abridge the Kings Patent under his Great Seal. You may be sure I endeavour'd, as far as I could, to prevent this, by speaking and

---

[276] Earl Cadogan. His position was thought to have been seriously weakened by the latest ministerial changes (TCD, MS 1995–2008/2024: Edward Southwell to Archbishop King, 2 Apr. 1724).

[277] William Conolly.

[278] George Byng (1663–1733), 1st Viscount Torrington.

[279] James Berkeley (c. 1680–1736), 3rd earl of Berkeley; first lord of the admiralty [GB]. The rumoured change did not take place.

[280] Macclesfield did not vacate the lord chancellorship until January 1725. The seals were first put into commission, and in the following June Sir Peter King was appointed lord chancellor [GB], after which Sir Robert Eyre took King's place as lord chief justice of common pleas, and Jeffray Gilbert, formerly chief baron of the Irish exchequer, who had moved to the English exchequer court in 1722, was promoted from baron to chief baron there.

remonstrating against it to the persons cheifly concern'd in the obtaining it; but received no other Answer, then that the Kings Prerogative was concernd, and that his Ministers could not sit by and see his own servants take upon them, without order or Authority, to controul his Patent; that Ireland was not concern'd in the present Question, since it was not intended to give the least sanction to the Patent, but only to leave it upon the same foot as it was before the Issuing that order.

Besides many other objections, I hop'd this might have some weight, that insisting on this order might possibly make it very difficult to meet this Parliament again, for that it was not to be imagined that both Houses could sit tamely by and see an order made, in the very Terms of their Resolutions, revok'd by persons whom they look upon as under their power, and some of them Members of one of the Houses, and as such certainly accountable to them for a breach or Contempt of their orders; but Arguments of this nature had very little weight, and to tell you the truth, I beleive concluded rather for, then against doing what was intended. However I cannot but be of opinion that our freinds at the Custom house will be under some difficultys, let them act in what manner they please.

I hope to settle my Affairs so as, if nothing extraordinary happen, to begin my journey towards Ireland the very beginning of next week; but as a good deal of the Term will be spent before I can possibly reach Dublin, and my wife no very good Traveller alone, I have thoughts of going over by Bristol, but am not yet come to any positive resolution …

[PS] Lord Hillsborough will soon be in Dublin.

595. *Alan I, Dublin, to St John III, 26 Apr. 1724*

(1248/6/13–14)

If I had not been more impatient to give you an account of what passed yesterday at the Castle then I needed, I had saved myself the trouble of writing a very long letter which I wrote last night after I returned from his Grace, and doe not think necessary to send forward to you: since I find by yours that you are all well aware of the consequences of the Kings letter for appointing Justices in the maner it is now came over viz. that my Lord C[arteret] is not Lord Lieutenant, but the Duke of G[rafton] continues soe till a patent shall be passed in England after his Graces landing there; and consequently that the entertainment of the Lord Lieutenant will belong to his Grace till that patent is passed.[281] The Duke shewed me the Kings letter dated 7 April,[282] in which there are very ample honourary clauses of his returning to receive farther marks of his Majestyes favour, of his Majestyes approbation of his services during his administration and of his being sent for over to give his Majestye a true account of the state of this Kingdome. When my Lord Carterets patent will passe seems to depend on the time of his Graces landing being notifyed at London, and that will be sooner or later as his Grace thinks fit to leave this place earlier or later, which he hath a very great latitude to doe, as he finds it for the Kings service, or for reason of state, or as

---

[281] It was passed on 6 May 1724 (*Lib. Mun.*, pt 2, p. 11).

[282] The royal warrant appointing Carteret in place of Grafton was dated 7 Apr. (TNA, SP 63/383/143–5). The decision had already been explained to Grafton (SA, 423/890: Townshend to Grafton, 1 Apr. 1724; Newcastle to Grafton, 2 Apr. 1724; TNA, SP 63/383/146: Grafton to Newcastle, 9 Apr. 1724).

his health will allow. I confesse I beleive it will not be long before he will think in earnest of going, having attained his darling point not to deliver the Sword into the hands of the Justices and out of his own. I write this before going out of my house this morning soe that I cannot learn what the men confided in say as to the time of his departure; but my servants have gotten it among them that Saturday next is to be the day. When the Duke shewed me the Kings letter yesterday I concluded that there had been one of another tenor sent by the messenger who brought the first intimation of the Kings pleasure in relation to Lords Justices, which was of too hard digestion to please here, and that to salve appearances his Graces applications had been complyed with by altering the form of it into what it now is; in which I cannot but think a certain person hath shewn more tendernesse and good nature then would have been shewn him on a like occasion. But I own you have undeceived me by your letter of the 21th; for till the receit of it I had no sort of doubt but that Lord C[*arteret's*] patent was actually passed, for which I had this foundation that I saw a letter under his Majestyes sign manual directed to John Lord Carteret Lieutenant General of Ireland etc and countersigned by the Lords of the Treasury for renewing the Commission of the revenue by inserting Mr Franklands name[283] into it in Mr Youngs room.[284] This mislead me to direct to Lord Carteret by the style of Lord Lieutenant even in a letter which went in the bag with the Dukes letters. Your freinds at the Custom house will find themselves under difficultyes when they received the order you hint at; but I am not soe much concerned what will fall on them as at the fatal consequences which may befall the rest of the Kingdome by that means. Sir O[*wen*] will keep his promises lately made just as he hath done formerly: If he can procure credit and faith he will betray every body to those whom he really loves, and whose measure and interests he is zealously and heartily in. In short nothing is aimed at by him but to continue himself in some tolerable esteem and to make use of what confidence may be reposed in him to doe all the mischeif he can. He hath done too many injuries ever to forgive the persons whom he hath insulted and treated most vilely; and he must be a very weak man who can be perswaded that he will ever forget his long practiced deceitful way of doing all the mischeif he can under the vizor of freindship. In publick affairs I will draw with those with whom his Majestye hath joined me, but I must be excused if I doe not take fair words for a sign of his fair intentions toward me. I am under great uneasinesse at the prospect I have that this damned project of Woods etc will tend to create uneasinesse in the next Session of Parliament, especially as I see it is now prosecuted with an appearance of leaving people at liberty to receive the Copper money or not: But every body reasonably thinks that Woods and his freinds expect some very great advantage by the intended order, or else they cannot account for the making such an order in his favor in direct opposicion to the sense of both houses of Parliament. I am sorry that you resolve to loose this whole term,[285] after so long and expensive an attendance in Parliament in England.

---

[283] Thomas Frankland (c. 1683–1747), of Thirkleby Park, York, MP [GB] Thirsk.

[284] A privy seal warrant to appoint Frankland was issued on 10 Apr.; the patent passed in Dublin on the 26th (*Lib Mun.*, pt 2, p. 34).

[285] The opportunity to practise at the bar during the current legal term.

596. *Alan I, Dublin, to St John III, 28 Apr. 1724*

(1248/6/15–16)

Since my last of the 26th there hath been a Councel held yesterday, in order to passe the new Commission to the Commissioners of the revenue which gave my Lord Abercorne oportunitye of renewing a mocion he had begun to make at the last sitting of the Councel before in relation to the paragraph in the prints about the proceedings before the Committee of the Councel about Woods patent. He yesterday moved the thing and said what is very true that the countrey is under the greatest fear and apprehension of their coming among us, and by his maner seemed to have more reason then other people to support him in the opinion that those fears had too much ground. His mocion ended in an order of Councel signed by my Lord Lieutenant and a very full Councel (as we reckon fifteen to be) referring it to the consideracion of a Committee of the whole board or any seven or more of them to consider of wayes to allay the fears of the people from the apprehensions they have of Woods money becoming current among us. And it is certain that from the time of the meeting at the Cockpit about Woods patent[286] we have been under much greater dread of their prevailing then before.[287] Nay his Lordship seemed to insinuate that he had grounds to think there either had or would be such methods taken by the Lords of the Treasury in England by order to the Commissioners here, as would tend to the making them as effectually current as a proclamacion could. This evening the Committee met to find out methods to allay these fears and after a great deal of time spent to very little purpose, at length my Lord Abercorne whose motion occasioned the appointing the Committee, being urged to shew what new grounds there were for those fears, of which some expressed they could see no cause after the Kings answer to the addresses of both houses of Parliament which ought to have more weight then a paultry news paper, his Lordship then said he had more reasons for his apprehensions then he was willing to mention, and such as would make some peoples hair stand on end; looking intently on Lord FitzWilliams I told Lord Abercorne that I thought it incumbent on him to give the Committee such light as he could of that matter that we might judge for ourselves. He then proceeded to tell us in a very warm maner something, which he by his way of speaking seemed to think had more weight in [?it] then his hearers did; of a story which he had heard from a Lord who landed lately out of England (Lord Limrick); the story was that the Lord who landed had been told something by a Bishop of this Kingdome now in London (Downe) which a great man in England had said about the half pence. At first I thought it might be Mr W[*alpole*] but I since hear it was a very near relation of his. But least my letter may be as tedious to you as the wrangle in the Committee were to me, I will conclude with telling you that we agreed to have a representation of the state of this Kingdome in relation to Woods patent and coyne framed on the debates of the Commit-

---

[286]See above, p. 10.

[287]Grafton informed Townshend in melodramatic tones, of an 'inconceivable alarm' in Dublin at this news, and of a 'terror' that had become 'almost universal' that acceptance of the halfpence would be forced on the Irish population. He thought 'all people' were 'united on this point', presumably including Speaker Conolly and his friends. (BL, Add. MS 32687, ff. 38–9: Grafton to Newcastle, 29 Apr. 1724.)

tee. But it was pressed prodigiously by Sir Owen Ralpho[288] Rugby etc that we might first frame the heads and particulars on which the representation should be founded; but people remembered what difficultyes the Commons brought themselves under by a like resolution and would not be caught twice in the same snare. After this the Committee adjourned till Fryday. What the event will then be time must shew; but I give you this true account of this matter by this post because I saw Jack step to the side table and write a letter (which I beleive was to somebody in England on this affair). And if that honest man be constant to himself you know how far he usually regards speaking truth upon subjects of this kind.

597. St John III, London, to Alan I, 29 Apr. 1724

(1248/6/17–18)

This will be the last letter you will receive from this place, which I resolve to leave to morrow, and go directly to Bristol, the Term being so far advanc'd that I should not overtake much of it if I went by Holyhead, unless I left my wife to travel alone, which I could not very easily do. I thought I had settled my own Affairs so as to have begun my journey a week ago, but have been appointed to attend one or other of our great men almost every day since, so that I could not possibly get away till now.

You will probably have a second Account in the Daily Courant of the Assay that was made at the Tower on Monday last of some of Mr Woods halfpence, pursuant to the order of Council. I was not there, nor indeed any body on behalf of Ireland, tho I hear there were letters or intimations sent to some Gentlemen from the Treasury to that purpose. What past there, as I was inform'd by one that was present, was no more then this. Wood produc'd 4 or 5 parcels of halfpence, which he said were taken out of the heaps of those coin'd at Bristol, which were Assayed as to weight and Fineness, and you may be sure, answer'd in both, only some were 5 or 6 Grains too light, which was made up by others as much too heavy, but in general 60 of them came up to a Pound weight. He then producd 2 or 3 sorts of those now Current in Ireland, which answer'd in neither when they were Assayed, from whence tis probable he and his Accomplices will frame their own Conclusions.[289] The value of the Copper was likewise enquird into, and appear'd to be between 12 and 13d per pound which will be reported by Sir Isaac Newton and Mr Scroop,[290] as well as the Quantity and Quality. They are very honest men and I beleive will state the facts fairly as they appear'd to them, and upon their Report, I take it for granted, the Treasury will issue the order I formerly mention'd, requiring our Commissioners of the Revenue

[288] An obvious reference to Conolly's lieutenant, the chancellor of the exchequer Sir Ralph Gore, MP [I]. 'Ralpho' was also the name of the squire in Samuel Butler's mock-heroic poem *Hudibras* (1663–78), a satire on the parliamentarian supporters during the English Civil War. Sir Hudibras, the eponymous hero, who in this analogy would correspond to William Conolly, was 'a Presbyterian true-blew', while Ralpho, with whom Sir Hudibras often bickered on matters of religion, was an ignorant sectary.

[289] Originally the privy council committee had asked Newton to order an official of the Mint to go to Bristol to assay Wood's coinage, but Newton objected and samples were instead sent to London where the king's assaymaster examined them, comparing them with copper coins issued for Ireland in the reigns of Charles II, James II and William III, and produced a favourable report (*Corr. of Isaac Newton*, ed. Turnbull et al., vii, 272–8).

[290] John Scrope (1662–1752), of Wormsley, Bucks., MP [GB] Ripon, senior sec. to the treasury [GB].

to recall theirs which forbid the several Collectors to receive or pay any of them. Those honest Gentlemen seem to be between the upper and nether Millstone, and by what I can learn, have represented the difficultys they are under, in very strong Terms; but without success.

Our freind[291] seems resolv'd to be perfectly passive in this Affair; beleiving, and not without reason, that some people hope to embarrass him by it, who may possibly be caught in the net they laid for another. Tis very difficult even to guess at what will happen 6 weeks hence; but as Affairs now stand, there is not the least reason to doubt his going over, unless he be kept here upon a much better Account. His Enemys would be very glad to see his back turn'd, and begin to find they have gain'd no strength by the late change. He is certainly as well if not better then ever with [*the king*]; constant in his Attendance at Court, and supported by almost all the foreign Powers. Tis said in the City that our Advices from Cambray are not very agreable, and that very unreasonable things are askt about Gibraltar etc. The late alliance too between the Czar and Sweden gives us some uneasiness;[292] tho there will not <u>probably</u> be any occasion to send another Fleet into the Baltick, nor for our freinds taking the journey I mention'd to you in my last. But these are only things in speculation, and such as I hope will never happen.

Tis impossible to express the kind behaviour of Lord C[*arteret*] upon all occasions, and the regard and freindship he always professes for you. One instance of these was his telling me tother day that he had spoke to the King, and resolv'd to begin his Government with doing me the only favour in his power, which was making me a Privy Councellor, and that he would send over the Letter for that purpose the Minute his Commission was under the Seal. I took occasion from hence to mention Harry Boyle[293] to him as from Lord Burlington, who had formerly spoke to me upon that occasion, and obtain'd his promise for him, so that I beleive the 2 letters will go over together.

When I see you we shall have an opportunity of talking at large about Affairs of this nature, and as you have it now in your power, I hope your inclinations as well as judgment will lead you to provide for some of your freinds who have serv'd you faithfully in times of Trial, and at the same time to return the Compliments of some of your Enemys, among whom I beg old Monmouth may never be forgot. Beleive me My Lord something of this kind is absolutely necessary.

My wife is extremely oblig'd to your Lordship for your kind intentions to supply her in the most expensive place in the world; but Mrs Courthope not having yet received your letter, we have made the best shift we could to discharge our Debts here, and hope we shall leave this Town without owing a shilling in it.

[291] Lord Carteret.
[292] The Treaty of Nystadt of 1721 had ended the Great Northern War.
[293] Henry Boyle, MP [I].

598. *St John III, Bristol, to Alan I, Dublin, 10 May 1724*[294]

(1248/6/21–2)

Yesterday I received your Lordships of the 26th and 28th April, which I immediately forwarded to my Uncle to be laid before Lord Carteret, that he might be sure to have a true Account of what past lately in Council about the halfpence. I am very glad that vile project meets with so much opposition in Ireland, which I beleive will have a good effect here; tho at the same time I must tell you my opinion, that if any body on behalf of Ireland had appear'd at a certain place, which I know was both expected and desir'd by Wood and his Accomplices, it would only have furnisht some people with a plausible excuse for doing what they were in all Events determind to do; whereas now all the world thinks and says the hearing was only ex parte. This I find is not understood by some of our freinds in Ireland, by one of whom I and all of that Countrey in London, were taxt with supine negligence, in not endeavouring to oppose the proceedings before the Council, of which I do not think one of us had the least notice till we read the Daily Courant,[295] tho if we had, I fancy we should have acted in just the same manner.

You may be sure Lord C[arteret] has been fully talkt to on this subject, and as he is perfectly free from all suspition of being concernd in, or wishing well to this base project, you may depend upon his doing what becomes him. Perhaps a time may come when a good use may be made of what is lately done; you will understand my meaning without further explanation.

You would not tax me with neglecting the last Term, if you know my only reason for doing so, was to see what turn things took. I assure you when our freind was first declard, they who procur'd him that honour, little thought of his going over; and I know the Duke of B[olto]n was promis'd his place, above 3 weeks after he was declar'd; but that matter is now settled, and you may depend upon it, he is at least as secure as some of his freinds are in their places.

I resolve to go Post to Chester on Tuesday if the wind be not fair before, and leave my wife here till tis so. She and I are much oblig'd to you for your kind offer, which I am afraid we shall be forc'd to make use of. The Post waits …

599. *Thomas to Alan I, 18 May 1724*[296]

(1248/6/23–4)

This will bee deliverd by Mr Tickle,[297] whoe will bee to attend the justices during the absence of Lord Lieutenant hee seems to have a true notion of the state of things with you.

---

[294] Partly printed in Coxe, *Walpole*, ii, 391–2. Letter endorsed by Alan I, 'Senny … about the proceedings before the Committee of Councel about Woods halfpence. Calls the patent a vile project. Glad of the opposicon it meets in Ireld'.

[295] See above, p. 109.

[296] Partly printed in Coxe, *Walpole*, ii, 392–4.

[297] Thomas Tickell (1685–1740), later of Glasnevin, Co. Dublin, appointed under-sec. [I] in May 1724 (*Oxf. DNB*; Sainty, 'Secretariat', 31).

I spoake fully to his Lordship upon the subject of Woods pattent, butt more plainely to Mr Tickle, desiring him to repeate to my Lord what I sayd, the substance of which was, that I could foresee nothing that would create trouble and uneasinesse to his Government except these halfe pence, that this was noe party cause, butt universally espousd, every man of estate being to bee affected as well as trade in generall, that among those whoe wisht best to his Government I did beleive a man would nott bee found soe hardy as to open his lips in favour of itt, nay nott to remaine neutor, unlesse hee could submitt to give up att once all his interest, and bee lookt upon as a betrayer of his country, I told him my Lord must judge for himselfe what part hee was to act, butt att the same time desired itt might bee remembred that I was of opinion nothing lesse then a vigorous opposition from his Excellency was hoped for, and I was very sure was expected.

That the pretence of limiting Wood to a small summe, would bee of noe availe for that none att all was wanted, besides that twould bee impracticable to discover what greater summe hee should coine, which without doubt hee would putt in practice, That unlesse timely precaution prevented itt, I was morally certaine twould produce such effects as I could nott thinke of, that people were nott to bee blinded with Woods name, that they full well knew the greatest share of the profitt was to goe elsewhere, and were sure such considerations ought nott, and they hoped would nott prevaile to the ruine of the Kingdom.

That an order to the Commissioners of the Revenue to recall or revoke their former directions to the Collectors against receiving them would bee interpreted an order to take them, which however would nott have the effect proposd, giving them a currency, for that none would take them in payment except the poor souldiers, whoe would very soone bee oblidged to live uppon free quarter, rather then starve, for that the pay in that coine would nott buy halfe enough in the markett to keep life and soule togather, that this would necessarily bring complaints from every part of the kingdom before the Government which would bee well improvd, and made use of here, by a sett of people whoe by a prophetick spiritt would foretell what might happen here. That I thought this would bee the first ill effect, butt that an utter losse of trade would soone follow, wherein twas very manifest England would thinke itt selfe, (as indeed itt will bee) immediately concernd. I mentioned what had happened in your Councill upon Lord Abercornes motion, asking him whither any Representation were come; I told him I thought nothing of that nature could adde force to the Representations of both houses of Parliament butt that I mentioned itt as what the Duke of G[rafton] could nott stem, for (as I heard) hee signd the order referring this matter to the consideration of a Committee of the whole board. Hee told mee hee heard his Grace had brought over something of this kind, for that the matter was soe managed on your side, and by one in perticular (whom hee named) as that twas carryd through before his Grace could bee ready to come away.

I concluded with taking notice of the essay made here, in order to lay that before the Councill here, for that I heard itt was to bee brought before the great councill, though hitherto itt had been onely before a Committee, I desird itt might bee considerd whoe brought the half pence soe essayed; every body knows twas Wood, was hee likely to bring the baser mettle, or lighter halfe pence, this essay would surely obtaine with nobody, and therefore I could nott butt thinke what was soe obvious to all others, would nott escape the notice of soe wise an assembly.

Whither what I have sayd and heartily endeavourd will have any effect I know nott, butt content my selfe with having to the utmost of my power with his Excellency (as well as elsewhere) endeavourd doing the best service I can to the kingdom, and if I can foresee any thing, to his Majesty for uppon my word I thinke twill bee made use of by those whoe doe nott soe heartily wish his ease and prosperity as I doe.

I ended with giving my opinion that if nothing were done, twould dye away silently, butt that if what might by implication or necessary consequence should bee atempted for giving countenance, a flame would bee raisd, nott easily to bee extinguish …

[*PS*] Recapitulate to Mr Tickle what I have mentioned, very breifely, for having had a pretty long conversation, hee may probably mention perticulars which I have omitted. Hee sayes twill bee difficult to write after Mr Addisons coppy,[298] in any perticular save that of integrity, which being in his power, hee will strictly adhere to.

I now take for graunted that the King does nott goe abroad for those whoe must know, are very positive in itt.

600. *Thomas to Alan I, Dublin, 19 May 1724*

(1248/6/25–6)

Late last night, after I had sent my letter which you will receive by Mr Tickle, (probably assoone as this) came yours to Mr Edgcombe, which cannott bee delivered, because your information of his being yett made a Peer, is a mistake, that affair is att present att a stand in general, for I suppose whenever there is a promotion hee may very likely bee one. Mr Tickle goes over to attend the Lord Justices as Secretary till Lord Carterets arrival, hee will informe you of things which I may have omitted, hee was to goe post very early this morning in company of Lord Forbes.

Your letter is dated the 9th instant which surely ought to have come sooner, is there still tricks in the office or did the Packetts lye on your side.

Madam Villat (whoe the world sayes is marryed to the late Lord Bullinbrooke) came to towne last night,[299] her errant may bee easily guesst, butt I thinke twill nott doe. Serjeant Miller[300] abruptly without the knowledge of any body mentioned calling for the pardon in the house of Commons, had hee been seconded, I am told twould have gone in a very very thin house, butt Lord William[301] putt an end to itt, by moving the question of adjournment which the Speaker immediately putt.[302]

---

[298] Pattern or example, now an obsolete usage (*OED*). The essayist Joseph Addison (1672–1719) was chief sec. [I] 1709–10 and 1714–15, and sec. of state [GB] 1717–18.

[299] Marie-Claire de Marcilly (1676–1750), widow of the Marquis de Villette, who had married Bolingbroke in 1719. Officially, Bolingbroke had been deprived of his title by the act of attainder passed against him in 1715.

[300] Edmund Miller (c. 1669–1730), of Petersfield, Hants, MP [GB] Petersfield; serjeant-at-law [GB] since 1715.

[301] Lord William Powlett (c. 1667–1729), MP [GB] Winchester; teller of the exchequer [GB].

[302] Sir Edward Knatchbull noted in his diary that on 20 Mar. Miller 'pulls out an old *Gazette* where it is said his majesty had granted his pardon to Lord Bolinbroke, and said it was the melancholiest news that ever came to England' and 'concluded the proper officer should lay before the House the pardon', but was not seconded, and the order of the day being called for the motion dropped. (*Knatchbull Diary*, 30.)

601. *St John III, Midleton, to Alan I, Dublin, 23 May 1724*

(1248/6/27–8)

After being 4 days at Sea we landed here on Tuesday last, but I was so extremely fatigued and out of order that I really was not able to write then. I wish I could have overtaken the Term, but in my last from Bristol I told you the true reason of my staying so long in London, nor indeed had I any reason to beleive our freind[303] fixt in the Government, till 3 or 4 days before I left it. You may be sure the Gentleman who helpt him to it, did not intend he should ever go over, and I have reason to beleive went so far as even to promise the Duke of Bolton he should be the man; but upon cooler thoughts I beleive he thought twould be pretty difficult to prevail with [*the king*] to go into that Scheme, and therefore all thoughts of that kind were laid aside. I find our freinds are a good deal apprehensive, even yet, that he will not come over; and tho tis pretty hard to guess what next Session may produce, or how far a certain persons hands may be yet further strengthned, yet I am sanguine enough to perswade my self that nothing but a better employment will prevent his coming over; and that there is a much greater probability of his being first Minister then of his being remove'd.

I wish you would please to order some proper person that you can confide in to make you a short Abstract of the charges of the several Establishments since the year 1715, and when the Additions were made to each of them. I promis'd Lord Carteret to send him over a particular State of them, and if you please to collect the materials, I will put them together as soon as I get to Dublin, where I will certainly be, with Gods leave, by the first day of next term …

[*PS*] Harry Boyle[304] and a good many of your freinds, are with me drinking your health.

602. *Alan I, Dublin, to Thomas, at his lodgings in the Privy Garden, Whitehall, 26 May 1724*

(1248/6/29–30)

I have your letter of the 19th instant by the post, but Mr Tickel is not yet arrived soe I must defer answering that which he brings till I see him. I could wish he had come over in other company; for the person you mention to be his fellow traveller is a man of intreague and entirely a creature of a certain D[*uke*] whom I take not to be at all a freind to Lord C[*arteret*].[305] You know too well how entire an agreement there is between that D[*uke*] and another person, and how far the later hath gone to encrease and support the others interest in that place where it may be of most use to both of them: soe that I have for some time past looked on them to be strongly linked together; and assure yourself Mr Tickels fellow traveller will not fail to make a fast freind in that engagement.

The Easterly winds kept our boat soe long on this side that I fancy my letter of the 9th came to you in due time. I cannot but beleive that Lord B[*olingbroke's*] freinds will find a

[303] Lord Carteret.
[304] Henry Boyle, MP [I].
[305] Possibly the duke of Grafton is meant.

favourable oportunitye to move what is intended in favor of that Lord,[306] and that it will find the same successe which every thing of that kind hath in the end mett of late. You may be sure we are under the utmost impatience to know what will be the last result of the ministry about Woods halfpence. If they do nothing in his favor it is impossible that coyne should ever find a currencye, and I much doubt whether the case will be much altered tho they should gratifye him to his wish. For he hath not the impudence to hope for a proclamacion to inforce their passing as Legal money, and without one he may keep them where they are. For Gods sake why doth not somebody tell what great person or persons are beleived in London to be the fortunate in that adventure: If the names were wrote in any loose scrip in a letter or at the bottom of one without referring any thing to the matter they are concerned in, it would be satisfactory and understood; yet lay the writer or receiver of the letter under no difficultye.

603. St John III, Midleton, to Alan I, Dublin, 29 May 1724

(1248/6/31–2)

I am 2 letters in your Lordships Dett; one I received this morning and the other by last Post, which should have been answer'd then, but that I had been abroad the whole day, and had not time enough when I return'd to do it, and overtake the Post.

If I had not expected to see you so soon I should have been more particular about many things which Lord Carteret did me the honour to talk to me of before I left London; but as he did not give me any directions to say or mention any thing in particular to you to which he desir'd an Answer, I thought it more adviseable to defer troubling you with many things which indeed could not so well be trusted to a letter which was to go thro honest Monmouths hands.

I resolve to begin my journey next Monday, so as to be in town by Thursday night, and beg you will speak to Arthur Hill to send a Coach as far as Naas to meet me, which must be there by Thursday noon. I hope he will not forget to hire me a footman as I desird by a letter last Post, for I shall be at a great loss if he does not, having discharg'd my own before I left London …

604. Thomas to Alan I, Dublin, 2 June 1724

(1248/6/33–4)

Last night I receivd yours of this day sennights date, and Mrs C[ourthope] another wrote the same day, I have nott seen Lord C[arteret] since my returne to towne, butt will in a day or two, I did nott read to him the letters which your sonne sent from Bristoll, there being some expressions in them, which might admitt of a double construction, butt recapitulated the whole substance of them, mine by Mr Tickle informes you how plainly I dealt in that matter; I thinke nothing will bee done therein which may enforce that ruinous designe, wherfore I thinke twill of course fall, and am confident twill, if people refuse becoming (by

---

[306] A pardon.

a ridiculous submission) partyes to what must unavoidably end in their own ruine; by the
first safe hand I shall acquaint you with what I doe nott care to venture by post, though I am
sufficiently empowered soe to doe, butt I thinke tis nott advisable. Mr Storer (just returnd
from Madrid)[307] tells mee the excesse of heat had brought the Locusts in great numbers
into Spaine, where the people were under terrible apprehension of the losse of their harvest,
should that prove the case, twill occasion a prodigious demand of corne, which I mention
that people (with you) may nott bee caught by the merchants whoe will have the earlyest
advice to buy.

605. Alan I, Dublin, to Thomas, at his lodgings in Whitehall, 5 June 1724[308]

(1248/6/35–6)

I have yours of the 18th of May before me and as soon as it was proper took occasion to
discourse Mr T[*ickell*] on the subject of it: he I find is entirely master of that whole affair,
and I think his wishes are for having the thing have the fate it deserves; but stil you must
give grains of allowance for his wishing it may be carryed soe as to give the least disturbance
to the measures and views of his Cheif, which I am soe far from blaming him for, that I
think it would be unreasonable and ridiculous to expect any thing from him that tended
not that way. I thank you for the prudent caution in your scrip by way of postscript, and
shal alway consider that great men and ministers of state act out of their province when
they cease to be Courtiers: but I had a letter from the person you mean last night, which
layes me under a necessitye of assuring him of all hints that I think may be useful and
necessary; but beyond those bounds my own prudence and your advice will surely prevent
me from going. I hinted to you formerly that two weak addresses from the grand Juryes of
the County and City of Dublin were laid before the Justices relating to Woods half pence,
and by them sent to my Lord Lieutenant, and I now find they have been laid before his
Majestye; whether they be soe framed as to serve the end for which they were intended or
the contrary I will not take on me to judge, for by speaking my mind I might contract a
suspition on my self as not having equal zest against base money with Colonel Bellers[309]
the foreman of the County Jury and Sir Nathaniel Whitwel[310] of that of the City.

[307]'Storer, the messenger' (HMC, *Polwarth MSS*, iv, 188).

[308]Letter endorsed by St John III: 'I would have wrote to you tonight, if my Father had not …'.

[309]No one of this name has been identified, although a Charles Bellers of Dublin did take out a marriage
licence in 1729 (*31st Report of the Deputy Keeper of the Records of Ireland* (Dublin, 1899), Appendix, p. 43).

[310]Sir Nathaniel Whitwell (*d.* aft. 1730), of Dublin and Curraghtown, Co. Meath; alderman of Dublin until
his resignation in 1730 on grounds of poverty and failing health, and lord mayor in 1727–8 (*Calendar of the
Ancient Records of Dublin*, ed. J.T. Gilbert and R.M. Gilbert (17 vols, Dublin, 1889–1921), vii, 512; Reg. Deeds,
31/163/18635; 62/133/43066).

606. *Thomas to Alan I, 6 June 1724*

(1248/6/39–40)

… Yesterday being Lord Lieutenants publique day, I did (contrary to my usuall custome) attend his Excellency and had in his private roome an oportunity of acquainting him throughly with Mr Bernards motion,[311] which afterwards I told to Lord Percivall and Mr Deering,[312] to whom the news was welcom enough. The company were generally officers, butt att lenghth Lord F[*it*]zW[*illiam*] and Mr Parry[313] came in, the latter advanct towards mee, which occasioned the mutuall stirring hats, butt went noe farther; A noble Lord to whom I since related the passage, made this observation that the turne which would bee given was that twas of your laying, my answer was, they might please themselves, since if twere soe twas a second proofe of that superior interest you have above those whoe would willingly beleivd others equalled itt, since the thing spoake itt selfe. I have nott seen the Representation from the Councill to his Majesty nor the letter to his Excellency upon the same subject,[314] butt am told both are strong and well worded, they have been layd before the King, and will before the Councill when Lord Townsend and Mr Walpole returne to towne; I cannott thinke any directions will goe hence to enforce, in any sort, their currency, and therefore thinke Mr Wood will find itt his interest to send his half pence after the rest to the plantations, unlesse hee should find them as ill relisht there as with you, which I hear is like to bee the case.

I cannott omitt mentioning what I hear of Lord Thomond, whoe speakes more plainly and with more spiritt against this cursed project, then any other nobleman of that Kingdom, butt comes even short of what (as I am informed and I beleive very truly) the Prince publiquely declares;[315] my opinion is, butt this I say onely as my thoughts, that the skill will bee how to have the matter fall soft, soe bee itt, and soe I thinke itt must and will end, if the people in Ireland stand their ground; I am never mealy mouthd in saying what I am convinct is strictly right, nor shall I faile doing itt in this instance, which I apprehend would in consquence prove a second South Sea scheme. Possibly those that are to be great gainers, (and such I assure your selfe there are) may struggle, in expectation thereby to carry their point, butt the more they labour itt, the more will they bee entangled, and forced att last to drop itt, when they find the mountaine cannott, will nott, come to Mahomet.[316] Irish understandings will cease (with some people) to bee a by word, as usually, for they say the

---

[311] Francis Bernard, MP [I], was described in February 1724 by Sir Richard Levinge as acting at the head of 'the Brodrick party' in the Commons in the absence of St John III, and as having been principally responsible for Alan's vindication in the lower house, from charges that his absence from the country had stopped the progress of public business (BL, Add. MS 9713, f. 15: Levinge to Edward Southwell, 10 Feb. 1723/4).

[312] Daniel Dering (*d.* 1730), who was both a cousin and brother-in-law of Viscount Perceval (John Lodge, *The Peerage of Ireland …*, rev. Mervyn Archdall (7 vols, Dublin, 1789), ii, 256).

[313] Benjamin Parry, MP [I].

[314] TNA, SP 63/383/229: report of committee of privy council [I], 15 May 1724; SP 63/383/233: address of lords justices [I] and privy council [I] to the king, 20 May 1724.

[315] The prince of Wales (the future George II).

[316] From Francis Bacon's *Essays* (1625), essay xii ('Of boldnesse'): 'Mahomet made the people beleeve that he would call an hill to him … The people assembled; Mahomet cald the hill to him, againe, and againe; and when the hill stood still, he was never a whit abashed, but said; If the hill will not come to Mahomet, Mahomet wil go to the hil'.

matter of the Representation (butt the timing itt more) was a damnd deep layd designe, which is wholly layd to one mans charge, I thinke much for his honour, and therfore I am far from making any Apollogy.

Tis with great pleasure I hear from gentlemen lately come over, as well as by letters which I have seen, the charecter your name sake has acquired, hee will lay such a foundation as necessarily must render him one day very considerable, unlesse his close attachment to truth, and just sence of honour, stand in the way, and that may bee case, for neither are much in vogue; hower I hope and doubt nott his perseverance *Quo semel est imbuta* etc.[317]

607. *Thomas to Alan I, Dublin, 13 June 1724*

(1248/6/37–8)

Last night came yours of the 5th wherein you mention having intimated the two grand jury addresses, if uppon recollection you are certaine you did soe, you may conclude that the trade of stopping letters is nott over, for I never heard of those addresses till now. When I spoake to a certaine person uppon that subject I told him I thought that matter att an end; his answer was, I hope soe, butt cannott say how far Mr —[318] may push itt when hee returnes; tis now sayd the two T[*ighe*]s[319] were to have £8000 between them.

His G[*race*] has been very smartly reprimanded; his pretended ignorance of an affair stands him in noe stead, because if true, tis such a failure as twould be a shame to own, butt the contrary is taken for graunted, I thinke this is very certaine, for I have itt from a very good hand.

An Aid de camp corresponds here, and does itt very sensibly.

Tis sayd Lord F[*it*]zW[*illiam*] is to be an english Peer, surely his Attendant may att least hope being an Irish one, both which will I beleive happen when the King goes to Mullingar.

Your new coine is peeping abroad here, which has occasioned advertisements (by way of caution against taking them) to bee affixt in several markett places, people here will nott bee imposd uppon. You may remember the Daily Courant (a paper of note) lead the dance, setting forth that they were nott of the vallue pretended.[320]

608. *Thomas to Alan I, 7 July 1724*[321]

(1248/6/41–2)

I purposd to have been going towards Bath next Munday, butt must putt itt of till I receive an answer to this.

---

[317]Horace, *Epistulae*, I, ii, 69: '*quo semel est imbuta recens servabit odorem; testa diu*' (the pot will retain for a long time the taste of what was placed in it when it was new).

[318]Presumably Speaker Conolly.

[319]Richard Tighe, MP [I] and his son William (1710–66), of Rossanna, Co. Wicklow, MP [I] 1734–*d*.

[320]See above, p. 109.

[321]Letter endorsed by Alan I: 'Thomas Brodrick … contains a proposal from Sir John Frederick for Ally. I answered and approved it. 12. July'.

This morning Mr Jennings came to mee,[322] att the desire of Sir John Frederick (Grand-sonne to the great Italian merchant of the same name)[323] whoe desired to know if hee might make a proposall of marriage with your daughter, whom hee has seen, and owns to have taken a liking to, though possibly shee does nott know him, butt this is onely my conjecture, You may bee sure I returned a civill answer, upon which hee sent to Sir John whoe lives in the neighbourhood.

Hee soone came; what I told him was that in your absence I could say noe more then that I would transmitt to you what hee should offer, and faithfully give him your answer; Hee is forty, a very well lookt man, and in my opinion genteele, what others may thinke I cannott foretell, butt though I was a stranger to his person, I know his charecter to bee very good, a man of sobriety and well principled. His first question naturally was her fortune, to which I answerd I knew you alwayes intended £10000 and I beleivd you continued of the same mind; hee told mee hee had heard soe, that the intent of his question was in order to his making a suitable proposall, which hee was willing to doe, That hee would make a jointure of £1000 per an payable outt of the long annuityes, which are payable quarterly, without taxes; that his mother (whoe was a great fortune)[324] has a jointure of twelve hundred pounds a yeare, to which hee would adde eight more making in the whole £3000 per an.

That as to younger childrens portions etc hee would refer to you whose interest twould bee to adjust those things reasonably, as much as his; hee askt mee whither the young Lady might nott expect being spoake to upon itt, I told him that I would nott doe till I had your directions, after which you would leave her free as to her liking, hee sayd hee hoped soe, for upon other termes noe happinesse could bee expected. I likewise told him the possibillity of a great additionall fortune, which I hoped however would nott happen; upon which hee hinted having more then hee had mentioned, and I am informd hee has what is very considerably soe; you will judge of the whole, letting mee have your answer assoone as possible, which I have promisd giving him.

I thinke his age nott unsuitable, nor indeed any part of the proposall, though I assured him greater offers had been made by very much, which went of by hers, nott your means. Hee has purchased the mannor of Hascomb (which you must surely remember)[325] the fine farme of Tewseley,[326] and a little one of £70 per an. adjoining to itt, the two latter within two miles of Pepper Hara, and has bidden vast prizes (in my opinion) for two other things in that neighborhood, being very desirous to lay as much as hee can, together.

---

[322] Possibly the barrister and former MP [GB] Philip Jennings (c. 1679–1740), of the Inner Temple and Dudleston, Salop.

[323] Sir John Frederick (c. 1678–1755), 1st Bt, of Burwood House, Surrey, was the grandson of Sir John Frederick (1601–85), of Old Jewry, London, lord mayor of London 1661–2 and MP [GB] 1660, 1663, who left an estate worth £42,000 (*The House of Commons 1660–90*, ed. B.D. Henning (3 vols, 1983), ii, 365). The proposed marriage with Alice did not take place, and in 1727 Sir John married Barbara (d. 1749), daughter of Sir Thomas Kynnersley of Loxley, Derbys. (*Cassandra Brydges, Duchess of Chandos, 1670–1735: Life and Letters*, ed. Rosemary O'Day (Woodbridge, 2007), 405).

[324] Leanora, a daughter of Charles Marescoe (c. 1633–70) of Bosse Alley, London: see *Oxf. DNB* (*s.v.* Marescoe, Charles); *Markets and Merchants of the Late Seventeenth Century: The Marescoe-David Letters, 1668–1680*, ed. Henry Roseveare (1987), 3–8.

[325] Hascombe, near Godalming in Surrey.

[326] Tuesley, Surrey, about four miles north-east of Hascombe.

You will write such a letter as may bee properly shown, taking notice of Mr Jennings in itt, and as you judge best, may write to Miss on the subject, unlesse you should thinke of coming over, which surely you may very well aske leave to doe for two or three months in order to spend some time att Bath for recovery of that health which has been somuch impaird by constant attendance, and the fatigue of publique business. Pray keep this matter entirely to yourselfe, for I experimentaly know what may bee the consequence of doing otherwise.

I have advisd your name sakes[327] spending as much time as the season will allow (for passing the Alps or Pyranease Hills) att Ratisbon, where all the Religious matters of Germany will bee taken into consideration,[328] the knowledge of which may hereafter prove of very great use to him, for his observations are soe just, and his way of reasoning soe strong, that what ever falls within his knowledge, will bee turnd to proper ends; for which reason I cannott butt thinke the time of his going abroad has proved extremely lucky, for hee will bee master of what some whoe hold their heads high, are wholly ignorant of. I am perswaded after our heads are layd low, hee will bee valluable.

609. *Alan I, Dublin, to Thomas, 1 Aug. 1724*

(1248/6/45–6)

Little did I expect on this day ten years that the representative body of the Kingdome (I mean the Lords and Commons in Parliament) should have had what they laid before the King as pernicious to the Kingdome left to be disproved by two or three fellows, in London: one of which (Browne) if he be the same person I beleive, is of soe vile a character that no sort of credit ought to be given to any thing he hath affirmed, or shal affirm: for the truth of which I refer you to a vote of the house of Commons, a copy of which I have sent enclosed. One would wish that Mr Wood and the freinds of his undertaking, could have produced men of better credit then such as stand branded, for having endeavoured to doe what he appeared to the house of Commons to have designed against innocent men, and for which the Attorney General was ordered by the house to prosecute him.[329] to avoid which I suppose was his cheif call to England. When the credit of the whole Parliament of Ireland, and the opinion of the Governement and Councel in a matter relating to the general good of Ireland, shal come to be put into a ballance with such a wretches affirmation, or his with theirs, people must think the Kingdome to be fallen very low: and will draw the natural conclusions from it. I do not think it will be much for his Majestyes service to disable a people (which hath at all times shewed the truest affection for his Majestyes person and Governement, to exert themselves in the support of either if there should ever be occasion, as (I doubt) impoverishing them will. For my part I cannot but think that there must be something more at the bottom of this affair then people are yet aware of; for hitherto mens

---

[327] Alan II.

[328] The Imperial Diet, which met at Ratisbon, or Regensburg, in Bavaria.

[329] John Browne (*d.* 1762), of The Neale, Co. Mayo, had fled Dublin for London in 1723 to avoid a prosecution ordered by the Irish house of commons, for conspiring against the life of John Bingham, the governor of Co. Mayo. His testimony before the British privy council in favour of Wood earned him further notoriety in Ireland, and a mauling by Swift. (*Drapier's Letters*, 37, 48, 50, 226–8, *DIB*, i, 916–17.)

conjectures have been that no more was in view then the getting soe much mony (as a boon for particular persons) as might be given by the undertaker for the benefit of the coynage, of a certain quantitye of Copper: but it is too well known by experience that greater summes have been obtained from this poor Kingdome by methods not soe disagreeable to it, as this half penny project, and people begin to fancy the determination in this affair may reach as far as the West Indies:[330] but I am not master enough of it to form any thoughts concerning it, and leave the consideration of things at so great a distance of time and place to those who will perhaps find themselves more concerned then they seem yet to be aware of. Pray let me know the name of the Lord who asked Mr Finlay at what rate he was to pay Wood for the £50000 for which he had agreed with him?[331] Methinks by his answer that he was to pay £70 per Cent for it, the Councel could not but see that an underdealer in this project was to have £15000 clear profit for laying at £50000. And they must at the same time perceive that Wood could afford to coyne and utter his halfpence soe as not to be a loser, if the patent had obliged him to coyne for the publick at the same price, as he could afford to take for his coyne from Mr Finlay. How this businesse will end I cannot foresee, but am apprehensive that it is carryed on with a view to make the Governement of our present Lord Lieutenant as uneasy, as the countenancing and supporting the project underhand rendred that of his predecessor. We have it among the intimado's that the naming the Bishop of Bristol[332] Primate, was done by ———[333] without the intervention of a freind of yours,[334] and that the vacancye on the Bench will be supplyed by the same hand, and entirely to the satisfaction of those here, who never desire to see his face in Ireland:[335] and who shewed great satisfaction at the news, as supposing they should attain their long desired end to gett one put on the Bench, whose great post at the Barre hath not influence enough to make his practice preferable to a puisne Judgeship. I have reason to apprehend that it is designed in England to give the refuse of the Cheif Justiceship to a freind of Lawryes,[336] but I am apt to think he will consider before he goes into a Court the practice whereof he is much a stranger to, and quit one where he hath by sitting some time acquired more knowledge then he brought over with him, I mean stil in reference to the practice of the Court: but indeed it is unhappy that the person recommended hence, of long experience and unquestionable abilityes (I mean Justice MacCartney[337]) should not have a prospect of

[330] See above, p. 61.

[331] Robert Finlay, a merchant and banker of Sherborne Lane, London (*Drapier's Letters*, 228; *Daily Courant*, 2 June 1720). In 1720 Lord Perceval described him as one of 'the two bankers for Ireland', and he seems to have operated with the Dublin banking firm of Burton and Harrison (BL, Add. MS 46971, f. 75: Perceval to Berkeley Taylor, 29 Sept. 1720; TNA, C11/2570/20: pleading, *Burton v. Hillsborough*, 1723). By 1724 Perceval was calling him 'our broken banker' (BL, Add. MS 47030, f. 74: Lord Perceval to Philip Perceval, 28 July 1724), and by February 1725 he was listed among recent bankrupts (*British Journal*, 27 Feb. 1725). Finlay testified to the council that he had contracted for £30,000 of the halfpence at 30% discount, on the assumption that Wood had obtained a proclamation for enforcing the acceptance of the coin; and also that a petition he himself offered for a patent some time ago was 'to be tied down to the making no more than £50,000 worth' (*Drapier's Letters*, 228; BL, Add. MS 47030, f. 74).

[332] Hugh Boulter.

[333] Presumably Robert Walpole.

[334] Carteret.

[335] Carteret's.

[336] Possibly Sir Robert Raymond, who was appointed lord chief justice of that court in March 1725. Raymond had been at Cambridge at the same time as Lawrence Brodrick.

[337] James Macartney (c. 1652–1727), of Belfast, MP [I] 1692–9, justice of common pleas.

successe to what he hath soe fair pretensions. I am sorry to tell you my apprehensions that Mr Browne will have more freinds for the part he hath lately taken, then enemyes for his past wickednesse. I mean on your side of the water.

610. *Thomas to Alan I, 1 Aug. 1724*

(1248/6/47–8)

I told you in my last that upon the 19th of last month I received yours of the 12th butt had nott then, nor have I since that which you promisd writing to your daughter by the succeeding packett, which I know nott how to account for, that letters were formerly intercepted I well know, butt I thinke I may very well conclude that practice, then carryd on att the post office, which I cannott thinke now the case, and therefore must conclude this failure comes from some other quarter, which concernes you to examine carefully, especially what relates soe nearly to your family, wherein I thinke your selfe alone concerned.

I have hitherto omitted breaking the matter to my neice, expecting each post that to her, butt being this morning to goe out of towne, without prospect of returning till I have spent some time att Bath, the necessity of which every day apparently encreases, I resolve to shew her your letter, and talke the matter throughly with her, after what manner shee relishes itt shall bee added att the end of this.

I mentioned already in grosse what the proposalls were, butt yesterday went more minutely into perticulars, which are what follows. The mothers fortune to bee setled on a daughter, if butt one, and noe sonne, if more and noe sonne £15000 if a sonne the same provision to bee made for younger children to bee apportioned by the father. The jointure of £1000 per an to bee out of the long annuityes, and £300 per an for pin mony, I demanded four, butt I thinke three sufficient. The jointure of £1000 with that of his mother being £1200 per an. to bee made up 3000 per an to bee setled on the 1st sonne etc. this to bee secured of other long annuityes unsetled, with a power to dispose of them for the purchase of lands of equall vallue to bee setled in the same manner, as shall bee most for the benefitt of the family, with the consent of Trustees of your naming. A Power to make a jointure to a second wife, £1000 per an was mentioned, butt I thinke that too much in case there should bee younger children, whose fortunes and maintenance may bear hard on an eldest sonne; this therefore remains ununadjusted, what is reasonable therein, being to bee considered, the fortune to bee payable on the marriage.

These being the materiall points were agreed to, other things which shall appear necessary to bee added.

In order to give you an oportunity of remitting the mony, I told him that Sir Thomas Pingelly (whoe is on the circuite) would I beleivd bee the councill you would pitch uppon, soe that till his returne nothing farther of this nature could bee proceeded uppon.

Hee then (very reasonably) desired hee might bee att liberty to make his application, I told him I would settle the time, and manner with her Aunts, and that my brother Lory (his old acquaintance att Cambridge) should informe him thereof, this way I chose in order to hear a little what her thoughts were, for I orderd itt soe as that shee has seen him, without knowing the reason, which had been needlesse, if I had been apprisd of her having seen him often.

Till very lately I know nothing of my Brothers acquaintance with him and then accidentally by his enquiry after him, the charecter is very pleasing which my Brother gives of him, that hee was a gentleman Commoner of Sidney colledge, where hee spent a considerable time, is a very good schollar, and livd soe regularly, as out of an allowance of £100 per an. hee kept a servant, without running six pence in debt, leaving behind him an honourable and good charecter.

His person is very good, and his deportment very gentlemanlike, soe that I hope there will bee noe objection to itt, butt this depending on her I can say noe more, then that I have done all in my power towards effecting what I hope shee may bee happy in.

I take for graunted that your Cheife justiceship will bee offerd to the chiefe Baron,[338] whoe (if hee accept) will bee succeeded by Mr West of our house,[339] otherwise heel I thinke bee chiefe justice, I doe nott know that this is fixt, butt I take itt to bee soe.

Thus far I have wrote att home, leaving as little as I could to bee added after talking with my neice, which you shall have as fully as I comprehend itt. I had forgott saying that I beleive your sone must have knowne him att Cambrige, from whom you may bee informd perhaps more perticularly.

Though tis out of place I must tell you I am very well informed that Wood will bee disappointed of his hoped for proclamation, nor will any thing bee done compulsary on his behalfe, I thinke falling soft is cheifly in veiwe with regard to the Prerogative, which hee endeavors to call in to his assistance, butt this will bee of little availe to him, since his pattent is for uttering to such as will willingly receive them, soe that the King is noe farther concernd, then leaving itt as tis purely in the people to receive or refuse them.

I have talked all that I thought necessary with my neice whoe expressess a great dislike, owning att the same time having frequently seen him, I presst her reason for itt, since that must arise from his person, to which I could gett noe other answer then that shee was sure shee could never bee happy with him, and would rather live on fifty pounds a yeare rather then marry him; I cannott guesse att the reason which none butt her selfe can unriddle, for after shewing her your letter I told her the proposals hee made were very honourable and great, to which shee answered that shee had heard hee was very rich, butt that did nott weigh, since shee could nott propose being happy from that consideration. You will now consider what will bee fitt for you to doe. I shall advise my brothers letting him know that waiting till you write to her will bee most advisable, since probably that would come soone, for that this day sennight I had given you an account of the miscarriage of your former letter, since I made nott the least doubt of your having wrote as you told mee you would. I have as near as I can told you every thing plainly, and therby faithfully discharged my part, what remains farther to bee done you will consider.

---

[338] Bernard Hale (1677–1729), of King's Walden, Herts., who had been appointed chief baron of the exchequer [I] in 1722.

[339] Richard West (c. 1691–1726), of Ridge, Herts., MP [GB] Bodmin and king's counsel [GB]. He was appointed lord chancellor [I] in 1725.

611. *St John III, Midleton, to Alan I, 9 Aug. 1724*[340]

(1248/6/49–50)

I am 2 letters in your Lordships Dett, one Dated the 28th July which I received the morning I left Galway, and the other the 25th, which I found here when I return'd last night.

As I am truly concern'd at having made a request which seems to you very unreasonable, so I own my self at a loss in what manner to answer the several objections you make to it, being apprehensive that many things which I shall offer in my own justification may be ascrib'd to my vanity, or fondness of being in a Station of power and grandeur, which however I must solemnly affirm were in no sort the Motives which inclin'd me to trouble you on this occasion. Tis now too late to consider the prudence of my desiring a Seat in the English Parliament, tho I think even that might be easily accounted for. I hope I have never misbehav'd my self there, nor given any of my freinds reason to be asham'd of my conduct since I sat there. The Question is whither since I am a Member, and as such oblig'd to attend the Service of the house, I might not reasonably hope, thro the Interest and intercession of my freinds, to have some Employment or mark of the Kings favour bestowed on me, and if so, whither what I mention'd was any way improper either to ask or be granted. I must surely have exprest myself in a very odd manner, far from my intention or thoughts, when after a second reading over that part of my letter, your Lordship apprehends I expected <u>an Equivalent from you</u> for the Expence which my attendance in England must necessarily occasion, or that you should make your self or wife uneasy on that Account, or disable your self from making such a provision for my Brother and Sister as is Suitable to your condition. Your Lordship best knows whither in any instance of my life I have acted towards you with so narrow, so self interested a veiew. No My Lord, the Duty, the Sincere affection and regard I shall always have for your Lordship proceeds from a much nobler Principle, a gratefull sense of the infinite obligations I lye under to you, whom I shall ever esteem and honour as the best of Parents.

I have not a Copy of my letter by me, but from the whole scope and tendency of it will venture to affirm upon my memory, that the Equivalent I mention'd could be no other then this viz. My attendance in Parliament not only occasion'd an immediate Expence, but likewise disabled me from practicing 2 of the 4 Terms, the loss of which was near equal to the money actually expended in London, and therefore I imagin'd it not extremely unreasonable to have some employment given me as an Equivalent for so great a loss, which my present fortune is not very well able to bear. This was my way of thinking; how far tis just or agreable I must submit to yours; but thus much I must beg leave to say, that I beleive there are not many cases like mine; especially considering my Relation and Attachments, (for I will say nothing of my own pretentions) who have not so much as once been thought of or recommended for any one Employment since the Kings accession, that of the Sollictorship excepted, which was hardly worth asking or accepting.

You tell me tis unaccountable in your way of thinking to hear one who is not satisfyed with his present income propose such a thing which will considerably lessen, and seem to think that my practice brings me in more money then the Emploiment I desire ever

---

[340]Letter endorsed by Alan I: 'Senny … seems to think himself neglected in not being recommended to succeed Sir Rich Levinge'.

would. If this were the case, which I assure you it is not, it might indeed be an objection to what I desire, supposing I had no avocation from my business; but while that continues, and is attended with the loss of half my practice, you will easily beleive that the profits of the office I desir'd are vastly greater then the other half of it, and consequently would be far from lessening my present income.

Tho I will not dissemble my satisfaction of being a Member of the English Parliament, yet I hope the fondness of sitting there has never betrayed me into a mean or unwarrantable Action, and I think may be easily reconcil'd with the request which my last letter carryed you. I am sensible had it succeeded my seat there had been vacated; but have had so many repeated assurances of Sir Francis Drakes and Sir John Hobards freindship in this or any succeeding Parliament,[341] that I should not have had the least doubt of being reelected; nor can I think the case of a judges of this Kingdom sitting there either extraordinary or new. If you please to recollect it was Sir Gilbert Dolbens for several Parliaments in the late Queens reign,[342] and seems not to be very unlike your own at present; at least I cannot see, why the objection is not as strong against a Judge of Equity as of Common Law.

The last part of your letter relates so immediately to my self, and I am so far conscious of the truth of what you say, that I shall not pretend to give it any other Answer but this viz. that a very little time would have worn off the objection to my Age, as a studious and diligent Application would that of want of experience in the Practice of the Court, which I certainly would have undergone had I been thought worthy to have presided there.

But all thoughts of that are now over.

I have now answer'd the Several parts of your letter in the best manner my confusion and the inexpressible concern your letter has given me, would allow. I can truly say this is wrote in the bitterness of my Soul, occasion'd, not by your refusing to gratifye me in the only request of the kind I ever made you, but by the severe and unkind manner of it. Prior obligations, and a conviction of the unreasonableness of what I desire, are certainly sufficient Causes for your doing the first; but then I should hope they might have been communicated with some expressions of concern and kindness, and a willingness to serve me upon another occasion, tho you might think it improper to do it upon this. But to be denied in such Terms as I am unwilling to mention, and such as I am perswaded, if you were to read your letter again, you would not repeat, this I confess greives me to the very Soul, and renders the disappointment, which I should otherwise have slighted, infinitely uneasy to me.

My Tears will not allow me to say more on this Subject; I hope you will not think I have said too much, or if you do, that you will attribute it to the concern I am now in, which is greater then I can express or you conceive.

---

[341] Sir Francis Henry Drake (1694–1740), 4th Bt, of Buckland, Devon, MP [GB] Tavistock, and Sir John Hobart (1693–1756), 5th Bt, of Blickling, Norfolk, MP [GB] St Ives, shared the proprietorial interest in the borough of Bere Alston, which St John represented (*HC 1715–54*, i, 225–6).

[342] Sir Gilbert Dolben (*c.* 1659–1722), of Finedon, Northants., justice of common pleas [I] 1701–20, sat in the English/British parliament for Peterborough and Yarmouth (Isle of Wight) between 1701 and 1715.

612. Alan I, Dublin, to Thomas, at his lodgings in the Privy Garden, Whitehall, 12 Aug. 1724

(1248/6/51–2)

I have your letter of the first instant which relates to the matter proposed by Sir J[ohn] F[rederick] and which contains more hopes of the matter of Woods Copper coyne ending without detriment to this poor Kingdome then the letters dated in London the 4th instant seem to give. The same maile give me an answer from Ally to the letter I had wrote to her, much to the same effect with what she said to you: she seems a good deal concerned for fear of having disobliged you in what she said to you in your last conversation: This maile I write my mind very plainly to her under cover to my sister, which I suppose she will communicate to you. I had a very long letter last post from ——. Pray recollect whether you have att any time (especially of late) said any thing as if the matter of Woods coynage would be brought before the Parliament at Westminster: For from an expression contained in a paper which I have lately seen I doe fancy you may be the person meant; altho it be said whatever people on this side of the water may think (the pronoun is on your side of the water) nothing will come of it and you will consider the words as spoken to conceal the person from my knowledge. Tho I alway knew ministers to be concerned in the main that others proceedings may not be brought on the carpet I hardly thought that those lengths would be taken as seem to be desired to be gone into in this affair. Perhaps I may soon have oportunitye to write to you by a private hand and then I will speake plainer. Probably this will not overtake you before you gett to the Bath which place (I hope) from long experience may be depended on to be of great use to you.

613. St John III, Cork, to Alan I, 16 Aug. 1724

(1248/6/53–4)

Last Post brought me yours of the 12th, with one Enclos'd for Collonel Bate,[343] which I immediately deliver'd, and discours't him and Fra[ncis] Bernard at large about a certain persons succeeding Hawley at Kinsale.[344] They both seem entirely dispos'd to serve him, and tell me that Mr Southwell has wrote very fully in his favour to his Agent;[345] notwithstanding which I am afraid we shall meet with very great difficultys in that Affair; and such as will not easily be surmounted. I find Collonel Bate has no thought of standing there, but he tells me that Jonas Stawell[346] has made such an Interest as neither Mr Southwell nor any body else will be able to shake, so that the only possible way of bringing what you desire

---

[343] George Bate (c. 1675–1725), lieut.- gov. of Charles Fort, Kinsale (*The Council Book of the Corporation of Kinsale …*, ed. Richard Caulfield (Guildford, 1879), p. xcv).

[344] Henry Hawley, MP [I] Kinsale, had died on 17 July (*Hist. Ir. Parl.*, iv, 385). The 'certain person' was Carteret's chief secretary, Thomas Clutterbuck (BL, Add. MS 605183, ff. 41–2: Francis Bernard to Edward Southwell, 25 Aug. 1724).

[345] James Dennis (?d. aft. 1735) (Toby Barnard, 'Wrecks and Reckonings in West Cork in the Early Eighteenth Century', *Skibbereen and District Historical Society Journal*, ii (2006), 7; *Coghill Letters*, 43, 45, 117, 167, 174).

[346] Jonas Stawell (1700–72), of Kinsale, Co. Cork, MP [I] Kinsale 1745–60 (*Hist. Ir. Parl.*, vi, 328–9). It seems likely that St John was confusing Jonas with his elder half-brother Anthony (*b.* 1685), who was eventually returned

to bear, is to endeavour, <u>by all means</u>, to prevail with him to resign, which I have done very heartily, but hitherto without Success. He is a man of a very easy fortune, perfectly independent, and a good deal positive, so that unless Mr Bernard has Credit enough with him to perswade him to decline, which he has promisd to endeavour, I doubt he shall never be able to carry the Election against him, nor indeed do I think it adviseable to put our freind upon standing a contested one. If therefore you ever write upon this Subject I should advise your doing it very cautiously, and in the mean to look out for another Burrough if a vacancy should happen, for to deal plainly I see very little prospect of success in this.

I am sorry to find your Sentiments about the result of a late hearing before the Council do not agree with those of a freind of ours, and fear you have too much reason to differ with him. Those who have drove this matter so great a length, will hardly be advis'd to stop short, and indeed every Step they have taken of late corresponds so exactly with what I was told they resolv'd to do, that I am confident they will at least make their words good in revoking a certain order, which the Gentlemen of the Customhouse are pleas'd to say was never made by them. This certainly will be going abundantly too far; however if nothing more be done, the people here and I beleive in every part of the Kingdom are so universally determind against receiving any of that vile Coin, that I hope very little if any of it will obtain a Currency.

You need not have been so cautious in describing Sir R[ichard] L[evinge's] Successor, there being at least 20 letters in town that name Mr West for it, particularly one of my Uncles to me and of Mr Southwells to Fra. Bernard. I am no otherwise concern'd at his promotion then as it convinces me — governs here as well as in England, and therefore I shall not be surpriz'd to hear that as soon as his Excellency arrives from Paris,[347] the Scheme, which I reason to think was long since concerted, is publickly avowed and declard.

Our Assizes end to morrow and I shall then go to Midleton, where I hope to continue till November, for I hear the Parliament is not to sit till after Christmas. I am sorry we are not like to have the pleasure of seeing you there …

614. *St John III, Midleton, to Alan I, Dublin, 17 Aug. 1724*

(1248/6/57–8)

… I saw Collonel Bate this morning who tells me he had talkt to Mr Stawell about resigning etc, but that he was determin'd not to do it, so that our only hope now is in Fra. Bernard, and I own I have very little hopes from his negotiations.

I am this minute landed from Corke …

---

but unseated on petition. Anthony Stawell had already engaged several voters (BL, Add. MS 605183, ff. 41–2: Francis Bernard to Edward Southwell, 25 Aug. 1724).

[347] Horatio Walpole (1678–1757), MP [GB] Great Yarmouth, British ambassador extraordinary to the French court; Robert's younger brother.

615. *Alan I, Dublin, to Thomas, Bath, 29 Aug. 1724*[348]

(1248/6/60–1)

I am just returned from spending six dayes at Mr Poles house in the Queens County[349] very agreeably with a great deal of company who loved and liked one another, and found yours of the 15th from the Bath: for which I thank you. In it you tell me that it will be the fault of Ireland if Woods halfpence prevail, because there will be no compulsory methods used to inforce them on us, nor encouragement given to them except by those who are in the bottom of the affair. I cannot tell how extensive this phrase may be; but can assure you that great earnestnesse hath been used to induce those here who have appeared most zealous against them to come into the grace and favour done us lately, by the consent of kind Mr Wood: viz to accept voluntarily £40000: and I have been soe urged to come into these sentiments, that nothing lesse then an unalterable resolution against this coyne in the maner it hath been endeavoured to be imposed upon us, grounded on a conviction of my judgement that my doing what was expected from me would tend to the hurt (if not utter ruine) of the Kingdome could have induced all the Justices to desire to be excused from issuing the orders required from them to be issued: As they did on 20th of this month, in a modest, submissive, and yet (in my opinion) a strong letter, the consequence of which we shal soon see and perhaps feel: but I think all the three are determined in the matter, and will adhere: but I can speak with certainty only for one of them. If you look into the beginning of Lord Clarendons history you may find a very judicious remark of the effect the judgement which was given in Mr Hampdens case about ship money had on the minds of people in general who had not soe much weighed the matter before.[350] And to the best of my observation what hath passed lately in relation to this Copper coyne seems to have a like influence here. I doe not find that the report hath made one convert, nor that the reducing £100800 to £40000 hath soe sweetened the draught that people are inclined to swallow it as altered and softned, which I confesse seems to proceed in a great measure from some severe passages in a certain paper, and from an opinion people may have that the same matter may be again thought useful or necessary for us, when we think we know the contrary, and could be very well content to be excused from having such a kindnesse done us against our wills. Others imagine that it will be impossible to prevent the imparting or uttering above £40000; which I own seems to me to be more difficult then the favourers of the project will allow it to be …

---

[348] Printed in Coxe, *Walpole,* ii, 394–5.

[349] William Pole (1680–1727) of Ballyfin, Queen's Co. ('Autobiography of Pole Cosby of Stradbally, Queen's County, 1703–37', *Journal of the Kildare Archaeological Society,* v (1906–8), 79, 81, 176).

[350] Edward Hyde, earl of Clarendon, *The History of the Rebellion and Civil Wars in England* … (3 vols, Oxford, 1707), i, 68–71.

616. St John III, Midleton, to Alan I, Dublin, 11 Sept. 1724

(1248/6/64–5)

… I find by the publick Prints Mr W[alpole] is gone into Devonshire,[351] which I suppose is the reason we hear nothing of the Resolutions taken upon the Receit of the Lords Justices Letter of the 20th of August. For my part I expect the worst, and know too much of the temper of some people to doubt their pushing this Affair to the utmost. All the advice therefore which I shall offer on this occasion is to remember and practice Lord Whartons Motto Expectes et Sustineas.[352]

Lord Barrymore and a great deal of Company are with me …

617. St John III, Midleton, to Alan I, 18 Sept. 1724[353]

(1248/6/66–7)

I am afraid your time is at present so taken up with Affairs of infinitely greater consequence then what I now write about, that you will hardly have leisure to read, much less to answer this letter.

I came this Afternoon from Corke, where I was employed 2 days together in a Hearing before the Mayor and Council upon a Complaint of the Misbehaviour of the Weighmasters in several Branches of their office.[354] You will easily imagine the City is very desirous to get rid of these Gentlemen who were put upon them in so extraordinary manner, but how far twill be prudent to pursue the measures that are now thought of to attain that end, I must beg your opinion when I have stated the case to you.

The charge against them consisted of these particulars. viz That they had appointed Deputys and Weigh houses without even asking the Approbation of the Mayor and Aldermen, as the Act directs; that they had branded several Hundreds of Unstatutable Cask, and

---

[351] Horatio Walpole: see for example, *Daily Post*, 15 Aug. 1724.

[352] 'Thou mayest hope and wait patiently.' The heraldic motto of Philip Wharton (1698–1731), 1st duke of Wharton and 2nd marquess of Catherlogh in the Irish peerage (*Symbola Heroica: or The Mottoes of the Nobility and Baronets of Great-Britain and Ireland; Placed Alphabetically* … (1736), 14).

[353] Letter endorsed by Alan I: 'Senny … about the complaint against the Weigh Masters of Corke. Answered 24 Sept. that in my opinion the first and last objections if true were good causes for removing them'.

[354] The corporation had lobbied in December 1723 against the Irish bill 'For continuing and amending the laws in relation to butter and tallow, and the casks in which such goods are to be made up …', which passed into law in February 1724 as 10 Geo. I, c. 9 [I]. This not only introduced new regulations for the work of weighmasters but sought specifically to deal with alleged abuses in Cork, by appointing as weighmasters the two MPs for the city, Aldermen Edward Hoare and Edmond Knapp, instead of permitting the corporation itself to nominate. Although there was a strong current of opinion in the county in favour of removing the right of appointment from the municipal authority (BL, Add. MS 46974, f. 56: Berkeley Taylor to Lord Perceval, 26 Dec. 1723), there was also a political context. Both Hoare and Knapp were associated with opposition to the Brodrick interest, and Speaker Conolly characterised the corporation's opposition to their nomination as politically motivated (TNA, SP 63/382/58: Conolly to [Charles Delafaye], 12 Dec. 1723; TNA, SP 63/382/64–5: Grafton to ——, 14 Dec. 1723). In August 1724 complaints were preferred in the city against Hoare and Knapp. On 27 Sept. the corporation determined that they had not complied with the requirements of the Act, but the final decision to remove them from office was not taken until 9 Oct., to give time for consideration of the implications. (*Cork Council Bk*, 438–40, 443–9.) St John was the first alderman after the mayor to sign the judgment (*Cork Council Bk*, 447).

that they had exacted a farthing for Stripping and heading every Cask, when the Act says they receive a Penny for their Expence and Labour <u>and no more</u>.

Their Answer to the first Article was that they had often desir'd the Mayor to call <u>a Council</u> in order to make a return of their Deputys and Weighhouses, but that he refus'd to do it, which I beleive was true, he conceiving the Return was to made to the <u>Aldermen</u> and not the Council. But little stress was laid on this Article by either side.

The second was prov'd by several witnesses who swore they beleiv'd almost all the Casks that were branded this Summer were made of unseason'd Timber, and were so far from being tight, as the Act requires, that they would hardly hold dry goods. To this it was answer'd, and I beleive very truly, that if the Act were strictly put in Execution, twould be in Effect a Prohibition to the exportation of Butter, for that there was not season'd Timber enough in the Countrey to make the 100th part of the Casks that were wanting; that tho those which had been branded were not entirely conformable to the Statute, they were however much better then usual; but that whither they had observ'd the directions of the Act in this particular or not; there was a Penalty of 5s impos'd by it for every Cask that was branded contrary to it, and therefore they were not liable to a double punishment; but that if any were inflicted they ought to be fin'd, if convicted, but could not be remov'd.

Their Answer to the 3d Article was that they were advis'd they were not oblig'd to strip and head the Cask, but only to weigh and try it, and that they never received the farthing, it being always paid to the Cooper, who appear'd however to be employed by them, and that their Deputys constantly refus'd to deliver the Countreyman his Butter, unless the Coopers Fee were paid as well as the weighmaster.

These are the Substance of the Articles and Answers, and I own I have a good deal of doubt about every one of them, and therefore entreat you will please to consider the Act, which is but short, and give me your opinion upon them, for I have deferr'd giving mine to the Mayor and Council till I hear from you.

In the first place I have some doubt whither upon considering the 2 Clauses in the Act about approving the Deputys and weighhouses, the weighmasters of Corke are oblig'd to have the approbation of the Aldermen. By the first Clause those in all other Corporations most certainly are; and then the Clause which appoints Hoare and Knap says they shall be <u>Subject to the Regulations of the Act</u>, and after those words power is given them to appoint Deputys, but no mention is made of their being approv'd; so that the Question is, whither the former words Subject to the Regulations of this Act, shall extend to the Subsequent Clause of the Deputys so as to put them upon the same foot with those in all other Corporations. The 2 other Questions are already Stated, viz. whither when the Act says they shall forfeit the Sum of 5s for branding a Cask made of unseasonable Timber, that be not the only Punishment that can be inflicted; or whither when it appears they have not pursued this part of the Act in any one instance, this be not such a misbehaviour as they may be remov'd for, notwithstanding the other Penalty.

The Question upon the farthing for Stripping and heading depends entirely upon the Clause which appoints their Fees, so that I need not say any thing further upon it.

I am afraid you will think these very impertinent Questions, and indeed so do I; but the expectations of people are so far rais'd, and the generality of the City have set their hearts upon the removing their new Masters to that degree, that I would gratifye them if possible; but will not do it at the expence of my Character, which I am sure will suffer if I should advise the doing it for any cause that is not justifiable, and therefore again entreat your opinion, whither those I have mention'd are so or not. We have deferr'd giving our Judgment till this day Sennight, and by that time, I hope to hear from you.

I received a letter lately from Jack Hasset[355] in which he desires me to recommend John Mason Esq,[356] as High Sheriffe and Mr Thomas Staughton[357] for a Justice of Peace in the County of Kerry. Mr Hasset is a very worthy Gentleman and very much your Servant, and has been hard born upon for being so; for which reason I hope you will gratifye him in the 2 requests he makes. You will think me troublesome, but now my hand is in I beg you will think of Coll Waller[358] for Sheriffe of the County of Limrick and Jack Colthurst[359] for our County, for the same reasons I gave you for obliging Jack Hasset.

618. *Alan I, Dublin, to Thomas, in the Privy Garden, Whitehall, 6 Oct. 1724*

(1248/6/72–3)

I am to acknowledge yours of the 26th of last month, and am as willing to give entire credit to what is said by a man whom I love and value as any man breathing: but I remember the prophet in the old testament declared that he had not power to speak more or lesse then what he was inspired with.[360] Time may reconcile these two things; which to me seem to carry in their natures a contradiction to one another viz a resolution not to use either art or force to reduce the people to alter their minds as to the receiving Woods halfpence, and at the same time an expectation that (considering the present temper of the people and the strong convictions they lye under that their being introduced would utterly ruine the Kingdome) they will yet be received, by the same people; unaltered in their resolutions either by art or force. Sure Wood is not the only person on your side of the water who is ignorant of what is intended; and how to reconcile his stil going on to coyne at a great expence (which you say in your letter of 24th Sept he stil does, and soe doth your Nephew in one of a later date from the report of ships lately arrived in the harbour of Corke from Bristol[361]) with a certain prospect that nothing will be done here to facilitate their currencye, surpasses my comprehension. But that which puts me more in doubt is a pamphlet lately printed in England in which the honest author hath introduced a Quaker to abuse the Parliament and people of this whole Kingdome, and at the same

---

[355] John Blenerhassett, MP [I].

[356] John Mason of Ballymacelligott, Co. Kerry (M.A. Hickson, *Selections from Old Kerry Records* (1872), 47).

[357] Thomas Stoughton (*d.* aft. 1735), of Ballyhorgan, Co. Kerry, a connection of Blenerhassett's (Hickson, *Selections from Old Kerry Records*), 104–6; Reg. Deeds, 111/39/75535).

[358] John Waller (bef. 1690–1742), of Castletown, Co. Limerick, MP [I] Doneraile 1727–*d*.

[359] John Colthurst (1678–1756), of Ardrum, Co. Cork, MP [I] Tallow 1734–56.

[360] Balaam in Numbers, 22: 38: 'Have I now any power at all to say anything? The word that God putteth in my mouth, that shall I speak'.

[361] The *Weekly Journal*, 26 Sept. 1724, reported that a ship from Bristol, loaded with Wood's coin, had lately arrived in Cork harbour but was met by several boats whose occupants warned them not to land for fear of suffering 'bad usage from the populace'. Seeing other boats approaching, the captain took fright and weighed anchor.

time deifyed Mr Woods Idol.[362] But indeed toward the later end of this scurriolous libel he seems to drop the argument of their being made current and contents himself they may passe as merchandize, and as your block Tin is disposed of in England.[363] No doubt somebody took the oportunitye of the resentments of people here against this coyne to inforce the necessitye of the Lord Lieutenants coming over forthwith, by which two ends were attained viz his absence from the Court, and the superseding the Commission of the present Lords Justices. The pamphlet I have mentioned before seems to me in page 18 to lay down a claim of a very extensive Prerogative to coyne Copper money for Great Britain (I mean by the Quaker) but not by the King or any of the ministers, for I will not goe into such a thought that any of them can countenance or be acquainted with the publishing such a scurrilous vile libel. My services to Lord Godolphin and if there be any other persons of qualitye or distinction whom I have the honour to be known unto, I desire you will give the same to them particularly to my Lord Dukes of Somersett, and Devon.

619. St John III, Midleton, to Alan I, 13 Oct. 1724

(1248/6/74–5)

I am to own the favour of two of your Lordships, of the 8th and 10th. The first should have been answer'd by last Post but being that day in Corke, I did not get home time enough to overtake the Post. Before I enter into other particulars give me leave to explain a passage in one of my letters, relating to C[ourthope] C[layton], and to assure you that I had not the least thought of him when I said I was surpriz'd at the silly groundless lye about our County and City Address,[364] which he had heard and told you. I knew it must have come from another Quarter, and never imagin'd he had any other hand in it then barely relating it to you, therefore pray do me justice, in your own thoughts, with regard to him.

I find by your letter to my Wife you have seen my letter to him, which contains every thing I can say about the villainous malitious Story of my having approv'd or encourag'd the Scheme of reducing Woods Coinage from £180000 to £40000, or lain my self under Engagements to any body that it would be submitted to here, so that I need not take up much of your time upon that Subject. I own, by your manner of expressing your self, I am a good deal concern'd for fear you should any way give into that groundless Calumny, or beleive me guilty of so weak as well as dishonest an Action; and therefore I do again in the most solemn manner assure you that I am so far from having consented to that Scheme, that it was never once propos'd in my hearing, nor was I ever talkt to upon that Subject by Mr W[alpole] or any man living. I will not say (tho I assure you I do not remember it) but that such a thing as lessening the Quantity might have been mention'd, when we were talking about the Patent; but that I either approv'd of or promis'd to go into it, I do again

---

[362] *Some Farther Account of the Original Disputes in Ireland, about Farthings and Halfpence. In a Discourse with a Quaker of Dublin* (1724). See Michael Ryder, 'Defoe, Goode and Wood's Halfpence', *Notes and Queries*, n.s., xxx (1983), 22–3.

[363] Tin of inferior quality cast into blocks (*OED*).

[364] The city address, in the form of petition to the king from the mayor, sheriffs, and commons of the city of Cork, is preserved in TNA, SP 63/384/137. See also SP 63/384/136: Carteret to Newcastle, 27 Oct. 1724.

most solemnly deny, and will put my veracity and Credit upon it, with you and every freind I have in the world.

I will make all the hast I can towards Dublin and hope to meet Lord C[*arteret*] there very soon after his landing, tho I shall hardly be in town till the latter end of this month. I intend to go into England after Christmas, if there be any thing to be done in Parliament. My Wife does not seem inclin'd to go over till Spring, and then only to the Bath; but when I see how the world goes here I shall be better able to determine my self in this matter.

The reason of my not signing our City Address was this. The Mayor[365] wrote to me to draw one and to send it by the messenger who brought his letter, that so it might be transmitted to Dublin the same Post; which I accordingly did, and as soon as he received it, he immediately order'd it to be Engrost, and it was sign'd and sent away that Evening. That for the County will soon be ready, and if the Gentlemen of the Countrey are not in hast to have it laid before the King, I shall with a great deal of pleasure bring it up and deliver it to Lord C[*arteret*], and shall never decline any opportunity of expressing my Sentiments against that detestable project.

We hear nothing of a new Parliament, nor can I imagine any body can be so weak as to imagine the Court will find their Account in changing hands; or that there can be a set of men found in Ireland that will not be at least as zealous against Mr Woods Patent as their Predecessors. I understand your hint about Sir Owen, and will endeavour to make the best use I can of it …

620. *Alan I, Dublin, to Thomas, in the Privy Garden, Whitehall, 20 Oct. 1724*

(1248/6/76–7)

I have yours of the 13th and must remind you that I have occasion to write too many letters to be able to keep copyes of them; and therefore am often to seek to understand your answers, particularly your last in which you tell me you read mine of the first instant to my Lord Lieutenant, and that he was pleased with it. I cannot recollect what it was which I said in it that hath pleased him, and desire you to give me an hint about it for my future conduct. The proceedings in Woods affair are soe double that I know not what to think of them: no force nor artifice is to be used, yet I see none omitted of the later sort; nor something of the former (or at least very like it) much wanting. But a very little time will put us at more certainty, my Lord Lieutenant being expected to land tomorrow or on Thursday at the farthest. We all seem to think the receiving the halfpence will not be more insisted on, when his Excellencye with his own eyes sees the temper and resolution of the people in that particular, which will convince him that their aversion to them arises not, nor is occasioned by the management of a few; but in the true sense of the people in general. As for my part I resolve to doe as you advise and to act upon principle whatever the consequence may be to myself but will use that temper and prudence in doing it, that I may not give an handle to my enemyes to doe me mischeif and to be able to justifye it after they have done it. I forget the reasons I assigned in mine of the 6th for sending Lord Lieutenant away in so much hast.

[365] George Bennett (*d.* 1743), of Cork (*Cork Council Bk*, 620, 645; Reg. Deeds, 111/296/76677).

621. *Alan I to Thomas, 31 Oct. 1724*[366]

(1248/6/78–81)

Instead of agreeable accounts of what passes here I shal be obliged to mention several things which I beleive will create you uneasinesse, because I am sure they doe soe to me in a great degree. The matter of Woods halfpence would have putt the Kingdome under difficultyes enough, tho our people here had acted with the greatest prudence and temper: for considering what steps have been taken in England in granting and supporting the patent, he must in my opinion be a very sanguine man who can hope for such an event in this affair, as I beleive might have been attained (before things had gone the lengths they have gone and before persons and things had been exasperated to that heighth which I fear they now are) if some people had spoke their minds as freely in that matter at the beginning as they have done since: but the game was plaid thus by a certain sett of men; they saw the carrying the point was much at the heart of the Lord Lieutenant and would be very well taken in England; they knew that the sense of the whole Kingdome was opposite to the receiving the halfpence; and consequently trusted that the majoritye in both houses of Parliament would be against them and prevent their obtaining a currencye, without their appearing in opposition to a darling point; and I am apt to think some Gentlemen (who have since thought it advisable to declare themselves as much against that coyne, as those who from the beginning honestly and publickly spoke their minds of it) gave hopes if not assurances that they would be for receiving them: This conduct I apprehend brought us in great measure to those difficultyes we now lye under and perhaps may be finally ruined by. For if the good of the Kingdome be concerned one way, I fear honour may be thought to be soe far concerned the other, that I confesse I hardly see what clue will lead us out of the Labyrinth we are in. But in addition to this misfortune, the behavior of some people who have thought fit to write against these halfpence hath given Mr Wood and his freinds great advantages, and may possibly turn to the great damage if not destruction of this Kingdome; unlesse prevented by the prudence and temper of others. On the day of my Lord Lieutenants landing there was a pamphlet published and cryed about by the Hawkers, one of which was brought to my Lord the next day; and on Saturday 24th October: his Excellencye shewed it to me and told me it struck at the dependencye of Ireland on the Crown of Great Britain.[367] I had not read it over but had one of them from Mr Tigh[368] in the Councel chamber who told me he bought two in the Castle from an Hawker; but after my Lord Lieutenant had mentioned the book to me under such a character, I read it over very deliberately; and when he asked me what my thoughts of it were I freely told him that I thought the pamphlet was highly seditious, and fit to be taken notice of in order to punish the Author and Printer. His Excellencye then declared he resolved to lay

---

[366] Printed in Coxe, *Walpole*, ii, 395–9.

[367] Swift's *A Letter to the Whole People of Ireland* (Dublin, 1724). For what follows, see Ehrenpreis, *Swift*, iii, 251–2.

[368] Richard Tighe, MP [I].

it before the Councel and to have the opinion of the Cheif Justice,[369] Cheif Baron[370] and Attorney General[371] as to the pamphlets being criminal; which he accordingly took and they were all of opinion that it was a seditious and vile libel and fit to be prosecuted. On 27th October my Lord held a Councel and in an handsome and strong maner disclosed the tendencye of the paper and expressed such a resentment of it as became a man in his Station upon such an occasion: but he spoke short and thought fit to select some few of the many exceptionable passages and to leave others to be enlarged upon by those who should speak after him. As I was convinced of the wicked positions contained in that libel, and how much the publishing such doctrines might and certainly would turn to the prejudice of the Kingdome, if such things should passe unpunished, I thought we should act wisely in taking the advice in the Communion service which directs us to judge ourselves, least we be judged of the Lord;[372] I then spoke pretty largely as to some points in the pamphlet viz. some of them which seemed to me to treat the King in an undutiful and dishonourable maner, others which asserted an independencye of this Kingdome, and one which in expresse words calls the power of the British Parliament to bind Ireland by Laws, a power <u>sometimes assumed in the memory of man</u>;[373] other paragraphs reflect on the wisdom of England, one insinuates (in my apprehension) that they I mean the Parliament are capable of corruption: Ireland is represented as in a state of slavery and treated as slaves by England;[374] nay when he mencions 50000 operators as a necessary number to distribute his fireballs[375] I doubt he means something which he dared not name, and insinuates as if we were to be born down with main force. I therefore moved that the Attorney General should be directed to prosecute etc. All the Lords of the Councel owned their abhorrence of the pamphlet as seditious and of dangerous consequence, nay soe did one who would not join in signing the order for a prosecucion,[376] for this reason (if I understood him right) least the prosecucion should fail of successe. Every body here knows the first contest between England and Ireland arose from the judgement given in the cause between the Societye of London against the (then) Bishop of Derry, now Archbishop of Dublin; in which the Lords in England voted that an Appeal brought by the Bishop against a decree in the Chancerye here was coram non judice:[377] This matter slept for several years till sett again on foot in the house of Lords

---

[369] William Whitshed (1679–1727), of Dublin and Killincarrig, Co. Wicklow, MP [I] 1703–14, chief justice of king's bench [I].

[370] Bernard Hale.

[371] John Rogerson, MP [I].

[372] 'Judge therefore yourselves, brethren, that ye be not judged of the Lord': from the exhortation spoken by the celebrant to communicants (*The Book of Common Prayer, and Administration of the Sacraments and other Rites and Ceremonies of the Church, According to the Use of the Church of Ireland* … (Dublin, 1722), unpaginated).

[373] *A Letter to the Whole People of Ireland*, 15: ''Tis true indeed, that within the memory of man, the parliaments of England have sometimes assumed the power of binding this kingdom by laws enacted there'.

[374] *A Letter to the Whole People of Ireland*, 14, 15.

[375] A reference to the assertion in one pamphlet that Walpole had vowed to 'cram this brass down our throats': Swift calculated that if it was intended to make the Irish swallow the halfpence as 'fireballs', this meant that government would need 50,000 'operators' to administer the dose – estimated at 17 balls per person, each made up of two and a half coins – to the Irish population (*A Letter to the Whole People of Ireland*, 21–2).

[376] Archbishop King (TNA, SP 63/384, f. 154: order for prosecution, 27 Oct. 1724; Ehrenpreis, *Swift*, iii, 268–9).

[377] The case of the *Society of London v. the bishop of Derry*, 1697–1704, for which see O'Regan, *Archbishop William King*, 97–111, 116–24. The archbishop was William King. *Coram non judice*, literally before a court without a judge, meant a legal proceeding without proper jurisdiction.

in Ireland in the Case of Sherlock and Aneslye in 1719 by means of the same man,[378] when the Barons of the Exchequer were proceeded against in an extraordinarye maner for acting as they were directed by the Lords of England in opposition to what had been determined by the Lords in Ireland;[379] but I am not at present sollicitous to tell you the circumstances of this Case. Only thus much I remember that it produced a certain representacion, which occasioned an English act of Parliament that hath declared that matter of jurisdiction.[380] The labour of supporting the jurisdiction of England fell a good deal to my share, and I was treated then as a betrayer of the libertyes of Ireland by some who beleived what they said and by others who had other views and knew more of the secret;[381] for the truth is if the jurisdiction of the house of Lords here could have been established to be the dernier resort; that house consisting generally of soe small a number of Lords present, it was alway in the power of one Bench to determine finally the propertye of every man in the Kingdome. This was a very desirable thing and much panted after, and I am much mistaken if I did not suffer for the share I had in this affair within one year last past. In this debate I used this argument to shew that appeals were not finally to be determined here, because they must necessarily have the power to expound Laws finally who have the power to make them; else another person may by expounding them contrary to the sense of the makers will enervate and in effect repeal them. This was an objection which could no way be soe fully answered as by resorting to Mr Molineux notion that they in England could not bind Ireland by any act made there;[382] which is one great position of our pamphlett and a darling point of his Grace; and from that quiver I take it the arrow originally comes, the author of the pamphlet having I think imbibed the principle from him. Now this is the man who was caressed to that degree in a late Governement that he had vanity enough to beleive he should at all times be courted in the same maner as his Grace of G[*rafton*] was pleased to doe. The late disappointment in the greatest Church preferment hath no doubt greatly irritated and exasperated the good man,[383] and hath occasioned the general reflection in the pamphlet as if no emploiments or preferments were ever to fall to the share of those of this countrey. That seems to be much insinuated, but no man can think the writer takes a way to mend matters in that particular, on the contrary is doing the most in his power to have all of this countrey for ever excluded from them. I will send you the pamphlet

---

[378]See *Anglo-Irish Politics*, ii, 8. Archbishop King is meant.

[379]By the Irish house of lords; see *Anglo-Irish Politics*, ii, 10–11.

[380]On 10 July 1719 the Irish house of lords agreed to prepare a representation to the king summarising the state of the case relating to their own claim for a final appellate jurisdiction over legal cases originating in Ireland. See *Anglo-Irish Politics*, ii, 12.

[381]See *Anglo-Irish Politics*, ii, 12–13.

[382]William Molyneux (1656–98), of Dublin, MP [I] 1692–d., in *The Case of Ireland's Being Bound by Acts of Parliament in England, Stated* (1698).

[383]The appointment of Hugh Boulter instead of King as archbishop of Armagh. King's reaction is illustrated in an apocryphal story retold by Lord Orrery, that on receiving the new primate King stayed in his chair, 'saying in his usual strain of wit … "My lord, I am certain your grace will forgive me, because, you know I am too old to rise"' (*A Great Archbishop of Dublin, William King, D.D., 1650–1729*, ed. Sir Charles S. King (1906), 321).

with lines under some of the passages of which I took notice when I spoke in Councel on this subject; and hope that your having this matter set in a just light may enable you to explain any thing that may be offered out of this writer to the prejudice of Ireland. The Councel also promised £300 as a reward to the person should discover the Author;[384] but in a little time after it was buzzed about that the writer would come in and own himself to be soe; and I had from my Lord Lieutenant yesterday that the Archbishop had been with him and spoke as if the Author would appear and own the writing the pamphlett; this to me was amazing, but I can never beleive it. I was this morning at the Castle and found the Archbishop in the Closett, but whether anything passed on this head before my coming in I cannot tell but beleive the contrary. The town concludes a certain Dean of the same name with our divine who lives beyond Shackleford to be the writer;[385] and indeed the maner and nature of it as well as the style bespeak him to be the Author. The Archbishop,[386] the Bishop of Elphin[387] and Dr Coghil[388] declined to sign the order for a proclamacion;[389] you know that the two later are the creatures of the former.[390] I wish this matter were once well over; and shal not be at quiet while I have any apprehensions of Woods importing his halfpence, which he may plainly seeth can never obtain a currencye with the consent of the people, but if he should stil opiniatre the thing and resolve to bring them in, I am in great doubt what may follow upon his doing soe. If the Mob should be soe audacious to meet in a riotous maner to obstruct the halfpence being landed and the Governement should think fit to oppose force to force, what a condition will this countrey be in? No body can tell what follyes the populace may be guilty of nor how far their behavior may provoke the Governement to proceed to chastise and represse them. But this is a subject of which I am weary, and will quit it. I have been very kindly treated by my Lord Lieutenant but I confesse nothing would have overjoyed me soe much as to have seen his instructions were to quiet our fears of the halfpence ever being brought among us; but this I am sorry to say I have not had the happinesse to be able to expect from anything which I have yet seen or heard. If things continue long in the uncertaintye they seem to be in at present I think the Countrey will suffer extremely in its trade and the Crown in its revenue, and I shal soon wish myself att Peperhara.

---

[384] *Proclamations*, ed. Kelly and Lyons, iii, 143–4.

[385] Jonathan Swift's first cousin, Thomas Swift (c. 1665–1752), rector of Puttenham in Surrey, close to Shackleford (Foster, *Alumni Oxonienses*, ii, 1447; E.W. Brayley, *A Topographical History of Surrey* (5 vols, 1841–8), v, 242). He had previously claimed some credit for the authorship of *A Tale of a Tub* (Jonathan Swift, *A Tale of a Tub and Other Works*, ed. Marcus Walsh (Cambridge, 2010), pp. xxxix, xli–xlvi, 237).

[386] King.

[387] Theophilus Bolton.

[388] Marmaduke Coghill, MP [I].

[389] Confirmed in *Proclamations*, ed. Kelly and Lyons, iii, 144.

[390] Bolton had previously been King's vicar-gen. in Dublin, as chancellor of St Patrick's cathedral, and in recommending him for preferment in 1716 the archbishop had written 'I know not his fellow' (*A Great Archbishop*, ed. King, 195). His continued closeness to his former patron was commented upon by Isaac Manley (TNA, SP 63/385/7: Manley to [Charles Delafaye], 9 Jan. 1724[/5]).

622. *Thomas to Alan II, Venice, 6 Nov. 1724*

(1248/6/82–3)

… I have nott had any letter from your father Since Lord Cartarets landing, I am sure Woods halfpence takes up his whole thoughts. Let them try what experiments (from hence) which they please, I am sure them [*sic*] will never bee able to prevail on the people of Ireland to take them. Itt is sayd wee are to have a very quiet easy Session, for that nothing extraordinary will be attempted, I hope tis true, for if there should bee any designe of engaging us as parties, to goe into a war, which may possibly breake out in Italy twill goe very hardly down if at all, my opinion is, itt cannot bee carried, for Ive noe reason for our engaging therein as principals, and I thinke wee shall scarcely as auxiliaryes.

623. *Alan I, Dublin, to Thomas, 7 Nov. 1724*[391]

(1248/6/84–5)

I have your two letters one dated the 24th, the other the 31th of last month; both which came to me under the same wrapper, which surprizeth me. I have at all times acted with the greatest respect toward my Lord Lieutenant and will continue to doe soe, it being my duty to him as Lord Lieutenant and what I personally owe him on many accounts: with which resolucion I hope it will not be supposed to interfere, if I continue to follow my own judgement in the matter of Woods patent; but I find the great difficultye is this, what temper is to be found in the matter. No body can be soe wild to expect that some people will put themselves in the wrong from the beginning by owning that the patent in the maner it hath been granted, ought not to have passed: nor consequently can reasonably hope for more then being delivered from the ill consequences which it is beleived will assuredly fall on us if that coyn ever shal obtain a currencye here, let the thing be done either by peoples willingly receiving them, or in any other maner. This is an end much longed for by every body: but then it seems to me as if some people thought the things dying of itself will look like a victory over the patent, and not consistent with the honour of those who were concerned in carrying it on. And if I understand Mr Woods letter to the Duke of Newcastle dated 29 Sept. 1724 right,[392] he seems to think it very hard to be soe great a sufferer as he is like to be by that which he saith was originally intended him as a mark of his Majestyes favour; this letter being transmitted to the late Lords Justices, I am apt to think speaks the sense of more people then Mr Wood: but I doe not yet see who the person will be that will think soe well of his own understanding as hope he can propose that which may be capable to remove this very great difficultye. I doe not find the least disposition in people to accept the £40000, nor that any body will venture to say such a thing may be an expedient, which (if accepted by those who appear for the patent) will be made good, if care be taken to prevail on or prevent Mr Woods bringing or sending over any of his halfpence. If anything of this sort should be proposed, I doubt we should

[391] Printed in Coxe, *Walpole*, ii, 400–2.
[392] TNA, SP 63/384/94: Wood to Newcastle, 29 Sept. 1724 (copy).

have it called undertaking for a Kingdome, which you know is the most likely method in the world to disappoint anything in a popular assembly:[393] since the merit of it will wholly redound to the honour of the proposers, and others will not readily contribute to that which may indeed be thank worthy, unlesse they can partake of the honour of having share of the thanks. I sent you this day sevennight an account of the pamphlet which was brought by my Lord Lieutenant in Councel under the consideration of the board. I did intend to have sent the book itself by Sir Gustavus Hume[394] for your perusal, with strokes pointing at many of the exceptionable passages in it; but far from all. But the Knight was sailed before I could send my letter to him, soe I am forced to doe it by post; which will be noe inconvenience to you since your privilege exempts you from paying the postage, which is indeed much more then the present is worth. I own upon reading it over more considerately and comparing it with a pamphlet supposed to be wrote by the same author some years since exaggerating the severityes this Kingdome lies under in point of trade from the Laws made in Great Britain, it is very observable that in that pamphlet he assigns the rise of them to have been much about the revolution, and I doubt intended by that means to insinuate prejudices against the revolution in the minds of the people here;[395] and for ought I know the Author retains stil some good wishes to his patron the Lord Bolingbrook and to that cause for whose service he wrote the Conduct of the Allyes:[396] It is plain that the matter of the Independencye of this Kingdome, the complaint of the Lords not having jurisdiction in matters of Appeal, and our not being bound by Statutes made in great Britain are the notions which have for several years past been propagated and avowed by a great Church man, who was lately thought fit to be taken into favor and to have distinguishing marks of being soe placed in him,[397] in the time of the Duke of G[rafton]'s administration, while I who alway opposed him in every one of those articles received usage which I cannot forget,[398] while I suffer under the effects of it. But why doe I mention my own little sufferings, when it is possible I may have strength enough to outlive the happinesse of my countrey; if this affair doe not take a more favourable turn then some people not only wish but expect. If this businesse were moved in parliament I am sure I would without reserve speak my mind without regard to popularitye and consider the service of my King and countrey only, in proposing what seems to me the only way which seems to be safe for the people and at the same time honourable for others: but least what I think right may not find the approbation of others, I am not very hardy to mention or propose it, for fear of falling under the odious name of an undertaker or having deceived people by my advice, if it should prove unsuccessful.

---

[393] For the opprobrium attached to the idea of 'undertaking' and 'undertakers' in parliament, see Hayton, *Ruling Ireland*, 115–17.

[394] MP [I].

[395] Presumably Swift's anonymously published *A Proposal for the Universal Use of Irish Manufacture …* (Dublin, 1720), though the statements mentioned by Alan are implicit rather than explicit in that pamphlet (see esp. 8–9, 12–13).

[396] Jonathan Swift, *The Conduct of the Allies, and of the Late Ministry, in Beginning and Carrying on the Present War* (1712). For the background to its publication, see J.A. Downie, *Robert Harley and the Press: Propaganda and Public Opinion in the Age of Swift and Defoe* (Cambridge, 1979), ch. 6.

[397] Archbishop King.

[398] See *Anglo-Irish Politics*, ii, 12–13.

624. *Alan I, Dublin, to Thomas, 17 Nov. 1724*[399]

(1248/6/92–5)

There are letters in this town of the 5th instant from London, which give me a good deal of surprize, for certainly mine dated either 29 or 31th October about what was done in Councel in relation to the discoverye of the Author and printer of the pamphlett intitled A Letter to the whole people of Ireland must have come to your hand time enough to have been owned in a letter of the fifth of this month; but I am yet in the dark whether that letter ever came to your hand. If it be stopped any where it is barbarous treatment: for I make no doubt that hot headed libel (for I cannot term it lesse) is handed about by Mr Wood and his freinds among the members of Parliament, and probably will reaise such resentment as may turn to the prejudice of this Kingdome, if care be not taken to have it understood that the Kingdome is in no sort of the mind of the Author, or his patron, whom I have pointed out in that letter. The Kingdome hath received and probably may receive more damage by the politicks and vainglory of those two men then it would ever have been in the power of its worst enemyes to have brought upon it without the assistance of indiscreet and seditious pamphleteers: but sure their follyes and crimes are not to be placed to the Nations account. There are now three pacquets due, and I have hopes you will by one of them put my mind at ease in this matter and be able to acknowledge the receit of the pamphlet itself with my marks on the margin of it, which I made as a guide to me in speaking in Councel against the most flagrant parts of the libel, in order to incline the board to order a prosecution.

The pamphlet went in a later maile, in a wrapper dated I think the 2 instant. I wish I could say any thing had been done here since my Lord Lieutenants landing which had quieted the minds of the people; but indeed I cannot with truth acquaint you that soe desirable an end hath been attained. It is true no compulsory methods have been taken to inforce the currencye of that coyne (for I will not with the Archbishop think the proclamation had a tendencye that way) but on the other hand no steps seem to me to have been omitted to create a willingnesse in people to consent to the receiving the summe proposed: but as far as I can make a judgement, people are at least as firmly determined as ever in that particular, and I cannot find by the discourse of the most temperate and prudent men in my sphere of conversation that anybody seems inclined to receive the reduced quantitye on any grounds whatsover; That really seems to me to be the sense of the people in general, but the grounds they goe upon have in my hearing been called nonsense; yet in our way of thinking (for we have a particular way of thinking from the rest of mankind if I understand that phrase in a late letter right) there is more sense in refusing that money for the reasons which move us, then others will allow, who no doubt have very different reasons from us on this occasion. I hear there is a paper called seasonable advice to the Grand Jurors,[400] to disswade them from finding a bill against the printer or Author of the letter, full of reflection on those of the Councel which voted for prosecuting and discovering the Author, and very liable to be called in question. But I have not yet seen it, tho I am one of the persons who are reviled

---

[399] Partly printed in Coxe, *Walpole*, ii, 402–6.

[400] *Seasonable Advice. Since a Bill is Preparing for the Grand Jury, to Find Against the Printer of the Drapier's Last Letter, There are Several Things Maturely To Be Considered by Those Gentlemen, Before Whom This Bill Is To Come, Before They Determine Upon It* [Dublin, 1724], the fourth of Swift's 'Drapier's Letters'.

in it, having heartily voted for a prosecution. You cannot imagine in what a condition this Kingdome now is; no doubt there are those who represent this affair in the strongest light they can to inflame peoples minds with an opinion of very hard treatment by this patent and the steps taken to establish it (as they think). I cannot but wish those who have it in their power to efface these impressions would think it deserved their care to do something out of hand in it; for the damage which acrews to the publick is very great while things remain in the state in which they now are; and the effects of this patents hanging over our head for about two years and an half, are throughly felt in the countrey already and will be soe in the revenue, when ever we come to meet in parliament. I doubt the demand will then be such as will not come within the compasse of the produce of the ordinary dutyes, and must be left unsupplyed, or new funds be found: now we have charged every thing that will bear it already, except one to which indeed some people insinuate this affair hath an eye: but indeed I cannot say I know one man in the Kingdome that will advise an attempt of that kind, as likely to have successe, or that will be hardy enough to propose it, whatever they may say privately in a Closett.

Our Lord Lieutenant doth not think fit or is not instructed to let anybody know what is expected to put this unhappy businesse at quiet, but seems to wait in expectation that proposals will come from the other side: but as far as I can judge, no man or number of men will venture on anything of that nature; soe that tho I think it is the inclination of everybody to come to a right understanding and agreement, yet I see no sufficient grounds to hope for success since neither side will begin; one side may, but seem not willing; the others think it not safe to doe it, but apprehend that their saying they have a readinesse to doe every reasonable thing in their power when they can doe it with honour and safety to themselves viz. when called together to advise on national affairs is all they can justifyably or in prudence doe at present; and think they ought to be beleived in their affirmation that they will meet in a disposition to act with great duty to the King and regard to the quiet and happinesse of the Countrey. As for my part I see soe many difficultyes that I have not a prospect to live soe long, till an happy end is put to them, and I see that I am not able to do any thing by my advice in this perplexing affair: and shal I think very soon retire into Surrey. My way of thinking is not such as is pleasing on your side and of consequence my advice can have little weight; and all that I am like to bring to passe is to be esteemed too stiff by some people and too condescending, or rather complying by others. Whichever of the two is my fault, ought to be imputed to want of better judgement: for I have done all in my power to discover what is the right thing to be done, and have an inflexible purpose to follow what I think to be soe. If I am soe unhappy not to be able to discover what is fit to be done, I ought to be pityed not blamed. I have thought soe much of this matter that I have really impaired my health by the uneasinesse of my mind and breach of my rest but will give over a matter in which I see my labouring is like to be successelesse; and where I reap no thanks for doing what I think right. I cannot but observe to you that the first time I heard there was such a paper printed as the seasonable advice was from my Lord Lieutenant on 15 November who told me the import of it, but I never saw it till 22 November at the Castle in the hand of Mr Tickel who read it to the Attorney General, Sollicitor[401] and me, who were talking of what had hapned the day before in the Kings Bench, when the

---

[401] Thomas Marlay, MP [I].

Court discharged the Grand Jury for not presenting that paper as seditious.[402] The maner of doing that I was told was what is contained in a paper which comes along with this, and was reduced to writing the same day the thing hapned. The town talks of that transaction variously and are far from being of one opinion about the discharging the Jury; for my part I will not presume to censure the proceedings of a Court of Justice, but will take it to be within their author[ye to doe it in the maner and on the occasion they have done it; because I am convinced that Courts have formerly exercised that power, and because I know no Law which restrains them from doing it: but then it is a power to be used with discretion and great consideration; and if what Mr Conelye told me last Sunday night be fact that 11 out of 23 were for presenting the paper, I confesse I could wish time had been given the dissenting 12 to have considered farther of the matter, and possibly one might have been convinced in two or three dayes time before their next meeting. This thought of mine I was rash enough to expresse to a certain person, who expressed himself soe warmly on the occasion that I cannot but fancy that this matter was settled and resolved upon beforehand: and if soe in taxing the discretion of the Court I fell into the absurditye of telling him that had before considered of it that the thing was misjudged. To conclude the town is in a prodigious consternation and ferment, and seem to be in the same condition as the disciples of our Saviour are mentioned to be in the 24 Chapter of St Luke verse 22.[403] I wish their surprize may be as happily removed as that of the disciples was, by seeing that thing effected by that person of whom they had almost given over all hopes of effecting the thing hoped for: I think it is usual with Physicians to change their course if upon trial they find the patient grows worse and the distemper increase upon using those methods which were at first thought the best: but my zeal for the service of my King and countrey, and the honour of my Lord Lieutenant have carryed me farther then one who had great concern for himself would have gone: Just now a very sober man of great fortune and well affected to his Majestyes person and governement expressed a good deal of surprize that no bill of Indictment had been drawn against Harding the Printer,[404] and seemed to hint if that had been done it is possible the bill might have been found which would have shewn how little influence the seasonable advice had on the minds of the Jurors; and indeed it is pretty unaccountable to me why that hath been not done in all this time, if there be sufficient for finding the bill; and this would have put the offence of printing into a Legal examination. If the receiving any of Woods coyne be finally on us I confesse noe prospect of its ever taken effect upon the terms of the Patent (<u>willingly</u>) and I hope it will not be a mark of disaffection in people to use that freedome which the Laws allow and his Majestye doth also in expresse terms. God help us, something is to be done and we find is expected, and I think everybody knows the nature of the expedient; but nobody will propose it, for reasons very obvious. I look on it as a great happinesse that I was [*not*] consulted about laying this paper before the Grand Jury, and consequently had no part in the advice given,

---

[402] Swift's *Seasonable Advice*, published in Dublin on 11 Nov. 1724, which on 21 Nov. the Dublin grand jury were exhorted to present as seditious. When they refused, Lord Chief Justice Whitshed sent them back to reconsider, and when they again refused he dismissed the jury and ordered another to be empanelled. (*Drapier's Letters*, pp. xlviii–lii; Ehrenpreis, *Swift*, iii, 279–80.)

[403] 'Astonished' on hearing the news that Christ's tomb was empty.

[404] John Harding (*d.* 1725), of Molesworth's Court, Fishamble Street, Dublin (M. Pollard, *A Dictionary of Members of the Dublin Book Trade 1550–1800* ... (2000), 274–5).

but from my being a stranger to the whole (which I hear was cheifly under the direction of the Cheif Justice and Secretary[405]) you will make your judgement in what degree of confidence I stand.

[PS] Gentlemen have expressed themselves disposed to consider of expedients to be offered them, if they might have any assurance that they should be freed from the fears of the halfpence, if what they offered should be reasonable; but nothing farther then the private opinion of a certain person (that it would be soe) could be obtained, because there was no authoritye to make such a declaration.

625. *Thomas to Alan II, 19 Nov. 1724*

(1248/6/97)

… For what hitherto appears I thinke we are like to have a short and Smooth Session, our ministers (as I am told) resolving to propose nothing butt what will goe easily, last it should prevent the kings going early abroad, your father is well, and strangely recovered.

626. *Alan I, Dublin, to Thomas, 23 Nov. 1724*[406]

(1248/6/98–9)

I am not at all surprized at your desire to be informed of every thing which passeth here in relation to Woods halfpence, considering the hopes you had given me in three several letters written soon after your return from Newmarkett that we should not be pressed in that very disagreeable affair, but left entirely to our own choice whether we would receive or refuse that coyne: I confesse I entertained hopes that in a little time all apprehensions of that money becoming current among us would have vanished, and people would have began to think of their businesse as formerly, and been free from their jealousies of this coyne obtaining a currencye in this Kingdome. This is so desirable a thing that every man who hath thought enough to conceive the prejudice which trade suffers while mens minds are in the same suspense about it as they have been for about two years and an half past, and how much the Kingdome and his Majestyes revenue suffer on that head, must earnestly wish it were settled. But alas! Brother, matters are much otherwise; and tho I cannot decline answering your expectations and letting you know the scituation we are in at present (since you desire it, and will make the best use of it for the service of the King and this unhappy countrey) yet I must take leave to protest you have imposed a very difficult task on me, and such an one as I would not undertake at the instance of any other man; for I beleive letters are sometimes opened, and am sensible that whoever writes on this subject will be found fault with by some whose resentments may not be easy to be born, what part soever he shal take in relating this affair; which will be thought favourable or unfair, as men are previously disposed, if not determined in their thoughts about the matter of Woods patent. However while I confine myself strictly to truth, as I resolve to doe (as far as my knowledge

---

[405] Thomas Clutterbuck, MP [I].
[406] Printed in Coxe, *Walpole*, ii, 406–9.

reaches) I think I shal only suffer in the opinions of others for not judging right, which I can easily bear; being for a long time accustomed to have greater and wiser men differ from me in opinion, as probably they doe and will continue to doe in this. I will not proceed to represent the circumstances in which I apprehend this City stands at this time. By a letter which the late Lords Justices received from the Duke of Newcastle dated the 3d October[407] they found that his Majestye had received repeated accounts as if Ireland were in such a condition as the quiet and peace of it was a danger (those are not the words but I take it is the sense of the letter) and they did think it was pretty strongly insinuated that they had been remisse in discouraging and preventing this evil, and in punishing persons guilty of publishing seditious libels, if not encouraging them in soe doing. This letter they answered and insisted on their having done their duty to his Majestye to the best of their power, and that the Kingdome was free from any disturbances and in perfect peace and quiet; and very well affected to his Majestyes person and governement.[408] When my Lord Lieutenant was sworn and the sword delivered to him by the Justices I did by their consent and direction of the other Justices tell his Excellencye that we did with great satisfaction deliver the sword into his hands and had great pleasure in being able with truth to assure him that the Kingdome was in perfect peace and tranquillitye: but we had acted very unfairly if we had said or insinuated it was in any measure disposed to receive Woods halfpence, or indeed any part of that coynage: for indeed we knew the contrary, and were sensible my Lord Lieutenant would be soon convinced that the aversion to that coyne was insuperable, as the Justices told the Duke of Newcastle in answer to his Graces letter of the 3d of October. The day my Lord Lieutenant landed, or very soon after, the letter to the whole people of Ireland came out, one of which I sent you with strokes under some of the exceptionable passages and seditious positions and insinuations contained in it, and must refer my self to my letter on that subject dated 31 October, which I find you had received on the 7th instant at which time the pamphlet itself had not reached your hand. The publishing this pamphlett shews that things of that nature might be printed and creep into the world without any neglect of the Governement, or encouragement given by it: for I think my Lord Carterett will not be suspected in that particular; and his Excellencye having one of them laid before him by some person, he called a Councel, and laid it before them for their consideration; if the Councel had not done what became them upon the occasion they had been highly accountable; but I confesse I think the Councel did as much as they could doe in justice or prudence; for which I refer you to my former letter. The proclamation agreed on in Councel had such an effect that Harding the Printer of that letter was apprehended and carryed before the Cheif Justice (as I hear) in order to be prosecuted for printing the letter; some time after there came out a paper called seasonable advice, one of which I send you under this cover: You will see the tendencye of it to be to disincline the grand Jury to find any bill of Indictment against Harding the printer, which I own I think to be a most imprudent and illegal practice, and punishable by Law, under the name of embracery of Jurors[409] (but perhaps I may mistake in this point of Crown Law having for some years past discontinued thinking on that part of my profession which relates to Criminal matters). The paper seems to me to goe farther and to endeavour not only to excuse but vindicate

---

[407]TNA, SP 63/384/ 96–105: Newcastle to the lords justices [I], 3 Oct. 1724.

[408]TNA, SP 63/384/112–18: lords justices to Newcastle, 17 Oct. 1724.

[409]The offence of attempting to influence a juror corruptly.

the Author of the letter for what he had said in relation to the dependency of Ireland, and to leave that as a doubtful point. I passe by that part of it which reflects most vilely on the persons who signed the order for prosecuting the writer and printer of the letter, considering that I am directly libelled by that paper.[410] These are some parts of that paper which appear to me to be highly criminal, but I doe not say or think they are all, for I doubt the tendencye of the whole is to create jealousyes between the King and his people of Ireland, and to forment divisions and misunderstandings between the people of Great Britain and us; of the consequences whereof I have fully spoken my sense in my former letters and tremble when they occur (as they frequently doe) to my thoughts.

627. Alan I, Dublin, to Thomas, Westminster, 8 Dec. 1724

(1248/6/104–5)

[*Copy of letter from Robert Hackett,*[411] *London, to [Alan I] in an unknown hand*]

Having for some time past observed with great concern the discontent, and disturbance occasiond by Woods Patent for Coyning of Halfpence, I made it my business to get acquainted with him, in order to use my endeavours to put a stop to the mischief which might happen on account of that Pattent; and have so far prevaild, as to get him to assign it to me, which I can then surrender or dispose of, as your Lordship shall direct.

I take the liberty of acquainting your Lordship with this matter, humbly entreating the favour of your Lordships advice how to behave in this juncture, believing it will be some pleasure to your Lordship to see an end put to an affaire which might be attended with very ill consequences, if there ben't already some measures taken for making that matter easy.

If your Lordship will be pleasd to favour me with a line or two directed to Young Mans Coffee house,[412] I shall Take it as a very great honour, and shall be sure to observe your Commands, and think my self very happy if my endeavours can be of any service to my Country, and in particular to your Lordship, for whom I shall always have, as I ought, the greatest Respect ...

[*in Alan's hand*]

The above is a true copy of a letter which I received on Monday last was sennight, when I also received your two letters dated 17th and 24th of November, which I would have answered sooner, if I had not thought it necessary at the same time to say something in relation to Mr Hacketts scheme. I communicated this letter to —— and afterward to my other freinds in whose prudence and freindship I could best confide: who all approved my having shewn it to —— as highly necessary, since to them as well as to me it seemed not at all improbable that he might have intimation of it from other hands, which however was

---

[410]The *Seasonable Advice* contrasted the members of the grand jury, who 'do not expect any employments in the state, to make up in their own private advantage, the destruction of their country', with those who signed the proclamation, who 'have great employments, which they have a mind to keep, or to get greater'.

[411]A wealthy attorney of Dublin and St James's, Westminster (Reg. Deeds, 20/377/10609; *The Parish of St James Westminster, Part 1: South of Piccadilly* (*Survey of London*), ed. F.W. Sheppard (vol. xxix, 1960), 120–1).

[412]Near Charing Cross (Bryant Lillywhite, *London Coffee Houses: A Reference Book of Coffee Houses in the Seventeenth and Eighteenth Centuries* (1963), 667).

not owned in any sort, but the question asked whether Hackett was sett on or employed in this matter by any private person, or otherwise. I said with truth that I knew nothing of the matter till I received the letter; which indeed I brought to him directly before I had soe read it as to consider and duly apprehend the import of it. Which seemed to me from one part of the first paragraph to import that Wood had actually assigned his patent to Hackett before the letter was wrote; but upon weighing the whole letter better I see now it is only a thing in agitation; and upon that foot I shal speak my sense of it in a letter which I intend to write to you of equal date herewith.

628. *Alan I, Dublin, to Thomas, 8 Dec. 1724*

(1248/6/102–3)

By the same pacquet you will have another letter of equal date with this, which brings you only the copy of a letter from Mr Hackett dated 24 Nov. with some short hints what I did on receiving it, to which I refer. But before I proceed to speak my mind more fully on that subject I will resume our correspondence where it broke off. I have formerly owned your several letters of the 7th 12th those of 17th and 24th I have not; my last to you being of the 23th of the last month. In it I told you how far matters had gone in relation to the discharging the Grand Jury on the 21th, and have to add that a thing pretty new startled people, and much was talked of the maner of doing it; not at all to the advantage of the Court: but I will not take on me to speak to that, not being certain I can inform you right therein; but by discourse which I had with some in Court at that time, I fear it was done with unnecessary warmth. This is a subject on which I resolve not to dwell considering how very much people differs in their thoughts about it: some justifye, nay seem to applaud it as an act of necessitye and a great indication of the courage and zeal of ——[413] while others speak altogether as ill of him as is possible for what hath been done: insomuch that I hear there is a bitter paper of half a sheet printed intitled a Letter to the right Honble [...[414]]. If I can get one before I seal this I will send it over to you. It is talked about town as if it were the language of those who are supposed to know, that it was the Act of the Court wholly, without any previous direction or signification of any bodyes desiring such a thing: this may be, but I doubt whether they who report this have authoritye for doing soe. But the consequence of impanelling a new Jury hath been a presentment indeed, but how agreeable it will be I cannot form a judgement, but leave it to you to judge for your self on reading it, which I send inclosed.[415] In short I doe not see that warm measures would have taken place if they had been thought advisable, not that I think those already taken ought to be called such by me: but I confesse if I had been previously consulted whether it would be for the Kings service to discharge the grand Jury in the maner and when they were discharged

[413] Chief Justice Whitshed.

[414] Space in letter, corresponding to a caesura in the title of the original, a single-sheet publication entitled *A Letter from a Friend to the Right Honourable* — — — (Dublin, 1724).

[415] SHC, 1248/6/96: a presentment of the grand jury of Dublin, 28 Nov. 1724, against those 'enemies to the people of Ireland' who are attempting to impose Wood's halfpence in defiance of the king's express intentions that accepting the coin should be voluntary; also acknowledging the services of 'patriots' who have detected 'fraudulent impositions'.

I think I should have given them time to consider better of the matters before them; but I would not censure the proceedings of the Court, upon which it may be supposed the thing came suddenly. To you I am free to give my sense of the matter, but will decline doing it here, because I know whatever my opinion shal be I shal disoblige abundance of folks, the great ones one way, the generalitye of the Kingdome the other. Thus far I went before I went abroad, and have since had the printed paper brought me, which I send to you not to spread the scandal but to shew you how inveterately the writer speaks of the Cheif Justice therefore I enjoin you to burn it as soon as you have read it over. Now as to Mr Hacketts letter; either he acts by direction or on his own head; if it be by direction, the intention then may be to try whether by this roundabout way I can be brought to advise or propose terms to accommodate matters; which the whole Councel thought to be a thing of such a nature that they dared not to intermeddle soe far in, as to give any advice; for I confesse I cannot understand the letters to the late Justices from the Duke of Newcastle one dated in August, the other in October last,[416] in any other sense, then in case the Kingdome should not be willing to receive the reduced quantitye of Woods coinage, upon what terms they would be content to gett wholly rid of them. This they thought to be a matter of such a nature as made it not advisable for them in any kind to intermeddle; and I confesse I was of that opinion; Would it not then be a most unaccountable act in me to give that advice upon Mr Hacketts letter which I had excused myself from giving when called upon to give it in a maner which required my best advice, if I had any to give or offer. But then take this to be the private affair of Mr Hackett (as perhaps it may). Doth not he desire my thoughts advice and directions how and on what terms to treat in which I am sure I am not in any wise qualifyed to give him advice; for he would reasonably think if I should think such terms might be reasonable, I had given him hopes that he should not suffer by his undertaking; or at least that I would use my endeavours and interest that he should not be a sufferer by going into a matter with a good intent and by my advice and encouragement. Nay his letter carries the thing farther, by saying the patent can be surrendred etc as I shal direct. Soe that it will look like a treaty carryed on by Mr Hackett as my plenipotentiary; and the event may probably be this; The Chancellor hath been one of the great opposers of this favourite scheme, and deserves to be mortifyed for the opposition he hath given. He or Hackett hath come to terms with Wood, let them make them good if they can, but we will not only not give them our assistance, but on the contrary will give him all the opposition we can, as he hath done to the currency of Woods coyne. This would be a sharp revenge, and be easily attained by some men with the assistance of those who are and have been all along of opinion that no compensation was to be made the patentee for the losse of his intended profit, which I take to be the sense of very many sober men, tho (since the madnesse of our pamphleteers) more seem to think terms are now to be gone into then formerly did. In few words Brother I think you may safely send to Mr Hackett and acquaint him that I thought it more reasonable to send you a copy of his letter, that he may explain to you whether he acts on his own head or not, and how far he hath proceeded with Wood; but yet in such a maner that you may not give him hopes of doing any thing in the matter any way inconsistent with the advice which you have all along given me in this matter.

---

[416]TNA, SP 63/384/112–18: lords justices to Newcastle, 17 Oct. 1724. Their letter of 20 Aug. to Newcastle does not survive in the State Papers, but is referred to in SP 63/384/56: Newcastle to lords justices, 8 Sept. 1724.

I once was of opinion not to take any notice of having ever received his letter, but resolved the contrary for reasons which seem to me to carry weight: The short is, that I apprehend this letter contrived to circumvent me into making a proposal, or saying what terms Ireland might in reason insist upon: and I thank God I have lived long enough not to be caught in such a trap, or to bring my [*sic*] under those difficultyes which I should lay myself under by advising, proposing etc. It was my forgetfulnesse not to insert in my last letter such an account as I had of the proceedings in the Kings Bench on the last day of the former Grand Juryes meeting and being discharged which I now send as they were taken by one in Court under a young Ladyes Cover.

629. Alan I, Dublin, to Thomas, 12 Dec. 1724

(1248/6/106–7)

This letter will come safe to your hand, since a man of Lord Forbes honour hath assured me he will deliver it. He also carryes a little pamphlet on the subject of the halfpence, which was the first that was wrote against that coyne that treated the subject seriously and without indecent reflections, and if it were not inscribed to me in a more complemental maner then I deserve I should be inclined to think that as it was the first serious paper wrote upon the subject, it exceeded the rest as much in weight as it preceded them in time.[417] It is from this paper that the Author of the Defence of the people of Ireland hath borrowed his notions,[418] and you may perceive he follows him almost in every instance; but I confesse there are some few material remarks and historical accounts in the later which are not to be found in the former. Sure you never received that Defence etc which I sent you under a cover (for so I did soon after it was publick) because I think you would have mentioned it as coming from me and not that you had read it by the lone of a Noble Lord. It is a poor thing to take out such a paper from a letter. Doe not omit letting me know when you received my letter in relation to Mr H[*ackett'*]s proposal; and let me know whether your neice or my sister sent you anything (which came to them by the same maile) together with your advice; for I never was more in need of it then at this instant having been told in expresse terms very lately that the advice of the Kings servants is expected and insisted upon, since there seems to be no prospects of the Councels giving any in this very difficult affair; and that possibly the ministry on the other side may tell [the king] that since his present servants will not advise him, it will be reasonable to employ such as will. And I was desired to consider the thing for a week or ten dayes, and then let my answer be known. Depend upon it I will act consistently with my duty to the King and my Countrey, and with regard to my own conscience and honour, which will determine me to act in no sort contrary to what have been my declared sentiments, and stil are the true sense of my soul. I say this to put your mind at peace that I will not give you reason to blush for or to reproach me. We are here in a terrible hurricane by my Lord Lieutenants looking into the money matters at the Custom house and Treasury; and I hear all hands are at work to borrow money to powre into the

---

[417] David Bindon, *Some Reasons Shewing the Necessity the People of Ireland are under, For Continuing to Refuse Mr. Wood's Coinage* (Dublin, 1724).

[418] *A Defence of the Conduct of the People of Ireland in Their Unanimous Refusal of Mr. Wood's Copper-Money…* (Dublin, 1724).

Treasury (the Army and some other branches of the establishment being vastly in arrear some say near 20 months without any visible reason, except some Kings letter and money given by the money bill and not provided for in the Aids). I hear Mr C[419] and Mr P[*ratt*][420] have their Agents very active to take up enough to stop the present gap: for this unexpected looking into the management was suddain as a thunder Clap on those who were not used in a late Governement to have their actions looked into; but every thing was taken on trust to be as they represented it. I must also tell you that I think the Castle is as desirous to have the affair of the half pence over as the Countrey is; the later neither doth nor I think need not aim at more then securitye from the evil; the former is I think under obligations to doe every thing which can be done to bring those who have taken very large steps in this matter off with honour: But how both can be compassed I confesse I am not sagacious enough to discern: Happy that man who could find out since a temper in the matter that might be proposed by an honest and <u>prudent</u> man.

I thank you for the Saffron which you gott for me and was brought by my Lord Cheif Justice Wyndham to whom I shewed all the respect that is due to his station person and character, and to so near a relation of my sister Courthopes[421]... I intreat you to present my services in a particular maner to Lord Godolphin, and the Duke of Somersett, and to my worthy freind the Master of the Rolls.[422]

630. *Thomas to Alan I, 15 Dec. 1724*

(1248/6/108–9)

Last week in a Committee of wayes and means, Mr Scroope moved a continuation of the maullt duty upon England leaving out Scotland, for that hitherto they had never payd to itt, under pretence of inabillity, therefore Hee should move something as an equivalent, which hee hoped might bee had without any additional charge for collecting, and that the house might bee apprized of what hee intended, mentioned an additional duty of six pence per Barrell on beer and ale, the which hee hoped the Committee would bee of opinion to augment by taking of the Bounty mony uppon corne exported, both which were oppos'd by the Scots, butt especially the latter.[423] This bounty mony is sweld from between four and five hundred, to very near two thousand pounds a year, and growing uppon us, in debating I tooke notice that an argument formerly made use of, that the reason why a mault duty ought nott to bee leavyd in Scotland, was that they had scarcely sufficient corne to serve their necessityes, which surely would nott now bee insisted on,

[419] Presumably Speaker Conolly.

[420] John Pratt, MP [I], deputy vice-treasurer.

[421] Thomas Wyndham (1681–1745), of Lincoln's Inn, appointed lord chief justice of common pleas [I] on 9 Dec. 1724 (*DIB*, ix, 1065–7). The family relationship between the Wyndhams and Courthopes seems to have been a distant one.

[422] Baron Berkeley of Stratton.

[423] John Scrope, MP [GB] Ripon, senior sec. to the treasury [GB], formerly a baron of the Scottish exchequer and an unofficial adviser to Robert Harley on Scottish affairs, 1710–14, who retained his influence after 1714 and was particularly close to Robert Walpole (P.W.J. Riley, *The English Ministers and Scotland, 1707–1727* (1964), 163–6, 280–2, 294). The nature and import of his intervention, on 7 Dec. 1724, is confirmed in *Knatchbull Diary*, 33.

since they exported soe great a quantity as that the bounty (being half a crowne a quarter) amounted to the summe before mentioned; Mr Dan Campbell,[424] turning his face from the chair, and looking directly on mee, sayd the encrease of the bounty was occasioned by the vast quantityes run in a clandestine manner from a country whoe would submitt to noe lawes, (hinting I suppose Woods coine) twas incumbent on mee to answer him, and indeed the Committee expected it.

I tooke notice that in a former session when upon occasion of a motion against allowing the Printing Irish linnen[425] I had sayd that gentlemen might fancy what they pleasd, butt that if the exception proposd should bee agreed to, there would nott bee a yard the lesse printed on that account for that the S[*cottish*] merchants would indeed buy itt att a low price in Ireland, and bring itt into England as the growth and manufactory of Scotland, to which hee might please to remember a name sake of his (Sir Ja. Campbell[426]) gave this answer, that if any Scots merchant should endeavour the bringing in butt of one single peice, the old women with their distress would beat out his brains, I wonderd therfore what was become of those old women when to the prejudice of Scotland such quantityes of corne was run in thither, unlesse they were employd in smugling Tobacco; butt that in truth hee had pitch upon a very ill time for that the westerne members[427] more especially the merchants knew that great quantityes of corne was then exported to the south parts of Ireland, nay and to Dublin, for which bounty mony was allowd in England, however I made noe doubt butt that whenever corne should bee very cheape in Ireland (where a bounty uppon exportation could never be obtaind) the Scots merchants would make their advantage by buying at low rates in Ireland, receiving bounty in Scotland, that therfore taking of the bounty would prevent what that gent complaind of, this occasioned a good deale of laughter, to which hee did nott thinke fitt to reply, nor did any of his countrymen. Mr Hungerford[428] then rose and sayd, that hee could nott butt make an observation on what had passt between the two gentlemen that spoake last, to witt that one of them was much a better advocate for Ireland, by setting this and other matters in their true lights, then the other for Scotland whoe seldom cleard up matters soe well; after a very long debate the Committee devided Yeas 136 Noes 91 Six of the latter English.[429] Itt is vissible to every body that Ireland gains ground in our house, to which Woods has a good deale contributed, for if (as some gentlemen say they will) a complaint bee brought in to the house, of the quantityes of halfe pence disperst here by his emissaryes, and those as a member assurd mee bought att 50 per Cent discount, hee will I beleive run the gauntlett; I gott the Poem of Prometheus from

[424]Daniel Campbell (1672–1753), of Shawfield, Lanarks., MP [GB] Glasgow Burghs.

[425]In the 1714 session, during the proceedings on the bill to amend the soap and paper duty act, in relation to the duty on printed linens, ordered on 1 May; or the bill to relieve importers of gold and silver thread and other fabrics, to which on 1 June 1714 was added a clause for the better securing the duties on printed stuffs; or the report of the committee of ways and means on 22 June, relating to the imposition of duties on imported linens (*CJ*, xv, 602, 655, 694).

[426]Sir James Campbell (c. 1666–1752), of Ardkinglas, Argylls., MP [GB] 1707–41.

[427]MPs from the English west country.

[428]John Hungerford (c. 1658–1729), of Lincoln's Inn, MP [GB] Scarborough.

[429]Given as 136–41 in *Knatchbull Diary*, 34, and as 138–41 by Dr William Stratford in HMC, *Portland MSS*, vii, 392. Knatchbull notes that about ten English MPs voted with the Scots, but only names four: John Barnard, William Clayton (one of two namesakes in the House), Velters Cornewall and Mr Plumer (either Richard or Walter). Stratford identified Barnard, Gilfrid Lawson, a Plumer, and George Wade, along with two others, unnamed. According to Knatchbull, this division occurred during a second debate in the committee, on 9 Dec. 1724.

Jemmy in C.[430] fifty coppyes of which att least have been taken, one reading whilst others writt in the Speakers chamber, tis what pleases, and has made way for what is more sollid, for the defence of the conduct is printed here, and bought by every body. Tis whisperd (butt whither true I cannott say) that some of our great men declare that instructions have been exceeded, which tis sayd tooke its rise from the account of discharging the G[rand] jury. Things hitherto have gone on very quietly in our house and will I hope continue doing soe, wee shall adjourne to the 11th of January. I have none from you, since my last to you.

631. *Thomas to Alan I, Dublin, 22 Dec. 1724*

(1248/6/115–18)

Your two letters of the 8th and that of the 12th instant came last night, the latter from the house box,[431] being post mark't, the other, by the usuall letter carrier. The long letter, (being the last wrote of the two former) will make this much shorter then otherwise itt would have been, for upon reading that with the coppy of Mr H[ackett's] (which I did first) every thing occurrd to mee, which the other expresses to bee your apprehensions, att least what you thought might possibly bee your case, if you should have entred into, or indeed answered the letter, which probably, (to say the least of itt) was wrote by concert, and direction of better heads then the writer, to mee itt appears very artfull, and I cant avoid thinking layd as a trap for you, which I am the more confirmd in, as I beleive you will bee, when I acquaint you that three or four dayes since I was askt whither I knew any thing of a letter wrote by a freind of mine to one here, hinting as if itt were of some consequence in relation to Woods coine, upon my saying I knew nothing of itt, the person replyd, then itt may bee a groundlesse story; from hence I thinke I may well infer, that the letter wrote to you, was knowne to more then the writer, and an answer expected. As I sayd before I need onely tell you in short, that I agree with you in every perticular of your long letter, except one, to witt that you thinke I may safely send for the writer, and enquire whither hee acts upon his own head, and how far hee hath proceeded with Wood, which I thinke by noe means advisable, for taking this (as I am sure I doe) to bee a baite layd for you, may nott some hereafter alleadge that you were treating, and as a proofe of itt, that I had conversation with H[ackett] about itt, and would nott this bear being calld artifice and management though you should never answer his letter, these are my thoughts, and therefore without your further direction ile make noe such step, and should rather thinke your owning to him the receipt of his letter, advisable, letting him know why you thinke advising nott proper.

Somuch for this perticular. You know I converse with noe great men (taking them for those generally meant by the words) butt others with whom I have talkt, looke upon discharging the G[rand] jury in the manner twas done, very extraordinary, and if creditt may bee given to common report, people on your side are acquitting themselves from

[430] Jonathan Swift, *Prometheus: A Poem* (Dublin, 1724): *The Poems of Jonathan Swift*, ed. Harold Williams (2nd edn, 3 vols, Oxford, 1958), i, 342–7. This was circulating widely in England (HMC, *Portland MSS*, vii, 393). 'Jemmy' is probably James Barry, MP [I].

[431] Letters sent to MPs at Westminster were kept in 'boxes at the lobby door' (*HC 1690–1715*, ii, 367).

having any hand in advising, nay, of somuch as knowing any thing of the matter, till after twas over. This morning two papers were sent mee by a freind of ours, the notes of what passed in Court uppon discharging the first jury, and the presentment made by the second. I had heard of them before, from people whoe condemne the one as rash and unwarrantable and applaude the other as cautious, modest and strong; I cannott omitt repeating what I formerly sayd, that in my opinion wee gain ground greatly. I have likewise the letter to Lord —[432] which I assure you I will nott shew, butt you may bee very sure twill come to other hands whoe will, for people of this country grow very inquisitive after Irish affairs.

I thinke you did right in shewing H[ackett's] letter to —— and should tell him, or shew him, what you write in answer, if you determine doing soe, as I thinke you will. Surely there can bee noe doubt with what intention the two letters wrote to the justices were sent, tis butt too plaine to admitt of dispute. Uppon the same foundation in part is H[ackett's] letter grounded, for the better attaining which, you are to bee circumvented, and afterwards exposd; for poore Wood and his accomplices are nott free from apprehensions of loosing the quarry by that affair being taken up here, which they may hope any comprimize would prevent; butt surely they are strangers to the present circumstances of Ireland, or a letter which was shewd mee this morning must bee ill grounded, if they can entertaine the least hopes of receiving any thing from that country. I cannott say whoe the letter was wrote by, for the name was turned downe, butt tis wrote to a man of good weight; itt sayes that both civill and military lists are prodigiously in arrears, and that the military contingencyes and Concordatum mony have swelld to a vast summe beyond the usuall allowances uppon those heads, where then will mony bee found for poore Wood, or how will a house of Commons bee prevaild on to thinke of itt. I am of opinion theyle fare well, if they gett of without a scratcht face.

I have nott yett reade the pamphlet inscribed to you,[433] butt have heard from those whoe have, that tis very well wrote, and agreed to bee the foundation on which the author of the conduct[434] built, I hear there is a suppliment to that calld further reasons etc butt have nott seen itt, or any body that has.[435] I am now drawing towards a conclusion, for I know nothing more to bee sayd by mee then in answer to what you say is demanded and insisted on, That since the Privy Councill will nott advise in the difficult conjuncture, those in the Kings service ought to assist with their best advice. In the time of the popish plott Mr Mallet whoe had alwayes been a warme man against the Court measures in favour of the Duke of Yorke and Popery[436] was applyd to by some (till then Courtiers) pressing him to exert in that time of imminent danger, to whom he gave this answer, you have knockt out the head of the Barrell, and now expect my endeavouring to stop itt by clapping in my thumb. However lett this passe, your advice is expected, give itt, and I am very sure youl doe itt very honestly, and as well as you can, better then I am capable of advising, butt were I in a station where I was to give itt, as I know you are, ile tell you what I should say.

[432] The Drapier's *Letter to the Right Honourable Lord Viscount Molesworth*, dated 14 Dec. 1724 (*Drapier's Letters*, 96–118).

[433] D[avid] B[indon], *Some Reasons Shewing the Necessity the People of Ireland are under, for Continuing to Refuse Mr. Wood's Coinage* (Dublin, 1724), was dedicated to Lord Midleton.

[434] *A Defence of the Conduct of the People of Ireland in Their Unanimous Refusal of Mr. Wood's Copper-Money …* (Dublin, 1724).

[435] Not recorded in English Short Title Catalogue: https://est.bl.uk.

[436] Michael Malet (c. 1632–aft. 1683), of Poyntington, Somerset, MP [E] 1660–78.

The Lords Commons Government and Councill etc have sayd there neither is or ever was a want of Woods Coine, against whose opinion and the many representations, hee, Browne and Coleby have obtaind creditt,[437] butt I was never convinct, I remaine still of my former opinion, and cannott thinke of any other expedient then putting an end to the pattent, as what alone will satisfie the nation, and cause the ferment to subside, which may bee done by directions against receiving them in the receipt of any part of the Revenue, and this I thinke the more necessary because tis very plaine Woods proposd their currency from their being receivd there, for what other veiwe could he have in that false suggestion of the Commissioners having issued orders against receiving them, then that by obtaining an order to them to revoke such their directions (if any they had given) to the end that lesse discerning people might apprehend this order to bee meant as obligatory on them to receive. Yes butt how will this looke, or how shall those whoe have gone the lenghts that some have done come of with honour; I know nott how to reconcile contradictions, I cannott stop the head of the barrel with my little thumb, if I am required to say my thoughts, and can comprehend noe other way then this, this must bee my advice, for I am of opinion an attempt for an equivalent will prove att least as unsuccessfull as others have hitherto done, and if soe, the longer things remaine in the uncertainty they now are, the more difficult will the applying remedyes bee found, this I say with respect to the Kings service in the first place, and the countryes in the next.

If my advice bee nott approvd of, I shall have the comfort of having given itt faithfully, when I can truly say Liberavi animam meam.[438]

This is on supposition that noe other way is proposed equally secure against the paying of this coine.

632. St John III, Midleton, to Alan I, Dublin, 26 Dec. 1724

(1248/6/119–20)

I came hither last night from Bennets bridge,[439] where I staid with Lord Meath Fox=hunting 10 days, and tho the weather was extremely bad, (I think worse then I ever knew it), we had very good Sport and kill'd 2 Brace of Foxes.

While I was there Jeremy Coughlane[440] deliver'd me a message from you, which I own gave me a good deal of concern, viz, That you were surpriz'd I did not call upon you before I went out of town, and tell you what past between ——[441] and me the morning I did so. You may remember I was appointed to be with him at 11, and accordingly I went precisely

---

[437] For John Browne see above, p. 120. Coleby was formerly deputy chamberlain of the exchequer in Dublin, but had been tried for embezzlement in Dublin in 1706, having stolen £1,200 from the Irish treasury and fled to England, where he was apprehended (HMC, *Portland MSS*, v, 305; *Drapier's Letters*, 37, 83, 226).

[438] 'I have freed my soul', a quotation from St Bernard of Clairvaux, *Epistles*, 371 (*The Oxford Dictionary of Quotations*, ed. Elizabeth Knowles (5th edn., Oxford, 1999), 69).

[439] Bennettsbridge, Co. Kilkenny.

[440] Jeremy Coughlan (*d.* 1735) of Lismore, Co. Waterford, an attorney and in that capacity one of Lord Burlington's agents (H.F. Morris, 'The "Principal Inhabitants" of County Waterford in 1746' in *Waterford: History and Society*, ed. William Nolan and T.P. Power (Dublin, 1992), 324–5; Toby Barnard, *A New Anatomy of Ireland: The Irish Protestants, 1649–1770* (New Haven, CT, 2003), 222–3).

[441] Lord Carteret.

to the time, but was not admitted till past 12, he having sat up later then ordinary the night before. He kept me with him about an hour, and the minute I left him I drove directly to your house, but found both you and Lady Midleton were gone abroad; upon which I made all the hast I possibly could back to the place from whence I came, in hopes of overtaking you there before you went in, but was told, you were sent for in some time before I came, so that twas not possible for me to communicate what past, without troubling you with a message, which you know would have been very improper at that time and place, and after your Conference with him would have been of little avail. Besides I take it for granted it was soon imparted to you, and for that, as well as other reasons, do not trouble you with it now.

I hope this plain short Account will satisfye you I was not guilty of any omission, at least, if I were so, that it was hardly in my power to avoid it, without being guilty of very ill manners to Lord Meath, by making him wait a day longer in town for me, after having kept him there the day before upon the same Errand.

I have a good many of your freinds with me, who are now drinking your health, and join with me in wishing you many happy new years.

633. *Alan I, Dublin, to Thomas, Westminster, 9 Jan. 1724/5*

(1248/6/121–2)

Yesterday my Lord Lieutenant read to me a letter he had received lately from my Lord Chancellor of England,[442] in which there is an expression to the purpose following: that things have been so managed in London that there is a great and general cry against the Masters in Chancerye, as there is here against Woods halfpence; but there is another part which occasioned the shewing it to me, viz. that my Lord Chancellors freinds are as warm as any people, and this I understand particularly to mean you. His Lordship adds that he had been freindly to me and thinks he had done me some service: which I take true thus far, (when he hath seen decrees made by me run in upon meerly upon that account) that he hath not gone with the current but supported them as far as his judgement lead him: and I own I think in such circumstances going soe far, is not only an act of justice but a testimony of freindship; for it is not alway that men in emploiment will oppose what is carryed on by the great ones, even tho they doe the right thing in doing soe. I promised my Lord I would write to my Lord Chancellor by this post, which I have done and told him that I understood by his letter that he thought, you (under the general term of my freinds) had appeared against him in a matter which related to him, and that as I had obligations of gratitude to him I should be glad every freind of mine would join with me in making the best returns. That I would write to you and put you in mind of the obligations I lay under to his Lordship, which I was sensible would incline you to act toward him with a due consideration what you as my brother and freind ought to doe with respect to those relations between us, and the acts of freindship which he had shewn me. I added that I was concerned at the difference between his Lordship, and an intimate freind of yours (the

[442]Thomas Parker, earl of Macclesfield, who surrendered his seals on 4 Jan. after a committee of the privy council had found evidence of malversation in the chancery masters' office. He was subsequently impeached. (*Oxf. DNB.*)

Master of the Rolls[443]). But as I know you too well to expect you would be induced by any thing I can say to act contrary to your judgement in a national affair (as the dispute about the Masters in Chancery seems now to be) I did not either in my letter to the Chancellor or discourse with my Lord Lieutenant say any thing to create unreasonable expectations: but this I cannot but recommend to you, not to let your zeal in this publick affair carry you to any warmth of expression or lengths which may give ground to my enemyes to say that you appeared in a particular maner opposite to my Lord Chancellor who had obliged your brother: Methinks too it may deserve consideracion whether prudence will not incline you to leave the person who is most certainly at the bottom of this removal (as well as of others intended) to make it his own act and not to strengthen his hands by the accession of its being done with the approbacion of etc ———. The letter to Lord Lieutenant in plain terms saith he[444] shal resign; now tho it may be in the power of a particular person (at present) to make him, and another in a great military post resign[445] (as he lately did one in a great Civil Station)[446] yet methinks I could wish it should be done meerly upon the irresistible prevalence of ——— without any concurring approbation of others which may be a good skreen upon occasion. And truly I am the more warm in this particular from an opinion I have that in an instance which immediately relates to Ireland some people will not fail to make use of their power in the utmost extent, if they can gett it. I have been of late perswaded that a method would be taken in England to ease this Kingdome of Woods coyne and the ministry of the clamor (as it is called by them) against the patent.[447] But I am not so sanguine, now, for if private letters have more truth in them then the London journal[448] or Goodwins letter,[449] Wood is not to be taken care of in England, nor the patent to be given up in that maner; and I own firm in my opinion that if nothing but a compensation made to Wood for his interest in his patent from Ireland will doe; they who are sanguine enough to beleive that will be compassed reckon without their [?—]: yet particular letters say it is expected something of this sort will be insisted on to be done for Woods. Perhaps the great ones among you may in time find that to be an impracticable scheme, and may be soon of other sentiments then to think it advisable to leave this patent in being when the parliament here meets next. If they doe, I own I think the Session will be very warm tho our meeting should be in the coldest month in the year. When I can doe it by a safe hand I [will] write more plainly and fully, and send you some papers which

---

[443]Sir Joseph Jekyll (1662–1738), of Westminster, MP [GB] Reigate.

[444]Macclesfield.

[445]William, Earl Cadogan. Swift informed a correspondent on 18 Jan. that 'They say Cadogan is to lose some of his employments' (*Swift Corr.*, ii, 543). See also HMC, *Portland MSS*, vii, 394. He was replaced as master-gen. of the ordnance [GB] by the duke of Argyll.

[446]Presumably a reference to the removal of Carteret as secretary of state the previous year.

[447]Carteret reported to Newcastle that same day that he had reassured people it was never the king's intention to enforce acceptance of the halfpence (TNA, SP 63 385/9–11: Carteret to Newcastle, 9 Jan. 1724/5).

[448]The *London Journal*, 2 Jan. 1724/5 reported: ''Tis said the affair of Mr Wood's patent … is as good as accommodated to the satisfaction of all parties; a stop being already put to the coinage, and Mr Wood order'd to give in an account of his expenses, etc.'.

[449]Robert, 1st Viscount Molesworth mentioned 'Goodwin's newsletter' in his correspondence in 1706 (HMC, *Var. Coll.*, viii, 234). He was a regular customer of the bookseller Timothy Goodwin, whose premises were in Fleet Street (for whom see below, p. 293).

you have not yet seen, worth your perusal. Hath Lord Forbes delivered you Mr Bindons paper.[450]

634. *Thomas to Alan I, Dublin, 16 Jan. 1724[/5][451]*

(1248/6/123–4)

The person whoe read the letter to you, spoake to mee uppon the same subject, and from the same person; without either of which I resolvd to act as becomes an honest man, as well as a prudent one, for nothing is prudent which is dishonest. You certainly judge right in thinking that being made the catts foote is in the wishes, and will bee endeavourd by some gentlemen, butt they will find themselves mistaken, the subject matter on which I am writing is of too much import for (even the [?screenes[452]]) to lett drop; tis grown too publique, and understood too well to bee palliated, they must therefore, (how unwillingly soever) apply a remedy, and to them, if none bee wiser then my selfe, the honour shall bee due, with them wee may, and shall (if they act fairly) concur, without putting our selves in the front of the battle nott out of servile considerations, butt to shew wee know how to act with more discretion then perhaps some people wish us masters of; rest satisfyed I concur with your notions, and will act accordingly.

I shall bee glad of hearing from you, when you have an oportunity of writing by a safe hand (the post I doe nott take to bee such) nott butt that I am perswaded I understand every perticular which you hint att; surely some people might from what is passt, reasonably lay aside all thoughts of a compensation to Mr Wood from Ireland, unlesse they argue as the gentleman of both our acquaintance did, in professing to putt the question to every fine woman he knew, for if shee refuse sayd hee, I am butt where I was, noe other motive can lead them into an attempt which common sence must tell them will prove fruitlesse, I thinke they are trying the depth of the ford, and will when they find themselves to the saddle skirts,[453] unwillingly turne the horses head. Lord [?F] left the paper with Mrs C[*ourthope*] which I have, and this day (in the house) the second letter to Lord C[*hief*] J[*ustice*] W[*yndham?*] was given mee; yesterday a parcell of the pamphlets (inscribed to you) were sent mee to bee dispersed among our freinds, this as well as the defence (which I formerly mentioned to have been soe) is reprinted here, and I doe assure you both the one and the other are approved; as far as I am capable of judging the pitt that was dug for Ireland will prove a receptacle for other people and that [?Bishop] Taylors motto[454] will prove applicable to that poor country. This alsoe for good.

---

[450]David Bindon MP [I] (see above, p. 148).

[451]Letter endorsed by Alan I: 'Tho Brodrick … will act the honourable part in Lord Macclesfeild affair by doing right to the countrey and not becoming any bodyes tool to do him ill offices'.

[452]Originally Robert Walpole had been nicknamed 'the screen' or 'screen-master general' for his role in sheltering ministers and courtiers from exposure for corruption in the South Sea scandal.

[453]Saddle-skirt: a flap on either side of the saddle seat which covers the stirrup-bars (*OED*).

[454]Jeremy Taylor, *XXV Sermons Preached at Golden-Grove* … (1653), 251: 'revenge … is like a rolling stone, which when a man hath forced up a hill, will return upon him with a greater violence, and break those bones whose sinews gave it motion'.

635. *Thomas to Alan I, Dublin, 16 Jan. 1724[/5]*

(1248/6/125–6)

Having wrote to you by last post, I did nott thinke of doing itt soe soone againe, were itt nott that a report spread about two months since, is revivd againe, I have nott heard itt from any body whoe must know, butt att the same time my intelligencer is one whoe I am perswaded hears and knowes most domestick things intended.

He sayes Lord C[*arteret*] is very soone to bee sent for, in order to goe embassador into France, that the D[*uke*] of Newcastle is to succeed him, and to bee succeeded by H[*oratio*] W[*alpole*].[455] This latter part has been often mentioned, and indeed I beleive for some time passt resolvd. Hee sayes likewise you are to bee removd, butt could nott, or would nott name a successor, butt from another hand I hear whoe has been in their thoughts, if I guesse right I fancy they must find out another, for if I can judge of the man, hee will desire to bee excused. You are nott from my information to conclude the thing certaine, all I can say is that I beleive itt, If itt bee soe youl retire with as much honour as ever man did.

636. *Thomas to Alan I, Dublin, 21 Jan. 1724[/5]*[456]

(1248/6/129–30)

You are entirely mistaken in the subject of your last letter, which I answered Saturday night, those whoe you apprehended would bee the promoters and drivers on of a certaine affair (att least underhand) are working like soe many horses to prevent any enquiry into the matter, butt neither their skill nor power will bee able to obstruct itt.

637. *Thomas to Alan I, 26 Jan. 1724[/5]*

(1248/6/131–2)

If you had been in the house last Saturday you would have been throughly convinc't how rightly I judged, what my last letter told you as my thoughts. I had noe share in the debate butt seconding,[457] which I barely did, without expatiating, itt lasted till halfe an hour past six, in which time more severe and bitter things were sayd then ever I heard within our walls, the consequence of which will bee (I am morally certaine) that all the mony, or att least very near all, belonging to the suitors, in the masters hands, will before this day fortnight (to which time the debate is adjourned) bee either payd into the Banke, or well

[455] The same misleading story had come to the attention of a London correspondent of Archbishop King (TCD, MS 1995–2008/2121: Francis Annesley to King, 26 Jan. 1724/5).

[456] Letter endorsed by Alan I: 'Tho: Brodrick …. that endeavours are used to prevent any enquiry in the matter of the Masters in Chancerye'.

[457] On 23 Jan. 1725, following a petition from the earl of Oxford and Lord Morpeth, trustees for managing the estate of the dowager duchess of Montagu, alleging corruption against one of the masters in chancery, a motion was made that the masters in chancery lay before the House the relevant documentation, which Brodrick seconded but which was frustrated by a counter-motion to adjourn the debate until 9 Feb. (*CJ*, xx, 379–80; *Knatchbull Diary*, 36–7).

secured, for in order to adjourning itt to that day, itt was almost sayd in plaine termes, itt would bee soe, without which, the main question would have gone, thus the most desirable part will bee attaind, nott butt that very probably some severe question may bee movd (and for which there is butt too apparent ground), I beleive I shall bee a hearer, as I was the last day.

The cause of putting of the report of the Stafford election, was an information given the house of a great summe given by the Pet[itione]r to the sitting member,[458] to make a faint defence, people were very warme, and will I beleive bee soe againe, what the consequence may bee I know nott, butt I thinke twill have some.

638. *Thomas to Alan I, Dublin, 28 Jan. 1724[/5]*[459]

(1248/6/135–6)

I wrote to you a post or two agoe (I know nott which) a very short letter, as this will bee, in relation to a perticular freind of yours, there is att this time a difference of opinion uppon that subject, att least in part, which you will I beleive understand mee in, which side shall prevaile I know nott, butt I thinke I shall bee acquainted with itt, assoon as determind, and you bee sure of the earlyest notice I can give.

639. *Thomas to Alan I, Dublin, 4 Feb. 1724[/5]*

(1248/6/139–40)

I have just time to owne the receipt of yours of this day sennights date, which came this morning. I cannott now doe more, having had a long day, uppon the matter of the Stafford election, youl see by the votes Mr Elds expulsion with the reasons of itt, and perhaps may bee surprizd that the noble Lord whoe was the Pet[itione]r should bee acquitted by a majority of about seventy, butt soe itt was;[460] I owne I thought a thing comprimisd imported that two persons att least must bee partyes, butt that went for nothing against the arguments

---

[458] The petition of Walter, Viscount Chetwynd (for whom see Appendix 3), against Thomas Elde, who had been returned at a by-election in November. The other sitting MP, Thomas Foley, who had defeated the Chetwynd interest in the 1722 general election, claimed to have evidence from the corporation of 'a bargain for money for Elde to resign his place to Lord Chetwynd' (*HC 1715–54*, i, 321; *CJ*, xx, 379; *Knatchbull Diary*, 36). According to one report 'the Tories upon Mr Ells [*sic*] being expelled the House and Lord Chetwynd's remaining, say it is a thing without precedent, saying that they ought to have ordered a new election. However, Lord Chetwynd has managed so well his affairs with the German ladies, that Lord Lechmere and some others were spoke to, and ... some great man, out of complaisance, has resolved to let that affair drop' (HMC, *Var. Coll.*, viii, 384).

[459] Letter endorsed by Alan I: 'Tho: Brodrick ... that the matter of recalling Lord Carteret and removing me seems to be in suspence, will give me the earliest account when things are determined'.

[460] A motion that Chetwynd was guilty of corrupt practice was defeated on a division 229–163, and he was then declared elected on the completion of the hearing of the petition (*CJ*, xx, 391).

of Coll Bladen,[461] Mr Ward of Hackney[462] and Mr John Chetwin[463], whoe were all that spoake against the question.

A certaine corner satt very firmly togather, and you may bee sure others might bee influenced thereby.

I will very perticularly answer the severall parts of your letter assoone as I can, butt beleive twill nott bee before Tuesdays post, for itt must bee long, and I thinke I shall nott have time this weeke, business of consequence being appointed for these next two dayes, butt Sunday I thinke will bee my own, when ile spend the afternoon in writing.

640. *Thomas to Alan I, 9 Feb. 1724[/5]*

(1248/6/141–2)

Yesterday was terrible till past seven uppon the citty Bill,[464] and this like to bee as bad, for I heare wee are to have the papers layd before us relating to the Masters with a message from the King, the purport I have nott heard, butt take for graunted that twill bee sharpe and popular,[465] I know tis intended to move an impeachment against Lord Macclesfeild, which probably will come from our leaders quarter for the reasons I mentioned in my last, for those are the true inducements, and understood soe by all indifferent men, lett them therefore play the game as they thinke fitt, wee shall I beleive sitt quiett.

I gott upp very early this morning being unwilling to loose a post in saying my opinion in relation to my nephew.

I agree tis now time to thinke of bringing him into the world, and consider with pleasure the expectation you very reasonably have uppon doing itt advantagiously by getting him a considerable fortune to which I assure you nothing will contribute more then the knowledge of him to the people you treat with, for I am sure (without partiality) hee will appeare in a bright light; hee has admirable sence, with the addition of modesty, such as will recomend him to those whoe have either the one or the other, his person and deportment are unexceptionable, and the charecter given of him by those whoe come from abroad, strangers as well as Englishmen leaves little doubt of his being a great and valluable man, when wee shall bee in our graves, unlesse the degeneracy of the age should make meritt a bar; I am nott apt to bee partiall, nor is my charecter sullyed with being soe, and if this bee truly the case, depend upon itt, you will have pleasure and the greatest satisfaction a parent can hope, for these reasons noe doubt his being with you uppon the place will bee most advisable, butt (in my opinion) nott in the manner you propose, of taking Ireland in his

---

[461] Martin Bladen, MP [I & GB] was one of the tellers against the motion.

[462] John Ward (*d.* 1755), of Hackney, Middx, MP [GB] Weymouth and Melcombe Regis.

[463] John Chetwynd (c.1680–1767), of Fullerton, Hants, MP [GB] Stockbridge, brother of Walter, Viscount Chetwynd.

[464] The bill 'for the regulating elections within the City of London; and for preserving the peace, good order, and government of the said city' (*CJ*, xx, 403–4). Passed into law as 11 Geo.I, c. 18. See I.G. Doolittle, 'Walpole's City Elections Act (1725)', *EHR*, xcvii (1982), 504–29; Nicholas Rogers, 'The City Elections Act (1725) Reconsidered', *EHR*, c (1985), 604–17.

[465] The various reports prepared by the privy council committee (*CJ*, xx, 405). The debate lasted till six p.m., before being adjourned (*Knatchbull Diary*, 38).

way hither, I thinke rather hee should first come hither, staying butt a very short time, then going towards you, when he does soe, surely his stay in Ireland will bee necessary, in order to accomplish what you have in prospect; Hereby by hee will have fresh opertunityes of continuing his former acquaintance, as well as making due acknowledgments to such from whom hee has received remarkable instances of respect abroad, and this I am sure alone determines my thoughts, butt for another reason I cannott bear a passage from Burdeaux, the Corsairs of Barbary[466] are in the ocean, and ply that coast, as well as Pyrates, whoe encrease in number every day, lett mee therefore desire your nott thinking of that, tis a hazard nott to bee run. You say you hoped his lott would have fallen in England, God forbid butt itt should, for what must bee apparently for his advantage must in consequence bee soe to those hee shall bee allyd to; noe fortune you can gett will bee an equivalent to the losse hee must inevitably sustaine by setling elsewhere, this I am perswaded you will bee convinct of after conversing with him a short time, youl find him nott of a common stamp, wherefore his candle should nott bee putt under a Busshell.[467] I thinke you may very safely turne your thoughts (and that assoone as you please) towards what you intend, for assure your selfe heele come out better in the eyes of any you treat with, then expected.

If possible ile adde our proceedings of this day, if nott ile give you the best account I can of them, assoone as possible.

Mr Comptroller[468] brought a message under the signe manual, importing in substance that all care had been taken for securing to the suitors their mony, and with itt, the severall Reports.[469] There was a deep silence for a time, noebody rising Mr Young movd taking the Reports into consideration on Fryday.

Mr Methuen was for reading them, the whole house gave into that, read they were, and then the motion for Fryday renewd. Mr Pultney was for referring them to a Comittee,[470] which was violently opposd by our Leaders, a great deale of sparring there was, att last the motion was agreed to without division.[471] Mr W[alpole] (by way of prevention) declared against a Bill, they have taken the lead, lett them doe as they please, I thinke they are a good deale perplext, and more are they like to bee.

641. *Alan I, Dublin, to Thomas, Westminster, 11 Feb. 1724[/5]*

(1248/6/143–4)

It is a pretty while since I wrote to you in so much that I doe not remember that I have owned the receit of yours of the 26th past. I confesse upon reading it I did apprehend that

---

[466] Ottoman or Berber pirates, based at various ports along the north African coast, from modern-day Morocco to Libya.

[467] Matthew, 5: 15: 'Neither do men light a candle, and put it under a bushel, but on a candlestick; and it giveth light unto all that are in the house'.

[468] Paul Methuen (c. 1672–1757), of Bishops Cannings, Wilts., MP [GB] Brackley, comptroller of the household 1720–5. Confirmed in *CJ*, xx, 405.

[469] The reports concerning the chancery masters' office.

[470] Confirmed in *Knatchbull Diary*, 38. Probably William Pulteney (1684–1764), MP [GB] Hedon, and cofferer of the household, rather than his brother and colleague at Hedon, Lieut.-col. Harry Pulteney (1686–1767), or their namesake Daniel Pulteney.

[471] The motion to adjourn until Friday, 12 Feb. Confirmed in *Knatchbull Diary*, 38.

the putting off the matter of the Masters in Chancery till the 9th instant (even in the maner and upon the terms yours mentions) was a great advantage obtained, and the rejection of Bennets peticion seems to me to be pretty much of a peice with it.[472] How popular and national soever this affair may be I think those who are unwilling to have misbehaviors in great ones punished (for fear of the precedent) will find out wayes and means to keep the game soe long on foot that the Dogs will be run off their noses. Your £20000 composicion for the North British tax on beer ale etc in lieu of their share of the Malt tax[473] is another indication of what I have long observed, that ——[474] power was increasing soe that it would [be] too late to think of putting any bounds to it. How far a freind and intimate of yours hath contributed to this, notwithstanding our great patriotism I must leave to his and your consideration. I am sensible Mr Southwel[475] hath in a letter written by him lately to a Gentleman here expressed him self in this maner, viz he inquires what my Lord Lieutenant hath done, or expressed to be the Kings resolution about Woods halfpence, and gives this for a reason why he expects to be informed from hence what hath been done that his Majestye hath more then once of late declared publickly that that coyne should not passe here.[476] Yet at the same time I doe not know any man so far confided in as to be intrusted with the secret. I wish our politicks in this particular may not be too finespun, but I vehemently suspect it. Last night Arthur Hill was marryed to a daughter of the late Lord Cheif Baron Dean, a very pretty girle and a good fortune.[477] My services to all freinds, particularly to the Lord Cheif Justice (shal I call him or Lord Chancellor)[478] and to the Lord Commissioner of the Seal (or may I stil venture to give him the Lower title of Master of the Rolls.[479]

642. *Thomas to Alan I, 18 Feb. 1724[/5]*

(1248/6/145–6)

Your observations are certainly well grounded uppon the generall practice, and that founded uppon the reasons you give, butt nott soe conclusive as to found a certainty uppon, there

---

[472]Thomas Bennett, a master in chancery: on 1 Feb. the Commons refused to hear a petition from him, 'wherein he charged lord chancellor with some facts as directing him to obey the order in chancery for fear of a parliamentary enquiry and likewise with the money received, etc.' (*CJ*, xx, 387, *Knatchbull Diary*, 37). Copies of Bennett's case can be found at Kent History and Library Centre, Knatchbull MSS, U951/C53/10, and Oxfordshire History Centre, Carter MSS, CJ/V/38: in it he asserted that on taking up office he paid £1,500 out of the suitors' money for the lord chancellor's use, while his predecessor retained a further £28,000, of which £7,500 remained unpaid.

[473]The Commons had agreed on 1 Feb. with a resolution reported from the committee of ways and means, that £20,000 should be raised in Scotland by a tax on malt made and consumed there, supplemented if necessary by a surcharge on the makers of malt (*CJ*, xx, 387).

[474]Presumably Robert Walpole.

[475]Edward Southwell, MP [I].

[476]Possibly in a letter to Marmaduke Coghill of 9 Jan., the original of which has not survived (*Coghill Letters*, 15).

[477]Anne (d. 1726), daughter of Joseph Deane (1674–1715), of Castlemartyr, Co. Cork, MP [I] 1703–14; chief baron of exchequer [I] 1714–d.

[478]Sir Peter King, who was a justice of common pleas, not lord chief justice: Alan had made this mistake before (see above, p. 78).

[479]Sir Joseph Jekyll had been appointed one of the commissioners of the great seal on 7 Jan. (*HC 1715–54*, ii, 174).

may bee (as you observe) somuch vertue as to cause a deviation from that general rule; or there may in some instances, bee an apparent necessity for soe doing, to which of these the great matter now under consideration ought to bee ascribed, ile leave to your judgment, being throughly convinct that the affair of the masters will bee carryed through, and indeed every day produces what confirmes mee herein; within the last forty eight hours a discovery has been made (nott by the Managers) that four onely of the Masters have, in their volluntary accounts given uppon oath, charged them selves with £37000 short of what they had in their hands of the suitors mony,[480] how much farther like discoveryes may bee made is uncertaine, that some will, is in my opinion most certaine; the South Sea affair was too Grosse to bee entirely bafled, screening perticular persons was the game next to bee played, in order to which some were to bee made Scape Goats, thus will itt fare in the present case, which I am soe strongly perswaded of, that I would (the Newmarkett way of argumentation) willingly lay five hundred pounds of itt, without the least thought of loosing. The person I formerly hinted, continues still of the same mind, to which I should most readily assent, did I nott apprehend some persons may consider that having too many Irons in the fire, might probably occasion some burning, which is all I argue uppon. If my nephew should come over with such veiwes as you expresse, hee will bee misserably disappointed, this I am most sure of. I saw Coll Piott[481] two dayes since going up the stairs to the house, pulld of my hatt to him, butt sayd nothing of papers to him, or hee to mee, perhaps his equipage might nott bee come.

As far as I can judge (and that very impartially) the people of Ireland have been soe far from loosing ground by their conduct in Woods affair, that they have gained prodigiously, with all impartiall men; in common discourse they are sayd to understand the interest of their country better then wee here, and spoake of as a steddy brave people whoe dare assert itt, if I doe nott grosly mistake, this will bee found whenever itt shall bee the hard fate of the country to be run uppon.

Reading over my letter I doubt you may apprehend my meaning to be that Lord M[acclesfield] is to bee screened, Noe noe that will nott bee the case, though others nott yett talkd of, may bee soe in time to come, for att present they are out of danger.

643. Thomas to Alan I, 20 Feb. 1724[/5]

(1248/6/147–8)

Yesterday I received by a servant the papers you sent, and att the same time your letter of the 11th. The enquiry which you mention to bee made by Mr S[outhwell's] letter has been the subject of wondering for a full month past, and I have heard some great ones pretend to bee surprizd when they are assurd by the people of Ireland that nothing satisfactory has been done or sayd in relation to Woods coyne, since orders have been soe long since sent for doing itt, I doe nott I confesse see the pollicy of omitting itt; when the late D[uke] of Devon was congratulated by a courrier, whoe told him the secret of King James

---

[480] The masters in chancery, whose activities were being investigated by the Commons in pursuance of the impeachment of Lord Macclesfield (*CJ*, xx, 405, 408).

[481] Richard Pyott (d. 1738), of Streethay, Staffs., lieut.-col., 4th troop of life guards (Dalton, *Geo. I's Army*, ii, 192–3, 371, 418–19; *Historical Register*, 1738, Chron., 7; TNA, PROB 11/691/78).

resolving to send him a pardon,[482] made answer your news comes late, for all the towne knowes itt.

I am told things will come out very black against Lord M[*acclesfield*]. His best freinds (whoe have been hitherto sanguine) begin to hang their heads, our Great men talke as bitterly as any others, submitting to swim with the streame.

Lord C[*hief*] J[*ustice*] King and the Master of the Rolls are in statu quo prius,[483] and I thinke like to remaine soe, for if I understand things right, termes in neither case are likely to bee agreed on.

Noe doubt butt the Zars death[484] wil bee sayd to create a necessity for his Majestys going abroad assoon as may bee, butt twill nott bee assoon as wisht.

644. *Alan I, Dublin, to Thomas, 21 Feb. 1724[/5]*

(1248/6/149–52)

This letter goes by Mr Andrew Crotty son of old William Crotty of Lismore servant to the old Earle of Burlington,[485] whom I dare trust for its going safe; and therefore I will speak more plainly in it then I should think fit to doe if I intended to send it by the post. As to your proceedings against Lord Macclesfeild I have in some measure told you my thoughts of the successe of them in a former letter and I confesse I continue in my then sentiments that he will come better off then you seemed to expect and beleived he deserved in the beginning of the Session. The steps taken by the examining that affair before the meeting of the Parliament seemed to me to aim at rendring a Parliamentary enquiry unnecessary and to give such redresse or remedyes as might incline people to think soe, and the natural consequence of that seems to me to be that the terriblenesse of a parliamentary censure was from the beginning designed to be averted by those who set that enquiry on foot, for I will not (with peevish people) term this proceeding anticipating the Parliamentary enquiry; but I must own I never apprehended that the only end was to redresse the injuryes of the suitors any more then I thought the enquiry of the Committee of Councel about the legalitye of Woods patent, and the abuses he had been guilty of in his coynage was meant for the releif of Ireland. And here I cannot conceal that it created in me a sort of sullen ill natured pleasure to see that the enquiryes at St Stephens Chappel[486] are becoming as insignificant as ours on this side of the water; but this is too melancholy a consideration to create one who loves the British constitucion soe well as I doe, any durable pleasure. Methinks your message too of the 8th of February by Mr Controller was pretty much of the same tendencye; but I find nobody took notice of it as any way intrenching on your right and methods of proceeding in such cases: soe that I ought to beleive I misjudge that matter, in fearing it seemed to prescribe to you, as if no more needed be done then had been, for certainly if all had been done which could be done etc it seems necessarily to follow that nothing more then all

---

[482] William Cavendish (1641–1707), 1st duke of Devonshire.

[483] Literally, 'are in the state they were before'.

[484] Peter the Great died on 8 Feb. N.S. 1725.

[485] Andrew Crotty (*d. c.* 1746) of Modeligo, Co. Waterford, one of the Irish agents of the 3rd earl of Burlington, was the son of William Crotty, who in 1694 served as bailiff of the manor of Lismore under Richard Boyle (1632–98), the 1st earl. Both were catholics. (Barnard, *New Anatomy*, 223–4; Vicars, *Index*, 114).

[486] Where the British house of commons sat.

could be done, soe that the doing any farther was impossible and soe unnecessary. The house indeed did not take it in this sense, but thought fit to proceed in the affair, but the great majoritye which was for proceeding by way of impeachment and not by bill[487] seems to me to indicate that Lord M[*acclesfield*] hath no reason to expect any unreasonable severitye from a certain quarter; and I am sure his freinds here take things in that sense and hope very well of the event and the more soe since they have seen the names of the Committee among whom one of them told me the only two men of weight were your Colleague[488] and Mr W Plummer,[489] and those two persons he said had expressed themselves to be, and were depended upon as, men of great moderation in this matter. The rest he said were young men,[490] by which I understood he meant that they could doe little mischeif tho it should be in their inclination when the other two were of the temper he described. If I had been in the house I think I should have been with the majoritye for proceeding by impeachment rather then by bill (not but that I am for punishing great offenders) altho I am sensible Lord M[*acclesfield*] hath a much fairer chance to come off clear and uncensured by this way of proceeding, then if it had been by way of bill: but I confesse I think a trial in the ordinary course of Law or of parliament is soe much every mans right that it to me appears a lesse evil that one real great criminal should escape unpunished, then that we should grow too familiar with bills of pains and penaltyes, which are of the nature of and introductory to bills of attainder. It is true both you and I were for the bills of pains and penaltyes in the case of the Bishop of Rochester and Kellye,[491] and soe I shal again be in any other mans case when it seems to me that the safety of the whole (the salus populi[492]) is at stake: and that I then thought to be the case, but here it is much otherwise. In short every thing that belongs to our Court here is entirely in the sentiments of the great ones in London and cannot conceal their inclination that Lord M[*acclesfield*] may reap the benefit of the Clerk of the Crowns prayer for the Culprits that God would send him a good deliverance,[493] and his particular freinds give themselves airs as if they had grounds to expect it from the letters they receive from your side. I told you formerly that the person who assured you that people should be left entirely at liberty in a certain affair had done the very utmost in their power to <u>create</u> a willingnesse to receive the halfpence; and I beleive the instructions were very strong to that effect, or else such large steps and warm methods would not have been taken to effect it, as I have formerly told you were taken. Soe that all is not gold that glisters.[494] I will here subjoin a late passage. Just before last Christmas last the Commissioners of accounts passed

---

[487] A bill of attainder, or of pains and penalties, such as had been used against Bishop Atterbury.

[488] Arthur Onslow (1691–1768), of Imber Court, Surrey, Thomas's parliamentary colleague at Guildford.

[489] Walter Plumer (c. 1682–1746), of Chediston Hall, Suffolk, MP [GB] Aldeburgh.

[490] The other MPs on the committee appointed on 12 Feb. to prepare articles of impeachment against Maccles-field (*CJ*, xx, 408), were George Bubb Dodington, Walter Carey, Mr Gore (Thomas or William), Phillips Gybbon, John Hedges, Henry Howard (Viscount Morpeth), Thomas Lutwyche, Sir George Oxenden, 5th Bt (chairman), Thomas Palmer, Sir Thomas Pengelly, Sir John Rushout, 4th Bt, Samuel Sandys, John Snell, Sir William Strickland, 4th Bt, Mr Thompson (Edward or William), Sir Clement Wearg and Richard West.

[491] Francis Atterbury, bishop of Rochester, and George Kelly (1688–c.1747), also the subject of a bill of pains and penalties in 1722 for his involvement in the same conspiracy.

[492] Literally, 'the health of the people'.

[493] The phrase 'God send thee a good deliverance' was commonly spoken by the clerk of arraigns to the accused at the beginning of a criminal trial.

[494] '… all that glisters is not gold' (Shakespeare, *The Merchant of Venice*, II, vii, 65).

the Vice Treasurers account of the publick money which came to his hand in the year ending 1722; and the ballance which appeared to remain then in his hand was 43000 odd hundred pounds; this was very surprising to us, who knew that the army is in arrear about twenty months; and people imagined that this ballance must have been otherwise employed then in paying the establishment, or else the military list could not have soe far run in arrear. But we were told that it would appear in the next years account (which should be ready as soon as we pleased) that ballance together with the accrewing revenue between 25 Dec. 1722 and 25 Dec. 1723 had been regularly applyed: Of this I immediately acquainted my Lord Lieutenant and received his strict commands to require that account to be forthwith put into such a method as to be examined and passed without losse of time, of which the Deputy Vice Treasurer[495] had notice and the Auditor[496] acquainted me before the end of last term that the account was ready: and the Commissioners appointed 28 February to examine it: but two dayes before Captain Pratt acquainted me he could not be then ready for want of some vouchers. I told my Lord Lieutenant what he said who seemed surprised at such a general allegation, and insisted on the accounts being passed before the Barons went their circuits; nay talked of stopping them from beginning their Circuit to attend it. But I received a letter on Friday from Captain Pratt that he could not be ready the next day and had also been with Lord Lieutenant. I sent this letter to my Lord yesterday, who sent me word he would order Mr Clutterbuck to call on me in the evening which he accordingly did and acquainted me that my Lord had upon what Captain Pratt told him, consented to have the examination of this account deferred till the Barons returned from their Circuits, and that the Commissioners should now appoint a day when they would proceed upon it; and that his Excellencye expected that they should prefix the same day for Captain Pratts lodging all his vouchers of payments within the year which begins on 25 Dec. 1723 and endeth on 25 Dec. 1724 with the Auditor General in order to have that account passed before the Parliament meets here. By this method his Excellencye attains two ends, he will have matters in preparacion for next Session, and prevents the Vice Treasurer falling under the difficultyes he might have fallen under of being forced to confesse that the publick money hath not been from time to time applyed in discharge of the Army etc whereby it would have circulated through the Kingdome and gives time to provide money between this time and that to pay off the debts to which that money ought to have been applyed in the years 1722 1723 and 1724. For you must know the course of our Treasury is this, whenever any man brings a debenture or other warrant for payment of money and carryes it to the Vice Treasurer in order to receive his money he is ordered to carry the warrant to the Clerk above stairs to deduct Pells[497] poundage[498] Hospital money[499] and other stoppages out of it. In order to the Clerks doing this, he calls for the warrant and will not give a certificate what the neat money payable to the party after such deductions

[495] John Pratt, MP [I].

[496] Charles Dering, jr (*d.* 1735), of Dublin (*Lib. Mun.*, pt 2, p. 54; *General Evening Post*, 19–22 Apr. 1735).

[497] The clerk of the pells had 'by ancient prescription' a right to retain 10s. per £100 in respect of all regular issues from the exchequer [I] (T.J. Kiernan, *History of the Financial Administration of Ireland to 1817* (1930), 239).

[498] Another of the ancient fees of the exchequer [I] (Kiernan, *Financial Administration*, 327).

[499] In the foundation charter of the Hospital and Free School, Dublin (the 'Blue-coat School'), Charles II had allowed £80 from the Irish exchequer for the chief schoolmaster (F.R. Falkiner, *The Foundation of the Hospital and Free School of King Charles II, Oxmantown, Dublin …* (Dublin, 1906), 41).

amounts unto until you lodge the warrant with him with the name of the party indorsed, and will not redeliver the warrant to the party, altho he alleges his name being indorsed on the back of it is a discharge of the whole warrant, if it remain in the Treasury; but is told that the Vice Treasurer enters in a book all payments really made on such warrant which fairly states the account between the party and Vice Treasurer on that warrant, of which he shal never want the use and benefit; and to say truth I never did hear that any person suffered by the Treasury pretending more had been paid on such warrant then had really and truly been paid on it. But the use of this course of the Treasury is easily to be comprehended: for the Creditor is told there is not money then in the Treasury but that he shal be paid when there is sufficient to answer his demands and those of preceding warrants. Thus there is an election given to the Vice Treasurer who shal be paid first who last; and the usual method is to pay the money by different payments at different times, but none of these are entred on the warrant, but the name signed on it when it is first brought to the office is a sufficient discharge to the Vice Treasurer and would be allowed a good voucher to him by the Commissioners of accounts, altho in truth the party had not then received one penny of the money. By this means you see that payment long after the money is due (and probably may be in the Vice Treasurers hand) will be a good discharge to the Vice Treasurer within the year when it becomes due, altho the money was at that time negotiated in other hands. And by this you see that it is impossible for the Vice Treasurer not to have vouchers for all the money he hath really paid, because the voucher (that is the full warrant with a receit on it) is lodged in his hand before he payes one penny of it, the consequence of which is that when he tells anybody he wants vouchers for such a summe he is to be understood that he pretends to have paid money which he hath not paid. People shrewdly guesse in whose hands this money lyes at an easy interest to answer the monstrous purchases made not long since; and that care will be taken to have it ready to pay the warrants which ought long since to have been paid with it before the next account passes; but it would be difficult with us to raise such a summe of ready money all on a sudden for we live cheifly on credit. For my part I cannot but think somebody hath been told in plain words how the matter stands and been prevailed on to give farther time for passing this account ending 25 Dec. 1723 to enable those concerned to provide the money by the return of the Barons etc. If this be soe sure the person will lye under great obligations to be very good in all events and no doubt hath promised to be soe; but in my sense the way had been to have put it out of his power to doe any hurt, as laying this matter open would have done: for (what ever promises may be made) his soul is in with Lord C[arteret']s enemyes. This is a long story and only fit for your own eye considering how plainly I speak of the great ones on both sides the water.

645. *Thomas to Alan I, Dublin, 27 Feb. 1724[/5]*[500]

(1248/6/153–4)

You cannott expect certainty from mee, in a matter which lyes in the breasts of soe very few, butt I was yesterday offerd by a very prying cunning man, a bett of a hundred pounds that what I formerly mentioned would soone happen.

---

[500]Letter endorsed by Alan I: 'Tho: Brodrick ... thinks Lord Lieutenant will be recalled and the giving up Woods patent be reserved (as a sugar plum) to sweeten people in the time of his Successor'.

I begin to think that Lord Lieutenant has noe positive directions for satisfying mens minds in relation to Wood's coine, from whence (if soe) I can infer nothing other then that itt is reserved for his successor, thereby to gild the bitter pill of great demands, concluding an expectation of the usuall Churchwardens presentment Omnia bene,[501] I really think this the case.

Our Managers (whoe are in the nature of a secret Committee) are very close, soe that I doe nott endeavour learning from any of them, butt hear from other hands, that severall new and very materiall discoveryes are made, the nature of the enquiry will take up time, and perhaps itt may affectedly bee made long, in order to have the Session goe over, for thus much I am well informed of, that ordering the chairman to move for a liberty to examine uppon oath, was warmely contested, and carryd butt by one, though after twas soe, all came into itt, youl easily guesse whoe were the opponents.

646. *Thomas to Alan I, Dublin, 2 Mar. 1724/5*[502]

(1248/6/155–6)

This morning Mr Crotte[503] gave mee (att the house) yours of the 21st of last month, your way of arguing has in most instances, provd a right way of judging, nor am I very cleare whither itt may nott in this matter, prove soe, though I am more inclinable to beleive itt may in this instance prove otherwise, unlesse what has been whisperd prove true, of a message to hasten, uppon account of the matter of Thorne,[504] and other things of moment, necessary to bee transacted abroad, if soe, itt will want noe explanation; a very little time will necessarily explain every thing; I cannott omitt informing you that tis sayd (and I beleive truly) that the Committee are a good deale divided; the reasons ile leave to your guesses.

Your letter needs noe other answer on the other head, then that the whole management (in my opinion) tends to what you guesse, and I verily beleive itt is well founded, butt surely somebody must bee mad, for I noe more beleive the end proposd will bee attained, then I doe that a certaine gentleman of the long Robes[505] complying in every case, will procure him a cusshion.

Lett mee advise your putting your affairs in the best order you can, and that without delay, for I am nott determined in my own mind, whither your coming soone over will nott bee more advisable then the thoughts of attending the Session, upon which I will soone write; Miss is nott well, I take good air and regular hours the likelyest method for retreiving health, wherefore I thinke your saying what you thinke proper, is very

[501] All is well; used if there was nothing to report.

[502] Letter endorsed by Alan I: 'Tho: Brodrick … thinks the Court will not be able to skreen Lord Macclesfeild but by putting an end to the Session which is talked of. Advises my going for England before the Parliament meets …'.

[503] Andrew Crotty.

[504] The events at Thorn (Torún) in Poland in July–December 1724, when the mayor and other Lutherans were executed following an attack on a local Jesuit college and repressive measures were instituted against protestantism in the town. This quickly became a *cause célèbre* and was widely denounced in the press as an example of catholic intolerance.

[505] A lawyer.

, .

necessary and that without losse of time. My head is disorderd, as youl see by writing confusedly.

647. Alan I, Dublin, to Thomas, 3 Mar. 1724[/5]

(1248/6/157–8)

Yesterday the pacquett boat came in and brought me two from you dated the 18th and 20th of last month: I will alway construe the actions of my freinds and superiors in the most favourable and candid sense they can be taken in; and never attributed the good things which are done to any other motive in the doers then the vertue of their minds. But I confesse I stil am a little diffident of that which you upon the spot think soe very certain, I mean the final event and upshot of this affair: you are soe very sanguine and clear in the matter in your first letter, that I began to waver a good deal in my thoughts about it, and reasoned thus with myself. He seeth with his own eyes and hath oportunityes of observing the turns the matter takes (which you promised to inform me of, but forgott to doe it) and how the great ones work and act. But I then considered what was said upon another occasion, that men are to expect very different events who live in republica Platonis, from what the same men would expect if they lived in Faece Romuli:[506] and this consideracion and a natural bent we have to beleive too well of our own way of thinking, inclined me strongly to differ with you in judging of the successe of this affair. I never took the person for a changeling,[507] who (you tell me) continues of the same mind as when you wrote formerly to me, and upon the principle which governs him he must never think of altering. But when you proceed to tell me that there will be a scapegoat found out; this plainly tells me that in truth the name of those concerned may be Legion (not for number but for their nature and power)[508] and consequently for the sake of others and to prevent getting too much light, it will be necessary to cover the nakednesse of ———. Senny began his journey toward Munster on Thursday last, after having told a certain person he intended for England (as he told me). We all know that orders are come about Woods coyne, but such are our politicks that nothing can induce us to own what they are in expresse terms, but in general it is said they are such as we wish to have them: If soe the sooner they are divulged the better; but truly the most I have been let into is this, that the King is very well pleased with our administration (you see I am taken into the part of merit) but I had much rather have the letter which relates to this matter communicated to me, then have all the fine speeches and caresses made me; and doe think I am not well used to be kept longer in the dark in this matter: You must have read over the papers which the Colonel sent you, and may probably have thought they would bear the reading of your freinds. Pray

---

[506] Cicero, *Letters to Atticus*, II, i, 8: '*nam Catonem nostrum non tu amas plus quam ego; sed tamen ille optimo animo utens et summa fide nocet interdum rei publicae; dicit enim tamquam in Platonis πολιτείᾳ, non tamquam in Romuli faece sententiam*' (Now you love our Cato as much as I do; and yet, with the best of intentions and in utter good faith, he sometimes does harm to the republic. For he expresses his views as if he were in Plato's *Republic*, not in the sewer of Romulus).

[507] A changeable person (a sense of the word described in *OED* as 'now somewhat archaic').

[508] Mark 5: 8–9: 'For he said unto him, Come out of the man, thou unclean spirit. And he asked him, What is thy name? And he answered, saying, My name is Legion: for we are many.'

how doe they and you bear <u>our way of thinking</u> (which his Grace of N[*ewcastle*] makes soe great a jest of) but the expression is his masters and not his own, and I can shew it in a letter of an earlier date from a man who thinks and knows himself able to prescribe to him, what he shal write and what style he shal use. You will observe we act and speak in a more Cavalier maner, and like men that think themselves to be in the right, and who are not to be frightned out of their sentiments, or be brought to conceal them when they are soe fully convinced (as we are) that we have all along acted for his Majestyes service and the good of our countrey, tho not according to the politicks att a certain place. This affair of the Masters, puts me in mind of the many wholesale deceits that have been practiced and carried to a great heighth, South Sea, Bubbles, Harburg Lottery,[509] etc and that which gives me the most melancholy apprehensions, is to be forced to own that every one of them took their rise within few years past; after mentioning these (in which Britain had its share) those which were peculiarly dedicated to the service of Ireland (I mean the Bank and Woods patent) are hardly worthy to be named; but we can never forget them; for they were sufficient to have done our businesse as effectually as the others were to have had their effect in the place for which they were calculated. In few words the Luxury into which we are fallen cannot be supported in the usual maner and must be furnished after a way to which former times were as much strangers as they were to our present excesses in all maner of vice Luxury and riot. You will say I am turning Enthusiast, but upon my word these are not the results of keeping a Lenten diet,[510] but what I have been fully convinced of the truth of for a long time.

648. *Thomas to Alan I, Dublin, 9 Mar. 1724/5*

(1248/6/159–60)

The whisper of this morning in our house, was that the Chancellorship of Ireland has been offered to Sir Wm Tomson (Recorder of London)[511] in order to make a vacancy for Mr Wests succeeding him,[512] this cannott faile of obtaining creditt with those whoe are

---

[509] One of the speculative enterprises that flourished in the wake of the South Sea Bubble. The Harburg Company, chartered to trade between Britain and Hanover, with Frederick, son of the prince of Wales, as its governor, was given the privilege of holding a lottery at Harburg (a port on the Elbe near Hamburg) from which the directors were able to make large profits for themselves. Against the advice of British government ministers, the company advertised the lottery in December 1722. The affair was then investigated by a house of commons committee. As it had involved a number of prominent individuals in England, including several MPs, it became a nine days' wonder. The Commons' report in February 1723 resulted in the expulsion from the House of one of the directors, John Barrington Shute, Viscount Barrington (*HC 1715–54*, i, 438; Cobbett, *Parl. Hist.*, viii, cols. 62–87). Alan had spoken in this debate: notes for his speech survive in SHC, 1248/9/117–18.

[510] Religious enthusiasm was deprecated in two letters by 'Diogenes' in the *British Journal*, 6, 13 Apr. 1723, repr. in *Cato's Letters* (4 vols, 1724), iv, 221, as 'a flaming conceit, that we have great personal interest in the Deity, and that the Deity is eminently employed about us or in us'. Subsequently there was a suggestion that this state of mind could be induced by diet, and in particular by fasting (230). The possible identity of 'Diogenes' is discussed in P.B. Anderson, 'Cato's Obscure Counterpart in *The British Journal*, 1722–25', *Studies in Philology*, xxxiv (1937), 412–28.

[511] Sir William Thompson (c. 1676–1739), of the Middle Temple, MP [GB] Ipswich, recorder of London since 1715; appointed cursitor baron of the exchequer [E] in 1726.

[512] The privy seal warrant for Richard West's appointment as lord chancellor [I] was dated 29 May 1725 (*Lib. Mun.*, pt. 2, p. 17).

throughly convinct that each of them are in all circumstances well quallifyed for such or any other promotion; you know them both, and cannott doubt of what most people agree in.

The four (Lawyer) Managers are by their brethren appointed to forme Articles against Lord Macclesfeild,[513] which I heare will bee presented to the house, the beginning of next weeke, nott sooner as I am told. I hope you are putting your affairs in such order, as to admitt of your coming over soone, for upon revolving things in my mind, I am (att present) of opinion that doing soe will bee most advisable, by the first safe hand I meet with, (which I hope to doe soone) ile write my reasons att large.

649. *Thomas to Alan I, Dublin, 11 Mar. 1724/5*

(1248/6/163–4)

I doe nott thinke taking a coppy of the Lords order necessary, for that you will certainly see, though possibly nott the Petition.[514] I am told the Pet[itione]r swore through stick to every Article, nott withstanding which I perswade my selfe you will bee able to give a full and satisfactory answer; with what intent this gentleman is spirited I thinke obvious enough.

I heare Sir W[illiam] T[hompson] desires to know what hee has done deserving transportation, till that appears, heel stay where he is.

How acceptable this restinesse may bee to Mr W[est] I know nott, for I thinke his cheife aime was att succeeding Sir W[illiam].

Tis sayd that an Additional sallery of £1500 per an is to bee to the Chancellor, which may make itt worth Mr W[est's] acceptance, or perhaps of some other person of meritt.

Our Managers will on Munday or Tuesday next, acquaint the house with their being ready to offer the Articles, att such time as the house shall appoint, which I suppose will bee on Wensday or Thursday following; I doe nott apprehend any debate can arise upon them, which will nott bee over the day they shall bee offered, consequently that they will bee sent to the Lords one day next weeke, I hear they will bee 12 or 14 in number.[515]

The towne talks of considerable changes here, that Mr P[ulte]ny[516] and Mr M[ethuen] are to turne out,[517] and Sir T H[518] to succeed one of them, and Lord T[orrington] to succeed Lord B[erke]ly,[519] how truly I know nott, butt shall nott bee surprizd if itt happen.

[513] Thomas Lutwyche, Sir Thomas Pengelly, Sir Clement Wearg, and Richard West.

[514] An order made by the Lords on 10 Mar., on a petition from Edward Edgeworth of Kilshrewly, Co. Meath (for whom see J.B. Burke, *A Genealogical and Heraldic History of the Commoners of Great Britain and Ireland …* (4 vols, 1838), iv, 756; *Hist. Ir. Parl.*, iv, 106) against the deputy chancery register in Ireland, alleging that he had been denied a copy of the minutes of the court in relation to a judgment of December 1720 continuing an injunction against him. The deputy register had claimed that he had acted under the instruction of the lord chancellor [I] (*LJ*, xxii, 445–6). For details of the suit from which this petition arose, *Swift v. Edgeworth*, see Josiah Brown, *Reports of Cases upon Appeals and Writs of Error in the High Court of Parliament …* (7 vols, Dublin, 1784), iii, 119–27.

[515] Sir George Oxenden reported on Thursday that the committee had prepared articles, which were read and agreed the same day (*CJ*, xx, 453–89). There were 21 in all.

[516] William Pulteney.

[517] As cofferer and comptroller of the household respectively. Both were removed, though Methuen became treasurer of the household and in May 1725 was named a knight of the bath.

[518] Presumably the tory Sir Thomas Hanmer (1677–1746), 4th Bt, of Mildenhall, Suffolk, MP [GB] Suffolk. He was not appointed.

[519] As 1st lord of the admiralty [GB].

My disorder (which appeard vissibly since last Fryday) encreases; I resolve going out of towne assoone as the weather alters, of which I have new hopes, the wind being come Southerly, and this day wee have had a little raine.

650. *Alan I, Dublin, to Thomas, 13 Mar. 1724[/5]*

(1248/6/165–6)

I have your two letters one of the 27th of last month, the other of the second instant. In the former you seem to beleive that the ministry in England had not yet communicated to my Lord Lieutenant the resolutions taken there in reference to Woods patent, but reserved the giving it up to some body whom they like better to ingratiate him and entitle him to make some unusual demands in the next session here with hope of successe. You have never told me that anybody in London pretends to say the patent was to be given up, or what that thing was which they said had been ordered to be done or published for the satisfying people here. And I can assure you from a very late conversation which I had (with one who must know) that every order is denied which hath been said to come over about that matter except that of publickly owning that the patent will not be endeavoured to be inforced, or any compulsory methods used to create a currency to Wood's Copper. If this be the truth of our case, we are as near attaining that which the nation will think to be satisfactory as we were in August last; for the Kings order in Councel is as full as possible upon that head. And I confesse I doe apprehend that those who talk, of orders being sent to Ireland which will be satisfactory to them, are to be understood to mean that such orders or declarations as I have mentioned have been sent, and that my Lord Lieutenant hath declared as much, which the Gentlemen in London are pleased to judge (for us) to be satisfactory, or such with which we ought to be satisfyed. If then this be the scheme (as I think it is) to let the matter sleep till the Parliament shal meet and to put it to an hazard what effects these measures will produce in the houses (if we meet while the patent subsists) no doubt but my Lord Lieutenant will doe a very acceptable service to those, who have been the instruments of bringing all the trouble and misfortunes and losse which hath fallen on Ireland through this project; if people can be brought to be silent and passive under the treatment the nation hath received in several instances on this head, and to goe on to give the usual supplyes in the usual maner, without complaint of any sort. That such hopes are entertained I am fully perswaded; but I have cautioned the person cheifly concerned not to undertake for any thing, and this I think I ought in justice to him and to my own character to doe. That there will be sycophants who will endeavour at any expence (even the safety of their countrey) to ingratiate themselves I am very sensible; and I think it will be notifyed that who ever fail in what is expected from them must expect no quarter, as on the other hand that men of merit shal not fail being taken full notice of. For my part I confesse I do not remember that I was ever in a more difficult scituation then I now am, and in which I more need your advice. My first resolution is that I never will doe any act which may contribute toward the introducing this vile coyne, or establishing a precedent that a patent obtained and passed in the maner this was and of such fatal consequence should obtain here; nay I farther resolve that whenever I am justifiably enabled to declare my dissent in Parliament I will not fail to doe soe: I have alway expressed myself to be of these sentiments and have never pretended the contrary to my Lord Lieutenant, in any letter acknowledging his favours and promising my services: and consequently he cannot call my acting consistently with myself a deviation from the professions I have at any time made to him which have constantly contained an exception (save in the matter of Uriah[520]). To me it seems as if he must be obliged to risque holding a Parliament without a previous giving up this patent (which you must know is in the language of some people here termed an entire victory over etc) and I wish he may not have entertained or given hopes of things ending well on that foot; I own I foresee more difficultyes and danger of the successe then other people apprehend, and am not of that mettal to wish for a storm at Sea meerly to shew my skill in sailing the ship or working her in great distresse. Tell me therefore whether it be your opinion that I should chuse rather to be on board only as a passenger, or to have a share in piloting the vessel. If you advise me to desire my quietus[521] I will follow it and I confesse I think I can (without doubt now) lay down with honour, but how to conduct myself in circumstances so perplexing as the next Session will (I think) be attended with I am in a good deal of doubts. We differ I see in our thoughts about the successe of the grand affair now on the carpet at Westminster, but you have better oportunityes of forming a right judging then I have, which I make from an old Maxim: Idem manens idem semper facit idem.[522]

[*PS*] Since writing what goes before I have been at the Castle and was there told by Lord Lieutenant that Mrs Duncombe (an English Lady) whom Lady Carteret brought over for a companion)[523] is told by a female correspondent that there will soon be great changes here, a new Cheif Governor but not who the man will be; a new Chancellor; Sir Wm Thompson late Recorder of London for so I take it the late shuffle or modelling the City hath or will make him. But Lord C[*arteret*] seems not to give credit to this, and looks on it only as female tattle: but there never is much smoke without some fire. For my part I think my freind Robin[524] is going in some measure to perform the large promises he made me in your presence att Chelsea of doing me all the good offices in his power: He knows I will not doe dirty work and gives me an oportunitye of being out of post at a time when I think it is very possible something of that nature may by order from your side be set on foot: I shal by this means be free not only from temptacion but delivered from a possibilitye of being supposed not to act toward one from whom I have received great civilityes and obligations in the maner I ought. When I [*am*] declared an enemy, they who make me so must expect that I will act as becomes the relation they have put me into as to them: that is that I will serve my King and countrey to the best of my power without regarding what will be agreeable to the men in power. I think I should have acted the part of an honest man in all events, but I am sure my good freinds are taking away all temptacion which too often misleads well meaning men in emploiment.

---

[520] Uriah the Hittite, the husband of Bathsheba, refused to obey King David's order to return to his wife from military service, and was killed after being placed in the front line of battle at David's direction. Alan may be alluding to his own refusal to abandon his patriotic duty in relation to Wood's halfpence, for which he considered himself to have been sacrificed.

[521] Release.

[522] That which remains unchanged always produces the same effect.

[523] Possibly Sarah (née Slingsby), wife of Thomas Duncombe (c. 1683–1746), of Duncombe Park, Yorks., MP [GB] 1711–13, 1734–41. Lady Bristol had reported earlier that she would be accompanying the Carterets to Dublin (*Letter-books of John Hervey, first Earl of Bristol* … (3 vols., Wells, 1894), ii, 366).

[524] Robert Walpole.

[*PS*] Let me hear fully and plainly from you. I write this post to your neice.

651. *Alan I, Dublin, to Thomas, at his lodgings in the Privy Garden, Whitehall, 13 Mar.
1724[/5]*

(1248/6/167–8)

This letter will be delivered to you by a Gentleman who is not personally acquainted with
you, but desires to be soe: I know I shal doe a pleasure to both by being a means of creating
a familiarytye between men of probitye and good understanding. I know not but he may
goe to the Bath before he goes to London, soe that possibly a letter I wrote this morning
by the pacquet boat of the same date with this may reach your hands before Mr Carter
seeth you, but I confesse I could be very well content his affairs would call him to London
pretty soon; for really if I were to recommend you to a man able and inclined to give you
a perfect state of our affairs here I could not think on any other man soe likely to doe it
perfectly. You knew his father in my Lord Romnyes time.[525] Ought not I to complement
my Lord Cheif Justice King upon his having the seal; for soe our news is here, tho you tell
me the contrary. Pray let me know whether it be true that your good freind and mine Mr
Serjeant Pengellye acts with great bitternesse in a certain affair?[526] Or only with becoming
zeal in detecting and bringing evil practices to punishment, which I take to be natural to
him. But the freinds of the person criminated pretend to say there is some private pique; if
there hath been any particular misunderstanding between them pray acquaint me with it. I
am certain that [*Carteret*] hath been told by his best freinds that they cannot foresee how he
can have an easy Session unlesse the patent to Wood be previously put out of the way; but
I am sensible he is pressed from your side the water to try what successe may be hoped for
without going that step (which will be looked upon as a victory over those who cannot bear
the thought of being put in the wrong by those whom they have treated in a very cavalier
maner witnesse the letter of 3 Oct. 1724 and the report of the Committee). And if I judge
right somebody is perswaded to promise himself successe in carrying on the other publick
affairs without touching at all upon Woods patent, which (they say) will consequently dye
away of itself and have no farther ill effects on the Nation. They who tell him this are sure to
attain one of their ends viz. either to have the Session break up without doing the publick
businesse and granting the necessary Supplyes in the usual maner, and consequently they
will be rejoiced to have his Administration unsuccessful; or (which some of them seem
to be sanguine enough to be able with the countenance of the Governement to carry) to
give the money, and not make any enquiry into or complaint of the halfpence, or take any
notice of any thing which hath passed on that head: they firmly beleive that those who
were in truth against them the last Session will be soe this, and will be openly declared
enemyes, while the others hug themselves in being moderate and willing to prevent things
from coming to warmth; and then they will pretend by this conduct to intitle themselves
to as much favor and credit as they were possessed of under the late Administracion. You
may depend upon it that this game is playing and thought very far from being a desperate

[525] Henry Sydney (1641–1704), 1st earl of Romney, lord lieut. [I] 1692–5.
[526] Sir Thomas Pengelly.

one. I long to have your sentiments of the freindly debate between three Gentlemen of this countrey and those in another place; for one time or other that affair will become more publick and not be wholly confined to a few hands who have the originals and may not be very fond of making things more publick then they now are. Should I not also complement my Lord Chief Justice Raymond[527] with whom I have a good deal of acquaintance and from whom I have received great civilityes.

652. Alan I, Dublin, to Thomas, 15 Mar. 1724[/5][528]

(1248/6/169–72)

My letter of the 13th instant which goes by the pacquet will certainly come to your hand before this can; which the Attorney General promises to deliver into your own hand as soon as conveniently may be after he gets to London; but I take it for granted that another letter of the 13th (which also goes by a private hand) will not be brought soe soon to you as this will. When a letter of that date is brought, it will presently occur to you that the hint I am now about to give you of the person who will deliver it) ought to put you upon your guard in your conversation and discourse with that person: for tho he very well deserves the character I have given you of him in that letter (for he is a man of good understanding and perfectly well apprised of the affairs of this Kingdome and hath appeared zealously in its interests) yet I know his attachments are such that when they are added to an ambitious temper, and an opinion of ones own sufficiencye may mightily encline a man to take the shortest way to attain his ends. But I think I can have no doubt of the bearers delivering this into your hands, and will therefore speak plainer English then otherwise I would venture to doe: yet not soe plain that everyone else shal know my meaning as fully as you will. This you may depend upon that the person who told you in soe solemn a maner that all people would be left at their own liberty etc thought it either necessary or convenient for him to use every way he could think of, that nobody should make use of that liberty to which they were to be left: No caresses were wanting to soften those who were supposed capable to be made pliant, nor was there any difficultye made of letting people know what was hoped (if not expected) from those who had dependancyes, and what the consequences of being refractory might (nay would certainly) prove. Those who were against warm methods at the beginning were not in so good grace as those who either advised, or were concerned, in putting them, in execution. To be short I cannot but think that a certain person knew ——[529] had the success of Woods coyne soe much at heart, that he was perswaded to undertake the businesse, as the man in the world most likely to effect it, and to deliver some people in London from those difficultyes they have laboured under by means of this patent; and I confesse it is my thought that more zeal and industry could not have been used to attain this end, then was employed, if the success of it were to be attended with an entire restitucion of the same favor and employment which he formerly enjoyed. You may be sure those who were most zealous enemyes to the project were first and most warmly applyed

[527] Sir Robert Raymond had been promoted to lord chief justice of king's bench [E] in February.
[528] Printed in Coxe, *Walpole*, ii, 413–17.
[529] Presumably Robert Walpole is meant.

to, and all they could be brought to was this: that they beleived, if the patent was surrendred by Wood before the meeting of the Parliament, and thereby the fears and dissatisfactions of people were dispelled, Gentlemen would not be fond of bringing that matter again on the carpett notwithstanding all the hard treatment and ill language the nation had receive; but that no body would go into the giving any thing to Wood in nature of a compensation for giving up the patent. People seemed to hope and promised to use their endeavours that on this foot matters of supply etc might goe on in the ordinary course; and I am convinced that a certain person[530] after having spent some time in Ireland, became so far sensible of the temper of the Kingdome, that he gave it to be understood in London as his sense that no endeavours that had been used had in any sort reconciled men to the receiving that coyne, nor had influenced their meaner passions to an acquiescence in the pleasure of those who in this affair seem (to me (at least) to act like our masters. I beleive also that he gave as little hopes of an easy Session of Parliament (unlesse the patent should be previously given up) as he reasonably might, and that he put the maner of attaining that end and bringing that about upon the English ministry. If my accounts from London be well grounded they pretended stil to beleive that the granting the patent, and all that [had] been done by the Lords to whose consideration Woods petition was referred, and Woods his maner of executing the powers granted to him and everything done in England in this matter were right and everything done here had been wrong from the beginning; and that even giving Woods (but not in expresse words or by name to him) a compensation for his patent was not at all agreeable to those at [the] Helm, and would look like a victory obtained by us here: and I fancy they insisted on Irelands being contented with the Kings not going farther to support the patent or create a currency for Woods coyne then had been done already, as enough to satisfye them, which is just what the order in Councel saith and was signifyed to the late Justices with directions to make it publick for which I refer you to some late papers delivered you by C.P.[531] from me. It was matter of amazement to those with whom a certain person advised, and pretended to be much influenced by their advice to be told every post that no orders were come about declaring what the King intended to doe to remove the difficultyes which Ireland laboured under from this patents stil hanging over our heads; but soe it was, only we were told that there would be time enough before the meeting of the Parliament; and that in the mean time no methods were used to bring them in upon us. Now I am pretty well convinced that the satisfaction (which Mr S[outhwell] and others in London had written was ordered to be given to Ireland) meant no more then letting matters remain quiet till the meeting of the Parliament; and I cannot but think that all hands have been at work to incline men to think it will be advisable to go on in the ordinary course of granting Supplyes, with out an actual surrender of the patent, or taking the least notice there ever had been such a thing in the world: However wild this scheme may seem to you, yet I am fully perswaded that it is hoped and expected that a push will be made to goe on with what we call the Kings businesse with all convenient dispatch, and if any thing of the halfpence should be mentioned to endeavour to postpone that till the other is finished, with full assurances of our having time enough for that and all other matters which relate to our Countrey. I have good reason now to be strong of opinion

---

[530] Probably the duke of Grafton.

[531] Charles Powell (*d.* c. 1653), of St James's, Westminster, one of the six clerks in chancery [I] (see *Anglo-Irish Politics*, ii, 329).

(which I confesse I was not of till very lately) that it is not in their thoughts to give up the patent before the Session, but fairly to try whether people can be cajolled or discoursed into the measures from the other side prescribed to us; and as far as I can judge there are some people here who give hopes that this scheme will succeed: but I own I am not of the number, yet cannot find reasons strong enough to think I have convinced a freind of yours that things will not answer expectation. It is very hard to perswade a man to beleive that will come to passe, which he hath a mind to have never happen. When I have spoke my mind freely on this occasion I have been asked who the people are who will create the opposition to things proceeding according to desire; and have been told that some people dare not after what they have done (whether it was meant in this particular or in other matters I know not, but beleive in other things which are come to the knowledge of a very discerning man) and that those who are not under any apprehensions from a sense of their past actions (whom I understood by the term used which was <u>others</u>) would not oppose the Kings affairs. You see that stil not giving opposition to Wood is called the Kings businesse, or that opposing the halfpence is to oppose the Kings businesse and consequently that those who will not oppose him are to be understood to doe it, as on the other hand those who will stil oppose that patent are to be deemed obstructors of it. Nay soe far have I heard matters carryed that no one body in the Kings service in any station removable at pleasure will be continued who shal not proceed in the method expected (not excepting even the most honourable the Privy Councel). I was on Sunday at the Castle and shewed my Lord Lieutenant your letter of the ninth by which he saw that Mrs Duncombes secret about Sir Wm Thompson was not so entirely new but that I had notice of it from you. He seemed a good deal surprized at the later part of your letter in which you tell me you hope I am putting things into the best order I can for going into England, and told me it would not be reasonable to desire or expect a licence of absence soe near before the opening of the Parliament; I told him I had no such thought; then saith he, you speak upon a supposition the King should dismisse you his service before that time (which I doe not beleive). To that I said it was not unlikely I should attend the Session in some capacitye either publick or private; and added that offering the Seal about from hand to hand, till somebody could be found to take it up, was certainly intended to lessen me, and in great measure did doe: the former he allowed but not in any sort the later, and added that my enemyes could not think I had lost any honour in this whole affair which had been so long between more then one ministry and me. To conclude this tedious scrawle I must tell you that my Lord [*Carteret's*] heart is bent on going through this session (as if there never had been such a thing as Woods patent in the Kingdome) and that he thinks I can and shal be an obstacle to their designs; thus far he doth me no injurye, for I have told him what I intend to doe in that matter; and hope shal not be disappointed in it. But if he beleives that the intimations given out that everybody in the Kings service shal be removed who will not comply, can incline me to quit or be silent in the interest of my Countrey he entertains thoughts lesse honourable then I apprehend my conduct hitherto in this and other affairs, have given him reason to have of me. I confesse that from his surprize at hearing what you mentioned in relation to my going over soon, and other circumstances I cannot but apprehend that his view is to have me passe the Session on the woolsack and there go through the drudgerye of it, and find the reward (which I have been so long and often told of) of my long faithful and painful services a supersedeas.[532] When that comes I shal cease to be the Kings servant, but not his loyal subject; but whenever that happens it will (in other peoples opinions) make me more Master of my self and my own actions, then when I was in emploiment. But I own I have alway looked on the salary and perquisites of my office as due to me for officiating in the Chancery and elsewhere as Chancellor; and I thank God I have alway thought my self at liberty to act vote and speak in Parliament (as a Lord) just in the same maner while I was on the woolsack as I should [have] done on one of the Benches. I have now done and am obliged to Mr W[*alpole*] for his honourable performance of all the promises he made me in England; but most particularly in providing me a Successor of such eminencye as Sir Wm. T[*hompson*] is known to be. I will not be longer in the power of an insolent man, but will in a little time save them the trouble of doing an act they have so often threatned me with but for other reasons then goodwill toward me have defferd the execution of their indignation.

653. *Alan I, Dublin, to Thomas, 18 Mar. 1724[/5]*

(1248/6/173–6)

Yesterday morning I received your letter of the eleventh, and have sent you inclosed the seal which was upon it. I doe not remember ever to have seen you seal with such an head; but if you have any such, I cannot but think upon looking on the wax and paper under it that the letter was sealed more then once; for there seems to me to have been a little flat wax put on at first and that afterward a good deal more wax hath been put on and then the visible impression made. Your own eyes and your memory of a thing which was soe lately done will give you an oportunitye to tell me whether any body hath peeped into that letter, which is a most unjustifiable practice unless when there is reason to suspect some thing is carrying on to the disturbance of the peace and safety of the Kingdome: and if that be your case and mine, that we are in the number of the supposed enemyes of the publick quiet I cannot but think those suspicions are very unsuitable returns for the services we have both done to his Majestye. Let me know your thoughts about the seal, for methinks from such a little incident one may make a judgement of mens being affected well or ill to us in greater matters. I come now to the subject of your letter. Soon after receiving it about eleven of the Clock I went to the Castle and was carryed to the Closet; my Lord Lieutenant was not then there, but followed me soon, and accosted me in this maner; that the pacquet was come in by which he found that the house of Lords had <u>mumbled</u> [533] one of my decrees; but that he had noe news in his letters, and asked me whether I had any. I told him I had received your letter of the eleventh and shewed it to him, in which you tell me Sir W[*illiam*] T[*hompson*] desires to know what he hath done to deserve transportacion and that he will remain where he is till he knows.

His Excellencye was pleased to say he did not beleive there was any foundacion to beleive the Seal had been offered to him, which I own surprized me a good deal, considering that

---

[532] In law a writ suspending proceedings: used here to mean Alan's supersession as lord chancellor [I].

[533] Mauled (*OED*; an obsolete usage).

Colonel Pyott had wrote a letter to Colonel Montague[534] in which he told him that Lord Lieutenant and the Chancellor were to be laid aside; and that Mrs Duncombe had also received a letter the post after from a Lady in which Sir Wm Thompson is named to be the person who is like to succeed me, both which letters his Excellencye knew the contents of, as he also did of yours of 27th Febr. in which you advise me to put things in preparacion to goe for England (if that should be found advisable) and also yours of the 2d March to the same purpose and that of the 9th in which you say the whisper of the house of Commons on the day before had been that the Seal had been offered to Sir Wm. T[*hompson*]. All this (added to the treatment I meet in other things from the same quarter) I say seems to me to leave very little room to doubt what is intended toward me. I make no question but that Mr Woods Patrons have been fully informed that the Chancellor is inflexible in that affair; that all the douceurs hitherto used have not had the desired effect; You are soe conversant in sailing to know that when the wind is bare the pilot is obliged to make tacks and trips, and alter the first intended course: and very probably those on your side of the water who doe not know my temper may fancy that giving out I am to be superseded may put me on thinking what that accursed thing is which hath raised the storm against me, and may put me on a resolution to cast it overboard. That my being unalterable in the matter of Woods patent (for I now chuse to use that phrase rather then his Copper or Coyne) is my great sin I am firmly perswaded: but till I can be convinced that I have hitherto been in the wrong in that matter I shal persevere in my opposicion to that affair, whatever the consequence shal be personally to me, even tho I should be deprived of what a man of much greater judgement esteems a punishment to him and soe I think transportacion to be, and soe he thought when he used the expression. Now to come to Mr Edgeworths appeal in the house of Lord; I confesse I am something surprized to find that some part of his peticion is true (which I doe not take to be alway the case in what some people say nay swear). He saith I refused to allow him to prove exhibits by witnesses viva voce on the hearing of the cause; soe far I beleive he may have said what is true, but he was pleased to conceal the reasons which induced me to leave him to prove his writings (or exhibits) by Commission or before the Examiner where the depositions of the witnesses are reduced into writing and signed by the witnesses: for you must know that every Court in Dublin, had been entertained with causes in which Edward Edgeworth (the Appellant) was concerned, and in all or most of them the matter in doubt was in relation to deeds or writings under which Edward Edgeworth claimed which his adversaryes not only alleged but gave shrewd reasons to induce other people at least to suspect of forgerye. I am mistaken if there were not trials in the Court of Exchequer and Common Pleas of issues wherein the matter left to the consideration of the Jury was whether the writings or deeds under which Edward claimed were real or forged. I confesse from the observation I could make in the cause wherein I made the orders complained of, I was soe unfortunate to have great suspicion that the writings by him sett up were not really executed: and if I am not misinformed, some witnesses produced by him and examined on his behalf in the Exchequer were tryed for and convicted of perjury by them committed in their examinations. These things weighed with me to leave Edward Edgeworth to proceed in the ordinary course to examine in writing and not ore tenus[535]

---

[534]Edward Montagu (aft. 1684–1738), MP [GB] Northampton, col., 11th Foot.

[535]Presented orally.

in open Court; and whereas he in his peticion saith that ex debito justiciae[536] the party ought to be admitted to prove writings by witnesses viva voce,[537] and complains as if that had been denyed to him which is never denyed in any other case: I must take leave to inform you that the ordinary course of the Court is to examine witnesses by commission or before an examiner in writing; not but that it is usual upon mocion to grant liberty to prove exhibits on the hearing by witnesses to be then produced viva voce: but sure this rule is not to be understood in that sense that the Court may not oblige the party to examine in writing, if it see cause for soe doing. And of my desire to have an examination in a cause of this kind to proceed in the most solemn maner induced me to deny the motion which was made that he might prove exhibits by witnesses viva voce on the hearing, I think my desire to find out truth, in the best maner, by letting the witnesses see that what they deposed was to be reduced into writing and signed by them and to remain in the office to be used as proof that they had swore such and such things, if hereafter they should be charged with having foreswore themselves, was sufficient ground to lead me to leave Mr Edgeworth to examine his witnesses in the ordinary course of the Court. But there is one part of Mr Edgeworths deposicion before the Lords, is plainly meant by him as a personal indignitye to me; he saith I was in a great passion when I denyed the motion, and that I shook my head: with what view this particular is taken notice of in the order I will not enquire but I can readily guesse at the inducement the Gentleman had to make it part of his examination; viz. that I was partially inclined to his adversarye. Now this gives me reason to call to mind a story which I have heard of Harry Mordant.[538] When Sir Henry Dutton Colt mocioned the house of Commons against an undue election and return of Mr M[*ontagu*] for the City of Westminster,[539] the sitting member applyed to Mr Mordant to be at the Committee and (as far as with justice he could doe it) for his freindship. Mr Mordant told him he would not fail to attend and assured him that he needed not be apprehensive of his favouring the peticioner, for (saith he) Sir Henry is the most worthlesse creature alive except one Mr M[*ontagu*] leaving it to the construction of the sitting member whether the words Mr M[*ontagu*] were to be taken as spoken in the accusative or vocative case. This is literally the case of the worthy appellant and appellee in respect to me; and I must own I think it is an happinesse to that part of the Kingdome where these Gentlemen have their lott fallen that they are not in league. But Mr Edgeworth hath attained two ends which he aimed at viz. the throwing dirt on me (who abominate forgery and may be apt to expresse my indignation where I see cause to suspect it hath been practiced, nay to goe soe far as to shake my head) and putting off, the hearing his appeal; Now as far I can carry the matter in my morye the cause was only thus far determined by me, that there should be a trial by leading order whether the writings under which he claimed were really executed by his father.

Upon this trial the appellant would have had oportunitye to produce his witnesses viva voce, and the truth of their testimonye would be weighed and considered by a Jury of their

---

[536] As of right.

[537] Orally.

[538] Hon. Harry Mordaunt (1663–1720), MP [GB] 1692–8, 1701–2, 1705–*d*.

[539] Sir Henry Dutton Colt (c. 1646–1711), of St James's, Westminster, petitioned against the return of Charles Montagu (1661–1715), later 1st earl of Halifax, after a particularly contentious election at Westminster in 1698, for which see *HC 1690–1715*, ii, 398–9.

neighbours who probably might know how far they were persons of credit much better then I could. If indeed I had decreed against the deed set up by Edward because not proved (after he had offered to prove it by witnesses viva voce) or if he had not had sufficient time to examine in writing, his complaint might have some reason in it; but the truth is this seems to me not at all to be levelled at as an error in the decree, but rather as a personal imputation of partialitye to me. I must alway beleive the highest judicature will not suffer any thing to be said or done before them which doth not consist with the respect due to the Court from whose decree the appeal is: And this is beleive may have been done, or may hereafter be done. But I confesse I shal not think that Lord Midleton suffers in case he be ill treated by Mr E[*dgeworth*] with impunitye but think the Chancellor suffers.

[*PS*] The order which was made in Dec. 1720 is alleged not to have been drawn up, but I am told by the Clerks on both sides (for the Register[540] is now unfortunately out of town) that fact is false and that the Defendant in the appeal hath it in England, and consequently the appellant might have it. If I understand the examination of Edgeworths sollicitor right he would insinuate that the Register had spoke to me about giving out the Copy of the minutes when I denyed the motion made to prove exhibits by witnesses viva voce, and that the Register had told him soe and that I directed the contrary. Now this must be understood as if the Register had applyed to me privately and received those directions from me, whereas he never once spoke to me in that or any other matter depending in Court but publickly in Court; it will import him to explain that matter; which I am sure amounts in truth to no more then this: I beleive Mr Edgeworth did by his Councel move the Court for an order to command the Register to deliver out a Copy of the minutes when the motion for examining witnesses in Court viva voce to exhibits was denyed; and as far as I can recollect I asked the Register why he had refused to make out a copy of those minutes, to which his answer was (to the best of my memory) but the course of the Court was contrary and that orders are never drawn up or copyes given of minutes, when the Court denyes the mocion: and the Register appealed to all the Clerks for his justification, and they (particularly Mr Gering who was Clerk for the Appellant[541]) owned that the course of the Court had been alway otherwise, upon which I thought there was no reason to vary from the constant course of the Court: But upon considering the matter now I doe not see upon what good reason that usage is founded; for a suitor may be as much injured by the Courts denying a reasonable mocion may [*sic*] on his behalf as by granting an unreasonable mocion made against him: and ought to be able to releive himself by appeal. When the Register comes to town I suppose he will by affidavit put the whole matter in a true light; and I will let you see what he saith of it.

654. *Thomas to Alan I, 18 Mar. 1724/5*

(1248/6/399–400)

This is the first time I have gone abroad for ten dayes, having in consequence of a shivering fitt, been seizd with an intermitting feaver, twas nott violent though probably itt might

---

[540]Richard Tisdall, MP [I].

[541]Richard Geering, MP [I].

have been soe, if an early stop had nott putt to itt, by what Dr Hales[542] prescribd, part of which I beleive was an infusion of the Barke[543] in a bitter tincture, which I have usually taken.

The Articles against Lord M[*acclesfield*] being this morning to bee reported carryd mee to the house, where some advocates for him, (tho alasse the honour of the house was the motive) endeavourd att a Recommitment, uppon suggestion that severall facts wherewith hee was charged were in point of time committed before the last Act of Grace,[544] in debating whereon, some things were sayd, which our leaders did nott relish, butt hop't wee should nott unnecessarily lett our selves into a matter of soe great consequence; To witt whither an Act of Grace were pleadable against an impeachment. This being gott over, wee proceeded to reading the Articles one by one, the question being putt uppon each Article; I hope in an hours time, which will bee soone enough for making up this, I shall have a short abridgment of them, to send you herewith. You must surely from every quarter have heard of your speedy removal, for tis become somuch the towne talke that I admire how the prints come to omitt itt, butt your successor is nott soe positively namd, though Mr West is sayd to bee the happy man, for I am pretty well assurd Sir Wm Tomson will nott touch, I hope you will prepare for coming away, wherein I thinke you should advise with those freinds whoe have stood by you.

I am almost of opinion that Lord C[*arteret*] will bee continued, att least till after the Session, which probably is the reason of his reservednesse in relation the Woods coine.

I am told that the Presidentship lyes between the D[*uke*] of D[*evonshire*] and Lord Trevor,[545] how twill bee orderd I cannott tell, nor must I say my thoughts uppon soe nice a subject.

I forgott to tell you that the Articles are orderd to bee engrossd, for that probably theyle goe to the Lords tomorrow.[546] Mr Conduite was the mover of a Recommitment,[547] Mr Young was for adjourning the debate till tomorrow,[548] Mr W[*alpole*] and the Sollicitor Generall for going on,[549] in short they were extremely disconcerted, which was what I founded my opinion uppon, that they would find themselves under a necessity of proceeding, for I never thought that any thing short of that would drive them into itt.

[PS] The number of Articles are encrease beyond what I thought by making each Masters case a seperate one, whereas I beleive joining them togather was att first intended.

---

[542] Richard Hale.

[543] 'Jesuit's Bark' or 'Peruvian Bark': a remedy against fever made from the bark of the cinchona.

[544] The Indemnity Act (masters in chancery) of 1724 (11 Geo. I, c. 2).

[545] Thomas Trevor (1658–1730), 1st Baron Trevor. On 22 Mar. it was reported in London that Devonshire 'may have it if he will' (HMC, *Var. Coll.*, viii, 389): he was appointed.

[546] The articles were engrossed on 18 Mar. (*CJ*, xx, 453–9); a clause was added on the 19th, reserving to the Commons the liberty of introducing further articles (*CJ*, xx, 460); and the Lords received them on the 20th (*LJ*, xxii, 459).

[547] John Conduitt (1688–1737), of Cranbury Park, Hants, MP [GB] Whitchurch. Confirmed in *Knatchbull Diary*, 42.

[548] William Yonge. He supported Conduitt (*Knatchbull Diary*, 42).

[549] Robert Walpole and Sir Clement Wearg. Walpole's position is confirmed in *Knatchbull Diary*, 42.

655. *St John III, Kilkenny, to Alan I, 21 Mar. 1724/5*

(1248/6/177–8)

I came to this place last night, and intend to stay here till Wednesday next, and from thence to go directly to Corke. This town is full of the news you gave me a hint of, and by some letters I have received both from Dublin and London, I doubt there is too much reason for the report. I need not say much upon this occasion, because I am sure you have too much Spirit and understanding to be concern'd at the loss of an Employment, which you have discharg'd and will part with the greatest honour, and reputation.

I am drinking your health with Will Flower,[550] Agar,[551] Weymes[552] and Dick St George,[553] the last of which began your health yesterday, at the Mayors Table, in a Bumper, and was pledg'd by the whole company. Mr John Cuffe[554] was the next person call'd upon, and began Mr C[onoll]ys in the same manner. I own I was always afraid he did not deserve the countenance you always shewed him, and could wish he had not been a witness to a conversation at which Lord Mountjoy, Mr Bernard[555] etc were present.

656. *Alan I, Dublin, to Thomas, 22 Mar 1724[/5]*

(1248/6/179–82)

Tho I wrote to you a very long letter of two sheets on Saturday, I find myself obliged to trouble you again now, cheifly to rectifye some mistakes in my former; which was wrote when Mr Cowper the Deputy Register[556] was out of town: He tells me that Mr Gering and Mr Powel[557] lay under a mistake (as he beleives) in saying that the order of December 1720 was drawn up; for that he cannot find it ever was, and therefore the notion they had (of its being drawn up) he beleives to be without ground: which matter he represents in this maner; that he is very certain if ever Mr Edgeworth or his Agent applyed to have it drawn up within a year and a day after making and pronouncing the order, he would have drawn it up; but doth not find nor beleive that any such application was made within that time, by which neglect of theirs it was (through their default) out of his power to draw up the order after the year and day was past, without a mocion made to the Court to empower and require the Register to doe it on the former minutes: and that no such mocion ever was made. This is a matter barely relating to the Register, and no way points to me. But as to that which seems to complain directly of me, that I had refused to allow Mr Edgeworth to prove exhibits by witnesses viva voce, he tells me that the notice and motion was to prove

---

[550] MP [I].

[551] James Agar, MP [I].

[552] Patrick Weymes, MP [I].

[553] Richard St George, MP [I].

[554] MP [I].

[555] Francis Bernard, MP [I].

[556] William Cooper (1689–1761), of Templeogue, Co. Dublin, MP [I] 1733–*d.*; a connection of the Hills (*Hist. Ir. Parl.*, iii, 492–3).

[557] Richard Geering, MP [I] and Charles Powell, two of the six clerks.

(not exhibits) but <u>a deed in the singular number</u>. And that the allegacion in the peticion that the Appellant (being denyed that liberty) suffered a condicional decree in expectacion that the Court would on farther consideration permit him to prove that deed viva voce, for which he had again moved (but without successe) Cowper saith that the first of these facts is impossible because the conditional decree was made in Trinitye term or the sittings after it and the motion for producing witnesses viva voce was not made till Michaelmas term following or after that term: Soe that his expecting to be admitted to prove his deed when he should again apply for that liberty could not be the motive to him to suffer a condicional decree, which was suffered before the motion was first made and refused; and he adds that upon search made in his books he finds not that ever any new motion was made for Mr Edgeworth to be admitted to prove his deed viva voce. He adds farther that it was urged at the bar that Mr Edgeworth had brought an ejectment on the title of Robert Adaire,[558] Lessor in ejectment in the Court of Common Pleas against one Smith for another parcel of Land (pretended to be conveyed by that deed to Adaire in trust for the appellant) and that the Jury in the Common Pleas after all Edgeworths evidence was fully heard to prove the perfection of that deed, found a general verdict for Smith who was either a purchaser or Lessee under Robert Edgeworth[559] (as Swift the defendant in the appeal[560] is) soe that the verdict given by the Jury against Adaire (whose name is only used in trust for the appellant and who knew nothing of the conveyance made to him) is in effect a finding against the realitye of the deed: for if that deed had been proved to the satisfaction of the Jury there was no room to find a verdict for Smith the defendant; but the verdict was entirely to the satisfaction of the Court and of all who heard the trial; You will see by the minutes of what I said when I refused to allow proving this deed viva voce that I expressed myself in this maner, that all the Courts rung of forgery and perjury in the suits between the two Edgeworths[561] and indeed the Judges in Commons in my hearing expressed themselves with the greatest detestation and abhorrence of the wickednesse which was either in Robert or in his son Edward (the Appellant) but they did not say in which the fault seemed to lye. These were my inducements to take the most wary steps in the examining the witnesses in this Case, and not to goe of the course of the Court, by making an order to examine viva voce. That the course of the Court is to examine by Commission or before an examiner in writing must be allowed and appears from this, that an examinacion viva voce can never be without a previous order; soe then it is not by course of the Court to be done. But the order of the Lords (as Cowper tells me) hath never been served on him by Mr Edgeworth; nor in my opinion ever will be; for he will consider that he hath already attained his ends viz. putting off the appeal from being heard at present, and throwing dirt on me as if I had done things very ignorantly (at least) if not worse. The order is that Mr Cowper shal <u>(when the appeal comes to be heard)</u> shew cause why he should not pay the Costs of not drawing up the order or giving the attested Copy of the minutes. Now I verily think the Appellant never intends to have the cause heard on the appeal, and consequently Cowper

[558] Robert Adair (c. 1682–1737), of Hollybrook, Co. Wicklow, MP [I] 1727–d., a trustee for a settlement made by Edgeworth's father on his wife Catherine (née Tyrrell) (Brown, *Reports of Cases*, iii, 121, 122–4; *Hist. Ir. Parl.*, iii, 55).

[559] Robert Edgeworth, MP [I], Edward's father.

[560] Meade Swift (1682–1738), of Lynn, Co. Westmeath, a first cousin of Jonathan Swift.

[561] For the case of *Edgeworth* v. *Edgeworth*, see Brown, *Reports of Cases*, ii, 326–33.

will never come to shew cause against his paying the Costs; and by this means the honest Appellant may propose to himself that the Lords will never hear the reasons why I refused to make the order moved for. It is true that Mr Swift is at liberty to move the Lords to assign a day for hearing, and I cannot but think that the affidavit which the Register saith he is ready to make may properly enough be used to induce the Lords to grant a short day for hearing the Appeal, at which time one would hope some one Lord might take the oportunitye of observing how well I have been treated by the Appellant in this whole affair. But I shal be pretty easy whatever they doe in that particular from a sense I have from the best witnesse that I acted as in the presence of God with uprightnesse, and (I think) with caution and prudence in this dirty affair. There came in a pacquet yesterday with letters of the 16th but none from you, which (I hope) proceeds from your resolution to write to me by some safe hand and not from indisposition. We here think Lord M[*acclesfield'*]s businesse is as good as over: if soe you see I have made a right judgement all along of the event of it.

[*PS*] Our minutes are not taken as fully as in England, for there is not any notice taken in them that the Councel for Swift mentioned the trial in the Common Pleas against Smith, or that a verdict had been found against the deed under which the Appellant (in the name of Adaires Lessee) made title, which however moved the Court in some measure to deny the motion, the Councel of the Appellant never gainsaying what was so offered by Swifts councel, and consequently the Court taking it for granted. Our news now is that we are to have Mr West (not Sir William Thompson) for our Chancellor: I wish my Successor more ease and satisfaction in his Station and that his services may find better acceptance with his Master, then mine ever have done with mine; but this I can say that mine began very early and that I served the Elector of Brunswick[562] at the time his Succession was not very zealously supported by others; and have never failed to doe the best in my power to serve his Majestye since his accession to the throne; tho I have not been able to bring myself to a slavish subserviency to the sentiments of some ministers (the rock I have split upon) but if I were to make the voyage again I would steer just the same course: I doe not find that the news which the last pacquet gives us of the death of a great countryman of ours much affects people, who cannot recollect any one good office he ever did to this Kingdome in his several Stations and Grandeur.[563]

657. *Thomas to Alan I, 27 Mar. 1725*[564]

(1248/6/187–8)

Last night came yours of the 12th 18th and 22d. I cannott account for the first nott coming sooner, for on Wensday wee had those of the 15th. I have nott been out since my last to

---

[562]George I.

[563]Henry Boyle (1669–1725), 1st Baron Carleton, died on 14 Mar. 1725 at his London residence, Carleton House in Pall Mall (*HC 1690–1715*, iii, 302).

[564]Letter endorsed by Alan I: 'Tho: Brodrick … that his former letter was sealed with my sister Couthopes seal and not opened. Presses me to lay down, without losse of time but not to come away till after the Session without consulting my freinds. Advises my telling Lord Lieutenant explicitly what I can and what I will not doe. Edgeworths peticion aimed at me. Addicional salary to be given a new Chancellor'.

you, butt hope soone to bee able to goe abroad, (which I will if I can) especially now that the weather is alterd, for when I rose, itt raind hard, the wind being come Southerly and the air warmer.

If I am able I will goe through the serverall parts of all three butt least I should nott, will begin with what most imediately relates to you; the head which you sent is Mrs C[*ourthope*] nott having my owne seale about mee, I made use of itt, making up my letter att Bond street, which I left open, in order to add anything I mett with, before I did soe, I beleive you had itt, as itt went.

I never heard any body speake perticulary of Woods pattent being to bee given up, butt that in general such orders had been sent as would give satisfaction, if they were communicated, butt these generals goe with mee for nothing, however I resolvd to lett you know what I heard. You desire my opinion as to laying downe, which you say you can now doe with honour, to which I can onely say, that in my opinion this mallicious turne will bee given, Hee layd nott downe till hee saw vissibly hee could noe longer hold; you are nott to understand mee as if I thought your holding either fitt or practicable, which brings itt to this short point, what method is most reasonably to bee taken. Surely the people of Ireland must bee strangely alterd, nay infatuated if a declaration (long since publisht) against compulsory means, will soe far prevaile as that this matter shall sleep, the Parliaments going on to graunt supplyes in the usuall manner; I doubt nott sycophants talking this language, butt will both houses come under the denomination, I thinke this was the intended scheme from the beginning, and the rather from any expression I heard made use of, to witt: Things can never bee sayd to bee safe till after an easy session of Parliament.

If this then bee the case your conduct is next to bee considered.

If you are layd aside (which I am very inclinable to beleive) nothing remains butt your coming immediately away or staying till after the session, my opinion remains what my last told you, that you ought to consult your freinds as to the prudentiall part, you owe itt to those whoe stuck by you, take their advice, and follow itt.

Take the matter now in another veiwe, you are to continue in order to become the catts foote, (butt assure your selfe) for noe longer time then till itt shall appear how far you can bee prevaild uppon, which to mee whoe know you is a sencelesse project, which may however possibly bee entertaind with some hopes, att least a possibillity of Successe. In which case I thinke itt incumbent uppon you as well on account of your owne charecter, as in justice to my Lord Lieutenant to desire plainly to know how far his orders reach, for that if they fall short of what in your opinion (nott that of others), will bee satisfactory, by making the nation safe, you freely owne your resolution of doing and contributing all in your power (in a proper place) towards making itt soe, [?then submitting] therefore to his Excellency whither hee thinks a man in your station acting as you determine to doe, can bee what will bee easy for him, that you thinke the Kings service and good of the country soe deeply as well as mutually concernd, that you are fixt.

This mankind must agree honourable, I am sure tis the honest part. I have sayd what occurs to mee as fully (though breifly) as I can. Can you rationally expect ever to live att ease (nott to say safely) with out sacrificing honour and conscience to those whoe have hitherto, (and I fear resolve persevering) made use of all their power for attaining their point, every day gives fresh instances how groundlesse such a thought would bee, this must bee obvious all first sight.

I come now to Mr Edgworths affair and should beleive as you doe, that hee will nott serve the order, if I did nott thinke more att bottom then his interest, butt this I vehemently suspect, and I thinke you may well conclude soe, if hee serves the order.

Surely the omission in the minutes of the tryall in the C[ommon] Pleas was a very greate one for the councill of the other side nott denying the fact would bee a reason (strong as mustard) for your refusall of the motion for examining Ore tenus, butt you say the minutes will shew what reasons you gave for rejecting the motion; the refusall of the coppy of them was certainly wrong, lett the practice bee what twill, itt will bee incumbent on Mr Cooper to sett things in a cleare light, (by affidavit) [?or] by coming over, as well for his own justiffication, as for doing you justice, for if I am nott misinformed severall of the Lords seemd to suspect Mr Edgworths having sworne largely,[565] and if that appear, may deale with him accordingly.

I doe nott wonder att the little regrett occasioned among you, by a late peice of news, if you knew what I doe, itt could nott happen otherwise. That the Seals were nott formally offerd Sir W[illiam] T[hompson] when hee mentioned transportation I beleive, butt that hee was sounded I am pretty confident; Hee is now spoake of againe and some doubt whither an additionall sallary, or a continuance of the pension of £1200 may nott overballance transportation. I thinke itt signifies little on which side the question goes, butt I beleive itt to bee true that Mr W[est] desired from Mr Gibbon (whoe was in the chair of the Committee) that hee might carry the citty Bill to the Lords,[566] which lookes to mee as if hee thought thereby to appear in the votes as having the cheife conduct of itt. Remember what the fly on the cart wheele sayd.[567]

658. St John III, Cork, to Alan I, 29 Mar. 1725

(1248/6/189–90)

… Just as I finisht this letter I received the favour of yours of the 25th, which I will not trouble you with an Answer to by this Post, further then by assuring you that if you think my going into England will, at this time, be of the least service or Advantage to you, which is not at all impossible, I am most ready and willing to do so, and will embark here in 6 hours after I receive your letter. I know my Uncle has infinitely more weight and Interest then I can ever pretend to; but perhaps his Indisposition or other reasons will not allow him to run up and down and attend great men, as I should do with pleasure upon this occasion, and indeed I cannot help thinking that something of this kind is absolutely necessary. When things are in Aequilibrio[568] a very small matter will turn the Balance …

---

[565] Loosely or inaccurately; defined in *OED* as an obsolete usage.

[566] Although Phillips Gybbon, MP Rye, had taken the chair of the committee of the whole house on the City Elections Bill, on 19 Mar. Richard West was ordered to carry the bill to the upper house (*CJ*, xx, 437, 462).

[567] From Aesop's fable, 'The Fly on the Wheel': a fly sat upon the axle of a chariot wheel and said, 'What a lot of dust I raise!'.

[568] In equilibrium.

659. Thomas to Alan I, 3 Apr. 1725[569]

(1248/6/191–2)

Though I have nothing to say other then repetition of what I have formerly told you, I choose to write, least you should thinke mee remisse, which may lay you under some concerne, though my being still confind (by illnesse) and like to remaine soe, for some time, may very justiably bee an excuse.

You may assure your selfe the honest part you have acted in reference to Woods pattent, is a mortal sinn, nott to bee forgiven, since I am pretty sure you will never repent of having soe done. If you judge (as you ought) by things and nott words, you cannott doubt my being in the right of what I have told you, and if more were required for your conviction, every day affords new arguments.

The treatment which your decrees meet with, surely is sufficient proofe; Lord H[arcourt] is a diligent attender, and you very well know by whose compasse hee steers; I am to beleive, (att least nott say otherwise) all the Lords doe, is right; however people without doores whoe are strangers to their reasons, fancy (groundlessly) that there is sometimes more then the merits, in veiwe. Submitt cheerfully, wishing Ireland an abler chancellor, for I thinke I may say noe body doubts your integrity.

I hope you have gone a great way in setling your own private affairs, finish itt assoone as you can, in order to come away assoone as you shall find itt reasonable soe to doe, though my health bee very uncertaine, my mind is perfectly att ease, and when you are out of businesse, yours will bee soe too.

660. Thomas to Alan I, 3 Apr. 1725

(1248/6/193–4)

I choose to write this in a seperate paper, because you say in your last (which I have owned) that you had shewn my severall letters to Lord Lieutenant and possibly may that which goes with this, wherefore I will not intermix any of my own affairs ... I hope before your coming away you will soe order payment of your growing rent as may make accounts plaine hereafter, for I suppose you nor I may possibly never take a journy for Ireland, after your coming over. You are certainly in the right that the share you have had in opposing Woods pattent is soe mortall a sinne as never to bee forgiven, the reason I thinke plaine. You cannott butt see by Lord H[arcourt's] manner of treating all your decrees how industriously faults are sought after, whither they are soe matters nott, hee represents them such, and soe they are to bee taken, I need nott tell you by what compasse hee steers.

---

[569]Letter endorsed by Alan I: 'Tho: Brodrick ... that I ought to lay down, since my opposition to Woods patent is unpardonable. That I am treated ill by Lord Harcourt in the house of Lords'.

I would nott for his pension of £5000[570] bee in his or your case, nott in his, because I would doe noe dirty worke, nor in yours because I would nott beare indignityes (as you doe) for nott doing itt.

I thinke what I proposd in my last letter, (take the matter either way) will attaine your end, for if uppon your declaring how you will act in parliament you shall bee remov'd, (which certainly will bee the case, unlesse they doe itt without such declaration) youl goe of with honour in every mans opinion, and nott lesse soe, if they are pleasd to remove you for a cause which every body will understand, I thinke this a happy incident which gives you soe fair an opertunity of doing what (in my opinion) you ought in prudence and reason to have done without itt … Mrs C[ourthope] … resolves setling in the country (which her circumstances require) having given warning for quitting Bond street att Midsomer; I thinke therefore, (without taking notice of being informd hereof) you should tell her you take for graunted shee will soone after your letter can reach her, bee getting to Pepper Hara, this is advisable for more reasons then one, though att the same time you may very truly hint the benefitt which your daughter will receive thereby, besides that I have wrote you word that I propose advantage to my selfe (in point of health) by ease and good air, both which I dearly want, for I remaine as yett confind, and nott like to bee better whilst I stay in towne; till I have itt, (which I hope will bee soone) ile give you the best accounts I can of what comes to my knowledge.

[*PS*] I heare that instead of confessing, Lord M[*acclesfield's*] answer will bee double the lenghth of the Articles, that tis ingrossing, and will bee putt in next weeke,[571] soe that probably the parliament will bee sitting, till, or after the middle of May.

Councill is to bee heard before the Lords next Tuesday for and against the citty Bill, which has already raisd a very greate ferment, and if I mistake nott likelyer to encrease then subside.

661. *Thomas to Alan I, Dublin, 6 Apr. 1725*[572]

(1248/6/195–6)

Last night I receivd yours of the 27 of last month, with the coppy of Mr Coopers affidavit, and of the certifficate of the Clerkes, which to indifferent men will appeare (in my opinion) very sufficient answers to Mr Edgworth petition, butt what signifyes that to such as resolve nott to see.

You mention the coppyes of the minutes to bee likewise sent, butt you either omitted putting them up, or they are taken outt, for none came; I am nott skilfull in discovering breaking open letters, and therefore send you the seale, which seems to have been crackt, and putt togather againe, tis a villanous practice, wherfore I will hope my suspition groundlesse.

---

[570]Originally awarded in 1720 when he was appointed lord privy seal and recently increased (Coxe, *Walpole*, i, 190).

[571]Macclesfield's answer, responding to each article in turn, was submitted to the Lords on Thursday, 8 Apr. (*LJ*, xxii, 487–94).

[572]Letter endorsed by Alan I: 'Tho: Brodrick … believes Lord M[*acclesfield*] not concerned in speaking ill of me in Dom. Proc. but my good friend Lord H[*arcourt*]'.

The last day I was in the house Ned Nicholas[573] told mee the story which you say current with you, butt sayd upon my pressing to know the certainty, that hee could nott vouch the truth of itt, butt would informe himself fully, since which I have enquird of some whoe came to see mee, and cannott by what I heare see ground to beleive itt of the person, butt am told twas sayd by a speciall freind of yours, whoe makes itt his businesse to say and doe every thing to your prejudice.

I hope you have by this time done what one way or other will sett you att ease, you see how necessary itt is, therefore loose noe time towards attaining what is soe desirable, remembring the fathers advice to a sonne, When a quarrell is unavoidable, bee sure give the first blow.

662. *Alan I, Dublin, to Thomas, 10 Apr. 1725*

(1248/6/197–8)

A Councel hath been summoned to meet this morning, cheifly to consider of the best methods to discover the robbers and murtherers of one Johnston a Quaker in the Kings County,[574] whom the villains put to most exquisite torture to oblige him to confesse where his money was by setting him on a grid Iron upon lighted coals; in so much that his privy parts being soe burned and swelled that he dyed in the greatest pain and misery imaginable.[575] It is earlier then [com]ports with the Castle people, who sate up late last night among the company (for Fryday is what we call a Castle night) then I did at home: soe that I take this oportunitye to own the receit of yours of the third, which I shewed to my Lord Lieutenant, who was extreamly startled at the advice you give me in it to lay down, and with the greatest earnestnesse disswaded me from it; and by his maner I think he spoke his mind; He told me that he had alway made his judgement how he should conduct himself when he had a struggle with enemyes, by considering in the first place what they wished he should doe; and unlesse there appeared better reasons then he thought were for my desiring to lay down he alway declined doing it upon this ground that they had reasons for wishing it, which were not at all for my advantage.

He said it was more advantageous to me in point of character to be laid aside without assigning any reason or perhaps being able to give any then to throw up in warmth. I urged that my continuing in emploiment continued me stil in some mens power to insult me, as I knew was done upon every occasion by a mercenary Sycophant, who knew what would be agreeable to the hand from which he received his daily bread,[576] I found by him that he hath thoughts entirely as honourable and favourable of that person as either you or I. When we were parting he conjured me not to doe any thing hastily or in passion, and (for more reasons then one I fancy) did very much in earnest urge my taking time

---

[573] Edward Nicholas (c. 1662–1726), of West Horsley, Surrey, MP [GB] Shaftesbury.

[574] Edward Johnstone of Carroe, King's County (R.S. Harrison, *A Biographical Dictionary of Irish Quakers* (Dublin, 1997), 66).

[575] A proclamation was issued on 10 Apr. for the apprehension of Johnstone's murderers (*Proclamations*, ed. Kelly and Lyons, iii, 146–7). Alan was among the signatories.

[576] Presumably William Conolly, in which case the 'hand' would be that of Robert Walpole.

before I determined any thing. I said I was already determined to doe the same thing in Parliament in reference to Mr Woods affair, either in or out of employment and that it must not surprise if I did soe, when that matter came on the Stage which I had hitherto done, in which I was unalterable. But I plainly perceive people entertain hopes matters may be soe ordered that things may goe on in the usual course without taking notice that ever that patent had been granted or was stil subsisting, upon a perswasion that the thing is wholly over and never again to be moved in, to bring that good coyne among us. The precedent is looked upon by those of this mind, either as a thing which will never arise against us in judgement, or rather as a peice of prerogative not to be receded from; but the great thing aimed seems to me to let things remain at present sub silentio; and then the good usage the people here have mett for having endeavoured to prevent that coyn to come among them, is to be passed over. How these things will end I know not; but this I am sure of that some of those who have hitherto appeared most violent against that project, seem to me to be complaisant in other matters as inconsistent with the good of the Kingdome as this either is or ever was thought to be; and I am apt to beleive from such observations as I have made of that sort that a certain person intends to play the same part the next Session which he did the last when Dr Boulter was Bishop of Bristol only. As to your Nephew he is not yet in town, but when he comes I will let him know what you say and give him my own thought of his conduct in the affair about which you write. If you turn to my letters dated about the time the thing which creates the dispute was first in agitation you will see that I cautioned you of what you say hath hapned. What you mention in relacion to my self in a post or two you shal see how that matter stands. I beleive you doe by this time think I gave a shrewd guesse what probably would be the event of a certain affair, for Idem manens idem semper facit idem.[577] Let me know what the Gentleman is about who gave you a letter dated 13th March, and whom I mentioned in another which went another way. His freinds here say he is like to attain his end upon which he went over, and I am much mistaken if he will not take all necessary measures to attain it. I will write to my sister by next pacquet: Lord Shanon lyes soe ill that I think he will not recover: I make no doubt his Successor will be one as much to be confided in by those in power as he was, and that was enough in conscience.

663. *Thomas to Alan I, 13 Apr. 1725*[578]

(1248/6/199–200)

Last night I receivd the minutes (without date) which your last mentioned, and which mine told you I had nott received. Mr Rogerson[579] on Saturday gave mee your letter, and this

---

[577]See above, p. 172.

[578]Letter endorsed by Alan I: 'Tho: Brodrick … suspects Tho: Carter to be wavering in the matter of Woods patent. Urges me to lay down it being intended only to make use of me in that matter in parliament and then to use me ill as hitherto. Hath been ill of the gravel but is easyer. Warm speeches against the supply for making good the deficiencyes of the Civil list. But carryed by a great majoritye, as all things proposed by the Court will be; particularly Lord Bullenbrooks bill'.

[579]John Rogerson, MP [I].

day Mr Carter[580] another; I thinke I see ground enough to apprehend what you hinted in the former of these butt of this I shall bee able to say more in a little time, for I will take some convenient opertunity of sounding that matter.

I perceive by that I had from Mr R[ogerson] that you had already taken the method I proposd, butt att the same time must observe that there appeard noe great likelyhood of attaining the end I intended; if you have nott already, repeat itt againe, for to mee the designe appears very plaine, and I thinke you cannott butt see through itt, one way or other disingage your selfe; if others will nott save you that trouble, which last I thinke the more eligible, if to bee compared.

Mr C[arter] in our discourse sayd hee hoped you would nott come away, (taking your removall for graunted) since that would bee depriving your freinds of such advice as they would rely on.

I was very explicit with him (which perhaps youl wonder att) in one thing, to witt, That in my opinion whilst the pattent subsisted, I thought the Kingdom could never bee secure against the halfe pence, which hee would nott allow, for that nothing butt force (even millitary) could make any body take them, which I told him I could nott agree to, for that artifice added to heare, might goe a great way, the inevitable consequence of which I tooke to bee a losse of fifty per Cent on all estates, this hee readily agreed to, supposing they obtain a currency, butt sayd the difficult part was how to manage this matter in Parliament whither before or after the supply, I told him my opinion was positively against coming after, and consequently must bee either before or att the same time, otherwise without the spiritt of prophecy I thought I might conclude their obtaining what hee seemd to beleive impossible, and thus wee parted.

I never shewd the papers brought mee by C[harles] P[owell] to more then one freind (you having cautioned against itt) whoe entirely agreed with mee that every part you had therein, was right, and I thinke all indifferent men must bee of that opinion. After I was in some measure recoverd after my feaver, I was seizd with a dreadfull fitt of the gravel; last Fryday a ragged stone came away as big as a large Pea, bloody water followd itt for four and twenty hours, attended with a great deale of paine, which I now apprehend to have been onely the sorenesse of the part, without any other to follow, for I am now in great measure att ease. I knew nott whither Mrs C[ourthope's] neighbour[581] did his part, butt make noe doubt that with pleasure hee held up a corner.

Sir T[homas] P[engelly] spoake very sharpely, butt without what is properly to bee calld bitternesse, concluding noe otherwise then what rightly flowed from indisputable premises.

You should certainly have complimented Sir R[obert] R[aymond] ere now.

Sir P[eter] King remains where hee was, butt possibly may nott long doe soe, if hee thinke fitt to change his post, for in my opinion the Com[mission] for the great Seale will bee changed, Sir J[oseph] J[ekyll] having spoake very strongly against the supply for making good the deficiency of the civill list. Mr T. did soe likewise.[582] However the question was

---

[580] Thomas Carter, MP [I].

[581] Possibly Lord Anglesey (Viscount Valentia in the Irish peerage), who may have influenced some tory MPs. In 1727 he lived in New Bond Street (*A True and Exact List of … the Present Parliament of Great Britain … Together with Their Houses, Lodgings, and Usual Places of Abode, in and about the Cities of London and Westminster …* [1729], 7).

[582] Given the context, this is probably George Treby, also a placeman, and a political ally of Lord Carteret (*HC 1715–54*, ii, 476–7).

carryd by a majority of above 100 which you may remarke uppon in your mind, butt I am sure ile make none in writing, save that twas soe late in the session as the ninth of Aprill, which noebody can deny, and the message brought to the house butt the day before.

I heard Lord Bullingbrooks Bill is to come in,[583] if soe tis plaine what game is playing, our great men can doe what they please.

664. *Thomas to Alan I, 20 Apr. 1725*[584]

(1248/6/201–2)

You know my opinion has alwayes been that turning outt was more eligible then laying downe, and consequently nott to bee done butt on failure of the other; if what I can learne bee true, you will soone bee putt att ease, butt soe little is to bee depended uppon (especially in cases where deceiving is the designe) soe that I must againe give my opinion for your doing (in case of failure) what others pretend saving you the trouble of. Whoe doubts butt that what you would avoid is what some people desire, and whoe doubts that their reasons are nott designed or intended for your advantage, what then remains for you to doe, butt consulting what will bee most for your honour. You cannott forgett the treatment you receivd when Lord S[*underland*] had (as hee thought) carryd his point, butt found the difficultyes to bee encountred by your removal; twas then lett fall, for their owne, nott your sake, though the world was perswaded to beleive your continuance the effect of your freinds sollicitation, the same game is to bee played over againe; will you bee caught a second time in that trap, I am well informd the judges have been consulted touching a successor in the fixing which more difficultyes appear then were expected, from whence I infer very strongly that making you the catts foote, is likely enough to bee their dernier resort; does nott every day give fresh proofs of the indignityes layd uppon you, and soe far was itt carryd (if I am informd right, and I thinke I am) that one day last weeke a noble Lord movd an Addresse to the King for your removal, twas nott indeed seconded, Ile leave you to judge the reasons, such presedents are nott perhaps liked.

What you say in another case is applicable to this of yours. Idem manens idem semper facit idem.

Twill in a little time bee sayd you tooke the opertunity of laying downe when there was nott reasonable time for considering of, and appointing a successor, and that you affectedly delayed declaring your intentions till the King should bee gon, or going, if you can beare every days insults, and reconcile those to your charecter I have noe more to say, butt if nott, act with that spiritt that becomes a man of honour and honesty. If I were in like circumstances Mr W[*est's*] employment should nott prevaile on mee. This relates ([?tis] true) imediately to your selfe, and therfore you must determine; butt att the same time our family is concernd, resolve as you thinke best, having soe done, putt your intentions in execution without losse of time.

---

[583] A petition from Bolingbroke, for restitution to his estates, was presented on 20 Feb. with an explicit endorsement from the king, and leave was given for a bill (*CJ*, xx, 499–500).

[584] Letter endorsed by Alan I: 'Tho: Brodrick … advises my laying down. That the ministry intend to make use in carrying through the Session and then turn me out. Presses my laying down'.

I cannott omitt acquainting you with what past in conversation with a person of the nicest honour, and your true freind, whoe vissited mee in my illnesse, Does your brother says hee intend to serve after the many indignityes putt uppon him, his bearing what hee formerly did (purely I know for the Kings service) has brought his charecter more in question, then can bee imagined, surely hee will consider this, when the use made by his enemyes will bee, that heel bear all for his places sake. You cannott forgett the speech you made on delivery of the Popery Bill (by order of the house) to Lord Lieutenant[585] and must remember what a speciall freind of yours sayd to a man of the first quallity, whose answer was, I had none of the mony wherefore I am for passing the Bill, – manet alto menti repostum[586]; tis in your owne power to putt your selfe out of his, which with the greatest pleasure heel alwayes make use of.

I am scarce able to tell you the numbers upon the mocion for leave to bring in Lord Bullingbrokes Bill Yeas 231 Noes 113 with the former the Court Toryes and Scots.[587]

665. *Thomas to Alan I, 20 Apr. 1725*

(1248/6/203–4)

Though I was really extremely sore on Saturday I would have made a shift to write, if before that time I could have seen the gentleman from whom I first received your letter; which I have since done; to him I frankly communicated what had passt between mee and another whom you will easily guesse, whereat hee was strangely surprizd, nott having the least notion of what I told him, butt was very well pleasd att my giving him so much light, for that hee resolvd to goe on with him as usually, taking for graunted his being of the same opinion hee alwayes had understood him to bee, and without discovering the least suspition of his being changd, assuring him of his owne being unalterably determined in a thing whereon hee was sure somuch depended; hee told mee one circumstance which hee ownd gave him great suspition, in confirmation of my suspition, and a strong one itt was, On Sunday, I was told (what you say has been wrote hence) that Mr C[588] had succeeded, having certainly been with W[alpole] and askt whither I knew the perticular, I answerd noe, nor doe I sayes the other, butt I thinke I shall soon learne itt, this was by one whose intelligence I know is good.

I now goe to another subject that of Woods pattent, Mr R[589] tells mee that having had conversation with men of figure uppon that subject, hee had honestly deliverd his opinion that if itt subsisted till the P[arliament] mett, hee could nott see the least probabillity of a succesfull session, butt beleivd the contrary, to [w]hich hee added that hee thought

---

[585] Presumably when Alan was Speaker of the house of commons: the reference would thus be to one of the three major popery bills prepared by the house of commons in 1703, 1707 and 1709.

[586] Virgil, *Aeneid*, i, 26–7: '*manet alta mente repostum iudicium Paridis*' (the judgment of Paris stayed deep in her heart).

[587] Figures confirmed in *CJ*, xx, 500. According to Knatchbull, 52 tories voted with the majority and only five against. He also recorded Thomas as saying in the debate that 'this was laying a foundation for a revolution and that we are as we were once under the influence of French ladies' (*Knatchbull Diary*, 48).

[588] Presumably the chief secretary, Thomas Clutterbuck.

[589] Probably John Rogerson, MP [I].

nothing soe likely to keep that cloud hanging over us, as giving (even faint) hopes that the point might bee weatherd without a surrender of itt, that hee would as often as opertunity offerd againe and againe repeat the same thing, declaring that hee should alwayes thinke himselfe bound (in duty to his country) to insist uppon what hee thought was the onely effectuall security, and would act accordingly, abstract from all private veiws whatever. I forgott to tell you in my last that Mr C sayd hee wisht hee could have seen your sone before coming away, in order to have known his sentiments butt that hee was out of towne.

How far people may bee prevaild uppon, and consequently how this matter may end, I know nott, though Mr R. thinks the thing impossible, butt in this wee entirely agreed, that the fate of the Kingdom depended uppon itt, for that although att present gentlemen might bee resolute, twelve yeares to come might bee time enough for working our destruction; this hee sayd in answer to the argument of security, grounded uppon the universall detestation of the people to the project. Though I write darkely you will I make noe doubt understand [?each point], to which ile adde any thing that occurs before sending itt away, for though I date itt as Tuesday tis wrote on Munday evening. I was this morning told (with assurance) that the designe of removing you att present is layd aside, uppon what has come uppon that subject from ———— you see how you are treated, and why.

666. *Thomas to Alan I, Dublin, 22 Apr. 1725*[590]

(1248/6/11–12)

The fatigue of Tuesday has rendred mee incapable of going abroad since, soe as to learne any thing more then that yesterday Edgworths case was before the Lords and (as well as my informer could tell mee) your D[eputy] Register examined, what immediately related to him I did nott enquire into, butt am assurd that in the debate all the severest things and reflections possible uppon you were plentifully thrown out.[591] That partiality might in some cases prevaile, butt that in others nott, which therefore would bee of lesse ill consequence then ignorance, or a resolution of preventing as far as in you lay Appeals coming hither, that they wisht some of the ministry had been there, that of [?ten] decrees nott any one affirmed, misserable therefore must bee the case of suitors; surely the Register, or some other whoe can better tell then my selfe, will bee perticular therein, in order to give you the best light they can.

Those whoe soe extremely compassionated the poore suitors, were Lord H[arcourt] Lord L.[592] and Lord B.[593] you cannott surely haesitate one moment uppon what you ought to doe immediately.

---

[590]Letter endorsed by Alan I: 'Tho: Brodrick … that I am ill treated in the house of Lords, presses me to lay down forthwith'.

[591]Edgeworth's complaint against Cooper, the deputy register, was dismissed, as were his allegations against Alan, for having instructed the deputy register not to provide Edgeworth with a copy of the court minutes (*LJ*, xxii, 513).

[592]Nicholas Lechmere (1675–1727), 1st Baron Lechmere.

[593]Allen Bathurst (1684–1775), 1st Baron Bathurst.

667. *Thomas to Alan I, Dublin, 24 Apr. 1725*[594]

(1248/6/207–8)

The Commons Replication to Lord M[*acclesfield's*] answer is sent to the Lords, itt concludes generally in the common forme, butt that is introducd very hansomly, though short.

I am told that Thursday sennight will bee appointed for beginning the tryall, you see I have judged rightly from the beginning, that itt could nott bee lett drop.

I say nothing of your owne affair because I make noe doubt butt you will have putt an end to itt, before this can reach you; If [*the king*] can bee brought into itt, yours will nott bee the onely remove, this youl assure your selfe of, for I have very good grounds for what I say.

I cannott yett send you a perfect list (butt soon will) of the negatives to the mocion uppon Lord B[*olingbroke's*] petition, when you have itt, youl see most of them are men of weight, whose being independent, bespeakes what probably others would have done, had they been under like circumstances.

The Toryes promise themselves (and I beleive uppon very good grounds,) a share in the administration ere long, which a very speciall freind of yours has for some time past assured them would bee brought about; I wish the very little which I sayd bee nott prophetick, that a foundation was laying for a Rerevolution, by the influence and power of French Ladyes.[595]

I thinke the list pretty exact.

668. *Alan I, Dublin, to Thomas, at his lodgings in the Privy Garden, Whitehall, 29 Apr. 1725*

(1248/6/213–14)

This letter will probably goe by the expresse whom my Lord Lieutenant sends to acquaint his Majestye with my having applyed to him to intimate my resolution not to serve as Chancellor in the approaching Session of Parliament. I attempted to see him yesterday after the Chancery rose, but he was gone abroad; but last night about seven I mett him and shewed him that part of your letter of the 20th and your entire letter of the 22th which relate to my quitting. He greatly disswaded me from doing it, urged that what H[*arcourt*] said was no more minded then the barking of a dog, and went not beyond the Lobby, that the mocion in the house not being seconded shewed that (indeed) the ministry were in the thing, but had not strength enough to carry it. That I doe not think to be the true reason, but the end was attained when I was named in the house in that ungracious maner and the making the motion was in the news letters and prints; as it is in one of the Dublin ones. He told me that no time was to be lost if I was determined; but that he must intimate it without losse of time that his Majestye might consider of a Successor, and that I ought to continue to act as hitherto till things were settled, which I think to be right and resolve to doe so. He was most

---

[594]Letter endorsed by Alan I: 'Tho: Brodrick … that the ministry will endeavour to bring the King in to remove Lord Carteret. Presses me to lay down'.

[595]See above, p. 113.

urgent in his disswasions that I had suffered no indignitye, and what H[*arcourt*] L[*echmere*] and B[*athurst*] said was not to be regarded, that he beleived they would not even after the Session here was over be able to remove me, which I wonder at his saying considering how many greater things W[*alpole*] hath of late brought to passe to his knowledge. But this is wrote in the morning before my going to the Castle which I resolve to doe as soon as I have closed this, and there tell him that my fixed and unalterable purpose is to quit. I am in a good deal of doubt as to the maner, whether to doe it by memorial in writing directly to the King, which may contain some things which I would have come to his knowledge, and never will any other way; nor even by that way if the memorial be sent to the Secretary; but that may be obviated by your delivering it with your own hand, and an audience will not be denyed you on that or any other occasion. But there is this objection to this way of proceeding, that when it is in writing it is liable to the criticisms observacions and cavils of my good freinds; and that tho you should deliver it with your own hand, it is very possible his Majestye may never give himself the trouble of reading it. Soe that which way I shal proceed I am as yet in doubt, but the next post will ascertain you; if that doth not bring you a draught of a memorial, you will rightly conclude I have dropt the thought of applying directly to the King.

Sure it will be advisable for you to make as early declaracion of my intencions and what I have done as is possible. You shal soon hear what I resolve to doe and how to dispose of myself for the remainder of my life: If I be advised by my freinds to remain here this Session I am fixed in two things, first, to do nothing which I think will hurt the publick, next, to serve the King (consistent with the good of the Kingdome, which I take to be one and the same). I put the publick before the King is named because I think he is alway included in it: but not with intent to be understood that I prefer anything to the Kings service, but if supporting Wood coyne shal be called the Kings service I shal be obliged to excuse my self from being of that number. I will here add that I resolve to act in every thing to the utmost of my power for the honour of my Lord Lieutenant.

[PS] Pray is the person you describe by the letter B. my Namesake, or some other Lord B.[596]

669. *Thomas to Alan I, Dublin, 1 May 1725*

(1248/6/215–16)

I should bee a good deale surprizd att your silence (nott having a word from you since yours of the 10th of last month) did I nott beleive itt was occasioned by your time being taken up in setling your owne affairs, as well as the business of the Court, and I am the more confirmed herein, because your freinds in Bond street have heard nothing, though I know you intended writing to them very soone after your last to mee.

I suppose you heare from other hands the fate of all your decrees as fast as they come before the Lords.

---

[596]By namesake, Allen, Lord Bathurst is meant. See below, p. 199.

I beleive you will very soone find, what I onely hinted in my last, to bee true; the Duke of Kingston[597] (nott mentioned till of late) is sayd to succeed Lord Carterett, and Mr Rogerson you, I owne for the sake of the country I am pleasd with the last, I know his sentiments in relation to Woods pattent, and have good reason to beleive hee has very fairly and franckly spoake his mind, from whence I conclude, what I have all along beleivd would prove the case, that the Duceur[598] of laying itt aside was reservd for a new Lord Lieutenant.

Tis intended (as I heare) to make a very short businesse of Lord Macclesfeilds impeachment, and that the King will soone after tis over, goe abroad,[599] you will therefore think my advice right, in nott giving opertunity to say that you delayd signifying your resolution till too late, by reason of the Kings absence.

670. Alan I, Dublin, to Thomas, 1 May 1725[600]

(1248/6/217–18)

The expresse which went hence yesterday with a letter to the Secretary of State from my Lord Lieutenant to notifye that I had applyed to him that his Majestye would be pleased to give me leave to surrender the Seal,[601] will have delivered also to you mine of the 28th of April by which you will see that I resolved (in compliance to your repeated advice and that of my freinds here) to lay down: No body was more warm or readier to give that advice, then the person, whose sense in the matter of Mr Woods coyne, Mr C[*lutterbuck*] told you he had so much desired but could not have by his being at that time out of town: from that and some expressions he lately used, I apprehend he may have entertained very vain expectacions; and if my conjecture be in any measure right, those probably must proceed from some words which may have been artfully let fall by a certain person on your side of the water to him to bring him into measures, which the Speaker of them never had the least thought of making good. My last letter told you that possibly I might desire the trouble of you to deliver a memorial directly to his Majestye, but on considering that matter again I thought it not advisable to proceed that way, which would put me under great difficultyes as to the maner of doing it. To have applyed to his Majestye in blunt terms to have leave to lay down the Seal without assigning any reason why I made that request would naturally imply a disinclination to serve the King of which I am sure I am not capable: If I resorted to the common motives for making such applications, indisposition of body, and my advanced age, this would have given some countenance to the revilings and lyes of Shimei[602] as if I

---

[597] Evelyn Pierrepont (1665–1726), 1st duke of Kingston-upon-Hull.

[598] *Douceur:* pleasure.

[599] On 22 Apr. Charles Delafaye had reported that 'Lord Macclesfield's business' would be completed quickly, adding 'So some talk of the king's going in three weeks. Probably it will not much exceed that time'. (HMC, *Polwarth MSS*, iv, 305.)

[600] Partly printed in Coxe, *Walpole*, ii, 417–19.

[601] TNA, SP 63/385/90: Carteret to Newcastle, 29 Apr. 1725.

[602] King David adjured Solomon: 'And, behold, thou hast with thee Shimei the son of Gera, a Benjamite of Bahurim, which cursed me with a grievous curse in the day when I went to Mahanaim: but he came down to meet me at Jordan, and I swore to him by the Lord, saying, I will not put thee to death with the sword. Now therefore hold him not guiltless: for thou art a wise man, and knowest what thou oughtest to do unto him; but his hoar head bring thou down to the grave with blood'. (1 Kings, 2: 8–9.)

acknowledged my self uncapable to serve the King in that office; whereas the truth is that I have health of body and strength enough to give me reason to beleive I should be able to discharge my duty on the woolsack this Session as well as I ever did in any former. To have told the truth, which is, that tho I am sensible of as much abilitye of body and mind to goe through with the businesse of Parliament and the duty of Chancellor as I ever have been since I came into that place, I did think my self to have been soe ill treated, that I did not look on my self in any sort obliged to run the risque of a fit of sicknesse after the Session, occasioned by the fatigue of the Session, this would or might put me upon explaining my self, whether I meant from [*the king*] or the Ministry, or any others and who in particular; and I doe not think it prudent to be in danger of making such explanacion as I must make if I told plainly what I resent (and I think very justly). These reasons and the advice of my freinds make me content myself with desiring my Lord Lieutenant to send no more in his letter then that I had attended him on Wednesday, and desired him to lay before his Majestye my humble request that I might have leave to surrender the Seal; and instead of a letter drawn by the Secretary, founded upon such expostulacions as I had made about my ill treatment at the time I waited on him, and which I then intended to mention in my memorial to the King, and told him soe the night when I first waited on him. The letter drawn by the Secretarye shewed me the difficultyes I should lye under, in such a maner that I could never agree it should be sent, as prepared. To say truth I am far from thinking Mr Tickel (who drew it) to have intended any unkindnesse to me in the draught (which mentioned ill treatment I had received <u>in England lately</u>) and that I found myself through want of health and my great age uncapable <u>to discharge the duty of my office</u>; I never did, or can yet with truth say soe: but my real resolution is that I will not wear myself farther out or run the hazard of sicknesse by the pains I shal take on the woolsack during the Session after the usage I have mett with, and when I know what I shal meet when the purpose of those by whose permission I yet continue in my employment, is effected by my assistance. But I beleive the letter was directed to be drawn by my Lord Lieutenant in such a maner that I might see how my resentment would look as put into writing by Tickel; and I think he took this to be as good a method to disswade me from using expressions of resentment, as persisting in giving me his expresse opinion to the contrary, which he fairly and strongly did. But I must be just to him in letting you know that he sent Tickels draught to me by Mr Clutterbuck who left it with me, to correct and alter and amend as I thought proper, since it was to contain my sense he desired me to expresse it in my own words; and on the best considerations of some of my most faithful and judicious freinds they and I thought it would be sufficiently understood by the world upon what motives I resigned without expressing them, so I went to the Castle and desired the letter might go in general terms, and soe it is sent. His Lordship I told you was greatly shocked at the resolucion I had taken; thought I gratifyed my enemyes in it, and should leave him under great difficultyes to hold a Parliament with a new Chancellor, who might prove a person not to be confided in, nor perhaps able to give him much assistance. This I though[t] proper to acquaint you with. Your Nephew[603] pretends to me that your demand on him will not come out such as you mention, but did not give me the satisfaction to see how the account stood by way of charge and discharge; and indeed I doe not find by him at what certain rent he holds

---

[603] St John III.

the Land or for what term. This confounded treatment hath prevented me from sending you an account how matters stand between us two. Our news here is that Batt Purdon is past hopes of recoverye,[604] and poor Harry Boyles Lady in extreme danger in a spotted feaver,[605] abundance of people have sickned and several dyed, who drunk Arack punch[606] at Corke Assises, and that country is represented to be generally sickly at this time …

671. *Thomas to Alan I, 4 May 1725*

(1248/6/221–2)

Att my returne from the house, I received (with great pleasure) yours of the 29th. ult. which I suppose (by nott being post marked) came by Lord Lieutenants expresse whoe came yesterday.

Lord F.[607] askt mee this day whither your good freinds had forc't you into laying downe, my answer was that I beleivd there needed noe compulsion, your honour being a sufficient motive, I then prayd him to tell mee whither hee knew the substance of what the expresse brought, for that I had great hopes that twas what I now find itt to have been, hee protested hee did nott know, butt from his question tis plaine, that other people have given that out, which I will confirme. I thinke the method you have taken much better then by a memorial in writing to the King, for though you might therein have layd before his Majesty what some people may nott bee very willing hee should know, you will have opertunity of acquainting him therewith after his returne home, for I am perswaded hee will bee soe gracious as to heare you, and soe good as to distinguish between misrepresentations and reall truths. I formerly told you my opinion of governing your selfe with respect to coming immediately away, or staying till after the session should bee over, I am still of the same sentiments that you ought therein to consult your freinds, butt I own I am for the latter for two reasons, If Woods patent bee to subsist, I make noe doubt of your doing all in your power to defeate that designe; in the next place you will in all reasonable and just things bee assistant to Lord C[arteret]. I know what my last told you was well grounded, with respect to him, though I am nott soe cleare with respect to your selfe, and therfore your laying downe may bee of use to him, since a new cheife Governor and Chancellor may bee thought too long a step, att the same time, for which reason onely, I am perswaded Mr R[ogerson] was thought on, for I thinke you may bee assured of his having very freely declard his opinion as to the pattent.

You very rightly interpreted the letter B to bee your namesake. The person whose opinion I told you, was your perticular freind att Midhurst,[608] and I am sure hee sayd what hee truly thought.

---

[604] Bartholomew Purdon, MP [I]. He survived.

[605] Catherine (née Coote), wife of Henry Boyle, MP [I], died on 5 May 1725.

[606] Arrack was a spirituous liquor distilled from sugar-cane, coconut or rice, and imported into Europe principally by the Dutch East India Company.

[607] See below, p. 203.

[608] The duke of Somerset.

Mrs C[*ourthope*] sent mee yesterday, a letter (to read) from my nephew,[609] which I hope shee will by this night communicate to you; I cant beare the thoughts of his embarking att Burdeaux, for the reason I told you, the danger of pyrates, butt am for his hastning to you after spending a very few dayes here, which makes your stay in Ireland for some time the more advisable, for I beleive (without partiality) hee will recommend himselfe to people there.

Yesterday two things (in my opinion) remarkable enough hapned in our house upon the (rejected) motion for incapacitating Lord B[*olingbroke*] sitting in either house, or holding any office, as youl see in the votes.[610] Mr W[*alpole*] sayd hee was positive that Lord B[*olingbroke*] had never since his being in the Kings service betrayd the Pretender, people were att a very great losse to find out then his meritt, which resolvd into his Majestys being best judge of that; this I take to have been extorted, by what was sayd that hee whoe had betrayd two, might bee reasonably suspected to play the same game with a third, a fair indication (as every body thought) that hee was againe to bee brought into businesse; and why nott as well as Lord H[*arcourt*].

The other notable speech fell from Pere Williams,[611] that if the instruction movd for, tooke place, the boone intended by the Bill would nott bee worth acceptance, from whence itt surely follows that Lord B[*olingbroke's*] interest somewhere must bee very strong, as indeed I beleive itt is, notwithstanding which if a whisper which went pretty glibly this morning prove true, hee may come short. Multa cadunt etc.[612]

Tis sayd the Emperors Resident[613] has (as from his master) represented the ill successe in Spaine, and losse of that Kingdom to the house of Austria, owing to this newly become favourite,[614] besides which wee hear of a memorial uppon subjects of more consequence, att the bare report whereof people seem a good deale startled, a little time will unfold these darke things.

The sixth of next month is talkt as fixt for the Kings embarking.

672. *Thomas to Alan I, 6 May 1725*[615]

(1248/6/223–4)

You may bee sure I made noe scruple of letting your freinds know what measures you have taken, and doe assure you tis applauded, this day, tis become coffee house newes.

---

[609] Alan II.

[610] On 3 May, before the House resolved itself into a committee of the whole to consider the Bill to restore Bolingbroke to his estates, a motion was made to instruct the committee to receive a clause to disqualify Bolingbroke from sitting in parliament or holding an office under the crown. This was defeated on a division, 154–84. (*CJ*, xx, 507–8.)

[611] William Peere Williams (c. 1664–1736), of Hoddesdon, Herts., MP [GB] Bishop's Castle 1722–7.

[612] The Latin proverb '*Multa cadunt inter calicem supremaque labra*' (There's many a slip 'twixt cup and lip).

[613] The Imperial envoy in London, Konrad Sigmund (1689–1727), Graf von Stahremberg.

[614] Lord Bolingbroke, in the Peace of Utrecht.

[615] Letter endorsed by Alan I: 'Tho: Brodrick … that my freinds applaud my having surrendred the Seal to which Lord Carterett recommended the Cheif Baron, but he declines it having a Cushion in England in view. The ministry under difficultyes whom to give it to and on other accounts.'

Lord Lieutenant recomended your cheife Baron,[616] butt hee has another veiwe, that of being brought hither, with prospect (as I suppose) of a vacancy on the bench, upon Sir P[eter] Kings being made Chancellor, whoe will bee your successor is (as yett) uncertaine,[617] butt negatively Mr Rogerson[618] (whoe is gone this morning with Mr Carter[619] towards Bath) will nott, I cannott say hee has been offerd itt, though I am pretty confident hee might have itt if hee pleasd, butt am very sure hee will nott accept itt, I thinke they are in some perplexity how to dispose of the Seale, which happens att an unlucky time, when the peace between the Emperor and Spaine has been declard by C[ount] Starembergh,[620] without the least previous intimation from any of his Majestys Ministers; what consequence that will have, time must determine, people are a good deale startled, and itt already affects the stocks, and consequently creditt. I suppose you know Mr Carters errant to bee, the purchasing from Lord B[erkeley],[621] the mastership of the Rolls, butt tis nott yett effected.

I take a motly ministry (very soone) for graunted; Lord B[olingbroke's] bill which yesterday passt our house, has entirely broken the Whigs, the independent ones leaving those of the Court to their new allyes, how long they will draw togather is uncertaine, butt I thinke may bee easily guesst, for I take our great mens dependance (generally) to bee uppon Lord H[arcourt's] fidelity, I say generally, because I know some of them have little dependance uppon itt, and I apprehend will nott long draw togather, though just att present, this may nott appeare vissibly to every body.

The farce of Lord M[acclesfield's] tryall is begun,[622] drop itt they could nott, how far they intend to carry itt, is yett a secrett, though I doubt nott its being long since concerted among themselves. Mr W[alpole] publiquely declard that the suitors were to bee noe loosers, nor the publique to pay any thing, butt wee are nott always tyed up to promises; this I am sure of, noe step has been yett made towards securing to the suitors what the masters prove deficient, which I thinke will appeare more then is generally imagined.

Your freind his Grace pushes earnestly for W[est] butt that meets with objections which arise from his own party, I am strongly of opinion that your Cheif Baron is wrote to, to know whither hee bee willing to decline his application for being brought over. Wee are extremely disconserted, how twill bee patcht up I cannott guesse, or whither (in earnest) itt can bee soe.

[616] Bernard Hale; Carteret sent this recommendation on the same day that he transmitted Alan's request to surrender the seal (TNA, SP 63/385/92–3: Carteret to Newcastle, 29 Apr. 1725).

[617] The duke of Rutland, for one, had already heard that Richard West had been nominated (TNA, SP 63/385/98: Rutland to Carteret, 6 May 1725). This was even before Carteret had been informed officially that Alan's resignation had been accepted.

[618] John Rogerson, MP [I].

[619] Thomas Carter, MP [I].

[620] On 5 May newspapers reported that Stahremberg had informed George I of the signing of a peace treaty between the emperor and the king of Spain (*Daily Journal*, 5 May 1725).

[621] Lord Berkeley of Stratton.

[622] On 6 May (*LJ*, xxii, 534).

673. *Thomas to Alan I, Dublin, 8 May 1725*

(1248/6/225–6)

I heare his Grace of G[rafton] sayes you are att lenghth turned out, butt that matter is throughly understood by every body.

I cannott learne whoe is to be your successor, nor doe I thinke tis determined, Mr W[est] is againe spoake of, butt as far as I can learne, hee is nott very fond of itt, hee certainly refused being Chief Justice. I am nott indeed sollicitous to know whoe is.

The evidence uppon the Articles of impeachment is soe very strong, that I heare the Lords are extremely incensed, insomuch that people begin to imagine the judgment will bee more severe then was att first expected; I allwayes told you itt could nott bee dropt. The Managers will finish their part on Munday, or Tuesday morning next, att farthest, what time his Lordship and his Councill will take up in the Reply is uncertaine, butt itt cannott bee very long, especially if the Lords should nott allow his giving evidence that former Chancellors have done the same things, which I beleive they will nott, for sakes sake, this would open a scene wee doe nott care to unfold.

I thinke the Parliament will rise the weeke after next.

I have had noe other letter from you since that dated the 10th of last month, except what came by the messinger, nor has Mrs C[ourthope] had any; you should nott have forgott writing to her.

674. *Alan I, Dublin, to Thomas, 9 May 1725*

(1248/6/227–8)

I am sure I received your letter of the 4th instant with as great pleasure as you expresse yourself to have been in upon reading mine of 29th of the last month, since it approves what I did both as to the matter and maner of doing it. I waited on my Lord Lieutenant and told him your thoughts and with what regard you had expressed your self toward him (in the whole tenor of it) and shewed him that part of it which related to my attending this Session here with a view of serving the King and him in all reasonable things, at which he expressed himself with great satisfaction and in a very handsome maner toward both; but seemed to doubt whether you reasoned right in your conjecture that what I had done would in any sort contribute to his service in the way you fancy, as if the removing a Cheif Governor as well as a Chancellor just before a Session of Parliament would not be thought too long a step to be taken at the same time. Doe not mistake my meaning, as if I would be understood that he thought he should be removed too, but I think he meant my giving up must not be understood as any way conducing to his being continued to hold the Parliament, which I think he looks on as a point wherein he shal not be disappointed by his enemyes, by reason [*the king*] will not be brought into it. But for my part I think men are but men and vary in their affections, however well founded: and I doe not see what can stem the torrent of power with which a certain person seems able to carry whatever he pleaseth. I am the more confirmed by the publick news of this pacquet that Mr H[oratio] W[alpole] is on his return from Paris, and he is a man of too much significancy not to be employed immediately, and nothing seems to me a post worth his acceptance but one of the first magnitude; and such an one is not (I doubt) now to be found without making a vacancye in one, whose present possessor cannot accept any thing lesse then this Governement in lieu of it: From this reason and the opinion I have of the good inclinacions which some in great power have toward my Lord C[*arteret*] I own I continue of the mind I have for some time past been, that we shal have a new cheif Governour before August. It is true there seems to me to be very good political reasons against recalling Lord C[*arteret*] before that time, but I cannot but beleive something will be of more weight then all those reasons seem to carry. I make no doubt but that before this comes to your hands you will be convinced that a certain affair, hath taken the turn I all along told you it would take in the end.[623] You misunderstood me if you beleived it would stop in the house of Commons to be my sense; no; I imagined it would finally come to nothing, I mean as to the condemnacion of what was imputed to the person, either by the facts not being proved or by their not being proved soe black as some people were pleased to think them. I have been a good deal puzzled to find out who the Lord F. is who asked you whether my good freinds had forced me to throw up. Is he a near relacion of my good freind Lord M[*ountjo*]y;[624] I beleive him to be the man; for by your maner I take it the words were spoke to you in the house of Commons, and I know none of that title in the house whose name begins F. but him; for I think Lord Fane is not a member.[625] Doe not feed yourself up with thoughts that they who have gone soe far in Lord B[*olingbroke'*]s matter will not be able to go through with all they intend in his favour, those are flattering and deceitful hopes and will disappoint those who take them up. For my part I begin to recollect and consider whether we have not been very injurious to two very great, and (for ought I can find if I can pin my faith on the sleeves of others) very good men I mean Lord H[*arcourt*] and L[*ord*] B[*olingbroke*] in beleiving of them as I own I have hitherto done, and I think such reflections ought to bring one to repentance, and yet that thought would lead me farther soe that I am not willing to pursue it farther. I am not surprised if the Imperial minister hath laid the losse of the Crown of Spain to the house of Austria, at Lord B[*olingbroke'*]s door; for I think the same thing was done in the beginning of his Majestyes reign; but I am much in the dark what that other memorial (which you say is talked of) can import, considering the description you give of its supposed matter in point of consequence to us: I resolve to proceed in the businesse of the Court,[626] in my usual maner, because I think it to be my duty. But it is not in complement to my Successor, to ease him of a good deal of trouble, or to give others any in correcting my mistakes, and rectifying what I doe amisse. I doe not beleive the Lord you named in your former letter will be Lord C[*arteret'*]s Successor, but rather another of the same Bench, who [you] will readilye guesse at. Nor have I the least thought of my Successor being the person you named in the same letter; he will be a man from another quarter of the earth. I am more lightsome then I was when I wrote last to you; for I find myself free from some uneasinesses that have too long been laid on me, and I rejoice in being discharged of what my enemyes would perswade the world I courted being under

---

[623] Macclesfield's impeachment.

[624] George Forbes (1685–1765), Viscount Forbes, 1st surviving son of the 2nd earl of Granard, whom he succeeded in 1734. His wife Catherine was Mountjoy's sister.

[625] Of the British house of commons. Lord Forbes was MP for Queenborough.

[626] Chancery [I].

the load of. I mean pretended favours and obligations, to be purchased at a rate I could not longer hold them at.

[PS] I will serve the King while I live to the utmost of my power with faith and zeal and be as much an humble servant to those who have been kind to me as they deserve from me. Pray tell me in plain words: Did Sir Tho: Pengelly at any time say in the house of Commons he would prove bribery and corruption on Lord M[acclesfield] for that seems to be a personal undertaking of facts within his knowledge: You call something a farce; I assure you we make it more soe here then you seem to doe. But I think it must have some consequences in the end which will be considerable, if the charge be proved, on Lord M[acclesfield] for he must be censured for them, if they be really crimes, and I think v. v.[627] if he be not punished (if the facts be proved) that can proceed from nothing but the things laid to his charge not being crimes. In the list you sent me I doe not find the name of your freind in Chancery Lane,[628] nor Mr Pultneys,[629] nor Mr Franklands[630] nor Sir Robert Riches,[631] were they in the house. Hath not your freind contributed hitherto too much to strengthen those hands, which neither he nor (for ought I see) any body can now in the least thing oppose. I was in the house when somebody in a former Session was against enquiring into the articles of the deficiencye of money to support the Civil list, least doing it should be made use as a reason why for the future we should be under a necessitye of supplying like deficiencyes: I suppose during the late debate on the Civil list money he was not of the same sentiments. At the time he declared himself in that maner I was surprized, as indeed I have been more then once at other compliances, without which I think matters could not have been carried to the lengths we have seen. I heard last night that the Cheif Baron will accept the Seal, but am not certain of it; but somebody must doe it, for I will not longer sweat under the load of it, when nothing but ill treatment can be the consequence of my doing soe. Harry Boyles wife is dead and I beleive soe is Batt Purdon both of the same distemper, a pleuritical feaver at Ballyclogh.

675. *Thomas to Alan I, Dublin, 13 May 1725*

(1248/6/231–2)

Your successor (Mr West) is this evening to kisse the Kings hand; the discourse of anothers successor is againe revived, H[oratio] W[alpole] being come to towne; I have hitherto guesst right, and beleive I have done soe in this instance.

I thinke your C[hief] B[aron] will bee brought over upon the first vacancy. The towne talke of many removes some as I told you there will bee (among them the two P[ulteneys][632]) butt I fancy nott to the number (att least att present) which is given out. Lord M[acclesfield's] tryall goes on slowly, though the Lords sitt every day till six, or near itt, the managers are

---

[627] *vice versa.*

[628] Sir Joseph Jekyll (*A True and Exact List …* [1729], 54).

[629] Daniel, Harry or William Pulteney.

[630] Thomas Frankland.

[631] Sir Robert Rich (1685–1768), 4th Bt, of Roos Hall, Suffolk, MP Bere Alston.

[632] Daniel, a lord of the admiralty, and William, cofferer of the household. Both lost their offices.

in earnest, att least most of them, how far others are soe, is passt my skill to determine; A noble Lord in high station sayd an odde thing in debating whither wittnesses should bee askt touching selling offices, whither doing soe had nott been usuall? What sayes hee can this question tend to, unlesse proving corruption to have been hereditary; the last word I suppose hee meant to bee synonimous with constant; a speciall freind of yours satt next him, when this Fo Pa[633] was lett slip. I long to heare how you intend to dispose of your selfe, I must goe into the country, for I gaine noe ground.

676. *Thomas to Alan I, 15 May 1725*

(1248/6/231–2)

Yours of the 1st came last night, I have often told you that your letters were soe made up, as that by drawing out one end of the wrapper the inclosd might bee taken out, that this was soe, I verily beleive, though the seale remain untoucht, butt itt matters nott a farthing whoe saw itt, tis every word truth; your reasons for applying as you did in general termes, was prudent, and the cause of your laying downe understood, and allowd sufficient, (to say noe more) by every impartial man whoe speakes of itt. I know twas surprising here to some, whoe thought you might have been prevaild uppon, to continue still the catts foote, and att the same time approvd by those whoe wish you well. I have had a message (by a freind) from your successor, to the effect following, that wee had alwayes livd well togather, and hoped the continuance of itt, aswell as of the rest of the family, to which end hee desird I would write by him to you; my answer was, that would bee needlesse, for that I was sure hee might depend uppon your assistance in every thing for the Kings service, and good of the country, since by that rule you had alwayes acted, and would continue doing soe, beyond which I knew noe perswasions of mine (if I would make use of any, which I never would) could prevaile.

I told you in a former the little I sayd uppon bringing in Lord Bullingbrooks petition, when I was scarce able to stand or speake; twas from the bottom of my heart I sayd I thought twas a step towards a Re=Revolution,[634] I pray God I may bee mistaken, butt I continue still of the same mind, and nott the lesse for the usage you mett with in a certaine place, principally by the means of one whoe I beleive has what I mentioned very much att heart, and might possibly thinke, and I verily beleive did, that the removal (which hee might well foresee would happen) of one whoe when others durst nott say their souls were their owne, had the courage and honesty to state a question for setting a price on the Pretenders head,[635] to this you may adde your speech (which I formerly mentioned) att the time of delivering the Popery Bill. Providence has often miraculously deliverd us, I hope the continuance of itt, for nothing lesse (in my opinion) can save us; I wish I could nott assigne too many reasons for this beleif; butt I can; old as I am I feare I shall live to see that day, or att least,

---

[633] faux pas.

[634] It had been reported a fortnight earlier that, on hearing a rumour that Bolingbroke was staying with an old political friend in Surrey, Thomas had sworn 'that he will commit him, if he can catch him where he has power to act as a justice of the peace' (HMC, *Portland MSS*, vi, 1).

[635] On 12 Aug. 1714, in the debate on the civil list bill, William Pulteney supported the addition of a clause offering a bounty of £100,000 for the capture of the Pretender (*HC 1690–1715*, v, 239).

a very hearty struggle for bringing itt to beare, since for damned lucre wee can goe into every thing that tends to itt.

I heare (how truly I know nott) that Bill is likely to come back to us from the Lords, with an amendment still more in favour of Lord B[*olingbroke*]. Mr P[*eere*] W[*illia*]ms blabd out more then hee should, butt if this happens surely twill open blind mens eyes, or Quos Jupiter vult perdere etc.[636] will bee very applicable ...Yesterday Lord M[*acclesfield's*] Councill summd up his evidence, his Lordship desired a day to recollect, in order to speake for himself what they had omitted, the Lords therefore adjournd to Munday.[637]

The Commons Managers will nott reply till Wensday att soonest, I beleive nott till Thursday, whither judgment will bee given on Saturday is nott very certaine, though I beleive twill.[638]

I know there are different sentiments in that house, touching itt, butt if I guesse right, the fine, whisperd for above a month past, will putt an end to itt, without sequestration from Parliament itt will and must goe as some people please, butt the publique will bee judges, when the tryall is printed, I am in this matter as indifferent as most men, never having opened my lips in this affair from its first beginning.

There has been a good deale of snapping and Repartees. Mr W[*alpole*] askt whither his Boyes (meaning the Managers) did nott behave well, to which Lord L answered, Yes, butt they will behave much better uppon the next occasion.

Wee are a good deale disconcerted, how things will end God knowes, butt I thinke plaine advantages are given to our enemyes. Tis sayd our thirty six knights will bee reduct to about a third of that number, for want of ambitious men, least the world should judge whoe have more mony then witt.[639]

677. Alan I, Dublin, to Thomas, 17 May 1725

(1248/6/233–4)

Mine of the 29th of April by my Lord Lieutenants messenger, and that which I wrote since upon receiving your letter after you had an account of my having laid down, told you all I knew when I wrote them; but I find since the return of that Courier that tho I had reason given me to beleive his Excellencyes letter of the 29th of April would contain nothing more then that I had desired him to lay my desire before his Majestye to have his leave to surrender the Seal, and that what arguments he had used to disswade me from that resolution had not prevailed with me to alter it (which he thought himself obliged to apprise the King of without losse of time) yet I now find that his Excellencye was pleased in the same letter to recommend the Lord Cheif Baron Hale for my Successor, and Sir John

---

[636] '*Quos Jupiter vult perdere, dementat prius*', the neo-Latin version of the classical Latin saying '*Quos Deus vult perdere, dementat prius*' (those whom the Gods wish to destroy they first make mad).

[637] Confirmed in *LJ*, xxii, 544–5.

[638] The Commons managers eventually began their response on Friday, 21 May, and judgment was given on Tuesday the 25th, when Macclesfield was found guilty (*LJ*, xxii, 549–50, 555).

[639] The founding knights of the order of the bath, promulgated by letters patent on 18 May. The proposed number of knights had been reduced from the original proposal of 100 to 52, and then to 36. (Andrew Hanham, 'The Politics of Chivalry: Sir Robert Walpole, the Duke of Montagu and the Order of the Bath', *Parliamentary History*, xxv (2016), 279–93.)

St Leger[640] to succeed him in the Exchequer,[641] whereas he very well knew that I had complained of ill treatment and that I was sensible the maner I was spoken of in a certain place was intended to force me to resign, to ease them of the invidious act of turning me out for the true motive which prevails with the men in power; and I told him before I waited on him about giving up, that the continuance of that usage would force me to quit before the Session of Parliament here; which my Lord Lieutenant seemed very desirous I should not doe; but when I consider that his good sense tells him that they who encouraged the Currs to bark, could with holding up their finger have silenced them, I confesse I am at a losse how to judge, whether it might not be thought to be a peice of refined policy on this side of the water to try whether I could be content to purchase my rest from the pursuit of the bloudhounds that were thrown off after an hurt deer, by a compliance in omnibus; and whether if I proved impracticable it were not better to have somebody else on the woolsack. If this be an ill grounded conjecture I can not hinder its coming into my head, for you must know I grow lesse confident of the fair intentions of Courtiers every day then the other, and am convinced very great men have their own grandeur and interest wholly in view, to which they think every thing ought to give way. The recommendacion of the Cheif Baron for my Successor took place for some time insomuch that my Lord Cheif Justice R[aymond] wrote to the Cheif Baron that Lord T[ownshend] had spoke to him about it as a thing agreed to, and the Duke of Devonshire (who is Hales true freind) as I hear wrote to him to accept, and this prevailed soe far, that his Officers were named, if not appointed viz. a Nephew to succeed Arthur Hill as Secretary[642] and Baron Pocklingtons son[643] to succeed Jemmy Barry as purse bearer.[644] Lord Lieutenants messenger is come back and brings a letter from the Duke of Newcastle[645] that Lord C[arteret']s letter of 29 April was laid before his Majestye who had accepted my resignation, but had not determined on the person to succeed me, but would declare his pleasure in a day or two, and with this letter was my Lord C[arteret']s messenger sent away at 12 of Clock at night; no doubt in hopes to prevent his calling for letters from private freinds. But alas! Lord T[ownshend] had not consulted his principal when he went into the scheme of the Cheif Barons being Chancelor, for you may depend on it that he hath received a letter from a freind who may be depended upon that the whole recommendation is overturned; and hath only served to shew that he had recommended the two persons I have named in the maner abovementioned; and now the town talks with more freedome then I think becomes them in respect of both; for you must know that our Countreyman happens not to be very gracious on this side of the water. How these matters will end time will shew; but I thank God I am gott safe on shore out of the shipwrack upon a plank, and pity those whom I see in the storm, which some have raised who perhaps doe not desire to see it allayed, and perhaps cannot quiet it, if they would. The

[640]Sir John St Leger (1674–1743), of Capel St., Dublin, MP [I] 1713–14, a baron of the exchequer [I] since 1714.

[641]TNA, SP 63/385/92–3: Carteret to Newcastle, 29 Apr. 1725. See also *Boulter Letters*, 114.

[642]Arthur Hill, MP [I]. These appointments were in the lord chancellor's personal gift.

[643]John Pocklington (c. 1658–1731), of the Middle Temple, baron of exchequer [I] since 1715. His son John (1690–bef. 1731) was a barrister in the exchequer court [I] (John Venn and J.A. Venn, *Alumni Cantabrigienses…* (10 vols, 1922–53), pt. 1, iii, 485; H.A.C. Sturgess, *Register of Admissions to the Honourable Society of the Middle Temple* … (3 vols, 1949), i, 261; *HC 1690–1715*, v, 163–5; Reg. Deeds, 57/250/38289).

[644]James Barry, MP [I].

[645]TNA, SP 63/385/109: Newcastle to Carteret, 10 May 1725.

letter saith a person is pitched on for my Successor whom the writer was not then at liberty to name but the rumor obtains that Sir Wm Thompson is to be the man. Whoever it is, I am confident care will be taken that he be an able man, and one who will supply those defects which have very lately been discovered in my understanding in a certain place. We are alarmed by a story which an Officer who came lately from Liverpool tells that he heard several members of the British Parliament say a bill would yet be brought in (as late as it was in the Session) to lay a duty of 6d per yard on Irish linen to be imported into England; this I suppose is to hang over our heads during our next Session to make us pliant to the orders which certain persons hope they may prescribe to us in relation to Woods patent. I am very weary of being alway in anxiety and trouble, and that which makes the thing insupportable is that no mortal hath yet been happy enough to light on any remedye, that is not as bad (if not worse) then the disease. When a Coach will overturn the best way is to fall with it in the softest maner; I will not contribute to the overthrowing it, nor venture my bones farther then others in struggling against an evil that sooner or later will fall out; I shal have my share of the misfortune when I retire to Surrey; for I think one that is in that part of the world may hope to be easy at least as long (if not longer) then he who resides here.

678. *Thomas to Alan I, Dublin, 18 May 1725*

(1248/6/235–6)

Yesterday when Lord M[*acclesfield'*]s speaking for himselfe was expected, his Councill movd being att liberty to examine witnesses, as to his estate; as well as his great charityes, his Lordship insisted on both points, butt being overruld, prayed further time, which was allowd till tomorrow; hee sayd his reall estate was no more then £3000 per an and that setled uppon his sonne, his personall butt £2000 the proofe of which would have been difficult, butt twill serve as a topick for his freinds to expatiate uppon.[646]

The Commons will reply uppon Fryday; this falls to the share of Sir T[*homas*] Pingelly and Mr Lutwitch,[647] a dry part they have, matter of law insisted uppon (by his councill) and remarking uppon their exceptions to the evidence, being what they are confined to.

I doe nott hear your successors kissing the Kings hand owned, least that should bee deemd an acceptance, and thereby his seate bee vacated, which might prove detrimental to the prosecution, by depriving the managers of his assistance; butt I am sure hee has deigned to accept, though nott in such forme. I have several times forgott mentioning the satisfaction I had in Lord C[*arteret*] making himselfe somuch master of the affairs of Ireland, as the towne sayes hee is become, I hope hee will continue doing soe, for without the spirit of prophecy one may safely conclude its being of use to him hereafter.

---

[646] Macclesfield's counsel having asked for the opportunity to bring in witnesses to attest the value of the earl's real and personal estate, the Lords decided not to allow it to be presented at this stage, whereupon Macclesfield requested, and was granted, an adjournment of proceedings for two days (*LJ*, xxii, 546).

[647] Sir Thomas Pengelly and Thomas Lutwyche (in that order) were the only managers to speak on the 21st, the last day of proceedings before the vote (*LJ*, xii, 549–50; HMC *Portland MSS*, vi, 5).

679. *Thomas to Alan I, Dublin, 20 May 1725*[648]

(1248/6/237–8)

Yesterday I receivd yours of the 9th. I suppose before this time Mr Wests pattent is past,[649] for I am told that this day sennight a new writt is to bee movd for, att which time twill bee incumbent on some body to informe the house that tis soe. I may bee mistaken in the judgment I make of your laying downe contributing to Lord C[*arteret's*] continuance, butt I am still of the same mind, though nott very certaine of that being sufficient.

The Commons reply tomorrow, and will I beleive doe itt sharpely, especially Sir T[*homas*] P[*engelly*] whoe never sayd (in the house) any thing like what you mention, for hee allways confind himselfe to points of law, letting himselfe very seldom and little into facts.

A memorial has been talkt of wherein was to bee demanded the restitution of Gibraltar and Port Mahon, with satisfaction for the losses the Spaniards suffered by our fleet.[650]

Sir J[*oseph*] J[*ekyll*] could nott bee in the list, nott being in the house, I very well remember what hee formerly sayd upon the motion for laying before the house the Pensions on the civill list,[651] hee then spoake his opinion, of which there needs noe other proofe, then his warmth, and strenghth in arguing against itt (I mean making good the deficiency) in this Session. Mr P[*ulteney*] was with the majority, Mr Frankland absent, and whither Sir R[*obert*] R[*ich*] were soe I cannott positively say. Lord Finch brought in the Peticion. The Lords this day read the Bill a second time, I left them in debate upon the question for committall, after standing a full hour and a halfe, which I could noe longer beare, I make noe doubt of the success, for the ministry are very warme.

Lord L[*echmere*] spoake near an hour against the question, went through every part of the Bill, spoake to the illegality of the pardon, from whence and several other premises strongly argued, concluded the dangerous consequences as well to his Majestys person as to the Kingdom, since people without doores could take itt in noe other sence then a conviction of the great wrong done to Lord B[*olingbroke*], for which this Bill was in some measure to

---

[648] Letter endorsed by Alan I: 'Tho: Brodrick … that a writ will be moved for on 27th of May to elect a new member in Mr Wests room he having been appointed Chancellor for Ireland. That Sir Jo[*seph*] Jekyl and Mr Frankland were not in the house when the mocion was made for bringing in Lord Bolenbrooks bill, nor he thinks Sir Rob. Rich. But Pulteney for the bill'.

[649] In fact the patent was not passed in Dublin until 23 July 1725, though the privy seal warrant was issued at St James's Palace on 29 May (*Lib. Mun.*, pt. 2, p. 17), and a new writ for West's parliamentary constituency of Bodmin was ordered two days later (*CJ*, xx, 543). West was obliged to seek re-election on accepting an office of profit under the crown under the terms of the Regency Act of 1706 (4 Anne, c. 8). He was re-elected on 28 June (*HC 1715–54*, ii, 205).

[650] As an ambition of the Spanish after the conclusion of the Austro-Spanish alliance, though in August Lord Townshend expressed the view to Newcastle that Gibraltar and Port Mahon were not 'the chief aim' of the alliance; they were 'pretences made use of to force his majesty into the Emperor's measures' relating to the Austrian succession (quoted in Jeremy Black, *Politics and Foreign Policy in the Age of George I, 1714–1727* (Aldershot, 2014), 181).

[651] On 9 Apr. 1725 in a committee of the whole house on the civil list, when a proposal was made to limit the number of office-holders in the Commons in return for granting the sum desired, and 'that it should be high treason to take a pension and not register it', Jekyll spoke 'against this demand till the papers were brought in' (*Knatchbull Diary*, 44–5).

attone.[652] His Grace of W[harton] spoake next,[653] begun with the highest panagirick on the Queen and her just and wise administration, to whose conduct the quiett and repose of Europe was due,[654] that Lord B[olingbroke] was nott attainted for any crime, other then for nott appearing to answer to what was nott soe, butt (as hee thought) great meritt. I stayd nott longer, the conclusion was very obvious, I must owne I thinke hee dealt fairly in saying plainly what other people thinke, butt will nott say, whilst those (att least some of them) whoe are of a contrary opinion, dare nott take measures to prevent, for feare of incurring the anger of more Ladyes then one. I suppose all this our ministry must allow for truth, because I doe nott heare of any of their denying itt.

[*PS*] I came away a little too soon, his Grace after bantering the ministry above half an hour concluded and divided against the question.

680. *Thomas to Alan I, Dublin, 25 May 1725*

(1248/6/239–40)

Yesterday the Lords read a third time, and passed Lord B[olingbroke's] Bill, there were two divisions, First whither the Bill should bee then read, Contents 55 Not contents 34. The second for passing the Bill Contents 75. Not contents 25.[655]

Before reading the Bill the Pardon was read, and the judges (whoe were all summoned) were askt whither the pardon were a legall one, Lord C[hief] Justice answered for all in the affirmative. Tis sayd their unanimity was grounded uppon these words contained in itt, Quantum in nobis est,[656] people generally thinke itt had been candid to have mentioned that reason, butt others thinke giving a sanction to the pardon (generally) much better. The Lords then proceeded on Lord Macclesfeilds affair, the question movd was that the Commons have maintaind their charge of High Crimes and Misdemeanours against him, which was agreed to Nem. Cont.

This day the Lords (The managers present) gave in their robes their votes seperatim,[657] each Lord being by name askt this question My Lord – Is the Earle of Macclesfeild guilty of High Crimes and misdemeanours whereof hee is impeacht by the Commons. Every Lord was in the affirmative.[658] Had his Lordship been in the house hee would then have been askt what hee had to say in bar of Judgment, butt hee wrote a letter to excuse his attendance by reason of sicknesse. The Lords have appointed proceeding tomorrow, when hee is to attend, notice having been given him that the Lords have found him guilty, if hee doe nott attend as I suppose he will nott his default will bee recorded, and probably the Lords proceed to consider of the Judgment which I beleive will bee given next day, butt

---

[652] Lechmere was said to have 'flamed with great vehemence, called him [*Bolingbroke*] that traitor to his queen, to his king, and to those to whom he had fled for refuge', provoking an angry exchange with Lord Townshend (HMC, *Portland MSS*, vi, 6).

[653] Confirmed in HMC, *Portland MSS*, vi, 6.

[654] Queen Anne and the tory ministry of 1710–14.

[655] Figures confirmed in Sainty and Dewar, microfiche.

[656] As much as is in us.

[657] Individually. Confirmed in *LJ*, xxii, 554–5.

[658] Confirmed in HMC, *Portland MSS*, vi, 7–8.

what that will bee is very uncertaine, the great question will bee sequestration or nott, in addition to a fine. Our leaders are very close and silent, butt the event will shew their minds, for if that bee carryd in the negative people will conclude the whole what many call itt, a perfect Farce. I thinke they are under a good deal of difficulty herein. Our Red Ribbons will bee disposd of the birth right.[659] The Session will not end till Munday or Tuesday, though Thursday next was the day fixt for itt.[660]

Just as I was making this up, came yours of the 17th. if my letters bee nott intercepted, you will find I told you all that you mention. Your Leverpoole officer, may have his lesson given him, butt I never heard any thing of itt spoake of here. Qui jacet in terris non habet unde cadet.[661] Lett them please themselves, and surmount difficultyes as well as they can.

681. *Alan I, Dublin, to Thomas, the Privy Garden, Whitehall, 26 May 1725*

(1248/6/241–2)

I have your letter of the 18th by which I find that Lord Macclesfeild seems only apprehensive of being heavily fined, since the motion made by his Councel and insisted also on by himself tended only to shew his fortune was not such as to make it reasonable to lay a very heavy fine on him. Before this can come to your hand his fate will be irreversibly determined, but I own I should rejoice if I were his most intimate freind to be assured that his punishment went no farther then a fine, if in the opinion of the Lords the articles laid to his charge have been sufficiently proved to be true. It is certain that Court had it in their power to have punished him in a maner, more greivous to a man of honour then the entire depriving him of his whole estate; if they had pleased: suppose they had added to a fine a vote or resolution that he should not sit in Parliament, as for ought I know they might have done, or be forever disabled to hold any publick office or place of trust: I doe not mean that you should understand me to intend that his punishment by fine (if the Lords shal take that way) is short of what he may have justly deserved: But I doe beleive that he is not soe great an offender as a certain person hath been, who you tell me was not thought fit to be unqualifyed for publick emploiment. But now to come to matters which more concern me then this doth. Upon my word we are here in a good deal of uncertaintye as to the scituation of our affairs here: whether [*Lord Carteret*] is to continue or to have a Successor; but a few dayes will put us at a certainty in that matter. As to my part, I will not give my self the trouble of hearing many causes, but leave them to one who will not determine them soe ill as I have done of late, which will save me some trouble and the countrey some money; for decrees well made will not be appealed from. But between freinds I am apt to think the same game is stil endeavoured to be carryed on which you have more then once called by the name of the Cats foot, but it will not doe. I intend soon by a private hand, to

---

[659]The new knights of the bath. Their investiture took place in private in St James's Palace on 27 May. Subsequently there was a second, public investiture on 17 June in Westminster Abbey. On the latter occasion the knights processed in order of precedence, from royal prince down to esquire, and presumably the same order was observed at the private ceremony. (Hanham, 'Politics of Chivalry', 291–2; *British Journal*, 29 May 1725.)

[660]The session ended on Monday, 31 May.

[661]'He who lies on the ground can fall no farther'.

send you a more particular account of some late management, then I will venture by post: He will deliver the letter with his own hand into yours.

682. *Thomas to Alan I, Dublin, 27 May 1725*

(1248/6/243–4)

Yesterday the Lords had under consideration the judgment to bee given against Lord M[*acclesfield*]. Thirty thousand pound fine was movd by Lord Finlater,[662] and agreed to by all.[663]

Two other motions were made uppon which there were divisions That hee bee declard uncapable of any office of profitt or trust, the numbers being equall, 42 each, by the rule of the house the negatives had itt, thus hee escapt uppon a planke.[664]

2ly That hee bee sequestred from parliament and nott to come within the verge of the Court Cont. 39 N contents 45.[665] The Lords whoe were the minority immediately quitted the house, and absented themselves this day when judgment was given.[666] The Commons debated three hours against demanding itt, uppon this principle, that twas nott adequate to the crime, if what was sayd without doores were true, and therfore insisted uppon appointing a Committee to looke into the Lords journals, which putt our great men under necessity of owning that twas soe,[667] several arguments were made use of by them against inspecting, among others Mr W[*alpole*] urged that the consequence would bee a dissolution from a rupture between the houses, I was of opinion that would compensate for the losse of the fine, butt they carryd itt two to one.[668] Both houses are adjourned to Munday, tomorrow being the Kings birthday, and Saturday the Restauration.[669] Lord Cheif Justice King will have the Seale by or before then, and I thinke will bee succeeded by Justice Tracy.[670]

Sir Wm Strickland comes into the Treasury in Bailyes roome whoe I suppose has a good equivalent,[671] and is succeeded as one of your Commissioners by Mr Tomson of Yorke.[672]

---

[662] James Ogilvy (1663–1730), 4th earl of Findlater.

[663] Confirmed in *LJ*, xxii, 559.

[664] Figures confirmed in Sainty and Dewar, microfiche. The phrase 'escaped on a plank' related to survival in a shipwreck, as happened to Odysseus in Homer, *Odyssey*.

[665] Figures confirmed in Sainty and Dewar, microfiche.

[666] The presence lists give a total of 97 on 26 May, and 74 on the 27th (*LJ*, xxii, 555, 559).

[667] Not recorded in *LJ*, xxii, 559–60.

[668] The division in the Commons on whether to demand judgment against Macclesfield was carried 136–65 (technically on a motion that the question be now put (*CJ*, xx, 541)).

[669] Restoration Day, commemorating the return of Charles II in 1660.

[670] Robert Tracy (1655–1735), of Coscomb, Gloucs., judge of common pleas [E]. He was not promoted on this occasion, and retired on 26 Oct. 1726 in return for being granted a pension. (*Oxf. DNB*.)

[671] George Baillie (1664–1738), of Jerviswood, Lanarks., MP [GB] Berwicks., lost his place on the treasury commission on 27 May, as part of the purge of Squadrone supporters from the ministry, being compensated by a pension equal to his former salary. He was replaced by Sir William Strickland (c. 1686–1735), 4th Bt, of Boynton, Yorks., MP [GB] Scarborough. (Sainty, *Treasury Officials*, 19; *HC 1715–54*, i, 428.)

[672] Edward Thompson (1696–1742), of Marston, Yorks., MP York, replaced Strickland on the Irish revenue commission.

Sir George Oxinden comes into the Admiralty,[673] a great many other changes are talkt of, butt I know them nott.

Mention was made in the house of Addressing that the fine might bee applyed towards the Masters deficiencyes,[674] butt the forme nott being throughly considered, twas lett drop till Munday, when twill bee done.

The house by the Speaker (whoe did itt very finely) gave thankes to the managers, which is orderd to bee printed,[675] the motion was made by Mr Poultney, itt went down (I thinke) like chopt hay[676] with some, butt all gave into itt; this does sufficiently shew what the house thought of the judgment for one sayd (nott very advisedly) that 42 Lords of honour were for extending itt farther[677] which att another time would nott passe.

683. *Alan I, Dublin, to Thomas, London, 5 June 1725*

(1248/6/247–8)

I desire you to put the inclosed under a cover with proper directions to my Lord Chancellor, to whom you will make my complements on your delivering it. I have very little to say, tho I might venture to say any thing which I would say to you at any time by this Gentleman whose honour I am safe in for the delivery of this letter into your own hand: but I have very little to say only that all is not gold that glisters[678] (it is your own expression and intended by mee in the same sense you wrote it). Our own personal regards are the only thing great men have in view; all that goes farther is meer grimace and not at all to be depended upon; but an acquaintance of yours and mine will not be undeceived till it is too late, and I have great apprehensions that notwithstanding all his art (of which he is sufficiently provided) he will be drawn in by those who are too cunning for him, and will not fail to make promises enough, which will be performed as they usually are by the Great ones, after their turn is served. My freinds here will not bear the thoughts of my leaving them before the Session is over; but when I see soe many now continue in England, I am not at all at a losse to guesse what game is playing. Pray how hath my Lord A[*nglesey*] his health; will his Ladyes[679] indisposicion admit of O[*liver*] S[*t George*] attending the Parliament here? Is the person whom I described to be very ambitious in my letter of 13 April determined? If you can inform yourself well let me know my Successors true character and dependance and his maner in the world hitherto. Let not A[*nglesey's*] peevishnesse in a former affair of the same kind restrain you from giving me and the party your thought upon a subject on which I wrote lately to Bond Street, which was imparted to you. Indefatigable pains are taken to

---

[673]Sir George Oxenden (1694–1775), 5th Bt, of Deane Court, Kent, MP [GB] Sandwich, was included in the new admiralty commission on 3 June (J.C. Sainty, *Admiralty Officials 1660–1870* (1975), 22).

[674]The funds missing from the accounts of the masters in chancery.

[675]The Speaker's speech of thanks (*CJ*, xx, 542).

[676]In relation to horses, food being swallowed without difficulty (P.R. Wilkinson, *Thesaurus of Traditional English Metaphors* (2nd edn, 2002), E.15b).

[677]See above, p. 212.

[678]'... all that glisters is not gold' (Shakespeare, *The Merchant of Venice*, II, vii, 65). Previously quoted above, p. 164.

[679]Mary (née Knox) was the wife of Oliver St George.

attain the end which hath been soe warmly pressed in relation to Mr W[*est's*] affair; but I fancy all will not perswade people to be silent while they see themselves in the way of ruine.

684. Alan I, Dublin, to Thomas, London, 8 June 1725

(1248/6/249–52)

This letter will be delivered into your hand by Arthur Hill, whose errand to London is to endeavour his being continued in the same emploiment of Secretary under my Successor as he enjoyed under me since Mr Lakes death.[680] I wish he may succeed according to his expectations, but am very apprehensive of it, and the rather since I hear Mr W[*est*] is special poor and consequently not unlikely to take all justifiable methods to fill his empty pockets; for (whatever Masters of Chancery may be) it is beyond all doubt, the Office of Secretarye to the Chancellor is not a judicial emploiment, nor within any Law (which I know of) restrained from being bought and sold: as most things seem now to be. You know his relation to my wife,[681] whom I would willingly oblige by any act of kindnesse in my power: and I am sensible it will be the highest obligation which I can place on her, if by my interposing with you in his favor I can induce you to shew him countenance and give him assistance in prosecuting his design with successe. He is newly married and very industrious, and I am desirous to see him make his way in the world, and shal be pleased to have been any way instrumental in his doing it because it will be understood one of the greatest proofs of kindnesse to one to whom I owe everything in my power that can be called kind. Your advice and assistance may stand him in great stead, and I desire you for my sake to afford him both … On Sunday an expresse landed with his Majestyes letter dated 29 May for constituting Mr West Chancellor here; My Lord Lieutenant did not let me know this, nor is it yet intimated to me directly; which I suppose proceeds from a sense he hath that when I have a formal intimation of his Majestyes having under his sign manual declared my Successor, it will be an unadvised act in me from that time forward to hear one cause or mocion or appear again in Court; as I have hitherto done and may stil justifiably doe till passing Mr West patent from which moment I neither will nor can so much as seal a writ or keep the Seal in my hands; but will on sealing that patent deliver the Great Seal into my Lord Lieutenants hand to be disposed of according to his Majestyes directions. It is plain that either the people concerned in this affair know very little what the consequences of sealing Mr Wests patent before he is ready to receive the Great Seal will unavoidably be, or that they take little care of us here. For the moment the patent shal be passed, my Commission to keep the Seal or affix it to any patent writ etc is at an end; and yet the Chancery must alway be open, that is, there must be a place to which the subject may resort for processe and justice at all times, which originally resides in the Chancery; soe that the blunder now committed in requiring Mr Wests patent to be passed during his absence is pretty much of the same nature with what was done in relation to my being made one

---

[680] Francis Lake (*d.* 1721), a Dublin solicitor (Vicars, *Index*, 275; King's Inns, Dublin, MS N3/3/4/4: notebook of Francis Lake, 1684–1721). Secretary to successive lord chancellors [I], and re-appointed when Alan I was raised to the lord chancellorship in 1714 (*Post Boy*, 9–11 Nov. 1714).

[681] Arthur Hill was Lady Midleton's son by an earlier marriage (see Appendix 2).

of the Lords Justices; but there I think the thing was a design in some people to keep me so long out of the Governement as till the Justices in Ireland should send back the Kings letter to passe a new patent constituting 4 Justices (without appointing that three or two of them might act in the absence of the others) as what would till my arrival leave Ireland without any Chief Governors at all; and that was true, for the patent to 4 would have superseded the Commission to the former three, so as they could not act under it till I came, nor three act by the new Commission which was directed to fowre; that is to empower no lesse then all fowre to act. I suppose my Lord Lieutenant will send this letter back and shew that without appointing Commissioners to keep the Seal till Mr West lands, all things will be at a stand.[682] It is not my businesse to go officiously to my Lord Lieutenant and tell him I hear of the letters being come over and what the consequences will be if it be putt in execucion, but will be so just to him to apprise him of them when he speaks to me on the subject, but presume his own good sense gives him already to understand the thing: when he doth soe I will obey his orders in passing Mr Wests patent when I receive them and leave the Seal with his Excellencye: but I think he will rescribere Principi;[683] and shew what will follow from executing the Kings letter immediately, and send it back for farther orders. If he had made use of the hints I gave him by shewing how I was treated in the [*British house of lords*] and what advice you gave me about laying down unlesse a stop were put to the ill usage: he would not have now been in the plunge he is; which will daily increase on him. But I am satifisfyed that from the time he found me inflexible in the matter of the half pence and that neither the good words he gave me, nor the more warm methods taken at the beginning of his administracion made any impression on me in favor of the patent (which he asserted and stil doth the Legality and reasonablenesse of as far as I beleive any man in England ever did) I plainly saw his favor run in another chanel and that Whitshed[684] and our late Cheif Baron[685] were the persons confided in, for they shewed more compliance toward his disposition to carry the thing on with an air of high hand, then I could think advisable: and from this time I am convinced he was very willing to part with me in hopes of having another person on the wool Sack who would give him all the assistance in his power to have the matter of the half pence sleep and never be taken notice of: in which perswasion he stil perseveres, and thinks he shal succeed; and he may for ought I know, if other people are as cool and temperate in this matter as your nephew who told me that my making opposicion now would be imputed to resentment at my being laid aside. You will be surprised that Mr Pratt our Deputy Vice Treasurer is not only superseded but arrested and in custody of the suit of the King [Lord Falmouth and Mr Edgecombe[686] *struck through*] for £43700 and odd pound.[687] My former letters have let you into the knowledge, how

---

[682] He did, pointing out that if Alan's patent were revoked before West arrived in Dublin there would be 'great inconveniences' as no writs could be issued under the great seal in the interim, unless commissioners were appointed (TNA, SP 63/385/138: Carteret to Newcastle, 8 June 1725).

[683] Literally, to petition the prince.

[684] Chief Justice Whitshed.

[685] Jeffray Gilbert.

[686] Hugh Boscawen, 1st Viscount Falmouth, and Richard Edgcumbe, the joint vice-treasurers (Pratt acted as their deputy).

[687] At the beginning of May 1725 Pratt had passed his accounts to June 1723. But he failed to comply with the lord lieutenant's directions to account by the end of that month for the period up to Christmas 1724, and the joint-vice-treasurers, Boscawen and Edgcumbe, arrived in Dublin to find him theoretically in possession of a

the ballances of the publick accounts appeared on 24 Dec. 1724 and 13 April 1725.[688] But I must break off being going to Court to act the part of Mr Wests Vice Chancellor for in truth I am no more.

685. Thomas to Alan I, 15 June 1725[689]

(1248/6/253–4)

I beleive the gentleman from whom I receivd your letter of this day sennights date, will succeed, and by the very means which you mention; Ile assist as far as I can, butt without appearing in itt; for uppon reflection you cannott thinke either your or mine doing soe, advisable; nothing that villanous mallice can suggest, will bee left unsayd, and that propagated by a sett of wretches in order to give creditt to what others say.

Assoone as I can (by a safe hand) ile explaine my selfe farther for you may assure your selfe both your letters and mine are opened; I should nott care if what att any time I write of publique affairs were fixt to the markett crosse, being noe more then what (without reserve) I say on every fitting opertunity, butt prying into private family concernes, by those who have nothing to doe with them, is very vexatious, butt soe itt is ... I doe nott att all wonder att the blunder (if such itt were, for the omission may proceed from another cause) of nott sending a letter for lodging the seals till your successor lands; I hear hee goes hence soone, butt know nott the certainty, for I have nott seen him. I acquainted you with the message hee sent mee by Mr Onslow,[690] aswell as the answer I gave, which was surely a proper one, for hee tooke noe notice to mee of his preferment (though wee saw each other every day in the house) till a fortnight after every Coffee house in towne had itt; perhaps hee expected my making advances towards him, which I really did nott thinke worth while, for I have nothing to expect or aske of great men, therfore I am quiett.

I suppose I need nott tell you either the addition made to his sallary, and equipage mony,[691] if you doe nott, youl soone know itt. Hee will shew himselfe an able Minister, and will deserve all hee shall have, if hee can contribute soe far to quietting the minds of people as to lett Woods pattent sleep, in order to which I suppose itt is that publique prints give an account of quantitys of his halfe pence being shipt of from Dublin, before which, there were sufficient numbers of them here, insomuch that I beleive notice will bee taken of them in our next session, and then (yours being over) they may bee carryed back againe, with profitt, for here they generally passe butt for farthings; I know your appearing vigorously for the good (indeed the very being) of the country may bee sayd to arise from pique att your

---

687 *(continued)* huge balance of funds (estimated at first as around £75,000 but in reality close to £97,000), for which he could not account. They were obliged to bring an action against him for his entire estate, real and personal, valued at over £43,700. In response Pratt 'did remove himself ... by habeas corpus out of the sheriffs' hands, into the ... Marshalsea'. He was immediately replaced as deputy vice-treasurer. (Barnard, *New Anatomy*, 162–3; Malcomson, *Nathaniel Clements*, 17–18; *Coghill Letters*, 21.)

688 Two of the quarter-days.

689 Letter endorsed by Alan I: 'Tho: Brodrick ... hopes Mr Hill will succeed in applying to be Mr Wests Secretary. Cautions me as to writing because our correspondence is pryed into ...'.

690 Probably Arthur Onslow, MP [GB].

691 A one-off payment made to each lord chancellor [I] for the expenses of his retinue.

removal, by those whoe doe nott know twas your own act, and might have been otherwise if you had thought fitt to hold, feare nott such sarcasms, butt goe on to endeavour the securing that poore kingdom against all the ill consequences which will certainly attend itt, if nott prevented. I suppose you have heard that one Mr Reynells is your Cheife Baron,[692] Hee has the place of Mr Marriott (lately deceast) in our Exchequer[693], generally thought worth £1200 per an. to which hee was advanc't from being Mr W[alpole']s secretary as Chancellor of that Court.[694]

I hope soone to gett into Surry, there to spend a little time before I goe to Bath, butt twill bee mostly att Guilford, since noebody is likely (for ought I see) to bee att Pepper Hara.

I labour att this time under a severe fitt of the gravell; if itt goe of by Thursday (when there is to bee glorious [?shew]), I shall spend that day in the citty, to settle some small affairs, soe as to leave mee att liberty to goe out of town when I please.

686. *Alan I, Dublin, to Thomas, 20 June 1725*

(1248/6/255–6)

Yesterday I received yours of the 15th and doe assure you I am altogether as unconcerned at curious peoples prying into my letters as you can be when yours find the same treatment, and for the same reason: for my actions words and letters are entirely of a peice and I never conceal that from you which I speak freely in the most publick places, and neither say nor write otherwise then I act. There are indeed some little familye concerns which one would not willingly have strangers (much lesse enemyes) be let into the knowledge of; but if great mens curiositye extends soe far, let them have the satisfaction of the knowledge they acquire of that nature, with the shame they must have of being led into such enquiryes by curiositye or malice which in honour they ought to desire to keep themselves wholly ignorant of. Soe much for that: My Successors intending soon to leave London is no news here; for my Lord Lieutenant owned he had a letter from him (full of complements and things of course as he termed them) in which he intimated that he should be at the waterside on the 15th July and desired to have the Yatcht attend him there on the tenth; but whether it be Holyhead or Chester I did not enquire.[695] I told my Lord that I alway knew he [*sic*] I was tenant at will to his Majestye of the Office, and consequently had a right to lay down when I thought convenient; but that I now found I was tenant at the will of one more, since it was expected I should drudge on and officiate till Mr Wests affairs or inclinations permitted him by landing here to determine my patent; for that if he did not soe, the Great Seal was

[692]James Reynolds (1686–1739) of Lincoln's Inn, MP [GB] Bury St Edmunds. Newcastle reported the following week that the Lord Chancellor King was still to 'pitch upon' a candidate for the post, though he had mentioned several names as possibles (BL, Add. MS 32687, f. 92: Newcastle to Townshend, 22 June 1725). Reynolds was not appointed on this occasion, but was made a justice of king's bench [E] in 1725, and eventually lord chief baron of exchequer [I] in 1730.

[693]Thomas Marriott of Lincoln's Inn, clerk of pleas in the exchequer [E] had died on 12 June 1724 (TNA, PROB 11/598/128; *Universal Journal*, 20 June 1724).

[694]Reynolds had succeeded Marriott as clerk of pleas in June 1724 (*Evening Post*, 18–20 June 1724).

[695]West left London on 9 July, 'with a great retinue', and arrived in Dublin on the 21st (*Daily Post*, 9 July 1725; *Parker's Penny Post*, 12 July 1725; *Evening Post*, 3 Aug. 1725).

not to be put to his Commission nor deferred longer then till he could be at leisure to accept it and have things got ready for constituting him Chancellor in my room.[696] His Lordship seemed to think I should goe on to hear the unheard causes, which I told him I had no disposicion to doe, since I thought it would only create businesse for some good freinds of mine at Westminster the next Spring, which I was not fond of doing, but he said he thought it to be for the Kings service and for the good of the people I should proceed in hearing businesse in Court after such intimacion of his Majestyes having determined his pleasure with respect to me, as the printed votes of the Commons import, I answered I would on his declaring him self in that particular goe on to act as he should direct and advise, but without his having said so much I should have looked on my self to have done my duty, if I adjourned over the unheard causes to hansel[697] my Successor in his seat of judiature who I hope and beleive will determine them more to the good liking of those who are to be final Judges of all proceedings in our Courts here: and I dare prophecye that this Kingdome will reap one good effect from his coming, that there will be fewer Appeals when he hears the causes and I doe not, then there have been of late, when I heard them: for I am very certain (I mean morally soe) that from a period of time (which I will not assign) I have not had the same capacitye of discerning between right and wrong as I once had; which I conclude from my not having been able (after my best endeavours to find out the right) to hit upon it, even by chance in one judgement in ten. [I] confesse it is amazing to me that the suitors and Clerks should be desirous to have the businesse now depending determined before I lay down the Seal; soe that I have been skilful enough or fortunate enough to have concealed my want of abilityes from the persons most concerned to have their causes heard by one who is (in their opinion at least) able and willing to doe right. It is no surprize to me to have Mr Wests salary and equipage mony augmented beyond what his predecessors (especially his immediate one) received: and I make no doubt the Kingdome (which is to supply that encrease of charge) will find its account in the services he will doe it; beyond what his predecessors have been able to doe. At worst, it will be but a little addition in comparison to some other charges which are upon the establishment, and be one means to convince men of the reasonablenesse of giving largely. I … am concerned to hear no body is at Peperhara, soe that you are like to spend most of your time before going to Bath at Guilford; I am to the last degree uneasy at that which I doe apprehend to be the true reason of your not going thither, and wish — were more reconciled to that place and lesse fond of another … Do not be surprized at what I am going to propose to you: I am sensible that a Sea voyage is in no [?rate] troublesome or disagreeable to you and cannot but be of opinion your coming from Bristol to Corke will be extremely for your service both with respect to one of your tenants[698] and indeed of your whole affairs; I had almost said that there is a prudential necessitye for your doing it at some time in your life; and surely this is the fittest time, when your health carryes you almost the whole Land journey, and when you can land at your own house. Methinks inclinacion to see your countrey, your freinds and tenants should induce to doe it; but when in addition to these consideracions your being here may be of great publick advantage I cannot doubt of your resolving on

---

[696] Carteret was informed by letter dated 15 June that Alan's patent was not to be revoked until West arrived, which he acknowledged on the 24th (TNA, SP 63/385/245: Carteret to Newcastle, 24 June 1725).

[697] Formally hand over to (*OED*).

[698] St John III.

it. How much better and more properly will that be done by you which you advise me to undertake? You see by what hath passed already that I have not declined your advice in any step yet taken and therefore ought to conclude I write this from a sense that your doing what I hint at will be of publick service: and I am confirmed in my opinion from the terror some people are certainly in least you should come over; for I was interrogated by a Court earwig upon this subject very narrowly of late. Pray consider this well, and doe not resolve hartily against it; if I thought it would prejudice you in point of health I would not mention it: But from what I have wrote formerly I beleive you think some people are rendred lukewarm; The Gentleman whom I lately recommended to you gives me reason to beleive some now in London (who were in appearance great patriots and whom he will name) are as cool as cucumbers,[699] and soe is one who came hither lately from that place.

687. *Thomas to Alan I, Dublin, 2 July 1725*

(1248/6/257–8)

Yesterday an expresse from Generall Wade (whoe comands the forces in Scotland in order to disarme the Highlanders)[700] with letters to the Duke of Newcastle, giving an account that hee had sent two companyes into Glascow to support the King officers in levying the mault tax, having receivd information that the inhabitants resolvd to oppose them:[701] The men after two days long march, in desperate bad weather, being come thither, demanded the keys of the guard house, to which the Provost[702] made answer, that the Townesmen had taken them from him; the souldiers were therfore forced to make the best shift they could that night, the next morning the keyes were deliverd, butt att the same time the townsmen seizd the magazine where the armes and ammunition lay; and surrounded the guard house; the officer sent to the Mayor to disperse the mob by reading the proclamation, which hee refusd to doe; the officer orderd his men to fire, butt to shoote over their heads in order to terrifie them, butt itt had a contrary effect, for they presst more uppon him, when our men fird Ball, and knockt downe half a dozen of them, upon which they drew to a greater distance, being about six hundred, armd with the armes they had taken out of the Magazine; the Provost (or Mayor) then sent to the comanding officer (whose orders were that hee should obey such orders as hee should receive from the Civill Magistrate) to draw his men out of the towne, which hee accordingly did, and in his marching of, was pursued six miles by the townes men, some on each side were killd; as far as I can learne the account goes noe farther.[703] The Regents this day mett uppon the occasion, what orders they have given, or what resolutions they come to I know nott.

---

[699] The first recorded use of the phrase in *OED* is from John Gay's *Poems* in 1732.

[700] George Wade (1673–1748), of Bath, Somerset, MP [GB] Bath; lieut.-gen. and col., 3rd Dragoon Guards. In 1724 he had produced a report recommending measures to ensure the pacification of the Highlands and in May 1725 had been appointed c.-in-c. of the forces in Scotland in order to carry it out (*Oxf. DNB*).

[701] In fact, in a letter to Newcastle dated 1 July (BL, Walpole papers, Add. MS 74066 (unfol.)) Wade stated that he was holding off moving troops till he received firm intelligence whether to send them west, to Glasgow, or north, to Inverness.

[702] Charles Miller.

[703] For the Malt Tax or Shawfield Riots, see Riley, *English Ministers and Scotland*, 283–4; John M'Ure, *The History of Glasgow* (new edn, Glasgow, 1830), 333–43.

The Townesmen being returnd went to Dan. Campbells house (one of their Represen-tatives) which they gutted, The commanding officer gave the Provost notice of an intention to doe this, and oferd to defend the house butt had for answer that there was noe need of his assistance, and therefore desird his leaving the towne; you must know they have entertaind a notion, that hee had advisd Mr W[alpole] to insist uppon leavying the mault tax; whither true or false I know nott.

I formerly gave you an account of the Scots members behaviour in the house when the matter was in agitation; one of them (Phrasier[704]) declard that hee in behalfe of his country protested against all they had or should doe uppon that occasion, for that twas never intended they should bee liable to this tax, though England was.

I beleive you may rely on this account as more authentick, then probably you will as yett receive from any other hand.

You know whoe has all along held them up under the chin, and now the consequence of soe doing appears, I hope an end wil bee soone putt to itt, butt that is more then any body knowes, for I thinke the late repeated favours to the party, likelyer to encourage then otherwise, I wish itt may nott prove soe.

688. Alan I, Dublin, to Thomas, 4 July 1725[705]

(1248/6/259–66)

From the repeated assurances you have given me lately that our little correspondence is thought worth prying into, I chuse to send this letter by Major Renouard[706] who tells me he will without fail deliver it into Allyes hand and when it once gets safe there I make no difficultye of her being able to convey it to you unexamined on your side of the water. We are now here upon a new scheme of politicks, which is not to be much wondred at considering the late alteration at the Castle by my laying down and anothers succeeding me. In consequence of which you may be sure I am trusted in the same maner as undeserving, disgraced, or disobliged people alway are at Court. I have all along acquainted you with every step I took to discourage my Lord Carterett from entertaining hopes of having a quiet and easy Session here, unlesse the Parliament were satisfyed as to the matter of Woods patent, (for soe I rather chuse to call it then Woods halfpence which I beleive every body seeth can not obtain a currency here, by reason of the resolution of those formerly in authoritye and the constancy of the people in their determination not to take them voluntarily, and that his Majestyes goodnesse and wisdome will not admit of his using any compulsory means to make them passe). No man can entertain a thought or apprehension that his Majestye will doe any thing inconsistent with the repeated declarations he hath made on this head. But in my opinion the tranquillitye and easinesse that the people hath shewn lately upon this matter proceeds not from their being told the King will not doe any thing to oblige the taking that coyne, nor from the sense they have that nothing but

---

[704] Hon. William Fraser (1691–1727), of Fraserfield, Aberdeenshire, MP [GB] Elgin Burghs 1722–5. He had been unseated on 23 Jan. 1725.

[705] Partly printed in Coxe, *Walpole*, ii, 419–23.

[706] Peter Renouard (*d. c.* 1763), major, Royal Irish Dragoons (Dalton, *Geo I's Army*, ii, 157–8; Vicars, *Index*, 397).

compulsion will give it a diffused currencye in the Kingdome; for his Majestyes patent and declaracion in Councel were as strong against using any compulsion to enforce that coyne on the nation, as anything which hath hapned since his Excellencyes landing, and the minds of the people were as well known to be very averse to receiving it voluntarily: nay soe averse were they, that Mr Wood and his freinds were pleased to argue that the people were on this score become disaffected to his Majestyes Governement. But in my opinion the seeming easinesse men shew of late by not talking at all about them ariseth from an apprehension that some publick act will be done or declaration made at the opening of the Parliament which may render it unnecessary to undeceive his Majestye and the Councel in England in a very material point viz. whether there was such a want of Copper coyne as was suggested to his Majestye to be in this Kingdome, without which suggestion there could not have been a pretence for asking or a ground for granting Mr Wood those powers of coyning which he hath by his patent. Mr Wood indeed was ready with his witnesses to swear there was a want of such coyne, and had the good fortune to obtain credit in that matter; for want of witnesses to prove the contrary; for the sense of both houses of Parliament, and of the Councel board were not of sufficient weight to shew the contrary; upon this principle (if I doe not mistake) that in matter of property, as Woods patent is, the votes of either or both houses or addresse of the Councel board are not Legal evidence, much lesse conclusive. But I doubt the Parliament may be inclined to lay the truth of that fact in another light then it seems to me to stand at present on your side the water, and perhaps they may fancy that when a thing is of so national consequence, as knowing whether there be occasion for 14 Tuns of Copper to be coyned into small money to be current for above £100000, this matter might have deserved the consideration of the representatives of the Kingdome or at least to have been referred to the Governement and Councel of it, and not to be finally determined at the Treasury upon the testimony of persons who might be either concerned in interest that Wood might obtain a patent to coyne, or be procured by him and his freinds. But my Lord Lieutenant seems to me not to expect he shal receive any orders to mention either the patent or proceedings had either in England or here on that head at the opening of the Parliament; and consequently that he shal not in his speech take any notice of that affair at all: and he also seems to beleive other people will be perfectly silent on that point too, and proceed in granting supplyes and other businesse of Parliament (if there shal be any other) just as if there never had been such a man as Wood in the world, or as if no patent had been granted or proceedings either in England or Ireland relating thereto.

If these be his real sentiments I freely own to you that I think he will be greatly mistaken. But I will now tell you my judgement on his conduct in this whole affair. I am well satisfyed that his own private judgement is that the patent obtained in the maner this hath been obtained, and when the Kingdome did not want (in reality) such a quantitye of small Coyne as Woods by his patent is authorized to coyne, and without enquiring into the truth of that matter (on this side of the water) I say that his opinion I beleive is that the patent is Legal (such a notion he seems to me to have of the Kings Prerogative) and that the King is by the Law the Judge of the conveniency to the Kingdome in granting power to coyne such quantitye of base money as he shal think proper, and that he is empowred to give currencye to a peice of Copper for an half penny which is not of such intrinsick value (allowing the necessary expences of coynage and other reasonable allowances). This I think to be his notion, but his good sense must tell him that such a concession puts the subject very much in the power of the Prince, if he be the sole Judge of the quantitye of

Copper to be coyned, and of what intrinsick value the peice to be coyned is to be of in proporcion to the rate it is to goe att. But I have no reason to say he thinks the King hath a right to inforce such base money to be received as current money by his subjects; by which added to the beleif everybody ought to have that the Crown will not use its Prerogative to the detriment of the subject I apprehend he thinks the subject to be sufficiently guarded against any great and greivous inconvenience from any excessive quantity of base coyne. 1. Because we should not think so ill of the Crown as to beleive it will for any private inducement doe any thing which may be prejudicial to the nation in general. 2. That there being no necessitye laid on the subject to receive this base money, they will be sure to refuse it when there is a superfluitye of it; and then there will be an end of coyning, when the trash cannot be uttered or received as money. But it is now time for me to proceed to unfold to you what I mean by our new scheme of politicks. You may remember the matter of Mr Hacketts letter to me:[707] and to speak plain English I am of opinion every thing is now kept perfectly a secret from my knowledge, which is really intended; for since I have from the beginning told Lord C[arteret] that I alway was and alway must be against Woods patent in the whole and in every part, and never could be prevailed upon either by the most artful and insinuating letters from England, or the great caresses used toward me upon his arrival to come into this [?darling] affair (in which I doe not find but that his Excellencye went as great lengths in the Committee of Councel as any body) and since the more cavalier methods taken by him soon after his landing to carry his point, had no more effect on me then his douceurs, I plainly discovered in him a coldnesse toward me; he alway treated me with great civilitye, and as far as good words went expressed himself to have a particular kindnesse for me; I should be glad to be able to give one instance of his favour unlesse his constantly advising with me in the most ticklish and dangerous affairs to advise in may be looked on as instances. From time to time I shewed him such parts of your letters as informed me of the maner I was treated in at a certain place,[708] and told him I understood very well the meaning of those who sett the chace on foot viz that they who could not assign a ground for removing me might put me on doing that from resentment which they wished to be done, but were unwilling to doe professedly. He could not but know from my telling him what I heard (to all which he alway professed he was wholly a stranger) that I intended to lay down that which only made me capable of being insulted in the maner I had been, and I told him, that I certainly would quit if it continued; without desiring him to interpose that I might have fairer quarter. Perhaps he did not think I was of so much mettle to doe what he afterward found I dared and resolved to doe; or to speak my mind clearly; he refined thus. This man will never come into my schemes, but Lord Cheif Baron Hale will; let them proceed to [?worry] in —— and let him be angry and throw up,[709] and then I shal have oportunitye of bring Mr Hale into his place to have a Chancellor as obsequious, as his predecessor hath been untractable. And I must neeeds say that upon the best consideration of things which I have been able to give them: My thoughts are that for some time it hath been wrote by Lord C[arteret] that its not to be expected things will doe in Parliament here without giving the people satisfaction in the matter of Woods patent, and I beleive he hath set that out soe strongly as to convince the ministry. I am also

---

[707] See above, pp. 145–6.

[708] The British house of lords.

[709] Resign.

apt to beleive that to bring them into the Kings giving him instructions or power to give the Parliament satisfaction in that particular he may have given hopes, nay assurances of being able on those terms to obtain great supplyes, and indeed of not being disappointed in any thing that is not very unreasonable in point of money, if mens minds can be made easy about the patent. But I am of opinion that he hath desired to be left at liberty not to mention it in his speech, out of hopes that no body will mention the patent in parliament; but if it be stirred and the Parliament shew a spirit that he may then have the patent in his power to qualifye their heats, and by this means he will come at the knowledge of the bold men who shal venture to appear in the service of their countery and not worship Baal, upon whom I have some reason to beleive as great marks of resentment will be shewn as men deserve who having emploiments doe not act as they are bid. On 25 June when the Commissioners for passing the publick accounts[710] passed two accounts one for the year ending 25 Dec. 1723; the other ending 7 April. 1724 (the day when Sir Wm St Quintin dyed)[711] I asked the Auditor whether the account from 7 April 1724 to 25 Dec. 1724 was ready; he told us not; and Lord Falmouth and Mr Edgecombe said they must desire us to allow them a little time to make applicacion for a power to be given to the Commissioners of accounts to give credit to the Vice Treasurers for paiments made on warrants not polled, or which perhaps they might object to, for their being ancient (but I think they did not expressely say what the objections were to the allowing those paiments by those who are now Commissioners of accounts). On 27 June Lord Lieutenant delivered into my hand a paper of which I send you a copy in the following words.

To his Excellencye the Lord Carterett etc. The humble peticion of John Pratt Esqr Late Deputy Vice Treasurer.

Sheweth That upon passing the Vice Treasurers accounts to the 7th April. 1724. there remained a ballance of 96148=9=5 and also upon the account from 7th April 1724. to the 7th June 1725. there may remain a ballance of about £30000 more which several ballances amount in the whole to the summe of 126148=9=5. which was occasioned by many vouchers being mislayd, most part of which are since found, and it is hoped the rest may be gott in some time. That the Commissioners of accounts think they cannot allow many of them because they are of old dates and not regularly entred with the Clerk of the Pells according to the usual forms of the Exchequer tho it plainly appears that the money hath been paid in discharge of the Establishment and other legal orders of the Crown. Wherefore your peticioner humbly prayes your Excellencye to be pleased to represent his Case to his Majestye that he may be graciously pleased to impower the said Commissioners of accounts to allow all such paiments as he shal from time to time make appear to have been made in discharge of the establishment and other Legal orders from the Crown and that the nation hath really and bona fide been discharged of so much money by the said paiments notwithstanding the regular entry of them in the Pells has been omitted and which can not now be supplyed by the forms of the Exchequer.

[710] According to the Irish act of 10 Hen. VII, c. 1, the vice-treasurer's accounts were audited by a board of treasury commissioners (the 'ancient board of accounts') comprising, *ex officio*, the Irish lord chancellor, chancellor of the exchequer, three chief justices, secretary of state, auditor-gen. and muster-master gen. (Kiernan, *Financial Administration*, 244, 271). In this case all three barons of the exchequer were involved.

[711] Sir William St Quintin died on 30 June but the new commission replacing him as joint vice-treasurer [I] with Richard Edgcumbe did not pass until 7 Apr. 1724.

This paper my Lord Lieutenant put into my hand in presence of Baron Pocklington and St Leger two of the Commissioners of accounts[712] and of Mr Bernard the Prime Serjeant[713] and desired our advice on it. I pressed to have an order from him in writing what on points we were desired to advise him, but this was declined:

On 28 June Mr Marley the Sollictor General delivered to Mr Bernard a draught of an opinion or report to be given on that peticion which Mr Bernard communicated it to me, and

On 29 June Mr Marley[714] and Sir John St Leger came together to my house and the former delivered me a like rough draught with that he had shewn to Mr Bernard which is in the following words.

In obedience to your Excellencyes order we have examined the allegacions of the peticion of J[ohn] P[ratt] late Deputy Vice Treasurer and do find that the said late Deputy Vice T[reasurer] hath paid several summes on account of clothing warrants for which he hath not taken credit in any of the accounts passed by us and that he hath paid several summes pursuant to Legal orders from the Governement for which he hath had no credit and cannot produce Legal receits tho we have good reason to beleive the same were paid. We farther find that some warrants of the Governement have been paid by the said late Deputy Vice T[reasurer] and for which he has legal receits have not been credited in his accounts and that none of the said several payments are entred by the Clerk of the Pells, nor can (as the said Clerk of the Pells alleges) be now entred by him, the ballance having been struck upon the accounts already made up.

We are humbly of opinion that your Excellencye may (if you think fitt) represent the peticioners case to his Majestye and that he may be graciously pleased by his letter to empower us to reexamine the peticioners account and to make him an allowance of such summes part of the ballance of 126148=9=5: as shal appear to have been really and bona fide paid and discharged by the peticioner pursuant to the establishment or other Legal orders from the Crown tho he cannot produce regular vouchers for the same aco[unt] to the course of the Exchequer.

This paper I no way liked containing matters which Marlay may know the truth of, but I doe not; and utterly refused to join in it. I doubt there have been paiments made on dormant warrants which have not been thought proper to be pelled, which gives publick notice there were such warrants, and that perhaps it was not advisable to publish at that time. And indeed St Leger blabbed it that Pratt would be able if such a letter were obtained to discharge £74000 of the ballance now standing on him and then the nation will appear to be by so much more in debt then was represented to them the Last Session, and the honour of this will fall to the share of those who advised this Commission; but if the letter can be advised and gott it may facilitate the ballance appearing £74000 worse on the nations side, then the Commons were told by the Governement last Session and then they apprehended upon their best enquiry: If this can be attained it will furnish some people with the popular argument that since the money hath been really paid pursuant to the Kings orders we must proceed to find funds for such deficiencye as will be created by allowing illegal payments on old or unpelled warrants, without considering the consequences which

---

[712]John Pocklington and Sir John St Leger, both barons of the exchequer.

[713]Francis Bernard, MP [I].

[714]Thomas Marlay, MP [I], solicitor-gen. [I].

this precedent will create or may have by procuring dormant warrants for payment of money (not appropriated) but given upon a confidence it would be employed in discharging the establishment, for which new supplyes must be provided in a succeeding Session. You have now part of the objection I have to releiving Pratt from the difficultyes he may lye under from having paid money where the warrants were not entred with the Clerk of the Pells; he sinned with his eyes open and may doe the same hereafter by which the Nation may greatly suffer by having the money they gave for other purposes misapplyed and the necessary paiments left in arrear, as the army now is. One great objection to releiving him where he may want releif, for payment on old warrants (of which I know not the instances) arises from the apprehension I have of seeing warrants now trumped up from those who were Justices in 1715 (Grafton and Galwey)[715] upon the Kings letter of the 9th of Febr. 1715 by which he was pleased to give a most unlimited power to those Justices that ever I saw viz. to appoint what part of his treasure (indefinitely) to any part of his service. And what warrants were then signed or may be now produced I doe not know, but I am sure the Cash of the Kingdome was put by that letter into hands who seem to me never to have been very careful how far the Kingdome was burthened. But the greatest objection to me arises from the payments made in discharge of the establishment <u>or other Legal warrants</u>. To what summes such paiments may amount I cannot tell; nor for what services such payments have been made, but give me leave to suppose a case, and that it should come out that there now should be in being a warrant which is not thought proper to be made publick for a very great summe payable to [—][716] and that this very warrant should be calculated to make amends to any body for a summe of money which they expected from some project which hath failed; will not this fall directly within the description in Mr Pratts petition of vouchers which he hopes he may be able hereafter to find? Will not the persons who advise the granting such a letter, as Mr Marlay thinks reasonable, be thought by the Commons to have too great an hand in bringing this charge on the nation; Will it not be thus understood that the Lord Lieutenant would not have applyed for the Kings letter to empower the Commissioners of accounts to make allowance of the payments of such after found vouchers and warrants, if he had not been advised to doe so by the Chancellor etc nay farther will not every abuse of the powers entrusted by such letter be placed to the accounts of those who advised the letter, and I should be unwilling to answer with my character for the actions of other men, tho never soe worthy. Upon this fact I now stand, and must be content to be reckoned very opposite rather then advise so new a precedent here, and which may have such consequences that perhaps are not yet foreseen: As for example, that no account hereafter shal need be passed in any other maner, or in the course of the Exchequer, but in the maner contained in that letter. By all conjecture I can make there is some dormant warrant in being, which being complyed with the Patent may be given up and truly this is the best explanacion I can give of this new scheme. But I resolve not to burn my fingers by coming into any advice for granting such letter and shal want the thanks I might be entitled to by such a compliance. Pardon the length and confused maner of this letter … Consider and doe not decline the service of a countrey which deserves your care and would be in great measure influenced by your example in this most critical juncture.

[715]The duke of Grafton and Henri de Massue (1648–1720), 2nd Marquis de Ruvigny and 1st earl of Galway, had served as lords justices from 1715 to 1717.
[716]Space in MS.

Have not some people [?deserved] at your hands to create them uneasinesse. If once it take air either here or in England that you have a thought of coming over, the great ones in both places will bestir themselves terribly to divert soe unexpected and disagreeable a visit. Try what turn the giving it out will take at London; or permit me to let fall an expression here that such a thing is not impossible: and take your measures afterward as you like the effects which such a peice of surprizing news will produce. After all I am yet in doubt whether the great ones with you are not soe bent to make ——— appear not able to doe service that they will not doe anything which may put him into a possibilitye of holding an easy and good Session of Parliament, tho by doing it they should attain one great end which I think is aimed at I mean a round summe for ———. Are not Lord Abercorne and Mr St George[717] very extraordinary men who were two of the warmest and earliest in bringing that which hath been the occasion of [?bringing] all the trouble we have had since the Duke of G[*rafton*]s leaving us on the Stage, and have very skilfully turned their backs on Ireland in the middle of the fray? Doe they intend to be lookers on at distance and is it expected by other Gentlemen of the Kingdome that some people must alway bear the indignation of the Court for opposing the measures which they apprehend will prejudice the countrey and others sit by at their ease. I have sufficiently bore my testimonye by laying down, and shal think myself at liberty not to live alway in hot water for a common cause when others equally concerned in the event seem soe indifferent.

689. *Thomas, Peper Harow, to Alan I, Dublin, 7 July 1725*

(1248/6/267–8)

This moment I received yours of the 15th which you know I cannott have time to answer by this post, butt intend doing itt by next if I am able, for the small motion (which I made soe as far as possible, for I was two dayes in coming) has throwne mee into a violent fit …

690. *Thomas, Peper Harow, to Alan I, Dublin, 9 July 1725*

(1248/6/269–70)

After having consulted all freinds and relations uppon the subject of a letter with a paper enclosd (uppon an affair which will most certainly readily recur to your mind) I thinke necessary to lett you know our unanimous opinion, which in short is, that wee doe nott thinke the thing in any sort advisable, if you insist uppon our reasons you shall have them, butt in the mean time I choose nott to defer giving our thoughts, since you say you shall in this (as formerly) have great regard thereto; I beleive another freind gave you this account before, butt I suppose the letter miscarryed, as you may assure your selfe severall both to and from you have done, a scandalous and villanous practice surely is this, of looking into private family affairs, in expectation of meeting with mens sentiments in relation to publique ones, butt more especially those of Ireland, which att this time they are very sollicitous to know. I resolve to determine nothing positively in relation to the latter part of your letter of the

[717] Oliver St George, MP [I].

20th of last month, which I just ownd the receipt of by last post, notwithstanding two difficultyes readily occur; the first more then a bare probabillity of itt being utterly out of my power to doe what you advise, the next the time when (if I should bee able) twould bee advisable to comply with itt, in order to my better information with respect to the latter, I have this day wrote to a freind whoe I know can informe mee (if hee pleases) by whose way of answering I shall bee able to forme some judgment. I intend towards the Bath the beginning of the weeke, in hopes of being able to beare going ten miles a day, which I assure you att present I am nott, for my paine has been soe very excessive since my coming hither, that I have nott yett had itt in my power to stand upright, butt itt decreases.

If my letters by the crosse post are intercepted, or opened, as others have hitherto been, or yours to mee directed the same way, there will remaine noe doubt where the foule play lyes …

691. *Alan I, Dublin, to Thomas, 17 July 1725*[718]

(1248/6/271–2)

I continue stil (as my wife once called me humorously enough) vice Chancellor to Mr West who is not yet landed, nor possibly may in two or three dayes, if his being unwilling to ride over the mountains of Wales, or any other consideration hath determined him to come directly from Chester water and not ride to Holyhead: the wind is now at West and may continue longer soe then he is aware of; but the Captain of the Yatcht will be able to tyde it down to the Head, and when he gets soe far, will be able to make his passage thence at least as well as any of the pacquet boats. Before you receive this I hope M. R.[719] will have delivered into your hands a long letter of three sheets, which I at first intended to have sent to you under Allyes cover: but altered my measures because it would then have gone first to Peperhara before you received it. I shal be very uneasy till I have your answer to each part of it, as well publick as private. Tho I have not received a line from you since yours of the second instant yet I am sensible you have had one from me, because my Lord C[arteret] takes notice of mine to him which went under your cover; In it he speaks to this effect: That he hopes I will continue to make use of my interest to keep things quiet here. This caution of his to me certainly arises from his having been told from this side, that such methods have been taken, to prevent the matter of Woods patent being brought upon the stage in our approaching parliament, as will attain the end if I doe not appear in the matter, and concert measures about it, and sett it on foot. As for my part in the affair I am kept entirely a stranger to what is intended; if any thing be yet determined: nay I am told my Lord C[arteret] hath not yet any orders in that particular, but he stil seems to hope that matter (with my assistance) will rest and that the Session will goe on very smooth without mentioning or thinking of the Copper money: I have alway told him he would find his mistake too late, and that unlesse mens minds were made easy in that particular it would certainly be taken up by some body; and when it should be soe that it would not

---

[718] Partly printed in Coxe, *Walpole*, ii, 424–6.

[719] No family member, friend or employee with these initials appears in the correspondence. It is possible, albeit unlikely, that the letter had been sent via the former Surrey MP, Morgan Randyll.

be in the power nor inclinacion of his sincere freinds to stop things from going farther then would have satisfyed mens minds at the opening of the Session. To fancy telling the houses from the throne that the King will not doe any thing to enforce a currencye of that coyne, is no more then the patent speaks and then is contained in the report of the Committee of Councel and the Kings order in Councel thereupon. This I think will be soe far from preventing the Parliament entring into the consideration of that matter that it seems to me to furnish an handle to those who have a mind to bring the affair on the carpett. And I confesse my thoughts to be that there will appear more Gentlemen in the matter then seems to be expected; I am very doubtful that encouragement is given from your side to the people confided in here to create my Lord C[arteret] all the difficultyes possible in the Session, and if a story be true, which I lately heard from noe ill hand, he will find not only little assistance but hearty opposicion from a quarter whence it seems to be little apprehended. Now methinks you might as you are going toward Peperhara call on a Gentleman who lives but a very little out of the road, and tell him that which I have often endeavoured to perswade his freind to be the truth of the case, that (unlesse it be resolved in England) that we shal speak our minds freely in what maner the Nation hath been treated in the matter of Mr Wood from the beginning to the end in the plainest maner, as well in procuring and passing the patent, as how the Parliament Privy Councel and nation have been used etc I say if this be not the wish of people some step should be made to quiet mens minds that neither this patent nor any obtained for the private benefit of any body without the application of the Kingdome or soe much as acquainting the Governement and Councel of this Kingdome, that it was suggested that there was a want of Copper money, or directing the truth of that fact to be inquired into, in Ireland; shal be used or put in practice. But if the long step taken at the T[reasury] in granting the patent upon such information as preceded the obtaining this, must in all events be supported and made a point of Prerogative, I can not but think the Parliament will look on their property to be touched too nearly by such a posicion as justifyes the maner of obtaining and granting this patent, not to doe their best to prevent their falling into misfortunes which they beleive will follow from this point being once insisted on in the maner it hath been (in my opinion) unlesse it be receded from. I know how difficult a thing it is, to bring great people to doe all that will be wished on this occasion: But I now write while there is time to doe what may prevent warmth in our approaching Session, and I confesse I doe not see that any thing lesse then what I have hinted at, can attain that desirable end. This, then, is the way and the only one I can think of to have things proceed smoothly in Parliament: Till we were blessed with a Bank and a Copper patent, every thing proceeded quietly here: the people gave what was demanded to support the establishment, nay ex abundanti[720] encreased their own expence by an addition to the pay of the troops. But when they found their money was going into private pockets (I mean the projectors of the Bank and Mr Wood and his partners) they could not digest those proceedings. Methinks you may better discourse this matter where it is proper, then that it should be done in a letter directly to the party; in which I should not be fond of speaking my thoughts soe plainly as to the Kings Prerogative and the proceedings at a certain place where you were a witnesse of what passed: as I reasonably may when I write privately to one whose estate lyes in this country, and to whom I have soe near a

---

[720] Out of abundance.

relation as I have to you, in whom I entirely confide that you will make no other use of what I write then to consider whether what my thoughts on this subject are, may be of any service to the King and this poor countrey in the very difficultyes we lye under; for it is certain, nothing can be soe fatal to our happinesse, as to lye or fall under the displeasure of the King or the resentment of the ministry. Now unlesse something can be done to prevent the heats, which I think will unavoidably happen in our Parliament, if it open without giving better satisfaction about Mr Woods coyne then (I fear) hath been yet given I confesse I have a very melancholy prospect of the Successe of the Session. You cannot imagine under what concern I am that I can not hear directly and positively from you or my sisters upon a familye concern which I wrote lately about to both in a most pressing maner: Whatever your thoughts are let me know them; for your silence gives too much handle for suspition that I doe not deal candidly or like a Gentleman, which as I never have yet been justly charged with, I should be very unwilling to give reason of being so much as suspected in this instance. Pray without losse of time let me hear expressely from you on this subject.

692. *Alan I, Dublin, to Thomas, Peper Harow, 20 July 1725*

(1248/6/273–4)

Last night there came in a pacquet against all our expectacions; occasioned I suppose by the messenger who came in her being very pressing to come over. We hear that his businesse is with orders to countermand our two regiments who were ordered to Port Mahon,[721] and I am told it is beleived they are already actually sailed, and that Captain Rowley who commands a small man of war here[722] is ordered to follow them with such fresh orders as have been sent from London. You may be sure mens thoughts are employed to find out the reason of this countermand, some pretend to say it is upon an apprehension of an attack upon Gibraltar, and that the regiments are instead of reinforcing Port Mahon to doe soe (where they are most wanted) at Gibraltar; while others fancy the stop proceeds from the disturbances at Glascoe: I confesse I doe not in any sort beleive this can be the reason, because there are other regiments here that might be employed there (if occasion required) without altering the resolucions which were soe long in taking about the number of regiments that should go to the Streights and which should be the Regiments. My Lord Lieutenant told me the expresse brought him indeed a letter from the Duke of Newcastle, but without any directions about our approaching Session.[723] If this be soe I think my Lords good freinds in England, will give him the honour and hazard of a good or a bad Session

---

[721] The *Dublin Journal*, 28 June 1725, reported that on 17 June three vessels had arrived at Falmouth to transport troops to Port Mahon, on Menorca.

[722] William Rowley (c. 1690–1768), captain of the *Lively*, a small frigate operating against smugglers and pirates off the Irish coast north of Dublin; later knighted, and made admiral of the fleet (*Oxf. DNB*).

[723] On 13 July Newcastle had responded to Carteret's request to prorogue the Irish parliament further, from 6 Aug., when it had been scheduled to meet, until 7 Sept. (TNA, SP 63/385/257: Carteret to Newcastle, 1 July 1725; SP 63/385/275: Newcastle to Carteret, 13 July 1725). But Newcastle offered no advice as to how the parliament was to be managed, in relation to the expected opposition to the halfpence. Instead, on 27 July he wrote to Carteret to ask if the lord lieutenant had any thoughts of an expedient that might put an end to the affair (TNA, SP 63/385/320–2).

as it shal prove without taking part in it. But I may reasonably guesse that this was only a courtly way of keeping me in the dark what the measures intended are; for being now out of all emploiment (as I shal be in two hours after this perverse wind will allow my Successor to set foot on Irish ground) and parted with in the obliging maner I have been, I make no doubt I am understood not to be the most zealous freind to the measures which the persons confided in shal think most practicable. If this be the case I am sure it will give me great ease, since nothing can be expected from a man in whom you doe not think fit to repose a confidence, or to think worth keeping a freind. Mr Hill gott to Chester on Wednesday last and writes to me from that place on the 14th that Mr West was gone forward to the Head where he proposed to be on Saturday night. The pacquet boat sailed thence about two in the afternoon, at which time I suppose he was not gott thither; but whether the Yatcht fell down from Chester water[724] to meet him at Holyhead I know not; but if that be the resolution I shal be kept longer on the uncertaintyes I now lye under (when I shal be able to goe into the countrey) for as soon as I am gott free from my trappings I will goe for a few dayes into the countrey, to lye stil and to be out of the way while my Successor receives the honours and respects due to his Station and merit, which I am sure will be very literally paid him by his freinds; and I wish him joy of them. I am extremely sorry to find your little journey into Surrey hath given you soe severe a fit of the stone as you describe, and shal be in pain till I hear again from you, which I hope will bring me the pleasure to know you are gott over it by voiding the stone which immediately occasions your torment …

693. *Alan I, Dublin, to Thomas, Bath, 22 July 1722 [recte 1725]*

(1248/5/227–8)

Yesterday I received your letter of the ninth, and one of the fourteenth from my sister, in which she tells me that you began your journey from Peperhara toward Bath on that day after the coming in of the post, and that you desire me to write to you by the crosse post; by which means we shal be able to discover where it is that the foul play is used in opening and sometimes stopping our letters: for that the later hath been done more then once I am sure, if there were two letters wrote by you (which she seems to intimate) in one of which you own the receit of the account of Ran[*dal*] Claytons death, and (in another as I take it to be) you owned my letter with one inclosed to my Lord Chancellor: now if you wrote two distinct letters, I doe assure you I received neither the one nor the other. I wrote to you on the 20th and directed it to Peperhara; and in it told you that my Lord Lieutenant assured me he had no directions in relation to Parliament businesse. I hope people on the other side of the water will find it to be prudent to doe something conformable to the little paper, which my sister sent to me dated 13 July and signed J.S.,[725] for indeed they who advise other methods will find themselves much deceived in their politicks; When ever he makes good his word in giving you farther light, I desire you will transmit a copy of what he writes to you by way of postscript, with this signature. J.S. which will make

---

[724]The Dee estuary.

[725]Possibly Jude Storer (for whom see above, p. 32).

me understand what it is and from whom it comes. We have not yet any account of the Yatcht; but Mr West is at the Head, and I suppose is not willing to doe the pacquet boat the honour of bringing soe great a man into the Kingdome, or perhaps he doth not think that kind of ship hath conveniencyes for himself and his Lady and whole familye; or he may (like other English men) think it to be dangerous coming in soe small a vessel as a pacquet boat.

As I am sensible your advice hath been ever given with the strictest regard to the good of your relation, it entirely shal take place and I have by this post already ordered things accordingly. I am greatly delighted to find by your letter that your pain decreaseth, and hope it will be to that degree that it will enable you to perform your intended journey to Bath without any great trouble, and that the waters there will enable you this winter to serve your countrey as you have hitherto done to the satisfaction of all unprejudiced persons. I cannot but repeat with utmost earnestnesse what I pressed you to doe in a late long letter (wrote in 3 sheets of paper) and sent by a private hand. The Gentleman did not goe in ten dayes after he first intended, soe that you had begun your journey from Peperhara toward Bath before he left Dublin, and this will account for the oldnesse of its date, which to the best of my memory is either on the 6th or 7th instant: the foul play our letters have mett with of late put me under a necessitye of saying what I did in that letter by a private hand: for I am sure nothing could be proposed that would more disconcert the measures now in the minds of the people confided in, then what is by me proposed and advised in that letter. There is one thing more in it, that doing what I propose seems to me to be the almost only thing capable of saving a certain persons character from suffering in the world. I am sure I doe not mean my own; for I am determined to combat Wm Wood in what shape so ever I meet him, and this I have at all times said and will at all times make good. It is with this reserve (of being against the Copper patent) that I have ever promised to serve or assist my Lord Lieutenant and this he will doe me the justice to own. But when I have told you how much it will import the publick that you comply in what is proposed, I need use no other argument. Upon reconsidering your letter of the 9th I beleive that is the letter which my sister M[artha] C[ourthope] means when she saith you had owned the receit of my letter with an account of Ran[dal] Claytons death; for you doe in the end of that letter mencion mine of the 2d, and one from Will Casaubon[726] about it; and this must be your letter which she mencions in hers of the 14th upon that subject. Soe here one of my letters is accounted for, but I never had any from you in which you acknowledged mine with an enclosed to my Lord Chancellor; but that the letter came to your hand I am sure, by having received my Lord Chan[cellor']s answer which I acquainted you with in my long letter by a private hand ... When your leisure will admit, pray let me hear from you, and you shal hear as often from me as my going into Munster will allow: for as soon as I can disengage my self from the Office I now hold (of being Mr Wests Vice Chancellor) I resolve to turn my back on Dublin and to breath fresh countrey air and see (what cannot soe easily be done here) honest undesigning Lovers of their countrey.

---

[726] William Causabon, MP [I].

694. *Thomas, Bath, to Alan I, 31 July 1725*

(1248/6/275–6)

Yesterday came yours of the 22d instant, I direct this to Dublin as I always shall, because your servants will know whither to send them, though I conclude your successor already arrived, for wee have had a bitter cold N. East wind for five dayes past.

You judge rightly in owning the receipt of one of the two which Mrs C[ourthope][727] mentioned, the other is certainly intercepted, butt for what reason detaind, I cannott guesse, unlesse that therein I told you some people must alter their measures, or would perhaps bee more embarrased then they expected, I am still of opinion they will be convinct that I judge right; and indeed every day confirmes mee in that opinion.

Your long letter is nott yett come, ile own itt, assoon as itt does. This will bee my second by the crosse post, which I doubt nott going safe, unlesse stopt on your side.

The waters (as usuall) have brought a way a pretty deale of gravel, butt the paine (from which I have never been an hour free for six months past) remaining, confirmes what I have for some time concluded, that there is a formed stone in my right kidney, the paine is of a different kind from that of the gravel passing the uriters, nott soe sharpe, butt continuall, and three or four inches higher, remaining still in the same place, I have a long time enjoyd tollerable health, and have noe reason to repine, when soe few reach my years; I can with great truth say I submitt without reluctance, to which my having acted alwayes honestly (according to the best of my understanding) does very much contribute.

I write by this post to a freind whoe I am pretty confident will shew my letter to ——. I intend hee should doe soe; youl easily guesse whoe I meane; and have assured him (whoe I am confident will beleive mee) that neither pique or resentment, or other motive then the hearty desire I have of discharging my duty both to King and country influences mee; whither twill have any effect I know nott, being very sensible that nothing butt conviction of its being somebodyes interest, will take place with him, and that very seldom failes of doing soe …

695. *Alan I, Dublin, to Thomas, 6 Aug. 1725*

(1248/6/277–80)

I formerly owned the receit of my sisters from Peperhara[728] on the day you left that place with the enclosed from my freind J.S.[729] (whom for the future I will call my freind without other addicion) and have good reason to beleive what he saith it is true. Everyday gives fresh reason to beleive the matter begins to be thought worthy of more serious consideracion and regard, then seems formerly to have been had of it. Mr West landed on 21 July and I supposed brought the holy Spirit (as was usual at the Councel of Trent) as they called the last result of the Pope and Cabinett at Rome, in his Cloakbag. Upon this confidence I

[727]Rachel.
[728]Rachel Courthope.
[729]Jude Storer.

ventured to ask one (who would have me understand that every thing relating to that affair, was and should from time to time be imparted to me as soon as it came to knowledge) whether any and what directions were come to put matters at quiet. The answer given was that none were come. I ventured then to congratulate him on the good news which I had received from a hand to be depended on, that something was resolved to be done to quiet the people before the meeting of this Parliament. This produced an acknowledgement that indeed he found by Mr W[es]t that something was to be done, and that the consideration what that something should be and the maner would lye in great measure on the opinion of a person to whom I wrote lately under your cover. But farther then this was not said. After I had given up the Seal I spent a week in the countrey, during which time my Lord Chancellor sent a servant to my house to know whether he might come to see me and when? The answer made at the door was that I was in the Countrey but should return soon; When I did soe, I sent him a message that I was come to town and should be glad to see him when his leisure would allow him to make me a visit. You know I am not a man of ceremonye and alway despised insisting on forms: but thought since he had not after landing visited me while Chancellor I ought to insist on the puncto[730] of not making him the first visit now he is Chancellor. Upon Sunday night he made me a visit, which I returned on Wednesday: At that interview we discoursed with a great deal of freedome and several civil things passed mutually between us. I took occasion upon his wishing an happy and quiet Session to say I did not see how it could be otherwise if one thing were removed out of the way, which he explained in the maner I meant, and added he beleived care would be taken that soe much should be done as would be to the satisfaction of every <u>reasonable</u> man. And this he spoke with a good deal of openesse and assurance that things would be as he had said: but confined himself to that general expression, beyond which I could not bring him. I confesse, that expression seems to me to leave room for others to be Judges whether we are reasonable men or not; and I doe not desire to have this expression used of the Parliament, which upon a certain occasion hath been used of another body of men of some consideration here, <u>according to their way of thinking</u>. The Duke of G[*rafton*] told us that the answer to the Addresses of both houses about Woods patent was such as would be satisfactory to all reasonable men. How many unreasonable men there must have been in Ireland by his rule, is pretty notorious: and I doubt the number [?of] reasonables would have been confined to himself and his Secretary and a very few dependants and creatures of his. On Monday last I had a great complement sent to me to be at the [*Castle*] the next day. I attended accordingly and was told that now at length there was an oportunitye offered to set a matter again on foot which had been written on formerly, but nothing of late, by reason that the former letters had no effect, in which state (as I understood it) things were like to have continued without saying any thing farther on this side of the water; if nothing had come from England till the meeting of the Parliament. But that —— had received a letter from a person who had been lately here Mr E[*dgcumbe*] to whom he had discoursed that matter at large that something was to be done to prepare things for an happy Session etc. That Gentleman writes that he had mentioned what had passed to his great freind: by whom he found it was desired or expected, or to that effect, that something should be proposed from hence, which [*Carteret*] said was sufficient foundacion for him to resume the

---

[730]The point of etiquette.

matter, and desired my advice, as a freind, what I thought would be satisfactory etc. I saw the danger I should be in of being either called an undertaker for a Kingdome or thought to be guilty of arrogance in prescribing to those who must be treated in another maner, and indeed ought to be soe. I said the thing was of great difficultye, and needed consideracion; added that my freinds on whose prudent advice and opinion I much depended were most of them out of town and that I must take time. The answer was that they were straightned in time, the Parliament being to meet soon, and that nothing being asked of me but my own private opinion what I should think absolutely necessary to be done previous to the opening the Session to give good hopes of people being satisfyed, notwithstanding what had passed, soe that in my opinion good men, and I in particular might think it to be a sufficient foundacion to expect an happy Session, and which (if occasion should require my doing it) would make me expresse myself satisfyed etc. I disclaimed speaking the sense of any man but my own in what I then should say, and that I must hereafter be understood to mean that such a thing is or is not reasonable in my private opinion only, altho I should not at the time of delivering my thoughts expressely then say that I doe not pretend to know or guesse at the sense of other men. I was then urged in the strongest maner to declare my own particular sense at that time. In answer to which I stated the much more intricate scituacion of that affair now then it was at the rising of the last Parliament by means of something which hapned at a certain place where you were present and of something done in consequence of that; which was far from being pleasing. After all I found the thing so intricate that I could not venture to give my own private opinion without taking some time to consider throughly of the thing; the next day was named and I promised to attend then. But indeed I had not considered at the time of making that appointment that my Physician had directed me to take Physick on that day, which I am obliged to doe oftner now then formerly, and more particularly of late for a great deafnesse which I have been [?seized] with, with an account of which I declined to trouble you till I had tryed such remedyes for the removing it as I should be advised to use. But I thank God I can now with comfort tell you by taking Physick and syringing my ears I have again recovered my hearing (if not in as perfect a measure as I ever enjoyed it yet) as well as I have had it for some years past. I sent Mr Hill to [*Lord Carteret*] to excuse my not attendance on Wednesday, as having taken Physick, which occasioned me a visit from Mr Cl[*utterbuc*]k, who told me his errand was to know my thoughts etc and indeed shortned the point viz: Whether in my opinion a surrender etc was of absolute necessitye to satisfye people; I said that in November last I had by [*Lord Carteret's*] permission or rather direction endeavoured to find the sense of some Gentlemen with whom I had acquaintance, which I had then told his Excellencye that I understood to be that no one of them would soe much as give their opinion or advise till the patent was given up. That I had not found any one of those Gentlemen to have altered their sentiments, that most of them were out of town and I had not seen the others but owned I continued of the opinion I then was and had no reason to beleive they had altered theirs, and could not say I beleived they had. He seemed to think this was saying nothing could (in my opinion) be done which would prevent this affair being brought into Parliament; I said I thought much otherwise viz that (tho there had been several steps taken which I wish had not been) yet if the patent was actually surrendred and that could be notifyed to the houses soe as they might to [*sic*] satisfyed of the truth, I did hope so doing might give satisfaction to several persons, and that nobody would be more pleased to have the occasion taken away of ever having that matter mentioned in Parliament then myself:

I also told him that in 1715 a patent had been granted in England for coyning half pence, which as I remembred had been taken notice of by the house of Commons,[731] and advised him to consult the votes of that Parliament and see what answer was thought advisable then and that I hoped the ministry now would in a like Cases apply a like remedye.[732] I write this before going abroad or having been at the Castle these three dayes. I refer my self to my letters written to you about or soon after the 17th of November last: for I am confirmed that my conjectures then were very well made and that some people were too sanguine at that time and gave more hopes of successe then perhaps they now see themselves able to make good.

[*PS*] Before sealing this up I received a letter from the Gentleman who carryed the long letter to you which he saith he left on this day sennight at the Privy Garden; soe as I make no doubt but that my sister hath forwarded it to you at the Bath and shal be very impatient till I receive an answer. Things now seem to be in some more hast then hitherto, and I can observe more sollicitude for the event of them then formerly. Perhaps it may take place that people would be found not soe ductile or to be managed as they may formerly have been apprehended, and that the character I gave of the Gentlemens temper and spirit in that particular is found to have been better founded then was thought at first.

696. *Alan I, Dublin, to Thomas, Bath, 12 Aug. 1725*

(1248/6/281–2)

I received by the boat which came last from the Head two letters from you dated at Bath, one of 31th July, the other of the third of August in the later of which you own the receit of a long letter from me of a very old date, and am glad to find the judgement I made of the care of the bearer proved true and that it neither had nor would miscarry. I thought your saying that you had not nor intended to make a secret of your intent to come over into Ireland would not only justifye but indeed in some sort require my saying as much at a certain place, which I did yesterday morning; but introduced it by prefacing that your private affairs here had suffered a good deal by your being absent from your estate so many years as you have been: which is too true. But I thought it modest to introduce it in that maner, least my telling him it abruptly, after he had entred on a discourse of Woods patent might seem to carry a sort of threat of what you would doe in Parliament when you came. And indeed I think when you have soe plausible a ground for doing it, there is no necessitye of saying it is upon the matter of Woods patent that you take the journey; tho let us say what we please both freinds and foes will beleive more lies at the bottom then barely your stating accounts with tenants. But I hope that the patent will be given up, and I hope we shal have such satisfaction that it is soe, that we shal be convinced we never shal suffer by it, or by the precedent. And if that shal prove to be the case both you and all good men will (I hope and think) be satisfyed, and not fond of mentioning any past rough or unkind usage.

---

[731] Among the materials which the Commons had requested in Sept. 1723, and which had been inspected by a committee which included St John III (*CJI*, v, 23, 26–7).

[732] Carteret replied cautiously to Newcastle, suggesting that the king send a message to the Irish parliament with reassurances that he would put an end to the affair, and adding that the surrender of the patent would be one sure way to achieve this (TNA, SP 63/386/5–8: Carteret to Newcastle, 6 Aug. 1725).

I take it for granted that the patent is entirely in the power of [*Walpole*] and the question seems to me to turn cheifly on this in what maner the Parliament shal be apprised that it is given up; for I doe not think, it is expected that promises of what shal be done hereafter will be very satisfactory; for the reason that the woman gave to her husband, who asked her why after he had promised her marriage she would not allow some freedomes which he would have taken, she told him for fear he might not have liked her well enough afterward to marry her, and that another Gentleman had forgott the promises he had made her after he had attained his end. I doe not compare the second husband to the first; there is a vast difference between the men; but sure play is good Play. I wish to God I may in your next hear a more comfortable account then your last gives of your state of health: for to me the thought of a stone formed in the Kidney gives the most dismal apprehensions and Ideas of miserye.

697. *Alan I, Dublin, to Thomas, 15 Aug. 1725*[733]

(1248/6/283–4)

When Woods patent was heard of first I cast about to find who the person was for whose benefit that worthy project was sett on foot, and truly the first way my thoughts turned was to consider whether this might not spring out of a former patent granted to Alderman Knox, the interest of which came to the late Earle of Arran; and I did fancy this might have taken its rise from that root, especially when I considered the relation that is between those who are descended from Lord Arrans heiresse and some persons in very considerable power at the time of the passing that patent. Under this mistake I continued till a freind of yours who is now on the continent gave me an account from the Court where he was at that time, that a certain person, to whom I recommendedd him, and who allowed him familiar accesse, seemed to espouse the patent in a warmer maner then I did beleive he would have done, as a matter which was undoubtedly the Kings prerogative etc. I then began to suspect that my first conjecture was wrong and, that any person representing Lord Arran or their freinds had the projecting or bringing the scheme to the perfection it came afterward: And I doe confesse that the judgement given by Solomon about the true mother of the child (which was grounded upon the real concern which appeared in one of the contending partyes, to prevent the death of the child)[734] hath influenced me a good deal in my opinion that the freinds of those who seem not to have half soe much concern for the event of this affair, as another person seems to me to have shewn for several months past are not so much at the bottom of it as I once beleived, and that this was the offspring of one (who is now in his grave) and for that reason, as well as to keep well with those who are to gett by it, hath been strenuously supported by his surviving freind. Of the truth of his endeavours to support it I need no proofs, but am to seek for a reason for a wise mans doing it soe far as I think this hath been carryed, unlesse there were some very strong reason to induce him to doe all in his power to endeavour it. This is most certain, that Mr W[*alpole*] disclaimed and

[733] Partly printed in Coxe, *Walpole*, ii, 426–8.
[734] King Solomon's judgment in the case of the two women, each claiming to be the mother of the same child, in 1 Kings, 3: 16–28.

doth disclaim having any hand in it, or other notice of it while it was in agitation then such as he necessarily must have by his Office, and I have it from a good hand that he declares he all along was in his judgement and declared himself against the thing as very unreasonable in it self. What I have already wrote I intend as a foundation for my following conjecture that all methods have been hitherto taken and I beleive will be used to have the fall as easy as possible, and perhaps the securitye of this poor countrey from any ill consequences which it may fall under by means of this patent or from such a precedent may be thought of lesse concern to be remedyed then the covering what hath passed in the maner of obtaining this grant. This consideration may lead you into conjectures what is advised from the freinds of the patent here, by which I think those on your side of the water will a good deal be guided in their measures to quiet this affair. How far such endeavours to cover etc will attain the end aimed at, which is said to be to quiet the minds of the people by giving them reasonable satisfaction etc I doe not know, but of this I am certain that a freind of yours seemed to me to be in great warmth when I discoursed him last on this subject and seemed to think the actual surrender of the patent would be insisted on; I say I observed a great deal of heat and dissatisfaction as far as I could judge by the maner in which he deported himself and some expressions which dropt. You will take your own measures as to your resolution contained in yours of the 3d (which is the latest I have received from you) and will consider when you know from your freind in London, what will be done, whether that will in your opinion [?*be*] safe and to the satisfaction of rational men who really have the good of their countrey, and not their own private interests in view, and take your measures accordingly: But the time is coming on very fast, and what will be done will be (I think) at the very beginning of the Session when not one man of the standing troops will venture to be absent (on pain which may ensue) and a vote then will determine the fate of this affair; and I think of our countrey too in consequence. Let me hear constantly from you as you shal from me …

698. Alan I, Dublin, to Thomas, 19 Aug. 1725[735]

(1248/6/285–6)

By a letter which I received from the person at Chester under whose cover I have sent my letters to you at Bath lately, I have reason to beleive that most of mine are come to your hand which went that way, because my correspondent owns the receit of them and assures me they from time to time were forwarded by the crosse post. I have given you the best and earliest accounts from hence that I can learn; for you may be sure I am kept entirely in the dark as far as possible; and yet there is not a movement they make, or any scheme undertaken by them but comes some way or other to my knowledge.

I have already told you that Mr C[*lutterbuck*] came to me on the day I took Physick and by that means could not attend at the Castle according to appointment, altho I promised to doe soe, and that the main of his businesse was to know my opinion whether nothing would doe but giving up the patent; and the answer I made, that in November last I had with the privity of my Lord Lieutenant discoursed several Gentlemen to know their mind and resolution in that particular, who had all unanimously declared their sense to be that

[735] Printed in Coxe, *Walpole*, ii, 428–30.

nothing but an actual surrender and giving up of the patent could prevent that affair being mentioned in Parliament; which was also my opinion at that time, and that I knew not that any one of them had altered his thoughts since, and beleived they had not, nor had I altered mine. Prodigious industry hath been used to soften this affair, as to the maner; and I must tell you that the person to whom your last letter seems to impute your not closing with Mr Hackett for the purchase of a certain farm, wrote to me lately to this purpose that for his part he thought a declaration from a certain place that we should never be troubled with the halfpence would be satisfactory to him; but that he was white paper[736] and if convinced that was not sufficient should be guided by his freinds; but said, he supposed it was not intended nor expected he should take the lead. If you turn to my letters you will find one dated in November which contains an account of a conversation between half a dozen Gentlemen of figure who dined at my house with the privitye of my Lord Lieutenant, that I might know what their sense was as to the maner of putting peoples minds at ease about Woods patent; and you will there find that not one of them thought of anything lesse then an actual surrender and giving up the patent. Upon this point I all along insisted and was accordingly treated; the same letter will also tell you the names of the Gentlemen who agreed in that opinion, no <u>one</u> dissenting. I beleive the English air really hath effect on most of our countrey who goe over, and I doe assure you it hath had very great influence on several, particularly on your tenant, and the Gentleman of whom I gave you caution under the character of a person very ambitious; of which he gave you a sample in his discourse whether the matter of the halfpence should be entred upon before other businesse. My last letter to you by the Crosse post … tells you how active —[737] is to ward against an actual surrender being declared from the throne: or being made (if I understand him right) but I fancy that point will be gott over; but am sure it will be with utmost reluctance and regret. But I now hear we are to have the old way of accounts being laid before the Parliament, which was condemned in the Session in 1703 for which we sent Sir Wm Robinson to the Castle and voted him uncapable of any publick emploiment, revived. His fault consisted in this, in striking a ballance by which the debt of the nation appeared to be one hundred and three thousand and odd hundred pounds more then it would have been if credit had been given for Cash in collectors hands, and for several solvend branches of the revenue that were not then collected.[738] I should be sorry any thing of this kind should be revived now or endeavoured to be brought again into practice; because I think the attempt will not succeed, and a disappointment will not be at all for my Lord Lieutenants honour; or if it should succeed I think it will be extremely hurtful to the Kingdome. I hear a certain person approves the thing extremely, and that the Officers who are to prepare the papers to be laid before the Parliament have directions to draw the demand at full without giving the nation credit, for somethings which I doubt the Parliament will think ought to have been brought to credit. This is an odd passage, but I verily think there is something in it, and sure you had

---

[736] In a figurative sense: a blank sheet on which one might write whatever one wished.

[737] Presumably Carteret.

[738] Sir William Robinson (1644–1712), of Island Bridge, Dublin and Sherwood, Co. Carlow, MP [I] 1692–d., dep. receiver-gen. and paymaster-gen. of forces [I] 1692–1703. On 16 Oct. 1703 the chairman of the accounts committee reported a resolution that he had misrepresented the debt of the nation, upon which the Commons declared him unfit for public office and committed him into custody (*CJI*, iii, 56, 162). For Alan's role in this affair see *CSP Dom.*, 1703–4, 157; C.I. McGrath, *The Making of the Eighteenth-Century Irish Constitution: Government, Parliament and the Revenue, 1692–1714* (Dublin, 2000), 169–70.

some hint of it when you say in a late letter that if you find schemes are framing to bring us into such a debt as must ruine the nation, you will come over to give your assistance to prevent it. For Gods sake (without the losse of <u>one</u> post) write to London for a copy of Woods last peticion which was referred to the Committee of Councel, and upon which they made the report which was the foundacion of the order about the Commissioners of the revenue recalling their orders, and the Lords Justices publishing the King would not force that Coyne; for much depends on it.

699. *Alan I, Dublin, to Thomas, in the Privy Garden, Whitehall, 23 Aug. 1725*

(1248/6/287–8)

I have yours of the 14th which mencions you intend to return to Peperhara the beginning of next month; this makes me conclude that you have stronger hopes of people on your side intending to make us secure from Woods coyne and the ill consequences we apprehend from that patent, as the matter the affair hath been managed on your side of the water, then I can yet perswade my self we shal find in the event; or else I did beleive you would have held your resolution and been here to help your countrey in the difficultest scituation (in my opinion) that we ever did see, or ever expected to see after his Majestyes accession to the Crown. The weather, and my fear of taking cold again to the endangering my utter losse of hearing have prevented my going to the castle for more then a week past; nor am I very fond of putting my self in the way to be catechised, having not been able to make the answers which are Orthodox or in fashion there in relation to what will be satisfactory in reference to Woods patent or what aids will be given. It is certainly true that the Master of the house where my wife and I retired after my ilnesse, and where we went when I laid down the Seal belongs to one Eustace, who is a Papist;[739] but it is as certain that he is by his wife a near relacion of my wifes and that it was impossible for me to goe down into Munster, and to return thence time enough to be up by the 7th of September; and that I had no house of my own nearer then the County of Corke; but Mr Eustace made us an offer of the use of his house, and that we accepted and carryed our Coach and six horses and servants fitting our condition: but I hope you doe not think we went thither to cosher[740] or to eat the Gentleman out of house and home. I doe not know what impression this matter may make with you, but I am not at all apprehensive that this or any other part of my conduct will draw into suspition of being a favourer of a Popish interest. When any person attempts to insinuate that I will answer what he objects, when he gives half as many and as significant proofs of being heartily in the English Protestant interest of Ireland, as I have done. It is very greivous to me to find you make such constant complaint of your pain in your Kidneys. God Almighty releive you from them. Depend on it, whatever is intended in this Session will be done early, soe that if you hope to come time enough to serve your countrey, and be not here before the first week of the Session is over, you will in my opinion come a day after the fair.

---

[739]James Eustace (*d.* aft. 1731), of Yeomanstown, Co. Kildare (Sir Eustace Tickell, 'The Eustace Family and their Lands in Co. Kildare, Part III', *Journal of the Kildare Archaeological Society*, xiii (1946–63), 374–5).

[740]To feast or to live at free quarters (*OED*).

700. *Alan I, Dublin, to Thomas, 27 Aug. 1725*[741]

(1248/6/287–92)

Yesterday morning my Lord Lieutenants private Secretary Monsieur Balaguier[742] came to my house to acquaint me Mr Edgecombe was landed and had brought dispatches concerning a matter of consequence and that my Lord intended to impart the news first to me; to which end he was ordered to call on me and tell me his Excellencye desired to see me at the Castle as soon as I could this morning. Before he came I had received my freinds letter of the 14th inclosed in yours of the sixteenth from the Bath. But by the by whoever recommended that messenger would hardly have thought him a proper person if he had been privy to the import of your letter; for that Gentleman withdrew from Ireland to avoid being examined as to his knowledge how far a certain great man knew of or was concerned in the procuring or supporting that patent: I mean he who said that Lord M[idleton] was at length turned out; if oportunitye offers, you or any freind of mine may say his favourite patent is brought to an end notwithstanding all the methods taken to reconcile people to it. The matter was imparted to me at the Castle under the greatest confidence as not having been communicated to any body before; but I could not conceal its being no news to me who had an account from another hand, and I can no more conceal from you that I mett the Speaker coming out of the Castle just as I came into the Yard, but possibly it was not told him. My Lord imparted the thing to the Councel which was said (by the Summons) to be called on extraordinary businesse. Every body you may be sure was extremely delighted with the news, and they seemed to me to shew most joy, who had hitherto never given that project any avowed opposicion. But the Speakers zeal carryed him soe far, as to use this overrhetorical expression that he beleived God Almighty inspired the ministry who advised his Majestye to the measures he had taken to have the patent surrendred, and as I understood he said he rose to congratulate or give thanks in the name of all the people (the last words he actually used) and should propose an Addresse of thanks to his Majestye, if he were not sensible that would more properly be moved elsewhere, and I think ventured to undertake for one if not both houses of Parliament that the thing would be done. Which put me in mind of a passage in one of Shakespeares playes, where Owen Glendower (a proud Welshman) in a rant said that at his birth the skyes were all on fire; to which Harry Piercy answered with just contempt that soe they would have been if his Mothers Catt had kittened at that time.[743] My Lord Lieutenant you may be sure represented the thing in the strongest terms as a great condescension, and an act of great goodnesse in his Majestye; and this I think might reasonably be expected to be his style; but the Archbishop[744] gave it the term of a peice of justice done by his Majestye to this Kingdome; I confesse that I apprehend the truth lies (as it often doth between disputants) in the middle, and that neither of them was in the right (to speak the real truth) if they confined their thoughts to the narrownesse of the expressions by them used; for my part I doe think the easing the Kingdome of that

[741] Printed in Coxe, *Walpole*, ii, 430–3.

[742] John Anthony Balaguier (1689–1764), who had been Carteret's private secretary as secretary of state 1721–4 and served as his private or second secretary throughout his viceroyalty (Sainty, 'Secretariat', 17).

[743] Shakespeare, *Henry IV, Part 1*, III, i, 13–20.

[744] Of Dublin.

patent was an Act which the King owed in justice and which they might with modestye hope from his Majestyes tender regard for and affection to them. But I doe not think that the King was any way obliged in justice to take those methods which brought Wood of his own accord without a judgement against the patent to surrender and give it up. And this certainly was a condescension in his Majestye and a great act of his goodnesse and a strong instance of that gracious disposition toward this Kingdome, which ought to remove all fears of his entertaining any other thoughts of us, then as of a very loyal part of his Dominions, to say noe more. My Lord Lieutenant told me yesterday he resolved not to make the Speech on the 7th of September, but that the houses shal meet then, and the Commons issue writs for new members, and the new Peers and Bishops be introduced; and that then the houses should adjourn for a week or ten dayes,[745] that the Kingdome might previous to the meeting of the Parliament be acquainted with the patent being laid aside. I foresee some difficultye that I doubt will arise about the maner of addressing; Everybody will with great duty and gratitude own his Majestyes goodnesse in what hath been now done; but how that will be done soe as not to give offence by mentioning the redresse to have arisen upon the Addresses of the houses complaining of the patent (which perhaps will not be liked) or else by making the thing a meer act of grace and favor, to which this strong objection may be opposed, that the Parliament hath by their several Addresses mentioned this patent (in the maner it was obtained) to have been unprecedented and very prejudicial to the Kingdome; to which his Majestye hath answered, that the patent he granted to William Wood was what his Ancestors had from time to time done etc these are not his words; but in my sense he by his answer claims it to be his right to grant a patent in the same maner, and upon the same information he granted this: and truly he hath been told all was right, that the Kingdome wanted small money, and that his Majestye had not been misinformed, etc but I confesse these are not the words of a certain report, but I take it to be the sense of it. If then we own the procuring the patent to be surrendred to be an act of mere grace and favor, is not that an allowance that in justice it might have been insisted upon as duly obtained and granted, and if that be soe; Will it not be in the power of the Crown at any time hereafter to doe the same thing, tho I own perswaded since this experiment hath hitherto had so ill successe, and met soe strong opposition, I doe apprehend the boldest minister will not think it advisable soon to steer the same course. But there seems to me an appearance that people may differ as to the merit of the thing; some will beleive they doe all that can be reasonably expected from them, if they forgett what is past (and that hath been a great deal) and proceed to businesse and give such supplyes as they should have judged reasonable, if the day of passing Woods patent had been (as Job wished the day of his birth had been) not joined to the dayes of the year.[746] But if I apprehend things right it is hoped and perhaps expected that in the joy of our hearts for this great condescension we shal supply very liberally, and perhaps be lesse strict in scanning and looking into money matters: but the Archbishop put the thing in this light the other day; A man (saith he) throws me into a mill pond and then pulls me out of it, all over wett: hath he done me a favor, taking the matter all together? I own if we can steer clear of the difficultyes arising from the maner of addressing I shal be

---

[745] Both houses met on 7 September. The Commons issued new writs, the Lords admitted six temporal lords, five bishops and the new lord chief justice of common pleas. Then both adjourned to the 21st. (*CJI*, v, 233–5; *LJI*, ii, 805–7.)

[746] Job, 3: 2–3: 'Job spake, and said, Let the day perish wherein I was born'.

inclined to wink at any <u>tolerable exceeding</u> in the supply, without enquiring with eagles eyes what is to be done or hath been done with the money. If I should suspect that it went a certain way, I shal consider whether in prudence we are obliged to be too inquisitive and to put this difficultye on Gentlemen who wish well to their countrey, to make them alway obnoxious and give others oportunitye of confirming the great men in England that they (and they only) now (as formerly) support the Kings interest. If you think I am wrong in this, you must not judge by the rules men are to take who expect to live in this world with any quiet; but I can not say that I think the thing strictly right. Farewell. I assure you I am glad the thing is soe well over. Pray God so unreasonable a supply be not pushed for as may divide men more then we have yet been.

701. *Alan I, Dublin, to Thomas, 1 Sept. 1725*

(1248/6/293–6)

I have in a former letter owned the receit of your letter of the sixteenth of last month (with the enclosed from my freind) by a private hand. An officious impertinent servant seeing my letter lye sealed on the table carryed it to the post office without my orders, for I intended to have sent it under the usual cover to Chester, to have gone by the crosse post thence to the Bath, as you will find by the direction all in my own hand: but possibly there was something in it which hath prevented its coming to your hand: yet I am under very little concern, tho that which I make no scruple to speak in plain words every day should be seen under my hand. The orders about Irish letters to the Bath being sent first to London is new, and must have some better reason for making it then readily occurrs to me; Att first I fancyed that letters which goe from Chester to Bath by the way of London pay more then when they goe by the Crosse post; but if that had been the inducement for making the order, sure it would have been more extensive and reached to the letters directly from Chester and the parts adjacent, as well as to those which came from Ireland; but I find by yours that my last which you received by the crosse post, came safe to you, being sent by my correspondent in Chester to whom I enclosed it under cover. You intimate to me who the person is that had the cheif hand in a late event: On the sixth day of July last that Gentleman wrote me a very handsome letter owning the receit of one I wrote to him under your cover, in which among other obliging expressions the following words are contained: viz

I doubt not but your Lordship will act the same honest and good part you have alway done, and by your great influence contribute to keep all things quiet. This freindly and honest advice and caution given in such a maner by a person of that value and honour would have had great weight with me, altho the thing advised had not suited my own sentiments and inclinations: but you are too well acquainted with my resolutions not to know that I alway firmly purposed to doe every thing to keep things quiet and easy, if insisting on Woods patent did not render it impossible to prevent that affair being mentioned in Parliament: but was of opinion that if that patent came ever to be mentioned in Parliament, that no body could expect to be able to doe any thing effectual to extinguish the flame it might raise. The great man who hath had the cheif hand in the late event hath shewn that he was in earnest in his wishes that things might continue quiet here by advising the most likely method to attain that end: and I am greatly delighted that this wise and temperate advise hath been hearkned to, because the surrender of the patent seems to me to leave people at liberty not to mention one word of the half pence or of the patent this Session, or of some proceedings which I am unwilling to mention, considering who the persons were who were concerned in them, and the nature and tendencye of them. Soe that I had great hopes that there would not be a necessitye for us to contradict and disprove Woods allegations, that the Kingdome wanted small base money,[747] for carrying on the retail trade; or to shew the unreasonablenesse and ill consequence of granting a patent for coyning halfpence for Ireland, upon the information of particular persons who might and probably were to be gainers if the patent was granted; and that the testimonye or judgement of any three or fowre private men in reason ought not to outweigh the sense of the Lords and Commons in Parliament, who (instead of beleiving the coyning such money would be of service) declared that doing soe would be destructive of the trade of the Kingdome: and the Justices and Councel in expresse terms assure his Majestye it was found by experience that we have a sufficient quantity of half pence to serve by way of exchange in the retailing trade. Yet soe hardy was Wood to bring these two points of fact in issue whether there was a want of those half pence, and whether it was the sense of the Kingdome or only of a few disaffected persons that importing his coyne would turn to the prejudice of the Kingdome. That he did insist on both these points is well known, and he took effectual care never to have it forgotten with what successe he for a time triumphed over all those who asserted and knew the contrary; by printing the report of the Committee of Councel; of which I will write here with the greatest deference considering the Sanction it afterward obtained; but if Mr Woods allegations are ever brought under the consideration of our Parliament, I make no doubt there will be people who will speak their minds very freely when they are called by his Majestyes writ to consult and advise about the ardua regni:[748] and will doe it in strong terms but with all regard to the King and such debates may probably produce mens thoughts of this matter in plainer English then will be agreeable. Perhaps too the treatment this Kingdome may be supposed to have mett in the maner Mr Wood hath gott that affair to be examined may be spoken of with freedome; but I forbear particulars for fear of making my letter vastly too long, if I should insert half that readily will occur to any man who intends to speak on this subject. Soon after my Lord Lieutenant landed he expressed himself to me in this maner, that he did not doubt to see a Session of Parliament in Ireland in which the affair of the half pence should not be so much as named. This was just after he had brought Swifts pamphlett before the Councel and they had agreed to issue a proclamacion with a reward to the person who should discover the Author and Printer:[749] and at that time his Excellencye seemed to me not to understand the temper and disposicion of the people soe well as (I beleive) he doth now. That time is I hope now come; for I doe own that the patent being actually surrendred, I doe not see there remains any farther danger of Woods coyne coming in among us, and that therefore I shal not be for mentioning any thing about them now; but go on in the usual methods. These are my thoughts and I did alway hope and doe now beleive that Gentlemen will not be fond of

[747] Currency of small denominations in base metal.

[748] Parliaments were summoned to debate 'ardua regni negotia' (the arduous affairs of the kingdom).

[749] The proclamation of 27 Oct. 1724 for the apprehension of the author of *A Letter to the Whole People of Ireland*, which was accompanied by an order from the lord lieutenant and council to the attorney-gen. [I] to prosecute the author, printer and publisher (*Proclamations*, ed. Kelly and Lyons, iii, 143–4; above, pp 134–7).

entring into the consideration whether the word and sense of the whole Parliament ought not to have obtained credit enough to put it into a legal way of enquiry, whether the King was not deceived in his grant by the misinformation of Wood that there was a want of halfpence without giving proof of this by witnesse at a certain place: for the people here, are not such Ideots as to beleive the King can revoke a patent (once granted) at his pleasure, without a legal trial. There is an expression in the report as it is printed, that supposeth us in this Kingdome to think in a maner different from other people (the words are in their way of thinking).[750] And if we whose estates cheifly depend upon a certificate and patent[751] should set up for assertors of the Kings being able to revoke his patent at pleasure; Our way of thinking is really as despicable as some people would willingly have it thought: but I can never take such an expression ill from a people who within fourteen or fifteen years past usually drunk this health, An Irish understanding to an English ———. This complement I think put us soe much in debt, that we may be content to think no more of having our way of thinking mentioned as it hath been. But I must deal plainly with you, in hopes you may be able to let others know, that to the best of my observacion there are people who would readily enough enter into the whole affair, now in the same maner as if nothing had been done for our satisfaction and securitye. My thoughts are that a great deal hath been done by procuring an actual surrender of the patent, but I find your last letter talks thus, that if any additional securitye shall be thought necessary to that which is proposed, it may be come att by us here. You say you presume that securitye will be imparted to both houses; but I have never heard one word of what securitye is proposed, other then the actual surrender of the patent; therefore let me desire you to explain yourself what that securitye is which you think will be imparted to the houses, and what farther securitye you in England think necessary after the surrender of the patent, that we may consider it well, and not through inadvertency apprehend that to be sufficient which in the event may not prove soe. You mentioning that my Lord Lieutenant will impart the matter to both houses makes me very apprehensive (from his maner of speaking of it in Councel) that he will doe in such strong terms as may draw on a debate how far what hath been done already is matter of condescension, grace and favour only, or of justice (as the A[rchbishop] of D[ublin] termed it) and if this happen, no man can tell how far the whole proceedings may be taken into consideracion and what the successe will be. Of this I have given his Excellencye my sense already but I find that he expects to have a vote just in the words of his Speech, of an Addresse of thanks for etc. I will endeavour not to have the halfpence mentioned at all in the house for fear of bringing on disagreeable debates and resolutions; but if the Speech doth mention them as we may addresse the King and thank him for what he hath done, in such a maner as may neither allow the necessitye of the patent, or the maner of obtaining and passing it, or that we have been well used since the last Session of Parliament (you see I chuse to speak in generals) I shal be as easy as any man in the house: but if occasion be given to oblige us to speak on any of these points I shal not refrain, giving my good freinds H[arcourt] and L[echmere] oportunitye of calling me the same blockhead in that profession to which I was bred, and by which I gott more money from Clients then either of them ever

---

[750] *The Report of the Committee of the Lords of His Majesty's Most Honourable Privy-Council, in Relation to Mr. Wood's Half-pence and Farthings … [1724]*. The phrase quoted does not in fact appear in the report.

[751] Those Irish protestants whose estates had been granted to them by the crown, in the various confiscations and plantations in Ireland in the 16th and 17th centuries.

did; and consequently the people beleived better of my knowledge in my profession, then either of these extraordinary men will allow me to have: but perhaps they kindly mean I once might have some knowledge but have outlived it. And if that be their meaning I shal be able in a more advanced age to doe little hurt to the patentee or patent against whom I shal be obliged against my will to speak, if we are pressed to say something in answer to what may be offered; And we shal think ourselves under a necessitye to shew our dissent to any thing that may be advanced in establishment of the patent being legal, as obtained, and of the reasonablenesse of the proceedings least our silence may be taken for a consent to what is offered. You talk of the London journals labouring this matter of the soft falling of Woods patent; but not one of the journals of that day is come into Ireland. Pray send me one and likewise that print in which Wood took care to have his victory over the Parliament of Ireland published in printing the report of the Committee at the Cockpit.

702. *Alan I, Dublin, to Thomas, 8 Sept. 1725*

(1248/6/299–300)

I am every day convinced more fully that the conjecture I made from Solomons judge-ment[752] was a right guesse. My freinds account was not more surprizing to me, then I think it was to others; and I doe assure you from the 28 July, on which day you may remember I told you I took Physick and was visited by [*Thomas Clutterbuck*] I have not been looked straight upon by [*Carteret*] which I know not how to account for but from the answer I gave my Visitant. By what I wrote formerly, you will perceive that it was not at all pleasing to be so tenacious in that point, as I had alway shewn myself, and that the thing by me insisted upon was greivous considering who were concerned in taking the large steps, that were taken in it at a certain place. But this letter comes to you upon another foot, to ac-quaint you that my long letter which I wrote to you lately directed to Peperhara was very ill judged; for I did not at that time think that there had been advice given and a resolution taken to insist on a certain question to be moved in one or both houses, as the foundation of Addresses on this occasion from the houses; much lesse could I have dreamed that the draughts of Addresses are ready drawn, and that in soe perfect a maner, that they are not capable of being amended in one word, without making them worse instead of amend-ing them. If this should be our present scituation (as I hear some people say it is) I much doubt it will have the same effect which the tenaciousnesse of our High Churchmen soon after the return of King Charles the second (to adhere to every title of our Liturgy) had; I mean that it will prevent some very worthy and good men from conforming, which they declared they readily would doe if some unnecessary things, which gave offence had been omitted or altered. But if any words in the addresse, or the tenor of it altogether, gives any countenance to or allowance of the Legalitye of this patent or the reasonablenesse to have the want of small money here, to be examined in England by the testimony of particular men (who may be and probably are concerned in interest) as a ground for the King to grant a patent for this Kingdome, or that such a patent obtained in England in deceit of his Majestye (by misinforming him that the Kingdome wanted small money) cannot or

---

[752]See above, p. 236.

ought not to be called in question in Ireland (where it ought to be inrolled) or that the King should not credit his Parliament here when they assure him the Kingdome is not in want of small money, till they have proved that matter to the satisfaction of a Committee of Councel in Great Britain, I say if the addresse intended point this way I fear I shal not be Orthodox, because my opinion in these points is so settled that I much doubt whether I shal hear any arguments of weight enough to convince my judgement, according to which I will advise when I am called by the King to doe it, and will never give my vote contrary to it. How many or how few vote the same way will not influence me, but I resolve to speak and act with all deference to the King and the house and with as much respect of the ministry as the nature of the thing will allow me stil speaking my mind with such freedome as the place where I am and the capacitye I act in will admit.

703. Alan I, Dublin, to Thomas, 16 Sept. 1725[753]

(1248/6/306–7)

I received yours of the tenth this morning, which was used as you (by my sister) told me my two letters to you of the 23 and 27th of last month were.

By my soul it is unaccountable that people should have soe much curiositye to know what you and I say to one another, when we speak the sense of our[?selves] to those inspectors in the most plain words possible. I had executed my promise to you in part before I received your last, by declaring I would with the greatest softnesse and duty to his Majestye acknowledge his goodnesse in easing us from the apprehensions and fears we lay under from Woods patent by his Majestyes interposing soe far as to have the patent resigned and surrendred, but at the same time I insisted on it that we should say it was done upon the humble representation laid before his Majestye by the Parliament: the person with whom I discoursed seemed much to dislike the later words, but was for our saying that the <u>Royal</u> condescension and goodnesse of the King in procuring the patent to be surrendred filled the hearts of his dutyful subjects with a deep sense etc and that the actual surrender etc had given us entire satisfaction. Much stresse was laid on this that it would not be said in the speech that it was the <u>meer</u> condescension and goodnesse of the King; but I could not understand that condescension (without any other word) meant any thing but meer condescension, or goodnesse any thing but pure goodnesse. I could not but observe great anxiety in the person with whom I conversed for the event of this affair: and I with all possible earnestnesse intreated that room might be left us who wished as well to his Majestye as any people in this or any other of his Dominions, to join in the addresse, because unlesse it were an unanimous one it would not be soe graceful, nor really soe much for his Majestyes service as if it was the unanimous act of every member of the respective houses, as I thought, it would or (at least) might be, if notice were taken that in condescension to the Supplications and representacion of his Parliament his Majestye had been pleased so to interpose as to obtain a voluntary surrender of Woods patent, and thereby had removed all causes of apprehension from any dangers which might fall on this Kingdome by means of itt. Every body seeth what the difference in the diction is, and with what views one seems

---

[753] Partly printed in Coxe, *Walpole*, ii, 433–4.

to be insisted on by some, and to be disliking to others. I know not what the event will be; but he with whom I talked seemed confident of succeeding in the method he liked best, but at the same time to tell you the plain truth I have great reason to doubt it. Time will try, for Tuesday draws on apace and that night will give a shrewd light into the successe of this Session, which I will endeavour to render an easy one, yet stil with a reserve that the snake that seems now to be frozen to death may not hereafter be found to have so much life left in him as will enable him to sting us to death.[754] I think very much depends on the prudence and temper of the houses in this great event and I assure you I will set a guard on my Lips that I offend not with my tongue: The ill treatment I have received shal not urge me to doe any thing from resentment, to the disservice of my Prince or the prejudice of my countrey: and I resolve to have a strict watch over the warmnesse of my temper, and not to permit it to carry me into any thing which is not perfectly consisent with the rules of vertue and duty: but stil my main point is to steer clear of any thing which will in consequence be prejudicial to this Kingdome and in these points I am unalterably fixed and determined. I wonder you take no notice of the copy of Woods peticion to the King in Councel upon which the hearing was in the Cockpit, when that peticion was referred to a Committee together with the addresses of both houses of Parliament here. That which makes me suspect there is some thing extraordinary contained in it is the maner in which it is mentioned in the report of the Committee: Pray do not forget to procure and send me one of them as soon as possible: for tho it can not be here the day of our meeting it will be of use afterward.

704. *Alan I, Dublin, to Thomas, in the Privy Garden, Whitehall, 18 Sept. 1725*

(1248/6/308–9)

My Lord Barrymore very lately related in my hearing a passage to this effect, that some time in the last Session he and you were together in the Speakers chamber and that Sir R[obert] W[alpole] passing through the room asked you what you thought of Woods patent and what would be done in it; and added with an asseveration that it either would not or should not be given up, to which your answer was that you did not care whether it was or not. He added that certainly it was soe resolved at that time: I told him something had occasioned those measures to be altered, which he said proceeded from the great deficiencye discovered in the clearing the establishment, and that without that, we should not have been eas[ed] of the patent. I can easily see the tendencye of this remar[k] viz. that those persons who by their resolution really were the true reason why that darling point was receded from, may not have the honour of it; or else to shew the reasonablenesse of being very complying in giving such supplyes as will be expected and said to be wanting. Pray recollect and let me know the time when this conversacion passed between you and the great man his Lordship named, for something may be inferred from being sure what he said was the then resolution; let me also know whether the person who asked your thoughts before you went to the Bath what the event of our approaching Session would be, and to whom you gave the answer

---

[754] In Aesop's fable, numbered 176 in Perry's index, a farmer discovered a snake that appeared dead and brought it home in his bosom, only for it to revive near the hearth and attempt to strike one of his children.

which yours of the 10th instant mentions was the same man, or another person and who. In your last you promise to say something which relates to your Nephew[755] and I should be glad you did it without losse of time that I might answer and give my thoughts of it and other things in one letter which I design he shal be the entire subject of; but at present I am not at leisure to answer his letter, which indeed is a very well wrote letter and shews a good of the man, and of the benefit he hath made by travailing, beyond what could be expected from his years. I doubt that the misfortunes of a disgraced father lay him under difficultyes and that he stands not now, in the Court where he is, upon the same ground he did before I was obliged to lay down, but he must bear it as I doe with patience and submission. My son is not yet come to town but stayes to see poor Major William Boyle buryed at Castlemarter where he dyed this day sennight.[756]

705. *Alan I, Dublin, to Thomas, 27 Sept. 1725*

(1248/6/320–3)

My last by post was dated on the 25th instant, and I beleive came to your hand in due time; nothing publick being contained in it: But now in performance of a promise which I made you I send you the enclosed history of the words (great wisdome) the inserting which words in our instructions to the Committee appointed to draw the addresse to his Majestye about Woods patent and into the draught of the addresse prepared by the Primate, who (being put into the Chair had the drawing and first framing it)[757] cost us a good deal of pains in the Committee; and occasioned as much trouble to the house to leave them out upon the report.[758] This letter goes by a Noble hand who voted in the house for having those words part of the instructions given to the Committee, and who in the Committee was one of those who was for amending the Primates draught (who had left them out, tho ordered to be an instruction to insert them upon a particular question whether they should be part of the instructions to the Committee) and voted in the house upon the report for their continuing a part of the Addresse. He assures me he will take care that this letter shal be delivered into your own hand; and is a man of nice honour not capable of doing a mean thing: soe that I resolve to tell you the whole truth in plain English. I chuse to draw the thing rather by way of narrative then letter, and have inserted a separate paper under this cover to which I refer you for this whole matter ...

[755] Alan II.

[756] William Boyle, MP [I].

[757] The address of thanks to the king for the surrender of Wood's patent was voted on 21 Sept. 1725, and the reference to his majesty's 'great wisdom' (alongside his 'royal favour and condescension') added after a vote. Primate Boulter, who had (as instructed by Carteret) made the original motion, reported on 23 Sept. from the committee to prepare the address, and again there was a contest over the words 'great wisdom'. (*Boulter Letters*, 127–8; *LJI*, ii, 809–10, 812.) Boulter wrote that, having 'brought into the committee an address somewhat differing in form from the resolution of the House', and in particular omitting the words 'great wisdom', he was overruled by the members of the committee and forced to add them (*Boulter Letters*, 128).

[758] Printed as Appendix 1 below.

706. *Alan I, Dublin, to Thomas, 2 Oct. 1725*

(1248/6/324–5)

I have yours of the 25th of last month; and should be shy of sending you the inclosed lines, considering the reason I have to beleive my letters to you are opened somewhere before you receive them, if the scurrilous paper (of which the lines on the back of this are a copy)[759] had not been brought into the house of Lords yesterday by Lord Altham, who complained of it to the house as containing in it scandalum Magnatum, but the Lord who seconded his complaint of it, considered it more properly as a great breach of priviledge (for I doubt whether an action of scandalum Magnatum doth lye originally in our house). Lord Altham said the Bench of Bishops was insolently treated in it, and soe were several Lords temporal, who having hereditary honours from their Ancestors, but their estates being greatly impaired his Majestye toward their supported allowed them pensions, which this paper represented as bribing them to give their votes to the undoing the Nation, which was an indignitye to his Majestye who was good to those Lords for supporting the Crown. He took notice too that my Lord Lieutenant had not escaped the virulence of the paper, contained in that line (Till positive orders was whisper'd from Court). Some Lords, who have no pensions seemed inclined to have said they hoped the Lords who had, did not pretend to be the only Lords who endeavoured to support the Crown; or to doe more toward it then they: but they declined it, for in the warmth the Lords were in who are ill treated in that paper, it might have been understood as intended to obstruct what was moved viz. that Sarah Harding (the Printer)[760] should be taken into Custody of the Usher of the Black Rod.[761] I fear our zeal was soe hot that we did not come to the vote, which (usually) precedes that viz. that a Paper intitled etc is a false and scandalous libel etc. If I be not mistaken in this point, I doubt we have first committed a woman for printing a Paper bearing such a title viz. On Wisdoms defeat without first declaring that it is a vile paper, and yet notwithstanding any thing appearing in the title the print may be an innocent one; for I take it for granted the libel will not be entred in our journal in haec verba; which is the way to perpetuate the scandal contained in it. After ordering the woman to be taken into custody, Lord Cavan moved two resolutions which I have not gott a copy of, but they are to this effect, that the Paper intitled etc is a scurrilous libel derogatory to the Peers and a breach of priviledge etc and that the Sherifs of Dublin doe on the following day burn it by the hands of the Common hangman at the door of the Parliament house and the Gate of the Tholsel.[762] I doe not hear on whom this wicked paper is fathered, and I confesse I expected some steps would have been made to find out the Author: But nothing of that nature hapned, probably because it is not beleived that the Author had soe little wit as to put it into the power of any body to discover him. The Clerk read it soe at the Table that

---

[759] 'On Wisdom's Defeat' (below, p 250).

[760] Sarah Harding (*d.* 1729), of Blind Quay, Dublin, widow of John Harding, printer of the 'Drapier's Letters' (Pollard, *Dictionary of the Book Trade*, 275–6).

[761] On 1 Oct. 1725 (*LJI*, ii, 815).

[762] *LJI*, ii, 815. The Tholsel, literally the 'toll-house', stood in Skinner Row, near Christ Church cathedral, and housed the offices of Dublin corporation, the Royal Exchange and the Trinity Guild of Merchants (Maurice Craig, *Dublin 1660–1860* (Dublin, 1952), 47). According to Swift, Primate Boulter and the earl of Cavan 'govern the House of Lords' (*Swift Corr.*, ii, 621).

I could not well understand him, and I heard a Gentleman of the house of Commons say at my house last night that he stood near him and imputed his not reading it better to his not being able to doe it for laughing. I confesse I could have been pleased our house had not been soe full as it was of Gentlemen, when this matter of privilege was moved; but by the favor of Lord Altham I gott one of the Papers, of which (after it hath been read and censured by the Lords in the presence of above 100 not of their own house) I think I may send you the following copy as a peice of news and as an explanation of our vote by which we have condemned it, which I make no doubt will be in all the newspapers; The paper is as follows.

On Wisdoms Defeat

In a learned Debate.

Quid est sapientia? Semper idem velle atque idem nolle.[763]

Minerva[764] has vow'd, since the Bishops do slight her

Shou'd the Reverend Peers, by chance ere invite her,

She's resolv'd never more to be known by the mitre.

The temporal Lords, who voted against her,

She frankly forgives, as not having incenst her,

For securing their pensions is best proof of their sense Sir.

At first putting the question, their Lordships were for't

And his Graces wise motion did bravely support.

Till positive orders was whisper'd from Court.

Soe this they allege in their justification

They vote for their bread in undoing the Nation

And the first Law of nature is self preservation

Rose Common

Shamelesse Woman

---

[763] Seneca, *Ad Lucilium*, xx, 5: 'What is wisdom? Always desiring the same things, and always refusing the same things'.
[764] The Roman goddess of wisdom.

The Lord who first brought this affair into the house was pleased to explain the fowre last words, as meaning a certain Earle whose title is in sound pretty like the first two of those words[765] for which I think that Lord is not much obliged to him.

The scrip which your last brought me relating to your Nephew was I suppose wrote by the husband to his wife who once lived in Bond Street with a relation of mine. There goes a merry story that a great man was speaking very warmly against the libel in the Lords, to which the person to whom he was speaking should answer, that it was true it was a severe libel, and that he must condemn it as such if brought before the house; but that the worst thing in it was that it was all ——— (I doe not find that people agree what the Epithet he gave it was; but I suppose it must be false, for nothing can make it soe bad as its being false.) and I think prudence would not allow his giving it any other Epithet.

You must be convinced before the receit of this whether what I wrote hath hapned, or whether the conjectures of greater men were soe well founded that matters would not be carryed in the maner I said they would. We are in great perplexitye how to lay the publick accounts before the house of Commons in such a way as may be agreeable, and yet attain the end in view viz. the payment of a debt which we never before heard of nor expected ever to hear.

707. *Alan I, Dublin, to Thomas, 8 Oct. 1725*

(1248/6/326–7)

I doe not remember that I have wrote any letter to you since that of the 28th of last month by a private hand, which I make no doubt you received in due time.[766] The truth is, nothing hath hapned here since worth your notice, for the Lords have so very little businesse before them that they adjourned from Tuesday 28 Sept to Saturday 2 Oct. and from that day to Wednesday the sixth, and from that day to Tuesday the twelfth.[767] The cheif businesse done in that house since the opening the Parliaments were the two Addresses one to his Majestye the other to the Lord Lieutenant, both voted the first day of the Session and reported on the Fryday following:[768] of which you have already had a full account, and of the debate, which the words Great wisdome created and of the fate of those words; you also are sensible that justice hath been done on the vile libel intitled (On Wisdomes defeat in a solemn debate) by its being burnt by the hands of the Common hangman, and that Mrs Harding the printer of it is committed to our Usher of the Black Rod and soe I presume will the Author be when he is discovered and can be caught. You may be sure as occasion offers we shal proceed to businesse of greater importance, when any thing of that nature is brought

---

[765] The earl of Roscommon.

[766] Later in October Alan wrote to his 'sister' Rachel Courthope that 'I wish I knew whether my brother received a letter dated on or about the 27th or 28th of last month, which I sent by a private hand …' (NLI, MS 41675/6: Alan I to Rachel Courthope, 20 Oct. 1725). A letter dated 27 Sept. is printed above, p 248. None dated 28 Sept. has survived in the Brodrick papers.

[767] In fact, from Saturday, 25 Sept. to Friday, 1 Oct., then to Wednesday, 6 Oct., Tuesday the 12th, and finally Friday the 15th (*LJI*, ii, 814–17).

[768] The addresses were voted on the second day of the session, Tuesday, 21 Sept., and reported and agreed on Thursday the 23rd (*LJI*, ii, 809, 812–13).

before us, tho I confesse I know nothing that is more soe then preserving the dignitye of the house and punishing insolent people who are soe audacious as to violate the priviledges of it in soe impudent a maner as hath been done this Session. On Wednesday the sixth (I told you) we adjourned to Tuesday 12 October, but the Commons having more businesse then we yet have, sitt daily; for the papers relating to the publick accounts were ready and laid before them on the second, when the house went into a Committee to consider the motion which had been before made that a Supply be granted to his Majestye, and that day the Committee came to a resolution that a Supply be granted to his Majestye; which was reported yesterday and agreed to unanimously by the house.[769] I wish I could with truth say that I foresee matters are like to goe on with the same unanimitye, as they have done there hitherto. Tho I cannot but think the Session will end happily. All people say they are ready to continue the addicional dutyes for two years soe that the establishment will be provided for in the usual maner, and this they are ready to doe without any losse of time (as I hear) soe that the bill may be sent over in a very few weeks from the date of this, and I see nothing that will hinder its being done in a fortnight, soe as it may be retransmitted before Christmas time enough to receive the Royal assent before the dutyes are expired viz. 24 December next: But I am told that it is expected the great debt which we are now (to our great surprize) assured the Nation owes shal be settled at least (if not provided for) at the same time, as the Committee votes the granting the addicional dutyes for two years. Gentlemen seem to think they ought to be allowed a competent time to apprize themselves of the reality of the debt, and to inform themselves how it hath hapned that they have been kept in the dark hitherto of their being so much in debt as they are said now to be etc one great reason of which is presumed to have been the precipitating the Committee of accounts to report, before they had sufficiently informed themselves of the truth of things; for Mr Warburton (who was chairman of that Committee)[770] told me it was usual to have a castle Brigade come down to the Committee and prevent their examining vouchers, by saying they were satisfyed, and calling for the question, upon pretence that my Lord Lieutenant was going for England and must not be detained etc altho in truth he staid till 8 May following, these transactions which hapned in November or December.[771] But I hope it will be thought advisable not to run the risque of the dutyes lapsing by waiting till the accounts can be fairly enquired into, and justly settled; which perhaps will appear to contain so many difficultyes as may not be removed to the satisfaction of men who wish very well to his Majestyes service and to the present administration in soe short a time as probably some people intend to allow for the doing it. The dutyes lapsing will be of terrible consequence to his Majestyes service and to the Kingdome by running it into a greater debt then we yet are, which we hardly know how to provide for, tho the funds should be continued: and I think —— is too good and wise to take the blame and

---

[769] The motion for a supply was made on 30 Oct., and referred to a committee, which reported on 7 Oct. a resolution for a supply, to which the House agreed (*CJI*, v, 245, 249).

[770] Richard Warburton, MP [I].

[771] The accounts had been laid before the house of commons on 12 Sept. 1723, and the committee of accounts reported on 9 Oct. (*CJI*, v, 19–20, 47–8). Carteret's own view was that 'I have laid before [*the house of commons*] a true state of the debt of the nation in as clear a light as the nature of the thing would admit, considering the disorder that has been in the treasury, and if they won't pay it now, they must pay it some other time; their own interest is at stake, and I fancy they will act prudently, notwithstanding the endeavour of some persons to mislead them' (BL, Add. MS 38106: Carteret to Edward Southwell, 14 Oct. 1725).

consequences of their lapsing on himself when he is assured he may (as I am told he either is or will be) have heads of a bill for continuing the additional dutyes for two years longer toward supporting the establishing and paying the debt unlesse at the same time a great summe is allowed to be a debt due by the nation; of which I doubt many people are a good deal in doubt as yet. How this matter will end God only knows, but I hear there are expressions used upon this head, which I have in a very long life been wholly a stranger to, and hoped should have dyed soe: — [?*Carteret*] cannot be more determined that things shal go to his wish then others seem determined to have things fully and fairly examined into before they ascertain and vote a debt. I suppose noses have been told and there must have been false musters; for (as far as one can judge) both sides are certain of a majoritye; It is plain there appears a great spirit in that which they call the country party, and the house is now pretty full: I hope things will not be carryed to extremitye and that men will be convinced where the majoritye is without a division: but things are coming to a crisis. I am happily out of all this bustle, by not being longer in the Kings service; but if I were my fate would be as it hath usually been, I should have had my opinion asked and I should have given it truly; but what I advised would have been overruled, and it would have been expected that I should endeavour to bring that thing about which was directly against my judgement, and I should have been in the black book for not being obsequious, I mean in another gove[m]ment. Poor Mrs MacCartney is dead,[772] but outlived Arthur Hills wife one night,[773] she dyed on Tuesday morning. The Commons have adjourned till Tuesday.[774]

708. Alan I, Dublin, to Thomas, at his lodgings in the Privy Garden, Whitehall, 12 Oct. 1725

(1248/6/328–9)

… This day will be a day of businesse in the house of Commons; I wish it may not be also a day of warmth. If some Gentlemen will in earnest join with others in finding out what is the real debt of the nation, and will be content that the true and real debt be made good, the others all declare they will provide for the real debt; but will be strict in examining the accounts to find out what is truly due and necessary to be provided for; Great professions are made that there will be no obstruction to their making the strictest enquiry to find out the truth, which I hope will be made good, for sure it is for the Kings service, the good of the countrey, the honour of my Lord Lieutenant and reputation of the Parliament to act in that maner; and this is the likelyest best way to cement a divided people. But I doubt there are those who propose to find their account in continuing us a divided people. God forgive them.

[772]Alice (née Cuffe), wife of James Macartney, judge of common pleas [I] (*Daily Journal*, 26 Oct. 1725; *Hist. Ir. Parl.*, v, 156).
[773]Anne (née Deane).
[774]From Friday, 8 Oct. to Tuesday the 12th: confirmed in *CJI*, v, 250–1.

709. *Alan I, Dublin, to Thomas 15 Oct. 1725*

(1248/6/330–1)

This goes by a private hand, the son of Archdeacon Hamilton[775] who promises to leave it himself in the Privy Garden, soe that I will speak plain English as I did in mine which my Lord Limrick carryed, of the receit of which in London I expect to hear by next pacquet. In my last I told you that I apprehended there had been false musters made, and that ———[776] depended on them; and was certain of succeeding in every thing he aimed at. When you read that letter over again and mind the maner of my expressing that matter you will plainly see, that his sentiments as to a certain majoritye in every thing that should be attempted differed widely from the sense of those who wish him well. The truth is, his aim seemed to be to have a summe certain (and a very great one) voted to be the debt of the Nation; I think he laid papers before the house of Commons, which (supposing them to be true) plainly shewed that there was as much money unpaid to some people as amounted to that summe;[777] but the way of convincing Gentlemen that the Nation owed soe much would have been, to have given credit for all summes which arose or were the produce either of the hereditary revenue, or the additional aydes, and to have deducted the total of them out of the charge of the Government, and whatever they fell short of making up the total of the charge would have been allowed to be a debt for which the Nation had not provided, and every body with whom I converse did and doe declare themselves ready to provide funds to answer a debt, soe appearing to them, to have not been already provided for: but truly they apprehended on Wednesday last after they had read over the papers delivered by the accountant General as containing a state of the revenue, receits, and payments, that they had only an account brought before them of what money was wanting in the Treasury to pay a great demand which had not yet been made good to the Army and civil list, without shewing what was become of the money given, and therefore they addressed the Lord Lieutenant to have an account laid before them of the produce of the hereditary revenue and aydes given since the year 1709 till the year 1725.[778] The reason of taking a rise from this period of time was this. In the Parliament held under Lord Wharton, the accounts given in to the Parliament allowed there was a summe of £71000 in the Treasury over and above the expence of the Governement till 24 June 1709 inclusive.[779] Soe that here is a fair rise for an account and the Commons seem to apprehend that the produce of the hereditary revenue and aids given since by Parliament being added to that summe will very near ballance the charge of the establishment and all the expences of the

---

[775] Henry Hamilton (1710–82), of Castle Conyngham, Co. Donegal, later 1st Bt, and MP [I] 1747–*d*., eldest son of Andrew Hamilton (c. 1669–1754), archdeacon of Raphoe (*Al. Dub.*, 360; Cotton, *Fasti*, iii, 365), and since May an undergraduate at Lincoln College, Oxford (*Hist. Ir. Parl.*, iv, 338).

[776] Presumably Carteret is meant.

[777] Various papers, as ordered by Carteret, were presented to the Commons on Wednesday, 6 Oct. by the accountant-gen., Matthew Pennefather, MP [I], and referred to the committee of supply (*CJI*, v, 246–7).

[778] On Thursday, 14 Oct., the chair of the accounts committee moved for an address to ask the lord lieu-tenant for an account of the produce of the hereditary revenues, additional duties and casual revenues between Midsummer 1709 and Midsummer 1725 (*CJI*, v, 255).

[779] This calculation had been included in the report of the Commons' accounts committee, made on 21 May 1709: McGrath, *Eighteenth-century Irish Constitution*, 214–15.

Governement from that time; and they think it was reasonable to supply any summe which that revenue and those aids doe fall short of paying the establishment and expence of the Covernement. They think they can not be wrong while Arithmetick is true; but they are for knowing what their real debts is and are not for lumping to save time: Perhaps you will think they goe far backward; but that objection is thus answered. Every account must have a period from which it is to commence; and the Commons would have been content to have begun the account from the ballance agreed in the last Session of Parliament to have been the debt of the Nation at that time; but truly after spending several months in dressing up papers which seem calculated to shew the account was not fairly laid before the Commons at that time, because there had been money paid out of the treasury which was not owned at that time to have been paid: the particulars of these payments doe not appear by the present account to the satisfaction of Gentlemen, but instead of it there are general articles of payments certifyed by the late Commissioners of accounts appointed to enquire into what equitable vouchers Mr Pratt had to justifye payments which he had made and had not yet credit for which I hear amount to upward of £60000, without mentioning to whom, when, by what warrant or for what service it was paid. This seemed to me to be soe improbable a story that I could not beleive it to be true, till one of the Commons shewed me the certificate of the present Chancellor, of the Chancellor of the Exchequer and of Baron St Leger dated 5th of this month viz that Pratt had produced undoubted equitable vouchers for several summes amounting to the best of my memory to upwards of £60000 for which he had not yet had credit in his account, without mentioning the times of payment, the persons to whom, the particular summes paid, or what warrant he had for soe doing. Soe that the applicacion for new Papers by the Committee on Wednesday last hath really sett the result of great Cabals how to dresse up an account that might passe (with willing people) without losse of time, soe as to be a foundacion for a vote that the debt of the Nation was just that summe which was made to be the ballance of that account, perfectly adrift. And now they must begin a new, unlesse they can perswade men that it will take up more time then the thing in dispute is worth to examine into the realitye of the debt of the Nation; I have some reasons to beleive that it was hoped, expected, and (I think I may add) depended upon that there would be a sufficient body of troops to have voted that the debt of the Nation was etc and too strong ones to be intrusted even to this paper. I was alway of another opinion and honestly declared myself to be soe, and did beleive I knew the temper of the house better then they did who gave such hopes, if they spoke their minds sincerely; which I much doubt, and am apt to think that there are some private directions from your side of the water, that a disappointment to [*Lord Carteret*] will not be unacceptable there. I cannot account otherwise for the behavior of some Gentlemen, who I am satisfyed were depended upon to carry things by dint of numbers; for I observed on Wednesday (while I was in the Committee) lesse zeal then the same Gentlemen had shewed in some former very late Sessions. But if [*Carteret*] can be content with the usual supplyes of two years addicional dutyes without stating the quantum of the debt this Session, and to leave it to another; or if he can be content to have the debt fairly stated this Session, after passing the bill for the addicional dutyes, and to lay such an account by way of debtor and creditor as the Parliament expects first before them, he may I think come of with honour, as having done as much as any of his predecessors had ever done before, notwithstanding it was his fate to hold a Parliament after the Nation thought itself very hardly used in the matter of Woods patent and by what hapned at the Cockpit[780] etc. But if he must and will insist on peoples giving great summes blindfold; I doubt his administracion will neither be soe honourable to himself nor satisfactory to the Kingdome as I wish. You may remember that about the end of June or beginning of July I gave you an account that Lord Falmouth and Mr Edgecombe applyed for a new Commission to allow equitable vouchers etc and that I never would come into the issuing such a commission; I now plainly see what that application was levelled at and rejoice at my having clear of it, and not having advised the Commission nor acted under it.

710. *Alan II, London, to Alan I, Dublin, 16 Oct. 1725*

(1248/6/332–3)

I am just arrived here from Hanover, and tho' it is so late that I have not time to write above three or four Lines, yet I thought it my Duty to let your Lordship know of my Arrivall.

His Majesty went this day fortnight to the Gôhre[781] in perfect good Health; and will be back in three weeks at Hanover, where He is expected to stay a Fortnight before He comes to England …

711. *Alan I, Dublin, to Alan II, 31 Oct. 1725*

(1248/6/334–5)

I received yours of the 16th from London with great pleasure and thank God for your return into your own countrey after the many dangers you must have gone through both by Sea and Land since you left it. I hope what you have seen abroad will make you more sensible of the happinesse we enjoy under the mild and free Governement both in Church and State at home, and particularly of our living where the religion established is that which our Saviour planted in the world and which is consistent with the reason of mankind when they are allowed to judge for themselves and not to beleive as they are commanded by their Preists; I cannot have the least doubt but that you have brought back the same principles of religion which you have been early and carefully instructed in; and that you have seen too much of the misery which the people of the countreys through which you have travailed labour under, not to be confirmed in your love to the Laws and constitution of your own countrey, where a due obedience to the Governement is enjoined the subject, but stil such as is consistent both with the liberty freedome and propertye of the Subject. Let nothing ever incline you to think well of the glittering shew that attends the Courts of Princes who govern in a despotick way; for you will find more true happinesse in those countryes where liberty and propertye are enjoyed by the subject then where there is a greater appearance of wealth and grandeur in the gay cloths of Ladyes and Souldiers and in the wealth of Churches in arbitrary Countreys. Your modestye as well as prudence will render you not inclined to

---

[780]The proceedings in April 1724 of the committee of the British privy council appointed to inquire into Wood's halfpence.

[781]Göhrde, for the hunting (*London Gazette*, 12–16 Oct. 1725).

make your travails the subject of your discourse, and above all things never officiously to make comparisons between foreign parts and your own countrey, much more you will be careful not to give yourself an air of liking things abroad better then those at home. But when you are urged to give your opinion doe it impartially and where you have observed things better ordered in foreign parts then with us, you will in a modest way own that in your thoughts the buildings Churches etc in one place, the painting sculpture etc in another, the regulation and emploiment of the poor in a third, and the industry in another State exceed anything you meet of the same kind in England: but this is to be done with great caution: for those with whom you will then converse are sure to be in opinion or at least in their wishes for their own countrey and will be apt to impute what you say to a vanitye in you of shewing you have seen and observed things which they never did and which they may surmise are due to your invention; and for these and other reasons there is no subject you ought to be lesse fond of discoursing upon then of your travails. My brother gives me an hint that you have thoughts of seeing us here soon; you are sure of an hearty welcome from your Mother and me; but pray let me hear some time beforehand at what time your freinds think it will be proper for you to begin your journey … Tell your Uncle that matters have been warmer in the house of Commons then they would have been, if granting the additional dutyes for two years would have pleased; but a resolution to supply deficiencyes was strongly insisted on at the opening of the Session and come into, and I confesse I thought the thing reasonable in the sense which I gave my Lord C[*arteret*] of the word deficiencyes; when this was obtained the next view to have the debt of the Nation stated and ascertained according to an account laid before the house by the Account General and other Officers; by which we should have been vastly more in debt then it was beleived the Nation was in realitye: This demand was very surprizing and not the lesse soe from the way of accounting in which there was much obscuritye if not contradictions. It was beleived (nay declared by some people) that there would be a grant of the additional dutyes for two years to carry on the establishment and some new tax for a fund to pay the supposed debt; and truly I did not ever hear one Gentleman speak against granting the additional dutyes for supporting the establishment for two years and toward payment of the debt when it should be ascertained (as far as they would goe) but some Gentlemen were soe sanguine to expresse themselves (as I have been told) in this maner, that there must be but one bill for the additional dutyes to support the establishment and the same must also contain a fund for the supposed debt: and it was talked that a little bill (which term your Uncle will explain) would be a good expedient, but this seemed not to relish, because it left the examining the accounts and stating the debt of the Nation to the house after the recesse, when it is alway very thin; but never fails to be attended by some Gentlemen. To avoid this and to bring things to a decision in a full house, the Commons have taken indefatigable pains and have come to several resolutions tending to the lessening the debt which are much complained of by those who were of opinion that the debt was such as the accounts laid before the house by order of the Governement returned it.[782] You may be sure some warmth might happen in canvassing these matters; I am sure my sincere wishes are and alway will be that this and all other matters in Parliament may be carryed on soe as will be for the service of the King and countrey and for the honour of my Lord Lieutenant.

---

[782]On 28 Oct. Sir Ralph Gore, MP [I], reported a number of resolutions from the committee of ways and means relating to additional duties, which were then embodied in the supply bill (*CJI*, v, 264–6).

I wish his orders or his judgement would have allowed him to accept what he might have had without a negative at the beginning of the Session, and which I think he stil may attain: But if somethings which are talked of (but whether with any just ground I cannot tell) of a lone or vote of credit shal be attempted I confesse the members seem to me not inclined to think there is either a necessitye or a good reason for either; and I cannot but wish their disposition in this particular may be understood any way rather then by a vote, which (there are a great many Gentlemen beleive) will passe in the negative ... God only knows what the event of this Session will be; whether greatly for the good of the Kingdome or the contrary; but the consequences of it will I think be very considerable one way or other. God direct and blesse us.

712. *Alan I, Dublin, to Thomas, 17 Nov. 1725*[783]

(1248/6/336–41)

Since this letter will be carryed by a private hand I resolve to put nothing into it but that which I am not very willing to commit to the common post ... From my late and former letters you have plainly seen what my sense was of the successe of the designs of the Castle. I was soe candid that I all along cautioned [*Carteret*] not to be too sanguine and confident of successe, and founded my advice upon these reasons that in my opinion that which was aimed at was against the opinion of the Countrey Gentlemen, and indeed in my own private thoughts what ought not to be pressed: but I had this farther reason that I verily beleived there were others upon whom there seemed to be an entire dependance, who would disappoint him, and in the event convince him that either they were not soe numerous, and strong in freinds as they pretended to be (which was true) or that they were not very sollicitous for his successe, which I confesse was then my opinion of them. But now to come to the point, on Fryday last the Committee of accounts came to a resolution, that the debt of the nation on 24 June 1725 was a summe not exceeding £119000, and some odd money:[784] Great endeavours were used to prevent their coming at that time to that resolution; it was urged to give farther time to enquire into the accounts, and it was alleged that the Auditor Generals office was the proper place where that could appear; but upon examination of Mr William Burgh (whom you know, and who had been Accountant General)[785] who attended by order to be examined to some other matters, it appeared to the satisfaction of the Committee that the Office of the Accountant General was the proper Office where that matter did appear: now the Committee had before them the account drawn up by the accountant General, among the papers laid before the house at the beginning of the Session. Burgh was asked whether an account might not be made up out of the Auditors office, he owned it might, since the account in the Auditors Office was in nature of a transcript of what was in the Accountant Generals office; but that it could not be made up in lesse then six weeks time. Gentlemen seemed to apprehend the

[783] Partly printed in Coxe, *Walpole*, ii, 435–7.

[784] The precise figure was £119, 215. 5s. 3⅜ d. The resolution, agreed in committee on Friday, 12 Nov., was reported on the following Monday, the 15th (*CJI*, v, 282).

[785] William Burgh (1667–1744), MP [I] Lanesborough 1713–14; accountant-gen. [I] 1695–1717 (*Hist. Ir. Parl.*, iii, 311–12; *Lib. Mun.*, pt 2, p. 137).

mentioning this new way of drawing up the account was calculated with a view of delay, and to beleive that when that account should be laid before the house, it would not be very full, which might not be for the service of the countrey: They also considered that the accounts formerly laid before the Parliament had been drawn up by the accountant general out of his own books, with out any notice taken of the Auditors Office; it was also said that the account might at the beginning of the Session, have been prepared out of the Auditors Office, and that therefore they ought to ascertain the debt of the nation from the papers laid before them by the Governement as the proper papers from which they might be ascertained what money was necessary for them to supply his Majestye with: and therefore moved to proceed to state the debt of the nation at that time. To divert this the question was proposed that the Committee should adjourn (for they had power to adjourn from time to time) but this question was carried in the negative Yeas 105 Noes 114.[786] Then the grand question was put and it was resolved without a division that the debt of the nation 24 June 1725 was a summe not exceeding £119000 odd money (which I omit). And yet so temperate and modest were the majoritye, that they consented not to report the resolution to the house immediately (which however is often done here, but I think very wrong) and they agreed to have it reported to the house on Monday: Great endeavours were used on Saturday and Sunday to convince people they ought not to agree on Monday, with the Committee; to attain this end after the resolucion was reported and the question for agreeing with the Committee was moved[787]; Mr Medlicoate (one of our Commissioners)[788] thought it to be Parliamentary and according to the form of proceedings to refer that resolution to the Committee of Supply; which would have gained time to give men new lights; but it was answered that by the report now agreed to, the debt appeared to be no more then £119000 and that the funds already given by the money bill for two years additional= dutyes were agreed to be estimated by the house at a summe cer= [*sic*] which would not only answer the money which the hereditary revenue fell short to support the establishment, but would also goe far in paying the debt of the nation due 24 June 1725 soe that the true meaning of the mocion must be to leave it to the Committee of supply to give farther aids then the two years additional dutyes already granted, which they said they hoped the house were not in a disposicion to leave room for. The question for referring it to the Committee of Supply was carried in the negative by 114 Noes against 93 Yeas.[789] Then a question was proposed by Jos: Allen[790] for adjourning the house, but carried in the negative by 122 Noes against 71 Yeas.[791] The third question; that the house agreed with the

---

[786] Proceedings in committee, including divisions, were not recorded in *CJI*. Lord Palmerston in London received information that the majority 'was but of ten on the first division, of more after' (NLI, MS 11478/1: Palmerston to William Flower, 27 Nov. 1725).

[787] The following events occurred on Monday, 15 Nov., when the report from the accounts committee was made (*CJI*, v, 282).

[788] Thomas Medlycott, MP [I].

[789] Confirmed in *CJI*, v, 282.

[790] Joshua Allen.

[791] This division in fact arose from an intervention by a treasury clerk, John Bayly, who informed the House that a sum of near £7,000 had been paid by the vice-treasurer but by mistake had not been charged against the public debt. The Commons voted nonetheless to agree with the accounts' committees statement of the debt, by 122 votes to 71, with St John III one of the tellers in the majority (*CJI*, v, 282).

report of the Committee was carryed in the Affirmative by 111 against 83.[792] The house came afterward to a farther resolution in the following words; That the hereditary revenue and present additional dutyes will support the necessary branches of the establishment, and be a sufficient provision for the debt of the Nation until the next Session of Parliament without any other aid or new tax upon the subject. It was not thought advisable to divide the house on this question.[793]

I have not been at the Castle since Sunday, when I was looked on very coldly, soe that considering how much worse matters have gone since that time I have no great ground to hope being better looked on when I go thither next then I was on Sunday. I was not thought worthy to be spoken to on Sunday, about what would or should be done the next day, tho Harry Boyle[794] was conducted into the Closet by the Bishop of Limrick[795] and immediately followed by ——. When he came out we found it was to endeavour to divert the storm the next day or to gett light into what was intended to be moved by the countrey Gentlemen. But no impression could be made on our Countreyman.

To come to a conclusion. I labour under very opposite passions, joy that my Countrey is (I hope) delivered from that which its representatives thought would be very pernicious, and concern for the uneasinesse which (I beleive) a disappointment hath given [*Carteret*] and least the ill success here may have a farther influence on him elsewhere. I will in few words tell you my thoughts about him, which must go no farther. He was at the beginning possessed with an opinion of the Legalitye and innocencye of the patent (as no way hurtful to us). He was as deep in the censure of the Parliament Justices and Councel and whole Kingdome as any one Lord at the Cockpit; he thought reducing the summe to be coined to £40000 was a matter of great grace and favor, and might have been represented in such a maner here, as that the summe would have been willingly received. He came over with an opinion that the Justices had been remisse in laying before the Country the matter of reducing the summe to £40000, and hoped by his addresse to have reconciled people to it, or if they should be refractory to have made it understood that it would not be for the service of those who made opposicion. Att his first coming he gave him self an air of letting people see he expected to meet no opposicion, or to surmount all he should meet and of making those who were so hardy to give opposicion, repent it. I beleive the prosecucion intended against the Drapiers (bad) letter,[796] was intended to intimidate him or any other person from writing on the subject of Woods coyne, and not only for those things which every body allowed the paper to be faulty in; and this I beleive from particular reasons. He found (in a while after the Grand Jury had refused to present the Letter and after he saw in what maner the discharging that Grand Jury was resented) that the temper of the whole people was averse to Woods coyne, and that it was not a faction or party only raised against it, that there was a necessity to doe something to pacifye peoples minds; but saw the method prescribed to the Justices (to publish the reduction of the whole summe to £40000) would be of no avail: his next thought was to order the Judges of Assize to assure the country in their respective Circuits and to satisfye the people the halfpence would not be brought in

---

[792] The third division was in fact on a motion to adjourn, which was defeated 111–83 (*CJI*, v, 283).

[793] Confirmed in *CJI*, v, 283.

[794] Henry Boyle, MP [I].

[795] William Burscough.

[796] *A Letter to the Whole People of Ireland.*

among them: and this they did so far that the countrey seemed easy and not to be under much concern on that account; but that proceeded from an opinion they had, that the patent would be called in or given up before the meeting of the Parliament, whereas it is very possible he expected the Parliament might be brought together and meet in such a temper as (if the halfpence were not brought into the Kingdome nor the patent given up) it might remain in being and all that had been done would have been passed over in silence. It is true that ——[797] read part of a letter to me, which (as it was read) seemed to me to import that it was his opinion the patent must be given up. But matters were so ordered between your side of the water and this, that we heard nothing of the resolutions taken in England till August last when the Parliament was near sitting and what passed then you will know. Then the giving up the patent and his Majestyes part in it must be represented as matter of condescension and Royal favor (against which I advised apprehending it was meant as a shooing horn for attaining somethings which could not with any good grace have been insisted on otherwise) and I much doubt some hopes if not assurances have been given by — that something very satisfactory to the persons who had obtained that boon should be found out. This I fear is at the bottom and if it be the disappointment will be as far fatal as the loosing the support of the persons who expect, can be soe.

[PS] The successe at the beginning of the Session in carrying the words Royal favour and condescension in the addresse to his Majestye and of supplying the deficiencyes in that to my Lord Lieutenant gave I beleive such hopes that it was beleived nothing could be proposed that would not be carryed: but men should distinguish between general expressions of complement in addresses, and votes for taxing the Nation: Men weigh the later more before they come into them then they doe.

713. *Thomas to Alan II, Peper Harow, 25 Nov. 1725*

(1248/6/343–4)

I have had noe letter out of Ireland, which I doe not wonder att, for whatever account should be given of their proceedings, tho never soe true and just, would bee liable to misconstruction, and according to the usuall method, have been unjustly and falsely misrepresented, butt I heare from other hands that my Lord Lieutenants private Secretary is come to the Regents, possibly to receive their orders, after what manner to proceed, having (as tis sayd) been disappointed in a Second attempt.[798] I very much doubt whither they will give any directions chossing rather to leave him to himselfe than intermeddle in Schemes which in the end I am perswaded will prove abortive; hee will probably (too late) bee convinct that relying on the advice of others there then hee does, would have been for the kings as well as his service.

I am told our Parliament will nott meet till the middle of January[799] …

---

[797] Presumably Lord Carteret.

[798] The lords justices appointed to act in the king's absence from England. It was reported in England that Carteret was 'in a rage as well as confusion' and that 'his private secretary has been sent over at an hour's warning, it is supposed to have instructions in some point of moment' (HMC, *Portland MSS*, vii, 404).

[799] Parliament was prorogued on 11 Nov. until 16 Dec., and then again until 20 Jan. 1726.

714. *Thomas to Alan II, Peper Harow, 4 Dec. [1725]*

(1248/6/100–1)

… I have no letter out of Ireland, Lord Carterets family expect him here in February; His freinds report that your father had promised, but broke his word, but nobody beleives them.

715. *Alan I, Dublin to Thomas, 12 Dec. 1725*

(1248/6/345–6)

The dreadful winds and stormy weather have kept us in the dark as to what hath passed in England of late, and soe I stil continue notwithstanding the arrival of a pacquet boat last night, which brought in three pacquets at least, for I have received yours of the 24th of November and my sisters of the 28th of that month and one of the first instant, but am as much a stranger to what hath been done in our affairs on your side of the water, as I was before its arrival for yours only tells me your conjectures that there will be a prorogation, in order to try what alteration time may make in peoples minds. I beleive this scheme was the occasion of a certain persons going over in very great hast about three weeks since; but I am an old Protestant, and have no faith that an intermediate estate between death and the day of judgement will purge away those sins which were not repented of before death; but this is a speculative point and some divines of our Church have entertained too favourable opinions of purgatorye; and call it a good natured error, if they can be brought to a allow it to be one. Long before this can reach your hands L. F.[800] will have sent or delivered you a short one from me, and C[ourthope] C[layton] a very long one to which (for its length) I ought not to add any thing, but indeed I knew nothing at that time which is not set forth at large and in very plain words in that letter … I will let your Nephew[801] know your thoughts of his or my going for England before the <u>final</u> end of our present meeting in Parliament: I call it final because in legal acceptacion our meeting will be ending by a prorogacion, if that be the scheme; but I cannot stil but look upon it to be in effect the same meeting of Parliament, and surely when the Commons voted that the dutyes given were sufficient to support the necessary branches of the establishment till the next Session of Parliament, they intended till the next Session at the usual period viz. the end of two years: and I think they will not be prevailed on to explain themselves in any other maner. For my particular, I really am weary, of going to Chichester house[802] to spend my time as I am obliged to doe some times in hearing things which no way suit with my slender understanding, and I am as weary of the cool looks I meet at a certain place where good maners sometimes call me: and I shal not be easy till I gett to Surry. But what I have said above you will understand that I have not been this morning at the Castle, nor doe I intend to goe thither tho Sunday is the usual day on which I make one of the Crowd generally to make my bow.

---

[800] Possibly Lord Forbes (see above, p. 203).
[801] St John III.
[802] The Irish parliament-house.

(1248/6/347–50)

I have acknowledged yours of the 28th of last month, but had not informed myself what
news the boat which brought that letter relating to this Kingdome afforded; but am now
satisfyed that there was no maner of foundation for the reports in the town of great alterations in the money bill made on your side of the water; the reports were that it was altered
in point of duracion viz. that the dutyes were granted only for three months, tho voted by
the Commons for two years; the consequence of which people apprehended would be to
make a new demand in another Session before the expiration of the three months; it was
also surmised that there was also an alteration in the dutyes granted by the bill, viz. whereas
the Commons had voted a greater duty on some goods to be imported, that the bill made
the duty lesse, and both these rumours created great uneasinesse; for people considered that
if once way should be given to the money bill being altered in England from a greater duty
given by the Commons to a lesser; that in time it would be carryed soe far to encrease
the duty given by the Commons to a greater summe then they had voted. But we are att
perfect ease in this matter finding there is no alteration at all except in spelling or the like:
You may be sure there are some here who impute the rise of these rumours to the malice
of those whom they doe not like: but the truth is (as far at least as I can guesse) that the
whole report took its rise from the White Hall letter which imported that the money bill
was passed the Councel of England <u>with some small alterations</u>. Every body depended on
it that some alterations had been made, and probably employed their thoughts in framing
conjectures wherein such alterations could consist; and possibly they might imagine from
the observation they had made what earnest endeavours had been used to gett more money
this Session then the Commons could be brought to grant, that the same vehement desire
continued of getting more money; which since there was no hopes of obtaining during this
Session, by reason of the vote to which the Common[s] had agreed that the aids already
given were sufficient to support the necessary branches of the establishment <u>till the next
Session of Parliament</u> there seemed no room for doing it soon without a short prorogation, which would make room for a new Session, tho not such a Session as the Commons
intended when they went into that vote, as divers Gentlemen in debating explained themselves, by saying the Supplyes would support the establishment for two years forward etc.
The conjecture of the summes voted being altered proceeded (I fancy) from a notion which
hath obtained too much among us of late that some people would be very glad to have us
taxed by others then our own representatives; for which notion I wish some Gentlemen
who are not perfectly acquainted with the constitution of Ireland, or the temper of the
people may not have given some ground. But I own that they were too blame who entertained a beleif that such alterations were made, when they had soe little ground for their
suspitions: but they certainly are without excuse who insinuated their own misgrounded
suspitions as truths, and yet I cannt but beleive there were such people; since I know not
how to account for those rumors of taxing for some time which were current among ordinary people before the money bill was brought into the house of Commons on Monday
last: We expect it to be sent up to the Lords to morrow, where it will receive all reasonable

dispatch soe that it is beleived it may receive the Royal assent on Monday,[803] and then we shal know whether the Parliament will be prorogued or adjourned. I am in no secrets, but doe own that I cannot but think by the earnestnesse which appears in both houses; and at the Council to passe the heads of bills from both houses into bills to be put under the Great Seal to be transmitted into England, and from other arguments that it will only be a recesse by adjournment to give time to send back those bills under the Great Seal of Great Britain to be passed after the adjournment. I think no one wise or good end will be attained by a prorogation, but rather greater disappointments then hitherto, to any person who shal be advised to hope something will be obtained in a Session after a short prorogation, that could be obtained in the present Session. But this is only the conjecture of a man who is kept as much as possible in the dark of all that is resolved on. I beleive they guessed right who told you with what persons [*Carteret*] consults. I doe not beleive he troubles himself to advise with any one person more then those your letter names. Our politicks are a good deal altered of late; you remember when it was the sense of our Parliament that one of the methods to prevent the growth of Popery was to prevent our having parish preists, and that none should officiate as such (under very severe penaltyes) unlesse such as should be registred within the time prescribed by the Act, which was intended (as it would effectually have done) to prevent a Succession of Popish Preists.[804] But truly on the 3d of this month the house of Lords came to the following resolution to agree with the Committee that the most probable way of restraining Popish Preists and regulars coming into this Kingdome will be to allow a competent number of secular Preists to exercise their functions under such rules and limitations as may be for the securitye of the Civil State.[805] And indeed the heads of a bill which we were then upon had an entire tendencye not only to allow but (as I did soe idly think) to establish the Romish worship and to provide for a constant succession of Parish Preists, to be licenced by the Governement etc. The bill is not gone through our house, and is unkindly enough talked of without doors; what the fate of it with us will be time must discover; but the Commons seem disposed not to perpetuate the succession of Popish Preists.[806] They have also agreed to heads of a bill to oblige converts to breed their children Protestants, which came to the Councel very imperfect with retrospective clauses but is now under the consideration of the Councel where much more pains are taken to digest it into a good bill then the first framer employed, and indeed the heads seem to me in some measure rather calculated to answer the private ends of some particular persons in one county, then to be suited to the circumstances of the Kingdome in general.[807] I write to you in a good deal of pains and weaknesse not being able to walk through a weaknesse in

[803] The money bill was brought in on Monday, 13 Dec., and passed through its various stages in the Commons in successive days, being sent to the Lords on Friday the 17th. In fact, it received the royal assent on the Saturday. (*CJI*, v, 372, 374–6, 379; *LJI*, ii, 381.)

[804] The act of 1704 'for registering the popish clergy' (2 Anne, c. 7) (*Catholic Ireland in the Eighteenth Century: Collected Essays of Maureen Wall*, ed. Gerard O'Brien (Dublin, 1989), 13).

[805] A resolution passed by the Lords on 3 Dec. 1725, on the report of the committee appointed to prepare a bill 'for restraining the number of Popish priests and regulars coming into this kingdom'. Alan had been a member of the committee. (*LJI*, ii, 827, 830.)

[806] Nothing more came of the bill (ILD).

[807] The bill 'For the securing and strengthening the Protestant interest in this kingdom, and to oblige converts to breed their children Protestants, and to prevent the occasional conformity of Papists', originating in the Commons, was approved by the Irish privy council but respited by the British (ILD).

my instep and ankle with a fit of the Gout in my right leg; soe that my poor left paralytick one is the strongest and best Leg I have left me to stand upon. But I am come to those years that I must expect to want supporters. I can come to no resolution about the time of our going for England, till I see what the upshot will be of our affairs at the end of our Parliament and of my Lord Lieutenants going. Before which time you will hear often from me.

[*PS*] Most of the countrey Gentlemen are gone into the countrey to keep their Christmas with their neighbours, and among them your Nephew[808] who left town this morning and assured me that —— was most outrageously angry with two of your freinds.

We are adjourned this day to 27 January after giving the Royal assent to the bill for continuing the addicional dutyes for two years.

717. *Alan I, Dublin, to Thomas, in the Privy Garden, Whitehall, 19 Dec. 1725*

(1248/6/351–2)

The postscript of my letter dated yesterday informed you that both houses of Parliament were (on message) adjourned to Thursday 27 January; no bill was ready for the Royal assent but that for continuing the additional dutyes to the 25 Dec. 1727.[809] The Speaker made a speech which will give you a better apprehension of its contents then any thing I can write; but you recur to your memory for the grace of delivery which attends every thing he saith upon soe solemn an occasion: only with this addicion that as in most instances he outdoeth others, in this he outdid himeself.

A more solemn silence I never observed in the house at giving the Royal assent or presenting the money bill, at which time it hath been usual here to shew our satisfaction with what the Speaker saith by humming. But there was a profound silence till the Lord Lieutenant went out, who made no speech.[810]

Pray doe not forgett to inform yourself truly and fully in what order the Prayer for the Parliament is read in the house of Lords and house of Commons; whether immediately after the collect for the Prince and Princesse and the rest of the Royal familye or whether the Collect for all Bishops and Curates and all congregacions committed to their charge takes precedence of that for the high Court of Parliament: Perhaps your houses may vary as I think they doe here; for I am told the Commons Chaplain vouchsafes to let the Lords and Commons take place of the Curates, but when he steps up into our house I make no doubt but he will take example by his predecessors in reading prayers there, who never fail to read the prayer for the Bishops and Curates next after that for the Lord Lieutenant and think the Parliament comes in time enough after the Preists: A freind of mine among them pretends it is ordered soe by the rubrick soe that it is not in their option to doe otherwise. Pray inform yourself fully herein and let me know how your course is. I have thoughts of going down to Munster during the recess to put matters a little to rights there which are

---

[808] St John III.

[809] These events occurred on Saturday, 17 Jan.

[810] The sequence of events is confirmed in *CJI*, v, 382; and *LJI*, ii, 840.

much out of order through an absence of more then years: for soe long it is since I was in that Province.

[*PS*] Your verses are not bad, but I think mean no more then what is contained in these few words, that he would convince Mr W[*alpole*] the Author will make a better S—[811] then Mr P—.[812]

718. *Alan II, Bond Street, to Alan I, Dublin, 25 Dec. 1725*

(1248/6/353–4)

… People here imagine that his Majesty came last night to Helveot Sluys,[813] if He did, He is still there, for the Wind does not serve to day, to bring a Ship out of the Maese,[814] but whenever it comes round, I hope He'll have a Quick, Pleasant, and Safe Passage into England.

We have no news but what comes from your side of the water; I am extreamly glad to hear from my Cousin Clayton that your Lordship is so well, and hope that I shall soon have the Happyness of seeing your Lordship, for I flatter my self that your stay in Ireland will be but very short after the Parliament there is up.

Poor Lord Mountjoy is retarded at Chester by Illness, and, as I hear, does not propose stirring from thence till the middle of next week at soonest …

719. *Alan I, Dublin, to Thomas, in the Privy Garden, Whitehall, 3 Jan. 1725/6*

(1248/6/355–6)

I have your letter of the 24th of last month, which owns the receit of mine of the 12th by the post, which you tell me was opened; and also of that of the 16th by a private hand. They who had the curiositye to peep into mine of the 12th would have been more edifyed if they could have had the examining the other: but neither the one or the other contained any thing which I am not free to tell a curious enquirer, if they would give themselves the trouble to ask the questions in which they desire to be satisfyed directly of me, for I make no scruple to say publickly anything which I think fit to be put under my hand. I am sorry to find by your last letter that the Lady who hath a demand on C[*ourthope*] C[*layton*] is in those circumstances which your last letter speaks of; but I can not wonder at any bodyes being undone that ever could be drawn into the damned S[*outh*] S[*ea*] scheme; for which I have that detestation that I can hardly pity those who suffered in it, because they by their money and example contributed to the carrying on that hellish cheat. We are here wondrous busy about forming bills for the second transmisse, which (notwithstanding all the care we use to dispatch them) will not (I doubt) be sent us back as early as is wished, for there will be at least a fortnight after they come back before they can passe the houses,

[811] Secretary.
[812] Pelham. Hon Henry Pelham, MP [GB], was sec.-at-war.
[813] Hellevoetsluis in Holland, the naval port of Rotterdam.
[814] The River Meuse, or Maas in Dutch.

tho they should have no other businesse; which will carry us farther into February then I think is wished at a certain place: the truth is, I cant wonder if my Lord Lieutenant desires to be at London soon after his Majestyes arrival. I cannot with any certainty tell you whether your Nephew[815] will take this town in his way to Westminster; tho I think he will, because I think he ought and know he promised his freinds to be up at the opening of the Parliament after the recesse; but others (who are not his freinds) say he will not be here and promise themselves some advantages by his absence. I write to him on this subject, and will not trouble you now with any thing relating to our Parliament here least it may prevent this (otherwise inoffensive) letter from coming soe soon to your hand as I wish.

720. *Alan I, Dublin, to Thomas, in the Privy Garden, Whitehall, 17 Jan. 1725[/6]*

(1248/6/361–2)

This letter will be delivered into your hand by one who I am sure will not permit it to be pryed into by any inquisitive person, of which sort there are too many both on this side of the water and on yours. No body hath a better memory, nor better understands what passed in the first part of our Session of Parliament, nor can give you a more instructive account of things or putt what passed in it, in a more agreeable light then the bearer; who hath behaved himself with honour and candor, and a great deal of spirit and brightnesse; soe that I desire you will forgett any past indiscretions in his conduct, and hope better of him for the future, then he gave his freinds ground to expect from the maner of his first setting out. As far as I can judge by the caballs and whisperings of the Castilians[816] they have something in agitation from which they propose some considerable advantage to their party; but this is not beleived to be practicable by a relation of yours and by others who have hitherto been of the same sentiments with him: they think that (after so many unsuccesseful trials) the ad[v]ersary will hardly venture at making any more. Now I confesse my way of reasoning is this: They cannot be in a worse scituation by being disappointed in any future attempt then they now are, if they acquiesce in things as they stand at present: Whereas all the regular troops are sure to be ready at any time that shal be appointed for their rendezvous, and on the other hand it is not only probable, but (I think) morally certain that very few of opposite sentiments will be in town when matters may be moved, and carryed in a thin house, nor will some people be much ashamed of doing things in any way which will attain the end. I confesse I have lived too long in the world not to observe that a mans despising his enemye often gives him such advantage over him which he could never have obtained any other way; and if I be not mistaken in the temper of him that hath the conduct and direction of the affair, he will, *Acheronta movere*,[817] rather then let things continue in the maner they were left att the time of the recesse. I did hope to have been able to have told my Lord Lieutenant yesterday (when he asked when I had heard from you) that I had

---

[815] St John III.

[816] The 'Castle party'.

[817] Literally, to raise up Hell; from Virgil, *Aeneid*, vii, 312: '*Flectere si nequeo superos, Acheronta movebo*' (If I cannot reach Heaven, I will raise Hell).

received some letter of a later date then your last was: But I reckon our next pacquet will bring us certain accounts whether the British Parliament will meet to doe businesse on the 20th instant or be adjourned to some farther day.[818] We talk of a farther adjournement of ours till about the middle of February,[819] because we think you will hardly be at leisure (in this busy season) to attend the affairs of poor Ireland: and I own the conjecture seems to be very just: But our men of speculation give a farther reason why our bills will not be retransmitted in great hast; since till they return a certain person cannot possibly goe into England. I doe not know whether the story I heard yesterday hath any foundation, viz. that the Primate and Chancellor are not upon a foot of freindship; how that will comport with the scheme of leaving them Justices is not my businesse to enquire: But this I verily beleive may be depended upon, that a Chaplain of the former, assured a Gentleman that the later had never been within the doors of the former since his landing: that the Doctor said soe I am convinced, being assured of it by a Gentleman of veracitye, but I confesse the story seems to me to be very improbable, in the great latitude of the expression (never since landing) unlesse by it he meant either seld[ome] or of late. The bearer goes over at a very improper time [?in my] mind and I wish it may not be upon an improper erra[nd]. He tells me it is upon some businesse of a freinds of yours in H[ano]ver square; Pray caution him how he engages too far there and upon what terms, and that he undertake nothing unfit or imprudent: his employer is a man upon whom nobody ought to depend farther then while he thinks them useful.

721. *Alan II, London, to Alan I, Dublin, 22 Jan. 1725/6*

(1248/6/363–4)

Inclosed I send your Lordship the Kings Speech, and the Address of the House of Lords; the Commons having presented theirs but this day, it is not yet printed. It is said to contain thanks to his Majesty for having communicated to Them the Treaties He has made, and the strongest Assurances of Duty, togather with a Promise of coming heartily into all Measures that may support his Majesty's Honour, and contribute to the Happyness of the Nation in Generall.[820] The Motion was made by Sir Robert Sutton,[821] and seconded by Mr Wyndham of Norfolk.[822] Mr Shippen,[823] as is said, took Notice of the Words no greater Number of

---

[818]The British parliament did indeed meet on 20 Jan., to which date it had previously been adjourned (*CJ*, xx, 544).

[819]In fact both houses met again on 27 Jan.

[820]Agreed on 21 Jan. and presented the following day (*CJ*, xx, 548).

[821]The motion for a loyal address in reply to the king's speech, made on 20 Jan. by Sir Robert Sutton (c. 1671–1746), of Broughton, Lincs., MP [GB] Notts., who subsequently reported from the committee appointed to prepare the address (*CJ*, xx, 545, 548; *Knatchbull Diary*, 49).

[822]Thomas Wyndham (c. 1686–1752), of Clearwell Court, Gloucs. (s. of Francis Wyndham of Cromer, Norfolk), MP [GB] Truro (*Knatchbull Diary*, 49). Named second to the drafting committee (*CJ*, xx, 545).

[823]William Shippen (1673–1743), of Norfolk St., London, MP [GB] Newton.

Forces [824]and Mr Pulteney[825] of these Viz <u>menaced and insulted</u>.[826] Messrs Hungerford[827] and Sandys[828] also spoke; but the Motion for the Address was carried, I think, Nem: Con?[829] which, as soon as it is printed, I will send your Lordship.

The Speaker presented a Bill to prevent Vexatious Suits and Arrests,[830] and, I think, some Writs have been ordered to be issued out, and this is the main part of the Business hitherto done. My Uncle has been very much out of Order, but is much better …

722. *Thomas to Alan I, 25 Jan. 1725[/6]*

(1248/6/365–6)

Of your fourteen publique Bills, twelve are referred to the Attorney[831] and Sollicitor,[832] the two Popery Bills to a Committee of the Councill, their fate you will easily guesse, among other exceptions to them one is, that very greate part is in substance the same which had been formerly transmitted, and rejected here; the Towne say (butt upon what grounds I know nott) that Mr W[*alpole*] had given assurances att Paris, that they would nott bee approved.[833]

A Privy Councillor (of note) told mee hee did nott see how those agreed to could bee retransmitted before the middle of March; I am of opinion they will nott goe back very soone; The D[*uke*] of Devon says hee supposes the Parliament will bee under adjournments from fortnight to fortnight till they come, soe that Lord Lieutenants family reckon without their [?fact] in expecting him here next month.

Wee have this day agreed to the Resolution for a Supply,[834] and shall with as little losse of time as possible goe through the Supply for the Current Service of the yeare.

I heare thirty men of war are to bee forthwith fitted out, part for the Baltaick, the others for the Mediteranean; wee have light frigatts enough att Sea for guarding the Coast, for any thing which as yett appears necessary.

You will observe the word Wisdom twice applyed to his Majesty in our Addresse,[835] one of our members upon being told what passt in a learned debate with you, replyed what then, can any more bee inferred from thence, or with more truth, Then that the

---

[824] The king's speech to the Commons had included the statement that the estimates to be presented to the House 'are formed upon the foot of employing no greater number of forces than was thought necessary the last year' (*CJ*, xx, 545). The fact that Shippen contributed to the debate (though not the content of his speech) is confirmed in *Knatchbull Diary*, 49.

[825] Presumably William Pulteney, the most prominent family-member in the House.

[826] The king had referred to the Commons being determined 'that you will not suffer the British crown and nation to be menaced and insulted' (*CJ*, xx, 545).

[827] John Hungerford.

[828] Samuel Sandys (his participation is confirmed in *Knatchbull Diary*, 49).

[829] No division is recorded in *CJ*, xx, 545.

[830] *CJ*, xx, 544, simply records that it was read the first time on 20 Jan.

[831] Sir Philip Yorke (1690–1764), of Carshalton, Surrey, MP [GB] Seaford; later 1st earl of Hardwicke.

[832] Sir Clement Wearg.

[833] Horatio Walpole, ambassador extraordinary to the French court.

[834] Confirmed in *CJ*, xx, 549.

[835] In fact only once, in relation to the forming of alliances to protect British interests (*CJ*, xx, 548).

Commons of England have more wisdom then the Lords of Ireland, and indeed tis become a Coffee house jest. I am sorry to bee the messinger of the terrible story of Jack Trevor (the ussher of the Rolls) having yesterday att four a clock shott himselfe,[836] hee was heard frequently to say that Lord Chancellor having putt him uppon an equall foote with a pack of knaves The Masters in Chancery, by ordering his paying into the Banke, as well as theirs, hee would sooner dye then submit to the reflection. The Preists are prayed for in our house immediately after the Prince etc. The Parliament follows them; I doe nott thinke worth while to enquire how tis with the Lords noe doubt in this (at least) wee agree. I am sorry you did nott take this oportunity of seeing your freinds in Munster, as well as setling your affairs there, for I thinke your time would have been much better employd then by attending in Dublin, where those att Helme will doe all the publique businesse to the satisfaction and for the advantage of the Country. When any thing worth notice happens ile write, otherwise nott.

723. Alan I, Dublin, to Thomas, Westminster, 26 Jan. 1725[/6]

(1248/6/367–8)

I am to own the receit of yours of the 20th, and have read over the Kings speech with great attention; but the vote I have not seen, but conclude that it is in the terms it was moved by Sir R[obert] Sutton; for I fancy the expression which I heard about the middle of September last (that a resolution for an addresse of thanks at the opening a Session ought not to vary from the words of the speech but only to Eccho that back again) was founded upon that which he had observed to be the usual and approved practice of another place. The Gentlemen who layd in their claim to examine the estimates very strictly were much in the right, for as I am sensible such a resolution (when put into practice) will be of use to the nation, soe I cannot foresee the making and declaring it can be of any immediate disservice to those who declare their intentions so early and in so publick a maner, on the other hand their doing a thing soe popular and right leaves them stil at liberty to hear all the arguments that can be produced to shew the estimates laid before the house to be very reasonable; and I cannot but call to mind the reasons given by a very worthy freind of yours against examining into the particulars which created the deficiencye necessary to clear the civil List when that matter came first on: you will understand me well enough. I am not at all uneasy at my being detained here by our Irish affairs, where I shal hear what you are doing att Westminster without being under the mortification of doing what possibly may be uneasy to some whom I greatly value. I confesse I am sensible such a war as I apprehend seems likely to happen will put us here in a sad way: Our Lands must fall prodigiously if it should fall out that the good of his Majestyes dominions should necessarily draw us into a war with Spain and Portugal which two countryes are the sources whence the little money arises which circulates among us.[837] but we must expect our little concerns should give way to those of more weight. When a nation is not engaged in a war it may more easily

---

[836] Alan's brother-in-law John Trevor, the 2nd son of Sir John Trevor, who held the office of usher of the rolls in chancery [GB] (*Daily Post*, 26 Jan. 1726; TNA, PROB 11/608/94).

[837] *Proclamations*, ed. Kelly and Lyons, iii, 81–3, 152–3.

keep out of it then it can procure a safe and honourable peace when a war is begun. But these are things in which I am no farther concerned here then as our little trade may be influenced by a war; and when I am in London I shal be better able to make a judgement after hearing the debates of the house. In the main I need not assure you that I shal be at all times for every thing which I think to be for the honour of the King and the good of the Kingdome, however I may suffer in my own private concerns. I hope you will from time to time give me such lights into what is doing as you think will be of use to me.

724. *Thomas to Alan I, Dublin, 27 Jan. 1725[/6]*

(1248/6/369–70)

… Last night the Attorney reported to a Committee of Councill some of the Irish Bills, butt which or how many I know nott.

A merry story is told concerning one of them, That for some crime mentioned (what I know nott) the offender should forfeite ten pounds, and loose both his ears, one moyety to his Majesty etc The other to such person as would sue for the same.

Wee have this day agreed to the Resolution of yesterday for ten Thousand sea men,[838] and tomorrow goe on the Land forces, possibly our Parliamemt may bee up before yours, unlesse something unforeseen happen to retard itt, for wee are in hast.

725. *Alan I, Dublin, to Thomas, 29 Jan. 1725[/6]*

(1248/6/371–2)

I propose to send this letter by a private hand and will therefore speak more freely then I will venture to doe when my letters may fall under the inspection of others before they come to your hands. As far as I thought it prudent, I in my last let you know my thoughts of our publick affairs in answer to yours of the 20th which gave me an hint of the matters debated in the house of commons upon the motion made by Sir R[obert] Sutton for an addresse to his Majestye,[839] and I made no doubt the successe of that motion would be the same as you foretold viz. that the resolution would be carryed in the very words the question was moved in; Tho you did not send me the Kings speech yet it came over in some of the prints of that day, and the addresse of the Commons followed soon after. I will not be so unfashionable to think that anything can be more for the good of his Majestyes service and the good of the Kingdome then the settling such a resolution to be proposed and insisted upon as will best answer and if I may use a term which I have had from a great man, eccho the very words of the speech: This I find to be in practice with you as well as elsewhere, which determines my doubts how far the method is Parliamentary: Yet perhaps a good many Gentlemen who were to give their votes on the question, were not at all upon an equal foot, with their fellow members who might have heard or been told what the

---

[838] On a report of resolutions from the committee of supply (*CJ*, xx, 553).

[839] The loyal address, in response to the king's speech: the debate on Sutton's motion occurred on 20 Jan. (Cobbett, *Parl. Hist.*, viii, col. 495).

speech would be: and consequently the others were not soe well able to frame a judgement how far the engagements they were moved to enter into by addressing extended: Now I desire to be informed whether this hath at all times been the course of Parliaments, and if not, I should be glad you would inform me when it first began, and upon what occasion. I make no doubt, if the method of such promisory resolutions by way of addresse, is not according to the ancient usage of Parliaments, that it was at first introduced, and hath often since been made use of very much for the good of the Kingdome, and particularly now: but I confesse that I have observed such use hath been made of engagements of that nature in a certain place which shal be namelesse that I could wish there may not be any need of peoples making promises or resolutions what they will doe, till the matters expected come to be proposed and actually done: this method would give Gentlemen more time to consider whether the things aimed at by the words contained in a general complemental resolution are reasonable to be complyed with in the latitude which may be expected, and whether more may not be couched in such general assurances, then what readily occurs to those who enter into the engagment. It is true, such general resolutions may be of use abroad by shewing the hearty zeal of the Parliament in his Majestyes and their countreys service and interest; but methinks the constant good affection and readinesse of the house on all former occasions should leave no room to doubt their continuing in the same good disposition.

You know we are fond of imitating you in the good precedents you set us,[840] and have given the most remarkable instance of it in the house of Commons last Thursday (as you will see by the inclosed printed votes) that I think can be given; for whatever may be said of going into addresses when his Majestye hath either by his Vicegerent spoken to the Parliament, or otherwise communicated any thing to them by message; I beleive our coming into the resolution and addresse contained in the votes, is not only copying after, but outdoing our elder brethren; for we have taken notice of a speech never made nor communicated to us, by answering it in our addresse paragraph by paragraph, which I think you have hardly ever yet done in England.[841] You will observe the amendment moved, and know no doubt from what quarter it came; the Addresse was moved by Mr Singleton, a Lawyer,[842] son of old Alderman Singleton of Droghedah whom you knew;[843] There were no words in the fourth paragraph (between the words We are firmly perswaded, and the words the steadinesse of your faithful subjects) in the resolution proposed and moved by Mr Singleton: So then the resolucion proposed was thus: We are firmly perswaded that the steddinesse of your faithful subjects etc without any mention of his Majestyes Councels or Administracion: I hear your Nephew[844] proposed the following amendment, that after the word perswaded these words should be added before the words the steadinesse etc viz. that the wisdom and prudence of your Majestyes present administration. Mr Singleton thought his Majestyes Councils should be also mentioned, to which no body made the least objection; but your Nephew was for

[840] Glenn McKee, 'Standing Orders and Precedents in the Irish House of Commons in the Seventeenth and Eighteenth Centuries', *Parl. Hist.*, lx (2021), 311–42.

[841] The address agreed on 27 Jan. to congratulate the king on his safe arrival in Britain and to thank him for his interposition in favour of distressed protestants abroad (*CJI*, v, 382–5).

[842] Henry Singleton, MP [I]. That he moved the address is confirmed in *Coghill Letters*, 33.

[843] Edward Singleton (bef. 1653–1710), of Drogheda, MP [I] 1692–d.

[844] St John III. Confirmed in BL, Add. MS 46977, f. 3: Berkeley Taylor to Lord Perceval, 19 Jan. 1725/6.

having both Councels and administration mentioned; but then there was great objection made to the epithet (present) and very many long harangues against Gentlemens insisting on that word.[845] I confesse if I had been of the house and had aimed at serving my Lord Lieutenants private interest, I should not have thought I did him any service in endeavouring to leave that word out upon a question, and if Mr S[ingleton] had readily owned that it was forgetfulnesse in him not to have made it part of his original motion, and had seconded the amendment I think the adding those words could not have done any body any hurt; whereas it now appears that the word (present) was left out on a question very much laboured, and every body on your side will conjecture out of what quiver that arrow came. On the other hand I confesse if I had been to speak my thoughts whether the word (present) should stand, I cannot but say that it was an unnecessary word, for the administracion must imply that adminstracion which was in being when the transactions hapned, and consequently the present, in which no alteration hath been made since that time. Methinks too my Lord Lieutenant might reasonably be thought to be meant by a Parliament of this Kingdome when they speak of the administration, and I would have taken it in that sense, or at least not understood it as calculated to exclude him. But the whole posse of a certain place were against the word (present) standing and the house was divided. Noes 103 Yeas 8 beside the tellers.[846] This was a suddain businesse, and I think not well weighed; but great endeavours were used not to have the amendment proposed and rejected appear in the printed votes; but the Yeas would not consent to leave it out; soe it stands, and now both sides may make the best use of it they can. Having said enough upon this head I will proceed to explain my thoughts of the condition in which this Kingdome will find itself if it fall out that there shal be a war between Great Britain and Spain: What little money comes hither we have from Spain and Portugal[847] and whenever we are deprived of the trade we have with those countryes, we are utterly undone; all other branches of our trade being to our losse. Now I confesse for this reason and for others I am extremely inclined to part with that estate which I have in this Kingdome and which is absolutely in my disposal, and if this be advisable in me, you will allow the same thing will be as much for the benefit of my younger son, who in conjunction with me, may turn his estate which he hath from his Mother into money and lay the money out in England: I doe not foresee that we are in any likelyhood of being incouraged in any branch of trade which may help to support or inrich us; on the contrary I think there are some who design to resent their not being complyed with in every thing, by doing us ill offices of more kinds then one. If then our trade shal fall under discouragement by a foreign war, or by clogs laid on it nearer home, must not the price of our Lands fall, and the rents sink in proporcion to the want of foreign markets for our goods. Add to this the prospect there is of new taxes. But so much for this very melancholy subject. When you have read this letter you may take and extract any part of it

---

[845] Marmaduke Coghill explained that the objection to the inclusion of the word 'present' was that it might 'look like a reflection on the past Adm[inistratio]n' (*Coghill Letters*, 33–4).

[846] *CJI*, v, 383 gives the totals as 103–8 including tellers, and the same numbers were recorded by Marmaduke Coghill, MP [I] (*Coghill Letters*, 34). However, another contemporary report records figures of 105–10, which would accord with Alan's comment (BL, Add. MS 46977, f. 3: Berkeley Taylor to Lord Perceval, 29 Jan. 1725/6).

[847] For evidence of the extensive circulation of Portuguese gold coins in Ireland at this time, and in particular the importation of large quantities through the port of Cork, resulting in a proclamation in January 1726 that they be accepted as legal tender, see TNA, SP 63/385/10: report of privy council [I] to lord lieutenant, 7 May 1725; SP 63/386/70–1: Carteret to Newcastle, 10 Sept. 1725; *Proclamations*, ed. Kelly and Lyons, iii, 152–3.

which you think fit; and then I entreat you to burn it: for you are the almost only man to whom I would speak in soe plain terms. Doe not speak to Senny, about this affair till you hear farther from me …

726. *Alan II, London, to Alan I, Dublin, 29 Jan. 1725[/6]*

(1248/6/373–4)

I am desired by my Lord Mountjoy to own the receipt of your Lordships of the second of this month for Him; which (by what Accident it happened He can not imagine) His Lordship did not receive till last Thursday Evening. He desires me to tell your Lordship that He is so lame that He cannot even write his Name, and that He did not think it fit to write to your Lordship by his Secretary, and therefore employed me.

He is very sorry to hear your dismal Account of the damage done by the Floods in Ireland; but I beleive they have not been worse there than here. Mr Payne of Easheen[848] says that Hee never remembers the Water so high there by some feet, in Perpendicular Height; and to give your Lordship some Idea of it, I must tell You that it ran over the very top of Somerset Bridge.[849] The Windsor Stage Coaches were stopped for more than a Week, and the farther one went westward, the greater were the Floods; insomuch that scarce any of the Somersetshire, Devonshire, or Dorsetshire Members are come to Town.

The Captains of the thirty Men of War lately put into commission meet with great Difficulty in their Search after Seamen; the Press Gangs have been out, but it is said that They have not yet been able to find near the Number of Sailors that They want for what Expedition they are designed is yet a Secret …

727. *Alan I, Dublin, to Thomas, 8 Feb. 1725[/6]*

(1248/6/375–6)

Yesterday our Parliament met after our three weeks adjournment from 27 January to the 17th of February.[850] The house of Lords did nothing but dispose of two orders on their book which required the attendance of the Bishops of Corke and Waterford, neither of which Prelates had attended the service of the house any part of this Session, nor indeed of a good many preceding it. We excused the Bishop of Corke who appeared to be really sick; but his Lordship of Waterford did not meet with the same favor, but was ordered to appear in his place on the 24th.[851] And then the Lord Chancellor by direction from my Lord Lieutenant intimated his Excellencyes pleasure that we should adjourn till that day sevennight, which was done accordingly.[852] The like message by Mr Clutterbuck had the

---

[848] The village of Eashing, near Godalming.
[849] A 13th-century bridge over the River Wey at Peper Harow.
[850] Confirmed in *LJI*, ii, 842–3; *CJI*, v, 386.
[851] Confirmed in *LJI*, ii, 843.
[852] Confirmed in *LJI*, ii, 843; *CJI*, v, 387.

like effect in the other house; but your Nephew,[853] and others moved that letters might be wrote by the Speaker to the several members to attend on that day,[854] and took their rise from reports which they said obtained abroad as if some thing very extraordinary was to be attempted at next meeting, and truly for ought I can find those who are in the secret doe not dissemble that they intend at the meeting to push for a vote to pay the interest of soe much as according to the ballance already struck by the house of Commons will be the debt of the nation at the end of the two years for which the additional dutyes are granted.[855] This is new, and I cannot see but that if we had so much ready money to lay down, that it would be very prudent to lodge it in the Treasury by way of advance ready then pay an interest for it. And yet nobody I think could have the face to move that money should [be] lodged in the Treasury to answer a debt which shal become due hereafter; for then the matter is in short this: That you put soe much into the hand of the Vice Treasurers which they may circulate for their own benefit till it becomes due. But they promise themselves successe, and I am not very clear that their indefatigable sollicitations may take place especially considering how far the late Addresse to his Majestye and his answer to it and the answer to it will be said to have engaged people. I formerly wrote at large the true account in what maner the words (present administracion) were left out of that Addresse in the house of Commons upon a question. Mr Carter told me a very odd story upon that subject yesterday in the house of Lords, and repeated it again this evening, viz. that there went an account from hence to a great man in London, that the question was carryed against those words standing as part of the addresse by those who were for inserting them; this he said from a very good hand with whom he corresponds, and that Mr W[alpole] took it in that maner till he was told the truth by his freind; at which he was very merry. You will easily know how far Mr C[arter']s correspondent had ground for what he wrote by speaking to Mr W[alpole] on the subject; whom you might and I beleive you did give to understand who they were that were for and against those words. But I cannot bring my self to beleive that the account could be sent by the hand named to me; the thing is too mean to be done by one of that figure and character; tho possibly a Custom house Officer might not think it below to ingratiate by such a paultry invention ...

728. *Thomas to Alan I, 10 Feb. 1725[/6]*[856]

(1248/6/377–8)

Yesterday came yours of the 26th. of last month. I thinke itt very plaine that what passed the first day of our meeting by the claime layd in of examining minutely into the several estimates had its very full effect, for uppon delivery of them wee were told that the calculations

---

[853] St John III.

[854] The House voted that there should be a call on the 24th, and the Speaker was instructed to write circular letters to county sheriffs to require the attendance of MPs on that day (*CJI*, v, 389).

[855] One Ulster MP reassured Speaker Conolly's crony Henry Maxwell of his determination to attend come what may, since 'A new scene offers indeed, which must make us exert ourselves, and follow the example set before us on the other side the water, and tho' not so able we must let the world see how willing we are' (PRONI, D1556/16/4/15: Samuel Waring to Maxwell, 12 Feb. 1725/6).

[856] Printed in Coxe, *Walpole*, ii, 496–7.

were made as low as possible, and soe itt proved, for I really thinke a thousand pounds could nott uppon the whole with colour of reason have been excepted against, soe that by common consent they were allowd, soe triviall a summe nott being worth contending. A very long debate happened yesterday uppon a motion of Mr D[aniel] Poultnyes[857] (which youl see in the votes) for appointing a Committee to examine the publique accounts from the year 1714 to which a negative was given by a majority of a great many above a hundred,[858] I was with the majority though some of my best freinds (from whom I seldom differ) devided for the question, because I thought itt extremely ill timed,[859] though the thing in itt selfe (generally speaking) is highly reasonable; taking itt in either veiwe was what I formed my judgment uppon. Supposing noe debt should have been incurred in that time which could possibly have been avoided, the enquiry was of noe use. Taking itt in another veiwe (which I beleive would have been the case) I thought itt very improper to shew the world our nakednesse, People abroad would naturally conclude us very willing the [sic] ruffle the Government when ever wee had opertunity for soe doing, and might from such a notion bee induced to goe into a war, which they would nott have adventured, uppon any other consideration. Creditt has for some time passt been in a sinking condition, and in my opinion would have grown worse, lett people thinke what they will this is our main support, take that away, our case will bee bad, I suppose I shall bee sayd to bee turned Courtier, butt I despise every suggestion of that kind, I never was for a ministry because they are soe, nor will I bee against them as such, which to deale plainly, was in my opinion the foundation of this matter. I contented my selfe with giving my vote, without speaking in the debate, the Toryes were generally with the minority, some few, butt nott many Whigs. You may perhaps bee surprizd by our votes, which you have and will see, whereby itt will appeare wee raise above three millions,[860] till you understand the matter, for above one third of itt is onely turning as much which wee owe into another shape, and this alteration is apparently a great saving to the nation, twere too long to enter into the detaile of itt, butt assure your selfe tis soe. I am told by an eminent merchant, whose correspondence is great and very good, that they are of opinion that there is noe likelyhood of the Empire or Spaine going into a war this yeare, whatever they may doe hereafter, for which they give this good reason, that they are in noe measure prepard for itt, I am fully perswaded wee shall nott bee the aggressors, for tis very plaine, that whatever our house sayes, wee are nott inclinable to itt, and I thinke twill bee in noe bodyes power to reconcile a majority to itt.

When ever it happens I am confident Portugal will nott bee partyes; they will find great advantages by a neutrality, and are nott overfond of rendering Spaine more considerable then itt is. The Dutch had long under consideration the same point, wherein their East Trade turned the ballance.

The Attorney Generall told mee that the three last Irish Bills were to bee reported this day. I thinke wee are winding up our bottoms as fast as wee can.

---

[857] Confirmed in *Knatchbull Diary*, 50. However, Cobbett, *Parl. Hist.*, viii, col. 501, attributes the motion to William Pulteney, and states that Daniel Pulteney seconded.

[858] 262–89 (*CJ*, xx, 566).

[859] Reports stated that there were 15 whigs in the minority (HMC, *Portland MSS*, vii, 423; Yale University, Sterling Library, MS 114: Delafaye to Richard West, 15 Feb. 1726).

[860] By now the committee of supply had reported three times, on 29 Jan., 7 Feb. and 10 Feb. The specific sums voted amounted to slightly less than £2,000,000, of which just under £1,000,000 was appropriated to paying off uncancelled exchequer bills. (*CJ*, xx, 558, 564, 567.)

Since writing I have been in company with a very knowing and considerable Tory (butt a Hanoverian) whoe desired mee to explaine the motion, which I did, and told him what induced mee to vote as I did, his answer was,

This is a very Ticklish time, I thinke you judged the matter perfectly right, for itt could now bee of noe use, butt might bee attended with fatall consequences, especially for that the commencement of the enquiry was to bee from the Kings accession to the Crowne. This was in my mind during the debate, and if I had spoake I should have mentioned itt, butt considering how apparent it was what would bee the successe of the question I was unwilling to say any thing of this kind, considering that some whoe had argued for the question are I am very sure as heartily in his Majestys interest as any subject hee has.

729. *Thomas to Alan I, Dublin, 19 Feb. 1725[/6]*

(1248/6/379–80)

The last long day of the Session I hope is over, Thursday in both houses the severall Treatyes.[861] The question for an Addresse (which you will see) upon a division of the Lords (att past six) was carryd ninety five against Fifteen.[862]

The Comons devided att ten 285 against 107.[863] Twas well debated on each side, all that could bee sayd was.

Your Bills being all gone, I suppose your Session will soone end, butt I beleive ours sooner, or in a very little time after itt.[864] Tis wrote from your side, that you will have a very full house and of a different temper from what they parted in, soe that little doubt is made of carrying that maine point (in another shape), which before they had rejected. I know assurances equally strong have been already given which have failed, as I beleive and hope these will.

I was told by a member of our house (whoe came nott long since out of Ireland) that a gentleman was come over whoe carryd a message to the Castle from Mr W[*alpole*] to the effect following, That if the house would nott come into what was expected, Hee and his party would change sides, by coming over.

I sayd (supposing the fact true) twould certainly make a difference of two, butt the word party I supposed signifyed very little for that I never heard hee had any; and thus wee parted, butt I must make this remarke, that after a good deale of blustering, I thought his last words shewd more despair then hope. Wee have taken a leape in the darke, if our vigorous resolutions prevent a war twill bee happy, butt if wee are att last forct into one, I thinke no man can foresee how twill end. Lett mee know when wee may hope to see you.

---

[861] The treaties between Austria and Spain (Apr. 1725) and Britain and Prussia (Sept. 1725), laid before parliament on the king's order and debated on Thursday, 17 Feb. in a committee of the whole house of lords, and on the floor of the Commons (*LJ*, xxii, 596–7; *CJ*, xx, 572–82).

[862] A vote for a resolution to address: Sainty and Dewar, microfiche gives the figures as 94 against 14, though another contemporary report also states the minority at 15 (Yale Univ., Sterling Lib., MS 114: Charles Delafaye to Richard West, 17 Feb. 1726).

[863] A vote for an address, the figures confirmed in *CJ*, xx, 582. Thomas was not appointed to the committee to prepare the address.

[864] The Irish parliamentary session ended on 8 Mar. 1726; the British not until 24 May.

730. *Alan I, Dublin, to Thomas, 26 Feb. 1725[/6]*

(1248/6/381–6)

I have yours of the nineteenth, and write this in answer cheifly to one paragraph of it, which is in the words following viz. It is wrote from your side that you will have a very full house, and of a different temper from what they parted in: soe that little doubt is made of carrying that main point (in another shape) which before they had rejected.

It is most certain that some people had very good ground for saying there would be a very full house; for it is beyond dispute all diligence was used to have a general rendezvous of all the troops that might be depended upon, and to doe them justice I cannot on the best enquiry find that any of those who it might be hoped would think otherwise now then they had done at the beginning of the Session, failed to be in town on Thursday; where sicknesse or other inevitable accident did not prevent their coming up. A freind of yours who was concerned by your means under the Lady who founded a school etc[865] hath justly deserved great applause for his successeful endeavours with his freinds to make their appearance for he was soe fortunate that I doe not think one individual man of his quota failed. But it happened unfortunately that several Gentlemen of real worth had occasions to goe out of town, very soon before the day the Parliament was adjourned to particularly Sir Arthur Gore, and Harry Brooke; and it also fell out soe that a good many Gentlemen whose estates lye in the more distant parts of the Kingdome, did not come to town at the time to which the Parliament was first adjourned; but (as they declared) they resolved to come up at the time when they should be informed by their freinds businesse would come on. In this number I reckon Col Hassett,[866] the honest son of an honest father (your old freind Jack Hassett of the County of Kerry[867]) and Sir Maurice Crosbye; and a good many of the County of Corke, as Redmond Barry, Anthony Jephson and Will Casaubon; all which I am satisfyed were wrote to by their freinds, and had prepared all things ready to begin their journey upon the first summons or notice from their correspondents. But no one of these five Gentlemen came up, whether for want of being written to, or for want of their letters coming in time to their hands I cannot tell, and am unwilling to suspect there was any neglect in the post Offices in the Countrey, if I could reconcile soe charitable a supposition with the characters of the Gentlemen who affirm they sent such letters, or with the honour of those to whom they were wrote, who (if they received them) broke their engagements to their freinds in not coming up upon receit of those letters. But be that matter how it will, certain it is that there appeared a very full house on Thursday last, who agreed upon an Addresse to his Majestye of which I hope to be able to give you a copy under the same cover with this.[868] But perhaps it may not be amisse to acquaint you with some things which passed before that time, since I think the knowledge of them will in some measure contribute to your better understanding the views and managements which seem to have been entertained and used in this affair. It was beleived that his Majestyes answer to the

---

[865] Lady Orkney, who founded the charity school at Midleton.

[866] John Blenerhassett, MP [I].

[867] John Blenerhassett (1665–1709), of Ballyseedy, Co. Kerry, MP [I] 1692–1709.

[868] On Thursday 24 Feb. the Irish house of commons agreed an address of thanks for the king's answer to their previous address (*CJI*, v, 387–8).

Addresse of the house of Commons congratulating his safe return etc and promising all that was contained in that Addresse come to Dublin by an expresse who arrived here on Thursday 10 February, but it was not owned soe early (unlesse to those who are in the greatest confidence, and in the secret of affairs) till a good while after: However it soe hapned that some who had the favor to know what it was, were too much elated with the honour done them in being made privy to that which others were kept in the dark of, not to give it to be understood that they were no strangers to it, and at length Gentlemen heard that in the Coffee houses which others knew sooner, and this (you must think) was not very agreeable to a good many to have such a difference made between them, in favour of men whom they did not think their superiors in any other respect. On Thursday 17th February the Parliament mett and it was (I hear) generally expected that the Secretary would have brought his Majestyes answer to the house of Commons; nay people went soe far in their conjectures as to beleive Mr Clutterbuck had his Majestyes most gracious answer in his pockett, and were a good deal surprised to find that the message he had to the house was only from the Lord Lieutenant, that it was his pleasure the house should adjourn till the 24th.[869] I heard some of those who expressed themselves resolved to continue in the same sentiments as they were before the recesse, say that they beleived there was a discretionary power left somewhere, either to have reported his Majestyes most gracious answer to the house on that day, or not, according to the opinion the persons confided in had of the complexion of the house: If this was the order, it is probable the great number of country Gentlemen who did appear beyond what was expected as it gave a deal of spirit to one side, soe it might a little check the assurances which others had framed to themselves and probably given at another place that things would goe entirely to their wishes; but the event was that no answer was then communicated to the house.

Whether the men of counsel judged right in postponing the matter (if all things were ready) or not, I will not too hastily give my opinion; for on the one hand those who were lately come out of the countrey seemed to be full of a sense what the countrey expected from them, and not inclined to doe any thing which should alter what they had done in the former part of the Session, or suffer that point to be carryed (in another shape) now, which they had on mature debate and deliberacion rejected in a full house. He would have been a bold man who would advise the bringing such a point to a decision till he had full orders, since there was a latitude (as was supposed) either to bring it on then or at a future time as discretion should direct; and a wise man would not make himself liable to censure for bringing it then on, if should not succeed. If I were to give my own thoughts, I confesse it seems to me that the diffidence which not doing it at that time shewed; did in some measure animate the opposite party, and give the freinds of the mocion intended to be made some diffidence of the successe, and I observed from that instant and I fancy from that cause *Ex illo fluere et retro sublapsa referris Res Danaum*.[870] But others say they beleive my Lord Lieutenant had not given any discretionary power to his Secretary but was either advised, or resolved of himself to try what influence his speaking to the members might have. It was thought that very few of the members had not been spoken to separately, I beleive hardly any except that number who voted for the words (present administracion)

---

[869] Confirmed in *CJI*, v, 387.

[870] Virgil, *Aeneid*, ii, 169: '*ex illo fluere ac retro sublapsa referri spes Danaum*' (From that time the hopes of the Greeks ebbed, and gliding away, were carried back).

being added to the addresse; and they I think were men of whom there was no expectacion. On Saturday 19 February I hear there met the number of 44 at the Castle, to whom his Majestyes most gracious answer to the Addresse was imparted, and your freind Anthony Shephead[871] (being then at the Castle on another occasion) was carryed in to or went in with the rest; but he hapned not to be wholly convinced of the reasonablenesse of coming to any resolution what addresse it was fit to make to his Majestye upon the occasion which ought in his sense to be debated and settled in the house. On Sunday the 20th I went to the Castle and having heard this story, I hinted to [*Carteret*] that I doubted making distinctions between Gentlemen by intrusting some with early knowledge of his Majestyes answer then others, to whom it was equally intended would not be well taken: by which I meant no more then that in prudence it should not have been shewn at all to particular persons of any kind till it was sent to the house. But whether what I said occasioned it, or whether it had another rise (as I beleive it had) [*Carteret*] caused Mr C[*lutterbuck*] to write letters to the members in town to meet at the Castle on Wednesday at seven in the evening; the Speaker and most of the members in town were there at the time appointed; but those of opposite sentiments to what was in agitacion, before their going thither, had talked together (or (to say it more truly) some of them had discoursed how far their appearing would be expedient, or was fitting. And as I hear they seemed to think it would be proper to goe, and after hearing and observing what passed and was proposed to declare one by one to a good number (about 7 or 8) in expresse terms that they did not like meeting to resolve on what was to be done in the house of Commons after maturely considering and throughly debating the matter, to which end they resolved to reserve themselves till they came into the house without coming there to any resolution, or declaring their then thoughts of what was proposed: But there was no room left for their doing this, by my Lord Lieutenants rising from his chair soon after he had ended the discourse which he made to the assembly without staying for the approbacion of any one of that great number, which several were ready to have given. Suspicious people fancy that some way or other the resolution taken by others of declaring as I have mentioned before, might have been carryed to the Castle and occasioned this conduct.

I was out of town when the meeting was at the Castle but heard it from one who was present, that things passed in this maner. The Speaker and members were carryed to the Councel chamber, and after they had been some time there the Lord Lieutenant came in and sate down at the upper end of a table, the members standing about the room. His Excellencye I hear in a very handsome maner opened to them the scituation of affairs abroad, and what the British Parliament had done; hinted that there might be reason to apprehend danger to this part of his Majestyes dominions in case of a rupture with the Emperor and Spain; but that he was not allowed to impart any thing particularly relating to this Kingdome, but seemed to insinuate there might be designs on us. That the way to prevent mischeif was to be provided against it if it should be attempted. That the force of Britain was but 18000 Men, and that of Ireland only 12000; that it would be reasonable to have them in readinesse for immediate service, but that there was due to the Officers of the Army to clear them no lesse then 22 months and 14 months to the half pay Officers.

He did not think anybody expected that they should raise money this Session to pay them such arrears, but that a trivial summe of about £8400 to be allowed as interest till the

---

[871] Anthony Sheppard, MP [I].

end of the two years for which the funds already given, would answer the emergencye and enable them etc which was such a trifle that he hoped no one Gentleman would scruple coming into, since it was to cease when the arrears should be paid off, which the Parliament judged would be done in two years. I am sensible I have delivered what I was told he spoke in a maner very far short of the accurate way in which he expressed himself: and mencion this to let you know that I am very far from meaning he used the expressions I have wrote or any one of them, nor am to account for them as if I said he said soe: but to the best of my sense the words I have wrote contain the sense of what I was told.

Having spoke he rose from his chair and used everybody in the handsomest maner, and several Gentlemen staid to drink his Majestyes health and eat a fine cold supper which was prepared. I cannot but think one great reason which might incline the Secretary not to deliver the message on the 17th, if he had a power to doe soe; was because he beleived a speech from his Excellencye with the advantages he gives everything he saith by the addresse and maner of his delivery might and probably would have good effect; and thus far the Secretary judged right, that it had great weight and influence on a good many Gentlemen, as I have been assured.

The Kings answer was laid before the house on 24th, and a mocion was made that the house addresse his Majestye to thank him for his gracious answer, but I have not the words of the resolucion as it was first moved by Mr Singleton,[872] but am promised it, and if I get it will enclose it under this cover. The substance was thought by some to be the very thing which your letter calls the main point (in another shape) which was rejected last Session. viz. That the money which remained unpaid to the Army but had been provided for by Parliament should be provided by the Kingdome once again.[873] The shape it was put in was that a summe of £8400 should be paid as interest for the debt due to the Army at such a time, till the principal should be raised out of the additional dutyes given this Session. This Gentlemen apprehended to be directly opposite to the resolucion that the money given was sufficient to pay the Army etc their meaning being not to provide it again if it had been misapplyed; and therefore they would not hear of the word interest standing a part of the resolucion, which must imply that they who agreed to pay the interest knew they were debtors for the principal, which they were sure they in noe sort were: they also apprehended from the way of debating used by some who were for the resolucion, that it was never intended to pay off that money by the Treasury but to have the annual interest of it to be charged as an increase to the establishment and consequently to be provided for every Session: by which means we were like to create such a load of debt on our selves as we should never be able to pay off. The word circulating the Officers warrants for their arrears which the Collector of Corke (Mr Maynard)[874] unadvisedly dropt made the thing better understood, and the bottom of the design to be beleived by a great many who did

---

[872] Henry Singleton, who subsequently chaired the committee to prepare the address (*CJI*, v, 388–9). St John Brodrick III was fourth-named to the committee.

[873] The resolution, as passed, emphasised members' 'zeal for His Majesty's sacred person and government, and … our firm resolution to promote such measures as the present situation and exigency of affairs may make it necessary to enter into', before agreeing that a sum of £10,000 from the current supply should be applied to clearing army warrants from 1 July 1724 to 30 June 1725, and providing for half-pay officers, and promising to make good any deficiency from the supply granted in the following session (*CJI*, v, 388).

[874] William Maynard, MP [I].

not before understand the tendency of what was moved and designed. Your Nephew[875] and some others had the night before come to a resolution that it would be advisable to doe something, considering what the house had promised by their addresse, and how artfully the ministry had laid hold of their assurances in framing his Majestyes answer. And determined to goe into that very summe which the house afterward came into, but resolved not to shew their intent early in the debate but by standing off to give the other side an oportunitye and to lay them under a necessitye of explaining themselves, which they did in so open a maner that every body saw the drift of the resolucion moved was to own the arrear due to the officers to be the debt of the nation, and that that debt should be turned into a stock and capable of being negotiated till the principal should be paid, which neither the Officers of the Army nor they who bought the arrears would ever be overpressing to have paid in, nor would the Governement make it their affair to doe it, nor would the nation probably grow soon into such condicion as to be able to doe it, so that it would increase our charge and introduce that ruinous way of taking up money at interest to support our establishment; This management had its intended effect to oblige the [*Speaker's*] people to explain them selves, but had another viz. that it gave an oportunitye to Mr Tho: Bourke[876] to make a mocion viz. to desire the King to give directions for the paiment of a summe not exceeding £10000 to be paid (or I think given) to the Officers of the Army and half pay officers, rather then have the word interest mentioned in the resolucion. Mr Maynard truly was soe very good an husband of the publick money that he was against giving £1600 more then was necessary, because no more was asked but £8400 which would arise out of the funds already given within two years. But the house were not so good husbands of the publick money nor soe great Patriots as that worthy Gentleman was, but said jocularly they would not goe so near the wind as he was for going; messages went from the house to the — and answers came to the persons confided in; at length Mr Collector who had used the term circulating, was pleased to say he would come into the assurances given for providing in the next aids for the paiment of the £10000 only desired it might be mentioned as a praemium to the Officers. Whether this proceeded from an old memory of that word which he frequently had heard in Exchange Ally in the South sea time,[877] or whether any of the messengers gave the hints that the word might be of use to the great design of this whole affair viz. to make this debt a circulating stock capable of being sold I know not; but the house did not like either circulating or praemium: and some proposed it should be called a bounty to the Officers but that word was as much disliked by the circulators and praemium men as the later terms were disliked by the men of bounty.

Soe that neither praemium nor bounty are any part of the resolution or addresse. The question passed unanimously, for indeed nobody ever intended to oppose giving the Officers a little ready money out of the Treasury, which might have been with some colour imputed to them as a token of disaffection to render it impossible for such regiments to march as might be found necessary to be employd immediately on service. I mentioned

---

[875] St John III.

[876] Thomas Burgh, MP [I].

[877] An alleyway in the City of London connecting Cornhill (where the Royal Exchange was situated) and Lombard Street. The coffee-houses on Exchange Alley, particularly Jonathan's and Garraway's, were a frequent resort of stock-jobbers.

above that Mr Bourke made the motion but must add that Mr Agmondisham Vesey was actually up at the same time with Mr Bourke, but the later was first up in the Sp[*eaker*]s eye (for V[*esey*] had been all along during this Session warm against the Kingdomes paying the money that had been misemployed). And soe the matter ended as we pretend to the great satisfaction of every body; each side say they have attained their end. But if I could send you the question first moved by Mr Singleton, and you will give yourself the trouble of comparing that and the resolucion and addresse together you will see whether the proposed end hath been attained. A fund of interest was in the question as proposed and circulating the Officers warrants was mentioned in the debate and in view and yet I doubt neither the one nor the other have been gone into, and indeed I cannot be of opinion that this resolucion or addresse will enable the Officers to take up more then £10000 in present; tho some people say they apprehend otherwise from some words contained in my Lord Lieutenants answer to the house of Commons yesterday when they delivered their addresse. But I have not seen his answer and consequently cannot form any judgement what his opinion may be on that point; but it will depend a good deal on the construction which those who are to part with their money give the addresse of what the Commons have engaged to make good in the next aids.

731. *Thomas to Alan I, Dublin, 3 Mar. 1725/6*

(1248/6/387–8)

Yesterday I receivd yours of the 18th of last month, and (att the house this morning) told Sir R[*obert*] W[*alpole*] what you had been informed, hee sayd your intelligencer was extremely mistaken, for that from the first moment hee heard of the words <u>Present Administration</u> hee understood itt as the truth of the fact was; I then told him that your letter giving an account of that transaction had been kept from my hands (as many others have) and the letter which came yesterday opened, his answer was, depend uppon my word neither the one nor the other is done on this side. Hee then told mee hee would tomorrow shew mee a representation (having left itt att Chelsea)[878] uppon the construction of the English Act[879] about which my nephew[880] wrote to mee last year, and askt whither I thought a short Bill to rectifie, were best to begin in the Lords house or ours, I was for the former, and soe I thinke twill bee. I see nott the least probabillity of setting the farme in your absence, for which as well as other reasons I wish you would come over assoone as conveniently you can.

The Spanish Minister att the Hague has deliverd a Memoriall reciting a memoriall given in here, about four or five years since (by his Masters order) against the Ostend Company, which hee desires may bee annext to that now deliverd, for that hee was still of the same opinion, and would act accordingly, you see our bullying has had a good effect, for the

---

[878] Walpole's town house was in Paradise Row, Chelsea.
[879] The Declaratory Act of 1720 (6 Geo. I, c. 5 [GB]).
[880] St John III.

danger of a war is over … Wee shall carry our bridge att Putney against all the opposition the citty or any others can give.[881]

732. *Thomas to Alan I, Dublin, 8 Mar. 1725/6*[882]

(1248/6/389–90)

I received yesterday yours of this day sennight date, opened as usually, where this practice has been carryd on, my last informed you, and that from a very good hand.

This trade has been too long driven on your side to bee soone left of, which perhaps they may hear of from hence, I shall nott scruple mentioning itt the first fair opertunity. I long for your letter by the private hand, because though I am told in generall, the result of the debate, I should bee very glad to know the particulars.

Uppon the death of the D[uke] of Kingston[883] the Coffee house pollititians gave the Privy Seale to Lord C[arteret] butt the King yesterday declard Lord Trevor; and Lord Godolphin to have the Garter. Lord Forbes told mee in the house that hee beleivd Mr Coakely[884] might have my letter, hee sayes hee came to towne last night. I saw Sir Robt Rich in the house, butt twas soe full (on account of Wallers petition against Captain Collyer[885]) that I could nott come to him, and did nott care to stay during a long debate, for I am by noe meanes well; lett them brew as they bake.

I thinke going into Munster will nott bee losse of much time, since your journy from Bristoll will bee shorter, and the road better then from Chester, I hope your stay wont bee long. The papers which Sir R[obert] W[alpole] sayd hee would shew mee, were nott (as hee thought) att Chelsea, butt given to the D[uke] of Newcastle; hee tells mee Lord T[ownshend] is for beginning in our house, whither twere a compliment to mee to make the motion, I know nott, butt I shall willingly undergoe the trouble, in order to have the thing done.

733. *Alan I, Dublin, to Thomas, 9 Mar. 1725[/6]*

(1248/6/391–4)

I have your letter of the third in which you mention the receit of mine of the 18th of February; which you say had been long kept from your hands. I cannot tell whether that

---

[881] The Fulham and Putney Bridge Bill was passed by the Commons on 10 May (*CJ*, xx, 696), and eventually reached the statute book as 12 Geo. I, c. 36 [GB]. Thomas Brodrick had chaired the committee investigating the original petition from gentlemen, freeholders and inhabitants of Middlesex. and Surrey for a bridge to replace the ferry crossing, from which he reported on 2 Mar. (*CJ*, xx, 596–7). He was not, however, present when the resultant bill was committed on 14 Apr. (*CJ*, xx, 665).

[882] Letter endorsed by Alan I: 'Tho: Brodrick … hath received mine of 1 March by the post (opened) longs for the account I mention in it by a private hand (Barrington) of what passed on the mocion for a fund of interest for the Officers arrears'.

[883] On 5 Mar. 1726 (BL, Add. MS 47031, f. 114: Daniel Dering to Lord Perceval, 7 Mar. 1725/6).

[884] Caesar Colclough, MP [I], who was seeking a private act of the Westminster parliament to break the entail on part of his estate (*Hist. Ir. Parl.*, iii, 447–8).

[885] The petition of Harry Waller (c. 1701–1772), of Grosvenor St., London, against the return of Charles Colyear (1700–85), Viscount Milsington, of Weybridge, Surrey, at a by-election for Chipping Wycombe. Waller was seated on 17 Mar. (*HC 1715–54*, i, 197–8.)

letter went by post or by a private hand; but I think it was by my Lord D.[886] which may in some sort account for its being longer on the road then it might have been if I had sent it by post. You also own the receit of one from me which came to your hand on the day before your writing to me, and was opened. I am in noe sort surprized at that, for no longer then since Monday morning, I was told by my servant whom I sent to the Post Office for my letters which I expected from London by the pacquet which came in on Sunday night, that the answer he received at the Office was that they were soe busy there in looking over papers that he could not have my letters (if I had any) in lesse time then an hour and half after, when he was desired to call again. I make my own judgement where the letters were at that time, and what was doing with them. These are little methods and shew that there is a good deal of uneasinesse and jealousy somewhere, least things may be shewn in another light by others then they have been by ourselves.

The Session is ended, and I think I may truly say to mutual satisfaction, for I really think the houses were as desirous to have things over as the Court: and both sides give themselves airs of being highly delighted with the successe and event of things. When I am informed by those who can tell me I will intimate to you which those bills are which have passed this Session that will contribute to the advancement of the Protestant religion, to the peace and tranquillitye of the Countrey and to the preservation and increase of trade. I suppose that to prevent running goods is meant by the last words,[887] for as matters were ordered between North Britain and the Isle of Man and the North part of Ireland I am told the fair trader could not possibly live and pay the duty, being undersold by those who seldome or never paid any. The Sherifs bill which is particularly mentioned in my Lord Lieutenants speech, will (I hope and beleive) prove useful to the Kingdome,[888] I wish I could say my thoughts were the same of all which our men of businesse had under consideration this Session. That of the poor house in this town and for regulating the deceits of Bakers were soe altered on your side of the water that the Commons who prepared the heads of them, say they would have been of worse consequence, then being without them, would leave them. Therefore they rejected both.[889] There was a great tax laid on the Inhabitants of Dublin by the former, and such taxes imposed by it as raised a very considerable annual income; which had been for upward of twenty years under the management and direction of those who were Governours of the poor house and work house. It was expected we should have been free from poor, and vagabonds and idlers, and that they would have been employed and supported by the poor house; but when a Committee of the house of Commons enquired into the management they found that the direction of the whole had fallen into the hands of some of the City, which had not been soe careful of their trust as they might have been; that a summe of money amounting to some thousands of pounds had fallen into the hands of a nephew of one of the Aldermen who had been employed (with taking securitye from

[886] John Bligh, 1st earl of Darnley (see Appendix 3).

[887] Presumably Alan means the bill 'to prevent the fraudulent and clandestine importing of goods' (enacted as 12 Geo. I, c. 2 [I]) (ILD).

[888] The bill 'for the better regulating the offices of sheriffs ...' (enacted as 12 Geo. I, c. 4 [I]) (ILD).

[889] The Dublin Workhouse Bill and the bill 'for preventing several abuses committed by millers, bakers and farmers'; both dropped in committee (*CJI*, v, 401–2, 405–6).

him to account for what came to his hands) and stepped aside.[890] The Commons altered the persons who were Governors formerly, and instead of making all the Aldermen and Sherifs Peers (who are of a Lower degree then Aldermen)[891] to be of the Governors, only left the Lord Mayor Sherifs, and fowre or five of the Aldermen of best character and figure by name and added to them several other persons of worth; they made no application to the Commons that they might be continued (as formerly) because their former management hardly left them room to hope for successe. But they petitioned the Councel to have all the Aldermen and Sherifs Peers inserted in the bill to be transmitted, and in answer to the objection made of their not having applyed to the Commons, said with a grave face that they had not time to doe it. But the Councel had more respect to the Commons then to the Aldermen and Sherifs Peers and were not inclined to vary from what the Commons had agreed upon; But the peticioners resolved to try their hand on your side, and did it with such successe that it came over, as they desired; but to their great mortification the Commons chose to reject the bill rather then to continue the tax under the management and in the hands where it would have been placed if the bill had passed,[892] which was originally a Job and contrivance of one now in his Grave, who shal be namelesse (for that reason) and hath served since to enable people to reward dependants and underlings, and been (I think) of little or no publick good. The Poor never were so numerous nor the Streets so thronged with idlers and vagabonds to my observation, as since that bill first passed.

We may hereafter have time to think of and digest things soe that there may be a Law for erecting a work house to employ vagrants and sturdy beggars and breed up children to work. And we may also think of a better scheme for the releif of the poor, then by making one Common fund for their support and carrying on the work house, which was one of the great defects of the former bill. You will have my Lord Lieutenants speech in the prints, in which you cannot but observe these words (whereby you have enabled his Majestye etc to give an immediate credit to the warrants for clearing the Army etc[893]). Before this can reach you, in all probabilitye you will have received a letter of two or three sheets sent by Mr B.[894] who left Dublin above ten dayes since, and you will then be able to judge for yourself whether what the Commons did (for which they are thanked in that paragraph) was intended by them for that end which the Speech seems to take it in. To that letter I refer you and will not inlarge here, for any other persons informacion … I cannot yet ascertain the time when I may hope to be in England, for I think it will be necessary for me first to take a journey into Munster …

---

[890] The committee had included St John Brodrick III (*CJI*, v, 254).

[891] Those who had served as sheriff of the city but had not subsequently been elected to the board of aldermen: their representatives formed a separate cohort ('the 48') in the common council (Jacqueline Hill, *From Patriots to Unionists: Dublin Civic Politics and Irish Protestant Patriotism, 1660–1840* (Oxford, 1997), 43, 129).

[892] The bill for the better regulating the workhouse of Dublin was amended at the British privy council and rejected by the Irish house of commons on its return (ILD).

[893] On closing the session on 8 Mar. Wording confirmed in *CJI*, v, 411.

[894] John Barrington (1666–1756), of Castlewood and Cullenagh, Queen's Co., MP [I] 1692–1714, 1727–*d*.

734. *Alan II, London, to Alan I, Dublin, 10 Mar. 1725/6*[895]

(1248/6/395–6)

I am ordered by my Uncle, (who has a great inflammation in his Leg, which is so painfull to Him that He can not write himself) to own the receipt of your Lordships long Letter to Him; and am commanded to say that He is very glad to find that every body is contented, and that the resolution lately taken in the House of Commons of Ireland, is such as gives both sides the Satisfaction of having obtained their Ends. He for his part thinks that there cou'd not have been a more proper Medium found out, and says that He can see no advantage obtained on either Side, unless it be by appropriating ten thousand Pounds, (part of a Supply granted in the former part of the Session) to the payment of the Army, preferably to the discharging Pensions or any other way of spending that Summ. He bids me moreover tell your Lordship that He will write to You as soon as He is able, and says that He by last post let You know of the Duke of Kingston's Death, and that He is succeeded by Lord Trevor in the Office of Lord Privy Seal. It is said now that the Garter vacant by his Death will be given to Lord Godolphin, and this I think the only peice of News to be picked up in London.

I am overjoyed to hear that your Lordship is so well, as I am informed You are by a Gentleman who saw You within these ten days …

735. *Alan I to Thomas, Westminster, 17 Mar. 1725[/6]*

(1248/6/397–8)

I am sorry to find by yours of the 8th that you were at that time out of order, and by your Nephews[896] of the 10th that it hath ended in soe greivous and dangerous a distemper as an inflammacion in your Leg. I think you are in the right when you agree with those here who doe not think the end designed by the mocion was attained viz. the fixing the original debt (which is certainly unpaid to the Officers) upon the countrey, as the granting them an interest for it would have plainly done if it had been gone into. On the other hand I doe not see that we have appropriated £10000 of the fund last given toward the paiment of the Officers arrears, the addresse being to pay them so much over and above their arrears due, soe that it is really a boon of £10000 instead of granting a fund of interest; which puts me in mind of a short Epigram in Martial.

Dimidium donare Lino, quam credere totum
Qui mavult, mavult perdere Dimidium.[897]

I need not english the two lines, but it is what you have I am confident practiced more then once, at least I am sure I have chosen to give five pounds to a man who would needs

---

[895] Letter endorsed by Alan I: 'Nally … that my brother hath an inflammation in his Leg, but hath received my letter (sent by Mr Barrington) giving an account of what the Commons had done on the mocion to give a fund of interest for the Officers arrears which he thinks is in no sort what Lord C. would have it beleived'.

[896] Alan II.

[897] Martial, *Epigrams*, i, 75: He who prefers to give Linus half rather than trust him with the whole, prefers to lose the half.

borrow ten of me rather then lend him ten upon promise of payment ... Let me have ... an account of your motions, and whether you intend for the Bath this Spring; for it is very possible we may make that our way to Peperhara. I long to see you, but must tell you that you will meet me in a worse state of health then I have formerly been.

736. *Thomas to Alan I, Dublin, 19 Mar. 1725/6*

(1248/6/401–2)

Yesterday I receivd yours of the 9th. I desired my nephews letting you know I had your long letter by Mr B[arrington] whoe had the ill luck to bee six days between Dublin and Hollyhead, becalmed all the time, the weather foggy to a great degree.

The French King caused Te Deum to bee sung after the battail of Ramelies,[898] others give themselves like airs, lett them goe on, for whilst the Kingdom can bee free from the designed cheats, itt matters nott (in reallity) what colour is putt on things.

Lottery Tickets (in the Ally) are att discount, butt I doe nott thinke buying ... there, advisable, the reason (as I apprehend) of the discount is this, People in that good place promising themselves profitt by a rise uppon Tickets have ingrosed a great number, the second payment draws near, and chapmen nott coming in as fast as they expected, putts them under a necessity of selling, in order to make the second payment to avoid loosing the first, I doe nott thinke itt improbable butt that the sellers after receiving good sumes of mony (many of them Bears,[899] id est, such as have noe tickets) may walke of, I will one way or other secure the six Tickets, lett mee know to whom they shall be deliverd, att least to whom I shall give an account of the numbers.

I am pretty well recoverd, butt nott yett gott out.

[PS] There is good reason to beleive (from the account brought by an Expresse) that the Zarina will accede to the Hanover Treaty.[900]

737. *Thomas to Alan I, Dublin, 26 Mar. 1726*

(1248/7/1–2)

Yesterday I receivd yours of the 17th. Two long days successively (yesterday till past seven) have been very hard uppon mee, butt I thought my attendance advisable; youl see in the votes our Addresse, which probably will bee deliverd this day; uppon a division the Yeas were 270. Noes 89[901] ... I hope to bee att Bath this season, butt att what time I cannott

---

[898] Marlborough's victory over the French forces at Ramillies on 23 May N.S. 1706. The *Observator*, 26–29 June 1706, commented that the duke 'has a dreadful enemy to engage, an enemy that, how much soever he be beaten, will cry Victoria and sing Te Deum'.

[899] One speculating for a fall in the value of stock.

[900] The Treaty of Hanover concluded in September 1725 between Britain and Prussia. The United Provinces and Sweden acceded to the treaty in 1726 and 1727 respectively, but Russia, then governed by Catherine I (1684–1727), widow of Peter the Great, did not.

[901] The address agreed on 25 Mar., and presented on the following day, in response to a message from the king concerning the increase in naval manpower and the need to make alliances and take other measures for the security of Britain's trade and the peace of Europe. The figures on the division are confirmed in *CJ*, xx, 640.

yett make a judgment. The inflamation in my leg is gone of, and the swelling almost (tho nott quite) abated. I am sorry to hear what you say of your selfe, Mr Coakely told mee hee thought you as well and hearty as you had been in seven years past.

I still continue my opinion, that wee shall have noe war, and thinke preparing the likelyest way to avoid itt. This will in great measure depend uppon the answer the Court of Madrid shall give our Minister,[902] whoe is ordered to demand a categoricall answer to severall points, our squadron for the West Indies will probably incline them to give such as well bee satisfactory.[903]

738. *Alan I, Dublin, to Thomas, 27 Mar. 1726*

(1248/7/3–6)

Tho several pacquets have come in lately, it hath not been my fortune to receive a line from you or any other of my freinds: Perhaps you have given over writing in expectation of our having left Dublin by this time; but this I can hardly beleive to be the cause of your silence, because I have in a former letter desired an answer to this question whether you intended to spend the Spring season at the Bath. I must now repeat my request to have your answer to that particular, and that you would ascertain the time you intend to be there: For your sister and I resolve to go directly to that place before we goe toward London; and hope to sail about the fifteenth of April for Chester … My Lord Lieutenant saith he resolves to go off hence tomorrow; I have already taken my leave of him, resolving not to be at the Councel when he declares the Justices in whose hands his Majestyes hath directed the Governement of the Kingdome to be put during his absence: I make noe doubt all things will be done during their Administration entirely to the satisfaction of his Majestye and of those who commended them to that great trust.

On Thursday I waited on my Lord Lieutenant and found by him (notwithstanding the good airs he hath given himself in relation to the closing the late Session of Parliament) that stil things have not been entirely to his mind. And he was soe free to tell me he would expostulate with me upon that subject in England, but that it should be before you; I told him I knew not that man upon earth before whom I should lesse desire to have it done then you, if I were not certain that I could give convincing proofs of any reasonable man that I had acted toward him, and indeed in every respect during the Session as I ought. But by his maner I plainly perceived that I am to be blamed, as greatly in fault, toward the Crown and his Lordship: for he told me as much by saying he expected to be asked by the King how <u>his freind</u> Lord Midleton had behaved; to which he should be obliged with some confusion of face to say indeed Lord M[idleton] was very well affected to his Majestyes person and house and the interests of the Crown, but was a man of great passions, and had through resentment taken a part since laying down the Seal, which he did not expect from him etc. He enlarged on having endeavoured to prevent my laying down; which is indeed true (for he did soe)

---

[902] William Stanhope (c. 1683–1756), MP [GB] 1715–22, 1727–30 and later 1st earl of Harrington; ambassador to Madrid 1721–7.

[903] A squadron of seven men-of-war under the command of Vice-Admiral Francis Hosier, sent to the Caribbean in order to blockade Spanish treasure-ships at Porto Bello (Nicholas Tindal, *The Continuation of Mr. Rapin's History of England* (5th edn, 7 vols, 1761–3), vii, 555, 558).

but his method was this: When I shewed the letters I received from you and from others in England which told me in what maner I was treated upon every occasion; he alway advised me to bear it without taking notice of it: But never was the man who said he either would or had intimated on the other side, that I told him if such ill treatment was continued I would certainly lay down whatever the consequence might be: and that I did tell him soe from time to time I appeal to the letters which I wrote in answer to yours which gave me account how I was used, and what I ought to doe in such circumstances. Soe that I can hardly refrain going now into the sentiments of my freinds here, who fancyed that from the time his Lordship found me unalterable in my resolution to oppose Woods patent (after his landing in Ireland, and using all the methods he could to reconcile people to the receiving £40000 of that trash) he determined and resolved to have a more complaisant person in my place. There is nothing which he more guards against then being thought to have been willing that I should be laid aside; for he would have it beleived to have been a rash and passionate act, and that I lay under no prudential necessitye to doe what I did: but I am soe much of another opinion that I declare, if all things were now in my power that were soe on 29 April last when I laid down I cannot call to mind any one step which I made, that I know how to have made for the better if to be determined upon now.

But enough of this subject: and I forbear to add that he was not at a losse to find out a Successor, the very morning after I had first intimated my resolution to quit viz. the then Cheif Baron Hale, who indeed shewed a very early zeal in Council in the Case of Woods patent and coyne and was highly applauded in my hearing for his very warm behavior in it, not to give it an epithet which I then thought it deserved much better. He told me indeed after my resolution to lay down he had taken other people into his confidence, and transacted publick matters with them (that is certainly soe if it did not begin earlier) and I congratulated him upon his new freinds and wished him joy of them and successe and honour to his Governement while it continued, which he seemed willing to perswade me would possibly be longer then was expected: Nay his freinds seem to expect he will hold another Session here. I know him to be an enterprizing man and of great spirit: but I am willing to beleive soe well of him that he will consider how far such a step may be for his Majestyes service, or his own honour. If he should fail in what he may be advised to undertake, or be ordered to push at, you cannot but think a disappointment may be of very ill consequence to him and you may remember my conjectures what would be the event of several things during the last Session have hardly ever failed to prove true in the end: and I own I much doubt whether it will be for his service to be the person who shal undertake such work as seems to have been cutt out for the next meeting by the motion made for a vote to pay interest for money due to the Army and half pay Officers and the resolution of the Commons thereon to give £10000 in the maner they voted it, and what hath been done since thereupon. I hear his Excellencye yesterday signed orders pursuant to the Kings letter relating to that affair but have not seen any copy of his Majestyes letter or of his Excellencyes orders thereupon; but hope to get both soon, which I will transmit to you. I am advised that great consultation was had with the men confided in and knowing in the Law in what form the orders should be conceived, and that the Prime Serjeant[904]

---

[904] Francis Bernard, MP [I].

Attorney[905] and Sollicitor General[906] were consulted, and have some reason to beleive one of them (at least) was advised with for he owned yesterday upon my asking him the question, that indeed the Kings letter had been laid before him. I confesse the scituation of these Gentlemen in this particular seems to me to be very hard: for as they are extremely well inclined to doe everything that may be for the Kings service, and agreeable to the Governement; soe their great abilityes and capacitye will make it very difficult for them to screen themselves from censure, if they should not be able to find out a temper which will comply with that which they <u>personally</u> know to have been the declared sense of the majoritye of the house of Commons when they came into the vote for £10000 at the passing of which every individual man of those three were present and also that which will be acceptable where they are willing to give satisfaction: I confesse I think they have a very base wind and whether they will be able to steer clear of rocks on one hand or sands on the other I cannot tell. But it pleases me that I am on shore and not concerned in the steerage. It will be an after game which three such prudent men will unwillingly depend on, that possibly matters may be soe ordered before next meeting, that a majoritye may then come to be of another opinion then the majoritye was most certainly of when the house came to that vote. Pray tell me whether I shal bring the £190 (which my son left a Cash note for in my hands for your use) shal be carryed over to you in specie to save exchange. He would have had the money back from me to send by Mr Clutterbuck as (he tells me) you directed him to doe; but that cannot be done: For I yesterday spoke to Clutterbuck in the Councel on that occasion and he very civilly excused himself (after making great professions of being ready to serve you) by telling me he had declined doing the same thing after being sollicited by several, because he travailed with a small retinue etc. Let me know whether I shal carry it in Guineas (which I hope to gett) but then it must be at your risque both by Sea and Land. Say this in expresse terms and I will not fail doing as you direct: but if I should give the money back to Senny to be sent by him (after having given an account by letter that I had received so much money for your use from him and thereby charging myself with it to you) it will be incumbent on me to shew that the person by him to be employed hath made you the payment or else I am still liable. You must before this time know that the Primate Chancellor and Mr Conelye are to be our Justices. This shews that they are mistaken who think the signing the Letter 20th Aug. 1724 about the then Justices obeying the orders received from Court for the circulating £40000 was an unpardonable sin; for Mr Conelye signed that letter as well as the late Chancellor and Lord Shanon,[907] and yet one of the three stands stil in the state of grace. The other two indeed (I doe not think) could hope for pardon, being I doubt hardned impenitent sinners. I doe not by this insinuate that any one of the three hath repented; but it is possible for great men to attone for false steps by greater services performed afterward, and this I am willing to beleive he may have done. I am in a good deal of doubt (considering the time of the year) whether this will overtake you in London or follow you to Newmarkett. But at which place soever it comes to your hand, let me intreat you to answer it without delay. Farewell.

Thus far I wrote in the morning, but have just now received your two letters of the 19th and 22th instant, and one from C[*ourthope*] C[*layton*] of the last dayes date. The singing Te

---

[905] John Rogerson, MP [I].

[906] Thomas Marlay, MP [I].

[907] See above, p. 128.

Deum after the battle of Ramelies is mightly apposite to what you apply it; if the conjecture made of the Czarinas being like to accede to the Hanover treaty be sufficiently founded, it is very good news; for I think it will be impossible we should have any disturbance given to our peace this year at least.

28 March. 8 in the morning. I hear the Drums beat to draw the militia together, so that I think Lord C[*arteret*] will go this day tho the wind be at S. E.[908]

739. *Thomas to Alan I, Dublin, 31 Mar. 1726*

(1248/7/7–8)

Meeting my Lord D[*arnley*] accidentally att Westminster Hall doore, hee told mee hee had a letter from you, which you desired him to deliver to my selfe, tis dated 29th of Jan. and I suppose his Lordship has been in towne more then halfe the time since. The former part relating to Parliamentary affairs your later letters, added to what I heard from others, gave mee fully to understand, and uppon which I have formerly told you my mind. The latter part is wholly new, notwithstanding which I thinke your reasoning soe strong as leaves little roome even for further consideration, butt if I should tell you the reason assigned for dropping a Bill, which I told you twas thought I ought to move for, and bring in, you would much more judge necessary to doe what you hint att, your stay in Ireland will nott allow of doing much in that affair att present, however you may perhaps bee able to doe something preparatory, and this I thinke of very great consequence, which makes mee write this hastily, being ready to gett into my Coach to goe to Kingston Assizes, att the earnest request of Ned Nicholas whoe has a tryall there, I thinke to goe thence to Pepper Hara though I am very ill able to doe itt.

740. *Alan I, Dublin, to Thomas, Westminster, 2 Apr. 1726*

(1248/7/9–10)

I have your letter in which you tell me that the Addresse was carryed in the house of Commons by 270 Yeas against 89 Noes: but I have not yet seen it, soe can only say that (with implicite faith) I congratulate the Yeas on their successe, of which number your maner of writing makes me beleive you made one. If what you have declared and done this Session shal be the means of preventing our being engaged in a war, your measures have been very useful to the publick and the event will justifye the wisdome of peoples going into them: but both you and I were in the house when we were told it was only voting and declaring our readinesse to doe soe and soe, and then the consequence would be that we should have no war with Spain. On the other hand it was said that we might begin, but possibly not soon see the end of a war which such proceedings might engage us in. Time hath shewn whether the event hath been such as was promised if we would goe into what was proposed. We did it; and yet a war did ensue which I doe not know to be yet at an end. Yesterday my Lord Lieutenant set sail with a very fair wind, the night hath been very

---

[908]Carteret sailed on 1 Apr. (*Boulter Letters*, 147).

calm, and the wind fair;[909] soe that I make no doubt the persons by him recommended to be entrusted with the Governement in his absence, will be sworn Justices some time this evening. Senny is now at my Lord Meaths house in the County of Wicklow[910] ... Pray when you doe come to the Bath, doe not forget to bring along with you the many letters I have wrote to you concerning Woods coyne. Upon what orders you have already given me without new, I will bring over as many Guineas as the £190 paid me (as I told you formerly) will purchase and deliver them to you in Bath with my own hand, provided no accident either by Sea or Land prevent it. I suppose as I am a member of Parliament I am intitled to one of the Trials of the Earle of Macclesfeild.[911] Pray order Charles[912] to call for it and to carry it to Valentines (Tim Goodwins partner)[913] to be bound for me, for I propose to read it over very carefully at Bath, as containing in it some thing extraordinary as well in the prosecution defence made by the Prisoner and his Councel as in the behavior of some witnesses and others and also in the upshot of the affair ... I hope to begin our journey in ten or twelve dayes from this time.

[*PS*] I heard it said last night that the British Parliament had not imitated ours in expecting an account what was become of money formerly given when we sent a fleet into the Baltick, and methought it was designed as an hint that for the future we should content ourselves with being told in general it hath been employed in the publick service, with out enquiring or telling us how. Pray how was this matter?

741. *Alan II, London, to Alan I, Bath, 30 Apr. 1726*

(1248/7/11–12)

I think it my Duty to trouble your Lordship with a Letter to congratulate You and my Lady on your safe arrivall in England; and shou'd have been overjoyed to have done it by waiting on You at Bath, as I designed, but was prevented by my Uncle, who told me, that your Lordships Orders were, that I shou'd not come till You and my Lady were actually on the Spot; He imagines that your meaning is, that soon after your arrival there You will give Orders for my coming, and therefore says I ought to wait in Expectation of Them. I therefore beg your Lordship not to deny me the Happyness of being able to pay my Duty both to your Lordship and my Lady as soon as possible; and to be assured that the Time will seem very tedious to me till I have your Lordships Commands to that Effect.

My Uncle orders me to say that He shall not write till I go, but that He will write in full by me. These are, as near as I can remember, the very words He said to me ...

[909] Having embarked on 1 Apr., Carteret arrived at Parkgate after 'a very good passage' on the 3rd (*Daily Courant*, 7 Apr. 1726).

[910] Killruddery House, near Bray, Co. Wicklow.

[911] *The Tryal of Thomas Earl of Macclesfield, in the House of Peers, for High Crimes and Misdemeanours ... Published by Order of the House of Peers* (1725).

[912] Powell.

[913] Timothy Goodwin (*d.* 1720) and Edward Valentine, his former apprentice and successor, printers and booksellers at the Queen's Head, Fleet Street (C.H. Timperley, *A Dictionary of Printers and Printing* (1889), 622–3; Alison Shell and Alison Emblow, *Index to the Court Books of the Stationers' Company, 1679–1717* (2007), 183–4, 402).

742. *Alan I, Bath, to Thomas, Westminster, 2 May 1726*

(1248/7/15–16)

Your Nephews letter of the 30th past hath undeceived me, who took it for granted from a letter which I received lately from you that you would have begun your journey toward Newmarkett on this day fortnight: but I find you have altered your measures. I am assured that Lord C[arteret] hath managed affairs soe as to be very well at Court; which you may be sure is pleasing news to me, who cannot but have a true and real personal regard and affection for him. But when I hear that two great men who have had different interests are reconciled and become again well one with another, I consider whether their interests are reconciled, which in the main direct and guide their inclinations. Your Nephew tells me you will let me know all you are able to inform me of by a letter of which he is to be the messenger. Particularly you will acquaint me what faults he layes to my charge in point of conduct in relation to publick affairs: I have from time to time wrote you the real truth and noe one thing that was not soe. Soe that you are able to form a judgement, which of us failed in doing what he ought to doe to the other. I wish I were able to answer as well for the conduct of the other parts of my life as I am certain I am in this: I would then despise every thing laid to my charge and call it by the true name of calumnye. I see several faces here which I used to meet at Westminster; The Duke of St Albans,[914] The Duke of Chandois,[915] Lord Abingdon,[916] Sir Montague Gerard Drake,[917] Sir Thomas Scawen,[918] Mr Plumptre,[919] and others; but in the main they complain that the town is not soe full of what they call good company as it usually is this time of the year: perhaps the fault lies in me who cannot find out as many beautyes now, as I have formerly done in a lesse number of Ladyes. Pray doe me the favour to send me by your Nephew the trial of Lord Macclesfeild, but bound up, with a few sheets of clean paper at the end of it; for I have very odd notions of that great affair; and such as I fear are not well grounded, because those who seem to speak their minds impartially have a way of thinking in that affair, and of the conduct of it very different from what I can bring myself to … My services to the few freinds which I have in London.

743. *Thomas to Alan I, 5 May 1726*

(1248/7/17–20)

Having this opertunity of writing what will nott bee lookt into before itt comes to your hands, I shall write more freely then I would by post. In order of time I am to begin with the Lords debate uppon the Kings message to the Commons.

---

[914]Charles Beauclerk (1670–1726), 1st duke of St Albans, died at Bath on 10 May (*The House of Lords 1660–1715*, ed. Ruth Paley (5 vols, Cambridge, 2016), ii, 100).

[915]James Brydges (1674–1744), 1st duke of Chandos.

[916]Montagu Venables Bertie (1673–1743), 2nd earl of Abingdon.

[917]Montagu Garrard Drake (1692–1728), of Shardeloes, Bucks., MP [GB] Bucks.

[918]Sir Thomas Scawen (c. 1649–1730), of Carshalton, Surrey, MP [GB] 1708–10, 1715–22.

[919]John Plumptre (1680–1751), of Plumptre House, Nottingham, MP [GB] Nottingham.

Lord Strafford[920] acquainted the house that having seen a printed paper entitled votes of the house of Commons etc hee thought himselfe in duty bound to take notice of itt, as very highly derogatory and prejudiciall to their rights,[921] concluding with a motion for appointing a day for taking itt into consideration, and that the Lords bee summoned, which was accordingly ordered;[922] This was seconded by Lord Letchmere.

The day being come hee after opening the matter in a very warme speech, (seconded as before) concluded with a motion, That an humble Addresse bee presented to his Majesty praying that hee would bee graciously pleasd to acquaint the house by whose advice that message had been sent to the Commons, without taking notice of their Lordships by message or otherwise. The two Secretaryes,[923] Lord Onslow, with some few others spoake, all after the same manner, in substance that itt was an omission and oversight, occasioned by want of thought etc.

Lord Strafford sayd (nott to the chair) soe loude as to bee heard by the Lords near him, that att first hee thought itt soe, and would have passt itt by, as such, had hee nott been informed, that the matter was under consideration, and carryd with a high hand, nott to send any message to the Lords att six a clock the motion for ajourning the debate to that day month was putt, and carryed by a majority of twenty nine,[924] the next morning a protest was entred of which I send a coppy enclosed;[925] I presume the parl will by that time bee prorogued to avoid entring a fresh uppon the adjourned debate. The 20 Bishops present with the majority.[926] I must now acquaint you with what in some measure surprisd mee last Fryday, when Sir Robt Walpole came to mee where I then satt, under the gallery, telling mee hee came to informe mee of what was agreed uppon a Representation of Lord Cartarets. After bantaring each other a little time, touching what would bee thought by the spectators, of the honour done, which both must suppose done to himselfe, Hee proceeded thus, and very near in these words. MacCartney is to bee superannuated, and therfore surrender his cushion, having a pension graunted him for life equall to his sallary,[927] and is to bee succeeded by Bernard,[928] and hee by Singleton as Serjeant.[929] The subsistence of the inferior Comission officers of the army to bee augmented to what tis in England, this sayes hee could nott bee thought unreasonable, since in truth itt is too scanty for gentlemen to live uppon, and noe way encreases the charge, for that the more subsistence they received, the lesse would bee due for clearings.

That this however was nott readily gone into by —— in as much as what was added to them must shorten others, (youl easily guesse whoe were meant) butt this Lord C[*arteret*]

---

[920] Thomas Wentworth (1672–1739), 1st earl of Strafford.

[921] Relating to proceedings on 24 Mar. 1726, when the treasurer of the chamber, Charles Stanhope, communicated to the Commons a message from the king relating to naval recruitment (*CJ*, xx, 638).

[922] Brought to the attention of the upper house on 30 Mar. The Lords then appointed the second day after the recess (20 Apr.) to take the matter into consideration and ordered all lords to be summoned (*LJ*, xxii, 637).

[923] The duke of Newcastle and Viscount Townshend.

[924] The Lords' own records give the figures for the division as 59–31 (Sainty and Dewar, microfiche).

[925] See *LJ*, xxii, 649–50. Eighteen lords protested, including Strafford and Lechmere, but no bishops.

[926] The printed presence list (*LJ*, xxii, 649) confirms that 20 bishops attended.

[927] James Macartney, who 'resigned for a pension of £600 a year' (NLI, Cooke MSS, mic. p. 1560, no. 34: H. Foster to Mrs Sweet, 7 May 1725).

[928] Francis Bernard, MP [I].

[929] Henry Singleton, MP [I].

undertooke to make easy, and will noe doubt (sayes W[*alpole*]) make meritt to the officers, tho had nott others cooperated, that scheme had been defeated.

The Dragoons whilst uppon duty in Dublin are to have an addition of a penny a day pay, which will amount to £1100 per annum; Two or three small pensions are added, none exceeding £100 a yeare. Three or four are added to the Councill (hee namd them nott),[930] butt none left out, the Emphasis hee putt upon the last words, was to mee a sufficient proofe of its being proposd, and I beleive twas intended I should soe understand itt; thus ended our conversation.

I had that morning (being the first publique day after my returne to towne) waited on Lord Cartarett, whoe told mee in substance what you by letter informd mee hee sayd hee would, adding thereto that hee had nott, nor would complaine to any butt mee, making great professions in particular to my selfe; tis very probable hee might nott thinke somuch opennesse as happened two hours after would have done soe; Hee sayd most extraordinary letters of a country to bee ruined and undone flew about to every part, my answer was very short, that I thought itt the duty of every honest man to consult the good of his country, and act conformably thereto. My visitt tooke up lesse then half an hour, being to goe to the house. I was told by a gentleman whoe assured mee hee was an ear witness to one of our great mens saying, that if Lord Bullingbrooks Bill were now to passe,[931] hee should nott have itt, whither this bee from his being extremely uneasy att nott being restored to his honour, or that they find him tricking, I know nott, butt thus much I am fully informed of, that Lord Harcourt is very frequently with him privately, and I very much doubt whither all their power would bee able to prevent what cost £14000, which I conclude the summe payd, because just att the time the Bill was in agitation, that summe was altogether taken out of the hands of Mead the Banker[932] where Madam Villats[933] mony lay. The resolution of a Bill against the D[uke] of Wharton is layd aside, and a Privy Seale either gone or to goe requiring his returne;[934] if I understand the matter right this will bee of noe farther use then being a foundation for a Bill next Session without disclosing the evidence against him, which I hear is very strong for I beleive neither the one or other will bring him into their powers, tis sayd hee is going back to Vienna, and will shift from place to place whilst

[930] Knightley Chetwode reported soon afterwards that Lord Charlemont was to be restored to the council, while Lords Kerry, Clanricard and Southwell, together with 'General Wynne, Sir Thomas Taylor and eight more' were to be added (NLI, MS 47891/1: Chetwode to Dr Mahon, 17 May 1726). In fact Carteret recommended Lords Charlemont, Clanricard, Duncannon, Kerry, and Newtownbutler, Bishop Nicolson of Derry, Sir Thomas Taylor, 1st Bt, MP [I] and Major-gen. Owen Wynne, MP [I], who were all appointed, with the addition of Lord Southwell, 'who had a promise of long standing'. Primate Boulter informed Newcastle that these additions had 'given very great uneasiness to several well affected to his Majesty here, on account of the characters of several of the persons' but was told that Carteret had pressed so strongly 'that it was complied with in pure deference to his opinion' (TNA, SP 63/387/184: Carteret to Newcastle, May 1726; SP 67/18/105–6: warrants for appointment, 9 May 1726; *Boulter Letters*, 150, 155).

[931] The bill to restore Bolingbroke to his estates.

[932] John Mead (c. 1662–1727), of Temple Bar, London, MP [GB] 1710–13.

[933] The marquise de Villette.

[934] Philip, 1st duke of Wharton, had left England in 1725 and, after a brief spell as the exiled jacobite court's plenipotentiary to Vienna, had taken himself to Spain, where he announced that he came with a commission from the Pretender, and was also seen in public wearing the insignia of the jacobite order of the garter. On 2 May George I issued a warrant under the privy seal demanding his return within a month. Supposedly Wharton 'threw the document into the street' and told jacobite friends he was 'now … banished England' (Lewis Melville, *The Life and Writings of Philip Duke of Wharton* (1913), 151–85).

any will subsist him, tis certaine hee publiquely wears the Blue garter and George, the late Duke of Ormond having installed him.[935]

You know how little notice is to bee taken of Courtiers behaviour in publique to each other, from what I have sayd before, youl infer I beleive, as I doe, that matters stand between them as they did, butt that his Excellencys freind (a noble Lady) uses her endeavours I make noe doubt, and that she will doe soe.

Yesterday the Duke of Devon fell in my way, butt a good deale of company being togather, I had onely an opertunity of asking his opinion whither the Parliament would nott bee up in a fortnight, the day to which the debate was adjourned, Hee told mee Sir Robt grumbled cruelly att our delatorinesse, and was very desirous of putting an end to the Session, butt that the Speaker never taking the chair till after one, hee did nott see how wee could possibly goe throught the private businesse before us, by that time, which says hee the Speaker insists on as reasonable and necessary, upon the whole I question whither these two act heartily in concert, and I have doubted itt for some time passt, butt theres noe forming certaine conclusions from any outward appearance, till ministers quarrell downright. In order to bee att liberty I yesterday petitioned Lord C[*hancellor*] setting forth how long my cause had been sett down for hearing, and my phisitians advising my going forthwith to the Bath, for recovery of my health, praying that a day might bee appointed for my hearing in this terme, butt could nott obtain that favour, hee really is soe very delatory in hearing causes that D. Burgesses observation will bee verifyed that a Chancery suit is for life.[936]

I thinke I am well informd that the King of Spaine and the Grandees are very averse to the thoughts of a war, butt the queen and the new great Minister Riperda[937] furiously for itt, the former openly owns itt on account of the indignity in sending back the Infanta.[938] I fancy Riperda will run Alberonis fate in contending with the Grandees.[939]

The Bill against Bribery was (by order) comitted for this day, the order being read,[940] there was plainly a designe to postpone itt, and indeed Sir Robt W[*alpole*] gave us to understand that nothing would come of itt, intimating the little likelyhood of its going through the Lords; Sir Wm Strickland acquainted the house that the Commissioners of Customs attended att the doore (uppon order relating to the Isle of Man) and desired they might bee calld in, which the Master of the Rolls[941] vigorously opposd, after which they

---

[935] Wharton had been invested by the Pretender with the garter in Rome on 5 Mar. N.S. 1726, though it was reported that his installation had been undertaken by James Butler (1665–1745), 2nd duke of Ormond, whom he had been sent to Madrid to assist (Melville, *Wharton*, 172; *Oxf. DNB*). The 'Great George' was an enamelled figure of St George, worn suspended from the collar; the 'Lesser George' was a gold badge, again depicting St George, worn from a ribbon tied around the neck.

[936] Daniel Burgess (1646–1713), presbyterian minister, of Boswell Court, Holborn, Middx. See John Arbuthnot, *Law is a Bottomless-Pit. Exemplify'd in the Case of the Lord Strutt, John Bull, Nicholas Frog, and Lewis Baboon … (1712), 21: 'Well might the learn'd Daniel Burgess say, that a law-suit is a suit for life'.

[937] Juan Guillermo, baron de Ripperdá, 1st duke of Ripperdá (1684–1737), a favourite of Elizabeth Farnese (1692–1766), the *de facto* ruler of Spain during the lifetime of her husband Philip V (1683–1746). Ripperdá's tenure of the office of chief minister had in fact come to an end on 14 Apr. N.S. 1726, with his arrest and imprisonment.

[938] The Infanta Maria Victoria (1718–81) had been betrothed at the age of seven to the young King Louis XV of France, but, as she was considered by the French to be too young, the marriage had been cancelled and she had been sent back to Spain.

[939] Cardinal Alberoni had been dismissed in Dec. 1719 after British forces had captured the port of Vigo.

[940] The bill to prevent bribery and corruption at parliamentary elections.

[941] Sir Joseph Jekyll.

gave up the matter and went into the Committee;[942] I make noe doubt of the Bills falling with the Lords, butt att the same time, cannott butt thinke twill prove a cruell thorne in the sides of the Ministry.

Whilst they were in the Comittee I tooke an opertunity of speaking to Sir Robt (whoe satt next the Master just under mee), uppon the Bill for selling Hambdons estate,[943] which is comitted for tomorrow, I told him I thought an amendment ought to bee made to the clause empowering the Commissioners to sell; by adding the words by publique auction to the best bidder, hee sayd hee thought the thing reasonable, and would direct Jacomb[944] to move it.

Before wee left the house hee told mee hee thankt mee for the hint, and beleivd hee understood what I meant by itt. I told him people spoake their minds with greater freedom to mee then they would to him; thus I made compliment to him, and att the same time attaind with ease the end I proposed. I was this day told in the house that a great man sayd wee should certainly rise Saturday sennight, which I beleive, if hee can bring itt to beare, which I extremely doubt, for wee have all along encouraged private businesse being brought in, contrary to the usuall method, the house having generally come to a resolution against private Bills and petitions some considerable time before the ending of the Session, butt noe such thing has been now done, which Hungerford tooke notice of lately with some bitternesse, our Session sayes hee I take for graunted is to bee held on, till wee see what the Zarina will doe with her Cockboats.[945]

You will I thinke bee fully convinct of my having made a right judgment of your sonnes great improvement by his travails, which I am the more confirmd in, from that character which hee has universally obtaind with those hee has conversed with since his returne, for more is sayd uppon the subject then usually happens to young men in like case, and this will every day encrease from his great modesty, for the more hee is knowne the better he is liked.

I doe nott utterly despaire of my cause coming before the sittings after this terme are over, for though my petition were nott answered to my expectation I have been told, and I take itt to have been from Lord Chancellor, that my cause would come on before hee closed, which you may bee sure ile endeavour to the utmost, in order to overtake you att Bath.

744. *Alan I, Bath, to Thomas, 6 May 1726*

(1248/7/21–2)

I forbore to give you the trouble of knowing the maner of our treatment by the Custom house Officers at our landing att Parke Gate: where my wife was forced to lye the first night after she landed in a wastcoat which she was obliged to borrow from her Land Lady, her

---

[942] Before the House went into a committee of the whole on the bill 'for the better preventing collusive seizures of foreign goods' the committee was ordered to receive a clause to enable the treasury commissioners to treat with the earl of Derby for the purchase of his 'estate and interest' in the Isle of Man. During the sitting of the committee the customs commissioners were heard in relation to their examination of a witness to fraudulent practices on the Isle of Man. (*CJ*, xx, 692.)

[943] Richard Hampden (aft. 1674–1728), of Great Hampden, Bucks., MP [GB] Wendover. The sale of the estate was necessary to settle Hampden's debt to the government following his misuse of funds as treasurer of the navy during the South Sea Bubble (*HC 1715–54*, ii, 104).

[944] Robert Jacomb (d. 1732), of Feltwell, Norfolk, MP [GB] Thetford; dep. paymaster-gen. [GB].

[945] A small boat, carried on, or towed behind, a larger vessel.

boxes with her own clothes and wearing apparel being all carryed to a little place which they have lately built there, and given to it the name of a Custom house. But truly, as far as good words went, no people could use others better then the Officers there used us, they made great professions of having inclinacions to act in the most civil and obliging maner, but we saw by their behavior that they either pretended they had those dispositions which they had not, or else that they lay under indispensable orders from above to act with the utmost vigor. As I doe not mention this by way of complaint of the poor fellows, soe I am sure I lye under noe obligation to them to take any pains to create or establish a good opinion of them in their employers; which I think will be the consequence of letting those in London know in what maner the custom Officers of the outports toward Ireland act in reference to us who are sometimes obliged to come out of that Kingdome into this: But the occasion of your receiving the trouble of this arises from the account we hear about the usage which Gentlemen and Ladyes meet at Bristol; My Lady Bingham[946] and her Neice came from Dublin to that port directly by long Sea and each of them brought over one dozen and an half of gloves for their own wearing; and both were obliged to make oath at the Custom house that those gloves were not brought over for sale: after doing which they had the favor of having their gloves delivered them, paying a duty of six pence for each pair. Without that oath I understand the gloves would have been condemned: Now who is able to make that oath but the owners of them, I hear the oath of the servant of the owner will not be accepted; soe that whenever the ship comes in from Dublin in which my wifes goods and mine are to be brought to Bristol, either she or I or both must take a rough journey to attend their honours at the Custom house at Bristol to make oath ourselves, or she will loose a dozen or two pairs of Gloves which she brought over that way for her own wearing, for want of her making oath in person that she doth not import them as a dealer and for sale. I am also told that two or three dozens of silver spoons and forks which she hath ordered to be sent the same way for the use of her house at Peperhara, will either be battered and defaced; or else that they must be redeemed by paying soe much per ounce duty. I confesse I am much a stranger to these sorts of dutyes, and wish other people were soe too. But the publick necessityes which may oblige the continuing them, may as well be answered by a lesse rough and haughty executing the Legal powers vested in the Custom house, and would allay a good deal of discontent which I hear arises from the maner in which Gentlemen are sometimes treated in some of those publick places. Pray let me hear from you that I may know in what maner I am to behave my self: For my part I have it in my thoughts to send orders to send back the forks and spoons to Dublin rather then land them and pay such duty as I am told will be demanded to preserve them from being broken and battered; but people here are in doubt whether paying the duty will save them from being bulged battered and defaced, for I hear Lady Tyrone[947] lately had a Silver Skillet which was made in Ireland battered and bulged at Bristol, and that she was obliged to pay the duty of soe much per ounce for it, before she could have it delivered to her after being battered. To prevent this I will order the box, in which the spoons and forks are, not to be brought on shore, but carryed back to Dublin, where the plate will be of use to me tho Irish made. I beleive your Nephew will be with us here before, or soon after this reaches your hands.

[946] Phoebe (née Hawkins), wife of Sir George Bingham (*d.* c. 1730), 4th Bt, of Castlebar, Co. Mayo.

[947] Marcus Beresford, 1st Viscount Tyrone (see Appendix 3).

[PS] Lord Montjoy gott an order from the Commissioners to discharge his plate at Chester; but his was a considerable quantitye which I mention to shew the thing is practicable; but whether it be worth while in so trivial a matter to apply I leave to your discretion. I will not seal this till I tell you that the fire here is putt out, after burning a few of the poorest houses without the South gate.

745. *Thomas to Alan I, Bath, 12 May 1726*

(1248/7/25–6)

... The Act against importing forreigne plate is extremely strict, drawne soe by the goldsmiths company, whoe upon laying the duty of six pence per ounce, alleadged their nott being able to pay itt, unlesse forreigne plate were (in effect) prohibited, for that the French (whoe generally worke finer) would otherwise become makers of great quantityes, and undersell them, the words are generall of which they take advantage, and allwayes will doe soe.[948] I beleive your best way will bee (as you say) to send itt back, unlesse you can bee better treated then Lady Bingham, you may consult Sir A. Elton[949] or some other merchant, for I am nott certaine whither being imported you can refuse landing itt; you will bee under difficulty in relation to the gloves likewise, for our worthy Commissioners in every instance support the impertinence of their officers, though one of them told mee those att Parke Gate were the greatest rascalls in any port whatever, and gave them more trouble then any others, butt these are butt words.

Wee whip and spur, butt I question whither wee shall bee able to gett to the ending post next Wensday.

Last night orders followd McCartny to embarque two more Regiments in addition to the four, to bee landed att Bristoll or Minehead.[950]

[PS] I forgott to tell you that yesterday the Lords obliged young Edgworth to enter into a Recognizance of £1000 to appeare within the first eight dayes of next terme in the Court of Chancery in Ireland, grounded upon a petition of his fathers, I heard a Lord say hee was the vilest fellow living, to whom I observd how greatly hee was alterd of late, for nott long agoe when hee petitioned against you, and was nott able to prove any part of itt, their Lordships in soft termes were pleasd to come to a resolution that hee had nott fully provd his petition, and this because hee was an injurd oppresst honest man, adding that I was sure hee well knew what varyed their opinions now, from what twas then.[951]

I made this day a motion for laying before the house a coppy of the proceedings upon an information in the Kings bench against John Ward (of Hackny) one of our members.

---

[948] The act of 1720 'for laying a duty on wrought plate' (6 Geo. I, c. 11 [GB]). See Jeremy Black, *Trade, Empire and British Foreign Policy, 1689–1815: The Politics of a Commercial State* (Abingdon, 2007), 66.

[949] Sir Abraham Elton 1st Bt, 'one of the greatest commercial magnates of Bristol' (*HC 1715–54*, ii, 11).

[950] Lieut.-gen. George Macartney (c. 1660–1730) (Dalton, *Geo. I's Army*, i, 253; *Oxf. DNB*).

[951] Edward Edgeworth, in relation to a lawsuit against his father, Robert, whose petition had been read in the upper house the previous day. Edward was questioned as to why he had failed to comply with an order of the Lords on 11 Feb. 1726 to deliver certain writings to the court of chancery in Ireland. He tried to explain himself and was obliged to deliver the papers concerned to the House and enter into a recognizance to appear in the courts of exchequer and chancery in Ireland at the start of the next legal term. (*LJ*, xxii, 677–9.)

The information was for forgery of which hee was convict upon the fullest evidence, butt had nott witt enough to gett out of Court before the verdict given, and went away for Holland.[952]

Wee shall have the proceedings tomorrow, when I intend to move his attending in his place on Munday, youl easily guesse the consequence. The Bridge Bill was read by the Lords a second time this day, and is comitted for tomorrow.[953]

The (now) D[*uke*] of St Albans has the smallpox att Windsor.[954]

Did Martyn and Olberry mannors (Mr Condringtons former estate was sold yesterday att the South Sea house for £16250.[955]

746. *Alan I, Bath, to Thomas, 17 May 1726*

(1248/7/25–6)

By the great fall of stocks for some time past, I cannot but with concern consider in how uncertain a scituation a great part of the propertye of that nation, which hath the best pretence to have what is called property in their estates of any people which I ever read of, some times is; I mean that of our own Kingdomes: and cannot but be under a good deal of concern to find the expectations of a war can have soe considerable influence on the minds of men to lower some of the stocks from 123 to lesse then £100 in lesse time then three months. If the fears of a war entred into on the terms and the steps on which that which seems to be near hath been undertaken (which I think to have been with the previous knowledge (if not advice) of the Parliament) can have so great an influence on credit, what may be the consequence of any ill event in the progresse of it? I cannot conceal my concern for the publick, when there seems to be soe strong a confederacy formed against us, and when one of the most potent of our freinds and Allyes, may have other views then the securitye of Great Britain. You know that I am not of those who will be immediate sufferers by the falling of the stocks (having little or nothing in them) But when the generalitye of the nation suffers by the fall of stocks, I think every individual man ought to be troubled at that which affects the rest of the nation. I hope it proceeds rather from the temper which one part of the Kingdome hath been heretofore supposed to be of then from any thing else, that people hereabout seem to me to be under great apprehensions; what the consequence may be of a war with soe potent adversaryes as we are to contend with, at a time when I doubt we are not in the best condition to carry on a successful war. But we have no more to doe then to exert ourselves to the utmost in support of what our good King with the consent of his people hath seen fit to engage in. Our poor countrey will most certainly be sufferers in having the pay of the regiments on the Irish establishment spent out of that poor countrey which must

---

[952] Ward was eventually expelled from the House on Monday, 16 May. For the proceedings against him, *see HC 1715–54*, ii, 519–20; *CJ*, xx, 698, 701–2.

[953] The Fulham and Putney Bridge Bill.

[954] Charles Beauclerk (1696–1751), 2nd duke of St Albans.

[955] Robert Codrington (*d.* 1717) of Codrington and Didmarton, Gloucs., had been obliged to sell off substantial parts of his estates, including the manors of Didmarton and Oldbury, Gloucs. (*HC 1690–1715*, iii, 640). These had passed into the hands of Robert Knight (1675–1744), the disgraced former cashier of the South Sea Company. Knight was now living in exile on the continent, while his confiscated estates were sold off (*Oxf. DNB*). The details of the sale of Didmarton and Oldbury are confirmed in *London Journal*, 14 May 1726.

pay them, with an increase of their pay to make it equal to the English pay, and exchange for the money not to mention that we are at the same time deprived of the securitye which those regiments remaining among us would be to that Kingdome. But when I consider they are employed in his Majestyes service and for the good of his Kingdomes, all that is answered.

Pray let me have the inscription which is put on the bust made for the late Lord Godolphin, of which your Nephew gave me an imperfect account: Praeter peculatum is a pretty thought and fine complement; but if the Author of it be known, it will not contribute to advance any pretensions he may otherwise have to preferment.[956]

Your purchase is in many of the Prints, and no doubt will be thought (in Ireland) to be made with some other persons money, then the Dutchesse of Marleboroughs, for whom I take it for granted your Name is used.[957] I am mighty desirous to know whether you intend to be at this place before we leave it, which probably will be about the end of this month. Pray let me know from you whether we can have good lodging and entertainment att Aldermaston. By entertainment I doe not mean high living (for I remember your story of the Cost of Lambe at that place) but whether we can lye clean and warm and have good hay and oates for our horses. Pray let me know what people think of matters: for I confesse the melancholy figures I daily see here, put me into more pain then I desire to continue in. Pray tell what was the name of the Noble Lord that is now of opinion the injured honest Mr E[dward] E[dgworth] is the greatest vllain; he was alway soe. When will the Parliament rise.

747. *Thomas to Alan I, 19 May 1726*

(1248/7/27–8)

I never yett thought the rise or fall of stock a certaine argument of danger or its contrary, since the variation is and will alwayes bee (in great measure) in the power of designing knaves in the ally; butt I have alwayes observd that they could with more ease frighten, then raise the spirits of people. The panick abates, and men begin to conclude rationally, which they cannott when feare predominates; nor is the fall of stocks a conclusive argument of danger to any one whoe (uppon considering) will find that fall to goe little farther then itt ought. For example, the true and reall vallue of South Sea is a hundred, because if you were to bee payd of, you would receive butt a hundred, for the interest of which (till payd) you receive this yeare five pound, afterwards butt four; tis true that a luxuriant creditt

---

[956] Sidney Godolphin (1645–1712), 1st Earl Godolphin. The duchess of Marlborough had commissioned busts of her late husband and Lord Godolphin from the sculptor John Michael Rysbrack (M.I. Webb, *Michael Rysbrack, Sculptor* (1954), 96). The inscriptions Thomas prepared for them did not find unanimous approval. The antiquarian Nicholas Mann, for one, thought they would 'not be admitted among us scholars' (BL, Add. MS 61440, f. 105: Mann to duchess of Marlborough, 6/17 Apr. 1726). Nonetheless, the bust of Godolphin, which is to be found at Althorp House, does contain the line '*peritus ut praetor peculatum nihil nesciret*' (skilled as a minister, he knew nothing of peculation) (Webb, *Rysbrack*, 70, fig. 28). The bust of Marlborough was destroyed in a fire at Wimbledon Park in 1785. Thomas's will (TNA, PROB 11/640/97, dated 5 Aug. 1728), includes the following request: 'I desire that the two marble bustos of the duke of Marlborough and earl of Godolphin be kept in my family in memory of two [of] the greatest and faithfullest subjects which any age has produced'.

[957] For evidence of Thomas's previous involvement in the duchess's business affairs, see BL, Add. MS 61476, ff. 70, 74–5, 83: Thomas Brodrick to the duchess of Marlborough, 8, 15 Dec. 1723, 21 Feb. 1723[/4].

may and will run the price to above a hundred, because by reason of the vast quantity of mony in the Kingdom you cannott by any other way make somuch interest as by this, butt carrying itt to twenty three is as notional and ill grounded (in proportion) as in the yeare twenty carrying itt to a thousand was, this is demonstrably true from the consideration of the rate which land bears, for instead of falling, itt growes dearer every day and this because the purchaser knowes (very near) the intrinsick vallue, by knowing what hee shall each year receive, whereas the fluctuation of stock makes such a judgment impossible. Thinking people argue this, lett what turne will happen, land will remaine, when possibly, and nott extremely improbable, a proportion of stock may bee pared of, if nott payd by a spunge, and indeed I have ever thought (and frequently hinted in the house, soe as to bee throughly understood), that the extortion and other indirect practises of the monyed interest, would earlyer or later bring itt to that, and for my own part I thinke with justice and good reason, for why should a Creditor of the publique whoe by his extortion has brought (in great measure) this load of debt on the nation, bee in a better condition then a private morgagee whoe after having receivd principall and interest is adjudged according to equity to have noe farther right. There is nott an instance to bee given when the Creditors of the publique have nott receivd four times their due, accounting according to this rule; noe says one of them for I bought butt a yeare agoe, and that att a vast price, this in reason as I conceive will nott differ the case, for you stand, and ought to doe soe, in the place of the first lender, you claim under him, and therefore ought to have considered what justly should have been his case if hee had still continued proprietor, and as to the heighth of price which you gave surely nothing is to bee sayd, for if you were soe mad as to give a Guinea for a Bath shilling, you cannott expect to find chapmen for itt att that rate.

What I thinke will greatly contribute to something like what I have mentioned is the prodigious summes which forreigners have in our funds, for they always take advantage of buying when (for different reasons and from different causes) stocks are low; what has within these three dayes caused a rise, is in some measure due to this, for tis known beyond contradiction that they have layd out vast summes, and are att this hour doing itt, this is a matter which cannott bee discussed in the compasse of a letter, and therefore tis time to leave, what indeed should nott have been begun.

Twould be as ridiculous in mee to justifie an opinion of our nott going into a war, when the generallity of mankind thinke otherwise, or att least would perswade the world they doe (for of that sort I beleive there are numbers) butt still in this aswell as other things I must and doe judge according to my own understanding, butt thus far I will goe, that unlesse some better security can bee found out, then att present occurs to mee, I thinke itt will bee absolutely necessary to doe itt before tis too late.

The inclosed comes from a very knowing honest officer, the person to whom twas writt (a member of our house) was soe kind as to lett mee coppy itt, after reading itt attentively consider itt well. I have from the very time of the Zars being in England,[958] expresst my thoughts (and that often) of what a few years might produce, and with the greatest concerne see itt come to passe.

In times like these I know nothing soe incumbent uppon an honest man, whoe loves his country, as acting steddily and uprightly, for private veiwes will (if pursued) soone

[958] Peter the Great's visit to England in 1697.

bring on our ruine; the subject is melancholy, butt ought nott therfore to goe out of our minds …

I send you both the inscriptions on the Busto's, that on the D[*uke*] of Marlboroughs was wrote by your sonne (whoe perhaps will nott tell you soe) I carryed itt to her Grace to bee perused by those shee thought proper judges, shee returnd itt in two or three dayes, with very little variation; I thinke itt full as well as the other, what is valluable (and very uncommon) in both is, that every word and sillable is strictly true.

The other I wrote my selfe in English, giving itt my brother to putt into good Lattin,[959] butt confining him to what I had sayd, soe that I am to answer for what may give offence which I am soe far from endeavouring to avoid, that I frankly own itt to every body.

They may in Ireland conclude what they please of my purchase, which every body in towne knowes was for the D[*uchess*] of Marlborough, nott that I should bee in the least concernd, if they beleivd itt my own for next to being rich, tis good to bee thought soe.

I see noe great probabillity of overtaking you att Bath, if you come away soe soone as you mention, nott that I am very sure of the contrary, for nothing shall detaine mee butt Lord Foresters tryall[960] … I hope you have presented your sone to the D[*uke*] of Shandois,[961] whose knowledge of him may one day bee of use, for if ever we grow honest that great man will certainly come into play, otherwise nott.

The time calls uppon mee to goe to the house …

748. *Alan I, Bath, to Thomas, the Privy Garden, Whitehall, 28 May 1726*

(1248/7/31–2)

Tho I am not now soe fond of ringing as I was when I was at Oxford, and a professed ringer, yet I confesse it pleased me to be waked this morning by the noise of the Abby Bells, considering that to be the way taken in the countrey to expresse the joy of the people and also considering what place I am in and what day this is. The ringers gave us two peales only, but I doubt we shal not scape soe easily to morrow: for I remember the difference which was made here foure years agoe between the 28th and 29th dayes of May in that particular. The ship in which our few goods came from Dublin is after being long expected is gott safe at length to Bristol; but Bull could not get an order to have our little plate, which was all made in England and carryed thence into Ireland, and paid duty at Chester (which my sister well knows) delivered out to us without paying some other duty on a late Act of Parliament,[962] as is pretended: For my part if I cannot have an order from above to the Officers at Bristol to deliver it me without paying again for it (which hath been done in favor of a neighbour of ours who hath an estate in Hampshire not far from the place where you advised us to lye instead of Aldermaston) very lately and to a much

---

[959] Presumably Laurence.

[960] George Forrester (1688–1727), 5th Lord Forrester, col. of the 4th troop of horse, Scots Guards (Dalton, *Geo. I's Army*, i, 352).

[961] The duke of Chandos.

[962] The British act of 1720 laying a duty on 'wrought plate'.

greater value (for ours is but little more then six hundred ounces) I hope we may have the favor to have an order to ship it back again to Dublin. For I resolve it shal not crosse the Sea soe often that the duty which it payeth to the Crown shal come up to the intrinsick value of the plate; and I must be content with lesse plate at Peperhara then I intended to use there. I will not complain of any sort of rough usage from the Officers at Bristol; but they seemed to doe what they were under a necessitye to doe in the civilest maner. Pray (if you can by speaking to the Commissioners of the Customs or any of them) obtain an order for the deliverye of this little parcel of necessary household plate that we may have the use of it in Surrey; but if that cannot be obtained, I hope it will not be refused that it may be sent back again to Ireland: for there is about £16 demanded for the duty of it, which added to what it paid when I first carryed it over, makes a round summe. The company grows thin here and I beleive will be all dispersed before the end of the next week, and I suppose we shal doe as others doe about the same time … Probably we shal leave this place on this day sevennight or on the Monday after, and steer our course directly to Peperhara …

749. *Alan I, Peper Harow, to Thomas, the Privy Garden, Whitehall, 13 June 1726*

(1248/7/33–4)

I have just rested my self enough after the fatigue of an excessive hot journey from the Bath to take pen in hand to tell you that your sister and I should be very glad to have your company for as much of your time as you can afford us in which we shal be very much delighted. I am sure this place hot as it is can not be soe much soe as London of necessitye must be, and you will be here perfectly quiet; but to tell you thruth I have an earnest desire to talk with you about matters both private and publick, in which your sense will greatly influence me: and sure your affairs will not detain you in town unlesse your suit in Chancery may in your opinion require your attending the hearing …

750. *Thomas to Alan I, Peper Harow, 18 June 1726*

(1248/7/35–6)

Wee mend our pace a little, this day four causes were dispatcht, my sollicitor gives mee hopes that those before mee will bee short ones, Lord Ch[ancellor] goes this evening to Ockham, Baron Price[963] sitts for him on Munday, and I hope will come early.

Ten of the Zarinas frigatts are accidentally burnt,[964] this I take to bee of noe great consequence, for I am confident shee has noe thoughts of sending them out, butt every little helpes.

---

[963] Robert Price (1653–1733), of Foxley, Herefs., MP [E & GB] 1685–7, 1690–1700, 1701–2, baron of the exchequer [E].

[964] The *Daily Journal*, 20 June 1726 carried a report from St Petersburg of a fire in the dockyards there on the night of 31 May N.S., which destroyed eight vessels and severely damaged another.

I heare your successors sallary is to bee augmented £500 per an. and Sir R[*alph*] Gores three; Ireland is surely very rich, however augmenting their sallaryes of whom they are sure, without itt, will nott doe as much mischeif as pensions to others.

I thinke there is noe manner of news stirring.

751. *Alan I, Peper Harow, to Thomas, the Privy Garden, Whitehall, 20 June 1726*

(1248/7/37–8)

I know too much the trouble and expence of a Chancery suit, not to pity those who are of necessitye engaged in one. But I confesse it is not on your account only that it greives me you are now in equitye, because I impute your not coming over hither to that attendance which being a suitor in that Court creates you. I never had soe much occasion for your advice and opinion as I have at this moment …

752. *Alan I, Peper Harow, to Thomas, the Privy Garden, Whitehall, 27 June 1726*

(1248/7/39–40)

I intended yesterday to have gone as this day to wait on my Lord Duke of Somersett att Petworth, and to have carryed your Nephew with me: but have upon second thoughts put it off till to morrow, for which I think my resolution will hold. For I resolve to have that complement over before the time of your coming hither, which your sister and I hope is near … Sure the time of your causes coming to an hearing draws soe near that you may be able to guesse the day now … If there were any probabilitye in the rumors which are handed about by Lord C[*arteret'*]s freinds in Ireland that he is to goe soon over thither, I think you would give me some intimation of an affair upon which our Countryes welfare soe much depends. If he proposes to be able to bring the noble scheme to perfection which he was perswaded to enter into with hopes of succeeding, by certain Sycophants, who told him they should be able to carry him through, but who were a good deal unconcerned what successe he had in the matter, provided they might attain their own end of having the Governement left in the hands of those who would be subservient to this scheme (which they have done) I say if the resolution of beginning where he left off is determined on, probably no body will be fond to take the work out of his hand, for he ought to be a man of spirit and warmth which shal undertake it with hopes of successe. But I am confident several people on the other side of the water are told with good assurances that the measures which were taken up the last Session, but not then brought to the desired perfection will be resumed and pushed with great expectacion of [———965] considering the favors and bountyes conferred on some and the mortification given to others in that countrey, for their good or disobliging behaviour …

965 Tear in MS.

753. *Thomas to Alan I, Peper Harow, 28 June 1726*[966]

(1248/7/41–2)

I am putt of till this day or tomorrow sennight according as Lord Ch[*ancellor*] shall appoint the seale day,[967] butt I am confident twill bee Wensday, because his Lordship intends to goe to Ockham next Thursday, and I am told will not returne till Munday.

Ile explaine to you when wee meet the occasion of being thus postponed …

754. *Alan I, Peper Harow, to Thomas, the Privy Garden, Whitehall, 4 July 1726*

(1248/7/43–4)

I must own that Ally did by her brother and otherwise make me understand that she was very desirous to have mett her Mother and me at the Bath; but to be free with you when I consider the great addicional charge which her last Bath journey was to the constant expence I am in her maintenance (which was not lesse then £168) and that my income is of late abated very much from what it was formerly; I thought it not fit to run into so much unnecessary expence … I wish Nally would buy and bring with him Mr Vernons Chancery reports.[968] I beleive your account of a certain person is truer then the news from Ireland, and think they hear there that they have been misinformed they will not be troubled …

[*PS*] Instead of going to make the visit to which you advised me on Fryday I sent over a servant and am glad I did soe, for I think by the answer he brought my dining there would have been unreasonable at that time, and soe I beleive you will beleive when you know it at large …

755. *Alan I, Peper Harow, to Thomas, 11 Aug. 1726*

(1248/7/48a)

I am extremely concerned at your telling me in what pain and apprehensions you are of an approaching violent fit of the Gravel, but I hope that neither your present indisposition is such, nor my sisters state of health soe bad as to hinder your taking your intended Bath journey, which having been at all former times of great use to you may perhaps be now not soe only but also necessary … We are very much alone in our retirement, and should be very glad of some company… Is there no news; for we are greatly in the dark.

---

[966] Letter endorsed by Alan I: 'Tho: Brodrick … that his cause with Lord Forester is postponed'.

[967] See above, p. 89.

[968] *Cases Argued and Adjudged in the High Court of Chancery. Published from the Manuscripts of Thomas Vernon …* (2 vols, 1726–8). The volumes were reprinted in Dublin.

756. *Alan I, Peper Harow, to Thomas, Bath, 1 Sept. 1726*

(1248/7/49–50)

I have yours of the 27th of last month, and am sensible that what you write concerning my coming to Bath again this later Season proceeds from your kindnesse to and care of me; But I doubt it will not agree with my affairs to take another journey thither this Autumn … Beside winter is coming on when we must return to London. The Duke of Somerset made me a visit and dined with me on Saturday …

757. *Alan I, Peper Harow, to Thomas, 21 Sept. 1726*

(1248/6/310–11)

I was extremely overjoyed to find by your letter from Bath to your Nephew, and by another to him from London that the waters had been of soe great benefit to you as you in both those letters mention. I hope you will find leisure between your going to Newmarkett and this time to spend some dayes with us at this place which you know to be a very retired one and such as needs and greatly recommends good company to every bodyes tast … On Tuesday we were surprised about fowre in the afternoon with a visit from my Lord Chancellor; who behaved with great civilitye and professions of freindship. He was very willing to enter into our Irish Parliament affairs, and seemed to beleive we had not in the last Session made such provision or granted such Supplyes as would answer the wants of the Crown, I insisted that if the money already given had been applyed to the uses for which it was given, it would on a fair statement of accounts appear there was a full supply given to support the establishment, but if the money had been applyed to other purposes, no body could tell what was wanting but they who had made the misapplications, for they only could inform us where and how they had disposed the money, and how much they had soe employed, which they never had done by making themselves Debtors for the revenue and aids given and shewing how the produce of both had been disposed of, which had never yet been done during the last Session; but the method taken was to return the unpaid debts due to several branches of the establishment as a debt to be provided for by Parliament without letting us know how that arrear became due and not paid since it might have been paid out of the hereditary revenue and additional aids:[969] and the only method of accounting given us was (There is soe much not paid etc therefore give us so much money) tho we have misapplyed or made other use of that which might have cleared the demand wholly if it had not been otherwise applyed. His Lordship owned we should have had an account by way of debtor and Creditor, and been told how it had been employed; but from that time he began to discourse what the Kings own revenue (which he thought consisted wholly in Lands or rents) amounted yearly to, and in such a maner as if he seemed to think the

---

[969]The crown was entitled to various 'hereditary revenues' Ireland by common law and statute (including tonnage and poundage, crown and composition rents, ale and aqua vitae licences, presage, lighthouse and aulnage duties, and other casual revenues). In addition a further set of revenues had been granted to Charles II and his successors in perpetuity (quit rents, customs, import and inland excise, hearth tax, and ale, wine and strong waters licenses). (Kiernan, *Financial Administration*, 79–86). The additional revenues were those time-limited taxes voted by parliament.

Crown had an absolute power of disposing this. He did not say soe in plain words, but his way of thinking seemed to me to be founded on that notion. I was not desirous to presse him to explain himself, but am fully satisfyed that the views at Court are, the enlargement of the Kings right to make such use as he thinks fit of the hereditary revenue and leave the charge of the Governement (I mean the Civil and military Lists) to be provided for by the Nation apart from the hereditary revenue, which consequently will be employed as men can make freinds with the great ones at Court. If this should be the scheme, here is a noble Privy Purse provided for the Crown out of a very poor part of his Dominions: and that this is and hath been in prospect for some years hath been my opinion from the best observation I could make during that time upon the conduct of those in power in both Kingdomes. He talked also of bringing in a bill about making judgements for personal debts, capable of being executed in either Kingdome; I spoke cautiously on this subject, and asked whether it was not as reasonable that a judgement obtained in Ireland should be executed in England against such as should remove into England, as that an English judgement should be executed against one who went into Ireland: he owned it equally reasonable: and I confesse I cannot see any good reason why a subject of the same Prince owing a debt in any part of his Dominions to a fellow subject of the same Prince should not be compellable to doe him justice in that part of the Dominions to which he is removed, in the same maner as he was obliged to have done in that part of them from which he hath withdrawn himself: but upon this head I spoke with more doubt then I really (from the nature of the thing) had in my own mind, because it occurred to me that in all probabilitye, the method which would be taken would be by bill in Britain, which would make the recovery of English judgements in Ireland compulsory on us, and soe he seemed to think they should be here (mutatis mutandis) but then they may hereafter think fit to alter that part in ease of them selves; whereas if it were left to us in Ireland to consider what the consequences of such a bill might be, we should have oportunitye of making an experiment by a temporary Law; and that in truth I have great apprehensions how far such an Act might affect Ireland with respect to demands from North Britain. He also was very inquisitive about your Nephew[970] and my attending the approaching Session of Parliament here …

758. *Thomas to Alan I, 24 Sept. 1726*

(1248/7/53–4)

I doe nott apprehend what can bee objected to Lord Ch[*ancellor's*] proposall of giving force to a judgment obtain in England, soe as to levy in Ireland, provided itt bee reciprocall, what you seeme to foresee that in future time one part of an act may bee repealed leaving the other in force, will nott beare, because itt must bee grounded upon a supposition of the greatest partiality and wrong imaginable; I doe nott conceive that much prejudice can come to Ireland from the North Britains making use of itt against their debtors, since generally speaking they will bee of their owne country; it may indeed hinder many of them taking sanctuary in Ireland, which I thinke will nott bee prejudiciall, for in my opinion there are already too many of them there.

---

[970]St John III.

I fancy nothing of this is in his veiwe, butt the notion instilld into him in the place from whence hee lately came, and this may, and I beleive will bee attended with worse consequences, you know Exeter, and the parts adjacent are cloathing countrys; the manufactorers whoe fall into decay often to avoid Goales [*sic*] fly into Ireland, these are englishmen, and such as carry on (tho poorly att first) the trade to which they were bred, the west of England must bee sensible of the losse of so many hands, and att the same time you may bee sure consider that those employ themselves in Ireland to the prejudice of their manufactory, this is a very tender point, and if nott thought of, ought nott to bee putt into their heads. Hee gave up the point of the proceedings in parliament last Sessions by owning that the accounts ought to have been made (merchant like) D[*ebto*]r and C[*redito*]r against which nothing can bee reasonably and honestly sayd. If what you apprehend bee in veiwe, the extending the Kings right of disposall of the hereditary Revenue in such manner and to whom hee shall thinke fitt, leaving the whole establishment to bee provided for by parliamentary aids, the answer to itt is obvious. If I doe nott mistake the first part of that Revenue is the quitrent,[971] and I beleive in the act mention is made of the necessity of providing funds to answer the charge, all the subsequent graunts must reasonably bee interpreted graunted uppon the same foote, and with the same veiwe, and to that end; I take itt that nothing soe fully interprets the sence of every law as practice, from the very time of its being enacted, and yett more strongly when for fifty years togather itt had been soe understood; for pensions and King's letters are of a very late date, I beleive twill bee found they tooke rise since the Revolution. There is an instance which to mee seems to carry great force; When King Charles the Second farmed out the Revenue, the then farmers were in the first place to defray the expence of the Establishment the quantum of which was reduc't to certainty, The surplus (if any) was to bee, and was in fact, remitted to the Treasury in England;[972] The farmers skilfully under pretence of nott keeping accounts reduced this surplus to a certaine summe of Thirty thousand pounds per annum. This they payd and itt was appropriated to the buildings att Windsor,[973] butt remember (as I sayd before) the establishment was first to bee provided for. Our great men would nott willingly have itt demonstrated that Pensions Kings letters Augmentations of sallaryes etc exceed even what is pretended necessary to bee provided for by Parliament.

After the Revolution (for some short time) the Revenue graunted to King James (though hee had abdicated) was collected; what did the Parliament then? Did they thinke King Wm entitled to this, soe as to have itt in his power to dispose of itt as hee pleasd, Noe Noe they ascertain his Civil list, and this to bee payd out of the dutyes etc appropriating all the remainder to the use of the publique, and thus wee all know itt has stood ever since.

The Deficiency of the Civill list has (as I take itt) been thrice provided for, uppon shewing that itt fell short, and this carryed by small majorityes, and nott without great grumbling and offence given;[974] I doe nott beleive how much soever they may want mony to supply great extravagancyes, that they will soone make the experiment of a like demand.

---

[971] A perpetual rent due for land granted by the crown (Kiernan, *Financial Administration*, 80).

[972] By leases, in 1669 and 1671 respectively, to two separate consortia. When both leases expired, in 1675, a third was granted, to a different group of farmers. (Kiernan, *Financial Administration*, 90–1.)

[973] Charles II's renovations at Windsor Castle.

[974] In 1711, 1715–16, and 1717 (C.I. McGrath, *Ireland and Empire, 1692–1770* (2012), 182–5).

Every body knowes how the numbers in the house of Commons are obtaind, and though itt serve a present turne, itt cannnott, itt will nott bee of duration. Having this morning to my selfe, I trouble you with this long letter. I thinke my selfe better then when I returnd to towne, in that the heat is abated, and my blood much quieter; my constitution is hott, and this raisd to a great degree by the Bath waters made the leaving them of, necessary; but they have had a very good effect. I am … designing for Newmarkett the latter end of next weeke.

759. Alan II, Drayton,[975] to Alan I, Peper Harow, 30 Sept. 1726

(1248/7/55–6)

I have, since I wrote last to your Lordship, been at London to see my Uncle before His Journey to Newmarket, which He intended to begin as to day; and am overjoyed to find that He has received so much Benifit from the Waters … I heard no kind of News in London, but what was talked of from the publick Prints, in One of which it is said that Sir Charles Wager is on the Point of returning home from the Baltick with the Fleet under his Command.[976]

760. Alan I, Peper Harow, to Thomas, the Privy Garden, Whitehall, 15 Dec. 1726

(1248/7/57–8)

I had letters from Dublin which give me the same account you doe in the end of your letter; that Mr West is dead.[977] I wish you would some way or other endeavour to let yourself into the secret who probably will succeed him: for it will be of consequence to a freind of mine (whom I wish very well to) if he can attain early notice who is likely to be the man, as it will in truth to the Kingdome that it be filled well.

By the late measures I think one may conclude that it is resolved at [the] Helm to fill every thing worth taking from this side of the water; unless the promises made by a certain person now in Ireland, of the great things he shal be able to doe in the next Session of Parliament prevail on Lord C[arteret] to push for him: It is the thing which he hath long panted after, but how far he will be supported here I cannot tell, much lesse whether the person on whom he depends hath power enough to recommend successefully. I rather beleive the Cheif Baron will be the man,[978] who hath not been long enough in Ireland to be esteemed

---

[975] Drayton (or West Drayton) in Middx. Alan II referred in another letter to staying with his 'Aunt Courthope' there (SHC, 1248/7/67–8: Alan II to Alan I, 17/18 May 1727). A Mary Courthope was buried in the churchyard of St Martin's, Drayton in 1729 (Daniel Lysons, *An Historical Account of Those Parishes in the County of Middlesex Which Are Not Described in The Environs of London* (1800), 38).

[976] Sir Charles Wager (c. 1666–1742), of Kilmenath, Cornwall, MP [GB] Portsmouth, vice-admiral and commander of the Baltic squadron.

[977] Richard West died on 3 Dec. 1726 (*HC 1715–54*, ii, 531).

[978] Thomas Dalton (c. 1682–1730). He had only been in Ireland since his appointment the previous year, and was one of two candidates recommended by Archbishop Boulter (*Boulter Letters*, 170). In fact, Carteret had immediately resolved to recommend Boulter's other candidate, the lord chief justice of common pleas [I], Thomas Wyndham (IAA, Conolly MSS, box 53: Thomas Clutterbuck to William Conolly, 12 Dec. 1726).

Irish: Pray endeavour to see our Surrey neighbour soon,[979] and learn in discourse from him whether the great ones (and one particularly) hath any person on this side the water in view; for I most earnestly desire to know that time enough, that application may be made in time for a little thing which will be in his Successors disposition: in which I should be very much greived to have my freind disappointed. I know you can with ease find from him whether the place will be immediately filled, and whether from this side of the water, of which I intreat you to give me the very earliest account possible. Nor doth my freind propose to himself to come in otherwise then people usually now doe into matters of that nature, for his money, but he would not loose it by coming too late; and all that is aimed at is to have an oportunitye of starting fair …

761. *Thomas to Alan I, Peper Harow, 5 Jan. 1726/7*

(1248/6/357–8)

The Session certainly opens uppon Tuesday sennight,[980] you may bee sure I would have given you notice if itt did nott, butt I thought itt unnecessary to say any thing uppon that subject, because when you expressed a resolution of being att itt, and twas therefore time to provide Lodgings my sister sayd twas early enough for doing that.

The Duke of Devonsheer nott long since askt whither you did nott intend coming over, I verily beleive hee knew as well as my selfe your being in England, I tooke itt (and I beleive very rightly) a Memento of your nott having waited on the King, I owne I thought the reproofe just, and was very sorry to find after my going to Bath you altered your resolution of doing itt, as you then told mee you intended.

Hee likewise att the same time sayd that circular letters were sent to all the Toryes to bee here the first day, soe that probably there will bee a very full house, and possibly some squabbling uppon an Addresse in answer to the Speech.

The Spanish preparations remaine yett in the clouds, how far they will proceed being altogather uncertaine.

762. *Alan I, Peper Harow, to Thomas, the Privy Garden, Whitehall, 14 Jan. 1726/7*

(1248/7/59–60)

I give you the trouble of this to let you know that your sister and I resolve to begin our journey next Monday toward London and lye at Cobham and propose to leave that place soe early on Tuesday morning as to be in town time enough to be at the house that day; you know that I neither have curiositye nor strength to goe to the house of Lords to have the pleasure of hearing his Majestye deliver his Speeech; It will satisfye me to have it at second hand when the Speaker reports it to the house: and that I hope to be early enough from Cobham to overtake: at least to come before the debates that you seem to think will arise upon it are over. The Duke of Devon might well enough think that I ought to wait

---

[979] The English lord chancellor, Peter, 1st baron King of Ockham, Surrey.
[980] The parliament had been prorogued until Tuesday, 17 Jan., when it reopened (*CJ*, xx, 707).

on the King before now, for he may be a stranger to the usage I have mett with. But you are not soe, and I suppose continue of opinion that I ought to resent it as I did by desiring to quit a service which I could not hold (under the usage I mett) with honour. Therefore I hope that you will beleive I come early enough to London now; and I confesse I think it will be a difficult task how I shal conduct my self when there. If I goe to Court I either shal mention to his Majestye something of what hath passed, and you know how hard a task it is to expostulate on such occasions or not. Or perhaps if I should be silent my silence will be interpreted as a proof of my being very easy; under what I have mett with. But you know that never was nor is the case; nor will any thing induce me to be soe but a sense that I have done something which deserved the usage I have mett with, of which I am not at all convinced nor ever shal be. Perhaps too some thing may then be said in reference to my future conduct, in which I determine to keep my self entirely at libertye. I shal not now hunt under a pole which I never could submit to when I was under some obligations from which I am at present wholly acquitted. But of this and other publick affairs we shal have time enough to talk when we meet in town. My wife and I have begged the favour of Lady Mountjoy to try to take us Lodgings, which she hath taken the trouble of doing on her. You will know at her Ladyships house where the little Lodgings are which she hath taken for us till we can fit ourselves better, and there you will hear of us, or at Lord Mountjoyes house in Brooke Street near Hanover Square.

763. St John III, Midleton, to Thomas, 15 Jan. 1726[/7]

(1248/6/359–60)

I wrote to you from Cove[981] about 3 weeks ago, where I had then hired a Ship to carry me over, but the weather has been so excessively stormy and the wind so contrary, that tho I have been ready and at Cove almost every day since in order to embark, yet the Master of the Vessel would not venture to Sail, nor indeed do I think twas possible to make a Passage. I was so impatient as to have resolv'd to go by the way of Milford[982] and ventur'd thro the Welch Mountains at this very bad Season of the year, could I have prevail'd with the Master of a vessel that was bound thither, and whom I met with accidentally at Cove, to have waited but one Tide for me, so as to have sent home for my Servants, Portmanteau etc, but he was in hast and unwilling to miss the opportunity of a fair wind, as he thought; but he had not been 6 hours out of the Harbour when it came about to South East, and blew the violentest Hurricane that has been known there many years, so that in all probability the poor man perisht, as I should have done had I been with him, there having been many wrecks on the coast that night, and 2 Ships having come in since from Milford, where they had no Account of him.

The weather continues as bad, and the wind as contrary as possible, so that I see not the least probability of making a Passage from hence, and therefore resolve to wait only a day or 2 longer, and then go away to Dublin, from whence I may reasonably hope for a Speedier, as I am sure I shall have a shorter and safer Passage.

[981] Modern-day Cobh, Co. Cork: a port on the south of the Great Island.
[982] Milford Haven, Pembrokeshire.

I have been and am very uneasy at this disappointment, having fully determined to have been at the opening of the Session, which, as it must be of the last importance to the Affairs of Europe at this time, so in all probability will it be an active and busy one; but there is no contending with the winds and weather, so I must submit.

As soon as I get to Dublin you shall hear from me; in the mean time, if there should be an immediate call of the House, I beg you will inform them of my case, which upon my honour is true in every particular; but if the call be not sooner then usual, I will, with Gods leave, answer for my self …

764. *Alan II, London, to Alan I, Bath, 13 May 1727*

(1248/7/65–6)

… It can be no News at Bath (tho' it was so to me till I came to town yesterday) that there are ten Thousand Men ordered to be ready in a Fortnight. They are, as I hear, to land at Calais, and to march from thence into Flanders; but to what Part I do not know.

It is now confidently reported here that the French have resolved on the Seige of Luxemburgh; and that They will have a strong Army in the Milanese, which is to march thither thro' Savoy and Piedmont.

I hope Your Lordship finds Benifit by the Waters …

765. *Alan II, London, to Alan I, Bath, 17 May 1727*

(1248/7/67–8)

… It is said here that his Majesty intends to set out on the 30th, but You know me to be so bad an Intelligencer, and that I must be particularly so at a time when I stir but very little abroad, that You will not depend upon it barely on this Information. I have not yet heard any time fixed for my Lord Carterets going into Ireland, but I think it is agreed on all Hands that He is to return thither.

I received a Letter last Monday from my Brother, dated the 8th from Dublin, which I intend to answer by tomorrows Post; He tells me no News, so I suppose most of what They have goes from hence. I hear there are many Competitors for the Place of Vice=Chamberlain, amongst Whom are Sir T Coke,[983] Sir J[ohn] Hobart, Mr Arundell,[984] Sir T[homas] Saunderson[985] and Mr Herbert;[986] my Cousin Clayton[987] goes into Flanders, the Lot having fallen on Col. Robinson's Company which He is in[988] …

---

[983] Sir Thomas Coke (1697–1759), of Holkham, Norfolk, MP [GB] Norfolk.

[984] Hon. Richard Arundell (c. 1696–1758), of Allerton Mauleverer, Yorks., MP [GB] Knaresborough.

[985] Sir Thomas Lumley Saunderson (c. 1691–1752), of Sandbeck, Yorks., MP [GB] Arundel.

[986] Hon. Robert Sawyer Herbert (1693–1769), of Highclere, Hants., MP [GB] Wilton, groom of the bedchamber.

[987] Courthope Clayton.

[988] William Robinson (*d.* 1741) (Dalton, *Geo. I's Army*, i, 303).

766. *Alan II, London, to Alan I, Dublin, 25 June 1727*

(1248/7/69–70)

I came to Town last night, and saw my Uncle; He says there is no News, nor any Certainty of the Disposition of great Places yet. Their Majesty's are now at Kensington, but come to St James's tomorrow, and the Parliament is to sit on Tuesday;[989] 'tis thought They will do nothing but settle the Civil List. Lord Scarborough and D[uke] of St Albans are the Masters of the Horse; One to his, and t'other to her Majesty;[990] Mr Schutz is Master of the Robes in the Room of all Malpas,[991] and Mr S. Cowper is said to be made Chancellor of the Dutchy of Lancaster vacant by the Death of Lord Lechmere[992] …

767. *Alan II, London, to Alan I, Chester, 29 June 1727*

(1248/7/71–2)

I was to wait on the D[uke] of Somerset yesterday; He asked me when He shou'd see your Lordship, and seemed surprized when I told Him You were gone for Ireland. He said (in the most obliging manner imaginable) that He took it for granted You intended to stand for Midhurst; for if He did not, He supposed He shou'd have heard from You; He ordered me to let You know that He had sent to the People to desire They wou'd not engage Themselves; he says, He beleives it will be a very easy Election; that He imagines Mr Knight will not try for two, and that the Electors will, without much Difficulty, choose their old Representatives.[993] Your Lordship will certainly write to his Grace immediately, and if You have any Orders for me I beg to have Them out of Hand …

768. *Alan II, London, to Alan I, Dublin, 4 July 1727*

(1248/7/73–4)

I wrote your Lordship two letters last thursday, One to Dublin, the other to Chester, to let You know that I had been with the Duke of Somerset the day before, and that I had

---

[989] Parliament had been prorogued to Tuesday, 27 June (*CJ*, xx, 866). The new king and queen, who were living at Leicester House when George I died, moved to Kensington first because St James's Palace was not 'ready … for receiving them' (HMC, *Polwarth MSS*, v, 5–6).

[990] Richard Lumley (1686–1740), 2nd earl of Scarbrough, became master of horse to the king; the 2nd duke of St Albans became master of the horse to the queen.

[991] Augustus Schutz (*d.* 1757), a Hanoverian who happened to have been born in England while his father was in London as Hanoverian envoy, replaced Sir Robert Walpole's son-in-law, George Cholmondeley (1703–70), Viscount Malpas, s. of the 2nd earl of Cholmondeley and MP [GB] East Looe (Beattie, *English Court*, 64, 179; TNA, PROB 11/831/40).

[992] Spencer Cowper (1669–1728), of Hertingfordbury Park, Herts., MP [GB] Truro. Lechmere died on 18 June 1727 (*HC 1690–1715*, iv, 606).

[993] Bulstrode Peachey Knight (c. 1681–1736), of West Dean, Sussex, who had acquired the Knight interest at Midhurst through marriage in 1725, had been elected alongside Alan I in 1722. Both were re-elected unopposed in 1727. (*HC 1715–54*, i, 336; ii, 327.)

his Orders to offer You his Grace's Interest at Midhurst for the approaching Election; He said He beleived Mr Knight wou'd stand alone, and, if so, He cou'd not foresee the least Difficulty in the Election. I now repeat this, for fear the others shou'd have miscarried; and expect to receive your Lordships Commands in this Affair as soon as You conveniently can send Them to me; the Manner in which the Duke offered this was really as obliging as the Thing itself; and I dare say You will have wrote to Him before this comes to your Hands.

I can not as yet give your Lordship any certain Account of the Success of any Applications; but this I may safely say, that I see no Reason to doubt but Things will be done, in their due Time, to your Lordships Satisfaction.

Elections engross all the Discourse of the Town; there are no less than seven Candidates at Haslemere; the 2 Present Members[994], Sir More Molineux,[995] Mr Folks a Relation of the D[uke] of Chandois,[996] Mr Essington of Wandsworth,[997] Lord Blundell,[998] and a seventh whose name I do not know. Mr Art[hur] Onslow and his Brother, the Colonell,[999] stand for Guildford; Mr Walters wou'd fain be excused standing for the County,[1000] but his Freinds urge Him to Joyn with Mr Scawen;[1001] 'tis reported that Mr Onslow will try his Strength for the County as well as Guildford; if He can be chose for both there will be a Vacancy for somebody or other at Guildford; but who They have in their Eye I know not.[1002] So far I am sure, that if They offer it to my Uncle, He will refuse it; for I will answer for Him, He will not take up with — any body's Leavings ...

769. *Alan I, Dublin, to Alan II, 4 July 1727*

(1248/7/75–6)

Your letters of the 25th and 29 June came not to my hand till this morning; no letter I ever read created me greater pleasure then the first of them by which I found you were gott over your feavourish indisposition.

I send under this cover a letter for his Grace of Somersett, to be sealed and superscribed by some unknown hand, and not in your own: To tell you the truth I could be very well content if his Grace could be prevailed upon to transfer his favour which he hath hitherto placed on me to one who I have reason to beleive hath more mind to a seat in St Stephens Chappel then I have; and who may be able to doe himself if not his countrey

---

[994] Peter Burrell (1692–1756), of Langley Park, Kent, and James Edward Oglethorpe (1696–1785), of Westbrook, Surrey. They were re-elected unopposed in 1727.

[995] William More Molyneux.

[996] A 'Colonel Fowke' of Elford, Staffs., was a partner in Chandos's mining ventures (C.H. Collins Baker and M.I. Baker, *The Life and Circumstances of James Brydges, First Duke of Chandos, Patron of the Liberal Arts* (Oxford, 1949), 347, 377).

[997] John Essington (1689–1729), of Wandsworth, Surrey, was returned for New Romney in 1727.

[998] Viscount Blundell (see Appendix 3).

[999] Richard Onslow (c. 1697–1760), lieut.-col., 1st Foot Guards.

[1000] John Walter (*d.* 1736), of Busbridge, Surrey, MP [GB] Surrey 1719–27.

[1001] Thomas Scawen (*d.* 1774), of Carshalton, Surrey, 1st surv. s. of Sir Thomas Scawen.

[1002] Arthur Onslow was returned for the county with Scawen, beating Walter (who stood on the same interest as Scawen) into third place. The seat at Guildford was then taken by Henry Vincent, returned in a by-election in 1728.

more service there then I shal be able to doe. But this is a tender point, and the person we have to deal with is very nice and great care must be taken least he should think it were transferring or [?r]ealecting[1003] his favour. But the conduct of this affair I leave to you and your Uncle, with a declaration that if it can be accomplished without disobliging his Grace and if it shal be agreeable to you and thought advisable by your freinds; I give my free consent to it, and will write a proper letter such as shal be advised from your side of the water. But if this scheme shal appear impracticable you are to deliver the inclosed to his Grace and make ackowledgements and complements for the very great favours I have already received and the continuance of them by this last act of his goodnesse and generositye. If this shal be determined on you must call on Mr Hoare and Mr Arnold[1004] and make use of the bill drawn by Mrs Brand on Nuttal in the entertainment of freinds in M[idhurst] which I freely empower you to doe, and they will on sight on this deliver you Mrs Brands bill on Nuttal with an indorsement to you. I doe not find that our men whose businesse it is have made the steps necessary for holding a Parliament here, not that any directions are come from your side in that behalf: but this is out of my province and the thanks which I have mett with in doing real service have warned me what I may expect when I take on me to advise in matters which belong not to me to intermeddle with.

The hurry people are here in about elections is hardly to be conceived and the heats in several corporations about their magistracye is not to [be] expressed. We really want a cheif Governor on the spot, but I mean a man of temper who will by a prudent and impartial conduct put things into a better scituation then they seem to me to be at present. Some measures within a few years last past have I doubt laid foundation for animosityes which every lover of his countrey must be greived at. I wish my Lord C[arteret] had not been laid under a necessitye of pushing the passing of Woods coine as long as he was (I doubt) obliged to doe. If that wrong step had not been taken this Kingdome would have been as unanimous now as I have had the happinesse to see it …

770. Alan I, Dublin, to Thomas, 9 July 1727

(1248/7/77–8)

… I wrote lately to your Nephew with an inclosed to his Grace of Somersett, which I confesse I thought ought not to be delayed one post; but upon second thoughts am very apprehensive his Grace may think I make too bold with his generous freindship if the scheme which I on a suddain proposed in your Nephews letter should be pursued, which I need not here repeat. It is true I wish my namesake[1005] could be brought in but I much doubt whether the way proposed by me will be advisable, and may not give offence. You will remember he and you had thoughts of his coming in nearer home, which I wish may be practicable: We are here in as hot water as ever I knew this Kingdome in: The new

---

[1003] Possibly used in the sense of assuming, or disposing (*OED*).

[1004] Henry Hoare (1705–85), of Stourhead, Wilts., MP [GB] 1734–41, had succeeded to his father's place as a partner in Hoare's bank in London. John Arnold was a salaried partner (H.P.R. Hoare, *Hoare's Bank, A Record 1672–1955: The Story of a Private Bank* (1955), 5).

[1005] Alan II.

elections put every body and thing and interest at work. They who rode us soe long are very unwilling to quit the saddle; as the rest of the Gentlemen are of being rode perpetually by a sett [of] men; Certainly there never was a better oportunitye for a great man to acquire all the honour that can be gott by putting this Kingdome into such a quiet disposicion and temper as it was in before some late mismanagements gave a good deal of cause of complaint. The scheme of the Bank and Copper patent and the warmth with which that last paltry wicked project was prosecuted in two late Governements, and the maner in which the governing part of this Kingdome at that time (I mean the Lords Justices and Councel) were used for not issuing a proclamacion to encourage the currencye of that base coyne, created a great deal of greif to the persons who in not answering the expectacions of the other side of the water, consulted the honour of his late Majestye and the good and happinesse of the Kingdome; and I cannot but be of opinion that as the Commons did not in that matter come up to the wishes of the then Governement, soe as by this disappointment Lord C[*arteret*] received a sensible mortification; I cannot I say but apprehend that his Lordship (if he comes again over) will push at carrying something here the next Session which will be as little agreeable (and perhaps attainable) as the last thing he so zealously pushed. Whereas a person who never was concerned in any of the late measures taken here to gett all our money into particular hands, will have the affections and assistance of every body in carrying on his Majestyes service. Especially if he shal be soe happy to bring over an establishment with him discharged of that load of pensions under which we groaned of late, and the many unnecessary payments to General Officers: prudence and temper in this great matter will be very necessary; and most particularly at this time when the Kingdome is almost wholly exhausted of its Cash by the ballance of trade running soe high against us the last year that people to save the exorbitant exchange of about £15 per Cent Chose rather to bring money into England in specie then by bills purchased at soe dear a price. I should also mention here what is too true the terrible scarcitye of all sort of grain (so as the worst wheat is now 25s per Kilderckin[1006]) almost to a famine and the dismal prospect of the approaching harvest through excessive rains and want of sun this whole Summer. There never was so much grasse on the ground as this year; nor did I ever see the poor in so wretched and starving a condition. If in these circumstances any thing be expected from us that is extraordinary I fear the necessitous condicion of the Kingdome must make those who are best affected, not willing (because not able) to answer those expectations. But if his Majestye shal be advised to ease and lessen the establishment (and sure there is room for it) the saving on that head may be applyed to purposes more for his Majestyes service then those to which they formerly went and much more to the satisfaction of his people. It would be of some service and ease to the revenue, if the Governement were obliged to specifye the particular services for which money is given out of the military contingencyes, in the warrants for paying such money; for if a favourite is to have a summe given him or her the method hath (some time) been to pay £100 to A. B. without saying for what and to place the summe to the account of money to be issued for military contingencyes. Now if the service which A B did for that money were named perhaps it would appear not in any sort to concern a military or perhaps civil affair. Corporacion matters have (I hear) sometimes reaped more money out of this fond then ought to have gone that way.

[1006] Kilderkin: a unit of measurement equal to half a barrel or two firkins.

The like for other contingent payments, why should not the service be expressed in the warrant and how and by whom the certificate was given. Indeed it were very desirable that some Gentlemen of Ireland now in London might be a little apprised of the nature of the intended establishment, before it is actually settled. I very much doubt whether our great men at the Castle are not now soe intent on the only businesse now on the carpet (I mean settling the Magistracyes of corporacions, in which they seem to be very intent, at least as much as ever I remember in my time[1007]) that they have not thought of doing those things which are necessary to precede our having a Parliament; I mean transmitting bills causes and consideracions for holding a Parliament with their advise of the necessitye: Without which by Poynings Law no Parliament can be here holden.[1008] And perhaps they may forgett this matter soe long, that we may be streightned in time for passing the bills for money, early enough before Christmas as to prevent the lapsing of the dutyes which are only granted until 25 December next, which (if it should be the case but for one week) would be a vast losse to the revenue by importing goods enough duty free as will in great measure answer the consumption of next year. Of this I think you may put that person in mind whom you have an inclination to shew the way unto, by which he may supply any neglect or forgetfulnesse of our great men here.

771. Alan II, London, to Alan I, Dublin, 11 July 1727

(1248/7/79–80)

I have received yours of the 4th, and set out for Petworth tomorrow morning to deliver that to his Grace. I can never sufficiently agknowledge my thanks to your Lordship for your offer of procuring me a seat in Parliament, even at the Expence of your own but sure You can never think that I cou'd have such a desire, or wou'd accept of it on those Terms, even tho' there were no other Difficulty. But, my Lord, I fear I can not propose that to my self, for there are such struggles every where, that there will be the strictest Scrutiny's into whatsoever may be disadvantagious to any Candidate.

I have only time to say that I will do every thing in the best manner I can at Midhurst …

772. Alan II, Peper Harow, to Alan I, Dublin, 16 July 1727[1009]

(1248/7/81–2)

I came hither last night from Midhurst whither I went by the Duke of Somersets Order; I found all Affairs there in a very good scituation, and the People peaceably inclined …

[1007] The approval by the privy council of the election of magistrates in certain specified corporations, according to the 'New Rules' of 1672 (for which see *Anglo-Irish Politics*, i, 30). Conciliar proceedings on this subject during the summer months were more extensive and prolonged than usual (TCD, MS 750/9, p. 7: Archbishop King to Richard Gorges, 19 Aug. 1727; *Dublin Intelligence*, 19–22 Aug. 1727).

[1008] One of the requirements of Poynings' Law (1494) was that before a parliament could be called in Ireland the chief governor and the Irish privy council had to 'certify the king under the great seal of that land the causes and considerations and all such acts as … should pass in the same parliament' (D.B. Quinn, 'The Early Interpretation of Poynings' Law, 1494–1534', *IHS*, ii (1941), 242).

[1009] Letter endorsed by Alan I: 'Nally … finds things in a good scituation at Midhurst and the people peaceably inclined. Scawen and Waters joined in opposicion to A[rthur] Onslow'.

Elections engross all Conversations; Mr Walters and Scawen are joined at last, which I beleive will hurt Mr Onslow.

773. Alan II, London, to Alan I, Dublin, 25 July 1727

(1248/7/85–6)

I wrote to your Lordship this day fortnight to let You know I was then going to Midhurst, where I found all things easy; I then called on Nuthall in my Way, who owned to me He had received the Money some time tho' He had neglected paying it to Mr Hoare; I insisted on his paying it immediately, which He has not done; this Neglect of his lay'd me under a Necessity of taking 40 Guineas of John Edwards of Oxenford,[1010] for which I gave Him a receipt for your Lordship's Use; and hope the Remainder of that money in my hands, with what I shall be able to get from the other tenants will be sufficient to defray the present Expences at Midhurst, whither I am going immediately by the Duke of Somersets Order, tho' there is no danger. He seem'd to say that if the People shou'd think themselves neglected when there is no opposition, They wou'd be less ready to Vote whenever there shou'd be any; and I am sure your Lordship wou'd have great reason to be angry, if I shou'd omit doing all in my power to support his Grace's Interest.

Lord Berkley is out of the Admiralty, which is to be offered to Lord Orford, who it is thought will refuse it on account of his Age and Infirmity's;[1011] if He does, Lord Torrington is to be the Man;[1012] Sir J[ohn] Hobart succeeds Mr C[harles] Stanhope as Treasurer of the Chambers; and Sir Or: Bridman is to be of the Board of Trade in Sir John's Place.[1013] Sir W[illiam] Strickland is to be Treasurer to the Queen, and Sir W: Yonge is to be out of the Treasury,[1014] so that there will be Room for Sir G[eorge] Oxenden and Mr Clayton.[1015] Sir G[eorge] Oxenden's taking this Place and Mr Chetwynds[1016] being out, make 2 Vacancies in the Admiralty, which are to be supplied by Lord Malpas and Mr Molineux.[1017] Lord Essex[1018] is to be ranger of the Park in the Room of Lord Chetwynd; Mr R[ichard] Plummer

---

[1010]The manor of Oxenford was part of the Peper Harow estate: it had been leased in 1712 for a rent of £120 p.a. to a farmer called James Edwards (SHC, G145/box1: book relating to Peper Harow estate).

[1011]Edward Russell (c. 1652–1727), 1st earl of Orford; 1st lord of the admiralty [GB] 1694–9, 1709–10, 1714–17. He died on 26 Nov. 1727.

[1012]Torrington replaced the earl of Berkeley on the new admiralty commission issued on 2 Aug. (Sainty, *Admiralty Officials*, 22).

[1013]Sir Orlando Bridgeman (c. 1679–1746), 2nd Bt, of Bowood Park, Wilts., MP [GB] Lostwithiel 1724–7, Bletchingley 1727–34, was included on the new commission issued on 8 Aug. 1727; Hobart and Richard Plumer were omitted (J.C. Sainty, *Officials of the Boards of Trade 1660–1870* (1974), 30).

[1014]William Yonge had been made a knight of the bath in 1725.

[1015]William Clayton (1671–1752), of Sundon, Beds., MP [GB] St Albans 1722–7 and Westminster 1727–41. Strickland was also a member of the previous treasury commission. The new commission was issued on 28 July (Sainty, *Treasury Officials*, 19).

[1016]William Richard Chetwynd (c. 1683–1770), of Chetwynd House, Staffs., MP [GB] Plymouth 1722–7.

[1017]Samuel Molyneux, MP [I].

[1018]William Capell (1697–1743), 3rd earl of Essex.

is to be succeeded by Mr Cary, whose Place in the mint Sir A: Fountaine is to have,[1019] and He to be succeeded as Vice Chamberlain to the Queen by Mr T. Smith.[1020] The Eight Lords of the Bed Chamber to his Majesty, who served Him in that Capacity when He was Prince of Wales, are sworn in to the same Places,[1021] and it is not known whether there are to be four or eight of the Late Kings continued. Mr Herbert (Lord Pembrokes 2d Son) is to [be] Commissioner of the Revenue in Ireland in the Room of Mr Medlicott.[1022] This is all the Publick News I yet hear, tho' I have good Reason to expect to know one Peice very much to my satisfaction, before my Return from Midhurst …

774. *Alan I, Dublin, to Thomas, the Privy Garden, Whitehall, 27 July 1727*

(1248/7/87–8)

By a letter I received some time since I was frightned with the account it brought of the two brothers being like to set up together in Gilford, by their joint interest there to overbear you. I heard afterward that the elder intends to set up for the County, but that Mr Scawen and Mr Waters are at length joined in opposition to Mr Onslow: how far the County election may influence that of the borough I know not: But probably their play will be first to have the County election over; and to delay that of G[uildford] till they see the event of that.[1023] But sure it will be reasonably expected in case he be chosen in the County that he previously declare he will rest content with that election, and not aim at being rechosen at G[uildford] to be able to make his election and bring in another on the issuing a new writ when he makes his choice to serve for the County. I had a letter from your Nephew[1024] which tells me he left things [in] a good scituation at Midhurst and people peaceably inclined: But what satisfaction can I have in being chosen, if I am not to meet my freinds in the house as they were when I sate there last. And yet I am frightned into a beleif that that may possibly be my case. For I understand by a letter from your Nephew[1025] that Sir Fr[ancis] Drake hath told him that he shal be obliged to bring Mr K. in at B[ere Alston] soe as he is like to be

[1019] Walter Carey (1685–1757), of West Sheen, Surrey, MP [GB] 1722–*d*., [I] 1731–*d*.; comptroller of the mint 1725–7. He was now appointed to the board of trade, and was succeeded at the mint by Sir Andrew Fountaine (1676–1753), of Narford Hall, Norfolk.

[1020] Thomas Smith (*d*. 1728), of South Tidworth, Hants., MP [GB] Tregony 1727–*d*. The impending appointments of Fountaine and Smith had been reported by Lady Bristol on 22 July (*Letter-books of John Hervey*, iii, 16).

[1021] The dukes of Richmond, Manchester, and Hamilton, the earls of Chesterfield, Essex, Albemarle, Selkirk, and Deloraine, Lord Clinton, Lord Henry Herbert, Lord Thomas Paget, and Lord William Manners (*The State of the Court of Great Britain* … (1728), 14).

[1022] A privy seal warrant was issued on 25 July for a new commission, in which Hon. Robert Sawyer Herbert (1693–1769), of Highclere, Hants., MP [GB] Wilton, replaced Thomas Medlycott (*Lib. Mun.*, pt 2, p. 134). The change was 'declared' publicly on 28 July (IAA, Conolly MSS, box 53: Theophilus Clements to William Conolly, 29 July 1727).

[1023] The Guildford borough election was in fact held first, on 18 Aug., when Arthur and Richard Onslow were returned unopposed. The county voters went to the poll on 30 Aug., with Arthur Onslow pitched against the combined interest of Thomas Scawen and John Walter. Onslow topped the poll, with Scawen also returned. Arthur Onslow then vacated his seat at Guildford and Henry Vincent was chosen in his place.

[1024] Alan II.

[1025] St John III.

out of the house, unlesse Mr K[*ing*] be able also to be elected at E[*xeter*] which he certainly might have been and stil may if he and his father bestir themselves in earnest:[1026] And he desires me to write to you on his behalf to speak to Lord Ch[*ancellor*] and to prevail that (if Mr K[*ing*] shal succeed at E[*xeter*]) he may have a positive and expresse promise upon the issuing of a new writ to be chosen in Mr K[*ing'*]s room. This promise he hopes you will bring Lord Ch[*ancellor*] into, and let it not depend on a bare hint which he hath given that it may be soe; but get his Lordship to promise that he shal succeed in that case without his familyes opposicion; and that he will push his sons interest and pretensions at E[*xeter*] to make this scheme practicable. You must be sensible how much consequence this affair may and probably will be of to his affairs during his whole life. You must also know how insolently the enemyes of our familye will triumph if any slur be placed upon him; and will endeavour to avoid it. Let me conjure you to bestir yourself on his behalf and not let him be trampled upon as he will be, if he be disappointed. This event may and (I doubt) will have ill consequences on this side of the water, where the countrey hath him in their eye for the Chair. But his conduct hath been too honest the last Session and too opposite to the vile schemes then on foot to begger the Kingdome by Woods money, and swelling the national debt, for him to hope for any quarter at a certain place; or from a certain person. This also will I hope have some weight with you [*to*] appear and exert yourself vigorously on his behalf …

775. Alan II, London, to Alan I, Dublin, 10 Aug. 1727

(1248/7/92–3)

I last night received your Lordships of the first, and think the most numerous Levee is where You imagine. I can not yet tell You the particular with any Certainty, for I do not know it my self, nor do I beleive it will be determined this fortnight; tho' I do not see the least room to doubt but something satisfactory will be done. Whatever it is, Every One concerned desires it may not be too little Work, for I will answer for the person cheifly concerned, that He will not complain of too much Employment, provided it is of a Nature to let Him into the Knowledge of what may be serviceable to Him hereafter … As the Writs bear Teste[1027] to day, I shall go to M[*idhurst*] in 3 or 4 Days; and must get some Money of my Uncle to bear the Expence of my Journey, and those there as soon as the Election is over, I will send your Lordship the Particulars of both the Accounts You ask for.

We have very little News except what relates to Elections; there are great Struggles almost every where. 'Tis said that their Majesty's intend to go to Richmond next tuesday for eight or ten days …

[1026] John King (1706–40), the eldest son of the lord chancellor. He did not stand at Bere Alston in 1727 but was elected for the Cornish borough of Launceston. In the next election, in 1734, he was returned at both Launceston and Exeter.

[1027] The word 'teste', literally 'witness', introduced the last clause of a writ, containing the name of the issuing authority and the date.

[*PS*] If your Lordship will please to direct for me at Mr Richard Fabian's in Old Bond Street[1028] (where I now lodge) my Letters will come safe.

776. *Alan I, Dublin, to Alan II, at Mr Richard Fabian's house, New Bond Street, 24 Aug. 1727*

(1248/7/94–5)

Last night I received yours of the 16th from M[*idhurst*] but can with truth affirm I had rather have had a prospect by it of having another freind of yours succeed in a matter of the same kind more Westward: and shal be much more pleased when my Sollicitor can give me an account of having been as successeful in another about which we have lately conversed by letter then in what immediately concerns myself. Your prudence will caution you of the maner you transmit me those papers which I formerly wrote to you about, after you had been at Oxenford, for letters sometimes fall into ill hands. Your Mother and I shal probably goe soon into Munster for three weeks or a month …

[*PS*] Make my complement in the best maner to his Grace to whom I resolve to write a proper letter by the very next pacquet; but will send it under cover to be delivered by you.

777. *Alan I, Dublin, to Thomas, the Privy Garden, Whitehall, 29 Aug. 1727*

(1248/7/96–7)

… I cannot but say that it greived me to read the name of the brothers in a certain return, and no doubt they will impute the successe to a superior interest in the borough, tho [?we] know the contrary.[1029] The death of Lord Cheif Justice Whitshed[1030] will make room for some grave Philosopher to succeed him, for I presume he will come from your side of the water: and perhaps he that was designed for the present Chancellors Successor in the Common Pleas may now be sent over,[1031] unlesse Lord C[*arteret*] hath or can prevail for his freind Bernard[1032] and will [*page torn*] for him; but how far he will thwart the wishes of some of our favourites here, who will doe all in their power to have Mr Justice Gore sett a pin higher,[1033] I cannot form a guesse.

[1028] A Richard Fabian (b. c. 1700), described as a haberdasher, of St James's, Middx., took out a marriage licence in 1730 (*Allegations for Marriage Licences Issued by the Commissary Court of Surrey between 1673 and 1770*, ed. A.R. Bax (Norwich, 1907), 46). The next letter in sequence gives Fabian's address as New Bond Street.

[1029] The election return of Arthur and Richard Onslow for Guildford.

[1030] On 27 Aug. (*Hist. Ir. Parl.*, vi, 538).

[1031] James Reynolds (c.1686–1747), of Castle Camps, Cambs., who was appointed in Whitshed's place (Ball, *Judges*, ii, 200–1; *Oxf. DNB*).

[1032] Francis Bernard, MP [I], appointed a judge of common pleas [I] the previous year.

[1033] In December 1726 William Conolly had recommended Gore to be promoted to chief justice of king's bench, as a means of bringing 'all his relations and friends (of which there are many) into all right measures' (IAA, Conolly MSS, box 53: Conolly to Clutterbuck, 22 Dec. 1726).

778. *Alan II, London, to Alan I, 31 Aug. 1727*

(1248/7/98–9)

… I will follow your Lordships Directions … with respect to … getting what Intelligence I can about Lord Carterets Journey … I will now give You account of what Money I have received for the Use at M[*idhurst*] and on the other Side transcribe an Account of the Expences

July the 13th: Received of J: Edwards	42=00=00
July the 28th: Received of J Goble	7=10=00
July the 28th: Received of Ed Garret	1=16=06
July the 31st: Received of my Uncle by H: Edwards	30=00=00
Aug the 10th: Received then of my Uncle the three following Summs	
A Bank Bill of	100=00=00
Ditto of twenty Pounds	20=00=00
60 Guineas in Cash	63=00=00
Totall	264=06=06

Expended	£	s	d
July the 11th: Horse Hire for 3 Horses five Days	02	12	06
13th: To the Ringers at Midhurst	01	01	00
15th: House Bill at the Angell	11	15	09
Given to the Servants	00	07	00
To the Bailifs Man	00	05	00
Tot[*al*]	16	01	03

	£	s	d
I left London again July the 25th.			
House Bill at the Angell during my stay there	15	08	09
To the Servants	00	10	06
Horse Bill	01	07	00
Aug: the 2d. Paid Richard Burly for meat delivered in for			
the Treats at Durmans and Marners	02	07	03
Paid Durman Expences of the Treat	12	01	06
Left with Mr Dawtrey to be spent at			
Marners on Aug: the 4th	12	01	06
To the Bailifs Man	00	10	06
Spent upon Burgers[1034] at Different Times, and at different Houses	00	17	00
Tot[*al*]	45	14	00

[1034] The franchise at Midhurst was in burgage-holders.

I left London again Aug: the 11th.

There was drank and Scored at the Angell in my Absence	1=03=06
at the White Horse	0=08=00
at the Boot	0=14=00
	2=05=06
To which add	16=01=03
And	45=14=00
Totall on this Side:	64=00=09

Paid at the Angell from the 13th to the 16th (the Day of Election)	04=06=06
Aug the 16th. To Mr Young for filling up the Return, reading the Precept and doing the Offices of Clerk of the Court (the Usuall Fee)	03=03=00
To the Ringers	02=02=00
To the Bailifs Man	01=01=00
Paid R. Burly for Meat delivered in the day of the Election	03=15=07
Paid the House Bill at the Angell the day of the Election	24=06=06
Paid for Horses the day of the Election	02=07=00
Breakfast the next Morning	02=03=06
To the Waiters and Servants	00=12=00
J: D[*awtre?*]y 20 Guineas	21=00=00
	64=17=01

Aug 17th at Petworth to the Ringers	01=01=00
for Servants and Horses	00=04=06
Brought over	64=00=09
Totall of All Expences	130=03=04

779. Alan I, Dublin, to Thomas, the Privy Gardem, Whitehall, 31 Aug. 1727

(1248/7/100–1)

…This morning I received a letter from Pettworth in very obliging terms, which I will answer very soon: but in it his Grace seems to expect my being in London at the very first meeting of the Parliament: Now to tell you the truth, I am soe far a stranger to publick affairs; that I doe not know when the Parliament is to meet; but I hope they will not meet to doe businesse before Christmas. A word to me on that head would be a great ease to my mind …

780. Alan I, Dublin, to Alan II, at Mr Richard Fabian's house, New Bond Street, 2 Sept. 1727

(1248/7/102–3)

Several packets have come in lately without a line from you or any other of my freinds in England, except Lady Montjoy to whom I wrote a letter in favor of Sir Edward Crofton,[1035] and to this I received an answer from my Lady Montjoy at the desire of her Lord, to whom indeed my letter was wrote, but his indisposition in his hands makes it impracticable for him to write himself. Your silence gives me a good deal of pain on account of my being at the same uncertainty in a certain affair, as I was when it was first hinted to me as a thing not far from receiving the finishing stroke: but in this case, no news is not good news … One Anesley[1036] is sett up in the County of Corke in opposition to your brother, no doubt by the encouragement of —— who I beleive hath applyed to Lord Anglesey to support and countenance him:[1037] He is a man not known soe much as by name or face in that County and I beleive hath not an acre of Land in it; but his Cheif is a bitter enemy of your brothers, I suppose pretty much because he was one and [sic] the principal persons who occasioned the sixpence in the pound to be taken off from the Vice Treasurer for the money which arose by the new addicional dutyes: which was a considerable losse to the then Vice Treasurers, and hath been soe to their Successors. But I think the County of Corke will not change their members for worse and I am confident they will not mend their hand by altering from their former members. The industry and zeal with which people sollicite elections here, is not to be described, much lesse beleived by those who measure their application by what hath been practiced in former elections. You would not beleive it, if I should tell you at what prices boroughs now are said to goe: indeed very infamous ones, and such as (I think) forebode something very ill to be not far off. Corruption hath ruined greater states then ours, and where ever it prevails will have the same effect; which God only can avert and may he doe it but how can we expect that while we are doing everything that naturally produces miserye and justly offends him? …

[1035] MP [I].

[1036] William Annesley (1709–70), eventually returned for Midleton in 1741 and later created 1st Viscount Glerawly.

[1037] Presumably Annesley's father Francis (1663–1750), of Castlewellan, Co. Down, MP [I] 1695–1703, 1713–14, [E & GB] 1705–15, 1722–34, a distant cousin of Lord Anglesey.

781. *Thomas to Alan I, Dublin, 7 Sept. 1727*

(1248/7/106–7)

I have never been able to learne with any certainty the time of the Parliament's meeting, I went this morning to a prime minister, in order if possible to informe you, butt found (what I before tooke to bee the case) that itt depended uppon what accounts should come from abroad, wanting these leaves us still under the same uncertainty; If good I take for graunted noe businesse will bee gone uppon before Chrismas, if otherwise itt is very probable twill sitt when the writs are returnable.

Some ships are already saild to reinforce Sir Ch[*arles*] Wager (whose men are very sickly) and others in readinesse to observe the first orders …

782. *Alan II, Drayton, to St John III, Dublin, 12 Sept. 1727*

(1248/7/108–9)

I am extreamly sorry to hear that You are likely to meet with Opposition for the County of Cork, even tho' my Father tells me He does not apprehend any danger of your losing the Election. I have just wrote to my Uncle Lawrence to do what He can with Lord A[*nglese*]y; but fear it is too late to hope for any great Success from that Application. However I have not omitted one Moment since I knew it; and am not without hopes that You took the same Method of applying to Lord A[*nglese*]y, upon the first Declaration of Opposition; for since my Father tells me your Competitor is not known either by Face or Name in the County, I flatter my self that He is no Relation (or at least a very distant one) of Lord A[*nglese*]y's. In this Election, and every thing else, my best wishes attend You; and I shou'd be happy were it in my Power to do any thing more than wish for You.

You know Sir F[*rancis*] D[*rake*] and Sir J[*ohn*] H[*obart*] are chose for Beeralson; Sir Francis is also chose for Tavistock and Sir John for Norfolk; now I always apprehended that Mr King was to come in at Beeralston; but He is actually chose at Dunhivid;[1038] so that Sir F[*rancis*] may, if He pleases, make his Choice for Tavistock; and I do not see what, in that Case, shou'd hinder You from being chose at Beeralston.

If You think this Hint worth your Consideration, You will improve it as You please; I will make it my Business in the mean time to endeavour to find out what Sir F[*ranci*]s's designs are, and to let You know them. My greatest fear is that L[*or*]d C[*hancello*]r's second son[1039] was not of Age at the time of the Election, but will by the meeting of the Parliament. I have however no ground for this Conjecture, but what my Apprehensions furnish me with; and if this is not the Case, I see no Reason to despond. There will in all probability be many Vacancies soon after the Parliament meets; if You will sett your self seriously to consider, I can not but think that You may come in some where …

[1038] Dunheved, otherwise the borough of Launceston in Cornwall.

[1039] Peter King (1709–54), who eventually succeeded his father and elder brother as 3rd baron King of Ockham.

783. *Alan II, Drayton, to Alan I, 13 Sept. 1727*

(1248/7/110–11)

I have received two Letters from your Lordship since I wrote last, and am going to answer them … The Duke of Somerset being at Petworth I cou'd not deliver your Lordships into his Grace's own Hands; but I gave it to his Steward at Northumberland House,[1040] and had his Promise that Care shou'd be taken of it … As for the M[idhur]st Accounts, your Lordship has I hope long had them, and does not think them dear; I am sure I did the best I cou'd; but I have lately received a Letter with a Demand from Mr Moore, as follows;

for 20 Pair of Blank D=ds	= 26=00=00
for a Man and Horse to Pepper=hara, and from thence to London, to let the D[uke] of S[omerset] know the day of Election	= 02=02=00
for my own Journey's Trouble and Expences	=

Your Lordship will observe that He leaves a Blank for the last Article, and He tells me in his Letter that He is willing to leave that to my Generosity, wisely avoiding to set a Price for what He knows does not deserve one Shilling.

I am very sorry to hear that there is likely to be a Struggle in the County of Cork; the Easiest Elections are troublesome enough, and I heartily pity any body concerned in contested Ones, even tho' they are sure of Success, which I hope and take for granted, is my Brother's Case.

Tis said that his Majesty will go to London next Fryday; and then People expect that the Warrant's for the <u>Commissioners of the Customs</u>, excise etc will soon be signed. These kinds of Places being inconsistent with a Seat in Parliament, the Commissions have not been yet renewed; for it was certainly highly reasonable to issue the other Warrants time enough to prevent Gentlemen the Trouble of Re'election, which was a great deal of Business; as much as cou'd well be done before the issuing the writs. I hear that the Civil List has been under Consideration since, and your Lordship knows that to be a Branch of such Importance as to require great Care and Exactness, and consequently to take up much time.

The Affair, in Relation to which your Lordship has more than once complained that You are as much in the dark as when it was first hinted to You, is of such a Nature as I can not well explain farther than I have already done; <u>and I hope 'tis unnecessary to do it</u>.

I do not hear one Syllable of News … my Uncle intends for Bath, and wou'd have been there before this time, did not a certain Affair keep Him in town.

[1040] On The Strand, the town house of the Percys, dukes of Northumberland. Somerset's wife (who died in 1722), *suo jure* duchess of Northumberland, was the last of the Percy line.

784. *Alan II, London, to Alan I, Dublin, 21 Sept. 1727*

(1248/7/112–13)

Sir R Baylis being appointed Receiver generall of the Taxes for the County of Midlesex and City of London has quitted his former Employment of Commissioner of the Customs,[1041] and his Majesty signed the Warrant for renewing that Commission yesterday, wherein He was graciously pleased to have my Name inserted in his Room. Nothing now remains but the Commissions passing the Offices, which I beleive will be done in three or four days. I hoped for the Honour of kissing his Majesty's Hand yesterday, but was informed that when Commissions are renewed, the Usual way is for all the Commissioners to wait on Him in a Body. I am throughly sensible of his Majesty's great goodness to me in complying with my Uncles Request in my Favour, and hope to behave my self in such a Manner as never to give my Uncle Reason to repent of having asked it, nor his Majesty of having granted it.

Your Lordship will pardon me that I have not, till now, expressly told what the particular Thing was; I was under Obligation to my Uncle not to do any thing that might make it publick; and it so uncertain into what Hands letters may fall, that I might have been worse than my word without intending it. Your Lordship will however perceive that I have not omitted the first moment to let You know the thing is done …

785. *Alan II, London, to Alan I, Dublin, 26 Sept. 1727*

(1248/7/114–15)

I told your Lordship in mine of last Thursday of his Majesty's great Goodness to me in appointing me one of the Commissioners of the Customs; this I now repeat to your Lordship, tho' I hope You will have received that letter; this Employment will oblige me to take a Journey to, and make a long Stay in Scotland; six months is the time People are told they must stay there, but They are seldom or never releived in less than eight or nine.

The Coronation is deferred till the Eleventh; the Reason of it was the Danger of the tide's coming into the Hall on the fourth.[1042] Mr Onslow being chose both for Guildford and the County, the Interest of that Family at Guildford is promised to Mr Vincent, a Son of Sir Francis Vincent;[1043] and Lord Baltimore is the other Candidate;[1044] the Event of this Election is very doubtfull, tho' I can not help thinking that Lord Baltimore has a very fair Prospect …

[1041] Sir Robert Baylis (1673–1748), of Watling Street, London, MP [GB] 1708–10.

[1042] Confirmed in *London Journal*, 23 Sept. 1727. A high tide was due on 4 October, and the coronation was postponed 'to guard against any inconveniencies that may happen about Westminster Hall'.

[1043] Henry Vincent (c. 1685–1757), eldest son of Sir Francis Vincent (1646–1736), 5th Bt, of Stoke d'Abernon, Surrey, MP [E & GB] 1690–5, 1710–13.

[1044] Charles Calvert (1699–1751), 5th Baron Baltimore, MP [GB] 1734–*d*. He was easily defeated by Vincent in the by-election in February 1728 (*HC 1715–54*, i, 329).

786. *Alan II, London, to Alan I, Dublin, 28 Sept. 1727*

(1248/7/118–19)

I write this to let your Lordship know that I am to have the Honour of kissing his Majesty's hand tomorrow, the Reason why I have not done it before, is that the Commission being renewed, it was thought proper that all the Commissioners shou'd go togather. I find I am to pass this winter at Edinborough, and am extreamly sorry that it shou'd fall to my Lot at a time when I might reasonably expect to have seen your Lordship and my Lady in England.

You must be sensible that (altho' the Income of this Employment is very considerable, yet) the Expence I must be at before I shall receive one farthing is very great; the Passing the Patent, my Journey to Scotland, and the living there many months before I shall receive any Money are great Articles. Your Lordship will also be pleased to recollect that the last money I had from You was £100 on my leaving Bath; which is now a good deal upwards of three months ago; and the Expence I have unavoidably been at since, is what I beleive I need not tell your Lordship has exceeded that summ. All these things considered I hope You can not think me Unreasonable in asking your Lordship to give me a summ of five hundred Pounds, to clear me hitherto, to set me out in the world, to pay the Fees of the Patent, to buy what is necessary for my Journey northward, and to maintain me there till Lady Day; before which time I can not expect to see one Shilling of the Salary of my Employment. Your Lordship by complying with this Request will put it in my Power to be very little troublesome to You on this Score as long as his Majesty shall please to continue me in his Service, which I shall always endeavour to deserve. Shou'd I be obliged to go to Scotland before I hear from You on this Head, I must be forced to apply to my Uncle to get me Credit for a Summ of Money, for tho' I have not spoke to Him on that Subject, yet I am very sure He has not a great deal by Him now, shou'd You think my Request extravagant and unreasonable (which I hope and beleive You can not) and refuse it as such, the Necessary and Unavoidable Consequence wou'd be that my Circumstances wou'd be very much streightned by my being obliged to spend my Income before I received it, and I shou'd consequently be continually in debt. When Your Lordship considers of all these things, You will, I dare say, be convinced that the Request I now make You is so far from being Unreasonable, that the present Circumstances of Affairs make it necessary for me to desire it of You …

787. *Alan II, London, to Alan I, Midleton, 30 Sept. 1727*

(1248/7/123–4)

The very first Syllable I heard of my Brother's Illness was by your Lordships Letter of the 16th from Ballyanan, and I am extreamly glad to find that the Height of that terrible Distemper was over at the time your Letter came away; I have wrote to Him this day on the Subject of his Recovery … I intend to go to Pepper=hara tomorrow, the Commission not having yet passed the Seals; so that I shall not be wanted in Town till the latter End of the week. I had the Honour of kissing their Majesty's Hands yesterday.

788. Alan I, Ballyannan, to Thomas, 6 Apr. [recte Oct.] 1727

(1248/7/61–2)

By a letter from your Nephew in London giving an account of his Majestyes goodnesse to him in appointing him one of the Commissioners of the Customs; I find he and I are obliged alway to own ourselves to be highly obliged to you. At the same time he gives me to understand that there will be occasion for an immediate summe of money which it is not easy for me to compasse immediately (it being no lesse then £500) but he may depend upon it that I will find a way to remit it as soon as possible, and if I had as much Cash in London to draw upon I would doe it by this very first post, but indeed I have not; his expences abroad and some other unforeseen ones having taken up all the money I had formerly lodged in London. If Mrs Brand will pay £500 of her morgage, I will be content to apply it to answer this suddain call: but probably she will be soe nice in having a formal discharge that she will not relye on my allowing it in part of the money she owes me on Mr Skippons morgage. There is another way by drawing on me for the money, which will subject me to English exchange, which one would avoid; but if no other way can be found out, and the exigence be soe great as not to admit of waiting for bills hence I must submit to that difficultye, and will find out a way to answer the bill punctually, but hope it will be drawn at one and twenty or one and thirty dayes sight. Soe much as to one of your Nephews. I must write something which concerns my eldest son, who is now in a very weak condition with his late pleuritical feaver, and tho the Doctors tell us his danger is over, I confesse I can not but be in great pain for him, least he should relapse, or his feaver return on him, which I doubt would prove fatal to him. I doe assure you all that were about him in his extream ilnesse observed a great heavinesse and weight on his spirits, proceeding from a deep melancholy which I doubt he labours under in great measure from an opinion that you have slackned your kindnesse toward him much of late, and particularly in the matter of Beralstone. I cannot give you stronger or better reasons for your interposing in his favor then I did in a former letter from Dublin; to which I will only add that he hath a certain account that Sir Francis Drake is twice Drake [*sic*] is elected at another place as well as Beralstone soe that if he make his election to serve in the other he will have it in his power to bring in Senny again.[1045] If you will be the means of accomplishing this, you will at once doe him a signal favor and service, and remove a deep melancholy which I see hath seised him, you willl doe him a great service as well in point of fortune, as reputation: and you will doe that thing which will be most grateful to me, as such I most earnestly intreat to bestir yourself in his behalf. I will only add that I shal look on this as the strongest instance of your brotherly affection to me and therefore intreat you not to deny me, nor to delay one moment in bestirring yourself in Sennyes behalf. Dear Brother grant me this last request which I shal make.

[1045] Drake was also chosen at Tavistock, for which he opted to sit. St John was put up for the vacant seat, but died a week before the election took place (*HC 1715–54*, i, 491).

789. Thomas, Newmarket, to Alan I, Midleton, 19 Oct. 1727[1046]

(1248/7/131–2)

Last night I receivd yours dated (by mistake) the 6th of April. I have very often observd people dissatisfyd with their freinds for nott accomplishing what they desird (though out of their power) because they flatter themselves with what they aime att being attainable, because they wish itt soe.

I have done all in my power (without saying I did soe) in the matter you mention and will continue my endeavors, butt cannott bee answerable for the successe.

Just before I came out of towne I receivd bills from Boles,[1047] which I indorsed to my nephew, nott knowing how soone hee might bee ordered to Scotland, whither of course hee will bee to goe being the youngest, those there, having already stayd beyond the usuall time, hee can (if there bee occasion) discover the bills, soe that hee will have noe occasion to draw on you, nor need you bee in hast to remitt, till you find an opertunity of the lowest exchange. In a day after getting hither I was seizd with a feaver, the Epidemical distemper which has carryd of numbers, butt nature made a stronger efort then what possibly art could have done, by a violent loosenesse, which lasted eight and forty hours, itt putt an end to the feaver, and then stopt gradually, I have nothing now to apprehend butt a relapse, which I will endeavour to prevent by taking what care I can and keeping warme, till I find my selfe in a condition to returne, soe that I know nott whither I shall overtake my nephew, for hee must goe assoone as hee is ordered.

790. Alan II, London, to Alan I, Dublin, 21 Oct. 1727

(1248/7/135–6)

I am to return your Lordship my most dutifull Thanks for the great Goodness You have been pleased to shew towards me in the severall distinct parts of your Letter of the 8th from Ballyanan, but more particularly for the Advice and Instruction You are so good to give me. The most convincing Proof I can ever produce of my due Sense of it, will be a constant Behaviour in Obedience to it; and I do not in the least doubt but that You will perceive from thence, that your Council and Pattern have not been entirely thrown away upon me. You are also extreamly good in complying with my request with respect to money; I shall not want above half that Summ before I leave England; which, when it will be I do not know; but I am certainly the next [?Oars]; and fancy I must move in a fortnight. I beleive it will not be possible for me to receive any Money from your Lordship before that time, but my Uncle will, I dare say, supply me in Case I am ordered away as soon as I expect … My Brothers Recovery is a great Pleasure to Us All;

[1046]Letter endorsed by Alan I: 'Tho: Brodrick … hath done what he can for Nally, but can not answer for the successe. Hath furnished Nally with money, being (for ought he knew) to go to Scotland out of hand. Hath had the feaver but is mending'.

[1047]Probably John Boles, Alan's tenant for Cahermone and Drumsarane, Co. Cork (SHC, G145/box 102/4, pp. 20–1, 34–5: rent rolls).

but nobody here knew one Syllable of his Illness till the Danger of his Distemper was over.

My Uncle was very well when He set out towards Newmarket the day of the Coronation …

791. *Alan II, London, to Alan I, Dublin, 28 Oct. 1727*

(1248/7/140–1)

… I have had Orders from the Treasury to set out for Scotland as soon as possible, and I hope to be able to obey them next week; I am sure that the less delay I make the more my Conduct will be approved.

I am very sorry You have the least Reason to apprehend any ill Consequence of my Brother's Illness; and hope the Symptoms are occasioned only by the Vast Quantity of Blood so terrible a Pleurisy must have made necessary to be taken from Him. Nobody doubted but his Election wou'd be very easy, even tho' his Antagonist had not desisted …

792. *Alan II, London, to Alan I, Dublin, 7 Nov. 1727*

(1248/7/146–7)

… tomorrow I set out on my Journey towards Scotland. T'is a great Affliction to me to think that your Lordship and my Lady will be in England this winter, and that I shall not have it in my Power to pay my duty to You; my Uncle Brodrick has been very much out of Order these three Weeks, and is not yet got out of his Chamber … I am extreamly sorry to hear that my Brothers Pleurisy has left so bad a Cough upon Him; and intend to write to Him by this Evening's Post

[*PS*] … I beg to hear often from your Lordship; a Letter shou'd be directed to me at the Custom House at Edinburgh.

793. *Alan II, London, to Alan I, Dublin, 8 Nov. 1727*

(1248/7/148–9)

My Journey northward being deferred one day, I have an Opportunity of troubling your Lordship once more before I leave London; and am now to write to You, by my Uncle's Order, in Relation to the Election in the County of Clare. Sir E: Obryan[1048] stood there in Lord Thomond's interest, who complains greatly of the Sheriff[1049], as having declared that if Sir E[*dward*] had every Voice in the County, He wou'd not return Him; and having actually returned Mr Purdon, tho' greatly outpolled by Sir Edward;[1050] this my Uncle orders me to write, and I do but set down what He dictates. I beleive You will have a Letter from Lord

---

[1048] Sir Edward O'Brien, MP [I].

[1049] Thomas Studdert (1696–1748), of Bunratty Castle and Kilkishen House, Co Clare.

[1050] George Purdon.

Thomond by this Post stating the Case, and desiring your Assistance, in obtaining Right, which my Uncle bids me tell You, He assured Him He shou'd appear to have. My Uncle likewise (who is not able to write) bids me tell You that You have never own'd the Receipt of a letter by Mr S;[1051] He was then confident He had good Ground for what He said in it, and is since confirmed in that Opinion from some Incidents; and therefore hopes that matter will not be let fall. These also are his own Words …

794. *Alan II, Edinburgh, to Alan I, Dublin, 18 Nov. 1727*

(1248/7/154–5)

I wou'd not defer one moment letting your Lordship know of my Arrivall here, tho' I have time for very little more. I will during my stay here be very carefull to observe the Directions You were so good as to give me in a late letter, and hope to shew your Lordship at least an Inclination and Desire of improving upon your Instructions …

795. *Alan II, Edinburgh, to Alan I, Dublin, 21 Nov. 1727*

(1248/7/156–7)

… I wrote to my Brother this day fortnight just before I left London, and am far from surprized that your Lordship's concern for his Illness shou'd prevent your speaking too Sanguinely on his Condition; I was therefore very glad of a Letter from You, out of the Country, telling me You was no longer in apprehension of any danger. I hope that He is by this time quite recovered, and that the Cough You formerly mentioned is entirely gone off.

If You will please to direct to me at the Custom House here my Letters will come safe. I can not yet say much of the Country in generall, or my own Business in particular; the One I am very lately come in to, and have not yet entered on the other, because the Gentlemen continue to act by Vertue of the old Commission till the Exemplification comes down, which We daily expect …

796. *Alan I, Dublin, to Thomas, 27 Nov. 1727*

(1248/7/160–1)

I received a letter dated the 8th instant in relation to the County of Clare election from your Nephew, written (as he Saith and I beleive) by your order. It complains of greivous injustice done by the Sherif of the County of Clare in prejudice of Sir Edward O'Bryen who stood on Lord Thomonds interest; if the Sherif (whom I never saw nor knew his name

---

[1051] Possibly Enoch Stearne, clerk of the parliaments (i.e. clerk to the house of lords) in Dublin since 1715, and a cousin of Jonathan Swift (Glenn McKee, 'The Operation, Practices and Procedures of the Irish House of Commons from 1692 to 1730', King's College London PhD, 2017, p. 272). Another possibility is the 'Mr Slatery' with whom Alan records dining (Coxe, *Walpole*, ii, 437).

till this occasion) was pleased to make such a declaracion as Nallyes letter imports (that he would not return Sir Edward tho he had all the votes in the County) he must be a very silly fellow, as well as a dishonest man. But that he hath returned Mr Burton[1052] and Mr Purdon as duly chosen Knights of the County of Clare is certainly true, and is complained of as well by one Ivers[1053] as by Sir Edward O'Bryen, but where the pluralitye of legal freeholders will appear to have been, I cannot yet tell; tho vox populi[1054] is in favor of Sir Edward O'Bryen. Howsoever matters will come out I know not, but this I am sure of; that if any thing very flagrant shal appear against the Sherif, it seems to me that he hath fallen into an unfortunate time to have a complaint brought against him before the house of commons when it will (probably) be greatly inraged at the wild behavior of several Sherifs; for I beleive it to be true that some Sherifs have refused to Indent with the returning Officers of several boroughs, or to return the Indentures signed by the returning Officers, but have returned Indentures between the Sherifs and some of the electors of the boroughs; which I hear is the case of Inniteague a corporacion in the County of Kilkenny, and the estate of your old freind Ned Deane,[1055] but now grasped att by my Lord Duncanon whose two near relacions (I think brothers) the Sherif hath returned an Indenture between him and some of the freemen of the election of;[1056] the same I hear is the case of Mulingar in the County of Westmeath, and other places; nay the Sherif of the County of Waterford (son of Tom Uniack whom you knew)[1057] hath returned an Indenture signed by himself and some of the electors for the borough of Dungarvon in the County of Waterford, by which Mr Uniack (himself) and Mr Wm Wall are returned to be members for that borough,[1058] altho Lord Burlingtons Seneschal Mr Coghlan,[1059] who is the returning officer tendred an Indenture signed by the Seneschal and the majoritye of the borough by which Mr Parry and Mr Carter are returned to have been chosen, as they certainly were, if report is at all to be credited.[1060] These are steps which you have not heard of in England, and such as strike at the root of our constitucion: The Crown appoints Sherifs, they are able to fill the house with representatives from every borough in the Kingdome as they please, and it is to be hoped that they soon may learn to doe the thing which will be best looked on at a certain place: and when an house is once filled with men thus chosen, thus returned; they may bring peticions who desire to be laughed at for fools. These things must, and I think will, be nipt in the budd, or farewel freedome of Parliament; farewell the vaunt we used to

---

[1052] Francis Burton, MP [I].

[1053] John Ivers, MP [I]. O'Brien and Ivers submitted separate petitions (*CJI*, v, 453, 528).

[1054] The popular vote (literally 'the voice of the people').

[1055] Edward Deane, MP [I].

[1056] Hon. Henry Ponsonby, MP [I] and his brother Hon. Folliott Ponsonby. Edward and his brother Stephen were returned by the portreeve (the returning officer); the Ponsonbys by the sheriff. On 20 Dec. 1727 the House voted that the Deanes were not duly elected, and seated Henry Ponsonby (though not his brother). In the several divisions Arthur Hill, and another connection of the Brodricks, Richard Bettesworth, acted as tellers for the Deanes. (*CJI*, v, 441, 463–4; NLI, MS 8470/9: account of Inistioge election petition [1727].)

[1057] Thomas Uniacke (*d.* 1734), of Ballyvergan, Co. Cork, s. of Thomas Uniacke (*d.* 1708), formerly customs collector of Cork (R.G. Fitzgerald-Uniacke, 'Some Old County Cork Families: The Uniackes of Youghal. Part III, The Uniackes of Woodhouse', *Journal of the Cork Historical and Archaeological Society*, ser 1, iii (1894), 183–8).

[1058] For committing a breach of parliamentary privilege in returning himself and William Wall, MP [I], Uniacke was ordered into custody on 13 Dec. 1727 (*CJI*, v, 442, 457).

[1059] See above, p. 153. Coughlan was seneschal of the manor of Dungarvan.

[1060] Benjamin Parry, MP [I] and Thomas Carter, MP [I].

make that we were bound only by Laws which we either in person or by representative consented unto. But whether these enormityes may not be soe great as to lessen the crime of a Sherif whose offence may appear only to be a beleiving a majorityе to have been for one competitor where it really was for the other I cannot tell. But I remember when you and I were at school at Kingston,[1061] that I was present [*when*] a Baronett pleaded a pardon for the murther of a Wandsworth Kedger in the water in the great road near Half way house between Kingston and Wandsworth. There were two high way men found guilty of robberye at the same Assises, and the Judges in abhorrence of the murther, repreived the highwaymen, and reported that they had done soe, to King Charles the second, giving this reason; that their crimes were no way commensurate to the Baronets and that they could not bring themselves to inflict that punishment on them which they could not give the other. Whether that repreive ended (as I heard) in a pardon I know not, but it softned the King soe far that he was not offended with the Judges. I have had a letter from Lord T[*ownshend*] and have answered it, and will doe all that I can justifye to shew my great regard for his Lordships interest, which I am personally inclined to doe; and lye under such obligations (which I never will or can forgett) to his Lordships great freind, that he may be sure to command my best services. We have had frightful accounts last week from Ballyanan, but we begin now to hope better of your Nephew then I did on receiving a letter of the 19th from Mr Chinery.[1062]

[PS] Mr S[*terne*] sent me your letter when I was in the countrey, which I would have communicated to a freind, but have not been able; the same reason makes it impracticable for me to saying any thing satisfactory now: If I were to speak my own sense I must say the remedye proposed is a desperate one, but perhaps the best if not the only one the case admits of. I will take occasion to write more at large about that matter in a few dayes.

797. *Thomas to Alan I, Dublin, 7 Dec. 1727, '9 at night'*

(1248/7/166–7)

I have this minute yours of the 27th of last month, and sitt up in my bed to owne itt. If Sir W[*illiam*] Parsons[1063] have shewn you a letter from mee with an anonimous one from another person to him, you will readily beleive that what is proposed will nott bee a desperate remedy in a certaine place, for surely hee cannott forgett whoe twas to whom hee gave the punch bowle made out of peice of a Yew tree, which grew in his parke.[1064]

The thing is wished for, I must say noe more.

[1061] Presumably Kingston Grammar School. Unfortunately no 17th-century registers have survived among the school records, so it has been impossible to verify this point.

[1062] George Chinnery (c. 1679–c.1755), who married Alan's niece Eleanor, the daughter of his sister Katherine Whitfield.

[1063] MP [I].

[1064] Parsons had received an anonymous letter from London dated 23 Nov., with a scheme to reduce the level of the pensions list on the Irish establishment, by means of a motion for an address to the king, offering to draw up heads of a bill to enable the king to disencumber his revenue of grants, pensions and bounties for lives and terms of years. Any reply was to be sent to 'Daniel Mussaphia, the Sword Blade Coffee House, Exchange Alley'. Thomas Brodrick then wrote Parsons a follow-up letter, explaining that the author was someone in London to whom he made a present of a wooden punch bowl. (SHC, 1248/7/177–8: Parsons to Alan Brodrick I, 23 Dec. 1727; 1248/7/171–2: Parsons to Thomas Brodrick, 20 Dec. 1727.)

798. *Alan II, Edinburgh, to Alan I, Dublin, 9 Dec. 1727*

(1248/7/168–9)

… I have received great Civility's from many People here, particularly from Lord March-mont's[1065] Freinds and Relations. The greatest Pleasure I have here is in hearing from my Freinds, and I therefore hope your Lordship will not deny me that Comfort when You have a little Leizure.

I shou'd rejoice to hear of my Brothers perfect Recovery, which I hope the next Letters I receive will assure me of … News is not the Commodity of this Country; but whenever I hear any that is likely to be so to You, I will not fail of writing it to You …

799. *Thomas to Alan I, Dublin, 21 Dec. 1727*[1066]

(1248/7/173–4)

I send this by a private hand, soe that I make little doubt of its coming to you, though I doe a great deale whither a letter I wrote to Sir W[*illiam*] Parsons on the 23 of last month, with another to him from an anonimous hand ever came to his, by the same post I wrote likewise to you, pray lett mee know whither they were stopt, which I am almost sure of, butt the certainty is of great import, they were upon the same subject of that by Mr Sterne, if they are stopt you will certainly judg why. If they came to you I shall need add nothing more butt that wee continue strongly of the same mind, for the thing will certainly doe, and uppon itt depends better and other consequences the[*n*] you think of.

800. *Alan II, Edinburgh, to Alan I, Dublin, 23 Dec. 1727*

(1248/7/175–6)

… I am glad to hear my Brothers Health is so perfectly reestablish'd; I write to Him to day, and direct to Dublin, because as the Parliament is sitting I take it for granted that He left the Country as soon as He found Himself able to undergo the Fatigue of the Journey. I hope He will be carefull enough of his Health not to risque a Relapse from too close an Attendance on Business. My Uncle has been much out of Order ever since the beginning of October, but by all the Accounts I have lately received, I find He is much better … the Members for this Part of the Country are looking southward, and most of Them propose to set out in a Day or two in order to be at Westminster by the 11th of next month …

[1065] Alexander Hume-Campbell, 2nd earl of Marchmont, lord clerk register [S].

[1066] Letter endorsed by Alan I: 'Tho: Brodrick … inforces the good effects of the scheme sent inclosed to Sir Wm P[*arsons*] in an an unknown hand that upon the successe of that scheme greater and better consequences will follow then I think'.

801. *Alan I, Dublin, to Thomas, the Privy Garden, Whitehall, 23 Dec. 1727*

(1248/7/179–80)

I formerly owned the receit of a letter by a private hand (I mean Mr S[*terne*]) when I was in the countrey, which gives you the reason of my not being more explicite in my thoughts of the matter which was the subject of your letter. The same stil continues, and God knows how long it may doe soe. But in the main I expressed my self a good deal doubtful how far the expedient hinted at ought in prudence to be gone into: and I confesse my doubts are not yet satisfyed. I have since received yours of the ninth instant, which gave me light into the meaning of a letter I had received from the person by whom the punch bowle was presented, in which he mentioned to have received two anonimous letters from me; which greatly amazed me who knew nothing of any such letters, and therefore had a letter sent to him by a freind for explanation of the matter. He hath this post sent me a copy of one, but omitted to send me that which was more material, viz. the form into which the Punch Bowle would have this affair cast; and when that comes I shal be able to form a judgement how far what is represented as feasible may be useful, I mean to the Kingdome in general, for I can easily foresee the advantages which may be made by particular persons on your side of the water, and the danger we should put ourselves into by going into soe general a method as seems to be thought advisable <u>by the former of the scheme</u>. The consequence must be that when applicacion is made, for what is proposed as the way, to releive the oppressed as far etc There must be an acquiescence under, and a confirmation of all from which we are not eased: and consequently an allowance of what was done, which may be repeated another time to other persons. But I shal understand this affair better when the Gentleman on this side of the water sends me a copy of the draught he had from the Punch Bowle, for which I write this night. I am sorry not to be able to give you a better account of your Nephew then I can in truth doe. My last letter from one of the Physicians who attend him stil (in answer to one by which I desired his sincere private thoughts of him) tells me in plain terms his case is very dubious; They all agree he had abscesse in his Lungs, which broke in a violent fit of coughing and since that he spitt up a vast deal of corrupted matter: but I doe not find he continues to expectorate in so plentiful a maner as he did: which were greatly to be wished. I thank you for the tendernesse you express for him and have let him know how zealously you have espoused his interests and put him in mind to renew his applicacion to Sir F[*rancis Drake*] which I am sure will be a vast comfort to him, as I think I may reasonably conclude from the dejection of spirits which he fell under when he apprehended your kindnesse for him was abated. Sennyes ilnesse hath had vast influence on this Session and given Mr C[*onolly*] and his Clan oportunityes to doe several things in matters of election etc which would certainly have received another turn, if both of the Knights for our Countye or <u>one of them in particular</u> had been in the house[1067] … I am sincerely troubled at the dismal condition you describe yourself in under the apprehension of a severe fit of the stone: but hope that proceeds from the lownesse of spirits which that distemper (I am told) usually occasions and that your [—[1068]] letter will bring an account of your fit being entirely over. Your sister hath been very ill but is better.

[1067] St John III and Henry Boyle.
[1068] Word missing.

802. *Alan I, Dublin, to Thomas, 26 Dec. 1727*

(1248/7/181–2)

Since my last I have received a copy of the punch bowle scheme, which I confesse was put a [*sic*] very fit hand, if it had needed nothing more but an honest and warm heart in the person who was to be concerned in the execution of it; but is there not more occasion of a good head, and tongue then our freind is master of? When you recollect what time is thought proper by the freinds of the scheme to put it in execution, you will find none is yet lost, for the preliminaryes are not yet over; nor can be in some time: The nature of the thing requires great deliberation whether the appearing conveniencyes which may attend it, be equal to the mischeifs which it may occasion. And in this particular I confesse I am far from being determined in my own judgement and should be very willing to have oportunitye to confer with one who (in my opinion) will be of greater significancye in bringing the affair to a good issue, then can be imagined by those whose distance from this place keeps in great darknesse of the present scituacion of affair and temper of people. If you shal hereafter receive from different hands, proposicions before which you see any figure or number prefixed keep them and perhaps you may receive others from different hands. Put them then in order according to the number prefixed to each proposition, and when they are read in that method they will explain the sentiments of freinds, which they may be unwilling to put into a continued discourse for fear of their falling into wrong hands, and making that no longer a secret which is desired to be made one, not for the writers sake but the sake of the schemist. Your poor Nephew is bitterly wanted here where matters (especially those relating to elections) are carryed on in a very new method. For example A and B. peticion the house that they were duly elected to serve as members for the borogh of R. but that the returning officer hath returned C. and D. to have been duly elected, their peticions goes farther that C. and D were guilty of briberye and corruption in obtaining the votes of some of the electors. The peticion is referred to the Committee of elections, and the Chairman of that Committee decides that by the orders of the house not only C must withdraw while the question is put on him, whether he was duly elected and returned; but also that D. must withdraw when the question is put whether C. was duly elected. Now till the sense of the Committee and also the resolution of the house hath determined it otherwise D seemed to several judgment to have a right to vote in all questions not concerning himself, and consequently in the question whether C was duly elected.

Upon the hearing there was such evidence given against one of the sitting members that he had bribed some of the voters that a good many seemed to beleive it; but a great many did not; and when the question was put in the house for agreeing with the Committee who had voted neither of the sitting members to be duly elected (tho not one sillable had been offered to prove one of them to have been concerned in the bribery supposed) and had gone farther and voted the peticioners to have been duly elected; tho it was fully proved that there was a majoritye of the electors (against whom no bribery was charged) voted against them and for the sitting members; this also seemed strange to several who thought that the corrupting some of the electors was no reason for depriving the uncorrupted majoritye of their right to elect burgesses, or to give the minoritye a power to send representatives to Parliament for them. Declaring it a void election did not serve the turn; but I think these points would hardly have been declared by your Nephew (if he had been in the chair of elections, from which absence only could exclude him[1069]) to be according to the course and order of Parliaments. Pray inform yourself from one who can and will honourably say what ought to be done in cases of like nature hereafter.

This cannot be a merry Christmas to me while I have such news relating to your ilnesse and your Nephews.

803. Alan I to Thomas, [c. 26 Dec. 1727]

(1248/7/223)

I have taken the Punch bowle sketch and transcribed it in 16 lines; each of which I intended should contain just nine words, but by mistake have in some of them put more; I presume you have a Copy of it, and therefore desire you will transcribe that in as many lines, and make each line to contain as many words as are added to the several figures following

1		9.
2 etc		11.
3	—	10.
4	—	9
5	—	7.
6	—	9.
7	—	8.
8		
9	—	10.
10.	—	9
11.	—	9.
12.	—	8.
13:	—	9.
14:	—	9.
15.	—	9.
16.	—	1.

By doing this you will be able to know peoples sense of that paper, for if it be intended to remarke on any word or part it may [be] done thus, viz. Line. 7. Words 3. 4. 5. soe that looking into that line and taking out of it the words which stand the third forth and fifth words in that line into a separate paper you will see what it is I am giving you peoples thoughts of as I apprehend them to be, and yet nobody but he who knows in what paper those lines are contained can tell the meaning of the first paper or the sentiments of people here.

Under this confidence I proceed to tell you what I have either observed myself or have heard remarked by other people. L[ine] 7 W[ord] 3 is a very comprehensive and indefinite word but as probably it was put in to prevent any thing of reflection upon what may have hapned lately, no objection would be made to it, but that L[ine] 5 W[ord] 7 is very extensive and L[ine] 13. W[ord] 5. hath the same term so that what is intended for

[1069]St John Brodrick III had acted as chairman of the committee of privileges and elections in the previous session but did not attend at the beginning of the 1727 parliament and was replaced by Thomas Trotter.

the benefit of the familye may be carryed soe far as to become its ruine: or of great part of it.

In line 7. W[ord] 9. there is an epithet which does not with truth belong to the substantive to which it is conjoined, and it may be of the last consequence to allow them that epithet which is really perfectly unnecessary unlesse it be to graft upon it a proposicion which we know not to be true, many of us with in our own memoryes.

L[ine] 5. W[ords] 4. 5. 6. 7. and Line 6. W[ords] 1. 2. 3. 4. 5. 6. 7. 8. 9. and line 7. W[ord] 1. contain the cheif things which seem desired, or rather at present expected; But then L[ine] 13. may extend farther then seems desirable considering that W[ord] 1. of the 14 L[ine] must be understood to be intirely left to the judgement of him whom you in your [...]¹⁰⁷⁰

804. *Thomas to Alan I, 30 Dec. 1727*

(1248/7/185–6)

I hope your next will bring a better account of your sonne, then that of this day sennights date, Mr Chinnery writes that there were thoughts of his going into France assoone as hee could beare the voiage; I will nott take uppon mee to advise butt am sure were the case my owne I should rather choose Lisbon then Montpelier, as being a softer air, for I have very often heard itt remarked that the keenesse of the latter has proved fatall (instead of beneficiall) to weake Lungs. God direct.

I have hitherto escaped another fitt of the stone, and hope (att present) to continue doing soe, having this last fortnight constantly taken gentle phisick which has brought away a good deale of gravell, I wish I were att Bath in hopes those waters would discharge the rest, butt when that will bee I know nott, for I have nott yett left my chamber, nott so much as going once down stairs, the Doctor apprehending that a fresh cold may occasion a return of my feaver. I agree with your way of reasoning, and the conclusion you draw from itt, butt you will surely consider that if the proposall bee accepted (as I hope itt will) the family cannott possibly suffer by itt, in as much as the Case (as itt now stands) is plainly against them, why then should they nott availe themselves of what they can. If you knew from whom this matter tooke its first rise, you would nott onely bee very sure of its successe, butt likewise bee convinct that nothing in substance, nay nott in words should bee altered, for reasons I have formerly given, lett itt bee done as is desired, and leave the rest to the share of those whoe (to speake plainly) will bee content to sinke under the load, butt lett mee againe repeate, that an alteration which att first sight may seem immateriall may bee soe turned as to defeate the whole, you cannott surely butt understand mee. I have hitherto maintained a charecter which I would nott in my old age forfeite, and uppon this ile putt itt, for in noe occurrence of my life was I ever more certaine.

¹⁰⁷⁰Remainder missing.

805. *Alan II, Edinburgh, to Alan I, 9 Jan. 1727[/8]*

(1248/7/189–90)

I am exceedingly sorry to see by your Lordship's of the 18th, which Mr Finlay delivered to me yesterday, that You was then under apprehension for my Brother; the two last I had received from your Lordship before that spoke of Him as past any the least danger, and as wanting nothing but strength; I hope however, (from what You say, that You expect to hear of his being out of Danger, by the next Post;) that You have had that good News long ago; and wou'd fain perswade my self, for my own Ease, that your Fondness and Affection for your Children makes You more apprehensive than is necessary. Your Lordship told me not long ago that I must not wonder at your having been far from sanguine in my Brothers Case; and I wou'd flatter my self, that your speaking with so much Uncertainty proceeds in great measure from the same tender concern. I must nevertheless beg your Lordship to give me the Satisfaction of a certain account of his Recovery, as soon as You can; and to assure Your self that there are but very few People to whom that News will be more agreable. I return your Lordship my Thanks for attempting to make me your Instrument in serving your Freinds. I shall think it an Additionall Happyness in the Place his Majesty has been pleased to give me, if it can ever furnish me with an Opportunity of obeying your Commands. Mr Finlay has as good a Character here as his Freinds on your Side of the water can give Him; but I am sorry to say that there is no great prospect of serving Him, to any purpose, on this Establishment. He is now Supervisor of the Duties on Salt at Prestonpans; now there is but one Employment in that branch of the Revenue worth more than his own; at least the Difference is so small that his Advantage in any other Change wou'd be very inconsiderable. Nor indeed are there above four Ports in this Country of which the Collectorship wou'd be worth his Acceptance; now the few Places of Value have so many Candidates of this Country for Them, the Moment they become vacant, that it is great Odds against Mr Finlay that He does not succeed, unless He obtains the promise of a Presentment to such a particular place; before it becomes vacant. Add to this that our Presentments are either warranted or superseded at the Treasury, as the Lords please; and the more Value a Place is of here, the more Sollicitation it occasions there.

I perceive however that Mr Finlay's Desire is to be fixed somewhere in England; now We (during the time of our Appointment here) have nothing to do with Presentments there; and Recommendations are not usuall from one Board (as a Board) to the other; but rather from Freind to Freind. He was recommended in the latter End of the Year 1723, or beginning of 1724, by the then Lord Cheif Baron Smith,[1071] to Sir J Evelyn[1072] and Mr Walker,[1073] by whose means He soon obtained the Post He now has; in which He has behaved in such a manner as gives Him good Pretentions to any Favour the Commissioners can shew Him. I therefore beleive many of them will be ready to Joyn with me in making

---

[1071] John Smith (1657–1726), of Frolesworth, Leics., lord chief baron of exchequer [S] until his death on 21 June 1726 (*Oxf. DNB*).

[1072] Sir John Evelyn (1682–1763), 1st Bt, of Wotton, Surrey, MP [GB] 1708–10, commr. of customs since 1721.

[1073] Thomas Walker (c. 1664–1748), of Wimbledon, Surrey, MP [GB] 1733–4, 1735–47, commr. of customs since 1714.

Application on his Behalf, to those Gentlemen, now in London, to continue their Kindness to Him; and it will certainly be in their Power to place Him more to his Satisfaction and Advantage, and probably to prefer Him sooner than We cou'd do here. If in the mean time any Presentment whatsoever, worth his Acceptance; shou'd happen to fall to my Lot, I shall immediately let your Lordship know that I have done my Duty by endeavouring to obey your Commands …

806. *Thomas to Alan I, Dublin, 15 Jan. 1727[/8]*

(1248/7/191–2)

My Lord Baltimore tells mee that Mr Ogle[1074] had a letter from a freind with the welcome news of my nephewes mending apace, and being in a very fair way of recovery, surely hee will assoone as able thinke of altering the climate, which every body must conclude absolutely necessary …

807. *Alan I, Dublin, to Thomas, 16 Jan. 1727[/8]*

(1248/7/193–4)

Since my last A is come to town, and I have discoursed him, from whom I find that he hath already given his thoughts upon a certain affair,[1075] approving it and expecting very good effects of it, and beleiving it to be feasible without great difficultye. But when we came to consider in what maner it should be conducted and what persons we[re] proper to impart the secret unto, I never saw a man at a greater losse then he then seemed to be. My advice was that he would take a certain list and mark those persons whom he thought fit to communicate the thing unto; some time after he returned and gave me the list with a mark by making a line in the margin before each name he confided in and desired me to crosse such of them as I did not approve. But I was unwilling to doe a thing so shocking to him who had made up the number of about a dozen, by naming the same man in different places as some of them hapned to be in the list, and the rest consisted cheifly of his own freinds, generally very honest and worthy men; but he named one who notwithstanding his freindship for A and a general character of being an honest Gentleman, lies under such attachments to that man in this Kingdome, who (in my opinion) is intended and ought to be kept a perfect stranger to the affair if it be intended to be brought to the desired issue, that it would be the same thing to consult the one, as to inform the other: which would be done in my judgement the very first oportunitye which offered, and by this means the thing would take wind, and lay C under difficultyes, which he in his paper to A endeavours to avoid. Now to give you my thoughts of the abilityes of the persons named by A for the work they were to undertake, and the prudence with which they would conduct it, I confesse I thought them so far defective in both, that I was not inclined to goe into what A proposed to me, with a frank readinesse to impart the matter to them. I saw the difficultye

---

[1074] George Ogle, MP [I].

[1075] The 'punch bowl scheme', to reduce the number of pensions on the Irish establishment.

I should be laid under if I should undertake that task, but seeing you expressed soe earnest a desire to have something done without losse of time I cast in my mind what persons I could find in the list whom I should think more capable to goe through with such an affair, then those whom A had pointed out and I formed a list of such whom I thought capable of conducting such a matter to a good issue if I found them of opinion with the thing; and talked with several of them how desirable a thing it would be to ease etc and after hearing their sense what way was to be taken to attain so desirable an end (as they all agreed the easing etc would be) I found them so very different from what a certain paper imports, as East is from West. I used the best methods I could to reconcile them to the method, which I by peice meales opened to them and heard their sense of the matter, but found it was irreconcileably dissonant from that form, which my freind approved. Soe that I could not propose those Gentlemen to A to be the men to whom the paper should be imparted with any hopes of their cooperating in bringing that to perfection of which others think very well. I used all the arguments I could to shew the good consequences which might be expected from approving, but doe not find I made more then two proselyes, who giving the reasons of their conviction gave such that one who was in opposite sentiments would have made advantage; When I consider how heartily B and C espouse this matter, and what B tells me in advising me to consult some late letters of his to find out the person there described, which I did immediately read over but found nothing there but what I understood before, I say considering all this, I cannot see that any thing can be done in the matter desired before you and others have an oportunitye of meeting: To have the thing known if not effectually proceeded on is not at all desirable: A is not able to goe through with it (I fear) nor doe I know anybody who will undertake a matter of soe delicate a nature and of so weighty consideration into his hand, so as to render himself accountable for accidents. A freind of yours is absolutely necessary to the conducting an affair of this difficultye through the several steps it must take, but alas! will not be able to doe that in any reasonable time if it please God ever to restore him to health.[1076] I am not vain in this but morally certain of its truth.

808. *Alan I, Dublin, to Thomas, the Privy Garden, Whitehall, 23 Jan. 1727[/8]*

(1248/7/195–6)

This morning I received a letter from Jo: Hoare in Corke,[1077] with a much more melancholy account of your Nephews condition then we have had for several posts past; but freinds seem not to have the same apprehensions from that letter, as I confesse it hath raised in me, which are (I confesse) very dismal. God is all powerful and good; and that seems to me to be the cheif (if not only) comfort left me that I shal again see him alive. The Doctors under whose

[1076] St John III.

[1077] Joseph Hoare (*d.* 1729), of Hoare's Lane, Cork, and Woodhill, Co. Cork, merchant and banker of Cork, brother and partner of Edward Hoare, MP [I]; a Quaker (Edward Hoare, *Some Account of the Early History and Genealogy … of the Families of Hore and Hoare* … (1883), 36; C.M. Tenison, 'The Private Bankers of Cork and the South of Ireland', *Journal of the Cork Historical and Archaeological Society*, ser. 1, iii (1892), 221–2). Hoare acted as the Brodricks' banker, receiving rents from their tenants in Co. Cork (SHC, G145/box98/1: Nicholas Greene to Alan I, 29 Mar., 14 Oct. 1720; Nathaniel Evans to Alan I, 25 Aug. 1727).

care he hath all along been have desponded much more of his recoverye then those here to whom we communicated the state of his case as drawn by the physicians at Corke, who from the beginning were for opening his side but those here not concurring that design was laid aside. If this letter be wrote in a disjointed, distracted style; it will represent the condicion my mind is in under this melancholy state of your poor Nephews health. God restore him and preserve him. Farewell. I am your disconsolate brother.

[*PS*] Since writing the other side I have received yours of the 15th and wish the account Mr Ogle gives Lord Baltimore of Sennyes prospect of a speedy recoverye, had as good a foundacion now as our hopes seemed to have about the time Mr Ogles letter was probably wrote I mean between a fortnight and three weeks agoe: but I must own I dread the receit of my countrey letters to morrow, least they bring an account with much lesse comfort then those which we have formerly had. As to his going into a warmer climate every body will judge it fit when the season of the year will admit his going abroad, or on ship board without taking cold, which is not now the case ...

809. *Thomas to Alan I, Dublin, 23 Jan. 1727[/8]*[1078]

(1248/7/197–8)

The dismal account given of my nephew in your postscript of the ninth, is soe very different from the preceding part of your letter which is dated the seventh, as leaves hope that your country accounts may represent his case worse then really itt was, though I shall dread the receipt of your next; however I shall nott enter into the objections mentioned, farther then that I thinke my former letters have fully answered them all; I have att all times and on every occasion endeavoured faithfully the service of my country, this was with the same intent, and will with great confidence affirme twould prove soe, butt every body is to judge for himselfe, and I shall satisfie my selfe in having done what I thought (nott to say sure) is right, the event will shew itt. Perhaps a dislike to both the persons whoe have been in great measure conveighors of the thing, may create an aversion to itt in somebody, if that prevaile God helpe us.

810. *Thomas to Alan I, Dublin, 1 Feb. 1727[/8]*[1079]

(1248/7/201–2)

I putt pen to paper with satisfaction from the last paragraph of your letter giving an account of your sonnes amendment. Surely you will nott lett him neglect the earlyest oportunity

[1078]Letter endorsed by Alan I: 'Tho: Brodrick ... persists in his opinion of the goodnesse of the scheme proposed to ease Ireland of Pensions. Expresses great concern for Senny. Thinks his former letters have answered all objections to the scheme about pensions; but I never saw anything that looked like an answer. Imputed the disapproving the thing to the dislike of the persons who have been concerned in conveighing the thing'.

[1079]Letter endorsed by Alan I: 'Tho: Brodrick ... very sollicitous to have the scheme for reducing pensions proceeded on. Hints at one who (being an enemy to B & C.) would be sure to obstruct it; that person I thought to be Mr C[onoll]ye; but I now think he must mean Senny'.

© *The Parliamentary History Yearbook Trust 2023.*

which the Spring will give, of altering the climate for in most cases delays prove dangerous, butt in his more especially.

I gave a darke hint in my last, of one whoe I was sure would doe all in his power to obstruct the treaty going on, though att the same time I doubted whither you would understand whoe was meant, by the description of his being an enemy to B and C butt now thinke you would guesse right, from your saying hee must bee kept wholly in the darke, till the bargaine was struck. If you knew how sollicitous a person principally concerned is from time to time, to know what progresse has been made in the affair, you would nott wonder att my desire to have itt brought to a good issue; for though I am nott personally interested, I cannott bee void of the greatest concerne for the good of the family, whose true interest I take this to bee; and thinke itt a greate happinesse when all sides have the same thing in veiwe, which I am sure is soe in this case.

I am still confind by the severity of the weather, and therfore know scarcely what is doing, butt am told by freinds whoe come to see mee that our greate men make nott the least doubt of a suddaine peace, notwithstanding the Kings speech leaves itt with uncertainty, butt this in prudence ought to bee soe.

811. *Alan I, Dublin, to Thomas, 2 Feb. 1727[/8]*

(1248/7/203–4)

I have your letter of the 23d of January, in which you tell me you think your former letter had fully answered the objections which occurred in a certain affair; I own it would have been much more to my satisfaction that you would have entred into those objections more particularly then I can find you ever did in any one letter wrote on that subject, and yet I have perused them all very carefully and weighed them: but our last accounts about D make the thing perfectly impracticable at this time; for I much doubt, whether tho he should be of the same sentiments with B and C; and as ready to goe into it as I beleive A hath told you he is, D and all his freinds (tho they should endeavour it) would be able to convince others of the expediency of the scheme: and I am sure a thing of that nature should either not be stirred in at all, or be effectually carryed through. If poor Sennyes condition of health would have admitted his attendance this Session, I think a good many of our late affairs would not have taken the turn they have, but I had such an account of his condition in a letter wrote from Corke on this day sennight that I verily expected to have had the certainty of his being dead by the letters of this day: but I thank God we had a more comfortable account from Robin Bettesworth in a letter dated 30 January[1080] in which he gives it as his opinion he may yet gett over his dreadful distemper; but as I know he hath very little judgement in the nature of his ilnesse and hath an extreme inclination that he should be continued longer among us, I doubt he rather speaks his wishes then his judgement: During his ilnesse he lay under great uneasinesse at the sense he had of your being displeased with him, and expressed it in terms that would move the hardest heart. The last part of your letter runs in these words; Perhaps a dislike to both the persons who have been in great measure

---

[1080]SHC, 1248/7/199–200. Robert Bettesworth (*d.* by 1756), of Cork, was the brother of Richard Bettesworth (1689–1741) of Dublin, MP [I] Thomastown 1721–7, Midleton 1727–*d*. (Reg. Deeds, 169/4/112549, 201/115/132015).

conveyers of the thing, may create aversion to it <u>in somebody</u>. If that prevails God help us. I think I need not tell you that I know who the conveyers were; but doe assure you I cannot frame a rational conjecture, who <u>the somebody</u> means in whom an aversion is supposed to be raised. I am sure the nature of the thing ought to determine people in their judgements in matters of this sort, and I beleive and am sensible doth and will doe soe. Pray explain yourself whether you can mean that there is a certain person who having an aversion, or a dislike (as you term it) to the conveyers, can thence entertain an aversion to a thing which they would otherwise approve. Indeed I neither know nor beleive there is any such person, not being able to think on anyone who hath a dislike to them; my acquaintance lying in a sett of people of another Kidney. Next Tuesday I intend to write my thoughts in a letter by a private hands in the plainest terms, and such as will fully let you into the true sentiments of my soul on this very nice affair.

[*PS*] I send Dr Gratton[1081] hence to morrow to your Nephew at Corke at a very great expence but his life is too valuable to me to consider that.

812. *Thomas to Alan I, 13 Feb. 1727[/8]*[1082]

(1248/7/207–8)

Last night (five packets coming togather) I receivd yours of the 29th of last and second of this month, which I am ill able to answer, having had a returne of the feaver, with a loosenesse, the former is in great measure abated, butt the latter remains, I should therefore have contented my selfe with ordering Charles Powell to have owned the receipt of them, were itt nott for a paragraph which I resolve to speake uppon, and shall therfore confine my selfe to that onely, hoping I may bee able to goe through itt without the losse of one post, if I am nott I must leave the finishing itt to another.

You say that my nephew during his illnesse lay under great uneasinesse att the sence hee had of my being displeased with him, and expressed itt in termes that would move the hardest heart.

This is a repetition of what in a former letter (some time since) you mentioned, to which you then added that you had told him you beleivd I was nott well pleased with his nott paying what hee owed mee, I cannott bee precise in the words, nott being able readily to turne to that letter, butt am sure of the sence, of this I tooke noe notice to you, judging itt such a reason as might by all mankind bee thought allowable, butt I very well knew this was nott the sore place as will appeare by what follows, which I thought I never should bee oblidged to mention, nor would I doe itt now, if itt were nott extorted from mee.

The last time I saw him when hee rose from his chair (after spending a quarter of an hour with mee) hee expressed himselfe with a good deale of passion to the following effect, I thinke I remember the words butt am sure I doe the sence and import of them.

[1081]James Grattan (c.1673–1747), the celebrated Dublin physician.

[1082]Cover endorsed by Alan I: 'Tho: Brodrick … a very unkind letter, containing unjust insinuations against my wife and reflections on her'.

I wonder sayes hee what I have done which should make you take part against mee: though I am going immediately away I have the satisfaction of leaving a freind behind mee whoe will take effectuall care that my interest in my father shall nott bee lessened.

I understood him very well, and could have given a full answer.

I have my share of satisfaction in having a witnesse to this (my Br[*other*] Lory being present) without which my veracity might bee questioned. I owne the charge right of taking part against him, which I did, and in this instance alwayes shall, because I am sure the thing was right and just; in addition to which I told you the sollemne obligation I lay under, to which you seemd to give little creditt, telling mee I was nott in Ireland when my sister dyed, butt I gave you several convincing instances of your being mistaken, to which you made noe reply, butt dropping that matter began talking uppon some other subject; I have in every instance relating hereto acted uppon principles of honour, and pursued the dictates of a clear conscience, and would if the whole were to bee gon over againe, doe just the same thing. I know nott how soone I shall bee to make a dreadful account, butt if this bee a crime I shall carry itt with mee unrepented of.

I can very certainly fix the Epoche of uneasinesse in our family, which till then wee were wholly strangers to, and can to a demonstration shew the foundation of itt. I dealt plainly with you on this head, and flatter my selfe that any impartial stranger would bee convinc't, butt how far Lady Midletons professing that shee never knew any thing of the matter may weigh with you I know nott, butt I am told shee does nott deny her knowledge of that groundles mallicious story (transmitted from Dublin) relating to C[*ourthope*] Clayton, which I should have thought you ought to have been acquainted with, if itt had nott been very well knowne that there was nott the least foundation for itt, butt doing soe would probably have disappointed the thing aimd att. The treatment of your daughter I thinke very fully warrants the conclusion.

I have acted as I thought right in every particular, I am extremely pleasd with having done soe, and shall persist, ending as I began.

I have with a good deale of difficulty gott thus far, would my strenghth allow itt, I could say ten times as much, butt thinke this enough.

My Br[*other*] W[*illiam*] lyes dangerously ill, wherfore I keep your letter to him till my B[*rother*] Lory comes to town, which I expect hourly.

813. *Alan I, Dublin, to Thomas, 24 Feb. 1727[/8]*

(1248/7/209–10)

Last night I received two letters from you dated the 13th and the 17th instant; the former tells me that Mr Chinery in a letter of the fourth doth not describe your Nephew to be in soe ill a condition as mine to you expressed him to be at the time I heard last out of the countrey; but that is not to be much wondred at, since after a free expectoration of the matter which loads his lungs, he seems to be in an hopeful way, and that account seems to me to have had great credit with you which Mr Chinerye sent, or else you could not but have expressed some sort of concern, for his very weak and dangerous condicion: which you may be sure we here thought to be so to the last degree when we sent a Physician from hence at a very great expence, in addition to that of three in Corke who have constantly attended him for more then five months past. I had letters from the Doctor whom we sent down dated in Corke 16 Febr. and one from Robin Bettesworth and another from Arthur Hill of the same date, which last inclosed one signed by his own hand, and expressed to be the last request of a dying son, but I will not say in how moving a maner he expressed himself for fear least those words should be construed to mean something far from my thoughts as I doe assure you, like words in a former letter have been by you: I had more reasons then one not to intend, what you seem to think I meant by them, which I will not trouble you with setting down here. But I cannot prevail with my self not to say that I think the insinuation of poor Allyes not being like to continue long <u>an eyesore</u>, to contain something in it which I did hope and beleive nothing could have brought out of your mouth, or into your heart. To me I am sure all my children (and she in particular) hath been most dear blessings and I cannot but be concerned that any of them should be thought eyesores to any thing which I love, or who by their relation to me ought to love them; and I shal be very little obliged to them who take the worst and wickedest way of expressing regard to and affection for them, by unjust suggestions of want of love toward them and too great partialitye in favour of others. I am equally related to them all and appointed an indifferent Judge between them, and will take leave to Judge for my self and them, according to what I think to be right; and have as little patience at the thought of any one of my children being an eyesore to any person related to me (and here you may be sure I cannot but mean my eldest son as well as my younger children) as any other person can be at thinking any other of my children is an eyesore to any body. These insinuacions beside being very unjust to the person intended, are very greivous and disagreeable to me: but I hope the life of my poor sick son and daughter will be continued by God to both soe long, that I may have oportunityes of silencing all murmurs and reproaches of this nature by such an equal deportment toward and just care of all, as may convince those whose prejudices and passions have carryed them greater lengths in these matters. But methinks you should have taken some notice of the subject matter of my two letters, they containing something relating to the affair you communicated to Sir Wm P[arsons] whom I have not seen these three weeks, nor expect soon to see again. Upon what foot that matter stands I know not; but this I know that it hath been soe wisely managed that (notwithstanding the caution given him to keep the thing secret if not found advisable) the matter is become Coffee house talk and two persons (now in London) mentioned as privy to the thing: This I was told some time since, and that Lord Santry said he had discoursed Sir Wm P[arsons] on the matter and convinced him of the unreasonablenesse of it: Whether he did soe or not I cannot tell; but I confesse he is as likely a man to be convinced by that noble Peers arguments on any subject as this Kingdome contains. I hear his Lordship heard and apprehended the grants to be called into question were those which concerned Lords and Gentlemen of Ireland only, of which number Mr Henry Barry (his Lordships son)[1083] is one; and the Earles of Roscommon, Cavan, and Lord Athenrye are also of the number. I formerly told you my fears of the consequence of this scheme, and cannot yet learn that it hath been put into such a light that it finds many who thinke (tho intended never soe well) it will in the event prove beneficial to the general good of the Kingdome. I have sent a letter to Corke to bring Senny up, which he earnestly desires and hopes (as

---

[1083] Hon. Henry Barry (1710–51), only son of Baron Barry of Santry, who eventually succeeded his father as 4th baron.

also doth Dr Gratton) to be able to accomplish in some time; for he cannot be easy in the daily conversacion [*of*] screech owles,[1084] as his Corke Doctors have all along been and given their thoughts to their confidents, that he is past hope of recovery but attend him as duly as the day comes, and swallow their fees as greedily as if they did something to deserve them.

814. *Alan II, Edinburgh, to Alan I, Dublin, 29 Feb. 1727/8*

(1248/7/211–12)

If your Lordship knew what an Happyness it is to me, to hear from my Freinds at Dublin, I am perswaded I shou'd not have been so long without hearing from You; and I beg leave to put your Lordship in mind that the Letter Mr Finlay brought me is the last Syllable I have seen from thence.

I hope there is no truth in an account I had this day from a Gentleman that my Brother is very ill again; He told me He had it in a Letter from Dublin, but I hope it is only a false report which some credulous person may have taken on Trust. Sure I need not tell your Lordship how greived I shou'd be were it true; nor how much I am concerned even at this uncertain report. But Uncertainty is one of the Misfortunes intailed on People at a distance from their Freinds; which I hope your Lordship will remove as far as You can, by letting me know, when You have Leizure, that My Lady, Yourself and my Brother and his Family are well … I apply my self closely to my Business here, and hope that time and practise will give me some Insight into it; at least I will not be ignorant for want of taking true Pains to be informed.

815. *Thomas to Alan I, Dublin, 5 Mar. 1727[/8]*[1085]

(1248/7/215–16)

Yesterday I receivd yours of the 24th of last month, and will in this speake to itt in the order tis wrote. You say Mr Chinneryes account seemd to have great creditt with mee otherwise I should have expressed some sort of concerne for his weake condition; I owne itt had somuch (hee being on the place) as gave good reason to hope I should in a short time congratulate, a much more pleasing subject then condolance, butt tis my misfortune to bee supposed to say too little or too much.

You next say words of yours were by mee construed to mean somthing far from your thoughts; if I guesse right the perticular you hint att, (for you doe nott mention itt) I can onely say I repeated your owne words truly, and beleive you know I did soe, a mans meaning may bee mistaken, butt words plaine and positive hardly can.

You say the insinuation of my neices being an <u>eyesore</u> containes something in itt which you did hope and beleive nothing could have brought out of my mouth, or into my heart.

[1084] The call of the barn owl, resembling a scream, was often considered an ill omen.

[1085] Letter endorsed by Alan I: 'Tho: Brodrick … persists in approving the scheme formed in London for easing Ireland of pensions but instead of answering objections saith he hath done it formerly'.

Cheif Justice Hales frequently sayd that concurring circumstances usually carryed conviction, I thinke (nay I am sure) I can instance butt too many to leave roome for doubting the truth of the insinuation, butt you give itt a turne as if meant to you, in which sence I would pawne my life you did nott understand itt, for the latter part of the paragraph evinces that, in the other sence I beleive itt, and that firmely.

You say you are equally related to all your children, the same I say of myselfe, and have shewne itt by doing what few unkles would.

You then say you will take the liberty of judging for your selfe between them according to what you thinke right. Say and hold without being influenced by any other person, for to speake plainly your resolutions have of late been very variable, as well as our way of thinking very different. I am sure I heartily joine in praying to God that both your sick sonne and daughter may live soe long as to give you opertunity of silencing what you call murmurs and reproaches, I saw her the morning after coming to towne, and omitt the surprize the doing soe was to mee, since which I have nott seen her, having suffered a good deale by going out that bitter morning, butt am assured by messages that shee is rather better then worse.

You end your letter with wondring that I take noe notice of an affair of a different nature from what preceded; to what purpose should I over and over againe repeat the same thing, if itt bee resolved against, I have done, having truly and faithfully delivered my opinion, if itt bee attempted (bee the successe what itt will) the event will shew whoe made the rightest judgment. Every one whoe may thinke himselfe in danger will use all means to divert the storme, your Lords therefore are in the right of representing itt as they doe.

I doe nott thinke more then two were entrusted herewith, and am ready to sweare for one of them that hee never heard or imagined any thing of what is suggested, and will goe as far as a compurgator can for the other, whoe is out of towne and has been for several days, att his returne I will acquaint him herewith, nott having seen him these 3 weeks …

816. *Alan I, Dublin, to Thomas, 14 Mar. 1727[/8]*

(1248/7/217–18)

By the letter which I wrote to Lawry on the second instant you will find that I had at that time ground enough for greif to the bottom of my soul by the account I had received the day before from Corke of Senny's death on the 26th of February: which neither needed, nor was capable of being increased (as I thought) but I must own that the very unkind and severe letter which I received soon after from you dated the fifth instant made me more sensible of an addition to the sorrow I was under, then I did beleive was possible. Indeed as the last pound, is said to break the horses back, which it would not doe of it self, if he had not had too great a load on him before to be well able to bear: I cannot conceal from you that instead of what I then much wanted (I mean comfort) it added to the sorrow that then afflicted me to the soul. But I will be silent on that subject, because I think it incumbent on me to comply with the dying request of your poor Nephew, which you see in the most moving paper my eyes ever saw, I mean his letter to me dated the 16th of February, just after his passing and getting over a fit of coughing which lasted between five and six hours and which he as well as every body about him thought he could not have survived; but it pleased God he gott over that fit to write the most melancholy, most submissive and dutiful letter that ever man wrote, in which nothing is contained misbecoming a man of spirit, but a great deal well becoming a good christian, a tender father and affectionate husband. If I had not been an eye witnesse in Autumn last of what he hath done at Ballyanan in making the place habitable, and beautifying it, and in planting and improving the Land I could not have entertained an Idea of it suitable to what the sight of it gave me. You see he mentions that he had been at very great expence in doing all that, and that he had at least encouragement if not a promise of having a farther and more continuing interest in that place as your tenant then he ever had, I mean for three lives. But his poor broken spirits made him apply to me to become an intercessor with you that his widow might be continued in that place by you as your tenant paying you the same rent which he saith you authorized him to set it to another tenant, at least during her own life: as a comfortable being for her and her fatherlesse children. I cannot decline laying his dying request before you that you will not let any body obtain a right under you in it to remove the widow of your Nephew and her helplesse children from that dwelling which he hath made comfortable, by laying out much more money on the house gardens and meadows etc then he could well spare which might otherwise have been some addition to the small provisions made for his children by the settlement on his marriage, in case he should leave daughters only. I am sensible how little interest I now have in you, and therefore fear my application to you may be of little use to those for whom I resolve (be the successe what it will) to become an intercessor. Read your Nephews letter deliberately over and it will melt your soul. Suppose him in the agonyes of death to have made you the same humble request which that letter makes, which you had heard him utter with his dying breath mixed with prayers for you and thanks to you for your intended kindnesse to his widow and children. All this you have in that paper but the affliction it would have been to you to see him in the pangs of death. You have this trivial addition, the request of a broken hearted brother that you would make my poor daughter easy in her mind that your (once) dear Nephews widow and children should not be put out of Ballyanan, to make way for another tenant to enjoy if not destroy the improvements he made there to a vast expence. You shal not be at any difficultye for the rent while the widow and my poor Grand children remain there: but if you please I will assign all my rents in Surrey to secure the constant payment of £160 a year for the rent of Ballyanan while Nancy and her children are continued there, and if you please I will become tenant to you to bind myself more firmly to the payment of the rent, and take with her for reimbursing or indemnifying me: but under a trust that while she continues there with her children she and they may be permitted to enjoy the Land at that rent, for which I will be bound. Dear Brother, I am now speaking to one who knew Sennyes value, who loved him, and will not in this last request of a departed freind disappoint the hopes and I think modest requests of one who never would have refused to undergoe any difficultye to shew his affection for and duty to you. Let me intreat an answer to this as soon as you well can after receiving it. And let it be such as will comfort one who needs some support to his oppressed spirits.

817. *Alan I, Dublin, to Thomas, 24 Mar. 1727[/8]*

(1248/7/219–20)

I have your letter of the ninth which expresses a just regard for the memorye of your poor deceased nephew, and your great concern for the losse of him. As for my part in that losse I will say little, for indeed words cannot expresse it. There are several pacquets due, the letters of the ninth being the latest date which we yet have from London. But the occasion of my writing now proceeds from a visit which my Lord Carterett made me this evening to condole me on Sennyes death. After he had sate near an hour with me he entred into discourse about the very respectful way in which he had been treated this Session by both houses of Parliament, insomuch (saith he) that no one thing disagreeable was stirred, or even thought of except one to wit, a motion Sir Wm Parsons intended to make in the house of commons about pensions, which however Sir Wm thought good to acquaint me of this [?way], before he would move it in the house. He said Sir Wm mentioned it as a thing transmitted to him out of England by some freinds there, and (as I understood his Excellencye) seemed determined not to stir in it, if he was against it: but of that part I am not certain his Lordship not speaking in a very clear maner, but he added that his answer was that every member was at liberty to move any thing which he apprehended would be for the service of his countrey, and seemed to me to leave him (as he found him) under a perfect latitude and at full libertye to act as he pleased; He added that he asked Sir Wm whether he had discoursed his freinds on this side the water and what their opinion was of it and that his Lordship asked Mr Shepheard[1086] and Mr Weymes[1087] what their thoughts were on that subject; to which either both (or at least the former) said it was a very wild and idle scheme. His Lordship was pleased to tell me farther that it was Coffee house talk here (which he did not beleive one word of) that you were in it, and named to be the person who had sett it on foot and then paused (in expectation I suppose of my giving my thoughts whether you knew or was privy to the thing) but added that he beleived I was one of the persons whom he had described under the name of Sir Wms freinds on this side of the water who did not readily come into the thing. By his Excellencyes conduct I found he was upon the pump to find out from me what had passed between people in England and others here in this affair, and I resolved to keep myself in reserve considering the great secrecye which was proper to be used in a matter of this nature, and which was soe strongly recommended by C in his letter to A. I chose therefore to answer in this maner, that his Excellencye[1088] would soon see you and might have full information of what passed between you or any body else with people here relating to that affair, I being sensible that you had not in that or any other instance done anything which you would deny or be ashamed of, and thought fit to remit him to you for informacion: not having any power from you or anybody else to communicate what I knew of it to his Excellencye or others: nor knowing what lengths Sir Wm had gone in letting his Excellencye into the knowledge of matters, only his Lordship assured me the Knight had shewn him the very resolution in terminis which was to be moved, and I beleive he did soe because the other

[1086] Anthony Sheppard, MP [I].

[1087] Probably Patrick Weymes, MP [I] rather than his son Henry, MP [I], a newcomer to the house of commons.

[1088] Carteret.

was perfectly possessed of the nature of the thing. And I did not know whether he had named names of people on your side of the water, or on this, and particularly mine, tho I beleive he had done soe, not out of any other motive but in cautiousnesse, but perhaps I may judge wrong in that conjecture and hope I doe. His Excellencye said jocularly and very merrilye (for it was an evening visit) that he would when he saw you acquaint you that Ireland was either very much altered from what it was when you left it, or that you had forgotten it because he was satisfyed the motion (if it had been made) would not have had ten votes on the affirmative side of the question. And he then seemed to resort back to know what my thoughts would have been in the matter. I was aware what use his Excellencye might and possibly would have made (if I had declared myself) of any answer I should have given; if I had declared against the thing I make no doubt but that would have been told where it might doe me or <u>those whom I am concerned for</u> the most disserve: If I had declared my opinion for the resolution, I think it would not have been made a secret, but have been told on this side of the water, where I think the sense of considering people is against it. And this you know to have been my opinion from the beginning. This is the last time I will trouble you with anything relating to this affair, to which I may add the epithet unfortunate; for soe I think it hath been to me in creating some coolnesse in you toward me, if not resentment, for not being able to find out the good consequences it would have produced to Ireland, or satisfactorye answer to the objections which seemed to me naturally to arise against it. I have looked over all your letters in no one of which I can find one word to those purposes, but in general that you had answered objections before and need not repeat them. Indeed you doe in one of your letters mention a letter to me dated 23 Nov. 1727 which upon my faith I never received; tell me if you are sure you wrote then.

818. *Alan I, Dublin, to Thomas, 5 Apr. 1728*

(1248/7/221–2)

… I am truly concerned to find by your letter that you think yourself to be in an ill state of health: My late losse makes such impressions in me that I cannot but dread the losse of any other friend, as well as foresee my own continuance is like to be very short after your poor Nephew in whose grave my heart is now buryed. But when I hear the ill state of health poor Ally hath been and continues in and how very weak my poor brother William is I own that the load I groan under is as great as my soul can bear. Dear Brother, doe not add to my affliction by thinking or saying anything that is unkind of one whom I am under all the tyes on earth to love, and who hath deserved it from me in as great a degree as ever wife did of an husband; doe not entertain a thought of unkindnesse toward her; for it is impossible to be unkind to her and kind to me at the same time: for whatever will shock her doth most sensibly afflict me, and perhaps more then any personal unkindnesse to myself. God preserve you and continue your health or restore you health …

819. *Alan I, Dublin, to Thomas, 15 Apr. 1728*

(1248/7/230)

… the death of poor Senny and of so many others of my acquaintance that have happened of late, viz. Col. FitzGerald of Castlemarter,[1089] Sir Piercy Freak,[1090] General Gorges and his wife the Countesse of Meath[1091] (in three dayes one after the other)[1092] have greatly alarmed us …

820. *Alan II, Edinburgh, to Alan I, Dublin, 18 Apr. 1728*

(1248/7/228–9)

I was prevented from returning your Lordship my thanks, for your's of the 27th of March, by last Post as I fully intended to have Done; it was a great Satisfaction to me to be assured that my Lady and Yourself were well, and I can not express the Happyness it was to me, to know that your Lordship did not dislike my Manner of shewing a small part of the great Greif my poor Brother's Death gave me. It shall always be my Endeavour to shew my Sorrow for, and Love of Him, in the Manner your Lordship directs, which is, I am sure, the only true One I now have left me to follow.

Your Lordship think's that I cou'd not employ my time more usefully here than by applying my self to the Civil Law. I am very sensible of the Use and Advantage of that Part of Learning, and at the same time know that it is a most pleasant and entertaining Study. The Turn I have taken since I came into this Country has happened to be quite of a different Nature from what your Lordship proposes, and is that which the Nature of the Business I am employed in, seemed not barely to point out to me, but in some measure to assist and instruct me in; I mean that the Business of the Publick Revenue, in it's different Branches, is what has taken up my thoughts of late more than any other Study; if your Lordship is of Opinion that the Civil Law, or any other Study whatsoever, will be more beneficiall to me, or more likely to procure me some little Character in the world; from the Instant I receive your Commands I will apply my self closely in the manner You shall direct. My Diligence in prosecuting whatsoever You shall judge to be fit for me to undertake, will, I hope, convince your Lordship of my ready Obedience, and at the same time let You see that I am resolved to use my best Endeavour's not to be a meer Cypher in the World.

I wait for your Lordship Directions on this head …

[1089]John Fitzgerald, MP [I].

[1090]MP [I].

[1091]Richard Gorges, MP [I]; his 2nd wife Dorothy (née Stopford) (*d.* 1728), was the widow of the 4th earl of Meath.

[1092]Freke and Lady Meath died on 10 Apr., Gorges on the 12th. No record of the date of Fitzgerald's death has been found.

821. *Alan I to Alan II, [Apr. 1728]*[1093]

(1248/9/140)

… You have turned your case [— — —] late into another way then that which I proposed to you, which was the study of the Civil Law, while you remained in Scotland, in which Kingdom it is very much professed as being in great measure the Law of the countrey, except where it is altered by expresse Acts of Parliament: That study I recommended to you as proper to the place in which your present residence is where you may have the advantage of books, and of instruction by the conversation of ingenious men learned in that noble and generous study. But I only recommended the thing to you as what might make you useful in publick affairs either at home or abroad without laying the least obligation on you, to apply yourself that way rather then another. I confesse what you mention to me as the matter about which your mind hath been of late conversant, I mean getting a through [*sic*] knowledge of the publick revenue in all its several branches, to be that which according to the present cause of things is most likely to put you into a way of enriching if not aggrandizing yourself: but whether the one or the other [1094] … free to caution you not to buy gold or preferment [*at*] too dear a rate; There will be a time when you will be convinced that the greatest affluence and grandeur are not worth what they usually cost us, at least not the price at which they seem to me to be purchased at. I will add no more on this head but leave you at entire freedome under this caution that he who aims at very great things must expect to goe great lengths to attain them: Before you determine or resolve on things of this nature know that he will be dropt whose mind will not allow him to goe all the greatest lengths which others are able without remorse of conscience to goe. Consider well and resolve vertuously and prudently.

822. *Alan I, Dublin, to Thomas, 30 Apr. 1728*

(1248/7/231–4)

… upon my word (Brother) this countrey is poor to a very great degree, and the common people in a starving condicion; nay I hear the want of corn in some parts is soe great that it amounts near unto a famine with which our late excessive rains seemed to threaten us by preventing our corn to take root in the ground and to come up … I … condole heartily with you for the losse of our truly valuable freind in Georges Street,[1095] and desire you to make my complements to good Lady Betty in the most respectfull maner on so dismal an occasion.[1096] This I desired Ally to doe in a former letter. Yesterday I had a visit from

---

[1093] The top half of this letter has been torn off.

[1094] Here Alan reached the bottom of the page. A large section of the letter is then missing.

[1095] Samuel Molyneux, MP [I]. Having collapsed in the Westminster house of commons, Molyneux died on 13 Apr. at his house in George Street, Hanover Square, Westminster (Paul Holden, 'Introduction' in *The London Letters of Samuel Molyneux, 1712–13*, ed. Ann Saunders (London Topographical Society, Publication No. 172, 2011), 15).

[1096] His widow, the former Lady Elizabeth Capel, daughter of the 2nd earl of Essex. She was a great fortune, having brought Molyneux some £28,000 in real and personal estate. Her younger sister Mary would marry Alan Brodrick II in 1729.

Dr Molineux,[1097] who attended me being a good deal out of order: He told me that he understood his Nephew had about ten years since made his will and by it left not only all his personal estate, but also all his real to my Lady Betty and the real to her and her heirs.[1098] And that her Ladyship had the day after Mr Molineux dyed made a will by which she disposed the real estate (after her own death) to the Doctor and his children etc and declared her resolucion to execute conveyances to that purpose and not leave it in the maner it must remain (while it depended only on a will) revocable at pleasure. He added that he understood Lady Betty was pleased to have some regard to your advice, and desired me to write to you to desire you to cultivate and continue those good dispositions in my Lady which she expressed for those who are nearest in bloud to Mr Molineux. I told him with truth that she was a Lady of that honour and goodnesse that I beleived he might assure himself she would in all her actions proceed with honour and goodnesse toward everybody, especially the nearest relations of her deceased husband.[1099] But that I could not pretend to doe more then lay his request to me before you who would act with great regard to his deceased freind and to Lady Betty, and as became you toward soe near a relation of Mr Molineux; who (you know) is in himself a very valuable man. I am greatly terrifyed at the state in which you describe your own and my sisters health to be; since the death of your poor Nephew my spirits are soe broken that any thing of the ilnesse of a dear freind touches me in such a maner that I sink under the thought of it; and then you may judge what effect my receiving every post letters in which I am either told of your, or Allyes or some other dear freinds ilnesse. Nay the same paper tells me you, my sister Brodrick, my two younger brothers, and Ally are all in a very ill way. But a little time will put me out of the power of feeling any impressions from such calamityes. We are but few of us left; pray let me have a constant account how the Bath agrees with you, and how those whom God hath hitherto spared are.

823. *Alan I, Dublin, to Thomas, 2 May 1728*

(1248/7/235–6)

… We are in a consumption and perfect decay and (as I apprehend) in great danger of a famine, if our excessive rain's continue a few dayes longer, much more if it prove weeks. Our importation this last year hath vastly exceeded our exportation, and our trade lyes under vast discouragements in all its branches but that of linen clothe in which our part of the countrey is not concerned … my infirmityes are soe increased on me since the last shock I have had by the unexpressible losse of your Nephew …

[1097] Sir Thomas Molyneux (1661–1733), MD, physician to the state [I]; MP [I] 1695–9.

[1098] Confirmed in the copy of Samuel's will, dated 15 Jan. 1717/18, in TNA, PROB 11/621/375. There were a few small additional bequests, including £50 to Sir Thomas.

[1099] In fact Molyneux's death was attended by scandal. On the night of his death Lady Betty eloped with the Swiss surgeon and anatomist, Nicholas St André, a close friend of the family who had treated her husband after his seizure and in some quarters was suspected of having hastened his death with a fatal dose of opium (Holden, 'Introduction', 15).

824. *Alan I, Dublin, to Thomas, Bath, 4 May 1728*

(1248/7/237–8)

… After reading and considering the report of the house of Commons about the payments made out of the sinking fund toward lessening the debts of the nation: I can plainly see that Sir R[obert] W[alpole] hath had the good fortune to have the approbation as well of his Majestye as of the house of Commons as to his managements in the Treasury; but what I would fain know is what the real debts of the nation at this time amount to in the whole; but that is left soe in the dark that he must have more skil in figures then I am Master of, and more leisure to goe through such an affair then I have that can find it out: but perhaps the question may be asked me, that a woman asked of a person who was very inquisitive to know what she had in a basket which she carryed covered under her Arm. Quum vides velatam, cur inquiris in rem absconditam?[1100] That I take to be the case; it is to be a secret to all profane eyes.

825. *Alan II, Edinburgh, to Alan I, Dublin, 4 May 1728*

(1238/7/239–40)

I wait impatiently for your Lordships Commands on the subject of mine of this day fort-night; if You shall think the Civil Law the most advantagious Study of the two, I will prosecute it, during my Stay here, with the utmost Diligence and Application.

My Uncle is, I beleive, at the Bath e'er now, and has no doubt great need of the Waters, for it is long since He was there, and nothing ever did Him so much good … This Place affords no News, or, at best, the Little We hear comes to Us when it is stale every where elce.

What sort of a Spring this may have been with You, or in England, I can not tell; but I never remember such an one as it has been here; I own I shou'd beleive that the Climate had a good Share in it, did not Every body agree that the like of it was never known.

826. *Alan I, Dublin, to Thomas, Bath, 16 May 1728*

(1248/7/241–2)

If your being in Bath doth not prevent my freind Capt Thomas Burgh from delivering this into your own hand, nothing else will; for his call into England is upon a pretty odd occasion; Tho he may be a stranger to you in person yet I am sure he is not soe in his character, for I think you cannot forget a Gentleman who served soe well under King William as to meritt from that discerning Prince such a marke of his favor as to make him Surveyor General of his works and fortifications in this Kingdome: which surely was

---

[1100]Plutarch, *Moralia*, 'De Curiositate', 3: The relevant section can be translated as 'It was surely a clever answer that the Egyptian gave to the man who asked him what he was carrying wrapped up: "That's why it is wrapped up." And why, if you please, are *you* inquisitive about what is concealed?'.

intended as a reward for his services, and never meant to place a slight upon him as it will; if the methods which have lately been taken shal succeed. A young Gentleman who hath ingratiated himself somewhere, hath pushed at that which Mr Burgh (as well as his freinds) doth beleive to be part of his Office of Surveyor General; in endeavouring to have his plan of a new Parliament house here to be approved of in England; and if that shal be determined in favour of that Gentleman, I suppose it will not be expected that the Engineer who hath a patent for his Office shal be only employed in supervising the others scheme, and executing his design.[1101] I wish you may be able to doe this Gentleman service with any freinds in England. We have an opinion here that our present Lord Lieutenant will succeed in his hopes of and pretensions to something on your side of the water which may better suit with his inclinations then any thing which is here. And the next thing which follows this notion is the thoughts of a person who is like to succeed him. Many who speake their wishes have entertained a thought that noebody is more likely to succeed Lord Carterett then the Duke of Chandois, and some have for some time past named him as a person very likely to be the man whom his Majestye may probably have in his eye for this great trust: for soe it is in more respects then one, and I wish our scituation may not need a man of his Graces great abilityes and prudence; perhaps you will be surprised at my saying this, considering the addresses of the houses, by reading which one would think there never had been soe firm a reconciliation of all partyes as at this time. To them I refer, tho I confesse were it not for the regard I have to what I see those great bodyes have said upon the occasion, I should be glad to see any thing which gave me those sentiments. Whether his Grace will be or now is at the Bath, I know not; but I resolve to trouble him with a letter (upon a supposition that he is like to be concerned in our affairs) which I resolve to put into Mr Burghs hand to be delivered by him to his Grace: and if he shal be at the Bath I hope you will doe Mr Burgh that freindly office as to introduce him to the Duke as a Gentleman of Ireland of value; You shal soon hear from me about your own affairs, but pray let me know whether the Bath hath had its usual good effects on you.

827. *Alan I, Dublin, to Thomas, Bath, 18 May 1728*

(1248/7/243–4)

… the whole Kingdome is in a languishing condition; tho some who have lately left this place will continue to pretend to beleive the contrary, and represent it to be in a very flourishing condition …

[1101] Edward Lovett Pearce MP [I].

APPENDIX 1: THE IRISH HOUSE OF LORDS AND THE SURRENDER OF WOOD'S PATENT

SHC, 1248/6/314–19: a 'narrative' included in Letter 705, Alan I to Thomas I, 27 Sept. 1725, and headed 'The Question in the house of Lords on 24th Sept. 1725 (Whether the words Great wisdome) should stand part of the Addresse of thanks of that house to his Majestye for putting an end to Woods patent arose in this maner'.

On the 26th of August (after I had received an account of it by your letter from Bath of the 16th which Mr Baily delivered to me) I was sent for by my Lord Lieutenant who imparted it to me as a great secret, and at the same time he told me he had summoned the Councel to meet on that day to acquaint them also with it. He added that he intended to mention it as an act of his Majestyes Royal favor and as a great condescension: I told him that in November last he expressed himself in this maner to me, that he did not doubt but he should see a Session of Parliament here, in which that patent should not be so much as mentioned: Of this I reminded him and told him (as I had formerly done) that he never would live to see that day in the sense he meant it; viz. that he should be able to quiet mens minds and reconcile them soe far to the patent etc that they would not complain of it, or of the usage they had received, unlesse the patent was actually discharged or surrendred. But that he had now thus far attained his wish to be able to hold a Session of Parliament, which might be carried on easily and not be interrupted in their proceedings by mentioning that affair at all; I added that if any body should be soe turbulent in his temper or indiscreet to mention it with a view to make men lesse inclined to goe on with the publick businesse in the usual method which I thought would not happen that his Excellencye had it perfectly in his power to put a stop to any such attempt by giving them to understand by his Secretarye (who is a member of the house of Commons) or by the Lord Chancellor in the upper house, that the thing complained of was entirely at an end by his Majestyes interposition in so effectual a maner that Wood had surrendred his patent, of which they should be fully convinced by having the ex[em]plification of the deed of surrender under the Great Seal of Great Britain laid before them which was all that was necessary to be done to prevent any ill bloud which might arise in either house; and this I said to prevent any difficultye which might arise from the maner of its being laid before them; for I well knew the part his Excellencye had taken in this matter at the hearing before the Committee of Councel at the Cockpit, and that he had repeatedly by letter and otherwise given me to understand that the King had not been deceived, nor any thing prejudicial to the Kingdome been done in granting the patent in the maner it was granted and upon such enquiry as had been made in England about the want of Copper money in this Kingdome. Hence I concluded that if he mentioned the thing at all, it would be probably in such a maner, as might bring the matter in question whether we wanted that coyne, and in consequence whether the patent was obtained in deceit of the King by misinformation given by Mr Wood that such coyne was wanting, as the Parliament asserted, or whether it was true as Mr Wood affirmed, and perswaded others to beleive, that the patent was advantageous to the Kingdome to supply a real want it had of halfpence and farthings to carry on the retail trade. But his Excellencye declared his positive resolucion was to impart the thing to the Councel and proceeded to expresse the maner in which he intended to doe it, which was much to the effect and very near the words in his speech. I told him that as he represented the thing, he made meer grace and favor and condescension, which left it indifferent and entirely in his Majestyes power whether he would ease us of that patent or not; soe that if he had not done it we should have no room for complaint, and consequently he may doe the same thing again and will then be at liberty how far he will condescend to extend his Royal favor for our releif; that the Parliament understood the thing quite in another maner viz. that the Nation did not want that Coyne which William Wood was empowred by his patent to coyne, and that the wants of the Kingdome should have been enquired into in another maner then they were, and the patent called in question by sci. fa.[1] upon the complaint of the whole Kingdome in Parliament without sending over witnesses to give evidence before a Committee of Councel that there was ground for a Legal prosecution; not that we here (whose estates depend on certificate and patent) had it ever in our thoughts that the King could avoid his patent without legal tryal, much lesse that the sense or vote of either or both houses of Parliament were sufficient to avoid a patent without giving evidence to the Jury who should try the issue on the sci. fa. whether the facts which were laid as misinformations of the patentee were true or not. We all knew that our saying they were false was not sufficient to avoid the patent, but thought we might be soe credited that the things which we averred would be made appear to be true beyond denial upon a fair trial would be proved on a tryal. These things I told him I beleived were as I have mentioned, in the opinion of the greater part of both houses of Parliament; but considering who had thought and said the contrary in a very strong and I think extraordinary maner I thought it prudent not to give an handle to bring these matters into debate, which I feared mentioning the putting an end to the patent to be an effect of his Majestyes Royal favor and condescension (without more) would draw on. But when I found him determined to mention it to the Councel (as I have said) I desisted saying more, considering that I was not in the Kings service nor consequently intitled to interpose my advice when I found my sense to be soe wide from his Excellencyes. Nay he went soe far as to presse me to represent the matter at the Councel in the strongest terms I could as an act of grace and condescension. I owned his Majestyes taking the method which was taken viz. his bringing Wood to a voluntary surrender at this time, to be soe; because else he might have kept this patent hanging over our head as long as the suit by sci. fa. for repealing it should remain undetermined, which might be a great while, and the event of that suit would depend upon the finding of a Jury, and consequently the successe was uncertain. But (supposing the patent was granted in deceit of his Majestye by misinformacion of the patentee, and that it was detrimental to the Kingdome) I could not think that it is discretionary in his Majestye whether he will or will not allow a sci. fa. to

---

[1] Scire facias (see above, p. 78).

be brought in his name to releive his people from the pressure they lye under by means of such a patent: and if the Law should be thus, it is as much as to say that the King can grant a patent in prejudice of his people in general; for if he can grant one, and is not under any obligation to bring it to trial whether the complaints of his people are well grounded that the patent is detrimental to the publick, which is only to be done on a sci fa in Chancerye the patent which ought not to have been granted must remain forever unrevoked if the King pleases not to permit a sci[*re*] fa[*cias*] to be brought. These are things which ought not to be unnecessarily brought upon the carpett; for it puts the subject under great difficultyes to be obliged to complain, and in the event is seldome of service to the Prerogative. But his Excellencye had come to a fixed resolution in what maner he would open the thing to the Councel, which he did on 26 August in words much to the effect with those of his Speech to both houses of Parliament. The news was very acceptable to every body; but more particularly one Gentleman seemed to be transported with it beyond measure, when he thought the good ministry which had advised his Majestye to doe what he had done were inspired by the Holy Spirit. The Archbishop of Dublin owned what the King had done was an instance of his Royal favor and condescension and of his justice, and added the passage which I mentioned formerly of a mans throwing another into a pond and after he had lain there for a considerable time in great danger and been very cold and wet, pulling him out again and telling him he was much obliged to him that he was not drowned. This I confesse was too homely a comparison but from his using it I took an oportunitye to tell my Lord Lieutenant in the Closett I did apprehend there would debates arise in the house of Lords on wording our addresse of thanks to his Majestye if he resolved to expresse the matter in the same terms which he had used in the Councel; and added that for my part I did apprehend our addressing the King and owning our having Woods patent put an end to, was favor and royal condescension only would leave a room to set up a right to doe the same thing in the same maner again; He told me that his words were not meer royal favour and condescension, or favour and condescension only; I then advised and beseeched him he would add these words that (upon the humble petition and representation of his Parliament of Ireland) he had etc which words left the matter in suspence how far the complaints were just, as the Crown had a right to doe the like again whereas I doubted acknowledging the giving up the patent to be an effect of his Majestyes Royal favor and condescension (without using any other words) was in truth owning it wholly due to favor and condescension, and that his Majestye might have refused to have done that, or to order a proceeding at Law by sci[*re*] fa[*cias*] to repeal the grant, which would I think have put an end to the patent, as fully (tho not as soon) as the surrender hath.

On 21 Sept. the Lord Lieutenant mentioned the surrender in the words contained in his printed speech, and the Lord Primate moved an addresse of thanks to his Majestye in the very words of the speech, and having mentioned the putting an end to Woods patent, owned it to be an instance of his Majestyes Royal favor and condescension without any other words; the Archbishop of Dublin moved this as an amendment to the instruction to be given to the Committee for preparing the addresse, viz. as an instance of his Majestyes great wisdom Royal favor and condescension etc the matter was debated a long time in the house whether the words (Great wisdome) should stand part of the instructions given to the Committee, and upon putting the question the Lord on the wool sack declared the not contents had it; whereas it was soe visible to every body that the contents were the majoritye, that the not contents would not divide the house, but Lord Santry (Governor of

Derry) called out that they yeilded, and indeed the majoritye that night was plainly with the Contents, for several noble Lords (temporal) had not received soe full information in the matter, as they did afterward. When this news was carryed to a certain place it occasioned abundance of heat as I am told; the particulars are not proper to be inserted here, but words of great warmth are said to have been used to or of some of the contents, and to have been returned with a great deal of spirit.

On 22 Sept the Committee mett and the Primate who had been put into the Chair brought in a draught of an address which he had prepared, and hoped would answer the mentions of the house tho he owned it did not come up to the instructions in words, but thought we were not tyed down by the instructions to the very words of the resolution; his Grace took care to leave the offensive words (Great wisdome) out of his draft of the Addresse. And some Lords much doubted whether these particular words, which the house had determined upon a question should be part of the instructions should be inserted as part of the addresse. At long run after a good deal spoken by the Archbishop of Dublin and others that the words ought to be inserted by the Committee, and if any Lord did not like them, that he was at liberty to move the question in the house whether (those words Great wisdome) should stand part of the addresse, or be left out, the Lords who were in the Committee for omitting them there, owned the proper place to leave them out was in the house and then the addresse was agreed to and inserted.

On 24th the Primate reported the draught with the words (great wisdom) as part of it, and an objection was made to those words as very improper by the Bishop of Elphin, who took notice this was an addresse of thanks and said we were thanking his Majestye for his Royal favor and condescension in putting an end to Woods patent; he added that thanks were never to be given but for some action, whereas we were now thanking his Majestye for a qualitye or virtue of the mind. He resembled it to a childs thanking his parent for a benefit done and telling him he was wise for doing it; which implyed the child was in the right in asking and the parent in the wrong for not doing it earlier. He went all along upon this supposition that the putting an end to the patent was an act of pure grace and favor and condescension, and soe did the Bishop of Dromore (Lambert). The Bishop of Meath gave a more extraordinary reason for leaving the words out, because they were not in my Lord Lieutenants speech, who knew as much of his Majestyes wisdome as any body, and would have mentioned it here, if he had thought it proper, and thought we might very well express ourselves in his words. I was a little moved at the reason given by the Prelate last mentioned, as not soe consistent with the dignitye of Parliament or the freedome of its debate which we ought alway to preserve inviolate.

The Lords who were of opinion that the words (Great wisdome) should stand part of the addresse endeavoured to convince the other Lords that the words of the addresse did not thank his Majestye for his wisdome, but acknowledged the putting an end to putt [*sic*] to Woods patent to be one instance of his Majestyes great wisdome, as well as of his Royal favor and condescension since it is plainly due to his Majestyes interposicion that such an end is put now to this patent which had hung soe long as a Cloud over this Kingdome; they thought that in an addresse of thanks the great qualityes of the person addressed to might very properly be mentioned and that it was an act of very great wisdome in his Majestye as well as the greatest instance of his favour and condescension to interpose between his people of Ireland (who thought themselves soe far greived by a patent granted to Wood as to make their humble application to his Majestye for releif) and William Wood who insisted on his right under the patent, to end this controversy to the mutual satisfaction of both partyes, and thereby to put an entire end to the disquiets which have been raised in the minds of the people ever since they were sensible that such patent had been granted. They thought it was very wise to doe it to prevent entring into the steps which had been taken, in appearance to avoid the patent, or to enquire what way should be taken to avoid it: but as they apprehended had no great tendencye that way; nor had in any sort conduced to the quieting the minds of the people. They expressed themselves unwilling to mention what had been done by Wood to misrepresent the Nation, and how far he had obtained credit that the Parliament (and not he) had misinformed the King, which they would not mention but to shew the necessitye of not leaving the patents being at an end as the effect of Royal favor and condescension only, but likewise of wisdome (for the word justice was of harder digestion then wisdome) and had been expressely and avowedly declared against by —— in my hearing with this addicion (backed by an asseveration) that he would put all his strength and interest on that point; which being known might be the reason of the Archbishops changing the word justice (which he used in the Councel) into great wisdome which he moved in the house. But at length the question being put whether those words should stand a part of the Addresse, the not contents were 21 Against 12 Contents.[2] Their names follow

Not Conts on 24 Sept 1725	Contents.
Lord Primate	Archbishop Dublin
E. Roscommon	Archbishop Tuam.
E. Cavan	E. Kildare
V. Fane Shanon.	E. Barrymore
Bishops Meath	E. Meath.
Kildare.	V. Midleton
Dromore	V. Allen.
Raphoe	V. Limrick
Elphin	V. Hillsborough.
Fernes	Bishop Ossorye
Derry	Baron Forbes.
Kilalla	Baron Bellew.
Clonfert	12.
Limrick	
Down.	
Barons Santy	
Ferard	
Newtown	
Southwel.	
21.	

[2]Confirmed in *Boulter Letters*, 127.

The Earles of Roscommon and Cavan voted on 21th for those words (Great wisdome) to be part of the resolution upon which the Committee were to frame the addresse) so did Lord Fane, Newtown and Ferard, and the Bishop of Raphoe. But they saw things in another light on the report; the Earle of Shelburne was also for having those words part of the resolution the first day, but hapned not to be in the house the second day. And I think some other Lords altered their opinions, but I am certain, not one of the Bishops except Rapho did; and I am as certain that neither Shanon nor Santry altered theirs for they voted against the words on both dayes. If the Archbishop of D[ublin] had not mentioned the report of the Committee at the Cockpit, I would not have taken notice of it, and so I declared in the Committee, but he having done it, I used some things contained in it as arguments why the matter should not turn upon the words Royal favour and condescension singly, because the King by his answer to the first addresse seems to me to claim a right to grant such a patent as that granted to Woods, and I doubt the Councel have gone a great way to inculcate into his Majestye that what was done was wholly right, and if soe may I think be put again in practice. It is true it is not likely that a thing which hath occasioned soe much trouble to his Majestye his Ministry and this whole Kingdome will soon be put again in practice: but I confesse I dread the consequence of our owning our being free from it to be only an effect of his Majestyes Royal favor and condescension.

This single consideration made me speak and vote for the words (great wisdom) standing part of the addresse; and if his Excellencye could have condescended to have mentioned that what his Majestye hath done was at the humble peticion and representacion of his Parliament, that should have satisfyed me without either the words (Great wisdome or justice) but without some words which might not make the matter to be meer grace and favor I thought it was a concession I ought not to goe into to expresse myself as the Primate first framed the addresse. This I write that you may let a certain know what were the motives which induced me to say what I did, and what it was that I really did drive at in my discourse.

After all it will not be easily gott out of peoples heads that there is now a new patent in agitation, to be granted to a certain Peer of this Kingdome; the probabilityes are, that the night bonefires were making here for the surrender etc there was news cryed of a new patent to be granted to the E[arl] of A[bercorn] and no longer since then last Wednesday the Archbishop of D[ublin] assured me that he had two private letters from London to that purpose. It is as certain that the Dublin print which mentioned this out of the London journal was very suddenly suppressed here by order;[3] and yet I doe not find the printer ordered to be prosecuted; and when I have mentioned this in a certain place I can gett no better answer that is not likely such a thing should be soe soon set on foot etc. But beyond this people will not be brought to goe.

---

[3] The *Dublin Journal*, 28 Aug. 1725, reported the news of the surrender of Wood's patent and a rumour that it had been granted to Abercorn.

APPENDIX 2: BRODRICK FAMILY MEMBERS AND CONNECTIONS MENTIONED IN THE TEXT

Barry, James (1689–1743), of Rathcormac, Co. Cork, 1st s. of James Barry (1659–1717), bro. of Catherine Barry, 1st w. of Alan I; unm.; MP Dungarvan 1713–14, 1721–7, Rathcormac 1727–*d.*; capt., Stanwix's regt. of foot 1706–12, Wittewrong's foot c. 1715–16, Lord Tyrawley's foot, 1716.

Barry, Redmond (bef. 1696–1750), of Rathcormac, Co. Cork, 2nd s. of James Barry (1659–1717) of Rathcormac; m. 1727, Anne Smyth of Coolmore, Co. Cork, *s.p.*; MP Dungarvan 1717–27, Tallow 1727–*d.*

Bettesworth, Richard (1689–1741), of Dublin, s. of Richard Bettesworth (see *Anglo-Irish Politics*, i, 326), MP Thomastown 1721–7, Midleton 1727–*d.*, 2nd serjt. [I] 1732–4, counsel to barracks commrs [I] 1733–*d.*

Brodrick, Alan I (1656–1728), of Dublin, 2nd s. of St John I; *cr.* Baron Brodrick 1715, Viscount Midleton 1717; m. (1) by 1684, Catherine, da. of Redmond Barry of Rathcormac, Co. Cork, 1s., (2) 1695 Lucy Courthope, 1s. 1da., (3) 1716, Anne Hill (*q.v.*), *s.p.*; MP [I] Cork 1692–10, Co. Cork 1713–14, and MP [GB] 1717–*d.*; recorder, Cork 1690–5, 3rd serjt. [I] 1690–2, solicitor-gen. [I] 1695–1704, privy councillor [I] 1695–1711, 1714–*d.*, Speaker of the house of commons [I] 1703–10, 1713–14, attorney-gen. [I] 1707–9, chief justice of queen's bench [I] 1709–11, lord chancellor [I] 1714–25, lord justice [I] 1717–19, 1719–21, 1722–3, 1724–5.

Brodrick, Alan II (1702–1747), 2nd but 1st surv. s. of Alan I by his 2nd w.; m. 1729, Lady Mary Capell (*d.* 1756), da. of Algernon, 2nd earl of Essex, 2s. (1 *d.v.p.*); commr of customs [GB] 1727–30, jt comptroller of army [GB] 1730.

Brodrick, Alice (1697–1780), only da. of Alan I by his 2nd w.; m. 1737, Rev. John Castleman, fellow, All Souls' College, Oxford.

Brodrick, Katherine (bef. 1665– 1731), 1st and o. surv. da. of St John I; m. William Whitfield (c. 1658–1717), rector, St Martin's Ludgate 1691–1714, prebendary, St Paul's 1695, Canterbury 1710, vicar, St Giles Cripplegate 1714–*d.*

Brodrick, Laurence (c. 1670–1747), 6th but 5th surv. s. of St John I; m. 1710, Anne Humphreys, 2s. (1 *d.v.p.*) 3 da. (2 *d.v.p.*); vicar, Sandon, Herts. 1697–1711, chaplain to house of commons [GB] 1708, prebendary of Westminster 1710–46, rector, Dauntsey, Wilts. 1712–14, Mixbury, Oxon. 1713–43, Turweston, Bucks. 1713–41, Islip, Oxon. 1741–8.

Brodrick, St John III (1684–1728), 1st s. of Alan I by his 1st w.; m. 1710, Anne Hill, jr (*q.v.*), 4 da.; MP Castlemartyr 1709–13, Cork 1713–14, Co. Cork 1715–*d.*, and MP [GB] 1721–7; recorder, Cork 1708–*d.*, privy councillor [I] 1724–*d.*

Brodrick, Thomas (1654–1730), of Wandsworth, Surr. and Ballyannan, Co. Cork, 1st s. of St John I; m. Anne, da. of Alexander Pigott of Innishannon, Co. Cork, 1s. *d.v.p.*; MP Midleton 1692–3, 1715–27, Co. Cork 1695–1713 and MP [GB] 1713–27; comptroller of salt duties 1706–11, jt comptroller of army accounts 1708–11, privy councillor [I] 1695–1711, 1714–27, [GB] 1714–*d.*

Brodrick, William (c. 1666–aft. 1733), of Spanish Town, Jamaica and the Inner Temple, 5th but 4th surv. s. of St John I; m. (1) 1693, Hannah (*d.* 1703), wid. of Capt. John Toldervey and Major Thomas Ballard, (2) by 1705, Ann (*d.* 1707), 1s. *d.v.p.*, 1da., (3) 1707, Sarah Ivey; attorney-gen. and judge adm., Jamaica 1692–8, 1715, attorney-gen. Leeward Is. 1694, member of council, Jamaica 1695, Speaker of house of assembly, Jamaica 1711–13, 2nd serjeant [I] 1718–21.

Clayton, Courthope (c. 1706–1762), of Mallow, Co. Cork, yr s. of Laurence Clayton (*q.v.*) of Mallow by his 2nd w.; m. Theodosia, da. of Edward Buckworth; MP [I] Mallow 1727–60, MP [GB] 1749–61; ensign, Coldstream Guards 1725, cornet, Royal Regt. of Horse Guards 1727, lieut., 2nd Troop, Grenadier Guards 1731, capt. 1740, lieut.-col. 1756–*d.*

Clayton, Laurence (1655–1712), of Mallow, Co. Cork, s. of Randal Clayton of Mallow, cousin of Alan I, St John II and Thomas; m. (1) Catherine, da. of Sir Henry Tynte, 1s. *d.v.p.*, (2) 1698, Ann Courthope, 3s.; MP Mallow 1692–*d.*; capt., Lesley's foot 1689, St George's foot 1689, queen's foot 1690–1.

Clayton, Randal (*d.* 1725), of Mallow, Co. Cork, 1st surv. s. of Laurence Clayton (*q.v.*) by his 2nd w.; bro. of Courthope Clayton (*q.v.*); m. Elizabeth, da. of Simon Gibbings (*d.* 1721), rector of Mallow, *s.p.*

Courthope, Martha (*d. c.* 1730), sis. of Sir Peter Courthope of Little Island, Co. Cork; unm.

Courthope, Rachel, da. of John Codrington of Codrington, Gloucs.; m. 1686, John Courthope (*d.* 1695) of Little Island, Co. Cork, *s.p.*

Hill, Anne (*d.* 1747), da. and eventual h. of Sir John Trevor (*d.* 1717) of Brynkinalt, Denbighs., Speaker of the house of commons [E] 1685–7, 1690–5; m. (1) 1690, Michael Hill (1672–99), of Hillsborough, Co. Down, MP [I] 1695–9, 2s. 1da., (2) Alan I, *s.p.*

Hill, Anne (*b.* aft. 1690), da. of Michael Hill of Hillsborough, Co. Down, and Anne Hill (*q.v.*); m. 1710, St John III, 4 da.

Hill, Arthur (c. 1694–1771), of Belvoir, Co. Down; MP Hillsborough 1715–27, Co. Down 1727–66; keeper of records, Dublin Castle 1719–33, registrar of deeds [I] 1734–48, privy councillor [I] 1750, 1753–*d.*, chancellor of exchequer [I] 1754–5, revenue commr [I] 1755–*d.*; *cr.* Viscount Dungannon 1766; 2nd s. of Anne Hill (*d.* 1747) (*q.v.*) by her 1st husband.

Hill, Mary (1684–1742), da. and coh. of Anthony Rowe (aft. 1641–1704), of St Martin-in-the Fields, Westminster (MP [E] 1689–90, 1693, 1701), and wid. of Sir Edmund Denton (1676–1714), 1st Bt, of Hillesden, Bucks., MP [E & GB] 1698–1713; m. bef. 1717, Trevor Hill (*q.v.*)

Hill, Trevor (1693–1742), of Hillsborough, Co. Down; MP Hillsborough 1713–14, Co. Down 1715–17, MP [GB] 1715–22; privy councillor [I] 1717–*d.*; *cr.* Viscount Hillsborough 1717; 1st s. of Anne Hill (*d.* 1747) (*q.v.*) by her 1st husband.

APPENDIX 3: MEMBERS OF THE IRISH HOUSE OF LORDS MENTIONED IN THE TEXT

Temporal Lords

Abercorn – *see* Strabane.

Allen: John Allen (1661–1726), of Stillorgan, Co. Dublin, *cr.* Viscount Allen 1717; MP Co. Dublin 1692–3, 1703–13, 1715–17, Co. Carlow 1695–9, Co. Wicklow 1713–14; privy councillor [I] 1714–*d*.

Altham, 14th Baron: Arthur Annesley (1689–1727).

Anglesey – *see* Valentia.

Athenry, 14th Baron: Francis Bermingham (1692–1750).

Barry, 3rd Baron, of Santry: Henry Barry (1680–1735); privy councillor [I] 1714.

Barrymore, 4th earl of: James Barry (1667–1748); MP [GB] 1710–13, 1714–27, 1734–47; privy councillor [I] 1714–*d*.

Bellew, 4th Baron: John Bellew (1702–70).

Blayney, 7th Baron: Cadwallader Blayney (1693–1733).

Blessington, 2nd Viscount: Charles Boyle (aft. 1673–1732); MP [I] Blessington 1711–18.

Blundell: Sir Montague Blundell (1689–1756), 4th Bt, of Blundell Manor, King's Co., *cr.* Viscount 1720; MP [GB] 1715–22.

Brodrick: Alan Brodrick I – *see* Appendix 2.

Butler of Newtownbutler: Theophilus Butler (1669–1724), of Belturbet, Co. Cavan, *cr.* Baron 1715; MP [I] 1703–14; jt clerk of the pells [I] 1678 (life), privy councillor [I] 1710–*d*.

Catherlogh, 2nd marquess of: Philip Wharton (1698–1731); also 2nd marquess of Wharton [GB], *cr.* duke of Wharton [GB] 1719; outlawed 1729.

Cavan, 4th earl of: Richard Lambart (*d*. 1742); lieut., Viscount Charlemont's foot 1694–8, capt., Gustavus Hamilton's foot 1703, lieut.-col., Dormer's foot 1715–26.

Chetwynd, 1st Viscount: Walter Chetwynd (c. 1677–1736), of Ingestre, Staffs., *cr.* Viscount Chetwynd of Bearhaven 1717; MP [GB] 1702–10, 1712–22, 1725–34; master of buckhounds to Prince George of Denmark and Queen Anne 1705–11, ranger, St James's Park 1714–27.

Darnley, 1st earl of: John Bligh (1687–1728), of Rathmore, Co. Meath, *cr.* Baron Clifton 1721, Viscount Darnley 1723, earl of Darnley 1725; MP [I] 1709–21.

Duncannon, 2nd Viscount: Brabazon Ponsonby (1679–1758), of Bessborough, Co. Kilkenny, MP [I] Newtownards 1705–14, Co. Kildare 1715–24; privy councillor [I] 1727,

1732–7, revenue commr [I] 1739–44, lord justice [I] 1754–5, 1756–7; suc. as 2nd Viscount. Duncannon 1724, *cr.* earl of Bessborough 1739.

Fane: Charles Fane (1676–1744), of Grange, Co. Limerick, *cr.* Viscount Fane 1718; MP [I] 1715–18; privy councillor [I] 1718–*d.*

Ferrard: Sir Henry Tichborne (1662–1731), 1st Bt, of Beaulieu, Co. Louth, *cr.* Baron Ferrard 1715; MP [I] 1715; privy councillor [I] 1715–*d.*, commr of great seal [I] 1716, 1717, 1721.

Fitzwilliam, 5th Viscount: Richard Fitzwilliam (c. 1677–1743); privy councillor [I] 1715–*d.*

Forbes: George Forbes, Viscount Forbes (1685–1765), of Castle Forbes, Co. Longford, 1st surv. s. of 2nd earl of Granard, summoned to Lords in his father's viscountcy, 1724; 2nd lieut., Holt's marines 1704–11, lieut., RN 1705, brigadier, 4th troop of Horse Guards 1708, major 1712–17, lieut.-gov., Minorca 1716–18, vice-adm. Austrian navy 1719–21, privy councillor [I] 1721, gov., Leeward Is. 1729–31, minister plenipotentiary to St Petersburg 1733–4, rear-adm. 1734, vice-adm. 1736; suc. as 3rd earl of Granard 1734.

Hillsborough – *see* Appendix 2 (Hill, Trevor).

Kildare, 19th earl of: Robert Fitzgerald (1698–1744); privy councillor [I] 1710–*d.*, lord justice [I] 1714–15.

Kilmaine: James O'Hara (c. 1682–1774), s. and h. of Charles O'Hara, 1st Baron Tyrawley (*d.* 1724); lieut., Royal Fusiliers 1703, capt. 1705, col. 1713, brigadier-gen. 1735, major-gen. 1739, lieut.-gen. 1743, gen. 1761, field-marshal 1763, a.-d.-c. to king 1717, ambassador to Portugal 1727, to Russia 1743, gov., Gibraltar 1756.

Limerick: James Hamilton (c. 1691–1758), of Tollymore, Co. Down, and Dundalk, Co. Louth, *cr.* Viscount 1719, earl of Clanbrassil 1756; MP [I] Dundalk 1715–19 and [GB] 1727–34, 1735–41, 1742–54; chief remembrancer of exchequer [I] 1742–*d.*, privy councillor [I] 1746–*d.*

Meath, 6th earl of: Chaworth Brabazon (1686–1763), MP Co. Dublin 1713–14; privy councillor [I] 1716–*d.*

Midleton – *see* Appendix 2 (Brodrick, Alan I).

Molesworth: Robert Molesworth (1656–1725), of Brackenstown, Co. Dublin and Edlington, Yorks., *cr.* Viscount 1716; MP [I] 1695–9, 1703–14 and [E & GB] 1695–8, 1705–8, 1715–22; envoy extraordinary to Denmark 1689–92, privy councillor [I] 1697–Jan. 1714, Oct. 1714–*d.*

Moore of Tullamore: John Moore (bef. 1676–1725), of Croghan, King's Co., *cr.* Baron 1715; MP [I] 1703–14; privy councillor [I] 1715–*d.*, commr of great seal [I] 1721.

Mount-Alexander, 3rd earl of: Henry Montgomery (c. 1652–1731); privy councillor [I] by 1711.

Mountjoy: William Stewart (1675–1728), 2nd Viscount; col. of foot 1694–8, 1701–13, dragoons 1715, brigadier-gen. 1703, major-gen. 1707, lieut.-gen. 1710, master-gen. of ordnance [I] 1714–*d.*, one of keepers of great seal [I] 1721.

Perceval: Sir John Perceval (1683–1748), 5th Bt, of Burton House, Co. Cork, *cr.* Viscount Perceval 1723, earl of Egmont 1733; MP [I] 1703–14 and [GB] 1727–34; privy councillor [I] 1704–*d.*

Roscommon, 8th earl of: James Dillon (1702–46).

Rosse, 2nd earl of: Richard Parsons (*d.* 1741).

Santry – *see* Barry.

Shannon, 2nd Viscount: Richard Boyle (c. 1675–1740); MP [GB] 1708–11, 1712–34; cornet, Horse Guards 1693, major 1696–1702, col. of marines 1702–15, brigadier-gen. 1704, major-gen. 1708, jt comptroller for clothing the army [GB] 1708, lieut.-gen. 1710, col., 25th Foot 1715–21, lieut.-gen. of forces [I] 1716, c.-in-c. [I] 1720–*d.*, col., 6th Dragoons 1721–7, Life Guards 1727–*d.*, privy councillor [I] 1721–*d.*, lord justice [I] 1722–3, 1724, gen. 1735, field marshal 1739.

Shelburne: Henry Petty (1675–1751), of Wycombe, Bucks., *cr.* Baron Shelburne 1699, earl of Shelburne 1719; MP [GB] 1715–27; jt prothonotary of common pleas [I] 1692–1700, jt ranger of Phoenix Park 1698–*d.*, privy councillor [I] 1701.

Southwell, 2nd Baron: Thomas Southwell (1698–1766), of Castlematrix, Co. Limerick; MP Co. Limerick 1717–20; privy councillor [I] 1726–*d.*

Strabane, 1st Viscount: James Hamilton (*d.* 1734), of Baronscourt, Co. Tyrone, 6th earl of Abercorn in the Scottish peerage; privy councillor [I] by 1711–*d.*

Strangford, 3rd Viscount: Endymion Smythe (*d.* c. 1724), of Westenhanger, Kent.

Thomond, 7th earl of: Henry O'Brien (1688–1741); MP [GB] 1710–14; privy councillor [I] 1714–*d.*

Tullamore – *see* Moore.

Tyrone, 1st Viscount: Sir Marcus Beresford (1694–1763), 4th Bt, of Curraghmore, Co. Waterford, *cr.* Viscount Tyrone 1720, earl of Tyrone 1746; MP [I] 1715–20.

Valentia, 6th Viscount: Arthur Annesley (c. 1678–1737); also 5th earl of Anglesey [E]; MP [I] 1703–10, and [E & GB] 1702–10; gentleman of the privy chamber [E] 1689–1702; jt vice-treasurer and paymaster-gen. [I] 1710–16, privy councillor [GB] 1710–*d.*, [I] 1711–*d.*, lord justice [GB] 1714.

Wharton– *see* Catherlogh.

Spiritual Lords

Bolton, Theophilus (c. 1578–1744), bp of Clonfert 1722–4, Elphin 1724–30, abp of Cashel 1730–*d.*

Boulter, Hugh (1672–1742), bp of Bristol 1719–24, abp of Armagh 1724–*d.*

Browne, Peter (c. 1665–1735), bp of Cork and Ross 1710–*d.*

Burscough, William (c. 1676–1755), bp of Limerick 1725–*d.*

Cobbe, Charles (c. 1687–1765), bp of Killala 1720–7, Dromore 1727–32, Kildare 1732–43, abp of Dublin 1743–*d.*

Crowe, Charles (c. 1656–1726), bp of Cloyne 1702–*d.*

Downes, Henry (c. 1667–1735), bp of Killala 1717–20, Elphin 1720–4, Meath 1724–7, Derry 1727–*d.*

Ellis, Welbore (c. 1661–1734), bp of Kildare 1705–32, Meath 1732–*d.*

Forster, Nicholas (c. 1673–1743), bp of Killaloe 1714–16, Raphoe 1716–*d.*

Hort, Josiah (c. 1674–1751), bp of Ferns 1722–7, Kilmore 1727–42, abp of Tuam 1742–*d.*

Hutchinson, Francis (1660–1739), bp of Down and Connor 1721–*d.*

King, William (1650–1729), bp of Derry 1691–1703, abp of Dublin 1703–*d.*

Lambert, Ralph (c. 1666–1732), bp of Dromore 1717–27, Meath 1727–*d.*

Lindsay, Thomas (1656–1724), bp of Killaloe 1696–1713, Raphoe 1713–14, abp of Armagh 1714–*d.*

Milles, Thomas (1671–1740), bp of Waterford and Lismore 1708–*d*.

Nicolson, William (1655–1727), bp of Carlisle 1702–18, Derry 1718–27, abp of Cashel 1727–*d*.

Price, Arthur (c. 1680–1752), bp of Clonfert 1724–30, Ferns 1730–4, Meath 1734–44, abp of Cashel 1744–*d*.

Synge, Edward (1659–1741), bp of Raphoe 1714–16, abp of Tuam 1716–*d*.

Vesey, Sir Thomas (c. 1672–1730), 1st Bt, bp of Killaloe 1713–14, Ossory 1714–*d*.

APPENDIX 4: MEMBERS OF THE IRISH HOUSE OF COMMONS MENTIONED IN THE TEXT

Agar, James (1672–1733), of Gowran Castle, Co. Kilkenny, MP Old Leighlin 1703–13, Gowran 1713–14, Callan 1715–27, St Canice 1727–*d.*

Allen, Joshua (1685–1742), of Stillorgan, Co. Dublin, MP Co. Kildare 1709–26; 1st s. of John Allen (*q.v.*); suc. as 2nd Viscount Allen 1726.

Barry, James – *see* Appendix 2.

Barry, Redmond – *see* Appendix 2.

Bernard, Francis (1663–1731), of Castle Bernard, Co. Cork, MP Clonakilty 1692–3, Bandon 1695–1727; solicitor-gen. [I] 1711–14, prime serjeant [I] 1725–6, judge of common pleas [I] 1726–*d.*

Berry, William (c. 1668–1739), of Wardenstown, Co. Meath, MP Enniscorthy 1703–13, 1715–*d.*, Duleek 1713–14; lieut., Inniskilling horse 1689, capt., St George's foot 1696, lieut.-col., Wolseley's horse by 1704.

Bettesworth, Richard – *see* Appendix 2.

Bindon, David (c. 1650–1733), of Cloney, Co. Clare, MP Ennis 1715–27.

Bindon, Samuel (1680–1760), of Rockmount, Co. Clare, MP Ennis 1715–*d.*

Bladen, Martin (c. 1680–1746), of Aldborough Hatch, Essex, MP Bandon 1715–27 and MP [GB] 1715–*d.*; ensign, Fairfax's regmt. 1697, capt., Hotham's regmt. 1705, col. of foot 1709–10, comptroller of the mint [GB] 1714–28, sec. to lords justices [I] 1715–17, privy councillor [I] 1715–27, 1733–7, 1739–42, 1745–*d.*

Blenerhassett, John (1691–1775), of Ballyseedy, Co. Kerry, MP Co. Kerry 1709–13, 1715–27, 1761–*d.*, Tralee 1713–14, 1727–60.

Bligh, Thomas (1693–1775), of Brittas, Co. Meath, MP Athboy 1715–*d.*; capt., 1717, major, 5th Dragoons 1719, col. 1729, lieut-col. of horse 1733–7, 1739, 1740–1, col., 20th Foot 1740, 12th Dragoons 1746, major-gen. 1747, brigadier-gen. 1747, lieut.-gen. 1754, capt., troop of horse guards 1755–74.

Boyle, Henry (1682–1764), of Castlemartyr, Co. Cork, MP Midleton 1707–13, Kilmallock 1713–14, Co. Cork 1715–56; Speaker of house of commons [I] 1733–56, chancellor of exchequer [I] 1733–5, privy councillor [I] 1733–*d.*, revenue commr [I] 1735–54, lord justice [I] with intervals 1734–*d.*; cr. earl of Shannon 1756.

Boyle, William (c. 1678–1725), of Castlemartyr, Co. Cork, MP Charleville 1715–*d.*; cornet, Schomberg's horse 1694, lieut., 24th Foot 1708, lieut.-col., Dormer's dragoons 1717–20; yr. bro. of Henry Boyle (*q.v.*).

Brasier, Kilner (*d.* 1725), of Ray, Co. Donegal, MP Dundalk 1695–9, St Johnston (Co. Donegal), 1703–13, Kilmallock 1715–*d.*; capt., Viscount Mountjoy's foot 1685, major, Peyton's foot 1689, lieut.-col. 1694, col. 20th Foot 1706.

Brodrick, St John III – *see* Appendix 2.

Brooke, Henry (1671–1761), of Colebrooke, Co. Fermanagh, MP Dundalk 1713–27, Co. Fermanagh 1727–60.

Burgh, Thomas (1670–1730), of Oldtown, Co. Kildare, MP Naas 1713–*d.*; capt. Royal Regt. of Foot 1692, engineer in king's own company 1696, surveyor-gen. [I] 1700–*d.*, lieut. of ordnance [I] 1706–14, lieut.-col., 20th Foot 1707–14.

Burton, Francis (1696–1744), of Buncraggy, Co. Clare, MP Coleraine 1721–7, Co. Clare 1727–*d.*; privy councillor [I] 1733–*d.*

Carter, Thomas (c. 1682–1763), of Robertstown and Rathnally, Co. Meath, MP Trim 1719–26, Hillsborough 1727–60; dep. master of the rolls [I] 1725, examiner in chancery [I] 1727, clerk of the crown [I] 1729–*d.*, master of the rolls [I] 1731–53, privy councillor [I] 1732–54, 1755–*d.*, sec. of state [I] 1755–60.

Casaubon (Causabon), William (c. 1694–1744), of Carrig, Co. Cork, MP Doneraile 1715–27.

Clements, Theophilus (1687–1728), of Rathkenny, Co. Cavan, MP Cavan 1713–*d.*; teller of exchequer [I] 1722–*d.*

Clutterbuck, Thomas (1697–1742), of St Martin-in-the Field, Middx, MP Lisburn 1725–*d.*, MP [GB] 1722–*d.*, chief sec. [I] 1724–30, lord of admiralty [GB] 1732–41, lord of treasury [GB] 1741–2, treasurer of navy [GB] 1742–*d.*

Coghill, James (c. 1677–1734), of Castleknock, Co. Dublin, MP Clogher 1723–7, Newcastle 1727–*d.*

Coghill, Marmaduke (1673–1739), of Drumcondra, Co. Dublin, MP Armagh 1692–1713, TCD 1713–*d.*, revenue commr [I] 1729–35, chancellor of the exchequer [I] 1735–*d.*; bro. of James Coghill (*q.v.*).

Colclough, Caesar (c. 1665–1726), of Rosegarland, Co. Wexford, MP Taghmon 1719–*d.*

Conolly, William (1662–1729), of Capel St., Dublin and Castletown, Co. Kildare, MP Donegal 1692–9, Co. Londonderry 1703–*d.*; customer, Derry and Coleraine, 1697–*d.*, revenue commr [I] 1709–10, 1714–*d.*, privy councillor [I] 1710–11, 1714–*d.*, Speaker of the house of commons [I] 1715–29, lord justice [I] 1717–19, 1719–21, 1722–4, 1726–7, 1728–*d.*

Creighton, David (1671–1728), of Crom Castle, Co. Fermanagh, MP Augher 1695–9, Lifford, 1703–*d.*; lieut. Levingston's dragoons 1692, Brudenell's foot 1702, lieut.-col. 1706, col. of foot 1708, brigadier-gen. 1711, major-gen. 1727, master of Royal Hospital, Kilmainham 1719–*d.*

Crofton, Sir Edward (c. 1662–1729), 2nd Bt, of Mote Park, Co. Roscommon, MP Boyle 1695–9, Co. Roscommon 1703–*d.*; privy councillor [I] 1714–*d.*

Crofton, Edward (1687–1739), MP Roscommon 1713–*d.*; s. of Sir Edward Crofton, 2nd Bt. (*q.v.*)

Crosbie, Sir Maurice (1690–1762), of Ardfert, Co. Kerry, MP Co. Kerry 1713–*d.*; cr. Baron Branden 1758.

Cuffe, John (1683–1740), of Desart, Co. Kilkenny, MP Thomastown 1715–27; cr. Baron Desart 1733.

Deane, Edward (1682–1748), of Dangan, Co. Kilkenny, MP Newcastle 1713–14, Innistioge 1715–27, 1728–*d.*

Delafaye, Charles (1677–1762), of London, MP Belturbet 1715–27; clerk in secretary of state's office [E] 1697–1706, chief clerk 1706–13, second sec. [I] 1713–15, gentleman sewer

[GB] 1714–27, jt. sec. to lords justices [I] 1715–17, jt. chief sec. [I] 1717, under-secretary of state [GB] 1717–34.

Edgeworth, Robert (aft. 1657–1730), of Longwood, Co. Meath, MP St Johnstown (Co. Longford), 1713–27.

Fitzgerald, John (c. 1648–1728), of Ballynacot, Co. Cork, MP Castlemartyr 1727–8.

Flower, William (1686–1746), of Castle Durrow, Queen's Co., MP Co. Kilkenny 1715–27, Portarlington 1727–33; privy councillor [I] 1735–*d.*; *cr.* Baron Castle Durrow 1733.

Fox, Patrick (bef. 1669–1734), of Fox Hall, Co. Longford, MP Kilbeggan 1703–13, Fore 1715–27; lieut., Charlemont's regt. 1694, capt., Caulfeild's regt. 1705, major, Creighton's regt. 1709, major, Will's foot 1715–16, lieut.-col. Palmer's regt. 1716.

Freeman, Samuel (1655–1732), of Esker Lodge, Timahoe, Queen's Co., MP Ballinakill 1715–27; col. 1716–19.

Freke, Sir Percy (1700–28), 2nd Bt, of Castle Freke, Co. Cork, MP Baltimore 1721–*d.*

Geering, Richard (bef. 1682–1742), of Dublin, MP Ballyshannon 1703–13, Jamestown 1721–7; one of the six clerks in chancery [I] 1701–34.

Gore, Sir Arthur (1682–1742), 2nd Bt, of Newtown, Co. Mayo, MP Ballinakill 1793–13, Donegal 1713–14, Co. Mayo 1715–*d.*; capt., Jones's regt. 1708–12.

Gore, Sir Ralph (1675–1733), 4th Bt, of Manor Gore, Co. Donegal, MP Donegal 1703–13, Co. Donegal 1713–27, Clogher 1727–*d.*; privy councillor [I] 1714–*d.*, chancellor of exchequer [I] 1717–*d.*, Speaker of the house of commons [I] 1729–*d.*, lord justice [I] 1730–1, 1732–*d.*

Gorges, Richard (1662–1728), of Kilbrew House, Co. Meath, MP Charlemont 1692–3, Bandon 1703–13, Ratoath 1713–27; cornet of horse 1685, capt., Viscount Lisburne's regt. 1689, adjutant-gen. of forces [I] 1696, quartermaster-gen. [I] 1701, col. of foot regt. 1703, brigadier-gen. 1704, col., 25th Foot 1706, major-gen. of forces in Spain 1707, lieut.-gen. 1710, major-gen. 1710.

Hawley, Henry (1657–1724), of Kinsale, Co. Cork, MP Kinsale 1703–*d.*; major, 19th Foot 1689, lieut.-col. 1690, lieut.-col. 33rd Foot 1691, Erle's foot 1695, gov., Kinsale 1701–*d.*

Hill, Arthur – *see* Appendix 2.

Hoare, Edward (c. 1678–1765), of Dunkettle, Co. Cork, MP Cork 1710–27.

Hopkins, Edward (1674/5–1736), of Coventry, Warws., MP TCD 1721–7 and MP [GB] 1701–2, 1707–10, 1713–27; revenue commr [I] 1716–22, chief sec. [I] 1721–4, privy councillor [I] 1721–7, 1733–*d.*, master of the revels [I] 1722–*d.*

Hume, Sir Gustavus (c. 1670–1731), 3rd Bt, of Castle Hume, Co. Fermanagh, MP Co. Fermanagh 1713–*d.*; privy councillor [I] 1714–*d.*

Ivers, John (c. 1650–1729), of Mount Ievers, Co. Clare, MP [I] Co. Clare 1715–27.

Jephson, Anthony (c. 1689–1755), of Mallow Castle, Co. Cork, MP Mallow 1713–*d.*; cornet, Wharton's dragoons 1710, half-pay 1713, capt., Fielding's dragoons 1716, lieut.-col., Lord Doneraile's dragoons 1716, col. 1740.

Knapp, Edmond (1659–1747), of Killycloin, Co. Cork, MP Cork 1715–27.

Levinge, Richard (1685–1748), of High Park, Mullalea, Co. Westmeath, MP Co. Westmeath 1723–7, Blessington 1727–*d.*; suc as 2nd Bt 1724.

Manley, Isaac (bef. 1682–1735), of Dublin and Manley Hall, Staffs., MP Downpatrick 1705–13, Limavady 1715–*d.*; postmaster-gen. [I] 1703–*d.*

Marlay, Thomas (c. 1678–1756), of Celbridge, Co. Kildare, MP Limavady 1717–27, Lanesborough 1727–30; king's counsel [I] 1715; solicitor-gen. [I] 1720–7, attorney-gen. [I]

1727–30, chief baron of exchequer [I] 1730–42, privy councillor [I] 1730–*d.*, chief justice of king's bench [I] 1742–51.

May, Edward (1673–1729), of Mayfield, Co. Waterford, MP Co. Waterford 1715–*d.*

Maynard, William (1690–1734), of Curryglass, Co. Cork, MP Tallow 1713–*d.*; collector of revenue, Cork port 1717–*d.*

Medlycott, Thomas (1662–1738), of Dublin and Binfield, Berks., MP Kildare 1692–9, Clonnmel 1703–13, Ballynakill 1713–14, Downpatrick 1715–27, Limavady 1728–*d.* and MP [E & GB] 1705–15, 1727–34; dep. steward of Westminster 1705–14, revenue commr [I] 1714–27, 1727–33.

Molyneux, Samuel (1689–1728), of Lowtown, Co. Kildare and St Martin-in-the-Field, Middx, MP TCD 1727–*d.*, MP [GB] 1715–22, 1726–*d.*; sec. to prince of Wales 1715–27; lord of admiralty [GB] 1727–*d.*, privy councillor [I] 1727–*d.*

Nesbitt, Thomas (*d.* 1750), of Grange More, Co. Westmeath, MP Cavan 1715–*d.*

O'Brien, Sir Edward (1705–65), 2nd Bt, of Dromoland, Co. Clare, MP Co. Clare 1727–*d.*, MP [GB] 1727–8.

Ogle, George (1704–46), of Dean's Castle, Co. Wexford, MP Bannow 1727–*d.*

Parry, Benjamin (1672–1736), of Dublin, MP Killybegs 1703–13, Limavady 1713–14, Tallow 1715–27, Dungarvan 1727–*d.*; register of memorials of deeds [I] 1707–*d.*, privy councillor [I] 1714–*d.*, keeper of Phoenix Park, Dublin 1722–*d.*

Parsons, Sir William (1661–1741), 2nd Bt, of Birr Castle, King's Co., MP King's Co. 1692–1713, 1715–*d.*; capt., Tollemache's foot 1688, major 1693, Fairfax's foot 1695, Jones's foot by 1710.

Pearce, Edward Lovett (c. 1699–1733), of Stillorgan, Co. Dublin, MP Ratoath 1728–*d*; cornet, Morris's regt. 1716, capt., Nevill's regt., surveyor-gen. 1731–3; kntd. 1732.

Pearson, Thomas (1678–1736), of Beamore, Co. Meath, MP Killybegs 1710–27, Ballyshannon 1727–*d.*; collector, Drogheda 1730–*d.*

Pennefather, Matthew (1675–1733), of Rathsallagh, Cashel, Co. Tipperary, MP Cashel 1710–*d.*; ensign, Ingoldsby's foot 1695, lieut. 1701, capt. 1704, commissary-gen. of musters [I] 1709, muster-master gen. [I] 1709–?

Ponsonby, Brabazon – *see* Appendix 3 (Duncannon, Viscount).

Ponsonby, Hon. Henry (1685–1745), of Ashgrove, Co. Kilkenny, MP Fethard (Co. Wexford) 1715–27, Inistioge 1727–8; capt., Inniskilling Regt. 1705, major 1711, lieut.-col. 1712–33, col., 37th Foot 1735–43, brigadier-gen. 1742, major-gen. 1743; 2nd s. of Brabazon Ponsonby (*q.v.*).

Pratt, John (1670–1741), of Cabra Court, Kingscourt, Co. Cavan, MP Dingle 1713–27; dep. vice-treasurer [I] 1716–25.

Purdon, Bartholomew (1675–1737), of Ballyclogh, Co. Cork, MP Mallow 1699–1713, Doneraile 1713–14, Castlemartyr 1715–*d.*

Purefoy, William (1660–1737), of Clonbulloge, King's Co., MP King's Co. 1717–13, 1715–27, Philipstown 1713–14; capt., Wharton's foot 1689, Ingoldsby's regt. by 1696, major, Brewer's foot 1697–1702.

Ram, George (1676–1725), MP Gorey 1713–*d.*; clerk of first fruits [I] 1716.

Rogerson, John (1676–1741), of Glasnevin, Co. Dublin, MP Granard 1713–14, Dublin 1715–27; recorder, Dublin 1714–27, solicitor-gen. [I] 1714–20, attorney-gen. [I] 1720–7, chief justice of king's bench [I] 1727–*d.*, privy councillor [I] 1727–*d.*

Rose, Henry (1675–1743), of Mountpleasant and Morgans, Co. Limerick, MP Ardfert 1703–34; judge of king's bench [I] 1734–*d*.

St George, Oliver (1661–1731), of Carrickdrumrusk, Co. Leitrim, MP Carrick-on-Shannon 1703–13, Dungannon 1713–*d*.; capt. of a troop of dragoons 1685, capt. Queen's Regt. of dragoons 1685–8, privy councillor [I] 1714–*d*.

St George, Richard (1670–1755), of Kilrush, Co. Kilkenny, MP Galway 1695–9, Carrick-on-Shannon 1715–*d*.; adjutant, St George's foot 1690, capt.1691, major, Lord Slane's foot 1708, lieut.-col. 1711, lieut.-col., Macartney's horse 1727; col. of foot regt. 1737; col. of dragoon regt. 1740, major-gen. 1744, lieut.-gen. 1747, major-gen. of staff [I] by 1755.

Sandford, Henry (bef. 1671–1733), of Castlereagh, Co. Roscommon, MP Roscommon 1692–*d*.; collector of excise, Dublin 1715.

Sheppard, Anthony (1668–1738), of Newcastle, Co. Longford, MP Co. Longford 1703–13, 1715–*d*.

Singleton, Edward (c.1674–1726), of Drogheda, MP Drogheda 1717–*d*.

Singleton, Henry (1682–1759), of Drumcondra, Co. Dublin, MP Drogheda 1713–40; prime serjeant [I] 1726–39, chief justice of common pleas [I] 1740–52; privy councillor [I] 1740–*d*., yr. bro. of Edward Singleton (*q.v.*).

Southwell, Edward (1671–1730), of Kings Weston, Gloucs., Kinsale, Co. Cork, and Spring Garden, Westminster, MP Kinsale 1692–9, 1713–*d*., TCD 1703–13, and MP [E & GB] 1702–8, 1713–15; clerk of privy council [E] 1693–*d*., jt prothonotary of common pleas [I] 1698–1717, judge of admiralty court and vice-adm., Munster [I] 1699–*d*., jt commr of privy seal [E] 1701–2, [GB] 1715, 1716, sec. of state [I] 1702–*d*., privy councillor [I] 1702–*d*., chief sec. [I] 1703–7, 1710–13, prothonotary of king's bench [I] 1715–17.

Stewart, Hon. Charles (1681–1741), of West Malling, Kent, MP Co. Tyrone 1715–27, MP [GB] 1723–7, 1737–*d*.; 5th s. of 1st Viscount Mountjoy; capt., RN 1704, plenipotentiary to Morocco 1720–1, c.-in-c., Jamaica station 1729–32, adm. 1729, vice-adm. 1734.

Taylor, Sir Thomas (1686–1757), 1st Bt, of Kells, Co. Meath, MP Kells 1692–9, 1713–*d*., Belturbet 1703–13; privy councillor [I] 1726–*d*.

Tighe, Richard (1678–1736), of Dublin, MP Belturbet 1703–13, Newtownards 1715–27, Augher 1727–*d*.; privy councillor [I] 1718–*d*; keeper of records in Bermingham Tower, Dublin Castle 1734–*d*.

Tisdall, Richard (c. 1698–1742), of Bawn, Co. Louth, MP Dundalk 1707–13, Co. Louth 1713–27; usher in chancery [I] 1714, 1734–5, registrar, chancery [I] 1716–44.

Trotter, Thomas (1684–1745), of Duleek, Co. Meath, MP Duleek, 1715–27, Old Leighlin 1727–*d*.; commr of appeals in revenue [I] 1728–*d*., master of chancery [I] 1732–42.

Upton, Clotworthy (1665–1725), of Castle Upton, Templepatrick, Co. Antrim, MP Newtownards 1695–9, Co. Antrim 1703–*d*.

Upton, Thomas (1677–1733), MP Antrim 1713–14, Co. Antrim 1716–27, Derry 1727–*d*.; king's counsel [I] 1715, commr of appeals in revenue [I] 1717–*d*., counsel to barracks commrs [I] by 1721–*d*., customer, Derry and Coleraine 1723; yr. bro. of Clotworthy Upton (*q.v.*).

Vesey, Agmondisham (1677–1739), of Lucan, Co. Dublin, MP Tuam 1703–*d*.; comptroller- and accountant-gen. [I] 1734–*d*.

Wall, William (bef. 1690–1755), of Maryborough, Queen's Co., MP Maryborough 1713–*d*.; master in chancery [I] 1742–*d*.

Warburton, Richard (1674–1747), of Donnycarney, Co. Dublin, MP Portarlington 1715–27, Ballinakill 1727–*d*.

Ward, Michael (1683–1759), of Castle Ward, Co. Down, MP Co. Down 1713–27, Bangor 1727; justice, king's bench [I] 1727–*d*.

Webster, Edward (bef. 1691–by 1755), MP Carysfort 1717–27; clerk, treasury [E] 1691–1755, chief sec. [I] 1717–20, searcher, packer and gauger, Dublin and outports 1718–43.

Weymes (Wemys), Henry (1703–50), of Danesfort, Co. Kilkenny, MP Callan 1727–*d*.

Weymes (Wemys), Patrick (1679–1747), of Danesfort, Co. Kilkenny, MP Gowran 1703–14, Co. Kilkenny 1721–*d*.; fa. of Henry Weymes (*q.v.*).

Whitshed, Samuel Warter (1685–1746), of Dublin, MP Wicklow 1715–*d*.; capt., Harrison's regt. 1706, Steuart's foot 1708, Hertford's regt. 1713, 15th Foot 1715, major, Mountjoy's dragoons 1716, a.-d.-c. to lord lieut. [I] 1718, major, 8th Dragoons 1718, lieut.-col. 1720, governor, Wicklow Castle 1726, lieut.-col. dragoon regt. 1729, 1733–6, 1738–41, col., 39th Foot 1740, 12th Dragoons 1743, brigadier-gen. 1745.

Wynne, Owen (1665–1737), of Hazelwood, Co. Sligo, MP Carrick-on Shannon 1692–3 Ballyshannon 1713–27, Co. Sligo 1727–*d*.; capt., Roscommon's foot 1689, major, Royal Irish dragoons 1694, lieut.-col., Ross's dragoons, 1695, col. of foot 1705–13, of dragoons 1715, of 4th Royal Dragoons 1727, of 5th Royal Irish dragoons 1732, of dragoons 1734–6, brigadier-gen. 1706, major-gen. 1709, lieut.-gen. 1727, privy councillor [I] 1726–36, lieut.-gen. of forces [I] 1735–6.

Wynne, Owen (1687–1756), of Hazelwood, Co. Sligo, MP Sligo 1713–*d*., ensign and lieut., Wynne's foot 1705–13, capt.-lieut. 1737, major of dragoons 1753–6, lieut.-col. 1756–*d*.; nephew of Owen Wynne (*q.v.*).

Index

This index covers all three volumes. Volume numbers are indicated in bold type.
Besides standard abbreviations, the following apply:

bro.   brother
d.   died
[E]   England
fa.   father
[GB]   Great Britain
[I]   Ireland
m.   mother
s.   son
sr   senior
w.   wife

Note that neither Alan Brodrick I nor Thomas Brodrick are indexed.

Abbott, Charles, **1**, 151
abduction, **1**, 151
Abercorn, 6th earl of *see* Hamilton, James
Aberdeen, **2**, 108
Abingdon, 2nd earl of *see* Bertie, Montagu Venables
abjuration oath, **1**, 272; **2**, 76, 84, 89–91, 98–9
accounts, public [GB], **3**, 276
accounts, public [I], **3**, 164–5, 223–4, 238, 251–2, 257
commissioners of, **3**, 164–6, 223–5, 255
accountant-general's office [I], **3**, 258
Acton, Thomas, **2**, 427
Adair, Robert, MP [I], **3**, 183
Adare, Co. Limerick, **2**, 40
Addison, Joseph, MP [I & GB] **1**, 268; **2**, 24, 27–8, 31–2, 34, 36, 42, 59, 187, 197–8, 208, 211, 213, 215, 219, 221–2, 233; **3**, 113
  The Old Whig (1719), **2**, 253
admiralty [GB], **3**, 213, 320
Agar, James, MP [I], **2**, 434; **3**, 182
Aislabie, John, MP [E & GB], **2**, 16–17, 233–4, 263–4, 268–9, 339–43, 347, 365, 381
Albani, Annibale, cardinal, **2**, 66, 79
Albemarle, earls of *see* van Keppel
Alberoni, Cardinal Giulio, **3**, 84, 297
Alcock, Charles, **1**, 90
Aldermaston, Berks., **3**, 302, 304
Aldrich, Henry, dean of Christ Church, Oxford, **1**, 10
Aldworth, Richard, MP [I], **1**, 16, 70, 72
Allanson, Charles, MP [GB], **2**, 277
Allen, family, **2**, 37
Allen, Mr, **2**, 156
Allen, Francis, **2**, 37

Allen, John, 1st Viscount Allen **1**, 154, 156; **2**, 37, 39, 195, 205, 405; **3**, 364
Allen, John, mayor of Cork, **1**, 313
Allen, Joshua, 2nd Viscount Allen, **1**, 256; **2**, 37, 122, 136, 208–9, 395, 410, 426, 432; **3**, 259
Allen, Richard, MP [I], **2**, 37, 432
Allen, Robert, MP [I], **2**, 37, 208–9, 432
Altham, 4th Baron *see* Annesley, Arthur
Altham, Lady *see* Annesley, Dorothy
Anderson, John, apothecary, **2**, 46–7, 50
Andrews, William, mayor of Cork, **1**, 182
Anglesey, **3**, 31
Anglesey, earls of *see* Annesley
Anne, princess, daughter of George II, **3**, 35
Anne, queen, **1**, 200, 233, 310; **3**, 210
Annesley v. *Sherlock*, **2**, 8, 10, 12–13, 216; **3**, 136
Annesley, Arthur, 4th Baron Altham, **2**, 92, 95, 99, 397–8; **3**, 81, 249–50
Annesley, Arthur, 7th earl of Anglesey, **1**, 32, 34–5, 157, 159, 182, 186–8, 190, 291, 294, 323; **2**, 89–90, 92–5, 98–9, 103, 105, 111, 149, 155, 190, 227–8; **3**, 191, 213, 326
Annesley, Dorothy (née Davy), Lady Altham, w. of 3rd Baron, **2**, 347–8, 366
Annesley, Francis, MP [I] **1**, 23, 97, 108, 110, 112–13, 117, 137, 141, 208, 239–40, 323; **2**, 73
Annesley, George, **1**, 108
Annesley, John, 6th earl of Anglesey, **1**, 239
Annesley, John, **1**, 108
Annesley, Maurice, MP [I], **1**, 69, 108, 193; **2**, 8
Annesley, William, MP [I], **3**, 326
Antrim, Co., **2**, 100, 128–33, 139, 142–3, 151
Antrim, 4th earl of *see* MacDonnell, Randal
Araglin, Co. Cork, **2**, 350
Ardee, Co. Louth, **2**, 194
Ardfinnan, Co. Tipperary, **2**, 350–1
Argyll, 2nd duke of *see* Campbell, John
army [GB], **3**, 3, 34–5, 271, 280, 314
army [I], **3**, 149, 165, 280, 282–3, 286–7, 290, 295–6, 300–2, 318
  see also quartering
Arnold, Edward, would-be assassin, **3**, 32
Arnold, John, banker, **3**, 317
Arran, 1st earl *see* Butler, Richard
Arran, 1st earl of (2nd creation) *see* Butler, Charles
Arthur, Daniel, **2**, 278
Arthur, John, **2**, 278
Arundell, Hon. Richard, MP [GB], **3**, 314
Asgill, John, MP [I] **1**, 197
Ashe, Richard, MP [I], **2**, 432
Ashe, St George, bishop, **1**, 126; **2**, 93, 95, 112, 120, 122, 144, 151

Sheres, Sir Henry, forfeiture trustee [I], **1**, 100

sheriffs, **1**, 242, 264–5; **3**, 66, 333–5

Sherlock, Eustace, petitioner to house of commons [I], **1**, 193

Sherlock, Hester, respondent in chancery case [I], **2**, 8, 10

Sherlock, Thomas, fellow of St Catherine's College, Cambridge, **1**, 87

Sherlock, William, dean of St Paul's, London, **1**, 75, 174

Shippen, William, MP [GB], **2**, 101, 232; **3**, 268–9

Short, John, MP [I], **2**, 436

Shrewsbury, 1st duke of *see* Talbot, Charles

Shuldam (Schuldam), Edmond, attorney, **1**, 250–1

Shuldam (Schuldam), Lemuel, clergyman, bro. of Edmond (*q.v.*), **1**, 250–1

Shute, John Barrington, MP [I], **2**, 69, 175

Silver, John, MP [I], **1**, 174–5, 178

Singleton, Edward, sr, MP [I], **1**, 125, 177–8, 193; **3**, 272

Singleton, Edward, MP [I], s. of Edward sr (*q.v.*), **2**, 436

Singleton, Henry, MP [I], s. of Edward, sr (*q.v.*), **2**, 153, 426, 434; **3**, 20, 73, 103, 272–3, 281, 283, 295

sinking fund [GB], **3**, 358

Skeffington, Clotworthy, 3rd Viscount Massereene, **1**, 122

Skeffington, Clotworthy, 4th Viscount Massereene, **2**, 99, 130–1

Skippon, Mr, **3**, 331

Skye, Isle of, **2**, 238

Slane, 17th Baron *see* Fleming, Christopher

Slieve Logher, **1**, 38

Sloane, James, MP [I], **1**, 50, 57, 64, 67

Sloper, William, MP [GB], **2**, 343, 346

Smalridge, George, bishop, **2**, 84

Smedley, Jonathan, clergyman, **1**, 283; **2**, 270, 272, 276

Smelt, Leonard, MP [GB], **3**, 37

Smith, ——, respondent in common pleas case [I], **3**, 183

Smith, ——, robber, **2**, 350

Smith, Boyle, MP [I], **1**, 316

Smith, John, lord chief baron of exchequer [S], **3**, 342

Smith, John, MP [GB], **1**, 91, 200, 203; **2**, 232, 251

Smith, Mrs, common-law w. of Christopher Wandesford (*q.v.*), **2**, 403

Smith, Peter, revenue officer, **2**, 325

Smith, Thomas, MP [GB], **3**, 321

Smith, William, **1**, 276; **2**, 40

Smyrna coffee-house *see* Westminster

Smyth, Edward, bishop, **2**, 93–5, 99, 128–33, 139, 143, 151, 220

Smyth, Francis, of Rathcoursey, Co. Cork, **1**, 195

Smyth, Grice, of Ballynatray, Co. Waterford, s. of Richard (*q.v.*), **1**, 266–7

Smyth, Percy, of Ightermurragh, Co. Cork, **1**, 194

Smyth, Richard, of Ballynatray, Co. Waterford, **1**, 266

Smyth, Thomas, bishop, **1**, 241; **2**, 40, 92–5, 99

Smyth, Sir Thomas, 2nd Bt, MP [I], **2**, 379; **3**, 69, 89, 99–100

Smyth, William, MP [I], **2**, 436

Smythe, Endymion, 3rd Viscount Strangford, **2**, 95, 405, 408; **3**, 80–1

Snape, Andrew, headmaster, **2**, 188

Snell, John, MP [GB], **2**, 232

Society of London v. *bishop of Derry*, **3**, 135–6

'sole right', **1**, 13, 15, 21–2, 27, 68–9, 142–4
    see also parliament [I], supply bills

Solórzano, José de Grimaldo y Gutiérrez de, Marquis of Grimaldo, **3**, 84

Some Farther Account of the Original Disputes in Ireland, about Farthings and Halfpence … (1724), **3**, 132

Somers, John, 1st Baron Somers, **1**, 14, 199–200, 226, 239, 299, 304

Somerset, **3**, 274

Somerset, duchess of *see* Seymour, Elizabeth

Somerset, 6th duke of *see* Seymour, Charles

Somerset Bridge, Surrey, **3**, 274

Somerville, James, MP [I], **1**, 199

Sophia Dorothea, queen of Prussia, **3**, 43

South, John, MP [I], **1**, 159

South Sea Bubble, **2**, 15–18, 279, 292, 294–5, 298, 303–5, 307–9, 311, 338, 340, 348, 354, 388; **3**, 2, 33, 36, 65, 118, 162, 169, 266

South Sea Company and directors, **2**, 261, 263–5, 268–70, 294, 300, 303–6, 314, 316, 318–21, 326, 330–1, 334, 336, 340–2, 346, 359, 362, 370, 380, 396, 413; **3**, 3, 36
    stock in, **2**, 284, 300, 303–4, 312, 324, 326, 330, 334–6, 342, 346, 411; **3**, 65, 302

Southwell, Edward, MP [I], **1**, 30, 68, 135, 138–9, 150, 165, 198, 212, 217, 259, 316; **2**, 13, 36, 179, 207; **3**, 127, 161–2, 175

Southwell, Thomas, 1st Baron Southwell, **1**, 68, 160–1, 194, 210, 234, 260; **2**, 122, 205, 271, 404, 408; **3**, 364

Southwell, William, MP [I], **1**, 290; **2**, 28, 199

Spain, **3**, 115, 200, 203, 270, 273, 276, 283, 289, 292, 312

Sparre, Carl Gustaf, Baron, **2**, 340

Spence, Elizabeth, **1**, 83

Spence, William, **1**, 83, 276–7

Spencer, Anne (née Churchill), countess of Sunderland, w. of Charles (*q.v.*), **2**, 141

Spencer, Charles, 3rd earl of Sunderland, **1**, 233; **2**, 4–5, 7, 9–11, 13–17, 39–42, 44, 49, 52–3, 64, 68, 76, 83, 85, 105, 116, 127, 158, 166–7, 180, 197, 213–14, 219, 225–6, 253–4, 290–1, 293, 296, 298–9, 307–8, 315, 318, 323, 344, 347, 375, 377, 380; **3**, 1, 3, 33, 39, 79, 192

Spread, William, purchaser from forfeiture trustees [I], **1**, 130

Spring, Francis, MP [I], **1**, 93, 170, 177

Spring, William, master of references to forfeiture trustees [I], **1**, 118–19

Squibb, Elizabeth, rape victim, **2**, 281–2

Stafford, Staffs., **3**, 158

Stafford, Edmond Francis, MP [I], **1**, 76, 111–12, 115, 120, 122, 175, 178

Stahremberg, Konrad Sigmund, graf von, **3**, 200–1, 203

Stair, 2nd earl of *see* Dalrymple, John

Stamford, 2nd earl of *see* Grey, Thomas